# Oil and Modern World Dramas

The first to focus on the (re-)presentations of oil in dramatic literature, theatre, and performance, *Oil and Modern World Dramas* is a pioneering volume in the emerging field of Oil Literatures and Cultures, and the more established field of World Literatures. Through close analysis, Fakhrkonandeh demonstrates how these dramatic works depict oil, both in its perceived nature and character, as an overdetermined matter/sign/object: a symbol (of freedom, autonomy, speed, wealth, modernity, enlightenment), a commodity, a social-cultural agent, a social relation, and a hyper-object. This book is also distinguished by its innovative and critically manifold conceptual framework, positing the petro-literatures and petrocultures an inextricable part of a global network. *Oil and Modern World Dramas* not only demonstrates how the chosen works of petro-drama manifest these concepts in their social-political vision, aesthetics, and historical-ontological dynamics, but also reveals how they deploy such assemblage-based approaches both as a cartographical means and aesthetic method for exposing the systemic (Capitalocenic) nature of petro-capitalist exploitation, and as means of proposing ways of resistance and producing alternative modes of subjectivity, community, relationality, and economy.

**Alireza Fakhrkonandeh** is Assistant Professor in Modern and Contemporary Drama and Literary Theory at the University of Southampton, UK. He has recently finished two books, titled *Body and Event in Howard Barker's Theatre of Catastrophe* (2019) and *Evental Ontology, Immanent Ethics and Affective Aesthetics in Howard Barker's Drama* (under review). He completed his PhD at Warwick University (2015). Fakhrkonandeh holds degrees in English Literature and Literary Theory (PhD), Continental Philosophy (MA), and Medical Humanities (MA). His works have featured in various journals and books, including *Symploke*, *Textual Practice*, *Comparative Drama*, *English Studies*, *JCDE*, *ANQ*, *The Edinburgh History of Reading* (2020), and *The Somaesthetics of City Life* (2019). He is also a professional academic translator. He is the sole authorized translator of Howard Barker's works into Persian.

Routledge Studies in World Literatures and the Environment
Series Editors: Scott Slovic and Swarnalatha Rangarajan

**Anthropocene Ecologies of Food**
Notes from the Global South
*Edited by Simon C. Estok, S. Susan Deborah and Rayson K. Alex*

**Literature Beyond the Human**
Post-Anthropocentric Brazil
*Edited by Luca Bacchini and Victoria Saramago*

**D. H. Lawrence, Ecofeminism and Nature**
*Terry Gifford*

**Religion, Narrative, and the Environmental Humanities**
Bridging the Rhetoric Gap
*Matthew Newcomb*

**Nuclear Cultures**
Irradiated Subjects, Aesthetics and Planetary Precarity
*Pramod K. Nayar*

**Contagion Narratives**
The Society, Culture and Ecology of the Global South
*Edited by R. Sreejith Varma and Ajanta Sircar*

**Women and Water in Global Fiction**
*Edited by Emma Staniland*

**Oil and Modern World Dramas**
From Petro-Mania to Petro-Melancholia
*Alireza Fakhrkonandeh*

For more information about this series, please visit: https://www.routledge.com/Routledge-Studies-in-World-Literatures-and-the-Environment/book-series/ASHER4038

# Oil and Modern World Dramas
From Petro-Mania to Petro-Melancholia

Alireza Fakhrkonandeh

Volume One

NEW YORK AND LONDON

First published 2023
by Routledge
605 Third Avenue, New York, NY 10158

and by Routledge
4 Park Square, Milton Park, Abingdon, Oxon, OX14 4RN

*Routledge is an imprint of the Taylor & Francis Group, an informa business*

© 2023 Alireza Fakhrkonandeh

The right of Alireza Fakhrkonandeh to be identified as author of this work
has been asserted in accordance with sections 77 and 78 of the Copyright,
Designs and Patents Act 1988.

All rights reserved. No part of this book may be reprinted or reproduced
or utilised in any form or by any electronic, mechanical, or other means,
now known or hereafter invented, including photocopying and recording,
or in any information storage or retrieval system, without permission in
writing from the publishers.

*Trademark notice*: Product or corporate names may be trademarks or
registered trademarks, and are used only for identification and explanation
without intent to infringe.

ISBN: 978-0-367-68204-0 (hbk)
ISBN: 978-0-367-68205-7 (pbk)
ISBN: 978-1-003-13466-4 (ebk)

DOI: 10.4324/9781003134664

Typeset in Sabon
by Apex CoVantage, LLC

To my country:

Iran

The land of the past, present and future

# Contents

| | | |
|---|---|---|
| *Acknowledgement* | | viii |
| *Prelude* | | xi |
| | Introduction: Modern and Contemporary Oil Dramas and Cultures | 1 |
| 1 | Oil, the Crisis of Representation, and the Dramatic Form | 35 |
| 2 | Conjonctural Cycles of Capitalist Oil Extraction in Western Peripheries: Leo Lania's *Konjunktur 1* (1928) | 66 |
| 3 | "On a Wave of Oil England Swam Towards Victory . . . Our Weapon of Choice Was Oil": Oil Monopoly, Petro-Dramaturgical Aesthetics, and Capitalocene in Leo Lania's *Konjunktur 2* | 134 |
| 4 | "Oil Is an Idea": From Production to Anti-Production in Leo Lania's *Oil Field* (1934) | 166 |
| 5 | "It's Not Easy to Make Oil and Love Run in Harness Together": "Petroleum Odes", "Oil Odour", and "Odious Coolies" in Lion Feuchtwanger's *Oil Islands* | 255 |
| | *Works Cited* | 367 |
| | *Index* | 382 |

# Acknowledgement

Time has been the toll of this book – but not just time. The loss of human and nonhuman life and nature should be included into the woeful annals and litany of such losses. This book was in gestation for nearly seven years, a period that proved replete with an array of personal and global trials and events, including the ravages of Covid, various natural and un-natural disasters across the world, including wars (and resource wars) across the world, various oil spills, and vast fires in forests across the world, including Iran, Australia, France, and various spots in Africa due to global warming and severity of summer heat. Add to this array of events a lukewarm and nearly impotent COP 27, the stipulations and promises of which barely amounted to anything tangible notwithstanding the exponential increase in the raging flares of global warming and its effects.

The writing of this acknowledgement, a few months subsequently to the completion of the book itself, coincides with the Russian invasion of Ukraine and the consequent, strategic food and fuel crisis (particularly targeting oil and gas) foisted both by Russia and the profiteering energy companies (such as BP) on other countries. Halting the exporting flow of already-contracted fossil fuels (gas and oil) into other European countries has been wielded by Russia as a strategic weapon to preclude and abort resistance, retaliatory measures, and sanctions against its continuous occupation of Ukraine. An occurrence that has yielded far-reaching ramifications by instigating global oil and gas crisis in terms of price spikes and shortage of supply – to say the least. Add to this Joe Biden's notorious trip to Saudi Arabia at the cost of tarnishing any remaining moral and political credibility (regarding the USA's claims to being the standard bearer of democracy, freedom, and human rights) only to ensure the uninterrupted and less expensive flow of oil into the veins of the American and global infrastructures. On the other hand, the heatwave in the UK – reaching the unprecedented record high of 41 C° – has not only been a testament to the earnestness of the climate crisis but has also come to induce grave issues with regards to water supplies. As tragic and lamentable as the aforementioned issues are, they at least coalesce to demonstrate the timeliness of the three volumes of this book on oil – I hope.

## Acknowledgement    ix

The act of writing this book proved a worldly experience. Whilst the main portion of this book was written in throes of my academic works and daily life in the UK, some of the parts were written during my sojourns in Germany, Iran, Turkey, and Canada. Consequently, the act of writing this book whilst a highly solitary experience incurred debts from various people.

First and foremost, I would like to thank a dear friend and colleague, Dr Yiğit Sümbül (at Ankara Hacı Bayram Veli University), who proved an unfaltering companion and a committed interlocutor in all stages of this project. Yiğit meticulously perused every single sentence in this book in its draft form and provided perspicacious feedback on them. Equally importantly, Yiğit's amicable banters and nearly blithe optimism about the destiny of this book buoyed me up whilst I was dismally floundering in the corrosive morass of various academic and non-academic plights.

In my extended and unceasing reflections on and engagements with the question of oil in its various representations and manifestations I have considerably benefited from my conversations and contacts with various friends and colleagues. In particular, I am immensely grateful to Peter Boxall, Jeff Diamanti, Stephen Morton, Stephen Shapiro, and Imre Szeman for their kind and gracious offer of invaluable and insightful conversation, feedback, support, and advice in various shapes and forms. Non-oil-driven conversations with some colleagues at the University of Southampton also proved helpful and galvanizing. I would like to particularly thank Stephen Morton, Stephanie Jones, Nicky Marsh, and Jakub Boguszak for their friendship and congenial companionship.

Above all I would like to express my profuse gratitude to Michelle Salyga and Bryony Reece at Routledge for their gracious patience, generous support, and perspicacious understanding in their treatment of this book and my need for more time at various junctures. I am obliged to them for their dexterous handling and expert care in the preparation of this book for production.

I gratefully acknowledge the support of the Faculty of Arts and Humanities at the University of Southampton for granting me a one-semester research leave which facilitated the completion of some of the remaining sections of this book by providing me with a sorely needed and vital respite from the onslaught of teaching, marking, and administrative travails thereby enabling me to fully dedicate my time to this project.

I would like to express my immense gratitude to the staff at Hartley Library at the University of Southampton whose kind and steadfast support proved vital and highly punctual. The library staff helped me to obtain access to a vast body of primary and secondary materials which would have otherwise been inconceivable, and sources which would not have been otherwise accessible.

x  *Acknowledgement*

Last but certainly not least, I would like to express my boundless love and gratitude to my family, my wife, and my son. Sara and Surena did not cease to nurture my oil-soaked mind and sun-seared spirit by their replenishing love, inspiration, and enthusiasm. Without being blessed with Sara's immense support and Surena's ebullient upsurges of beauty and his barrage of insatiably curious "whys", this protracted book project would have been a far more strenuous, arduous, and dreary undertaking. Sara and Surena remain the balmy beacons of my hope.

# Prelude

## I.  Adding Fuel to the Fires of Petrocultures?

In June 2015, a large throng of people comprising 75 individuals, all clad in black garments and black veils and carrying books in their hands, entered Tate Britain Gallery intent on conducting what turned out to be a 25-hour guerrilla protest to Tate's ties with BP as a sponsor (from high tide on 13 June, 11.53 a.m. until high tide on 14 June, 12.55 p.m.). The performers/demonstrators then started scrawling cautionary and foreboding passages about global warming from a selected number of works – including Naomi Klein's *This Changes Everything: Capitalism vs the Climate*, the UN's latest climate report, and Margaret Atwood's *Oryx and Crake* – in charcoal on the sloping, 500-foot-long floor of the Turbine Hall, which once accommodated the oil-fired turbines of the Bankside power station. Gradually the visitors/audience gathered that this unsolicited intervention was actually a performance event, called *Time Piece*, undertaken by the group Liberate Tate to urge Tate to rescind its BP sponsorship deal prior to the Paris climate summit in December.

Nearly three months later, in September 2015, the expectations of the visitors of Tate Britain were yet again given an astonishing twist by the presence of 30 or so individuals all dressed in black and wearing black veils marching through the hallways and galleries of Tate (littered with the BP logo). The solemn, elegiac procession suddenly halted to affectively-cognitively douse the visitors with an aurally viscous experience, that is, by reading out the Intergovernmental Panel on Climate Change (IPCC)'s report – a text replete with dense, complicated scientific details – in a precipitous monotone. This unsanctioned intervention was later revealed to be another performance initiative – titled 5th Assessment – conducted by Liberate Tate. These two 2015 performance events, however, were not singular events but rather part of an array of extended series, initiated in 2010 when the Liberate Tate group was founded. Here, however, I will confine my discussion to two of their most conspicuous performances.[1]

In June 2010, some visitors casually rambled into the hallways of Tate Museum for the lack of a better pastime and some as afficionados with xii *Prelude*

strictly premeditated plans. What struck both groups with consternation was the advent of a quasi-funereal procession of persons, some of whom were vested in black, monastic garments (evoking abstinence, mourning, and loss), whilst carrying oil cans and exercising "obstinate silence" as a communicative means which is "more truthful than any discourse proffered by a mouth" (Rancière 2007, 13). Some other members of the procession are robed in nylon and plastic overalls emblazoned with BP's imprint/insignia sullied all over with oil stains whilst their pants and overall are rolled up from the foot upwards, laden with grubby blotches of oil. As the event unfolded the audience was afforded glimpses into the nature of the event. The event, called *Licence to Spill*, was conducted by Liberate Tate group and intended as a counterpoint to the summer party celebrating 20 years of BP support of Tate by choosing the performance to run parallel with the summer event. Here the world opened up by the performance erupted into the world of the oil-sponsored art institute, thereby fostering a jarring heteroglossia by finding a non-normative and non-standard language to reveal a devastated world hitherto occluded by oil corporations and their industrial and ideological associates. In the event, the performers/activists poured oil and feathers outside the entrance to Tate Britain, in Pimlico. As is semiotically evident, the oil cans (bearing BP's eco-friendly "helios" logo), staining and spilling on the gallery floors, all constituting crucial components of the performance, symbolized the sordid affairs of oil and BP's being redolent of off-shore scandals, one of the most outrageous of which was the Deepwater Horizon oil spill (in the Gulf of Mexico) and its pernicious effects on human and nonhuman environments and ecosystems. This semiotic-discursive measure was taken to counter BP's own "curatorial" presence in the gallery spaces, conducted through schemes such as the "BP Walk Through British Art" at Tate Britain – which entailed the corporation's sunflower logo being placed on walls as a repeating way-finder around the gallery (see Evans 2015, 38). Liberate Tate's manifold acts of visual and discursive disruption were a means of deconstructing the white mythology – which both BP and Tate had spun around themselves and their extractive acts as institutes. The group accomplished this deconstruction by, in this case, restoring visibility to what has been rendered invisible – whitewashed and artwashed[2] – in the pristine, humanistic building and art-studded walls of Tate Gallery: to wit, the lethal ecological, social, and political-economic cost and effects of oil extraction by the global petro-capitalist system. As the group explained: "it is the sacredness and neutrality of the gallery that we are able concurrently to utilize and disrupt" (Liberate Tate 2012, 138).

The most emblematic example of Liberate Tate's performances is, perhaps, the "Human Cost" – conducted on 20 April 2011 to mark the first anniversary of the disastrous Deepwater Horizon explosion that spilled 4.9 million barrels of oil into the Gulf of Mexico over 87 days. During the 87-minute performance event that unfolded viscously and poignantly

*Prelude* xiii

on the floor of Duveen Gallery before the audience's eyes, two members of the group poured oil/petroleum on the naked body of another member of the group lying on the marbled floor leaving him petroleum-slathered and in a creaturely state: reduced to bare life by the toxic effects of oil extracted and spilled by oil companies and petro-capitalist regime. The resonant cynosure of this site-specific performance was indeed the sight of a naked, oil-soaked body of a human huddled up in a foetal position reminiscent of the poignant image of the oil-soaked pelican in the Gulf in the aftermath of the spill – a haunting reminder of human-nonhuman vulnerability in the face of natural or otherwise catastrophes. This striking image can also be construed as an attempt to render the human in all his/her *homo sacer* condition as an animal, thus symbolizing nature (and animals) and their exposure to the pernicious effects of pollution and oil spills. Importantly, and perhaps as a tentative testimony to the political efficacy of Liberate Tate's energy/ecologically oriented performances, this array of performance-interventions ultimately led to the annulment of Tate's contract and sponsorship agreement with BP. Whilst any claim regarding a direct or non-mediated relationship between the artwork and the social-historical context (and at the expense of sacrificing the "autonomy" of artwork – see Adorno's *Aesthetic Theory*, 23, 109–110, 228–235) would be naïve, this effect can be argued to have partly been achieved through the activities of environmentally focused artists and activists – such as Liberate Tate and Platform – which were aimed to draw attention to the politics underlying these acts of "artwashing", thereby subverting the oil companies' attempt to establish their "social license to operate"[3] by sponsoring arts and art institutes.

If oil is as much a political-economic matter as a matter of sense-making (of oneself and one's personal-national place in the world), sensory perception, and habit (of identification, consumption, communication, and mobility); in other words, if oil is as much a lifestyle as a form of life, then Liberate Tate's performance events can be argued to be efficacious means of un-making that sense and sensory perception by exposing the audience – at cognitive and affective levels – to not only how fossil fuels and fossil capital act as the conditions of possibility of the visibility of art and artforms mediated by the institutions but also how most of the audience's aesthetic experience is indeed a petro-aesthetic experience in far subtler ways than they would reckon or imagine – that is, embedded into the fabric of their sense and sensibility (including their cognitive-affective habits, norms, and patterns of determining aesthetic, moral, social, and economic value and meaning in relation to life and art). More specifically, Liberate Tate achieved this not through "rhetorical persuasion about what must be done" but by rendering visible "a multiplication of connections and disconnections that reframe the relation between bodies [and] the world they live in" (Rancière 2009, 72). By lodging their counter-discursive performance within "a multiplicity of folds in the sensory fabric of the xiv *Prelude*

common", which "passes itself off as the real" (Rancière 2010, 148), and by creating the environments of "dissensus" (see Rancière 2010), Liberate Tate fostered the possibility of the re-"distribution of the sensible",[4] which in turn engendered a possibility for the emergence of new communities of sense – where sense tries to be driven less by fossil fuels in its dynamics. Liberate Tate countered the aestheticization of the politics not through a direct politicization of their (performative and ecocritical) aesthetics. Liberate Tate's creation of a theatrical sphere is markedly political whilst attempting to retain its theatrical-aesthetic autonomy; a move which in effect enhances its political potency by showing how "there is no 'real world' that functions as the outside of art" (see Rancière 2010, 148).[5]

What is of particular significance to the social-political efficacy and visual-kinaesthetic dynamics of Liberate Tate's performances is their mobilization of a politicized phenomenology of spatial-temporal experience where the "worlded" space and ecosystem of the performances are foregrounded only to reveal how both such art events/exhibitions and the audience's position in relation to them are being traversed and determined by Capitalocenic time-space coupled with the uneven, extractive logics steering the Capitalocene (including Capitalogenic ecological and economic crises otherwise excluded from the museumified space of the institute). Their "worlded" space is also reflected in their decision to hold their performance events concurrently with and spatially adjacent to the BP-sponsored events, exhibitions, or workshops run at Tate. As such, they also sought to demonstrate how the otherwise politically neutral and autonomous space of art belies the deep-seated co-implications and complicities between the art institute and the petro-capitalist corporation. Acutely cognizant of the "considerable discrepancy between the explanatory heart of energy geography in urban centres and at the campuses, and the messy, remote and unstable resource fringes where these situations take place" (Pendakis 2017, 507), Liberate Tate sought to debunk the "artwashed" myth/picture of BP (as the third largest oil producer in the world and liable for numerous pernicious spills around the world), a myth/picture concocted for the public consumption, by countering the political-economic entanglements between corporation petro-capitalism and public-facing art institutions. They accomplished this move not only by presenting performance events that sear into public consciousness the *enmeshments* (see Morton *The Ecological Thought* 124) between the human-in-nature and nature-in-human – which involves the contemporary climate crisis as well as the dystopian future that awaits them if no remedial or pre-emptive action is taken on a global scale – but also by making their performance act as an imperative to humans to enact their "ethical agency" in relation to nonhuman natures.[6]

These reverberating artistic critiques of "artwashing" exhibitions were not the only events (cast in the form of performance and/or theatrical/dramatic works) that made the 2010s a distinct decade in the cultural-social

*Prelude* xv

history and memory of environmentalist movements/activism concerned with climate change and global fossil capitalism. Far from constituting an isolated series of oil-focused and climate-conscious performance events in the scene of contemporary British culture, the aforementioned interventions were accompanied by an array of other unprecedented events – particularly in 2015. Not only did 2015 anticipate the emergence of unprecedented plays in British dramatic history in that they took the question of oil as their sole and sustained crux/focal point – namely, Ella Hickson's *Oil*, Ben Harrison's *Crude: An Exploration*, Clare Duffy's *Arctic Oil*, and Sulayman Al-Bassam's *Petrol Station* – all of which constitute the focal points of analysis in this book in its extended three-volume form. Indeed, 2015 also marks a critical juncture not only in the history of the largest public media in the UK, the BBC, but also in the cultural history of the country, in that in 2015, unprecedented in the history of any public media in Britain, the BBC dedicated one whole series of radio plays to one single topic: oil. Whilst this event attests to the considerable extent to which the ecological and political-economic ravages of a fossil-fuel-driven – and, above all, oil-driven – mode of life in conjunction with the mode and logics of their extraction (the petro-capitalist global system) had gained a prominent position in cultural consciousness and public media discourse, this should not be considered in isolation from the broader global context. This series, whilst significant and encompassing in its historical scope in its own right, was not an isolated event but rather part of a constellation of energy-conscious and oil-oriented events during the 2010s. The impetus underlying dramatic-cultural enterprises with such social-political magnitude can partly be explained by reference to the global event (consequential event: the Paris Agreement). On 12 December 2015, the Paris Agreement – as a legally binding international treaty on climate change – was signed and adopted by 196 Parties at COP 21 in Paris and took effect on 4 November 2016 though it was partly unravelled due to Donald Trump's withdrawal from it in November 2020.

This seven-episode series of radio dramas titled *The Price of Oil* takes oil, its global history, and the world-systemic nature of its extraction, circulation, evaluation, and consumption as its focal points. The seven petro-dramatic radio plays were written by various writers and produced and broadcast by the BBC in 2015. The series seeks to span the genealogy and history of oil and accordingly takes the geopolitical hotspots or pivotal extraction sites of oil as its geographical settings. The series treads a far-reaching historical-geographical trajectory spanning a period from 1951 to 2045, and spots from around the world ranging from Iran to Alaska, Libya, Nigeria, Turkmenistan, Washington, and onto Scotland's offshore rigs, to explore the role oil has played in shaping our world. The titles of the plays include: *Stand Firm, You Cads!* (Jonathan Myerson), *Looking for Billy* (Nigel Williams), *The Weapon* (Jonathan Myerson), *Baby Oil* (Jonathan Myerson), *Someone's Making a Killing in*

xvi  *Prelude*

*Nigeria* (Rex Obano), *No Two Days* (Joy Wilkinson), and *Blood From Stone* (Tamsin Oglesby). Apart from its significance in terms of its foregrounding of the emergence of an oil-focused historical consciousness in the British cultural consciousness and media discourse particularly since 2014, what makes this series crucial to this book is the way the series in its totality depicts a distinctive geopolitical aesthetics: an act of cartography or "diagramming" which not only exposes various oil frontiers (or zones of extraction) to be systemically related rather than being historically-geographically and politically-economically isolated and unrelated spots. It also reveals the uneven relational dynamics and logics informing the relationship between these oil frontiers, but more importantly between the core (the global north) and the peripheries of the petro-capitalist system. The series thus foregrounds the causes and histories underlying the imaginative epistemological and social-cultural limits of the possibility of moving beyond oil ontology and oil's global hegemony.

One of the most intriguing aspects of this series of seven petro-dramatic radio plays is not what was included in them but what was excluded. More specifically, as Myerson recounts, Nick and Myerson had conceived of the project as encompassing the longue durée of the modern oil world – spanning nearly two centuries of oil extraction and dependency (the 1850s–2050s period).[7] The initially conceived project was intended to begin with the discovery of oil in the US and conclude with a speculative vision of its continued hegemony. Evidently, this insightful initial plan was intended to reveal the inherent links between climate catastrophe, the extractive logics and core-periphery dynamics informing the world-systemic operations of the production of oil as a globally strategic commodity. Equally importantly, this longue durée vision of oil history would have included the globally extensive and fundamental role of the British Empire in the emergence of oil as the hegemonic and globally strategic commodity. This would include the colonial role of British Empire in the formation of new nations – in geopolitical, infrastructural, and political-economic terms – merely due to their possession of oil, including Iraq and Nigeria. Encountered with the BBC's uncompromising request that they set the historical point of departure of their project in the post-World War II period, however, Myerson and Nick were left with no remedy but to truncate the original scope of the project and tailor it to the demands of the BBC. Such a revision, however, curtailed and clipped short the longue durée vision of the global history of oil (informing the original version of the series) into a censored and whitewashed history where the role of British Empire – in the development of the petro-capitalist system and the *conjonctural* dynamics of the cycles of oil extraction and production of sites of oil along with all the attendant racial gender and class dynamics – were nearly entirely elided. Consequently, by taking 1951 as their point of departure, after much of Britain's overtly imperial activity in the Middle East was drawn down, the petro-dramatic series leaves the genealogy, dynamics, and consequences of imperialism under-explored and inadequately delineated. Furthermore, the series despite the variety of visions and styles informing it due to its being written by five different playwrights – Myerson single-handedly wrote three of them – remains largely conservative in vision. This conservativeness comprises the near lack of a vision or suggestion of a horizon beyond the oil ontology. Besides, apart from plays such as *Blood from Stone* and *No Two Days*, the plays remain less formally-aesthetically innovative and more thematically oriented (with a specific focus on the history as well as the social-cultural and political-economic facets of oil). The series thus falls short of presenting a longue durée vision of oil.

The BBC event needs to be considered as part of a worldly extended constellation. This was partly instigated by an array of international decisions and events concerning climate change in conjunction with environmental disasters that had coalesced/mounted to an alarming peak. A detailed exploration of the BBC's seven petro-dramas is beyond the scope of this prelude; however, suffice it to state that *The Price of Oil* – in its overarching vision and trajectory – does not prove radical enough: the ecological effects of oil on this planet are now so well established, as they were in 2015 when the plays were broadcast, that a requirement for a literary engagement with such a toxic substance should, as Imre Szeman argues, be engaged with challenging the listener/reader to thinking provocatively what the world would look like without oil.

## II.   Towards a World-Ecological Theory of Oil in World Dramas

### A.   *From Petroculture to Petro-Aesthetics to Petro-Drama*

Resonant with the events and issues delineated earlier, two looming issues have recently urged scholars and artists to deliberate on the role and nature of energy – particularly fossil fuels and, above all, oil – in relation to the life of contemporary humanity in almost all its dimensions, namely, "environmental catastrophe and capitalist crisis" (Bellamy and Diamanti 2018, ix). They have tackled these coterminous issues, not only by critiquing the means and modes of production, consumption, and extraction of energy/oil, but by proposing and promoting alternative energy forms and models and manners of consumption and extraction (Petrocultures Research Group 2016, 13–25, 55–64). The field ever since has come to be almost unanimously designated, more broadly, as "Energy Humanities" and, more specifically (focusing on oil), as "petrocultural studies". Energy Humanities has been defined as a project that "aspires to provide a speculative impulse as well as a critical diagnostics" – informed with a materialist and world-systemic approach and devised as a means of

xviii  *Prelude*

future-thinking and worldmaking in an era of climate chaos. Petroculture, on the other hand, as Petrocultures Research Group propose, is intended to illuminate the magnitude of the oil effect:

> [petroculture designates] the ways in which post-industrial society today is an oil society through and through. It is shaped by oil in physical and material ways. . . . Even more significantly, fossil fuels have also shaped our values, practices, habits, beliefs, and feelings.
> (Petrocultures Research Group 2016, 9)

Of particular relevance to the disciplinary context and conceptual approach underpinning this book is the recent emergence of the Energy Humanities, a field of study premised "on an appreciation of culture's role in establishing, maintaining and transforming resource and work/energy regimes" (Westall 2017, 269). The task the Energy Humanities sets itself is to "first, grasp the full intricacies of our imbrication with energy systems (and with fossil fuels in particular), and second, map out other ways of being, behaving, and belonging in relation to both old and new forms of energy" (Szeman and Boyer 2017, 3).

Deriving its premises and insights from various strands in petrocultural studies and beyond, this book attends to scrutinize our "energy unconscious" through a critique of the "fuel apparatus of modernity, which [is] all too often invisible or subterranean, but which pumps and seeps into the groundwaters of politics, culture, institutions, and knowledge in unexpected ways" (Szeman and Boyer 2017, 9). Following Brent Ryan Bellamy and Jeff Diamanti's argument concerning resource aesthetics, I do not distinguish between economic and aesthetic production.[8] Instead, I will seek to demonstrate how these plays (across the three volumes) recognize and render visible the materiality of petroculture. Such a consideration is in keeping with Patricia Yaeger's thought-provoking question: "what happens if we sort texts according to the energy sources that made them possible".[9] That is, we ask "how . . . might one best begin to use energy as the lens through which to view culture".[10] Oil culture has been defined by Ross Barrett and Daniel Worden as "the broad field of cultural representations and symbolic forms that have taken shape around the fugacious material of oil in the 150 years since the inception of the US petroleum industry" (269).[11] Sourayan Mookerjea, on the other hand, conceives of petroculture as one which is critical and post-oil-oriented, rather than merely representative of the hegemonic presence of oil in contemporary life and the socio-cultural sphere: "petroculture is nothing less than a generalized need for new kinds of people dispossessed of the habits of the recent past and so able to live together in new ways and to invent the rationalities with which a new mode of social reproduction may be built" (*Petroculture* 338). By the same token, the term "petroculture" can be argued to designate the logics of identification, dynamics of relationship

*Prelude* xix

with human-nonhuman other, cultural forms, and social imaginaries constituted by the knowledge, practices, and discourses which not only emanate from the extraction, production, consumption of and subsequent addiction to oil; it is also the very discourse that then comes to propel the aforementioned phenomena. Put pithily, one of the principal designations of the petroculture is the fossil-intensive and carbon-heavy habits of urban and suburban life in modern and contemporary history, along with the attendant narratives of identity, mobility, futurity, and freedom – habits which are no longer confined to the bounds of the bourgeois family and entrepreneurial subject in the global north.

This petrocultural turn has been paralleled in the field of literary studies (see Balkan and Nandi, *Oil Fictions*, 2021), preceded with the consolidation of environmentalist and ecocritical paradigms, where the scrutiny of the works of petrofiction has been pursued as their crux and a key to the lived and imagined lives of the subjects and cultures of the time. However, there has been no parallel attempt to extend this petrocultural approach and exploration into the field of drama and theatre studies until very recently (see Fakhrkonandeh *Textual Practice* 2021; Fakhrkonandeh 2022). As a petrocultural study of modern and contemporary drama, this book undertakes an exploration of the ways in which these petro-dramatic works manifest ethical, psychological, and social-cultural aporias and contradictions of a world where oil acts as its ontological principle, its political and economic impetus, and the premise of value, as well as a matter indispensable to the materiality of commodity culture, to modes of subjectivity, and to forms of relationality. Conjoining eco-materialism and world-systems analysis, this book conducts its exploration of the selected works of petro-drama under the two premises that, firstly, "energy is dialectically bound to economic history – not a concept or variable independent of it, but a structuring force without which capital could not operate" (Bellamy and Diamanti, 1) – and, secondly, that energy, in the form of oil (and fossil capital, more broadly), expresses itself aesthetically in ways that subvert dominant generic categories and formal paradigms.[12] Whilst the analytical framework in each chapter has been immanently developed in light of the distinct aesthetic-thematic subtleties of each play, a world-systemic approach constitutes the analytical crux of this book's engagement with the selected dramatic works. Such an approach entails attention to the questions of core-periphery dynamics and combined and uneven development.

This book situates itself in the newly emerged context of petrocultural studies with a specific focus on the representations of oil and an oil-driven world in dramatic works. In this light, this book is the first to undertake an energy-intensive scrutiny of oil-focused drama and theatre, in its various modes, genres, and geographies-histories in an attempt to present a petrocritical analysis – comprising the eco-materialist and world-systemic approaches – of the most prominent, yet highly under-explored, works of

xx *Prelude*

petro-drama. In so doing, this book seeks to demonstrate how, through successive periods, particularly embedded modes of oil-dependent and oil-driven subjectivity, cognitive-affective habits, personal and collective imaginaries, social ethos, and ecological morality create a predominant culture of being and imagining in the world. Accordingly, in the ensuing sections of the introduction, primarily, I will seek to establish some of the features and facts about oil and its significance in the contemporary works and theories of petroculture as recognized and delineated by the scholars from across various disciplines. Secondarily, I will delineate the conceptual premises of my eco-materialist (or petrocritical) approach which will underpin my exploration of the oil-focused plays across the three volumes of this book. I will also explicate the formal and aesthetic challenges posed to drama as a medium and genre in its attempt to tackle the manifold question of oil as a volatile biophysical matter, as a strategic energy resource, as a temporally overdetermined object, as a global commodity muffled up in metaphysical associations, and as the symbolic motor of civilization, modernity, and progress. Far from intending to collapse the noteworthy differences between the new materialist and world-systemic discourses, my dialectical synthesis of the two discourses will strive to maintain an acute cognizance of their mutually critical stances regarding such issues as the nature and dynamics of climate crisis, resources, extractivism, human-nonhuman relationship, and subject-system relationship, among others. As such, adopting either of these two approaches in isolation would have led to a restricted and non-dialectical approach. In critically conjoining these two paradigms, I intend to develop a conceptual framework that would not only enable me to redress the problematic of scale variously informing both approaches – particularly as regards the effects of oil upon the modern world and subjectivity at the macro-scale (of the world and world systems including the climate, planet, and capitalism) and micro-scale (of the word, individual psyche, affect and interpersonal relationship) – but also enable me to effectively probe the relational dynamics between these two scales.

The crux of this book is to demonstrate how the critical vision informing the selected works of petro-drama here, in conjunction with their symptomatic presentation of the various facets of oil and its effects on the human-nonhuman life in modern and contemporary oil order (global petro-capitalism), can be characterized – among other ways – as a Capitalocenic vision. As such, it will ponder and probe the ways in which a world-ecological vision and a world-systemic logics of the production, extraction, and consumption of oil foster not only new dramatic forms and aesthetic features but also new modes of subjectivity as well as new ways of relating to time, space, the socio-symbolic order, and human-nonhuman others.

One notable point worth elucidating concerns the mode and dynamics of my analytical engagements with the selected plays. As the reader will

*Prelude* xxi

have noticed, the chapters here tend to be fairly extended and present detailed explorations of the petro-plays. They also incorporate ample textual evidence to illustrate the points and establish the arguments. Apart from arising from the thematic and aesthetic complexities of the petro-dramatic works at stake here, such a move stems from the fact that out of the four plays scrutinized in this volume three are my archival discoveries which are not only not widely available to the public reader at all, but, more importantly, never formally published either in their time or more recently. Notably, out of these three archival and unpublished plays, two are originally in German and have never been translated into English, to my knowledge. Consequently, in order to provide the reader with abundant insights into the narrative and thematic details of these plays, I deemed it essential to provide extended accounts of the subtleties and details of the characters, thematics, and form in these dramatic texts.

## B. *Towards an Infrastructuralization of Critical Analysis of Oil Drama and Energy-Intensive Aesthetics*

As indicated, one of the distinct features of this book is its nuanced and critically manifold conceptual framework. To tackle various facets of oil, as particularly depicted in the selected plays from world dramatic literatures, this book develops a "systemic", or systems-based, eco-materialist conceptual framework. A concise elucidation of the conceptual underpinnings and methodology of my eco-materialist analysis of the works of "world petro-drama" is necessary. My eco-materialist or world-ecological framework, far from being restricted to one specific critical stance, includes the following theoretical approaches: (1) theories of petroculture and ecocritical studies as variously elaborated by Imre Szeman, Matthew Huber, Jeff Diamanti, Rob Nixon, and Dipesh Chakrabarty, among others; (2) world-systems theory: Immanuel Wallerstein (2000, 2006, 2011), Giovanni Arrighi (1999, 2003, 2007), and Jason Moore (2013, 2017a); (3) Leon Trotsky's Theory of Combined and Uneven Development and David Harvey's *Theory of Uneven Geographies* (2017). As regards the literary hermeneutic methodology, I shall draw on a number of congruent strands in the theory of world literature – particularly the ones elaborated by David Damrosch (2003), Franco Moretti (2000), WReC (*Warwick Research Collective; Theory of Combined and Uneven Development* 2015), Pheng Cheah (2003, 2016), and Fredric Jameson (2005, 2008, 2015, 2019).

By the term "worlded" (which I will be utilizing in short-hand form of "world" throughout this book), I have specifically in mind the way the concept has been elaborated by the World-Systems school of economic thinkers, such as Wallerstein and Arrighi – extended accounts of whose theories have been provided in Chapters 1 and 3. But equally pivotal to my adaptive development of the notion of "world petro-drama" have been xxii *Prelude*

the revisionary takes on world-systems theories undertaken by various scholars in the field of political geography, political economy, ecological studies – most prominent amongst whom, for the purposes of this book, has been Jason Moore with his significant expansions and elaborations of this theory in terms of the notions of the world-ecological, the Capitalocene, and metabolic shift. (I have provided explications of these terms in the second part of the Introduction.) The third noteworthy strand is my adaptations of the appropriations of the aforementioned theories in the field of world literature by scholars such as Franco Moretti and WReC (Warwick Research Collective).

To succinctly delineate the premise of this worlded dynamics, suffice it here to refer to two salient strands in this field mainly represented by Franco Moretti and Pascale Casanova, respectively. In a bid to establish a dialectical way beyond the binary of internal and external criticism, Casanova wonders: "Is it possible to re-establish the lost bond between literature, history and the world, while still maintaining a full sense of the irreducible singularity of literary texts?" (2005, 71). The solution Casanova propounds takes the aesthetic autonomy of literary works in a problematically ideal "meridian" of the world republic of letters as its pivotal criterion. For Moretti, on the other hand, it is the heteronomy of literary work and the dynamics of production amidst the asymmetrical political-economic relations informing the world market that constitutes the core value. Moretti's characterization, as I will argue, has a close bearing on the historical-geographical characteristics and the petrocritical vision underpinning the dramatic works under consideration in the three volumes of this book. As he explains:

> I will borrow [. . . my] initial hypothesis from the world-system school of economic history, for which international capitalism is a system that is simultaneously one, and unequal; with a core, and a periphery (and a semi-periphery) that are bound together in a relationship of growing inequality. One, and unequal: one literature (Weltliteratur, singular, as in Goethe and Marx), or, perhaps better, one world literary system (of inter-related literatures); but a system which is different from what Goethe and Marx had hoped for, because it's profoundly unequal.[13]

Critically deriving elements from the world-systems theory not only enables us to recognize and analyze petro-capitalism in its broader historical-geographical scope and cycles of resource extractivism; it also allows for the recognition of what Jameson terms the "simultaneity of the non-simultaneous" (derived from Ernst Bloch's notion of *leichzeitigkeit des Ungleichzeitigen*[14]), thereby enabling readings of texts in relation to the multiform (often resource-determined) violence of incorporation into the world system. Another prominent instance of a rigorous deployment of

*Prelude* xxiii

the world-systems theory for the analysis of works of world literature has been WReC's book. Deriving their premises from an array of existing sources – including Franco Moretti's and Pascale Casanova's respective definitions of world literature as a singular and uneven field, WReC define world literature "as the literature of the world system" (2015, 8); or more strictly, "as the literary registration of modernity under the sign of combined and uneven development" (17).[15] In WReC's account, works of world literature are not "only those works that self-consciously define themselves in opposition to capitalist modernity . . . [or which] stage a coded or formally mediated resistance to capitalist modernity" (15–20). Rather, as they elaborate,

> the literary 'registration' of the world system does not (necessarily) involve criticality or dissent. Our assumption is rather that the effectivity of the world system will necessarily be discernible in any modern literary work, since the world system exists unforgoably as the matrix within which all modern literature takes shape and comes into being.
>
> (2015, 20)

WReC's statement further elucidates the issue and its dynamics: world literature reveals "the literary registration and encoding of modernity as a social logic" (2015, 15). More recently, Michael Niblett combines the conceptual premises of world-systems theory with Jason Moore's notion of the world-ecology to develop a hermeneutics or analytical framework for the exploration of certain Caribbean works of narrative fiction in a bid to reveal the manifestations of the world-ecological dynamics in the themes, forms, genres, production practices, and circulatory networks of these texts. Here he posits the capitalist world system as "not just a world-economy but also a world-ecology", such that world literature is also "the literature of the capitalist world-ecology" (Niblett 2020b, 16).

Such a conception of the world literary text as one which registers the capitalist world system, however, as Michael Walonen (2016) and Melissa Kennedy (2017) variously discern, is beset with its own inadequacies. Prominent among the problematic implications of WReC's definition is its evocation of literature as a material surface for the registration of the traces and effects of the unequal structures, historical forces, and social-economic relations of the capitalist world; literature is thus relegated to a secondary position, thereby becoming a pheno-text of a more fundamental economic geno-text. By the same token, Niblett, for instance, supplements WReC's characterization by adding the ensuing qualification: "world literature will necessarily register ecological regimes and revolutions (. . ., even if only negatively)" (Niblett 2012, 20). Furthermore, whilst the world-systemic facet of the theoretical framework underpinning this book is predicated primarily on Wallerstein's notions

xxiv *Prelude*

of *conjoncture* and *longue durée* along with Jason Moore's notions of metabolic shift, the world-ecological, and the Capitalocene and far less on Arrighi's theories, it is worth indicating that I have been acutely cognizant of the issues identified in Arrighi's theories by other scholars and have incorporated them into my process of developing the analytical framework here. In addition to Moore's incisive revisionary take on some of Arrighi's world-systemic insights, one of the rigorous critiques of Arrighi's model from a materialist perspective has been articulated by Shapiro and Deckard. Their critique can be distilled into three principal points. Firstly, they contend that Arrighi's model has become "a machinic reading devoid of class struggle" in the hands of his followers. Secondly, they argue that it tends toward "theological" rather than "analytical" modes of interpretation. Thirdly, they claim that it overlooks the expanded model for capital reproduction (M – C . . . P . . . C′ – M′) developed by Marx in Volume Two of *Capital* (see Sharae Deckard and Stephen Shapiro 2019, 11–13).[16]

Accordingly, partly in a bid to eschew and transcend the aforementioned fault lines and partly due to the distinct material and ideological features of the crux of this book – oil, that is – the conceptual framework here, far from being invariably fixed and confined to the rigid boundaries of one theoretical approach or trend, encompasses a broad range of often consonant and supplementary theories without any attempt to collapse the historical, ideological, or conceptual differences between them. Such a move stems from my attempt to conduct a nuanced analysis of the selected works where I have striven to adapt the analytical framework in each chapter in an immanent relation of resonance and forced movement[17] with the specific problematics informing each petro-play at thematic, aesthetic, psychodynamic, and ontological levels. Accordingly, in my engagement with each play, the reader will notice extensive deployment of the theories of psychoanalysis, deconstruction, feminism, and race studies, amongst others. Given the crux of this book – oil as a manifold, and globally strategic energy resource – in conjunction with its focus on the formal and aesthetic registration of the psychological, petrocultural, ethical, and political-economic implications of oil which are primarily driven by a systemically uneven dynamics, I will seek to demonstrate how oil enters the dramatic/theatrical text or performance as "a field of forces" and an overdetermined object-idea thereby destabilizing the established generic boundaries and tropes and thus reconfiguring them within new hybrid shapes and energetic textual forms. This three-volume book demonstrates how a critical appropriation of insights from the world-systems and world-ecological approaches – in conjunction with the theories of world literatures – will enable us to move beyond (the currently prevalent) ethnographic reading of oil towards a reading of oil cultures/literatures and oil-determined socio-historical consciousness that is situated in a global network and global sign system (symbolic order) as an immanent part. This is an eco-materialist analysis that probes the aesthetics and

*Prelude* xxv

economics of dramatic forms in their interaction with petro-capitalism's "world-ecological revolutions" (Moore 2015, 20).

The third strand in my conceptual framework is the notion of "petro-cultural criticism", which put succinctly, can be defined as "a methodology [. . .] for reading, historicizing, and politicizing the ubiquitous but avisual force of fossil fuels across social, economic and physical environments" (Diamanti 2021, 28). The foregoing conceptual steps towards an eco-materialist exploration of oil in drama are also an attempt to fulfil the necessity of what Szeman and Diamanti (2020) call "infrastructuralizing critique" in literary and dramatic criticism. As Szeman and Diamanti expound:

> A critical theory attentive to the historicity and materiality of energy sifts through infrastructure, because it is in infrastructure where one encounters the dusty, bloody, and sedimented archive of capitalism's longue durée over the bodies and resources of the planet. The critique of energy infrastructure makes available a presentism that refuses the terms of the present.
>
> (154)

Accentuating the critique of the "ongoing violence that grids infrastructure in the present and future" as a crucial task of Energy Humanities, they proceed to elaborate that "a critique of infrastructure also needs to be an *infrastructuralization of critique*: not more of the same . . . but a materialism both new and historical, intimate to what makes infrastructure dizzying and dazzling" (154). This book is an attempt to put such a demand and insight into critical practice. There are two pivotal points worth elucidating here. First, far from intending it to evoke a mode of logical or ontological dualism – exemplified by the crude Marxist binary of base and superstructure – my development of the term "infrastructural criticism" posits an immanent ontological relationship between the phenomena that have traditionally been cast in binary terms: between the human and the nonhuman, between the subject and the object, between the core and the periphery, between the local and the global, between the conscious and the unconscious, and between the individual and the collective. Even in the cases where the differences and uneven modes of production and relationship lead to transcendental (or ontological) divisions between races, classes, and genders, these divides can be characterized (borrowing a term from Deleuze) as a form of immanent transcendence (see Deleuze 1994, 46–48; Deleuze and Guattari 1994, 142). Second, in my elaboration of the term "infrastructural criticism", infrastructure has three designations: political-economic, socio-cultural, and existential-psychological (this facet can include such categories as the political unconscious and the energy unconscious, among others). As such, "infrastructural criticism" not only serves to expose and deconstruct the "produced" intersections

xxvi  *Prelude*

and entanglements between the abstract and the material, form and matter, the subject and object, the human and non-human, the conscious and unconscious, and the core and periphery but also reveals the processes and dynamics through which such logical-ontological transformations and occlusion between ostensibly antithetical categories are "produced".

# Notes

1. For an extended account of the details and history of their ecocritical performances see their website; see also Mel Evans, *Artwash* (London: Pluto Press, 2015), pp. 2–3, 103–118, 141–152.
2. See Evans, *Artwash*, pp. 140–165.
3. A term coined by the marketing company Fishburn Hedges, for their work with Shell.
4. Rancière defines his concept of "the distribution of the sensible" thus: "the sensory self-evidence of the 'natural' order [which] destines specific individuals and groups to occupy positions of rule or of being ruled" (Rancière 2010, 139).
5. Jacques Rancière, *The Future of the Image*. Trans. Gregory Elliott (London: Verso, 2007).
   Jacques Rancière, *The Emancipated Spectator*. Trans. Gregory Elliott (London: Verso, 2009).
   Jacques Rancière, *Dissensus: On Politics and Aesthetics*. Trans. and ed. Stephen Corcoran (London: Continuum, 2010).
6. See Keith Ansell-Pearson, "Deleuze and New Materialism Naturalism, Norms, and Ethics," in *The New Politics of Materialism*, ed. Sarah Ellenzweig and John H. Zammito (London: Routledge, 2017), pp. 88–108.
7. As Jonathan Myerson mentioned to us in an interview we conducted with him, "Nic (Kent, the creator of the series) did originally approach the BBC wanting to effectively do oil from the beginning, but they came back and they only wanted to do post war" (interview with the author).
8. Brent Ryan Bellamy and Jeff Diamanti, *Materialism and the Critique of Energy* (n.p.: MCM, 2018).
9. Patricia Yaeger, "Editor's Column: Literature in the Ages of Wood, Tallow, Coal, Whale Oil, Gasoline, Atomic Power, and Other Energy Sources," *PMLA*, 126.2 (2011), pp. 305–326.
10. Imre Szeman, "Conjectures on World Energy Literature: Or, What Is Petroculture?," *Journal of Postcolonial Writing*, 53.3 (2017), p. 278.
11. Ross Barrett and Daniel Worden, "Oil Culture: Guest Editors' Introduction," *Journal of American Studies*, 46.2 (2012), pp. 269–272.
12. Brent Ryan Bellamy and Jeff Diamanti, "Phantasmagorias of Energy: Toward a Critical Theory of Energy and Economy," *Mediations*, 31.2 (Spring 2018), pp. 1–16, www.mediationsjournal.org/articles/critique-of-energy.
13. Franco Moretti, "Conjectures on World Literature," in *Debating World Literature*, ed. Christopher Prendergast (London and New York: Verso, 2004), pp. 149–150.
14. Ernst Bloch, *Heritage of Our Times*. Trans. Neville and Stephen Plaice (California: University of California Press, 1991), pp. 266–267.
15. Seeking to find a middle ground between postcolonial and world literature, Casanova in "What Is a World?" observes: "Is it possible to re-establish the lost bond between literature, history and the world, while still maintaining a full sense of the irreducible singularity of literary texts?" (2005, 71). In the

*Prelude*  xxvii

same vein, she attempts to mend the rupture between an "internal, text-based literary criticism [which posits] the total rupture between text and world" and an "external criticism that runs the risk of reducing the literary to the political" (71). However, as will be explicated later, I do not agree with the viability and cultural politics underlying Casanova's proposed term.

16. "World-Culture and the Neoliberal World-System: An Introduction," in *World Literature, the Neoliberalism, and the Culture of Discontent*, ed. Sharae Deckard and Stephen Shapiro (London: Palgrave, 2019), pp. 1–49.

17. See Deleuze, *The Logic of Sense*, pp. 239–249.

# Introduction
## Modern and Contemporary Oil Dramas and Cultures

### I.  Oil as Energy Resource, as Global Commodity, and as an Aporetic Object of Desire

Oil has not only been described with epithets as diverse as "black gold",[1] "devil's excrement",[2] "a prize from a fairyland",[3] "capitalism's life-blood",[4] and a viscous, nonlocal, and uncanny "hyper-object".[5] Oil has also been referred to as "the most powerful fuel and versatile substance ever discovered"[6] – thereby being unanimously recognized as the most vital, valuable, ubiquitous and yet, paradoxically, invisible commodity of modern and contemporary global economics and history.[7] In *Carbon Nation* (2014), Bob Johnson confirms the point at issue: "we industrial peoples have preferred to keep our energy dependencies out of sight". He adds how "mineral rights" highlight the "embodiment of fossil fuels, including our affective attachments to them".[8] Similarly, Ruth Salvaggio argues that oil has turned out to be a "spectral substance" due to its being "curiously concealed" through various ideological-discursive or infrastructural means, including the politics of representation (such as media discourse), political hegemony, pipelines, storage containers, and car engines.[9] Oil has also been referred to as "the machine of destiny"[10] and "the mediator of futurity"; that is, "a vanishing mediator between industrialism and family life", and "a singular force capable of produc-ing singular effects – oil wars, oil addiction, and oil states" and – we might add – palpable *cultural affects*.[11] Yergin draws our attention to how oil has proved not only "the lifeblood of suburban communities", but more importantly, the "very nature of civilization".[12] Underscoring the significance of oil by referring to it as the "ur-commodity", Imre Sze-man explains why this viscous shape-shifter should be distinguished from other fuels: oil literally "drives" our world of liquid modernity and fluid (post-)modernity; "[oil is] the substance on which the globe depends to heat its homes, to move bodies and goods around, to build and maintain infrastructure – the substance that, for better and for worse, makes the world go round" ("Petrofictions", 3, The editorial introduction to the special section of *American Book Review*. March – April 2012). The idea

DOI: 10.4324/9781003134664-1

## 2   *Introduction*

of making "the world go round" is key. It is this movement and speed that is the mark of globalization and development in the context of Western modernity towards and beyond the "Age of Great Acceleration".

On the other hand, oil is also catastrophic. While it enables social relationships and empowers the individual, it also has the capacity to dismantle them. "[A] black and cruel demon" is what a character in Upton Sinclair's *Oil!* calls crude oil, continuing to describe it as an "evil power which roams the earth, crippling the bodies of men and women, and luring nations to destruction by visions of unearned wealth and the opportunity to enslave and exploit labour" (Sinclair 2007, 548). Accentuating the fundamental ways in which oil undergirds our modern life and subjectivity/selfhood, Stoekl simply states that "in some ways we are oil".[13] The long 20th century has, accordingly, been defined as "the century of oil".[14] As Stephanie LeMenager observes: "while the extraction of oil cannot be performed without labour, the spectacle of its gushing from the earth suggests divine or Satanic origins, a givenness that confers upon it an inherent value disassociated from social relations" (2012, 92). Most recently, seeking to present a genealogical account of the ways in which the contemporary petrocultural lifeform (our historical present and also the modality of anticipation) and its continuation into the future was produced by techniques of future-thinking and scenario-making through subtle discursive and speculative measures developed/devised by the Shell experts in 1970s, Diamanti writes: "oil is more than one kind of thing in the figuration of the future. Oil is the primary medium in which the very thinkability of economic futurity is made possible" (2021, 41). In light of the foregoing point, Diamanti proceeds to sound an alarming note by elaborating how such a hegemonic domination of petroculture poses crisis at cognitive, affective, and imagination levels: "the ostensible impossibility of imaging a future without oil (even when, as was true on April 20, 2020, oil becomes cheaper than free) is a signal crisis of the petrocultural penumbra" (25). The key to the critique of the current, hegemonic petro-capitalist order and to envisioning an alternative energy order resides in the identification of what Diamanti calls the "petrocultural penumbra". Defining the petrocultural penumbra as "an important space in need of critical mediation where capitalism reproduces itself materially, discursively, and culturally", Diamanti argues that we can discern the presence, magnitude, and effects of the petrocultural penumbra by "looking for oil between the ubiquity of its presence in the lifeworld of contemporary culture and the 'avisual' force it exerts over the *longue durée* of capitalism" (29).

The undeniably prevalent role of oil in human life and culture has urged critics such as Szeman, LeMenager, Nelida Fuccaro, Carola Hein, and Barret and Worden to define the present era as one of "petroculture", "petro-modernity", "petroleumscape", and "oil culture" respectively. Discerning the far-reaching effects of oil on the way modern and

*Introduction* 3

contemporary humanity has come to perceive both itself and its world, Szeman re-frames the question in terms of oil-world, rather than articulating it merely in terms of oil-culture. Szeman thus proposes that we should reconceptualize our understanding of the history of capitalism on the basis of what he calls "oil ontology". As he provocatively asks: "What if we were to think about the history of capital not exclusively in geopolitical terms, but in terms of the forms of energy available to it at any given historical moment?"[15] This ontological conception of oil is further expanded on by LeMenager when she observes:

> The historical question that I see as relevant to Herbst's and Soper's concerns, as well as to the creative ventures of peak-oilers like Kunstler, is why petromodernity has enveloped the Euro-American imagination to the extent that "oil" has become implicitly synonymous with the world, in a large, Heideggerian sense of the human enframing and revealing of earth, thus the world we know.
>
> (61)[16]

Oil, and by extension energy, has, accordingly, come to be ascribed such a pivotal role in recent literary and cultural studies that some scholars have gone so far as to insist on the necessity of presenting a new periodization of literary forms on the basis of energy regimes. More recently, Yaeger (2011), in her provocative *PMLA* editor's column, has embarked on refiguring literary history by recasting it around energy-based eras defined by wood, tallow, coal, whale oil, oil/gasoline, and atomic power. In so doing, Yaeger is contending that, instead of considering literary trends and generic forms through such divisions as romanticism, modernism, and postmodernism, we should predicate our categorization and inquiry around topics specifically concerned with and driven by energy regimes of that period or beyond. She thus suggests that we recognize such energy-based categories as oil and nuclear literature, or speculative forms of literatures concerned with renewable energy regimes (solar and wind) still to come.

The extent and intensity of the considerations, conceptualizations, and representations of the relationship between oil, literature, cultural ecologies, and economies of an oil-addicted world (debates over how history gets told) is testament both to the severity of the current ecological crisis and to the cumulative momentum gained by petrocultural studies since the 2000s in putting petrocultural issues on the agenda. As Moore acutely writes: "By the dawn of the twenty-first century, it had become increasingly difficult to address core issues in social theory and social change without some reference to environmental change" (2013, 1). It also throws into relief their multidisciplinary nature. Predicating their argument on the "insight that culture is entangled with the infrastructure of energy", Szeman and Diamanti affirm that "the operations of energy

4   *Introduction*

in shaping contemporary culture, and our critical ability to grapple with this as we attempt to move away from fossil fuels exceed the analytical capacity of any one discipline or conceptual approach" (2019, 2).[17] LeMenager sheds further light on other crucial dimensions of the contemporary subject's relationship with oil by more specifically focusing on the lived and phenomenological facets of it – hence according primacy to the psychosomatic and cognitive-affective aspects of the lived body and the category of habit and the unconscious. Such a symptomatological and phenomenological account demonstrates the efficacy and unique contribution literature and creative arts can make to an exploration of oil given the epistemological, imaginative, and embodied capacities of literature as a medium. As LeMenager explains:

> the petroleum infrastructure has become embodied memory and habitus for modern humans, insofar as everyday events such as driving or feeling the summer heat or asphalt on the soles of one's feet are incorporating practices . . . decoupling human corporeal memory from the infrastructures that have sustained it may be the primary challenge for ecological narrative in the service of human species survival beyond the twenty-first century.
>
> (26)

It is in this regard that drama/theatre and literature more broadly can play a crucial role, that is, not merely as a surface for the registration of the political-economic logics and dynamics of the extraction and production of oil and perpetuation of oil hegemony but also a material-agential space of intervention into the socio-symbolic order, a space not only for exploring the lived and unlived effects of oil on the body, mind, and imagination and relational dimensions of the subject; but also for practicing post-oil economies, selfhoods, and ecological relationalities at the level of social-cultural and artistic imagination (see Geo 2016). The aforementioned are among the focal points of this book in its extended three-volume scope.

Despite persistent market upheavals and the wide acknowledgement of a planetary ecological crisis instigated by the expanding consumption of hydrocarbons, the alarming fact, as scientists alert us, is that there are no realistic alternatives to crude oil (or natural gas) on the immediate horizon. "Crude oil", Hitchcock thus notes, "remains a dominant symbol of contemporary global capitalism for now".[18] The reifying cultural logic of oil as a commodity has affected not only the knowledge of the self, nation, nature, and the world, but also the means and modes of such knowing: "oil dependency is not just an economic attachment but appears as a kind of cognitive compulsion that mightily prohibits alternatives to its utility as a commodity and as an array of cultural signifiers".[19] The role of oil in the production and determination of selfhood and nationhood would be more palpably perceived if we were to consider that the nation, as Anderson

*Introduction* 5

and Wenzel both posit, is not only a polity but also an ecology or life-world. Literary representations of the political ecology of oil can reveal how "national imaginings . . . also depend on the very materiality of the nation as a life-sustaining habitat – on differing modalities of configuring the metabolism between society and nature".[20] More importantly, however, beyond the imagining of the nation, "nationalised petroleum produces a state (as the owner of the means of production) that . . . mediates the social relations by which oil is exploited . . . and . . . is simultaneously granted access to the world market".[21]

Humanity's fundamental dependence on oil has not been confined to the industrial, economic, and social aspects of life, but has rather come to assume psychological and emotive-affective dimensions too. One such dimension is to be found in the ostensibly abstract ideas of freedom and selfhood. As Szeman observes: "Despite being a concrete thing, oil animates and enables all manner of abstract categories, including freedom, mobility, growth, entrepreneurship, and the future in an essential way".[22] Significantly, this profound attachment does not involve an attachment to the substance itself but rather to "all of the things that oil makes possible".[23] Discerning the "ultra-deep"[24] nature of this dependence-attachment, LeMenager describes this dynamic in terms of "loving oil" – albeit qualifying it as a "bad love".[25] The modifier "bad" can be construed here as involving disastrous and detrimental moral, existential, and ontological implications, not only for humanity and nature but for social and interpersonal relations. This affective relationship, however, as our exploration of the selected works of petro-drama will demonstrate, can be toxic, not only due to the nature of oil itself but also because of both the traumatic and categorical conflating the finite with the infinite and of the sometimes uneven dynamics and irrational means through which oil is extracted, produced, abstracted, and consumed.

Drawing on Latour's idea of "natureculture"[26] (designating the "inevitable intermixture of the self-generating (organic) and the made"), LeMenager pushes the argument concerning the vital and pervasive role of oil, particularly in the late capitalist, technologically advanced Western societies, to the point where she contends: "the human body has become, in the wealthier parts of the world, a petroleum natureculture".[27] Furthermore, as many scholars have noted, petroleum products provide the supplementary materiality for a neoliberal cultural politics of "life".[28] As Huber notes, the most salient manifestation of this neoliberal cultural politics of subjectivity is discernible in the hegemonic promotion of "entrepreneurial life", both as the norm and the ideal image of citizen-subject. The rise of this neoliberal hegemony accompanied by increasing suburbanization, single-family homeownership, and widespread automobility in the post-World War II United States and, more broadly, in the global north – all enabled by cheap fossil fuel garnered under duress from around the world (particularly countries "peripheral" to the world

## 6 Introduction

system or "zones of sacrifice"). Finally, oil has been the primary cause of major wars and revolutions across the world over the last five decades: the revolution in Libya (1970), the revolution in Iran (1979), the war between Arabs and Israelis (1973), between Iraq and Iran (1980–1988), between Iraq and Kuwait (1990), between America and Iraq (First Gulf War 1991), along with the USA's invasion of Iraq (Iraq War 2003). These issues, coupled with economic and environmental crises across the world, make oil the burning issue of our time.

Oil, importantly, is an overdetermined material replete with structural contradictions or aporias. The Drummers' reportage-like description of oil – in Duncan McLean's *Julie Allardyce* (1999) – sheds light on some of these aporetic attributes:

> Oil is god. / Oil is power. / Oil is the devil. / Oil is the biggest of the world's big industries. . . . Oil is used to light the fuels of hell; / . . . Oil is the blood of the living planet / . . . Oil is John D. Rockefeller. Oil is Samuel Samuels, Henri Deterding . . . Calouste Gulbenkian, Josef Stalin, Saddam / . . . Oil is me. / Oil is you.
>
> (34)

Whilst I will elaborate on some salient instances of these aporias, suffice it here to indicate one of them. Whilst oil incarnates both the historical and the transhistorical times (given its formation over millennia preceding human history), and even as it has been the most historically invested and determining energy resource (or commodity) in modern and contemporary history, revealingly, "oil" has often been utilized as "the vehicle of escape – from history, from others, from oneself, from nature" (Willmott 2017, 194). Willmott proceeds to add a crucial feature of oil which is resonant with my identification of its aporetic features – including oil as the impossible object of desire and oil as *objet petit a*. As he argues: "Oil is totemic held in fear and reverence, in a society devoted to virtual and violent pleasures and addicted to amnesiac drugs" (Willmott 2017, 194).

What distinguishes oil from other energy regimes and resource-phases in human history, however, is the extent, scope, and depth to which it has come to penetrate, permeate, and constitute our civilizational, social-cultural, and technological infrastructures, logics, and logistics, but, more ontologically, the meaning and value of the human as we hegemonically know and live it. As Vaclav Smil points out,

> lessons of the past energy transitions may not be particularly useful for appraising and handicapping the coming energy transition, because it will be exceedingly difficult to restructure the modern high-energy industrial and post-industrial civilization on the basis of non-fossil – that is, overwhelmingly renewable – fuels and flows.
>
> (2010, 105)

*Introduction*   7

This feature has come not only to accord oil a unique and hard-to-supersede status, but to pose a daunting challenge to imagining and conceptualizing alternative energy cultures and non-oil-dependent human futures. A consequent concern of the cultural critics (such as Szeman, LeMenager, Diamanti, and other critics of petrocultures) has thus been to envisage and conceptualize the conditions of possibility of a transition beyond fossil-dependent horizons of meaning and being. That is, they strive to, psychologically and existentially, wean the people (particularly Western people and their modes of consciousness and identity) away from oil-addiction (social-cultural modes of communication, knowledge, relationality, and identification) towards alternative, non-fossil-fuel paradigms. It is with this attribute of oil in mind that Peter Hitchcock refers to "oil's generative law", by which he means that it is "everywhere and obvious[;] it must be opaque or otherwise fantastic" (87).

This energy dependency (on oil) has long been elided from the cultural imagination and historical consciousness through various hegemonic means, including media and public discourse. Jennifer Wenzel, in the Introduction to *Fueling Culture*, calls energy "a great not-said" in the cultural productions of the twentieth century and beyond (Imre et al. 2017, 11); and Vivasvan Soni refers to the "unsignifying opacity" of energy in critical and cultural discourses (2017, 133). Yaeger, by the same token, wonders whether "energy invisibilities may constitute different kinds of erasures" (2011, 309). Notably, Yaeger coins the term "energy unconscious" as a way of probing the presence and absence of energy within a given text or generic form (2011, 309). Yaeger also underscores the role of energy/oil as a force field, both at local (personal and textual) and global (social-cultural) levels: "energy sources also enter texts as fields of force that have causalities outside (or in addition to) class conflicts and commodity wars" (309). The question of the near-invisibility of oil has not only been posited as a symptom of the late capitalist petroculture, but has proved to pose aesthetic and epistemological challenges for both creative writers and critical thinkers in their attempt to ponder oil in all its socio-historical and infrastructural complexity. Andreas Malm, for instance, couches this as a "crisis of the imagination", caused by the material fugitiveness and infrastructural disguise of oil (Malm, "This Is the Hell That I Have Heard Of", 126.). Ursula Biemann discerns "this level of abstraction in the representation of oil as yet another way to keeping it firmly in the hands of market dynamics" (8).[29] In their petro-capitalist approach, Andrew Pendakis and Sheena Wilson accentuate that "the problem of visualization . . . is not specific to oil, but one politically structural to a system that is at once spectacularly consumerist and fully globalized on the level of production" (Pendakis and Wilson, "Sight, Site, Cite", 4).

Analogous to the social-cultural (and even historical) invisibility of oil indicated previously, oil seems to have remained the glaring "invisible"

8  *Introduction*

in modern and contemporary Anglo-American drama until very recently. In keeping with the rise in public awareness of ecological questions and environmental issues, and along with their conspicuous media coverage, there has been an upsurge of various dramatic trends and theatrical forms seeking to contribute to the discourse on climate change, global warming, the relationship between human and nonhuman beings, and also between nature/ecosystem and technology/science. In these Anglo-American works, the foregoing issues are particularly approached and articulated through the discourse of the Anthropocene. This is attested to by a tidal rise in dramatic works that revolve around environmental-ecological issues. Yet, despite this growing interest, there has been a dearth of plays taking oil as their focal point. Oil drama – what I will call "Petro-Drama" – has indeed, until very recently, been conspicuous by its absence from the stage. In the context of the European and Anglo-American drama, in addition to Ella Hickson's *Oil*, there have been barely more than ten other works which, to varying degrees, tackle the question of energy and energy politics, namely *Konjunktur* (1928) and *Oil Field* (1932) by Leo Lania and *Petroleuminseln* (or *Oil Islands*) (1927) by Lion Feuchtwanger, John McGrath's *The Cheviot, the Stag and the Black, Black Oil* (early 1970s) and *Boom* (1977), Duncan McLean's *Julie Allardyce* (1993), Leigh Fondakowski's *Spill* (2014), Annabel Soutar's *The Watershed* (2016), Clare Duffy's *Arctic Oil* (2018), Sulayman Al-Bassam's *Petrol Station* (2018), a fascinating play: *Crude: An Exploration* (2016) by Ben Harrison (produced by the Scottish company Grid Iron), along with a whole host of American plays on oil. This volume undertakes an exploration of *Konjunktur* (1 and 2), *Oil Field*, and *Oil Islands*. The second volume has been dedicated to the analysis of the remaining plays indicated earlier. And the third volume is dedicated to the scrutiny of works of petro-drama from Persian, Arab, and African dramatic canons.

Nevertheless, the neglect of the vital relevance of oil to the modes of subjective-political economy, and to the modes of social-cultural relationality of lived experience in contemporary life, does not betoken a lesser degree of socio-cultural or political urgency or significance – at least for the Anglo-American public and life. Instead, I argue, it demonstrates the symptomatic invisibility of oil from literary and dramatic discourse. Indeed, "the history of oil", as Amitav Ghosh – writing in 1992 on the "missed encounter" between oil and the modern American novel – contends, "is a matter of embarrassment verging on the unspeakable, the pornographic" (1992, 29). Peter Hitchcock compounds the issue of the aforementioned missed encounter by adding: "But what if the very structure of the oil encounter compels the suppression of a missed encounter?" (2010, 89). In making the latter statement, Hitchcock hints at the traumatic structure of the oil encounter and, to derive our terms from Jacques Lacan, the role of oil as an *objet petit a* in such an encounter. Whilst a number of literary scholars have sought to rectify Ghosh's limited vision/

account of works of petrofiction by drawing up an extended roster of works and presenting analysis of them, such an attempt has been largely absent in the field of drama studies. This book is the first full-fledged and extended attempt to fill this lacuna. What the selected works of petro-drama under scrutiny in this three-volume book seek to present is the frame of this missed encounter. These plays accomplish this, by, on the one hand, exposing the political economy, cultural politics, and ethics of the traumatic encounter/experience or touché in the Real of oil's meaning, both for the peripheral countries and Western modernity, and, on the other, by showing how the political economy of oil in globalization is contingent on a transnational division of labour. As Hitchcock explains: "The unpleasant truths of wars that kill innocents and produce environmental disasters are much easier to explicate than the touché stitching these truths together into the fabric of the modern state" (2010, 87).

Accordingly, deriving some of its mooring points from the literary-critical possibilities propounded by the Energy Humanities, the present volume responds to Yaeger's injunction by conjoining her emphasis on the recognition of the aesthetic, historical, and epistemological ramifications of incorporating energy sources into the genre of literature and the literary discourse with the conceptual rubrics provided by the world-ecology and materialist ecocritical perspectives. In so doing, this book posits the necessity of understanding oil as an agent, a world-ecological force, and an energy resource extracted from the peripheries and frontiers, coupled with the cultural forms and values with which oil is imbricated, in terms of the uneven extractivist logic and structural relations of capitalism as a world system.

## II. From the Anthropocene to the Capitalocene

As a term coined by the ecologist Eugene Stoermer in the 1980s and popularized by the Nobel-winning chemists Paul Crutzen and Will Steffen in the 2000s, Anthropocene is utilized to declare the end of a geological era (Holocene) and to name a new anthropogenic reality which is simultaneously geological, historical, and ontological (see Zalasiewicz et al. 2017, 55; also see Lewis and Maslin 2018). In stratigraphic terms, the proposition of the term has been based on the evidence showing how the sedimentary patterns of the last 250 years are distinct from the antecedent geological period (the last 10,000 years: Holocene). Anthropocene designates how this new reality – and the sheer scale of biophysical change – is a consequence of devastating upheavals instigated by human agency/intervention on the planet and natural world. Attested by the use of "anthropo" as the root word in the term "Anthropocene", this human-wrought reality is unprecedented since in all the previous periodization paradigms of geological ages the cause or the agency underlying the planetary transformations was ascribed to natural causes. The term

10 *Introduction*

"Anthropocene", in the formal geological sense of the word, was defined by the Working Group on the Anthropocene (2016, n.p.). Their definition is predicated on the stratigraphic signals which indicate that the Anthropocene is, will be, and will have been a distinct stratigraphic unit whose distinctiveness stems precisely from its being anthropogenic in nature.[30] Some of these are enumerated in Crutzen's rather elegiac litany:

> About 30–50% of the planet's land surface is exploited by humans. Tropical rainforests disappear at a fast pace, releasing carbon dioxide and strongly increasing species extinction. Dam building and river diversion have become commonplace. . . . Energy use has grown 16-fold during the twentieth century, causing 160 million tonnes of atmospheric sulphur dioxide emissions per year, more than twice the sum of its natural emissions. More nitrogen fertilizer is applied in agriculture than is fixed naturally in all terrestrial ecosystems; nitric oxide production by the burning of fossil fuel and biomass also overrides natural emissions.
>
> (2002, 23)

Consequently, as climate scientists explain, by "unwittingly destroying the artificial but time-honored distinction between natural and human histories, . . . the human being has become something much larger than the simple biological agent that he or she always has been. Humans now wield a geological force" (Chakrabarty 2009, 206). Ever since its introduction, however, there have emerged intense debates not only concerning the efficacy and validity of the term "Anthropocene", but also some other facets of the term – including the questions of agency and periodization at stake in it. As regards the latter problematic, for instance, some literary and critical theorists have discerned the various ways in which the notion of the Anthropocene compounds the hegemonic conception of time/history since the advent of modernity – namely, history/time as following a linear-progressive and teleological trajectory. Jeremy Davies, for instance, argues how the concept of the Anthropocene "requires a certain indirectness [because] one must imaginatively transfer oneself to the far future" to see "how readily discernible [environmental change] will be millions of years from now" (66–67).[31] Amitav Ghosh presents a more materialist vision of this temporal-historical complication fostered by an Anthropocenic lens: "The Anthropocene has reversed the temporal order of modernity" because "those at the margins are now the first to experience the future that awaits us all" (2016).

Relatedly, and further compounding the definition, scope, and implications of the notion of the Anthropocene, the ways and methods of marking or determining a date for the commencement of this geological era have proved volatile and a moot point. Theorists of the Anthropocene have propounded numerous different historical narratives with their own

*Introduction* 11

respective ascriptions of agency and time (regarding the historical point of origin) of the Anthropocene in their attempt to identify the historical, political-economic, ecological, and ethical implications of the term. As specifically regards the dating and periodization of the Anthropocene, there have been four proposals that have gained wider consensus and authorization among scholars. Paul Crutzen proposes the first Industrial Revolution as the start date of the Anthropocene where alterations of the earth system (including relentless rise of atmospheric carbon dioxide levels) become quantifiably visible. More specifically, Crutzen refers to James Watt's invention of the double action steam engine in 1784 as an event that instigated the transition to coal fuel that powered the Industrial Revolution. In Crutzen and Steffen's quantitatively based approach – where the role of technological innovation is given methodological-causal primacy over capitalist dynamics – the criterion for the determination of epochal-geological shifts is primarily "energetic efficiency". As they observe: "industrial societies as a rule use four or five times as much energy as did agrarian ones, which in turn used three or four times as much as did hunting and gathering societies" (616). The Anthropocene Working Group proposes the post-Second World War period as a more appropriate marker thereby attributing determining agency to the so-called Great Acceleration, and the concomitant rampancy of an expansive consumer capitalism that exceedingly spans the globe. Similarly, since 2017 the World Geological Society has concurred on the date of 1945, set from around the end of World War II, because it marked the beginning of the Great Acceleration, the explosion of the atom bombs, and the intensification of nuclear activities by the competing superpowers of the 20th century. Finally, proposing a more politically-economically oriented account of the Anthropocene, Lewis and Maslin locate their genealogical account of the Anthropocene in a colonial-imperial context by identifying 1610 as the date for its onset; a date that marks a historical juncture in its reference to the European conquest of the Americas and the emergence of colonialism and global trade.[32] And there are also accounts where even the most ostensibly innocent and least aggressive forms of resource extraction and nature cultivation (such as farming and human settlement) are deemed as contributing factors to the emergence of the Holocene. For instance, the Ruddiman hypothesis contends that pre-industrial agriculture (nearly 8,000 years ago) emitted enough greenhouse gases to preclude a new glacial episode and contributed to the moderation and stability of the Holocene.

One of the most conspicuous deficiencies of the term Anthropocene is the forms of agency encoded in it and the narratives evoked by it. Accordingly, many of the debates concerning the Anthropocene revolve around the identification of a more accurate sense of agency. For instance, whilst confirming the characterization of the contemporary geological-natural alterations as "anthropic", scholars such as Ziarek find the term

## 12  Introduction

Anthropocene at best flawed since it does not reflect technology as a crucial constitutive element. Therefore, he suggests some hybrid alternatives such as the "Techno-Anthropocene or the Techanthropocene" (9; Ziarek 2011). The introduction of the term Anthropocene has from the outset been coterminous with the recognition of its ethical implications. As Jason Kelly acutely notes, the term Anthropocene "serves the dual functions as an 'is' and an 'ought'" (2018, 11). As he further explains, the Anthropocene

> nearly always serves as a metanarrative of modernity – a narrative in which energy- and resource-intensive industrialization and capitalism have been accompanied by population booms, increased flows of goods and peoples, the central role of nation-states, and demands for improvements in quality of life.
>
> (Kelly 2018, 11)

Elaborating on other ethical implications of the Anthropocene, Van Dooren explains that

> the Anthropocene is inescapably bound up with an ethical demand: it announces our need to inhabit this world in a spirit of mindful accountability, not just to those that happen to live amongst us now but rather to all those multispecies generations who have come before and all those who might yet still come.
>
> (Van Dooren 2012, 232)

The questions of agency and ethics raised by the Anthropocene includes two corollaries. First, the term "Anthropocene" accords primacy to the human as the agent or cause of the climate catastrophe, thereby inadvertently reiterating the violence inflicted by humans on nonhuman natures at conceptual, ontological, and biophysical levels. Eileen Crist indicts the "narcissistic overtones" that the "naming of an epoch after ourselves" (2016, 24) carries, indicating how such a gesture is self-reflexively "anthropocentric" and mutually co-extensive with the "worldview that generated the Anthropocene . . . in the first place" (2016, 14). The second problem as discerned by the eco-critics is the problem involved in the high-stakes "we" inherent in the notion of the Anthropocene both in terms of its semantic content (the "transcendent, humanistic "we" it signifies) and historical-cultural associations. In its evocation of a general, neutral, and collective "we", the Anthropocene has been contended to be ethically disarming, historically-geographically misleading, and economically-ecologically diffuse. In Anthropocene thought, agency becomes particularly high stakes – particularly given the specific and different manifestations of the social-economic and ecological effects of the Anthropocene in each geographical and social setting context. The Anthropocene reveals the

*Introduction* 13

detrimental effect of not the Anthropos or humanity but a geographically specific and historically clear part of humanity. The latter critique is worth a brief elaboration since it is highly consonant with the idea of Capitalocene. In brief, according to various critics of the term who have approached it from various political, social, and conceptual/philosophical perspectives, the term Anthropocene is beset with two fundamental problems: first, its erasure of difference at various levels; and secondly, the overweening pride tacit in the term. In consequence of these two deficiencies, the scholars argue, the term Anthropocene (however unwittingly) reiterates the ecological, socio-historical, and ontological violence it intends to critique and tackle by centralizing the human over the nonhuman and sub-human and erasing ethical, historical, and agential differences.

Two prominent critical voices who have acutely elaborated on the inadequacies besetting the Anthropocene have been Chakrabarty and Nixon. Both scholars repudiate the Anthropocene narrative of the species-level, singular "human" as responsible for the earth's deteriorated condition and, instead, accentuate the necessity of taking into account the root cause of such a multi-scalarly uneven dynamics, that is, the prevailing political economy of capitalism. Significantly, Chakrabarty argues that a critique of capital in and of itself is "insufficient to account" for the processes of the earth's changes, as these require "geological and paleoclimatological knowledge" (Szeman et al. 2017, 41). He notes that what specialists need to dwell on, however, is the "uneven responsibility" it places on the generic term "man" – the Anthropos being attributed with a geological force, a fact, he notes, that needs to be addressed within a framework of justice and away from the levelling, universalizing tendencies (42; see also Klein 2014, 1–28). This universalizing discourse of the Anthropocene ramifies in at least two ways. First is the entity humanity – or Anthropos – around which (or more precisely, around whom) the Anthropocene discourse is organized. It is a term much despised, notes Chakrabarty, because of its unresolved historical baggage and "ideological trappings" (42). Chakrabarty takes issue with the universalizing predilections and their moral ramification/extrapolation tacit in the discourse of the Anthropocene that the whole humanity should be held accountable for the resource-extraction and resource-consumption activities and habits that have instigated and precipitated irreversible geological-ontological alterations to the biosphere and the earth's climate.

Chakrabarty identifies three fundamental problems – ontological, structural, and historical – that beset the notion of Anthropocene. At a structural level, the term Anthropocene occludes and implies a systemic violence and misrepresentation – hence Chakrabarty's indication of the "ideologically suspect" trappings attached to the Anthropocene (2021, 17). Whilst acknowledging the Anthropocene as "a crime", he accentuates the necessity of exposing the geographical-historical roots, causes,

## 14  Introduction

and agents of such a crime. As he contends, the ostensible democratization of this crime (committed by a few industrialized countries) by accentuating the necessity of equal distribution of its moral-historical burden and its ecological-existential consequences amongst all nations (thereby including the poor in the global south which barely had any contribution to its emergence during the 19th and most of the 20th centuries) is merely a reiteration of the same imperial-colonial logics and another instance of epistemic, representational, and historical violence inflicted by the core countries on the peripheries (2017, 61–66). At a historical level, the problem with the Anthropocene's assumption of humanity as one unified whole or monolithic constituency is its elision of the ontological and social-economic divisions and differences between individual subjects and national-local levels and scales along the lines of race, gender, class-traversing modern and contemporary histories (2017, 36–41). In his distribution of moral-ecological responsibility on a global scale and within a longue durée span, Chakrabarty adds a third group of people – the other (non-Western) humans – who were chiefly mere spectators to the "men's" systemic and cyclical onslaught on the earth and its resources. This is consonant with Rob Nixon's argument that "homo sapiens may constitute a singular actor [in the Anthropocene] . . . but it is not a unitary one" (2017, 44). As Chakrabarty more specifically elucidates, only "one fifth of humanity" (2021, 57), chiefly concentrated in limited parts of the global north, and not humanity at large as a universal category and globally extended phenomenon, is mainly responsible for the climate catastrophes characterizing the Anthropocene. Chakrabarty's contention alerts us to a crucial point egregiously neglected by the science and politics of global warming who either abstract, de-subjectify, and hence mystify the fundamental material changes in the earth's climate by analyzing and presenting them through the processes of charting and scientific modelling, or promote the techne or the instrumental rationality of the Anthropos or Homos by valorizing scientific methods (such as bioengineering) – rather than systemic or structural alterations at infrastructural, political-economic, and social levels – as the remedy for the current ecological disasters (see Jon 2015; see also Orsato 2016). And, finally, at an ontological level, "the science of anthropogenic global warming has doubled the figure of the human – [now] we have to think of the two figures of the human simultaneously: the human-human and the nonhuman-human" (Chakrabarty 2012, 11).

As both Nixon and Chakrabarty aver, another instance of structural inequality inherent to the term "Anthropocene" concerns not merely its causes, but its aggravated effects on a certain portion of humanity due to the latter's lack of equal access to the means of mitigating or reducing the devastating effects of the climate catastrophes. Nixon posits the recognition and establishment of the dialectical relationship between the human and nonhuman (the social-cultural and the natural), the local and the global, the individual and the collective, and the core and the periphery as

Introduction 15

essential to a more rigorous and nuanced conceptualization of the genealogy as well as the moral and historical implications of the Anthropocene. Hence the necessity of pondering the ways in which "the Anthropocene's grand species perspective" can be adopted without suppressing the "much more fractured story that acknowledges dramatic disparities in planet-altering powers." (Nixon, "Promise and Pitfalls" 2018, 8; Mitman et al. 2018). He articulates this problem in the ensuing terms: a "crucial challenge facing us is this: how do we tell two large stories that can often seem in tension with each other, a convergent story and a divergent one?" (2011, 8). Nixon proceeds to elaborate a twofold solution to this quandary: "first, a collective story about humanity's impacts that will be legible in the earth's geophysical systems for the millennia to come. Second, a much more fractured story that acknowledges dramatic disparities in planet-altering powers" (Nixon 2017, 8). Nixon posits the necessity of negotiating "the complex dynamic between a shared geomorphic narrative and increasingly unshared resources" for elaborating a more nuanced and credible conception of the Anthropocene thinking (2017, 8).

Equally crucially, many critics have accentuated the absence of a structural critique as one of the main drawbacks of the Anthropocene position. Jason Moore has proposed the notion of the *Capitalocene* as an alternative, to account for the role of capital in forcing anthropogenic changes, whereas Anna Tsing's Plantationocene explores the legacies of colonial land use in contemporary resource extraction. Moore underscores the necessity of developing a conceptual (dialectical and historical-materialist) framework that situates the anthropogenic effects on the earth's ecology within a critique of capitalism in its longue durée cycles of accumulation and abstraction. The emphasis on "history in nature" rather than on a dichotomous view of "history and nature", is also crucial to Jason Moore's formulation of the "ecological" as offering "a holistic perspective on the society-environment relation" (2011, 114).[33] But for Moore, such a perspective also questions how "master processes of colonialism, etc." remain "resolutely social", always "ceded to the Cartesian binary" (2011, 115–116). As one of its conceptual premises, and in keeping with its world-ecological approach, this book deems Capitalocene a far more rigorous, efficacious, and holistic concept in tackling the intertwined subtleties and complex dynamics of oil in its various manifestations and its various stages of extraction, production, evaluation, and consumption. This valorization of the Capitalocene over and above Anthropocene chiefly arises from numerous structural inadequacies besetting the latter – as already extensively elaborated by numerous scholars. Whilst rehearsing the details of the debate between the two critical approaches is beyond the scope and economy of this introduction, suffice it here to succinctly delineate the pivotal characteristics of the Capitalocene in conjunction with the two concomitant notions of the world-ecological and metabolic rift.

16  *Introduction*

Accordingly, it is my argument here that the notion of Anthropocene due to the inherent flaws delineated earlier is an inadequate means of achieving such a twofold aim in the exploration of various facets of an energy resource that is a capitalist commodity through and through: oil. Instead, as I will explain, I will delve into the logics and dynamics involved in oil (including its extraction, production, and consumption), along with its ecological and other effects, through the lens of the notion of Capitalocene as a far more rigorous and potent conceptual and historical framework. Notably, with regards to art and both the Capitalocene and the Anthropocene, literary critics have extensively discussed fiction, but drama/theatre remains a widely neglected genre and medium. As I will argue in Chapter 1, drama/theatre, in its temporal and ontological mode of existence (its evanescence and its eventual nature), offers a unique epistemological and phenomenological opportunity to think through, and imagine beyond, the pressures and challenges of the Capitalocene as well. In brief, and as will be demonstrated in this volume, thinking of oil and other fossil fuel sites in relation to the *Capitalocene* involves thinking of the environments where the voracious overreach of human agents from the core areas of the imperial-colonial and capitalist system (the Global North and more recently China, Russia, and India) has been most extensive and visible.

## A.  *The Capitalocene*

The Capitalocene is Jason Moore's term proposed as a corrective alternative to the inadequacies of the notion of the "Anthropocene". Moore's sustained and rigorous critique of the Anthropocene is directed at various facets of the term along with the historical, ontological, and structural assumptions underpinning it. Suffice it here, however, to indicate two pivotal instances of such flaws. Firstly, whilst acknowledging that the "Anthropocene helpfully poses the question of Nature/Society dualism", Moore finds such a conceptual move inadequate and adds that it "cannot resolve that dualism in favor of a new synthesis" ("Anthropocenes & The Capitalocene Alternative" 74). Secondly, identifying the politics of the Anthropocene as "an anti-politics in Ferguson's sense", or, more strictly, one which is "resolutely committed to the erasure of capitalism and the capitalogenesis of planetary crisis" (74), Moore proceeds to explain in what respects the Anthropocene proves also politically inadequate:

> Popular Anthropocene is but the latest of a long series of environmental concepts whose function is to deny the multi-species violence and inequality of capitalism and to assert that the problems created by capital are the responsibility of all humans.

(74)

Nevertheless, Moore contends that the Anthropocene cannot adequately ponder the expansive historical questions it raises because it remains conceptually bound to Cartesian dualism – above all, the duality of Nature/Society – according to which nature and humanity are ontologically discrete (2016, 84). Similarly, the other facet of Moore's critique of the Anthropocene is his contention that the Anthropocene tends to produce narratives of historical change in which humanity, a "homogenous acting unit" or an undifferentiated whole (the Anthropos), is identified as the propelling force behind environmental crises, while questions of capitalism, class, and power are elided or occluded (2015, 170).

Recasting the past five centuries as the Capitalocene, the "age of capital", Moore establishes two intertwined arguments. First, the exploitation of labour-power depends on a more expansive process: the appropriation of unpaid work/energy delivered by nature, colonies, and women. Second, accumulation by appropriation turns on the capacity of state-capital-science complexes to make nature legible. Moore's argument, in this regard, shares notable imbrications with Wallerstein's world-systemic critique of capital in its various historical-structural permutations. More specifically, Moore's argument here is highly akin to what Wallerstein calls an "unequal exchange" (Christofis 2019, 4) and "systematic transfer of surplus" (ibid., 4) meaning the boundary between the "labour intensive" and "capital intensive" come together, unveiling the social and economic inequalities in the core.[34]

Taking the Cartesian revolution and the "age of exploration" in the Atlantic world as one of the historical junctures in the beginning of a new cycle of resource extraction, Moore explains how this period ushered in a new episteme and political-economic discourse whereby knowledge production and environment-making both produce and are produced by processes of primitive accumulation and imperialism. Historically, relations of appropriation facilitated the expanded accumulation of abstract social labour. Prominent components of the longue durée history of such surplus extraction practices are cheap labour and cheap nature. For Moore, at the heart of capitalism's law of value is the contradictory dialectic of exploitation and appropriation. Gleaning his insights from Marx, Moore is concerned with how the capacity to do work (by human and extra-human natures) is transformed into value, measured in terms of socially necessary labour time. However, such relations of exploitation operate properly insofar as their reproduction costs can be held in check (Moore 2015, 16). According to Moore, labour exploitation is contingent upon "the historical-geographical connections between wage-work and its necessary conditions of expanded reproduction. These conditions depend on massive contributions of unpaid work, outside the commodity system but necessary to its generalization" (2015, 16–17). Hence, in Moore's account, the contradiction at the core of capitalism's law of

## 18  *Introduction*

value (between exploitation and appropriation) hinges on the disproportionality between "'paid work,' reproduced through the cash nexus, and 'unpaid work,' reproduced outside the circuit of capital but indispensable to its expanded reproduction" (Moore 2016, 92). Given capitalism's tendency toward rising labour productivity (which implies accelerating biophysical throughput) the system "must appropriate ever-larger spheres of uncapitalized nature" (Moore 2016, 92). More explicitly establishing the correlation between nature and labour in terms of the nearly identical and coterminous extractive logics to which they are both subjected under capitalism, Moore writes, "Great advances in labor productivity, expressing the rising material throughput of an average hour of work, have been possible through great expansions of the ecological surplus" (2015, 96). He further elucidates the other facets of this multivalent extractive process thus: "the whole system works . . . because capital pays for only one set of costs, and works strenuously to keep all other costs off the books. Centrally, these are the costs of reproducing labor-power, food, energy, and raw materials" (Moore 2016, 92). While such costs can be externalized in the short-term, Moore notes that "ultimately new sources of work/energy must be found, and appropriated. Thus, every long accumulation cycle unfolds through new commodity frontiers" (2015, 95–96).

According to Moore, not only is the Nature/Society dualism inherent in processes of extractive violence and exploitation carried out by modern capitalism as a historical project with immanently uneven political-economic logics. Such Nature/Society duality also occludes the history of the modern world (2016, 79). In a bid to transcend the impasse of Cartesian dualism (endemic to the capitalist practices), Moore advances a "world-ecology" approach. Central to Moore's world-ecological approach is the concept of oikeiosis, denoting "the relation through which humans act – and are acted upon by the whole of nature – in our environment-making" (Moore 2015, 4). Situating the oikeiosis at the core of his narrative strategy, Moore reconceptualizes historical change in terms of a double-internality, couched in chiasmatic terms and relations: "humanity inside nature, nature inside humanity" (Moore 2016, 79), to illuminate how capitalism works through nature (and vice versa). Therefore, by articulating his argument in terms of this immanently chiasmatic dynamics – or the double-internality – Moore presents a world-historical reconstruction not of the Anthropocene but of the Capitalocene. As he explains:

> My central thesis is that capitalism is historically coherent – if "vast but weak" – from the long sixteenth century; co-produced by human and extra-human natures in the web of life; and cohered by a "law of value" that is a "law" of Cheap Nature. At the core of this law is the ongoing, radically expansive, and relentlessly innovative quest to turn the work/energy of the biosphere into capital (value-in-motion).
> (Moore 2015, 14)

Notably, Moore dispels any reductionist conception of the nature of Capitalocene by strenuously underscoring that capital's law of value is not solely economic, for its "accumulation (as abstract labor) is historically materialized though the development of scientific and symbolic regimes necessary to identify, quantify, survey, and otherwise enable not only the advance of commodity production but also the ever-more expansive appropriation of cheap natures" (2015, 191). Premised on this point, and expanding the historical-ecological scope of his analysis of the Capitalocene far beyond the historical primacy Crutzen et al. accord to the 18th-century Industrial Revolution, Moore instead draws attention to antecedent transformations (of land, labour, science, and knowledge) during the "long 16th century" that laid the ground (by establishing a globally oriented capitalist extractive logics) for the emergence of the "Age of Coal" (2015, 191). Elaborating on the historical and structural dynamic of such a globally extended process, Moore articulates three interrelated historical processes (ca. 1450–1640) pivotal to the rise of industrialization: (1) primitive accumulation; (2) new forms of territorial power and imperialism; and (3) new ways of knowing and making the world. Moore stresses the dialectical relation between these three historical processes as science, the economy, and the state emerge to serve capital accumulation (2016, 85–86).

To Moore, conceiving of capitalism as a civilization – that, for the first time, "mobilized a metric of wealth premised on labor rather than land productivity" (2016, 110) – enables us to account for the most conspicuous transformations in the early modern landscape – ranging from the appropriation and exhaustion of forests and soil in Brazil, Scandinavia, and Poland in the long 17th century; and from the sugar and slave frontiers in the New World, to the expansion of the fossil fuel frontier from the 19th century onward (Moore 2016, 110). Moore first delineates his account of the dynamics between capitalism and nature by characterizing it negatively, to wit, by elucidating what it is "not". Initially, Moore repudiates a functionalist account of capitalism's production of and extractive relation with nature. As he explains: "Capitalism does not produce an external 'historical' nature according to its needs. . . . Nor does capitalism simply respond to external changes in nature" (200). Moore then proceeds to identify his dialectical account of this relational dynamics thus: "successive phases of capitalist development are at once cause and consequence of fundamental reorganizations of world-ecology" (200). He then specifies the epistemological and political-economic advantages of such a dialectal method: "Both 'capital' and 'nature' acquire new historical properties through these reorganizations: this allows us to give the differentiated unity – historical capitalism/historical nature – real historical content" (200). Further accentuating the indelible intertwinements between human history and nature, Moore elucidates how these "reorganizations" take effect and unfold through the "interpenetrating

20   *Introduction*

patterns of planetary change – forged over Braudel's 'very longue durée' of geological time – and capitalism's configurations of power and production forged across long centuries of accumulation" (200). Rejecting a dualistic account of history, nature, or capitalism and establishing a causal link between "climate and the rise and demise of great civilizations", Moore proposes the alternative notion of "historical nature" as a means of showing how "the layers of historical time shape each other" (200). Calling historical natures "a dance of the dialectic between part (modes of humanity) and whole (the web of life)", Moore explains how such an approach reveals the way the "cascading movements of the web of life enter into particular historical geographical configurations of power and production" (200). Positing "biosphere" as "the integument" of "human sociality", Moore cogently expounds his dialectical vision thus: "[h]istorical natures are those specific part-whole combinations in which specific 'geological, hydrographical, climatic, and [biogeographical]' conditions enter into the most intimate, and also the most expansive, domains of human history" (200).

### B.   *The World-Ecological*

The second pivotal component of Moore's theory is the notion of the "world-ecological". Moore theorizes "world-ecology" as a corollary to the notion of the world system; it refers not (necessarily) to "the ecology of the [entire] world", but rather to how capitalism

> progressively deepens the world-historical character of microlevel socio-ecologies in the interests of the ceaseless accumulation of capital. With the rise of capitalism, varied and heretofore largely isolated local and regional socio-ecological relations were incorporated into – and at the same moment became constituting agents of – a capitalist world-ecology.
>
> (Moore 2003, 447)

Indeed, one of the pivotal concepts through which Moore elaborates the uneven extractive and dualistic dynamics informing the Capitalocene is the "world-ecology" or "world-ecological" – which he identifies as a new paradigm. Moore defines this "new paradigm" as one that considers capitalism as "a way of organising nature" (2015, 2–3), that is, capitalism as a world-ecological regime of world-historical import. Moore expounds his "central thesis" for world-ecology thus:

> capitalism is historically coherent . . . from the long sixteenth century; co-produced by human and extra-human natures in the web of life; and cohered by a "law of value" that is a "law" of Cheap Nature. At the core of this law is the ongoing, radically expansive,

*Introduction* 21

and relentlessly innovative quest to turn the work/energy of the biosphere into capital (value in motion).

(14)

In his attempt to conceptualize "the historical reality of successive reorganizations of world-ecology in the capitalist era", Moore synthesizes classical Marxist and world-systems concepts (developed by Wallerstein and Giovanni Arrighi). The thrust of Moore's argument can be summarized thus: "each phase of world capitalist development is at once cause and consequence of a fundamental reorganization of world-ecology" (2015, 200). Moore calls the successive reorganizations of world-ecology by its various permutations "systemic cycles of agro-ecological transformation" (2015, 36, 55, 138, 253). For Moore, world-ecology names both "a method of bounding and bundling the human/extra-human/web of life relations" and "a framework for theorizing the manifold forms of the human experience, past and present" (2015, 36). Pivotal, here, is the jettisoning of Nature versus Society in a sophisticated new dialectical vision of "capitalism-in-nature/nature-in-capitalism" (2015, 33–37), where nature is understood as a "web of life" that includes all human and "extra-human" forms in their messily complex interrelations, and where the "web of life" must be historicized in relation to capitalist modernity and capitalism's peculiar "law of value" – that is, its creation of "Cheap Nature" (2015, 37).

Significantly, in his post-Cartesian critique of capitalism as ecological history, Moore argues that the term "ecology" should not be conflated with "the environment". Rather, ecology designates "the matrix of dialectical relationships and processes through which species (including humans) make environments and environments make species" (2011, 5; 2015, 7). In Moore's world-ecological vision, history is defined as invariably co-produced by humans alongside the rest of nature. Historical systems (such as capitalism, feudalism, or the slave-based societies of antiquity) are bundles of human and extra-human relations and activities, woven together in such a way as to instantiate definite law-like patterns of wealth, nature, and power over a long time and large space (180–181, 197–200, 208). The differently specific ways in which these natures are woven together within successive epochs are determined ultimately by the prevailing mode of production, itself constituted through a particular set of dialectical relations between human and extra-human natures. On this view, capitalism is a "world-historical matrix" that "knits together humans with the rest of nature . . . within a gravitational field of endless accumulation" (2012, 227). Accordingly, the processes through which this mode of production develops (including, say, colonization, industrialization, and financialization) are to be grasped as not merely having consequences for the environment, but as ecological projects – as both producers and products of specific forms of life- and environment-making

## 22  Introduction

(Moore 2015, 82, 291–292). Notably, the identification of nature as a "matrix" within which human activity unfolds by Moore foregrounds his insistence on the affirmation of a *dialectical unity-in-difference* – humanity-in-nature/nature-in-humanity – where neither collapses into the other to form an undifferentiated monism or holism. Moore accentuates the necessity of retaining such distinctions because humans are the only species particularly equipped with the historic capacity for environment-making whereby nature is harnessed to the dynamics of accumulating wealth and power (Moore 2015, 9).

Moore emphasizes the inadequacy of what Bourdieu calls "substantialist" thinking which, in its fetishizing conception, resources are simply deemed material "stuff". Such a substantialist approach denies the "relationality of material flows and class relations" (2015, 182) and considers "substances as prior to, and independently of, events and fields of relations", thereby enabling human exceptionalism and reifying or mystifying unpaid work/energy as "free gifts" of nature (2015, 178). By the same token, Moore contends that a world-ecological (which is always already cultural materialist) approach requires "a relational rather than substantialist" perspective since the movement of "resources, the circuits of capital, and the struggles of classes and states form a dialectical whole" (179), and "what 'counts' as a resource shifts as . . . new historical natures emerge" (196). In Moore's view, the "historiography of resource extraction has seldom taken the relational point seriously", notwithstanding resources being "actively co-produced" as "markers and creators of the historical natures that help to define the scope of opportunity and constraint in successive eras of capitalist development" (196). This world-ecological and thus necessarily relational perspective is perhaps best illustrated by his example of coal:

> By itself, coal is only a potential actant; bundled with the relations of class, empires, and appropriation in the nineteenth century however . . . it becomes a way of naming a mass commodity whose presence was felt in every strategic relation of nineteenth-century capitalism.
>
> (196)

To firmly establish the importance of resource-relations (rather than resources per se), Moore propounds a dictum: "Shut down a coal plant, and you can slow global warming for a day; shut down the relations that made the coal plant, and you can stop it for good" (172). To unravel the implications embedded in Moore's dense contention, for Moore any non-dialectical ecocritical or anti-capitalist attempt that seeks to decry the ecologically pernicious effects of a certain energy resource, particularly fossil fuels and above all, oil – whilst neglecting the more complex web or systemic dynamics that inflicts such a dispossession and destruction on human-nonhuman nature – would be inadequate: "These too – states,

*Introduction*   23

classes, commodity production and exchange – are bundles of human and extra-human nature. They are processes and projects that reconfigure the relations of humanity-in-nature, within large and small geographies alike" (Moore 181). An effective step for overcoming such historically entrenched Cartesian dualisms (of nature-culture, human-nonhuman, science-history) is the recognition of their dialectically determining relations: "geology co-produces energy regimes as historically specific bundles of relations; geology is at once subject and object" (Moore 181).

The key strengths of the world-ecological method are worth enumerating here. First, predicating his conceptual framework and historical-hermeneutic vision on the methods and insights elaborated by Immanuel Wallerstein and Giovanni Arrighi, Moore explains how world-ecology allows us to historicize capitalism's longue durée and its century-long cycles of accumulation in relation to long-wave energy and "ecological regimes" (2015, 53). Second, the world-ecological foregrounds the "commodity frontiers" (10) and "ecological surplus" (95) created, primarily, from "the Four Cheaps of labour-power, food, energy, and raw materials" (17). Third, it has a clear sense of how these and other "cheap" resources have enabled the world-historical cycles of mutation, expansion, and unabated "deepening" of capitalism's systemic "appropriation of unpaid work/energy" (29), especially through the history of imperialism. Fourth, the world-ecological offers a "worlded", webbed and multi-scalar way of grappling with human and "extra-human" relations, overturning the empty and dualist abstractions of Nature and Humans/Society that characterize capitalism's ability to plunder and exploit. And finally (for now), it recognizes that, as a system of "endless accumulation" (91), capitalism is a system of "cyclical" and "cumulative" crisis-formation (11), unfolding through world-ecological revolutions and resulting in the signal crisis of the neoliberal regime – a potentially epochal (rather than developmental) crisis because capitalism has, in effect, destroyed its own mechanisms for self-renewal.

Crucially, Moore's systemic and Capitalocene-based approach is reflected in his conception of various forms of resource crisis – above all, the crisis of the scarcity of access to cheap oil and the end of the era of "easy oil" and the advent of the "Tough Oil World".[35] Rather than confining his vision to the crisis signalled and instigated by individual resource peaks, Moore posits the current global crisis as a token of a system-wide crisis of "negative-value" (266–278). More specifically, this crisis stems from "the transition from surplus value to negative-value" where "the 'old' contradictions of depletion are meeting up with the 'new' contradictions of waste and toxification" (267). If the old contradictions comprised the problem of "peak appropriation" (105–106) – where further appropriation of cheap resources and labours are impeded by the exhaustion of capitalism's ability to appropriate what previously constituted world-ecological surplus – the new contradictions of capitalism partly arise from

24    *Introduction*

the "closure" of capitalism's geographical, ecological, and commodity/ waste frontiers – due to their saturation and undergoing metabolic rift – this crisis marks a situation where accumulated ecological debts result in diminishing returns.

Accordingly, this book argues that a Capitalocenic or world-ecological (which is inherently also world-historical) understanding of the importance of oil – an understanding which is (new) materialist, relational-dialectical, and world-systemic – potently reveals the dynamics of capitalism's total-izing logic where both old and new contradictions are revealed. A world-ecological consideration of oil and global petrocultures accomplishes this task by shedding light on the subtle yet structural ways in which the "new kind of global history" inaugurated by capitalism is inextricably intertwined with an epochal reorganization of global natures such that "varied and heretofore largely isolated local and regional socioecologi-cal relations were incorporated into – and at the same moment became constituting agents of – a capitalist world-ecology" (Moore 2003, 447).

## C.   *Metabolic Rift or Metabolic Shift?*

### 1.   *The Metabolic Rift and Its Critique*

The third pivotal component of Moore's dialectical or eco-materialist approach is the notion of "metabolic shift" – which is posited by Moore as one of the crucial ramifications of the hegemonic rule of the Capi-talocene. The notion of "metabolic shift" is indelibly linked with, and has been devised as a critical response to, the notion of "metabolic rift". "Metabolic rift" designates the effectuation of an ontological and epistemic rift in the immanent relationship between human (social) and nature (natural or extra-human) but more importantly also between some humans (from the core regions of the petro-capitalist system) and other humans (from the peripheries produced by core as zones of extraction). The notion of the "metabolic rift" has turned out to be one of the central concepts amongst contemporary critical environmental scholars and has become shorthand for capitalism's crisis-ridden relations in the web of life. Developed in preliminary form by Marx and reconstructed recently by Foster, the concept of "the metabolic rift" signifies the rupture in nutrient cycling between the country and the city in historical capital-ism. The "metabolic rift" designates the breaking of the human-nature metabolism or a rupture in the human-social relationship to nature. Two emblematic examples of the metabolic rift can be found in, first, the dis-ruption of the cycle of soil-nutrients-produce-consumption-waste-soil, and second, in the carbon cycle and the accumulation of carbon dioxide in the atmosphere. The latter, more strictly, involves the whole biosphere – arising from excessive burning of fossil fuels, industrialized agriculture, and industrial forestry practices (see Foster et al. 2010).

*Introduction* 25

John Bellamy Foster, later joined with Jason Moore, is perhaps the most prominent exegete or theorist of the notion of the "metabolic rift". Criticizing Western Marxism for banishing nature from dialectics, Foster established a new Red-Green canon and elaborated a new cognitive map for ecological Marxism. More specifically, Foster conceptualizes the notion of "metabolic rift" in his attempt to elaborate on the so-called Marx ecology where Marx is posited as a social theorist preoccupied with the fundamental metabolism between humans and nature (Foster 1999, 2000a). Here, Foster develops the concept to characterize the nature-society interaction within capitalist society. Foster explains the theoretical premise of his approach as follows:

> It was in *Capital* that Marx's materialist conception of nature became fully integrated with his materialist conception of history. In his developed political economy, as presented in *Capital*, Marx employed the concept of "metabolism" (Stoffwechsel) to define the labor process as "a process between man and nature, a process by which man, through his own actions, mediates, regulates and controls the metabolism between himself and nature." Yet an "irreparable rift" had emerged in this metabolism as a result of capitalist relations of production and the antagonistic separation of town and country. Hence under the society of associated producers it would be necessary to "govern the human metabolism with nature in a rational way," completely beyond the capabilities of bourgeois society.
>
> (Foster 2000, 141)

In his analysis of the origins of agricultural land rent, Marx expands the critical-geographical scope of his exposure and analysis of the metabolic rift – which he had associated with capitalist industrialization – to encompass the global where extractive capitalism seeks to find new cheap homes (Marx 1981, 949).

The emergence of capitalism causes a fundamental reorganization of world-ecology, characterized by a "metabolic rift", a progressively deepening rupture in the nutrient cycling between the core and periphery, between countryside and the city. The transition to capitalism brought about not only new forms and modes of alienation (abstract social labour, abstraction of value, and alienation of the labour from nature); it also instigated a new division of labour between core and periphery, between town and country – on both regional and global scales. Such a rift or division of labour and its inextricable intertwinement with metabolic rift involved a process whereby the products (and nutrients) extracted from the ecosystems in the peripheries and the countryside flowed into the core cities and metropolises in a unilateral and irreversible logic, to wit, without returning those extracted resources and nutrients back to the point of production in any form. Consequently, the land and its subterranean

26　*Introduction*

resources were progressively pumped to the point of relative exhaustion which in turn feted surplus extraction and profitability. Foster's explanation can be illuminating:

> The coevolutionary relation between human society and nature, as organized under capitalist production, is creating an ecological rift that is generating numerous changes in environmental conditions, some of which threaten to hasten the accumulation of carbon dioxide in the atmosphere and wreak social havoc.
>
> (2010, 147)

Notably, the aforementioned dialectical domination with its extractive and surplus-driven dynamics led to a situation where the localized ecological problems of both the feudal and capitalist era were conducive to the globalizing problem of the metabolic rift (see Foster 1999).[36] When faced with such an impasse, natural exhaustion, and economic contraction, capital has no resort other than seeking out and developing new ways of exploiting territories which were deemed to lie beyond the reach of the law of value. This process of geographical expansion and social innovation instigated a new phase of capitalist development (Arrighi 1994; Moore 1999, 2000; see also Moore 2017b, 285). The capitalist system continued to function smoothly due to the incessant process of accumulation and surplus production, resulting in exceedingly alienated and divided human beings, as well as globally extended cycles of the destruction and disruption of the ontological and relational co-dependency and dynamic co-implication not only between humans and nature, but also between core humans and peripheral humans and extra-humans (natural resources). In other words, the conquest of nature was concomitant with the conquest of human. As Foster and others expatiate:

> At the planetary level, ecological imperialism has resulted in the appropriation of the global commons – the atmosphere and oceans, which are used as sinks for waste – and the carbon absorption capacity of the biosphere, primarily to the benefit of a relatively small number of countries at the center of the capitalist world economy. The core nations rose to wealth and power in part through high fossil fuel consumption and exploitation of the global South. Anthropogenic greenhouse gases emissions, while stemming from localized sources, are distributed throughout the atmosphere and accumulate as waste, which degrades the atmosphere and leads to further alteration of the biosphere, creating a global crisis.
>
> (2010, 145)

To sum up, then, the "metabolic rift" is generally conceived of in two overlapping senses. In the first sense, rift designates separation in

*Introduction* 27

a historicized ontology where capitalism "continuously . . . separate[s] the social metabolism from the natural metabolism" (Clark and York 2005, 417). In the second sense, rift is conceptualized as an agent of disruption. As Foster indicates, capitalism's "global metabolic rift" has "disrupted the 'eternal natural condition' of life itself" (Foster 2015 quoting Marx 1977, 637).[37] As Foster elaborates, one of the critical consequences of the metabolic rift is "alienation". It is in fact alienation in conjunction with alienated labour[38] (which subtly mediates the relationship within the capitalist relations of production) that partly accounts for the inabilities of societies to tackle the various contemporary ecological crises – hence the ceaseless continuation of the fossil fuel (particularly oil and gas) consumption despite human societies being on the verge of their extinction.

## 2. *Jason Moore's Critique of Metabolic Rift Discourse*

Foster's elaborations on Marx's incipient conceptualization of "metabolic rift", whilst receiving wide approval, have not been left unscathed. Perhaps the most cogent theoretical critique of Foster's "metabolic rift" has been that of Moore's. Here, I will succinctly delineate both his critique and his alternative concept – "metabolic shift" – since not only is it pivotal to my exploration of the ecological effects of oil on human-nonhuman nature. It is also integral to a rigorous understanding of Moore's theory of the Capitalocene and the world-ecological. The three notions in fact constitute the conceptual premises of my analytical engagement with almost all the petro-dramatic works under scrutiny in this book.

Far from dismissing metabolic rift thinking, Moore "affirm[s] its dialectical core" (Moore 2017b, 285–287) whilst arguing it to be inadequately dialectical. The rampant "sense of urgency" to develop modes of thought appropriate to "an era of deepening biospheric instability", rift thinking (as a salient strand in environmental sociology) has recognized – "but inadequately internalized" – the understanding that "humans are part of nature" (Moore 2017b, 287; see also Moore 2015). Nevertheless in its theorization of this crisis, rift thinking is beset with an "impasse" (Moore 2017b, 285–287). Moore, however, is suspicious of the previously mentioned popularity of the rift analyses and attributes it to its over-flexibility and the fact that "Rift analyses have rarely theorized capitalism's socio-ecological contradictions – beyond marxisante axioms that (rightly) say capitalism does terrible things to nature" (2017b, 286). Moore critically calls metabolism "a plastic category" through which rift analyses have combined "the Green emphasis on modernity's environmental consequences and the Red focus on capitalism's political economy", but, crucially, "without synthesizing" the two (286). In other words, Moore argues that a less obtrusive form of non-dialectical dualism is still discernible in the notion of metabolic rift. That is indeed why Moore contends

28   *Introduction*

that the notion of metabolic rift "represents the highest stage of 'Green Arithmetic': Society plus Nature equals Crisis" (286, 305).

One of the reasons Moore finds Foster's method inadequate is on the grounds that it forces Marx's "interdependent process of social metabolism" into a dualist frame: the "metabolism of nature and society" (Marx 1981, 949; Foster 2000, Chapter 6).[39] Moore argues that whilst Foster's re-reading of Marx and the former's articulation of social metabolism as a rift of "nature and society" (rather than society-in-nature) importantly revealed hitherto latent facets of Marx's socio-ecological thought, it nevertheless made Marx's ecological thinking to be "narrowly understood" – particularly due to Foster's inadequate attention to the "critique of political economy". As Moore explains: "'The' environment became just another – albeit a major – analytical object for Marxists. It did not compel a fundamental rethinking of how capital accumulation works, how it booms, and how it develops through accumulation crises" (2017b, 286–287). To Moore, Foster's account of metabolic rift falls short of establishing a relational "cross-fertilization" between "the theory of monopoly capital" and "an ecologically-informed historical materialism" (2017b, 287).

Moore contends that Foster's method falls short of "mov[ing] beyond re-branding Society as 'human nature' and Nature as 'extra-human nature'" (2017b, 290). Moore discerns a trace of dualism persisting in Foster's notion of metabolic rift, and thus argues that Foster's method does not manage to eschew and transcend the polar/dual perils of environmental determinism and social reductionism. In Moore's view, Foster's method proves inadequate for understanding the complex ways in which "human society" is "simultaneously a producer and product of the web of life, unevenly co-produced and symbolically enabled" (290). As such, whilst metabolism seems to have the potential synthesizing power for bridging the Great Divide (Nature/Society) through which "the specific forms of human sociality could be distinguished and analyzed in much more complex and nuanced ways", it fails to propound a full-fledged dialectical-relational synthesis and method. In his reconstructive and revisionary critique of the concept of metabolic rift, Moore deliberates on two pivotal questions which are "implicit in – but not engaged by – Rift arguments" (287). The first chief question turns on Nature/Society dualism and the problem of post-Cartesian thought. And the second one concerns a debate on "whether or not one may abstract geographical relations, configurations, and conditions from conceptualizations of historical change". In this regard, Moore poses a determining question, by which he means to unveil a lacuna in rift theory as well: "Can one dispense with geography in conceptualizing capitalism's histories, or are such geographies an ontological condition of historical change?" (287–288).

Moore contends that one of the drawbacks of the notion of metabolic rift lies in its over-emphasis on disruption and separation, "rather than

*Introduction* 29

reconfiguration and unity". In so doing, the metabolic rift has come to signify "a disruption in the exchange between social systems and natural systems" (Foster 2013, 8; see also Moore 2017b, 292). Implicit in such a conception is a "violent [undialectical] abstraction" complicit in the creation and reproduction of two separate epistemic domains: Nature and Society. Such violent abstractions involve an "epistemic rift" not only between nature and society but also nature and capital as "two separate epistemic domains" (293). Such a practical-epistemic rift is based on the assumption that nature is external to capitalism thus neglecting the real dynamics underpinning the process: the recognition of how "capitalism and its limits [are] co-produced through shifting configurations of human and extra-human nature" (292). The abstractions are "violent" because "they remove essential relations from each node in the interests of narrative and theoretical coherence" (293). Moore counterpoises such abstractions with "dialectical abstractions" that "begin with historical movement and strategic historical relations – something conspicuously absent from Nature/Society" (293).

Moore, therefore, discerns a subtle lapse or disparity at the core of metabolism-centred studies. To Moore, this "unresolved contradiction" exists "between a philosophical-discursive embrace of a relational ontology (humanity-in-nature) and a practical-analytical acceptance of Nature/Society dualism (dualist practicality)" (292). To Moore the challenge resides in "how one move[s] from seeing human organization as part of nature towards an effective – and practicable – analytical program" (292). On this premise, Moore contends that Foster's strenuous emphasis on rift and disruption has two adverse implications: Firstly, abstraction and, secondly, an exclusion of geography from his analysis, which, in turn, leads to an inadvertent divorce between history and geography. As Moore explains: "Foster's expulsion of geographers from his version of ecological Marxism is tightly related to his procedure of abstraction. For Foster, Society (and capitalism) can be conceptualized abstracted from geographical relations and conditions" (2017, 291). Moore elaborates how in rift models, the relations between basic units – Nature/Society and their specifications – may shift, but the constitution of these units remains outside their interaction. Calling such a procedure "dualist practicality", Moore contends how in "their embrace of Green Arithmetic – Nature plus Society – Rift analysts are at least indirectly, and in effect, 'accepting' the [intellectual] framework" of modernity, even as they seek to challenge it" (2017, 287).

Elsewhere Moore is more explicit in his critique of the notion of "metabolic rift" and calls it "the metabolic fetish" contending how deceptively easy it is to demonstrate its historical factuality and "justify [it] quantitatively", particularly by placing it within "its manifold resource- and energy-determinisms" (2015, 182). Moore adds a crucial caveat: "But numbers are tricky things. They easily entrain an empiricist logic that

## 30   *Introduction*

blinds its handlers to alternatives capable of enfolding quantitative data within world-relational processes" (2015, 182). Averring that such a poignant "confusion of numbers for explanation" tends to ensnare "interpreters [in the logic of] their own rhetoric. They [tend to] believe in their own objectivity, and fail to discern the prejudice that leads them to one interpretation among many [others] consistent with their numbers" (182). Moore mentions the "Anthropocene line of thought" as an emblematic case in point where every conceivable periodization has been propounded except one which takes account of the longue durée of its chief cause: capitalism. As he explains: "that has given rise to many possible periodizations, with the exception of one: the turning point of the long sixteenth century" (182).

Adopting a world-ecological and post-Cartesian perspective on both metabolism and historical change, Moore argues that a more adequate conception would entail a consideration of the social-natural or human and ecological "as a relational configuration" where primacy is accorded to "how humans have mixed their 'labor with the earth'" (2015, 128). Moore describes the epistemic and conceptual deficiency of the "Rift arguments and models" in terms of "dualist practicality" according to which "the relations between basic units – Nature/Society and their specifications – may shift, but the constitution of these units remains outside their interaction" (2017b, 287). Moore defines metabolism as "a means of unifying humans within nature, unfolding through combined and uneven metabolisms of power, wealth, and nature" (2017b, 292). Moore's valorization of the historical-geographical materialism "privileges the relationality of humanity-in-nature (and nature-in-humanity) in which material and cultural transformations are entwined – without succumbing to idealism" (2017b, 291).

Moore delineates the contours of his synthesis-based account through "a reconstruction of metabolism as a means to unify, methodologically, the differentiated flows of capital, power, and life in historical capitalism" (2017b, 288). Moore accentuates the necessity of conceiving of metabolism as "a process of life-making within the web of life" rather than an exchange between quasi-independent objects (Nature/Society). This conception of "a singular, internally diverse, historically variant and geographically uneven, metabolism of humanity-in-nature" opens up new possibilities by "allow[ing] us to chart a course beyond dualism" (2017b, 288). Inherent in Moore's revisionary conception of the metabolic rift (which he terms the "metabolic shift") is an immanent relationship between nature and society attested by his use of terms such as society-in-nature and nature-in-society. Akin to Foster who posits "human society" as "internal to and dependent upon [the] larger earthly metabolism" (Foster 2013, 8), Moore argues that the "totality of nature is immanent in every human thought, organization, and movement" (2017b, 289). In Moore's account, "the metabolic moment of class and capital cannot be

*Introduction* 31

abstracted"; and when conceived thus, metabolism can "bridge the Great Divide" between the social and ecological, between human and extra-human nature as both immanently embedded in the web of life (290). Dwelling upon the subtle yet significant differences between "global metabolic rift" and "ecological imperialism", Moore explains how these two issues or areas are often "conflated" in Metabolism theories. Such a conflation indeed illuminates "the disjuncture between the Rift's dialectical claims and its dualist practicality" (308). What is "conspicuously absent in most Rift analyses", according to Moore, is the "crucial dialectical procedure of sorting out the relation between the concept of a relation and the relation it-self" (308–309). To Moore, any theory of metabolism – whether called metabolic rift or shift – should be characterized by three features: first, it should be capable of accounting for the ways in which "[m]etabolism operates simultaneously as outer and inner moment of capital accumulation" (309); second, it should be amenable to historical-geographical adaptation and specificity such that "the incorporation of new empirical phenomena allows for conceptual reflexivity" (308); and thirdly, it should be predicated on "a world-historical method that grasps the messy and porous interpenetration of human and extra-human natures" (309).

As such, and as will be demonstrated in the ensuing chapters, the term has a revealing bearing on all the petro-plays under scrutiny in this book. In most of the plays, as a consequence of the infliction of the metabolic shift on human-nonhuman natures, carried out through both violent and subtle discursive means, the natives and the peripheral regions and peoples are associated with nature as mute, objectified, and extractable matter – hence their association with instinct, non-rational passivity and primitiveness, pre-modern animality, and barbarity. Given the recurring and reverberating presence of "barbarity" in plays such as *Oil Islands* and *Petrol Station* – invoked in relation to not only nature and native people (as well as the stateless Bedouins) but also oil and oil industry (embodied by Miss Grey, the Chimpanzee) – it is worth noting how such violent abstractions, as Moore expatiates them, are conducive to the reproduction of these violent and alienating dualisms. As Moore explains:

> Nature and Society have been real abstractions – abstractions with operative force in the material world. These and cognate terms, clustered in early modern Europe around "civility" and "barbarism" or "savagery," implicated a new ways of thinking and a new civilizational praxis: Cheap Nature.
>
> (2017b, 293)

Moore further notes how the birth of these real abstractions, Nature and Society, was consolidated in early capitalism (Moore 2015). In the

32  *Introduction*

centuries after 1450, capital, science, and empire enacted a series of socio-ecological and symbolic revolutions aimed at the creation of an "external" nature as a source of cheap inputs Moore (2015). What is crucial to understand is that "Nature" in the rise of capitalism and the heyday of petro-capitalism came to include the vast majority of humans within its geographical reach (293). In a similar vein, in *Oil Field*, *Oil Islands*, *The Watershed*, and *Petrol Station*, this dynamics is evidenced not only by the treatment of natural resources and the natives, but also by the pervasive presence of transnational labour transportation, importation of cheap labour and treatment of them as exchangeable commodities. As Moore argues:

> The contradictions – the "laws of motion" – of such bundled processes are not rooted in an abstract Society [but] rather, rooted in the mosaic of modernity's "double internality" – that is, in the ways that power and re/production are specifically bundled within a web of life that makes humans and that humans make.
>
> (2017b, 289)

## Notes

1. Ed Kashi, *Curse of the Black Gold: 50 Years of Oil in The Niger Delta* (Brooklyn, NY: PowerHouse Books, 2008). See also Federici, p. 11.
2. Juan Pablo Perez Alfonso in Michael L. Ross, *The Oil Curse: How Petroleum Wealth Shapes the Development of Nations* (Princeton and Oxford: Princeton University Press, 2012), p. 1.
3. Winston Churchill's remark on the oil extracted by British Petroleum from Persian/Iranian oil resources/wells; see also Michael J. Watts, "Oil as Money: The Devil's Excrement and the Spectacle of Black Gold," in *Money, Power and Space*, ed. Trevor J. Barnes, Jamie Peck, Eric Sheppard and Adam Tickell (Oxford: Blackwell, 1994), pp. 406–445.
4. See Matthew Huber, *Lifeblood: Oil, Freedom and the Forces of Capital* (Minneapolis, MN: University of Minneapolis Press, 2013), particularly Chapter 1 and 2; see also Ted Atkinson, "Blood Petroleum: True Blood, the BP Oil Spill, and Fictions of Energy/Culture," *Journal of American Studies*, 47.1 (2013), pp. 213–229 (p. 215).
5. Timothy Morton, *Hyperobjects: Philosophy and Ecology after the End of the World* (Minneapolis and London: University of Minnesota Press, 2013), pp. 28–40, passim.
6. Tyler Priest, "The Dilemmas of Oil Empire," *The Journal of American History*, 99.1 (2012), pp. 236–251 (p. 236).
7. See Stephanie LeMenager, *Living Oil: Petroleum Culture in the American Century* (New York: Oxford University Press, 2014), pp. 1–6; see also Timothy Mitchell, *Carbon Democracy: Political Power in the Age of Oil* (London: Verso, 2011), pp. 4–9, 23–31.
8. Bob Johnson, *Carbon Nation: Fossil Fuels in the Making of Modern Culture* (Lawrence: University of Kansas Press, 2014), p. xxix; see also Ernst Logar, *Invisible Oil* (Vienna: Ambra Verlag, 2011).

*Introduction*  33

9. Ruth Salvaggio, "Imagining Angels on the Gulf," in *Oil Culture*, ed. Ross Barrett and Daniel Worden (Minneapolis and London: University of Minnesota Press, 2014), pp. 384–403 (p. 386).
10. Peter Maass, *Crude World: The Violent Twilight of Oil* (New York: Vintage, 2009).
11. See Matthew Huber, "Refined Politics: Petroleum Products, Neoliberalism, and the Ecology of Entrepreneurial Life," in *Oil Culture*, ed. Ross Barrett and Daniel Worden (Minneapolis and London: University of Minnesota Press, 2014), pp. 226–243 (p. 226); see also Maas, *Crude World*; see also Peter Hitchcock, "Oil in an American Imaginary," *New Formations*, 69 (2010), pp. 81–97.
12. Daniel Yergin, *The Prize: The Epic Quest For Oil, Money, and Power* (New York: Simon Schuster, 1992), p. xiv.
13. Allan Stoekl, "Foreword," in *Oil Culture*, ed. Ross Barrett and Daniel Worden (Minneapolis and London: University of Minnesota Press, 2014), pp. xi–xiv (p. xiii).
14. Kaveh Ehsani, "Disappearing the Workers: How Labor in the Oil Complex Has Been Made Invisible," in *Working for Oil*, ed. Touraj Atabaki and Kaveh Ehsani (Basingstoke: Palgrave, 2018), p. 11.
15. Imre Szeman, "System Failure: Oil, Futurity, and the Anticipation of Disaster," *South Atlantic Quarterly*, 106.4 (2007), pp. 805–823.
16. Stephanie LeMenager, "The Aesthetics of Petroleum, after Oil!," *American Literary History*, 24.1 (Spring 2012), pp. 59–86.
17. *Energy Culture: Art and Theory on Oil and Beyond*. Ed. Imre Szeman Jeff Diamanti (Morgantown: West Virginia University Press, 2019).
18. Hitchcock, "Oil in an American Imaginary," p. 82.
19. Ibid., p. 82.
20. Benedict Anderson, in Fernando Coronil, *Magical State: Nature, Money, and Modernity in Venezuela* (Chicago and London: University of Chicago Press, 1997), p. 8.
21. Ibid.
22. Imre Szeman, "How to Know about Oil: Energy Epistemologies and Political Futures," *Journal of Canadian Studies/Revue d'études canadiennes*, 47.3 (2013), pp. 145–168 (p. 146).
23. Jennifer Wenzel, "How to Read for Oil," *Resilience: A Journal of the Environmental Humanities*, 1.3 (Fall 2014), pp. 156–161 (p. 156).
24. Stephanie LeMenager, *Living Oil: Petroleum Culture in the American Century* (New York: Oxford University Press, 2014), p. 3.
25. Ibid., p. 11.
26. The concept of "natureculture" has also been elaborated by Donna Haraway in a fairly similar context. See Donna J. Haraway, *The Companion Species Manifesto: Dogs, People, and Significant Otherness*. Vol. 1. (Chicago: Prickly Paradigm Press, 2003).
27. LeMenager, *Living Oil*, p. 5.
28. Huber, *Lifeblood*, pp. xv–xx, 19–25, 97–128.
29. Ursula Biemann and Andrew Pendakis, "This Is Not a Pipeline: Thoughts on the Politico-Aesthetics of Oil," *Imaginations: Journal of Cross-Cultural Image Studies*, 3.2 (2012).
30. "Working Group on the 'Anthropocene'." Subcommission on Quaternary Stratigraphy, 23 Feb. 2016, quaternary.stratigraphy.org.
31. Jeremy Davies, *The Birth of the Anthropocene* (Berkeley: U of California P, 2016).
32. Simon Lewis and Mark Maslin, "Defining the Anthropocene," *Nature* 519 (2015), pp. 171–180.

## 34  *Introduction*

33. J. W. Moore, "Ecology, Capital, and the Nature of Our Times: Accumulation & Crisis in the Capitalist World-Ecology," *Journal of World-Systems Research*, 17.1 (2011), pp. 107–146. https://doi.org/10.5195/jwsr.2011.432.
34. See Jason W. Moore, "The Capitalocene, Part I: On the Nature and Origins of Our Ecological Crisis," *The Journal of Peasant Studies*, 44.3 (2017), pp. 594–630; see also Jason W. Moore, "The Capitalocene Part II: Accumulation by Appropriation and the Centrality of Unpaid Work/Energy," *The Journal of Peasant Studies*, 45.2 (2018), pp. 237–279.

    See also Jason Moore's "Capitalocene" (2015) as a way of reinstating capitalism's extraordinary co-optation and exploitation of human and nonhuman life into discussions about the "Anthropocene".
35. See Michael T. Klare, "A Tough Oil World: Why Twenty-First Century Oil Will Break the Bank – and the Planet," *Huffington Post*, posted March 13, 2012, www.huffingtonpost.com//.
36. J. B. Foster, "Marx's Theory of Metabolic Rift," *American Journal of Sociology*, 105.2 (1999), pp. 366–405.
37. J. B. Foster, "The Great Capitalist Climacteric," *Monthly Review*, 67.6 (2015), pp. 1–18.
38. An important instance of which is "fixed labour" as incisively elaborated by Stephen Shapiro. See Stephen Shapiro, "From Capitalist to Communist Abstraction: The Pale King's Cultural Fix," *Textual Practice*, 28.7 (2014), pp. 1249–1271, DOI: 10.1080/0950236X.2014.965889.
39. J. B. Foster, *Marx's Ecology* (New York: Monthly Review Press, 2000).

# 1 Oil, the Crisis of Representation, and the Dramatic Form

## I. The Sublimities of Oil and the Questions of Form and Genre

One of the pivotal concerns of this book is the question of form and its various modifications and manifestations both in relation to the idea of "world dramas" and the primary thematic concern of the selected plays: oil. If, as Imre Szeman and Dominic Boyer emphasize, one of the key concerns of resource/energy-oriented artists and scholars should be the critical depiction and exploration of "the structure and function of energy epistemologies",[1] then one of the foremost aims of the selected dramatists' works can be argued to be the exploration of how oil – and the consequent social-political formations, linguistic-cultural paradigms, technologies/facilities, and affective-cognitive bonds – come to determine not only the characters' self-knowledge, but also their knowledge of the world and others (of the same nation/community and outside nations/communities) in conjunction with the means of obtaining both forms of knowledge. Nevertheless, as the aforementioned scholars alert us, "our epistemic tools for revolution and redemption are deeply entangled with the magnitudes of energy promised by fossil fuels".[2] Such epistemic tools, as underscored by Szeman and Boyer, include *form* and *structure*. By the same token, it can be argued that one of the central points every artist/writer concerned with the history, ethics, and political economy of energy and material resources (particularly oil) should preoccupy themselves with is the question of *form/structure*. A fleeting survey of the plays under scrutiny in the three volumes of this book will make evident that among their most pivotal concerns are the questions of form, structure, and language – particularly in tackling the questions of time-space complex, economy of desire and structure of phantasy, as they inform the individual's relation to oil and oil ontology, subjectivity, relationality, and history with regards to an always already acculturated and vibrant matter – oil – that resists representation by remaining, both literally and discursively, largely invisible.

The chief challenge this energy consciousness poses for the arts and literature concerns the concomitant questions of representation, aesthetics,

DOI: 10.4324/9781003134664-2

## 36  *Oil, the Crisis of Representation, and the Dramatic Form*

and form. As Andrew Pendakis and Ursula Biemann acutely observe: "Is there an aesthetics of oil or are its cultural manifestations too diverse or localized to be usefully generalized?" (2012, 8) If in the contemporary era of late petro-capitalism oil is always already as much naturalized as it is capitalized (Morton 2007, 16–17), the crucial task left to arts and literature then is to deconstruct or denaturalize such an association or logic through various aesthetic means. Oil, and by extension energy, has come to be ascribed such a pivotal role in recent literary and cultural studies that some scholars have gone so far as to insist on the necessity of recognizing the inherent link between race and energy, between the "rapidly rising temperatures and rapid advances of the far right" (see "Introduction" in *White Skin, Black Fuel*); but also the necessity of presenting a new periodization of literary periods and forms on the basis of energy regimes. In the same vein, Szeman discerns a critically neglected yet "foundational gap" in the history of literature – namely, its relation to and engagement with the question of energy (particularly oil). Accordingly, he contends that this gap stems from "the apparent epistemic inability or unwillingness to name our energy ontologies" (Szeman and Wenzel 2011, 324).

One aspect of this formal challenge was discerned by Brecht early on. Delineating the steps for an effective development of a theatrical work (new subject matter, new human relationships, new form, etc.), Brecht states: "The first thing to do, then, is to identify the new subject matter, and the second to map out the new relationships" (Brecht 56). Significantly, in his elaborations on the reason why such an aesthetic line should be pursued, Brecht refers to "oil/petroleum" as an illustrative example:

> Because art follows reality. Here is an example: the extraction and use of *petroleum* represents a new thematic complex within which, upon closer inspection, entirely new kinds of human relationships become apparent. Both the individual and the masses display certain modes of action, which are clearly specific to the *petroleum complex*. But the new modes of action were not what created this particular way of utilizing petroleum. On the contrary, the *petroleum complex* came first, and the new relationships are secondary. The new relationships represent the answers people give, the solutions they find, to question of "subject matter". The subject matter (the situation, as it were) develops according to definite rules and simple necessities, but petroleum creates new relationships. These, as I have said, are secondary.
> (ibid.; italics added)

As contentious as Brecht's Marxist-materialist claim here concerning the precedence of the infrastructural and social-political over and above the consciousness, forms of social action and relationships, and the formal-literary is (more strictly, the historical event as the impetus or condition of possibility for the creation/emergence of new forms or dynamics), what

*Oil, the Crisis of Representation, and the Dramatic Form* 37

is of foremost concern to us here is Brecht's use of oil as a paradigmatic example – in terms of the historical relationship between cultural consciousness, petro-modernity, and theatre history.

Equally significantly, Brecht proceeds to establish an aesthetic and epistemological link between form and content generally, and dramatic form and oil (as a subject matter or content) more specifically. Implicit in Brecht's argument is the notable repudiation of a binary relationship between form and content: the former as abstract spirit and the latter as historical material basis. Rather, Brecht argues that both form and content are inherently at once aesthetic and political. The following elucidation confirms this point:

> In order to embrace the new subject matter, a new dramatic and theatrical form is needed. . . . Petroleum balks at five-act form, today's catastrophes do not proceed in a straight line but in cyclical crises, the 'heroes' are different according to the different phases, are interchangeable, etc., the graph of human actions is complicated by human error, fate is no longer a coherent category, instead we find force fields with opposing currents, and the power blocks themselves show movement not only against one another but within themselves.
>
> (ibid.)

As will become evident in our scrutiny of each play, the formal concern in relation to oil as articulated by Brecht is shared by all the dramatists across the three volumes. Accordingly, one of the principal concerns of this book is to explore and expatiate the formal (dramatic and linguistic) techniques and aesthetic idiosyncrasies developed by the works at stake here in their attempt to express the specificity of their characters' encounter with and experience of oil as registered in/through the characters' cognitive-affective dynamics, economy of their relationality, and their mode of identification.

The crisis of form in its encounter with the overdetermined and manifold topic of oil, as I will explicate and demonstrate in my exploration of the petro-dramatic works, stems from two issues. Firstly, it arises from the twofold challenge posed by oil itself: the historical-temporal features and biophysical properties of oil as an energy form and natural matter/substance, on the one hand, and the distinctive and aporetic attributes of oil as a commodity in global politics and economics as well as in modern petroculture, on the other. Secondly, it arises from the now widely recognized problems of pondering the ecological, political-economic, and ontological consequences of the establishment of oil as the dominant mode of energy and form over the long 20th century. The second reason includes the questions of time, space, scale, and measure in relation to oil as a problematic. It is worth briefly pondering on each of these two challenges and/or reasons underlying the crisis of form.

## 38   Oil, the Crisis of Representation, and the Dramatic Form

Let us start by scrutinizing the second reason or challenge first. The problems besetting any literary-artistic engagement with, or representation of, oil – as one of the chief causes of global warming – are indelibly imbricated with the challenges posed to similar attempts at thinking and representing the Anthropocene. Timothy Clark argues that the Anthropocene – as a *threshold concept* or a "necessarily vague but insidious border" (2015, 48) – constitutes a brink where "modes of thinking and practices that were once self-evidently adequate, progressive, or merely innocuous become, in this emerging and counterintuitive context, even latently destructive" (2015, 21). By the same token, Clark – along with a number of prominent eco-critics such as Claire Colebrook, Maggie Kainulainen, and Bernd Herzogenrath – endorses and valorizes the development and deployment of non-linguistic art forms (184–186). One of the principal reasons underlying such a critical stance towards anthropocentric literary forms is that the pivotal features of the narrative form – namely, discursive language, linguistic representation, and narrative – have been traditionally inclined to assign ontological priority, (rational or otherwise) agency, (moral, actional, or emotional) centrality to the human subject. More importantly, such anthropocentric forms – and above all "narrative" – not only as a means of organizing knowledge (historical or scientific) and identity (self-understanding), but also as a means of imagining, in the mode of teleological speculation, on the possible end of human life[3] – are mired in dualistic ontological assumptions where humans assume a subjective and the nonhuman an objective position. Consonantly, Colebrook poses the question as to whether discursive language and traditional forms of narrative and representations are adequate media and apposite modes for thinking about climate change: "one might say that climate change should not require us to return to modes of reading, comprehension and narrative communication but should awake us from our human-all-too-human narrative slumbers" (2014, 25). It is on this basis that she critiques one of the dominant trends in literature and film: the post-apocalyptic genre. As she contends:

> [a]n entire genre of what has come to be known as post-apocalyptic literature currently and repeatedly, with ever increasing verve, plays out a fantasy of human near-disappearance and redemption, and does so precisely when our energies ought to be focused on what humans have done to the planet and how they might desist from so doing.
>
> (Colebrook 2014, 197)

Defining Anthropocene as "a threshold at which all 'our' concepts of horizon, milieu, ethos and polity are voided" (188), Colebrook contends that Anthropocentric forms and genres – those forms and genres where primacy is accorded to narrative, to discursive techniques, and to human(ist) language, namely fiction and (particularly realistic-naturalistic modes of)

## Oil, the Crisis of Representation, and the Dramatic Form    39

drama – are inadequate to tackle the agentially, temporally, and spatially complex relationship between the human and nonhuman operative at various levels of ecosystem (including biosphere, lithosphere, etc.), non-human scales, and the demands of the Anthropocene. Colebrook deems linguistic narrative ill-equipped since "linguistic narrative [is] seemingly more allied with forms of anthropocentric thinking to be overcome, or as an art of sequences of human action geared to a definite significant end in some fulfilled or unfulfilled intention" (Clark 187).

Many literary eco-critics have underscored not only the inadequacy of existing literary forms to tackle the temporal, agential, historical, and political-economic challenges captured and posed by the notion and phenomenon of the Anthropocene. Some critics have even celebrated such a failure by valorizing disjunction or mismatch between the human and the nonhuman, between the representing "subject" and the resistant-to-being-represented "object" as an affirmation of ontological difference between human and nonhuman, but also an index of the success of the literary form in maintaining this otherness by refusing to anthropocentrically reduce it to recognizable bounds of recognition and comprehension (see Levinas, 194–195). Furthermore, such a resistance to human forms of representation and epistemic appropriation is a testament to the agential power of what was previously presumed to be an inert object (see Harman 2017; Latour 2002; Jane Bennett 2010;[4] Timothy Mitchell 2002, 38; see also Karen Barad's theory of agential realism 2007).[5] On this basis, they promote works whose "material and formal qualities . . . come to displace and overwhelm" established forms of expression and representation (Clark 2015, 183). It emphasizes "disjunctiveness, a being-overwhelmed by contexts in which the human perceiver is deeply implicated but cannot hope to command or sometimes even to comprehend" (184).

With a specific focus on the realist novel as it developed over the past two hundred years, Amitav Ghosh deliberates on a rather different kind of failure: the failure of the modern literary imagination to recognize, accommodate, and respond to the questions of energy (particularly fossil fuels) and environmental calamity – issues which are at the forefront of the discourse of Anthropocene which alerts us to a "renewed awareness of the elements of agency and consciousness that humans share with many other beings and even perhaps the planet itself" (*The Great Derangement* 2016, 63). For Ghosh, the realist novel, in its preoccupation with the quotidian life of the bourgeoisie, relegates to oblivion, if not denying it altogether, this intimacy of shared agency and consciousness between the human and the nonhuman (including energy resources such as oil). Ghosh, consequently, calls for an alternative history of the carbon economy (2016, 114, 124–134). Upon scrutiny, Ghosh's contentious claim (about the missed encounter with oil in American fiction) not only evinces his neglecting of a number of significant works of petrofiction in American literature and beyond (including Sinclair's *Oil!*, Edna Ferber's *Giant*, Ross

## 40  *Oil, the Crisis of Representation, and the Dramatic Form*

Macdonald's *Sleeping Beauty*, and Raymond Chandler's *The Big Sleep*). Ghosh's claim also tends to conflate, or reduce, the literary imagination to a novelistic one. In other words, Ghosh entirely overlooks drama.

Such concerns over form in its encounter with the Anthropocene and ecological crisis are further compounded and pushed to extreme when it comes to the matter of "oil". Consonant with the foregoing concerns over form and climate crisis, and having characterized the notion of the Anthropocene (for which fossil fuels such as oil and coal are primarily accountable) in terms of "slow violence" at the levels of causes and effects, Nixon discerns how such a temporal-epistemological dynamic poses a representational quandary:

> how to devise arresting stories, images, and symbols adequate to the pervasive but elusive violence of delayed effects. . . . How can we turn the long emergencies of slow violence into stories dramatic enough to rouse public sentiment and warrant political intervention.
>
> (2011, 3)

As Szeman and Boyer observe, "If it has been so difficult to grasp and grapple with so important an element, it is in many respects because fossil fuels are saturated into every aspect of our social substance" (2017, 6). Recognizing the glaring lacuna of oil in the literary-cultural imaginary of the long 20th century, MacDonald perceives this ubiquity of oil as an opportunity rather than an impediment:

> All modern writing is premised on both the promise and the hidden costs and benefits of hydrocarbon culture. If this proposition seems unwieldy – preposterous even – it is still worth thinking [about] how oil's sheer predominance within modernity means that it is every-where in literature yet nowhere refined enough – yet – to be brought to the surface of every text. But it sits there nevertheless – untapped, bubbling under the surface, ready to be extracted by a new generation of oil-aware petrocritics.
>
> (Macdonald, "Oil and World Literature", 31)

This formal challenge in conjunction with the complexities, subtleties, and challenges of the context of oil ontology (its spatial historical scope, its complex dynamics, its invisibilities, the oil's volatile life and shapes) has led to the emergence of numerous forms such as petro-magic real-ism, capitalist realism, peripheral realism, and irrealism (see Niblett 2020, 61–65).

Whilst bearing in mind our deconstructionist and poststructuralist caveats regarding the prevailing conceptions of theatrical performance as a non-iterable, material-real, in-persona event – where deconstruction alerts us to the questions of iterability, spectral materiality, and mediation

## Oil, the Crisis of Representation, and the Dramatic Form 41

as invariable ontological and historical conditions of production (given the late capitalist society of the spectacle or the age of simulacrum)[6] – it is worth also acknowledging that such ontological and historical conditions, however, are shared by all genres. What distinguishes drama – particularly in the form of theatrical production and live performance – is the more immediately felt presence of such phenomena as materiality, energy, force, and crisis as a situated experience where our being caught in the web of life at natural-ecological, social-communal, and political-economic levels reaches higher thresholds of our sensorial dynamics and consciousness. Equipped with such means and features, theatre/drama can render visible – or, more strictly, perceptible – the temporal, spatial, and material conditions that have been informing and determining the economy, ethos, and ecology of our individual and social being over the course of the long 20th century which has been unanimously identified as the era of oil or Petrocene. Such a move is also in keeping with Bruno Latour's description of global warming as an ontologically multivalent phenomenon and a quasi-object (1993, 13–15, 50) which is "simultaneously real, discursive, and social" (1993, 64). As will be demonstrated in my exploration of the petro-dramatic works in each chapter, each play develops a hybrid form in a bid to not only effectively overcome these challenges, but to transcend the limits of anthropocentric forms in its encounter with the intricacies of such an energy resource as oil which has been identified at once as an *objet petit a* and a hyper-object.

Indelibly intertwined with the concerns and debates over the efficacy of various artistic media, literary forms and genres, one of the practical concerns of energy-conscious writers and critics has been the material social-cultural effects of literature and critique on the improvement, deceleration, or partial transcendence of the ecological and energy-related issues. Notably, theatrical/dramatic form has already been hailed as a form that embodies and keeps alive the sense of situatedness, shared agency, and material conditions of individual-social consciousness. As Benjamin Wihstutz states, "actors and spectators gather together for a period of shared time, which, due to its liminal and transitory quality, means that every performance bears the potential to trigger reflections on time and temporality" (2009, 110). Ecologically oriented critics, such as Baz Kershaw, have demonstrated how the very process of staging drama underlines the extent to which drama is constituted by "unavoidable interdependencies between every element of a performance event and its environment", – conditions which make "theater ecology a matter of living exchange between organisms and environments" (2007, 12). Oddly, however, Kershaw almost entirely neglects the questions of energy, energy form, energy resources and above all fossil fuels (including oil).

Finally, for sometime now one of the foremost concerns of both eco-critics and petrocritics has been to find – through various formal, aesthetic, discursive-epistemic, and epistemological manoeuvres – the ways

## 42  Oil, the Crisis of Representation, and the Dramatic Form

in which literary-artistic works can exert real effects on the audience's/ readers' consciousness, their embodied ethos, and their socius as specifically regards their relationship to energy, fossil fuels, climate crisis along with their habitual patterns of consumption and exert material changes in the extra-textual world. Most recently, David Thomas discerns a "common tendency . . . to subtly overstate contemporary literature's attentiveness to the history and politics of energy and infrastructure" in literary criticism (115). Stressing the importance of maintaining some vigilant scepticism towards the material and social-cultural efficacy of literature and literary criticism in its engagement with energy and fossil fuels, Thomas indicates how "our readings [literary-critical analyses] are often carried off with such skill and dexterity that all concerned can lose track of the heuristic struggles that generated them, struggles in which the critic is engaged actively, if silently" (116). Thomas sounds a caveat concerning the efficacy of any literary or intellectual attempt at critiquing the current petrocapitalist hegemony or conceptualizing the possibility of transcending it, given the infrastructural and epistemological limits posed to any such representational-critical attempt by the petrocapitalist organization of knowledge:

> the profound changes taking place within the late capital's knowledge production networks, changes that are incrementally shifting the content of our debates [about literary representations and cultural critiques of the socio-economic order driven by oil and other fossil fuels] and the nature of audiences,
>
> (132)

Nevertheless, he maintains: "we may have little option but to go on tilting at windfarms, acting in the quixotic conviction that other, wiser worlds will eventually begin to drag themselves from the husk of this dying one" (133). Roberto Schwarz's argument is a noteworthy case in point. Schwarz argues how and why the "material constraints of social reproduction" should be considered as

> fundamental forms that, for good or ill, are impressed on the different areas of spiritual life, where they circulate and are re-elaborated in more or less sublimated or falsified versions: forms, therefore, working on forms. Or better – the forms discovered in literary works are seen to be the repetition or the transformation, with variable results, of pre-existing forms, whether artistic or extra-artistic.
>
> (2001, 25)

Consonantly, and broaching this problem in the context of the representations of ecological and energy issues in the Caribbean literature, Michael Niblett draws on Raymond Williams's expansion of Marx's

*Oil, the Crisis of Representation, and the Dramatic Form*   43

notion of "productive force"[7] to articulate his position thus: "Cultural forms, including literary works, can be grasped as productive forces in this sense, then: as a species of social knowledge fundamentally interwoven with the reproduction of material life" (2020, 3).

Considering the relationship between materiality, matter, materialism, on the one hand, and cultural-literary forms engaging with the question of energy and fossil fuels in the context of Energy Humanities and petroculture on the other, Szeman (1999) seeks to expand the common conception of materialism as a "critical practice that focuses on matter" (1), often associated with reductive readings of literary and cultural texts as mere registrations of the world. In contrast, Szeman defines materialism as an attempt to "understand the processes of literary and cultural transubstantiation" (3), where a concentration on the "material conditions" (3), that are all-too-often relegated to the sidelines, can be "concrete without being reductive, determinate without being determining" (6). The Energy Humanities aims to enact this kind of materialist vision by subjecting to critical-materialist scrutiny what Macdonald calls the "hierarchy of material . . . forms" within petroculture (re)materializing petro-modernity's immaterial self-presentation, and accentuating its material implications and potentials for society, culture and individual's relation to themselves and nature in their ability to redefine their relationship with "a material life sustained and underpinned by hegemonic forms of energy extraction, production and consumption" (2013, 10, 3).

More recently, Szeman and Wenzel (2021) more extensively delve into various facets of the question of "extractivism" as a recurring theme and topos in literary-cultural discourses in their introduction to a special issue dedicated to the exploration of the question of (energy, mineral, and labour) resource extraction and extractivism as they feature in various literary canons of world literatures in relation to various energy modes and resources (including coal and oil).[8] Here, Szeman and Wenzel express a similar concern about both the necessity of attending to the materiality of energy and the practices of extractivism (along with the political-economic and ecological logics and dynamics underlying them) and alert us to the deficiencies and drawbacks involved in metaphorizing the term and processes of extraction and extractivism in the field of literary research. Expressing reservations about some of the ways in which extractivism tends to be invoked in literary and cultural discourses, Szeman and Wenzel sound an earnest cautionary note about two problematic or symptomatic facets of the appropriation of the terms extraction and extractivism through a process of abstraction, metaphorization, or generalization. Here, Szeman and Wenzel, as part of their argument, attend to what they describe as "the dangers of conceding too much conceptual ground to a concept of extraction that has become generalized and generalizable" (514). Further elucidating the semantic and material reach of the term "extractivism" in its metaphorical reincarnations and adaptations, they explain how extractivism "enables extraction to become a process

## 44  Oil, the Crisis of Representation, and the Dramatic Form

writ large, the name for any kind of taking out or drawing out – whether of iron ore and oil, value, work, data, or meaning, or indeed any other process that appears to fit the mould" (515). Whilst acknowledging the material effects and nature of metaphors and their psychosomatic nature ("There's no problem per se with the metaphoric or rhetorical use of extraction to speak to the outcomes of different practices"), Szeman and Wenzel contend that collapsing the boundaries between the two carries at least two determining "perils". The first peril of such a metaphorical appropriation of the notion of extraction/extractivism is that

> it tends to flatten the ground, collapsing historical, geographical, and cultural distinctions that should be important to fully understanding the specific operations of extraction, including the ideologies and imaginaries that surround it at any given time and in any given space.
> (514–515)

The second peril, according to Szeman and Wenzel, "emerges out of this generalisation of extraction, in what might seem at first glance to be a contradictory process" (515). Crucially, however, they add,

> The problem we are pointing to emerges only when an equivalence is drawn between extraction of this kind – meaning, via the reading of a literary text – and a very different mode of extraction of different sorts of objects: mining coal, drilling for oil, harvesting timber.
> (515)

What Szeman and Wenzel diagnostically describe tends to be rather one of the pervasive symptoms of analytical methos and approaches informing literary studies where the boundaries between the material and metaphorical are blurred – for the benefits of a hermeneutic practice – to the point where the materiality of energy resource and its distinctive "material" effects – at political-economic, ecological, and affective-cognitive levels – are elided and/or conflated. This crucial materialist caveat is one which this book takes seriously and implements in its exploration of the selected works of petro-drama.

One of the prominent eco-critics who has explored the relationship between literature, nature (including ecological issues), and socio-cultural dynamics has been Hubert Zapf. Pondering the possibility of literary space not only as a sustainable cultural space but also a space for promoting and representing ecological sustainability, Zapf argues that "imaginative literature acts like an ecological force within the larger system of culture and of cultural discourses" (Zapf, 4). What Zapf describes here constitutes some of the main goals and intentions of the dramatic works and dramatists I am scrutinizing in this book. In his attempt to account for the material effects of literature in relation to ecological questions, and

## Oil, the Crisis of Representation, and the Dramatic Form    45

predicating his argument "on a functional-evolutionary view of cultural and literary history", Zapf explains how literature (including theatre/drama) can contribute to the development of a cultural ecology and cultural ethos "in which literary texts as imaginative and artistic forms of textuality have acquired specific qualities, modes, and features of writing that are both interrelated with and different from other forms of writing" (4). Basing his argument on a biological definition of the notion of "sustainability" – as "the ways in which living systems remain alive and productive over time" – Zapf elaborates how "the cultural ecosystem of literature fulfills a similar function of sustainable productivity within cultural discourses" (4). As such, Zapf valorizes literature (and we can say, drama/theatre, by extension) "as a transformative force of language and discourse" (4) where sustainability can be practiced and promoted. Positing "sustainability" in a cultural sense as "the ways in which the life of culture can be kept in 'equilibrium with basic ecological support systems'", Zapf argues that this criterion is particularly applicable to "literary culture, which is characterized in its functional dynamics by maintaining a deep-rooted affinity between its modes of (re-)generation and the ecological processes of life that it both reflects and creatively transforms" (4). Whilst I find Zapf's insights rigorous and illuminating and find myself in concurrence with many of them, the issue with Zapf's argument is not only its (nearly Habermasian) assumption of a politically-economically neutral and ideal ground on which such a sustainable practice in the literary space can be accomplished – hence devoid of any cognizance of the historically uneven (or core-peripheral) relational dynamics between various producing and reading parties. The issue also stems from a lack of sustained engagement (on his part) with the questions of energy culture – with a specific focus on the globally hegemonic energy modes and resources, particularly the fossil fuels (coal, oil, gas) and above all: oil. In fact, what has considerably suffered neglect – particularly in the field of drama/theatre studies – has been the material question of fossil fuels – along with their ecological and political economy.

Bursting the bubble of culture (and literary culture) as an autonomous realm untraversed with and un-implicated in the uneven dynamics of energy extraction and consumption, dramatic/theatrical scenarios of ecological and infrastructural disasters enhance the audience's ability to experience culture as an energy-intensive and at once material and discursive process. Performances of ecological and oil-related catastrophes emerge "as something that arises from the complex and sometimes chaotic interaction of a diversity of human and nonhuman factors and actants, rather than as something that is neither divinely orchestrated, purely natural, or exclusively societal in its etiology" (Rigby 2015, 50).[9] Theorizing performance in relation to energy (with a specific focus on fossil fuels and, above all, oil) as well as ecology "is important, because art sometimes gives voice to what is unspeakable elsewhere" (Morton 2010, 12). More

## 46  *Oil, the Crisis of Representation, and the Dramatic Form*

recently, in considerations of the materiality of the social-cultural effects of ecocritical thinking and ecologically oriented works of literature, there have emerged attempts at articulating the relationship between drama and energy, particularly fossil fuels such as coal and gas. A prominent case in point is Sabine Wilke's attempt to show "how the theatre functions as a laboratory for exploring the Anthropocene" (2021, 132), through a close examination of Kaiser's *Gas* and Müller's *The Task*. Such an approach, according to Wilke, "encourages us to go beyond humanism [and] explore greater complexities" such as the question of energy and "stage as a system of cultural ecology" (136). Sabine then suggests that we conceive of literary imagination in relation to energy and fossil fuels (as they feature in dramatic works), and the literary-imaginative mode of engagement with them, in terms of "laboratory". Thus couched in terms redolent of Zola's naturalism, I would argue that the notion of laboratory – as utilized by Wilke – reiterates the dualist ontological and epistemological assumptions inherent in the term the Anthropocene. More strictly, the term "laboratory" not only reiterates the anthropocentric conditions – by placing us into a human and human-made environment where nature or energy is at best the object of the human subject's observations. More importantly, retrogressively, it takes us back to the epistemic and subjective logics of Western modernity and Enlightenment in that the situational dynamics of the trope of "laboratory" entails the adoption of an impersonal, objective, detached position by the rational human subject thereby stripping nature and energy of their "agency". In addition to the foregoing inadequacies of Wilke's proposed approach (that of "laboratory"), although Wilke's move seems a step forward – compared with drama-focused ecocritical studies that entirely neglect/ignore the question of energy (particularly fossil fuels: coal, oil, gas), nevertheless she tends to neglect the logics and dynamics of the extraction of these fossil fuels and particularly the "world-systemic" nature of such these extractive practices – hence remaining inured to the aesthetic and epistemological confines of the Anthropocene. This lapse, in turn, involves a neglect of the questions of political ecology, political economy, and the concomitant issues of race, gender, and class as embedded in the extractive practices of these systems.

Instead, deriving my mooring points from Jason Moore and later Adorno,[10] I suggest we conceive of it in terms of the "labour" of imagination in a world-ecological and negative-dialectical mode. The notion of "labour" wielded in the phrase "the labour of world-ecological imagination" has six advantages over and above other notions, including "laboratory". Primarily, engaging with works of petro-literature – particularly in the genre of drama/theatre – in terms of the "labour of world-ecological imagination" enables us to grasp the engagement as an affective-cognitive exercise in recognizing the political-economic conditions of possibility of not only the production of the work by the writer and producers, but also the condition of possibility of the act of reading/witnessing by

## Oil, the Crisis of Representation, and the Dramatic Form 47

the audience/reader. Such an approach places the petro-dramatic work and the act of reading in a worldly context where the reader becomes aware of their embeddedness in an uneven economics of production-consumption. Secondly, the experience of engaging with petro-dramatic and petro-literary works as the "labour of world-ecological imagination" enables the recognition of the Capitalocene dynamics and logics of the globally extended system – through a cognitive-mapping aesthetics – a system that has caused climate change and ecological disaster. Thirdly, the signifier "labour" – as a concept and praxis – throws into relief the materiality of the act of imagination as it acknowledges the embeddedness of the cognitive-affective act of imagination in its historical, geographical, ecological, and ethical aspects of the extraction, production, and consumption of fossil fuels – and particularly oil. Fourthly, the word "labour" accentuates the energy required for such an engagement by the reader/audience, thereby foregrounding the cultural and political economy of the energy required for the act – and its conditions of possibility – of reading/witnessing the literary-theatrical works as well as the ethics involved in obtaining access to cheap energy (derived from oil, primarily). The fifth advantage is that the word "labour" designates the necessity of adopting an immanent and embodied (or cognitive-affective) mode of involvement in the act of reading, representing, and interpreting energy and fossil fuels (including oil) as a critical hermeneutic process of reconsidering the questions of matter/materiality, value, meaning, and action in relation to ecological and petrocultural plights and our infrastructural complicity with them. And finally, the term "labour" highlights the epistemological and cognitive-affective affinities between social form and aesthetic form. The negative-dialectical facet of the notion of the "labour of world-ecological imagination" foregrounds the co-implication of the subject and object, the human and nature, and the human and nonhuman in one another in a mutually determining, agentially co-extensive and co-constructive dynamics which precludes the subsumption of the Other (human and nature) into the terms of a rational ostensibly "autonomous" self as part of the logic of the petro-capitalist and Anthropocenic systems (see Adorno, *Negative Dialectics*, 52–63, 138–143, 174–178). Whilst drama/theatre (including both play and performance) has, by and large, received short shrift in petro-literary scholarship, it is my aim, through the three volumes of *Oil and Modern World Drama*, to demonstrate how drama/theatre – as illustrated by the emblematic instances of petro-drama included here – can act as an effective means of addressing and conveying the aporias of producing and living in the era of oil at the various stages of its development. It can also serve as a means of fostering new economies and ethics of relationship between human and nonhuman but also between energy (fossil fuels, particularly oil) and culture, energy (fossil fuels) and the future, and energy and agency.

## 48 Oil, the Crisis of Representation, and the Dramatic Form

## II. Aporetics of Oil and the Crisis of Representation: Four Premises

Let us now turn to an explication of the first reason underlying the formal crisis posed by oil. Upon closer inspection, the crisis of form or representation – nearly rendering oil a sublime object – can be argued to arise from four pivotal features of oil in its various forms and the various phases of its existence: time, space, scale, and measure. Each of these four attributes or problematics concerns oil at the level of cause and effect. And any intersection or imbrication of the four issues can induce a crisis at the levels of knowledge, action, representation, perception, and imagination. The fourfold challenge throws into relief the particular difficulty of perceiving and representing oil – or more broadly energy-related crisis (including global warming or climate change and disasters such as explosions and spills): a difficulty that, I would argue, emanates from the four critical vectors delineated next.

*(1) Space:* The first formidable challenge posed to any attempt at representing oil and imagining beyond oil is the question of space or, more specifically, the spatial geographies of oil extraction in conjunction with the political economy of not only the visibility of extraction sites but also the concomitant visibility of climate change. As important to the problematic of space (and the concomitant problematic of scale) as the sites of extraction are the systemic and petro-capitalist networks of circulation and transportation which are internationally and globally extended networks paradigmatically illustrated by pipelines, tankers, shipping containers dotting the unseen shores of the world – most of which remain outside the purview of the ordinary citizen-subject.[11] Such spatial dynamics and politics of visibility impose discursive and legal limits on the visibility of and the media and public access to the sites of oil extraction and of oil-caused disasters.[12] Such visual-spatial politics not only grant the citizens of the global north and metropolitan centres the illusion of them occupying a rarefied position unsullied by the practices through which their access to cheap oil is made possible. These spatial features also coalesce to make oil feature as the limit of perception, imagination, and any remedial or critical action regarding not only the uneven and exploitative logics of the extraction of oil but also its pernicious effects on peripheral peoples, natures, and geographies. Furthermore, these politics of space and visibility make oil-related disasters appear as something happening to other people in ontologically vague hinterland areas far from metropolitan centres, where the ravages of extractivist petro-capitalism (such as social-economic dispossession and ecological degradation) appear as one more disaster added to the disasters of poverty, colonialism, and underdevelopment.

What further compounds the infrastructural dynamics of oil in its various stages (of extraction, production, distribution, and consumption) are

## Oil, the Crisis of Representation, and the Dramatic Form    49

the politics of visibility. Most of the sites of oil extraction and production are not only beyond the visual-perceptual limit and purview of the individual citizens of core countries (Anglo-American and European countries – global north), but also the locals and national citizens of the countries that own the resources. Equally notably, these sites of oil extraction often transcend the national borders and territories located in far-flung regions and nations (that is, in occluded resource frontiers in peripheral countries) – regions which are barely media-covered and at best occupy a vague place in the psycho-geography of both core and peripheral countries.[13] This prevents the national individual citizens of both core and peripheral countries from perceiving – at affective and cognitive levels – the effects of oil order, but also the degree of their own unwitting complicity in it. As such, the inadequacy of ordinary or conventional means of representation in exposing both manifestations of the spaces and scales of oil extraction (and the inhuman and uneven dynamics governing them) – delineated earlier – prevents it from being amenable to an effective perception and representation by the individual viewer/subject.

Crucially, even when located within the bounds of a nation-state, such sites of oil extraction either are situated in places barely accessible to the ordinary citizen-subject (deep-water drilling, off-shore drilling, etc.) or due to the sheer physical-spatial scale of them defy the individual's limited sense of spatial and scalar measures (this applies to the major-ity of oil extraction sites – but paradigmatically Alberta Tar Sands and Niger Delta); or are simply camouflaged by various petro-architectural strategies. As regards the world-ecological approach of this book, any exploration of the political-economic and social logics informing the spaces of oil extraction, production, and consumption – in conjunction with the relational dynamics between them – needs to be premised on the recognition of the uneven, core-periphery dynamics informing such sites and spaces both locally and globally. This dialectical, cognitive-mapping method enables us to expose and establish the vertical-hierarchical logics informing the interaction of spaces and forces both within the local and between the local and global.

*(2) Time:* The second feature of oil that poses a formal crisis to the attempts at its critical representation is the complex temporality – given its longue durée, multi-scalar dynamics –informing the processes and phases of its formation, extraction-production, consumption, and future implica-tions: a future projection that lacks any punctual event or finite end (in terms of its toxic effects on human-nonhuman natures). Thinking of oil and its temporal-historical dynamics – particularly in relation to climate crisis and the Anthropocene – demands that we at once contract our temporal-historical span (by restricting it to the start of the extraction/ production and consumption of oil since nearly 1850s) and consider-ably expand it beyond the customary dates and periodizations commonly associated with the Anthropocene – given that the sheer amount of energy

## 50  *Oil, the Crisis of Representation, and the Dramatic Form*

that oil releases stems from the burial, absorption, and sedimentation of two millennia of solar and biotic material and energy in it. Hence the description of oil as the container or embodiment of "buried sunshine" and "biotic concentration of time" (see Huber *Lifeblood* 9). The formation of oil predates the human life on earth by almost 450 million years. Approximately 10% of the oil extracted today was formed during Palaeozoic – 541 and 252 million years ago – and the rest was formed during the Mesozoic era, which happened between 252 and 66 million years ago. The other facet of oil that compounds it temporally is its being a capitalist commodity and petrocultural phenomenon. Indeed, the consideration of the specific historical span within which oil has risen to prominence as the dominant energy resource and strategic global commodity (since the early 20th century) – as the means and premise of value, producing a certain (neoliberalist and petro-capitalist futurity) and social-cultural ethos – entails a recalibration of historical scale too.

On the other hand, the exhaustion of oil and the full-fledged manifestation of its devastating effects on human and nonhuman life on earth will only appear as a too-far future, a horizon barely to be experienced by the contemporary dweller of the earth. Accordingly, one of the chief challenges posed to any critical thinking about the temporal-historical dimensions of oil (and its cultural, social, and ecological life) concerns the dynamics of the manifestation of its ecological and ontological effects.[14] Not only does the formation of oil predate and by far exceed the history of human life on the planet but also the longevity of hitherto discovered oil (by any speculative calculation) and its full-fledged manifestation transcend the lifespan or lifetime of a single human individual. Consequently, not only are attempts at enlightening the public or the audience/reader about the ecological and social-political ravages of the oil order impeded and blunted by the aforementioned temporal dynamics, but so are the attempts at raising ethical obligation and ecological consciousness in individuals concerning their implication in the chain of the petro-capitalist consumer culture. It is such an invisibility and near-imperceptibility of the effects of oil consumption and petroculture (arising from the aforementioned temporal dynamics) that leads to, and subverts any remedial action against what Rob Nixon calls "slow violence", a term which designates forms of attritional violence affecting humans and the environment"; forms of violence that are "typically not viewed as violence at all" (2). For Nixon, slow violence is "a violence that occurs gradually and out of sight", by contrast with an event or action that is immediate in time, "explosive and spectacular in space, and as erupting into instant sensational visibility" (2). The challenge of slow violence is thus precisely its resistance to becoming spectacle, a resistance that leads, in turn, to a "need to engage the representational, narrative, and strategic challenges posed by [its] relative invisibility" (2).[15] It is the coalescence of the previously mentioned features that undermines attempts at the representation

## Oil, the Crisis of Representation, and the Dramatic Form 51

of oil and enhances its temporal complexity. The ontological ramifications of this temporal subtlety incarnated by oil has been cogently captured by Andrew Pendakis who incisively discerns and articulates part of oil's temporal and ontological complexities by referring to it in terms of arche and telos:

> Oil is an arche. . . . To posit oil as an arche is not a matter of abstruse cosmogony, nor some immemorial origin of things, but to thread the domain of appearance to its occluded, undemonstrable first principle. Oil is that upon which an enormous mass of extended, plastic Being directly relies for its beginning: it renders not just thinkable, but actualizable its very existence. There is an important double function here, at once epistemological and metaphysical.
>
> (Pendakis 2017, 382)[16]

The works of petro-drama under consideration in this book, as will be demonstrated, demand us to imagine the relationship between past, present, and future as a chiasmatic, unfinished, and ongoing process, rather than presenting us with an apocalyptic or post-apocalyptic future where the present audience is left with no function but to engage in brooding over the catastrophic future awaiting them. The latter approach or dynamics shares some affinities with the position produced by what Timothy Morton calls "ecological elegy" that is, mourning for "events that have not yet (fully) happened" (2010, 254)[17] – a position described by Greg Garrard as "proleptic mourning" (n.p.).[18] According to Morton, in the ecological elegy, the reader has "to occupy two places at once: projecting through imagination into the future, looking back on the present; and reading the elegy, in the time of reading, the 'here and now'" (Morton, 254). Notably, however, Morton contends that such a "double position" blunts the evental force or galvanizing edge of the question of climate crisis as an urgent plight besetting us here and now. As Morton explains, such a double position

> reproduces dualism, as we look back upon ourselves from the vantage point of the imagined future perfect. From this imaginary vantage point, ecological rhetoric struggles to posit the ecological crisis as an event – since things only happen when one looks back at them having happened.
>
> (Morton, 254)

If the mode of the "future perfect" inherent in ecological elegy "hollows out time" and "undermines this weeping at the very moment of weeping itself", according to Morton, then we need to ponder the possibility of a more effective alternative. Equally importantly, if mourning according to Freud designates a normal process of recognizing the loss of a loved and intensely cathected object of desire – whereby the now-lost object

## 52 Oil, the Crisis of Representation, and the Dramatic Form

undergoes a process of being de-cathected – then this proleptic mourning will be conducive not only to the confirmation of the reality of the loss (of nature) but also to establishing its irremediability, its inevitability, and its irreversibility. Hence, it will be debilitating and disarming rather than invigorating and enabling thereby precluding any possibility of change or remedial praxis at habitual (social-cultural and cognitive-affective) and infrastructural levels. As such, I would argue that whilst a melancholy mode of the recognition of ecological loss is certainly more productive and ethical, the ecological and aesthetic approach that may enable us to reach more praxis-oriented and interventionist modes of petro-drama involves uses of "the future anterior" that do not confine us to the psychological-ontological dichotomy of mourning and melancholia. It is my argument that the use of "future anterior" does not have to be confined to an elegiac mode, but can instead be recast as internally heteroglossic and hybrid in terms of form, tone, and ontology. Such a petro-dramatic form involves a threefold position which includes that of "future anterior" (see Lyotard 1993)[19] or an at once proleptic and analeptic vision of history and one's immanent relation to it in the here and now of the theatre space; a position that not only can be both narrative-enabling and praxis-enabling, but can take both the artist and the audience beyond that of an "ecological elegy" (Morton 254). If, as Claire Sagan argues, "capitalocentric temporalities" (conceptualized as uchronia) "disconnect us from our times (ou-chronos)" by "fetishiz[ing] time as capitalist futurity (eu-chronos)", I would argue that irrealist and non-naturalistic treatments of time/history in theatre/drama act as a potent move to counter such capitalocentric temporalities and their conceptions of futurity.[20] What makes theatre a particularly well-equipped medium for an efficacious engagement with the complex temporality of oil is the temporal multi-dimensionality of theatre as a genre and medium. This is evidenced by how theatrical performance is simultaneously characterized by its capacity for the creation of an event in the moment of now through the live transmission of immediate affects and occupying a shared communal space in the liminal ontology of the performance (see Alain Badiou, *Rhapsody for the Theatre* 2013). What further compounds this temporal dynamics – and concomitantly the question of agency and memory – is theatre's unique possibility of incorporating modes of embodied memory accomplished by placing archive, repertoire, and evental nowness (see Lyotard Jean-Francois Lyotard, "The Sublime and the Avant-Garde," 1984) into a dialectical relation in a way that past, present, and future are rendered uncannily and simultaneously present.[21] Such a dynamics is manifested in such forms as docudrama, reportage, petro-magic realism, and irrealism. In addition, what distinguishes the temporality of petro-drama – as well as the dynamics of the practice of embodied memory (in relation to various layers and histories of oil) from that of fiction is that the former involves the co-presence of the source (the narrator) and the receiver (the audience).

## Oil, the Crisis of Representation, and the Dramatic Form   53

*(3) Measure:* The "measure" facet of oil poses an insurmountable challenge to any representation of or thinking about and beyond oil in literature and theory. The measure facet of oil concerns the indeterminate amount oil existing in the world – an indeterminacy that not only occludes our knowledge of the past and current ravages of petro-modernity, but precludes the possibility of developing a however scientific or speculative account of the duration of the oil era or imagining a future, post-oil social-ontological order. This measure-challenge is further corroborated by the phenomenon of so-called peak oil – where even establishing certain crucial points such as peak oil on which numerous scholars concur has lurched into muddy waters (see Campbell 2005; particularly see Chapters 1, 6, 7) because it is common knowledge that the states and governments do not provide real and accurate information about the amount of their existing oil resources due to the issues of national security and strategic political-economic reasons (such as oil price and global competition over monopoly). This point hurls us into a situation which, deriving our term from Szeman, can be described as antinomial where we find ourselves in a liminal situation stretched between the antinomies of the finite and infinite, between limit and limitlessness. This fluid, volatile, and elusive informational and petro-political situation regarding the measure of oil resources in the world (along with its historical and ontological corollaries) also arises from the fact that new reserves of oil keep being discovered and, more crucially, new technologies have been developed which make possible the production of oil from materials which were formerly reckoned unextractable. This issue partly accounts for scholars' indication that we have now entered the era of tough or unconventional oil: including offshore drilling, deepwater extraction, hydrofracking (in Alberta's tar sands, for instance).

Another important aspect of the "measure-related" facet of oil – which is indelibly intermeshed with the question of time – is the question of measuring its effect: a nearly impossible act given the historically extended emergence of the effects of oil on human-nonhuman natures and their biophysically-causally complicated nature. In fact, any attempt at representing and measuring the effects of oil (quantitatively and qualitatively) is susceptible to suffer the same fate as an attempt at measuring the scale of the effects of the Anthropocene. This challenge is highly resonant with the notion of "slow violence" articulated by Nixon. The differentiated violence of climate change is difficult to conceptualize for those who are not experiencing it directly. Nixon (2011) describes climate change and other ecological slow-moving crises as "long dyings" (*Slow Violence and the Environmentalism of the Poor* 2). This is the kind of violence that is often unseen or misunderstood because it happens gradually over a long period of time, "a violence of delayed destruction that is dispersed across time and space, an attritional violence that is typically not viewed

## 54  Oil, the Crisis of Representation, and the Dramatic Form

as violence at all" (2). Nixon argues that this slow violence has consequences across geographies, race, gender, and economic mobility, as "it is those people lacking resources who are the principal casualties of slow violence" (4). The magnitude of this slow-moving and cumulative "violence" is far greater for the peripheralized and marginalized peoples, species, places, and nonhumans.

*(4) Scale:* Part of the failure to perceive and represent the ecological-ontological effects of oil stems from the question of scale in terms of depth, expanse, and scope of oil fields, on the one hand, and the extent to which oil permeates the capillaries of our daily lives at psychological, infrastructural, ecological, social-cultural, and political-economic levels, on the other. The other complication oil poses in terms of scale is its double effect at micro and macro levels. The former includes the biochemical effects of oil on human-nonhuman organisms at cellular and other biological levels. And the latter includes the effects of oil on such phenomena as the climate systems, weather patterns, territorial, and geopolitical phenomena. One paradigmatic example of the problematic of scale in relation to oil is how the discovery of oil can be conducive to the emergence of a country (Iraq, Nigeria, etc.) or to the elimination of a people, a community, and one entire natural habitat (Niger Delta, for instance). Another emblematic example of the challenge posed by the question of scale of oil is the sites of oil extraction that are often sprawling, multi-layered, expansive fields which defy visual-perceptual and rational mastery as well as the measuring methods used by ordinary means and embodied experience. As such, to register the temporal and spatial complexities of such sites, hybrid and multi-media means of representation are pivotal to capturing the two scalarly different levels or faces of oil – where apprehending the macro-level scale is only possible through adopting an aerial, sublime-like (though impersonal, affectively detached, nearly partially historicized view and devoid of sensory details and experience) and apprehending the micro- or ground-level (of lived, perceived experience of the individual) proves equally myopic, partial, and blind to the global, nonhuman, longue durée facets of oil-induced Capitalocene. Such hybrid and multi-media aesthetics are also necessary for capturing the dialectical relationship between the two scales. A third aspect of the problematic of scale regarding oil is the corollary of the first two aspects: the sheer scale of structural, infrastructural, and socio-psychological changes needed to transcend the current global hegemony of oil (and fossil fuels, more generally) and move towards a post-oil order. Allan Stoekl's argument that the other side of peak oil will not simply involve an inversion of the order of petro-modernity: "It is tempting to assume a simple reverse dialectic: the return of the feudal" (199).[22] However he adds the caveat that such a process will comprise far-reaching structural and infrastructural adaptations which pose impediments to such an inversion model:

## Oil, the Crisis of Representation, and the Dramatic Form    55

> But there is more than an energy blip that separates us from the Middle Ages. . . . We cannot simply flip over the dialectic and predict a decline where previously there had been an advance . . . the unknowable future will not be conceivable as the simple downside of a bell curve. . . . We cannot assume that we will be forced into any given social regime by any given energy regime.
>
> (203)

Specifically focusing on the "hyperobjects of the petro-modern state form – such as global climate change, landscapes erased and refashioned by infrastructure, and durable forms of industrial toxicity", Michael Truscello acutely alerts us against any hasty assumption in our speculative accounts that a peak oil era and/or a post-oil era may involve "a return to technosocial assemblages of earlier stages of capitalism, perhaps even to a neo-feudal order defined as much by its technologies as by its wealth disparity" (185). Instead, Truscello insists that a more realistic account of the post-oil era can be envisioned if the aforementioned infrastructural elements are "factored into any consideration of the coming assemblages" (185. Michael 2020). Consonantly, Am Johal accentuates the question of "scale" in envisioning any such transition to a post-oil era: "Change . . . requires a rupture with the existing order, even of forms of resistance and how they conjure up a relationship to energy at the scale of the state and capital" (*Energy Culture*, 2019, 153).

Therefore, broaching oil from the perspective of "scale" entails a consideration of the ways in which oil has come to determine not only the dynamics of our relation to such fundamental phenomena as space, time, labour, and freedom, but, equally fundamentally, our form of life (at individual and social levels) and the forms of political governance. As Mitchell argues: "Fossil fuels helped create both the possibility of modern democracy and its limits" (2011, 1). Pondering the question of scale more specifically in the context of the petrocultural studies, Szeman identifies scale as a crucial component of any discursive or artistic engagement with the question of oil. He identifies the emphasis on scale as a "dominant aesthetic strategy in reference to oil" (361). Focusing on a number of oil-focused documentaries, whose aesthetics Szeman described in terms of "failed sublime" and "scalar aesthetics", Szeman ponders the antinomies not only informing these documentaries but also antinomies deconstructively exposed by them. Szeman also identifies unanticipated affinities between environmentalists and anti-capitalists in terms of their shared antinomies and symptomatic lack of a post-petro-capitalist vision at analytical and ontological levels. Dwelling on the use of scale in these documentaries, Szeman explains how the deployment of scale "is intended to add to knowledge and to generate an affective response. Is this not an appeal to the Kantian sublime in both of its aspects, the mathematical

## 56    *Oil, the Crisis of Representation, and the Dramatic Form*

and the dynamical?" (361). Reflecting on the aforementioned facts about the (infra-)structural scale of our dependency on oil and its devastating ecological-existential ravages – to the extent where even the formation and dynamics of our social "commons" depend on this "commodity" – Szeman wonders if the "evaporation" (that is, "depletion") of oil should be considered an auspicious sign portending the possibility of the emergence of less pernicious energy resources (2012, 364).

Consonantly, ruminating on the related notion of the Anthropocene, Timothy Clarke recognizes scale as one of the crucial sites of knowledge, praxis, and representation. Clarke elucidates a significant point by underscoring an ostensibly absurd proximity of the macro and micro levels involved in any engagement with the question of global warming and the Anthropocene: "a bewildering generalizing of the political that can make even filling a kettle as public an act as voting" (Clark 2012). His more extensive elaboration is worth quoting in full:

> One symptom of a now widespread crisis of scale is a derangement of linguistic and intellectual proportion in the way people often talk about the environment. . . . Thus a sentence about the possible collapse of civilization can end, no less solemnly, with the injunction never to fill the kettle more than necessary when making tea. A poster in many workplaces depicts the whole earth as giant thermostat dial, with the absurd but intelligible caption "You control climate change".
> (Timothy Clark 2012)[23]

As such, the question of scale when considered specifically in relation to oil – and issues concomitant with it (such as climate crisis) – raises a number of crucial points. On the one hand, the scalar consideration of oil confronts us with a traumatic experience of rift, limit, and non-relation. This emanates from the manner such a scalar consideration yields two correlative conceptions: oil as *hyperobject* and oil as *objet petit a*. What connects these two extremes of scalar perception and effect is the manner both, in varying ways, pose crises of knowledge, relationality, representation, and action thereby instigating a humbling sense of sublime awe, an experience of de-subjectivation, and either a reminder of non-relation or, ideally, an intimation of an immanent, non-hierarchical relation with the other – in both of its (peripheral) human and nonhuman senses. On the other hand, a focus on the question of scale in relation to oil can indeed enable us to think in trans-scalar and non-transcendental terms. Such a trans-scalar approach entails an epistemological and affective-embodied dynamics that enables transversal and *trans-corporeal* experiences across various boundaries (including human-nonhuman, human-nature, racial, gender, class, and geographical) – which were traditionally deemed ontologically binary and transcendental. In my deployment of the term *trans-corporeality*, I have Stacy Alaimo's elaboration of the term in mind to whom it designates a state in which the individual is traversed with the invisible micro-materialities where "the figure/ground relation between the human and the environment dissolves" (Stacy 2018, 435), thereby accentuating the "material interchanges between bodies (both human and nonhuman) and the wider environment" (Stacy 2010, 16). Finally, and in the light of the foregoing points, such a consideration accentuates the ethical and epistemological necessity of developing a negative-dialectical (or world-ecological) thinking for a robust scalar and trans-scalar understanding of the issues at stake in an oil – or fossil fuel – ontology.

*(5) No End of Oil Aporias?: The Worlding of Oil Dramas:* Last but not least is what subtends the aforementioned fourfold reasons underlying the formal-representational crisis posed by oil and an encounter with it, that is, oil as an aporetic limit. This feature of oil makes it act both as the fourfold's a priori and ontological condition of our immersion in oil and its petrochemical and petrocultural implications to the point where feeling, imagining, living, and relating to ourselves and to the world would otherwise be inconceivable. LeMenager and Szeman have consonantly captured two dimensions of this ontological and discursive condition. This situation, according to Szeman, accounts for the energy impasse with which we are currently confronted: "Oil capital seems to represent a stage that neither capital nor its opponents can think beyond" (Szeman "System Failure"). Similarly, LeMenager contends: "To step outside of petromodernity would require a step outside of media, including the modern printed book" (2012, 70–71). Apprehending, representing, and transcending the effects of petro-modernity (at the levels of cognition, affectivity, phantasy, and the economy of desire) has proved a highly challenging task given "how deeply embedded in our very sensorium and modern ways of seeing the Anthropocene-aesthetic-capitalist complex of modern visuality has become" (Mirzoeff, "Visualizing the Anthropocene", 213). Consonantly, Donna Haraway indicates how petro-modernity should be perceived as the motor and the burning heart of the Anthropocene, the continuous era of human-induced environmental change whose "scale of burning ambitions of fossil-making man . . . is hard to comprehend" (2016, 49). As was explicated earlier, in conjunction with the biophysical and historical-temporal features of oil, such a condition arises from the status of oil as a strategic global commodity and the magic transformer. Matthew Huber ascribes the crisis posed by oil and petro-modernity at the levels of representation and perception to the perceived status of oil as an overdetermined object-commodity, that is, oil as a "thing-in-itself" (see Matt Huber, *Lifeblood*, 36): a description that adumbrates the uncanny agentialness and performative thing-power of oil as an uncanny actant and an *objet petit a*. This has led to the formation of the phantasmatic and mysterious qualities surrounding oil and their concomitant aporetic psychodynamics.

This ontological aporia or problematic is saliently discernible in the conceptions and imaginations and perceptions of the future – a future

## 58   *Oil, the Crisis of Representation, and the Dramatic Form*

which, in the context of the global hegemony of the oil order – to many scholars portends an impasse. Even more resistant to social-economic and infrastructural thought have proved the period and implications of the transition stage which is supposed to take us beyond oil and other fossil fuels. As Boyer and Howe argue, "energy transitions are ambivalent: both anticipatory and unknown, where hope and caution are equally gathered" (xii). Significantly, however, such a "transition away from fossil fuels" – a transition that "has no template" – demands an alternative way of thinking about energy (Wilson 379). Accordingly, literary works concerned with various aspects of energy resources – particularly fossil fuels and above all oil are charged with the task of creating a means of "fram[ing] the unimaginable" (35) – that is, of telling stories not merely confined to the horizons of apocalypse, whether ruminations on "peak oil" or any of a number of climate collapse scenarios (Petrocultures Research Group). Thus, the *After Oil* collective asks: "Is there a useful 'utopian' counter-narrative to the dystopic or catastrophic one"? (40). Additionally, an attendant preoccupation of the artists and scholars working on oil has been a consideration of how various discursive modes and literary-artistic forms might help to shift popular thinking about the putative impasse that we face as critics, readers, and consumers of oil-produced energy and as energy consumers (see *After Oil* 16). Defining energy impasse as an "outcome of a complex set of contradictions inherent to the political economy of fossil fuels" (Wilson 379), Sheena Wilson contends that one pragmatic and affective-cognitive route towards a post-oil horizon is one that must be weaned away from the sources of contemporary energopower, which is to say the "political power [derived from] electricity or fuel" and the narratives that champion its extraction (Wilson 379).[24]

These ontological and formal challenges – in conjunction with the contextual and spatial subtleties – have led to the emergence of numerous forms such as capitalist realism, peripheral realism, petro-absurdism, and irrealism (see Niblett 2020). Consonantly, Nixon discerns how such ecological and ontological dynamics – particularly given the longue durée nature of their causes and the "slow-violence" dynamics of their effects – pose formal and representational barriers:

> how to devise arresting stories, images, and symbols adequate to the pervasive but elusive violence of delayed effects. . . . How can we turn the long emergencies of slow violence into stories dramatic enough to rouse public sentiment and warrant political intervention.
>
> (2011, 3)

Indeed it has been in response to similar challenges at the level of scale – that is, historical, geographical, political-economic, and ecological scale – that critics such as Fredric Jameson, Rob Nixon, and Elizabeth DeLoughrey, in their engagement with such issues as global capitalism

Oil, the Crisis of Representation, and the Dramatic Form    59

and the Anthropocene, have valorized the deployment of dialectically oriented forms and aesthetics – such as allegory – as an effective means of capturing and critiquing these scalar issues. As delineated earlier, many of such scalar subtleties apply to the question of oil too, not only due to its unique biophysical and historical features but also because oil is both the prime mover and prime cause of capitalism and the Anthropocene respectively. A salient instance of a theoretical attempt to ponder the possibility of a more efficacious representation of oil – in light of the aforementioned fourfold complications – with a specific focus on dialectical and world-systemic approaches is Szeman. Consonantly with Jameson and DeLoughrey, in the literary and artistic engagements with (or representations of) oil, Szeman valorizes a dialectical aesthetics in which various antimonies involved in the extraction-production-consumption of oil are exposed and deconstructed. Defining antinomy as a "stark social contradiction that emerges out of the messy activity of innumerable social systems" (360), Szeman explains how the "productivity of antinomy is that it gestures to an overcoming that is present in the terms of the structuring division – one that requires only the right insight into the dynamic that produces the division to begin with" (361). Szeman calls oil an "unresolvable social contradiction" and posits oil "as foundational to contemporary social form" (351). Szeman argues how the "insights offered by these films suggest that the problem of oil has the potential to destabilize the aims of both [anti-capitalist and environmental] movements" (362). Accentuating how both anti-capitalist and environmentalist positions – notwithstanding their apparently different agendas and goals – have failed to earnestly ponder and self-reflexively take into account how both movements share the condition of being complicit in and dependent on fossil fuels (particularly oil) and ineluctably petro-capitalism: "As surprising as it may sound, it is the socially taken-for-granted physical substance of oil . . . that has to be placed conceptually and discursively at the heart of both movements if either is to realize its ambitions" (Barrett and Worden 2014, 352; in *Oil Culture*). Equally notably and resonant with the earlier arguments by Clarke and Morton (regarding the positive value of failure of form and the adoption of disjunctive form), Szeman in his reflections on these oil documentaries explores the social-cultural, representational, and political efficacy of their aesthetics of oil. He concludes his reflection by contending how most of the considered oil documentary works fail in critical and creative respects – where a part of the failure of efficacy lies in their failure to instigate remedial action and praxis which is, in turn, rooted in the discursive and social-cultural conditions of the production and perception of oil and partly resides in the biophysical and political-economic attributes of oil. Having explicated how his selected oil documentaries "struggle with Hardt's antinomies and the political antinomies of crude aesthetics", Szeman emphasizes how these oil documentaries "leav[e] open the question of how to resolve them (or even if they can be resolved), and

## 60   *Oil, the Crisis of Representation, and the Dramatic Form*

refus[e] to offer solutions that would do little more than affirm that which they would seek to deny" (364). Subsequently he proceeds to ask: "Does this constitute a form of political success or failure?" (364). However, approaching the same social, epistemological and aesthetic problematic from another perspective, Szeman proposes that we may consider this failure as revelatory and a step forward:

> perhaps their politics [of these documentaries] lie in the evidence they provide of the limit of what can be said about a socially ubiquitous substance that remains hidden from view – even today, and even in the process of bringing it to light.
>
> (364)

By the same token, as I will demonstrate in my exploration of each petro-dramatic work in the ensuing chapters, the selected dramatists in their acute awareness of the challenges delineated earlier develop dialectically oriented and hybrid aesthetic means to capture the scalarly complex dynamics of oil and the processes of its extraction, production, and consumption. The petroscapes that emerge in these plays signal a new – Capitalocenic or world-ecological – imagination, figuring a critical account of the petrocultural life across many scales. Through their recalibrations of scale, in their treatments of the effects of oil and petro-capitalism – these petro-dramatic works prompt us to rethink the questions of agency, relationality, and belonging by revealing the footprints of such hyper-objects as oil and climate crisis in every fibre of our being.

The aforementioned complications of oil – in conjunction with the ways in which they pose daunting formal-aesthetic and epistemological challenges to any attempt at literary-cultural representation of them and the imagination of a beyond – have been rigorously broached by Szeman in his essay titled: "Systems Failure". As a point of departure Szeman alerts us to a prevailing social-cultural symptom or predilection, to wit, we think of remedying or replacing the detrimental existing political-economic and social-cultural systems only after we are confronted with their ravages and their encroachment on our immediate personal life; in other words, only when these systems fail. Here Szeman undertakes an elaboration of a typology of the prominent discourses that seek to tackle and conceptualize the questions of oil politics, oil cultures, and environmental crisis induced by fossil fuels (above all, oil) – along with the ideological underpinnings, discursive limits, and historical visions sedimented in each of them. Szeman articulates the three most prominent schools of peak-oil discourse in the following terms: "strategic realism, techno-utopianism and eco-apocalypse" (2007, 808). Techno-utopianism is premised on the assumption that the predicament of oil depletion will be resolved through technological innovation, while strategic realism is a realpolitik approach which considers only the management of a nation-state's geopolitical position

## Oil, the Crisis of Representation, and the Dramatic Form    61

as a relevant concern. Both discourses "remain committed to capitalism" (Szeman 2007, 815) in their shared assumption that capitalism will remain in place indefinitely and that its maintenance is a desirable goal. The eco-apocalyptic approach, contrarily, recognizes that "social and political change is fundamental to genuinely addressing the disaster of the end of oil" (815), and that these alterations are impossible "while we retain the present consumer-capital economic system" (816). Importantly, Szeman contends how these three discourses or positions – notwithstanding their considerable social-cultural and ontological differences – confront us with an energy impasse and fail to provide an efficacious critique of petro-capitalism and a vision of the transition stage that would usher in a post-oil horizon. Szeman, however, accentuates the necessity of finding a "fourth" or alternative epistemological and discursive method and framework in order to move beyond the impasse and move towards a more socialist (and non-capitalist) topos if not u-topos. Szeman does not dismiss the possibility that the end of "surplus energy" will result in the collapse of "surplus profit" (as one of the principal characteristic of capitalism); nor does he neglect to acknowledge that "the disaster of oil is already prefigured in the temporal shift of the capitalist economy that goes by the name of neo-liberalism" (817). He underscores how these two aforementioned points have already transpired, evidenced by capitalism's regressive movement into a mode of primitive accumulation. Indicating "Retort" collective as a group whose critical views pivot on the aforementioned points only to propose the possibility of a move towards a non-capitalist utopia, Szeman pauses to exercise some caution and pragmatic scepticism towards such utopian hopes. This stance is reflected in the sombre and stern note on which he concludes his reflections:

> It is not that we can't name or describe, anticipate or chart the end of oil and the consequences for nature and humanity. It is rather that because these discourses are unable to mobilize or produce any response to a disaster we know is a direct result of the law of capitalism – limitless accumulation – it is easy to see that nature will end before capital.
>
> (821)

When juxtaposed with one of the long-standing preoccupations of scholars concerning the efficacy of the plethora of the representations of natural and social-economic disasters wrought by oil and other fossil fuels at the levels of affect and praxis – where they believe the excess of information and representations leads to disaffection and benumbed sensibility,[25] Szeman's argument, prima facie, prompts us to wonder if the utmost efficacy that critical engagements – in literary and cultural discourses, with the questions of oil, fossil capital, and climate crisis – can achieve is barely consequential, why the writers/artists and scholars should ever bother to

## 62 *Oil, the Crisis of Representation, and the Dramatic Form*

undertake their epic-scale or otherwise representations and critiques of oil, petro-capitalism, and their pernicious ecological and social-economic effects. Szeman, however, is not striving to sound a dystopian note or a note of cynical reason (Slavoj Žižek) at all. Upon closer inspection, Szeman's incisive argument intends to alert us to the necessity of (infra-) structural and systemic thinking and critique if creative and critical writers ever intend to achieve meaningful effects on their audience and in socio-symbolic reality.

By the same token, in scrutinizing the dramatic aesthetics and rhetorical codes in selected instances of modern and contemporary petro-drama (including the questions of form, time-space, scenography, narrative conventions), then, one of the focal points of my analysis – over the course of this book in its extended three-volume form – is to explore how genre (and other aesthetic features) mediates different aspects of petro-modernity. More specifically, I consider how engaging with different dramatic-theatrical genres through the lens of the Capitalocene, the world-ecological, and the energy unconscious enables us, firstly, to deconstruct both the core-periphery dynamics linking the resource frontiers and the global north and the combined-and-uneven logics of extraction/production of oil across the globe; secondly, to de-mystify the abstractions of oil through the subtleties of monopoly and finance capitalism; and thirdly, to defamiliarize the rhetoric of petro-fetishism that aids and abets common sense and good life assumptions about petro-modernity. Such a triadic orientation – informing my formal and thematic exploration of these petro-dramas – invariably entails a scrutiny of the ways in which the petro-capitalist extractive paradigm produces ontologically uneven or unequal structures at the levels of gender, race, and class.

Premised on the conceptual framework delineated, I will argue that an infrastructural or eco-materialist mode of world drama – one which is not only conscious of the ecological and material conditions of its own production as a "worldly" and "worlded" phenomenon (see Szeman and Moretti earlier) but one which is attentive to the material conditions of the production of the human-nonhuman world in an ontologically intertwined and a dialectically co-producing dynamic (as delineated previously in my accounts of Jason Moore's concepts). In an eco-materialist or world-ecological approach to petro-drama, not only are the social-machinic hyper-objects amongst the main focal points of analysis where the ecological and political-economic features of energy and fossil fuel production and consumption are treated as potent means of registering the different meanings of "oil" available in different historical moments, social systems, and world cultures. Such a world-ecological approach also provides a rigorous means of gaining a symptomatological insight into our habitual and historical modes and manners of investment in and attachment to various forms of energy and oil above all. If oil is

## Oil, the Crisis of Representation, and the Dramatic Form 63

simultaneously symbol/metaphor, commodity, and matter, when considered in its petrocultural and infrastructural accoutrements, oil transpires as a paradigmatic performative phenomenon with material, affective-cognitive, and narrative agency exerted on nature, culture, and subjectivity. The manifold dynamics of the (bio-)performativity of oil make drama/ theatre a highly apt and effective medium for engaging with it. What further renders theatre/performance an apt medium for "speculative" and "critical" engagements with oil is their shared "uncanny" nature. More strictly, the uncanny nature of oil – as simultaneously abject and sublime, abstracted commodity and toxic matter, the condition of possibility of the idea of modernity and the magic transformer, metaphor and material – is congruent with the uncanny nature of theatre/performance as an agon for the coalescence of abstract forces and concrete presences, lived and unlived histories, spatially-temporally conscious modes of presencing and absencing (Heideggerian terms).[26] Add to this the synaesthetic nature of theatrical performance where the gestural, visual, dialogical, and narrative modes of communication coalesce to render theatre the place of living, witnessing, and speculating about the sustainability of the vibrant matter of oil. Finally, if "form [is] the most profoundly social aspect of literature: form as force" and if form is an "abstract of social relationships",[27] it is one of the goals of this book to demonstrate how one of the chief ways through which the systemic nature of oil-capitalism and "the worlded" nature of critical representations of it in dramatic/theatrical literature is manifested through the "form" of the play. More specifically, I will be probing not only the meanings of oil – under a range of rubrics, including oil as commodity, as social agent, as cultural signifier, as hyperobject,[28] and as impossible object of desire – but, equally importantly, the manifestations of oil, as an overdetermined force and vibrant matter, in dramatic and theatrical forms.

## Notes

1. Imre Szeman and Dominic Boyer (eds.), *Energy Humanities: An Anthology* (Baltimore: Johns Hopkins University Press, 2017), p. 6. Energy epistemology designates the complex manners our ways of knowing, figuring, representing, and figuring energy are limited and determined but also the way those very energy resources (most prominently fossil fuels including oil) have come to affect the limits of and means of access to our knowledge of the essence effects and experience of these energy resources . . . and inflect our knowledge. (See Szeman and Boyer, *Energy Humanities*, pp. 4–9.)
2. Ibid., p. 8.
3. See Paul Ricoeur, *Time and Narrative, Volume 1*. Trans. Kathleen McLaughlin and David Pellauer (London: The University of Chicago Press, 1983).
4. *Vibrant Matter: A Political Ecology of Things* (Durham, NC: Duke University Press, 2010).
5. *Meeting the Universe Halfway: Quantum Physics and the Entanglement of Matter and Meaning* (Durham, NC: Duke University Press, 2007).

## 64   Oil, the Crisis of Representation, and the Dramatic Form

6. Derrida on performativity and iterability (see *Signature Event Context* 17–18) "Signature Event Context" (MP, 307–30; LI, 1–23). Adorno's argument in this regard can be illuminating.
7. See Raymond Williams, *Marxism and Literature* (Oxford: Oxford University Press, 1977).
8. Imre Szeman and Jennifer Wenzel, "What Do We Talk about When We Talk about Extractivism?," *Textual Practice*, 35.3 (2021), pp. 505–523, DOI: 10.1080/0950236X.2021.1889829.
9. Kate Rigby, *Dancing with Disaster: Environmental Histories, Narratives, and Ethics in Perilous Times* (Charlottesville: University of Virginia Press, 2015).
10. As Adorno explains, negative dialectic is that extreme form of dialectics in which the alterity of the other (including nonhuman nature, other – or non-hegemonic – races, genders, and classes) is not sublated or assimilated into the homogenizing dynamics of Hegelian dialectics. (see Theodor Adorno, Negative Dialectics, trans. E. B. Ashton. London: Routledge, 1973. Particularly see 85–149.)
11. See *Our Extractive Age: Expressions of Violence and Resistance*. Ed. Judith Shapiro and John-Andrew McNeish (London: Routledge, 2021); see Chapter 2 and 3 in particular.
12. See Adam Thomlison, "From Pipeline to Plate: The Domestication of Oil Sands through Visual Food Analogies," in *Rhetorics of Oil* (London: Routledge, 2020), pp. 189–210. See also Roberta Laurie, "Still Ethical Oil Framing the Alberta Oil Sands," in *Rhetorics of Oil*, pp. 169–188. And, finally, see Graeme Macdonald, "Containing Oil: The Pipeline," in pp. 36–77 in *Petrocultures* McGill University Press, p. 208.
13. See Synnøve Marie Vik, "Petro-Images of the Arctic and Statoil's Visual Imaginary," in *Arctic Environmental Modernities* (London: Palgrave, 2017), pp. 43–58.
    See Roberta Laurie, "Still Ethical Oil Framing the Alberta Oil Sands," in *The Rhetoric of Oil*. See Georgiana Banita, "Sensing Oil: Sublime Art and Politics in Canada," in *Petrocultures*, pp. 431–457.
14. Petroleum trade journals like *Esso Oilways* featured "educational" cartoons that equated petroleum consumption with a high "standard of living".
    One 1950 cartoon featuring the image of a horse and buggy (1900) contrasted with the automobile (1950) and asked, "Did you know that a nation's progress (and its standard of living) can be measured pretty well by its consumption of petroleum?"
15. Michael Ross, for instance, identifies two effects of oil on politics and forms of political governance: the rentier effect and the repressive effect. See Michael Ross, "Does Oil Hinder Democracy?," in *World Politics*, 53.3 (2001), pp. 325–361.
16. "Being and Oil: Or, How to Run a Pipeline through Heidegger," in *Petrocultures*, ed. Sheena Wilson, Adam Carlson and Imre Szeman (Montreal: McGill-Queen's University Press, 2017), pp. 376–388.
17. "The Dark Ecology of Elegy," in *The Oxford Handbook of the Elegy*, ed. Karen Weisman (Oxford: Oxford University Press, 2010), pp. 251–271.
18. Greg Garrard, "Climate Change and the Art of Memory," *The Memory Network*, 18 March 2014, thememorynetwork.net/ climate-change-and-the-art-of-memory-greg-garrard/.
19. Jean-François Lyotard, *The Postmodern Explained*. Trans. Julian Pefanis and Morgan Thomas (Minneapolis: University of Minnesota Press, 1993), pp. 14–15.
20. Claire Sagan, "Capitalist Temporalities as Uchronia," *Theory & Event*, 22.1 (January 2019), pp. 143–174.

## Oil, the Crisis of Representation, and the Dramatic Form   65

21. See Diana Taylor's distinction between the archive and the repertoire. Diana Taylor, *The Archive and the Repertoire: Cultural Memory and Performance in the Americas* (Durham: Duke U P, 2003).
22. Allan Stoekl, *Bataille's Peak: Energy, Religion, and Postsustainability* (Minneapolis: University of Minnesota Press, 2007).
23. T. Clark, "Derangements of Scale," in *Telemorphosis: Theory in the Era of Climate Change*. Vol. 1 (Open Humanities Press, Michigan Publishing, 2012), http://quod.lib.umich.edu/o/ohp/10539563.0001.001/1:8/-telemorphosistheory-in-the-era-of-climate-change-vol-1?rgn=div1;view=fulltext.
24. Sheena Wilson's "Energy Imaginaries at the Impasse," *Materialism and the Critique of Energy*, ed. Brent Bellamy and Jeff Diamanti (Chicago and Edmonton: MCM Prime Press, 2017). See also Sheena Wilson, "Oil Ethics," *American Book Review*, 33.2 (2012), pp. 8–9.
25. See Roman Bartosch, *Literature, Pedagogy, and Climate Change*; particularly see Chapter 3.
26. In Heidegger's vision of Being, Heidegger argues "simultaneous presencing/absencing as an uncanny and inherent feature of Being." As he explains, this is

> the essence of uncanniness itself, namely, presencing in the manner of an absencing, and in such a way that whatever presences and absences [das An- und Abwesende] here is itself simultaneously the open realm of all presencing and absencing [der off ene Bereich aller Anwesung und Abwesung].
>
> (Hölderlin's Hymn "The Ister" 75/92)

27. Moretti, *Graphs, Maps, and Trees*, p. 23.
28. Timothy Morton, in his object-oriented ontology, opens his delineation of what he terms "hyperobjects" by providing a number of examples notably including a black hole. See Morton, *Hyperobjects*, pp. 1, 49.

# 2 Conjonctural Cycles of Capitalist Oil Extraction in Western Peripheries

## Leo Lania's *Konjunktur 1* (1928)[1]

### Introduction

No other play in this book (perhaps except *Oil Islands*) presents such a detailed account of the nuts and bolts of the oil industry and the mechanisms of petro-capitalist system as *Oil Field* (1934) and its predecessor, *Konjunktur* (1928), do. *Konjunktur* and *Oil Field* depict the emergence of both oil industry and the concomitant monopoly petro-capitalism – in its two manifestations or stages: imperial-national (or competitive-monopoly capitalism) and a nascent form of multinational corporation capitalism. The oil boom depicted in *Konjunktur* and *Oil Field* occurs on a seemingly bare and barren landscape located in a peripheral European country: Albania: a former colony of the Ottoman Empire for more than five centuries (1385–1912).

In 1920s – the date in which *Konjunktur* is set – Albania was still recovering from the ravages of its colonial state and was in the throes of constructing a modern democratic state. The state building process, as Austin notes, requires a domestic source of stable income, international loans, and foreign investment. The latter three, in turn, require national political stability which Albania egregiously lacked.[2] The most famous political struggle of the 1920s over the establishment of a national democratic state is perhaps the one between Fan Stillian Noli and Ahmed Bey Zogu, which I have covered in the ensuing sections. The establishment of a national democratic state proved a path replete with impediments due to (apart from internal/national reasons) both explicit and subtle ways in which regional and global powers sought to impose their will and interests on the country and its resources by exerting various kinds of national and international pressures. Furthermore, such a complex national and international condition also raised the necessity of maintaining the balance between protectionism and free competition (Jean Batou and Thomas, David (eds.). *Uneven Development in Europe*. Geneve: Libraire Droz Sa 1998, p. 292). A testament to the inefficiency of Albanian political, social, and economic systems is the observation by Albert Calmes, the representative of the League of Nations, in 1921: "[whilst] Albania's economic life

DOI: 10.4324/9781003134664-3

Conjonctural Cycles of Capitalist Oil Extraction    67

depended on agriculture, its economic system and methods of cultivation were primitive, leading to Albania being forced to import foodstuffs" (in Austin 2012, 16). Prospecting for national mineral wealth (including oil, coal, and metals) – mostly conducted by international agencies and global powers such as Britain – was part of finding a stable source of domestic income. It is in this context that the discovery of oil in Albania assumes a national and global significance.

*Oil Field* and *Konjunktur* depict how, due to the discovery of oil, Albania is hurled into a transitional state or a passage from a mainly agricultural society and agrarian land (in its various forms, including fishing, herding, and farming) to an oil-intensive site of extraction and production on the global map of the petro-capitalist system. Consequently, not only does oil become the national commodity of the country, but the country is expected to undergo rapid industrialization and consequently achieve economic prosperity. Both expectations, as the two plays demonstrate, are, ironically, brought to a grinding halt and nearly nipped in the bud. The inversion of the anticipated developmental logic – the social-political and economic boom – can be considered to partly arise from what has come to be called "resource curse" (see Ross 2012, 246;[3] see also *101 Words*, 185–188) for the peripheral countries, since such an inversion (and its concomitant crises) is inflicted on Albania primarily due to the very intervention of the global-imperial powers of the petro-capitalist system in quest for a monopoly over its fossil and mineral resources. As such, both *Oil Field* and *Konjunktur* provide a valuable account of the political economy and social ecology of extraction in a peripheral nation (Albania) in the 1920s, tethered to the logics and dynamics imposed by the global petro-capitalist system (led by countries such as England, Italy, USA, and France). With the speculation about the existence and the subsequent discovery of oil in certain lands in Albania, we witness the step-by-step emergence and influx of all these contending international countries/ corporations at a time when an American Empire and the American century had not yet appeared – as a full-blown force and hegemony – on the scene of world politics and the Anglo-European Empires had not declined yet (see David Harvey 2003, 1–26). Consequently, in both plays we witness the intense competitiveness and complicitous entanglements among Anglo-American and European powers – including Britain, Italy, France, Russia, and the Netherlands (as a main stakeholder of the Royal Dutch Company) – over the monopoly of Albanian resources and markets.

The discovery of oil, as both *Oil Field* and *Konjunktur* illustrate, immediately lures in all the global and regional powers. These global or regional powers – and, above all, the delegate of the allegedly neutral League of the Nations – are shown to be implicated in a crisscrossing tangle of complicities between the ostensibly contending parties (which often contradict and nullify each other) even as they are embroiled in a ruthless competition to gain and exert monopoly over Albanian resources. Interestingly, all

## 68 _Conjonctural Cycles of Capitalist Oil Extraction_

these international representatives and Western powers are proven to be willing to connive at the violation of all the social-political values (such as democracy, human rights, etc.) they otherwise promote and claim to incarnate as long as their resource monopoly over oil (and other chief resources, labour, and markets) is guaranteed. This is attested by their endorsement of the suppression of people's, and particularly workers', demonstrations and discontent by the Albanian non-democratically appointed ruler; their support of the dictatorship, corruption, and of the continuation of the authoritarian reign of the central national government as long as the monopoly and interests of one global-imperial power or their merged representative (the merged, multinational oil company which emerges later in the play) are maintained, among others.

In _Oil Field_ and _Konjunktur_, therefore, we are still evidently in the world of competitive capitalism. The latter is marked by struggles towards monopoly capitalism, characterized, according to Jameson, with a "new interest in the properties of the object" – as opposed to its successor "finance capitalism" which is characterized by "exchange value and monetary equivalence" where "equivalence has as its result a withdrawal from the older notions of stable substances and their unifying identification" ("Culture and Finance Capital" 258).[4] Towards the end of _Oil Field_, we witness the emergence of monopoly capitalism[5] – in the guise of multinational corporation capitalism – as an intensification of the tendencies inherent in the capitalist mode of production towards the centralization and concentration of surplus value and wealth. What instigates this considerable structural shift is the presence of oil as a strategic global commodity and the petro-capitalist world system's reliance on it. This thematic and political-economic aspect of the play is corroborated by Mandel's argument. To Mandel, what facilitated the transition from market to monopoly capitalism was the invention of combustion – what he describes as a "fundamental revolution in power technologies" – and hence the global accessibility of the fuel (oil) that made them possible and functional (see Mandel 118). As will be delineated next, it was this very recognition of the strategic significance of the objects, energy resources, and commodities (particularly oil as the "ur-commodity") in the monopoly capitalist system that led to drastic alterations in the plot, aesthetics, and politics informing the initial versions of Lania's play.

The choice of an ostensibly empty landscape, by Lania, is intentional. The landscape is described – both by the, mainly foreign, contenders to the proprietorship of the land and by the media controlled by the hegemonic powers (and in both cases disingenuously) – as a barren, useless "nonplace" located apparently far from centres of human habitation. In reflecting such colonially inflected misrepresentations of the land, Lania intends to expose the politics of representation of the resource frontiers – underpinning both of the aforementioned groups' discourses – as devoid of modern civilization, education, and culture and the local-national

## Conjonctural Cycles of Capitalist Oil Extraction 69

people and state as lacking technical knowledge and technological means to transform the wild (un-extracted) nature (in their own national territory) into an acculturated (cultivated, to wit, technologically tamed) resource. This racialized political economy of relationship coupled with the racialized relation of production between the core and the peripheral nations is a staple of imperial-capitalist and (neo)colonial discourses and a condition of possibility of their extractivist logics and exploitative dynamics.[6] Notably, what this juxtaposition of an obscure (peripheral) place and the apparently adventitious presence of foreign (European and American) visitors is intended to evoke is a spirit of American-European frontierism indelibly associated with the colonial-imperial history of core powers (of the world system), including Britain, America, France, Spain, and Portugal (see Peter Taylor "History and Geography: Braudel's 'Extreme Longue Durde' as Generics?" 35–65. See also Jason Moore, "Dutch Capitalism and Europe's Great Frontier" 65–96. Both chapters appear in *The Longue Durée and World-Systems Analysis*. Edited and with an Introduction by Richard E. Lee. New York: SUNY, 2012).

Initially, in *Oil Field* (and *Konjunktur*), the land seems to be an abandoned wasteland with no ownership claims; gradually, however, we glean inklings to the contrary. The debunking of such a misrepresentation (or myth) of the periphery is introduced almost in parallel with the advent of the neo-colonial misrepresentation. This is conducted through counterpointing each misrepresentational claim (made by the foreign and corrupt domestic contenders) with a statement either made by the actual owner of the land, lady Oxhumani (which also contain references to her memories of this traditionally inherited land and the histories embedded in it) or made by the shepherds who used this land for the feeding of their herds.

In both versions of *Konjunktur* (here called *K1* and *K2*), the imperial global powers attempt to install a protégé through whom to implement their (neo-)colonial extractive practices (of oil). However, in both cases the protégé (Goldstein/Trebitsch) fails miserably and the national scene ends up with the, however transient, triumph of the nationalist-socialist revolutionary and popular forces led by Claire-Barsin. The imminent future prospect portends yet another imminent war (over oil as a strategic resource) between the national and global-imperial forces, that is, a longue durée of further misery for the peripheral Albania as long as the country owns the resources. *Oil Field* also culminates in a cul-de-sac where despite the choice of an ostensibly nationalist leader (who is actually corrupt and willing to readily buckle and be bribed into a cash sum) the anticipated prosperity of the oil industry leads to the stagnation and standstill anti-production because the global powers (Britain and US in particular) use their hegemony over Albania and other peripheral countries in order to fix the prices (prevent the price decline) and manage the market and maintain their monopoly.

70  *Conjonctural Cycles of Capitalist Oil Extraction*

The textual history of *Konjunktur*, in both of its manifestations and versions – *Konjunktur* (1 and 2) and *Oil Field* (which are genealogically intertwined) – is one of the most intriguing and complex among the texts under scrutiny in this book. A brief consideration of the textual history reveals the complexities and intricacies of the scene of the 1920s Germany – including the contending social-cultural histories, politicized aesthetic trends, and cultural politics – as well as various discursive-ideological tensions and power struggles amongst the contending parties permeating it. Since I have delved into this textual history relatively extensively later, suffice it here to indicate that this process resulted in two final texts: one in German (*Konjunktur* 1928, referred to in this chapter as *K2*) and one in English (*Oil Field* 1934). *Konjunktur* (literally meaning economic, including oil, boom or prosperity) was premiered in Berlin in 1928. Erwin Piscator directed the play and Kurt Weill composed incidental music for it. In *Konjunktur*, put crudely, three oil companies undertake a ruthless competition over the rights to oil production in a pre-modern Balkan country, and in the process not only exploit the nation and its people but inflict metabolic rift and ecological degradation on its environment.

The other integral component or feature of the textual history of *Konjunktur* and *Oil Field* is their collaborative nature – involving Erwin Piscator and Charles Duff respectively. As Lania avers (see later), the collaboration with Piscator (and his distinctive dramaturgy) exerted a considerable formative influence on the text in various respects (thematics, aesthetics, and politics). Finally, *Oil Field* and *Konjunktur* are further distinguished by two concomitant facets: their generic hybridity and aesthetic (and dramaturgical) complexity. As will be demonstrated, *Konjunktur* and *Oil Field* variously partake of various aesthetic and formal features and techniques including reportage, documentary realism, dark comedy, and some Brechtian techniques such as alienation effect.

But before embarking on a detailed engagement with the other distinctive facets of *Konjunktur* (1 and 2) and *Oil Field*, we need to capture a glimpse into the professional and literary life of Lania, particularly given that he is a rather obscure figure in the Anglo-American dramatic tradition. My own three-year quest for obtaining the playscripts of his mostly unpublished plays is another testimony to this glaring gap. When fleetingly mentioned, Lania's name is mostly invoked in the context of more prominent dramatists' and theatre directors' engagement with his work – including Brecht and Piscator (see, for instance, John Willett, *The Theatre of Bertolt Brecht* 64–65, 167–168). Whilst Lania's reputation arises as much from his prolific work in various genres and media – including fiction, drama, film, and documentary-drama – as his extended and pioneering enterprises and activities in journalism, both his dramatic work (with the possible exception of *Die Wupper*) and his prose have tended to be overlooked.

## Conjonctural Cycles of Capitalist Oil Extraction    71

## I.   Leo Lania in the World and the World in Lania's Work

Leo Lania (1896–1961), whose real name was Lazar Hermann, was a journalist, playwright, and screenwriter. Lania was born to a Jewish family in Kharkov (located in then the Russian Empire). Emigrating to Vienna and serving in the Austro-Hungarian Army during the First World War, Lania became increasingly involved in far-left politics and political theatre. His most prolific years were spent in Germany, France, and the USA where he worked with such famous theatre directors as Erwin Piscator, Bertolt Brecht, Max Reinhardt, and Alexis Granowsky (see Tatjana Röber 204–225, 247–302; see also Michael Schwaiger 244–282, 303–340).[7] Lania needs a special treatment not only on account of his literary-dramatic achievements but also his leading role in the development and deployment of reportage theory arising from his extensive engagement in journalistic activities and historically accurate and revealing accounts of historically significant events (see later). The sheer extent of Lania's exposure to and engagement with historical events of national and global consequence – not only in Germany and across Europe (Ireland, Italy, England, France, Latvia, Albania, etc.) but also beyond (including Russia) – is astounding. Such a critical immersion in historical currents surrounding him afforded him a unique artistic and historical vantage point at the level of lived experience and critical detachment. A noteworthy event in Lania's professional life is his role as Mowrer's assistant, who puts him in touch with many American journalists and writers (such as Sinclair Lewis and Dorothy Thompson) with whom he developed durable friendships. These local-national and global engagements, in conjunction with his insight into the dialectical, yet uneven, ways in which the core and the peripheries at both intra-national and international scales were connected, consequently coalesced to constitute his "worlded" and "world-systemic" stance – manifested in his dramatic and journalistic work.

The 1920s and 1930s were among Lania's most prolific years. It was during this period that most of his prominent works were published, including *Konjunktur* (1928), the communist-affiliated *Prometheus Film* and *The Shadow of a Mine* (1929) for the Volksfilmverband. He also produced the screenplay for G. W. Pabst's *The Threepenny Opera* (1931). As a journalist, Lania travelled a lot in the 1920s, at home and abroad, in the provinces and in the metropolises. He wrote for various Leftist journals, theatre companies, and social-political institutes and supplied more than 15 newspapers and magazines with journalistic material, including *Die Weltbuhne, Das Tagebuch, Die literäre Welt*, and *Prager Tageblatt*. His articles during this period encompass a broad spectrum of topics: politics, economics, travel reports, court reports, feature sections (theatre performance reviews, book reviews, film reviews, portraits, cultural-political articles), miscellaneous, sports, technology. In early 1924 Lania reported as a correspondent for various newspapers – *Arbeiter-Zeitung,*

## 72  Conjonctural Cycles of Capitalist Oil Extraction

*Willi Munzenberg, Wieland Herzfelde, Vienna, Prager Tageblatt, Montagmorgen, Berlin, Das Wort, Halle* and others – mostly under the abbreviation L.L. He also reported on the "Der Hitler-Ludendorff-Prozess", the trial against Hitler, Ludendorff, and others involved in the coup (see Gewehre auf Reisen 1925).[8] In 1926 Lania went on a trip to the Balkans by ship and was in Athens and Albania, where he met the dictator Ahmed Zogu and observed the start of the oil demand ("In the Land of the Silver Crown", 1926, LLC, 814 / F3). Hence Lania's dramatic depiction of the social and political-economic situation in 1920s Albania around the question of oil can be argued to be extensively based on historical facts and rigorous personal observations (see Ronald W. Ferrier, J. H. Bamberg, *The History of the British Petroleum Company* 172).

One of the intriguing aspects of Lania's professional life is his interviews with nearly all the world-leading political figures of his contemporary history including Hitler, Mussolini, and with the "leadership staff" and also some "conversations" with Hitler, whom he portrays in his book The *Hitler-Ludendorff Prozess* (1925) as a smear actor and mad fanatic.[9] He deftly manipulated his way into these interviews either through a disguised identity (as an admirer/advocate of the leader's causes) or as an undercover journalist. During the 1920s, feeling alarmed by the cumulative body of evidence about an upsurge in the anti-democratic and hypernationalist sentiments (particularly fomented by the national socialist party), Lania wrote a number of background articles, which clarified the danger from the right and alerted the readers to the activities of popular circles, anti-democratic sentiments, and activities in ministries and imperial institutions, about the support of popular circles by the judiciary.[10] Above all, Lania was interested in finding out about the Nazis' next plans and their weapons depots.[11] In the winter of 1923/24 he spent several months researching the mafia-like structures of the gunslinger circles, thereby uncovering some of their secret weapons depots along with the complicity of some shipping companies and the entanglements between popular circles and the Reichswehr.

During the 1920s, he wrote numerous politically engaged and scathingly critical plays concerned with historically topical issues such as energy crisis, working-class people, the moral and financial corruption of political figures – these were predominantly incendiary pieces which involved the censorship interventions by the authoritarian national state and foreign (imperial) forces. The emblematic examples include: *Die Friedenskonferenz* [The Peace Conference] (1926) about his experiences as a journalist during the Genoa Conference (1922); *Generalstreik* [*General Strike*] (1926) about the industrial action in England in 1926; *Konjunktur* (1928); *Emigrants* (1929, directed by Alfred Braun, one of the pioneers of German radio); *Der Mensch No. 17381* (1929, a radio play directed by Max Bing). One of the recurring preoccupations of Lania's work during the 1920s is the First World War. One salient example of this vexing

## Conjonctural Cycles of Capitalist Oil Extraction    73

concern is his docudrama *Gott, König und Vaterland* [*God, King, Fatherland*] (1930) which is concerned with the situation in the Balkans before and during the First World War. *Gott, König und Vaterland* features Dragutin Dimitrijević, called Apis, who was one of the key figures in the Serbian struggle for unity and independence between the turn of the century and the World War, co-founder of the legendary secret organization "Black Hand" and also the alleged commissioner of the murder of Franz Ferdinand in Sarajevo – and thus indirectly also the trigger of the First World War. Another noteworthy work of this period is Lania's translation and adaptation of Tretyakov's docudrama "Roar China!" which was based on an allegedly true historical event that Tretyakov claimed to have learned during his stay in Beijing in 1926. The theme of the play is the oppressed working class's and, generally, people's struggle for freedom against their exploitation for cheap resources and cheap labour by European (and American) imperialism.

Lania's attention to peripheral European countries is not confined to Albania (the setting of his play *Konjunktur*). Rather, it includes numerous other peripheral countries, Latvia, Lithuania, and Ireland. Visiting Latvia from November 1928 to January 1929, for instance, Lania stayed in Riga for the tenth anniversary of the Republic of Latvia and reported, among other things, on the power of Royal Shell in the country. There are discernible traces of his experiences during these journeys in some of his literary works including his novel *Pilgrims Without Shrine* (1935). Lania paid visits to England and Ireland (Dublin) in 1930, collecting material for a planned book on the Irish rebellion – which would never appear. One interesting detail of this journey to Ireland is his expression of simultaneous bafflement and fascination with the "fanatical sectarianism" of the Irish (WiU, 278).

Lania had extensive collaborations with Brecht – including 3-Groschenoper, a book project that Lania joined at Brecht's request where he was entrusted with the task of adapting it as a film script. This latter project however never materialized as a collaboration due to the disagreement between Brecht and the director Georg Wilhelm Pabst in the preparatory phase (see Tatjana, 202–225). Consequently, Lania had to finish the project with other collaborators: Ladislaus Vajda and Bola Baldzs. He also worked and was in close professional communication with many well-known writers, including G. W. Pabst, Thomas Mann, and Sergej M. Eisenstein (see Schwaiger 68–72, 344–346). Lania is one of the few writers/journalists who has a law named after him: "Lex Lania" – a law passed by the Reichstag Court according to which journalists were given the right to refuse to admit the allegations and enforced divulgence of information and were thus treated on an equal footing with doctors, clergymen, and lawyers (see Schwaiger 262–263).

Lania felt compelled to emigrate from Germany in the wake of the Nazi takeover in 1933. What instigated his escape to France was an alarming

74 *Conjonctural Cycles of Capitalist Oil Extraction*

personal incidence, to wit, finding himself as a target of a rampant Jew hunt and antisemitism. Put briefly, in mid-February 1933 on his return from Berlin, whilst staying in Dresden, he found in an article titled "The Jewish War Begins" a strident indictment of himself (due to his critique of Hitler in an article published under a pseudonym) and the exposure of his pseudonym (see Tatjana Röber 29; in the appendix to her thesis: *Band II, Anhang, Dokumentation*). Both his trip to and his extended stay in France proved replete with agonizing vicissitudes. On his arrival, he was kept as an internee in a camp along with hundreds of other refugees without access to basic amenities and in wretched conditions. He appealed to the authorities to release him based both on the Nazis' imminent occupation of France by Germans and his being a provocative Jewish journalist and writer; but his efforts proved futile. He eventually had to flee the camp along with some friends. In France he felt isolated and alienated although he spoke fluent French and wrote in French. This overwhelming sense of being unrooted in France partly stems from the slim chance of working as a writer in France.[12] He eventually settled in France. He worked on several screenplays, including fellow emigre Robert Wiene's *Ultimatum* (1938). Following the outbreak of World War II, Lania was interned by the Daladier government. During his three-year stay in Paris (1936–1939), whilst also engaging in various collaborative theatrical productions, Lania directed all his creative-critical energies towards cinema and the writing of movie scripts, some of which were produced. Stylistically, these pieces diverge from Lania's ardent socialist values and aesthetics and tend to be commercially appealing melodramas. Lania adopts this stance chiefly due to commercial reasons and for making them financially rewarding. During 1933–1935, Lania received numerous commissions for writing film scripts and even for writing a book on the Far Eastern border areas of the Soviet Union from the London publisher Victor Gollancz. Most of these potential projects, however, proved abortive and unviable due to particularly practical or political reasons.

Obtaining a visa for the USA proved an ordeal. Managing to get his visa at the last minute, Lania went to the United States. Following the United States' entry into the war, Lania was employed by the Office of War Information. He later returned to Germany and settled in Munich. Lania would always fall back on this republican-democratic foundation of his thinking, especially from the 1940s in American exile and later after the Second World War. After the conclusion of the Hitler-Stalin pact in August 1939, Lania had finally lost his former sympathies for the communist Soviet Union, which were still very much alive in the 1920s and 1930s.

Lania underwent a socio-cultural and political upheaval in the US. Not only did he come to gradually relinquish his convictions about communism and radical socialism, he also started adopting a hybridized

## Conjonctural Cycles of Capitalist Oil Extraction  75

(that is, liberalist) version of socialism. The ensuing statement by him is illuminating:

> Adjusting to American life is the crucial test that Europeans have to pass – especially the European intellectual. I and a thousand others had hardly passed it unless a fundamental change had taken place in America during the twenty years of the Roosevelt era, which I might call the "Europeanization of America".
>
> (WiU, 331)

Notably, whilst Lania harboured an ardent admiration for America, it took him almost two decades to obtain American citizenship (even as his wife was granted the same status far earlier). This might have partly arisen from the suspicions concerning his past associations with communist and socialist causes and groups.

Having already expressed his profound suspicions, in 1941, about Hitler, denigrating any business with Hitler, and underscoring the necessity of the US entering the war and confronting Hitler (Leo Lania Center at Wisconsin Historical Society, B12/F24), Lania joined the Office of War Information (OWI) in New York in February 1942. From September 1944 Lania embarked on extensive travels across the USA as a speaker for the JDC (American Jewish Joint Distribution Committee). As early as 1941/42 he was one of the "speakers for democracy" and a member of the "American Lecture Bureau". The cosmopolitan manner of his appearance, his commitment, his good knowledge of the situation in Europe, and his analytical skills were also famous. He was recommended as a "stroke of luck" and better than all previous speakers. His work for the JDC – as well as his work as a "roving editor" and special European correspondent for the United Nations World Magazine (UNW) – also drove him back to Europe. In the last two decades of his life, Lania worked as a mediator between the old and the new world. He travelled to Europe almost every year and then stayed there for months. As a special correspondent for the UNW in the second half of 1948, he visited all the countries of Europe for five months, both those west of the Iron Curtain, as well as the Eastern European people's democracies and the Balkans.

Lania discerned a crisis in the West. It was his conviction that hopelessness was not rampant for economic reasons, but because new principles and guidelines were missing for a spiritual and political recovery. In the East, he notes, people would no longer see communism as a concept of a social system, but as an expression of Russian imperialism, the imposition of the will of the Kremlin. The book *The Nine Lives of Europe* emerges as a balance sheet of these trips, an inventory of the situation in Europe on both sides of the Iron Curtain, in which Lania allows his thoughts on international politics and his diverse experiences with Europe to flow. He also processes his assessment of the situation in Eastern Europe for Radio Free Europe in the form of satires about life in the real socialist countries.

## 76   Conjonctural Cycles of Capitalist Oil Extraction

Notably, in the German edition of his biography published in 1954, he introduces himself as an American citizen (WiU, 340).

Although Lania did not manage to have any of his plays produced and staged (ever since his Weimar years) in later phases of his life, during the 1950s he wrote a number of radio plays, including his radio series *As the Comrade Sees It* (1950/51), his *Ivan's Travels and Adventure* (1952), and his sketches for Radio Free Europa and Voice of America. He also wrote a number of biographies: most prominently, *Hemingway: Eine Bildbiographie* (1960) and a biography of Willy Brandt, the social democratic politician and the then Berlin mayor, who was very popular in America. Lania died holding a pen in his hand whilst in bed in the hospital and still engaged in completing the manuscript of his last book *The Generals* – as his wife reports (B18/F2, letter of 20 August 1966). *The Generals* is an epochal novel spanning three periods from the First World War to the first years after the Second World War, with the careers of a few fictional and historical military at its centre.

## II.   The Argument

The argument in the ensuing sections of this chapter is fourfold. First, given the structural way reportage and documentary elements inform both *Konjunktur* and *Oil Field*, a concise account of Lania's reportage theory will be provided. Here we will explore how a central part of Lania's career – as a socialist and theoretically sophisticated journalist/reporter – proves pivotal not only to the thematics and aesthetics of his plays, but also to their historical-political and economic vision. In this regard, I will not only try to establish (methodological) parallels between Wallerstein's quasi-journalistic activities/writings and those of Lania's; I will also show the affinities between Wallerstein's and Lania's respective conceptions of history (as driven by a cyclical or conjonctural dynamics within a capitalist world) pervading Lania's journalistic and literary-dramatic writings – and, above all, *Konjunktur* and *Oil Field*.

Following the insights delineated in the first section,[13] the crux of the second strand of argument is the exploration of the subtle ways in which a world-systemic vision pervades both *Konjunktur* and *Oil Field*. As will be demonstrated, this world-systemic vision is vividly reflected not only in the thematics, aesthetic, and political economy of oil (as depicted in the plays). It is also discernible in their geopolitical and global scopes which feature all the major imperial-global powers of the global capitalist system, including the UK, the USA, France, Italy (with Russia as the glaring absence). A cogent testimony to the prevailing presence of a world-systemic vision in the plays is the choice of a peripheral European country as the main setting of the play. Albania is depicted in *Konjunktur* and *Oil Field* as a site where the extractivist logic of the global petro-capitalist powers – driven by a combined and uneven development and a

*Conjonctural Cycles of Capitalist Oil Extraction*   77

core-periphery dynamics – is thrown into relief. Such a choice of setting (or geographical location) – Albania as a zone of extraction – evinces an acute cognizance of the subtle ways in which the combined and uneven development and the core-periphery dynamics of the petro-capitalist system are not confined to the non-European parts of the world. Rather, such dynamics come to inform the relationship between the core and peripheral parts of Europe where the periphery (here Albania) is utilized as a zone of extraction (or resource frontier) for sustaining the "energy security", "strategic ascendancy", "sustained political economy" of the colonial-imperial core based on a finite, exhaustible, and rare substance (or energy resource) lying mostly in non-national regions and realms, driven by accumulation through dispossession. As Lania's explanation of the reasons underlying the choice of Albania evinces his consciousness of the core-periphery dynamics: "I chose Albania as the setting for the play, . . . because it is precisely here that the outer stages of the global political struggle can be followed on a small scale from the very beginning" (Leo Lania in "Programmheft zu Konjunktur").

My usage of the terms "frontier" in the context of oil cultures and oil-focused extractivist practices within the petro-capitalist system derives from Jason W. Moore's definition of commodity frontiers as

> bundles of uncapitalized work/energy that can be mobilized, with minimal capital outlays, in service to rising labour productivity in the commodity sphere. Such frontiers can be found on the outer geographical boundaries of the system, as in the early modern sugar/slave complex, or they can be found within the heartlands of commodification, as in the proletarianization of women across the long twentieth century.
>
> (Moore 144)

Considering the ontologically hierarchical and socio-economically uneven dynamics of the relationship between the core and periphery pervading the commodity frontiers, it can be characterized as zones of extraction and/or production that restructure and reorganize human and biophysical natures based on a dynamics that facilitates the extraction and global circulation of vast reservoirs of the four cheaps (and seven cheaps as identified by Moore in his more recent work): "cheap" energy, raw materials, food, and labour-power into the capitalist world-economy (Moore 2015, 53).

The crucial point concerning the term "frontier" (particularly given its use and applicability to many of the plays under scrutiny in the three volumes this book) is that, "frontier", as Michael Niblett elaborates, should not be restrictively utilized in reference to only non-European countries. Rather, not only can each nation, whether they belong to the Anglo-American and European world or not, contain its peripheral

## 78  *Conjonctural Cycles of Capitalist Oil Extraction*

regions and parts (based on the capitalist logic of combined and uneven development), but also the larger geopolitical entities in the global north – such as Europe – can include their own peripheral and semiperipheral regions; for instance, technologically or economically less developed countries which are used by the central countries as sources of "seven cheaps". As Niblett explains: "the term 'frontier' could be said to name less a geographical space . . . than the complex of relations between humans and the rest of nature through which the moving borderline between commodified labour and uncommodified work is constituted" (Niblett 2020a).

Similarly, my usage of the terms "core", "periphery", and "semiperiphery" derives from world-systems theory. In this theory, the constellation core-periphery-semiperiphery is a principal way of producing structural inequalities at both local and global levels. Crucially, these three terms designate not only "spaces", but also "processes" (see Deckard and Shapiro 2019, 5–10). Given that I have elaborated on these three terms extensively both in this and other chapter(s), suffice it to indicate here that the core zones and states are characterized by their tendency

> to have multiple production processes, involving secondary or finishing processes. Core regions tend to implement potent state sovereignty, which, in turn, enables them to enact decisions about the trans-boundary movements of goods, people, and capital. Peripheral regions, in contrast, have weak sovereignty and are characterized by the dominance of extractive industries of single export commodities (such as oil, coal, or minerals) or monocultures of cash crops.
>
> (Wallerstein 2004, 46)

In this triadic dynamics, the semiperipheries, combining the two processes, act as a calibrating zone that can "translate" the social action and commodities extracted from peripheries to cores (see Shapiro 2008, 33).

By the same token, I will argue that Lania shows how, despite the global wave of decolonizations sweeping across the previous colonies, the ontological and political-economic hierarchy – between core and periphery or the imperial power and former colony – returns through the back door in the guise of the global powers' providing technological-industrial means necessary for infrastructural development. Such a relationship ushers in the reproduction of the colonial and extractivist dynamics under the new rubrics of neo-colonialism and the rentier states. The return of such a relational logics (between the core and the periphery) under new discursive terms and political dynamics attests to the continuation of the longue durée of petro-capitalist extractivism – a situation that confirms Braudel's contention that "mental frameworks are also prisons of the longue durée" (Braudel 2009, 179). Whilst it is not my argument that Lania whether in his plays or in his meta-dramatic (and authorial) vision

## Conjonctural Cycles of Capitalist Oil Extraction    79

explicitly invokes the longue durée but rather that he evidently accentuates the significance and necessity of establishing a dialectical link between the short-term, event-driven facet of history and its longer – *conjonctural-cyclical* – dynamics. Similarly, by setting *Konjunktur* (1 and 2) and *Oil Field* in a peripheral European country, Lania draws our attention to the core-periphery logic (at political-economic and social-cultural levels) as a premise of the extractivist mode of relationship between the petro-capitalist powers and a peripheral country (Albania) which is rich in all cheaps: natural-mineral resources, energy resources, labour, and nature.

Thirdly, given that *Konjunktur* (as it was performed in Germany and directed by Piscator and as it appeared as a text in German), which constitutes the focal point of this chapter, remains untranslated and unpublished in English, in conjunction with the fact that *Oil Field* is in effect an adaptation of *Konjunktur* (in both of its main versions *Konjunktur 1* and *Konjunktur 2*), providing a succinct account of the principal preoccupations of *Konjunktur* in conjunction with a brief comparative analysis of the thematic, aesthetic, and political-economic imbrications, additions, and removals (excised sections) will be highly illuminating regarding the reasons underlying the alterations – in aesthetic, stylistic, and political respects – Lania made to the text with a specific focus on how the history, politics, and economics of oil is depicted in the plays both in a national and global context. Crucially, one of the preoccupations of the chapter, closely interlaced with Piscator's objective and materialist dramaturgy and its influence on the rewriting of *Konjunktur 1* – is the materialist aesthetics of both plays. In *Konjunktur* and *Oil Field*, the dramaturgical methods, semiotic elements, diegetic agency, and dramatic dynamics revolve around and are determined by the magic substance – oil, to wit – that has entered the text as a force field or magnet around which the political-economic and cognitive-affective forces of the play are reconfigured. As will be established, such a materialist aesthetics is also in keeping with the *conjonctural* (systemic) and materialist conception of history pervading Lania's plays (though untainted by any sense of historical determinism in the crude Marxist terms) attested by its configuration of the dynamics around and attributing central agency to oil. The materialist aesthetics underpinning both plays is thrown into relief if we juxtapose the earlier version (*Konjunktur 1*) with the later ones (*Konjunktur 2* and *Oil Field*). Later, I will also demonstrate how the inclusion of oil, in all its material-physical, ontological, and economic-political volatility, instigates a generic alteration, reflected in the movements from a piece of salon comedy with stereotypical characters into a reportage-like and nearly epic-style piece informed with a dialectical and materialist vision. We will probe how this materialist approach exerts an influence on the ethics of interpersonal relations, international politics, identity politics, and the economy of one's desire, practices, identity, and ideological allegiances.

80    *Conjonctural Cycles of Capitalist Oil Extraction*

## III.  Lania's Materialist Aesthetics, Reportage Theory, and Journalism in *Konjunktur* and *Oil Field*

No account of the aesthetic techniques, historical vision, and world-systemic dynamics (of the political-economic complex) informing *Oil Field* and *Konjunktur* would be adequate without a consideration of the role of journalism in the plays. Journalism is not only a thematic concern in *Oil Field* and, more extensively, in *Konjunktur*; it also constitutes a determining diegetic and dramatic element in them. The crucial social-political role of journalism – as a (counter-)discursive tool – is prominently reflected not only in the recurring radio/loudspeaker announcement of the news of Albania and the world but also in the newspaper run by Pusspad and commissioned by Brown. However, any attempt to delineate the various functions of reportage and journalism both in the plays and as a constituent of Lania's aesthetics, more generally, would primarily require a consideration of Lania's own long-standing professional engagement with journalism and reportage/reporting.

Notably, as a tool of social-political critique and a means of historiographical praxis, journalism not only provides a significant link between Lania (and his world-systemic vision, as argued in this chapter) and the main founders of world-systems theory: Fernand Braudel and Emmanuel Wallerstein. Upon closer inspection, journalism (and reportage) also reveals more striking affinities between Lania's historical method and social-political vision of the world affairs, as reflected in his journalistic and artistic-creative works, and those of Braudel and Wallerstein as elaborated in their works. Therefore, before delving into the role and functions of journalism in *Konjunktur* and *Oil Field*, it will be illuminating to consider the nature of journalism and the historical method journalism involves as propounded by the principal exponents of this theory. I will then juxtapose the world-systems theory's conception of journalism with Lania's account of journalism/reportage's functions in a bid to demonstrate considerable imbrications between the two approaches.

Fernand Braudel – whose chief writings in *Annales* have instigated a paradigm-shifting alteration in both the genre and institutional practices of history since the 1940s – recognizes the significance of journalism for a world-systemic account of history and society. A conceptually sophisticated mode of journalism is discernible as one of the components of Braudel's recasting of historiography's central tenets through his world-systemic geographical-historical analysis. This is attested by the leading role Braudel played in transforming the journal *Annales* (as a prominent periodical in France) into a paradigm-shifting school of thought. As Immanuel Wallerstein recounts: "The Annales School asserted holism against 'segmentalized thought' – the economic and social roots against the political façade, the longue durée against événementiel, 'global man' against fractional man" (Tim Kaposy, 401 in *Petrocultures: Oil, Politics,*

## Conjonctural Cycles of Capitalist Oil Extraction 81

*Culture* edited by Sheena Wilson, Adam Carlson, Imre Szeman).[14] Braudel's identification of "event" as the focal point of journalistic activity should not mislead us into presuming that Braudel is disparaging "event" as an epistemologically and historically unimportant category. Braudel's 1958 article on the longue durée makes a brief reference to journalism:

> [T]o put things more clearly, let me say that instead of a history of events we would speak . . . above all [of] the time of the chronicle and the journalist. . . . side by side with great, historic events, the chronicle or the daily paper offers us all the mediocre accidents of everyday life: a fire, a railway crash, the price of wheat, a crime, a theatrical production, a flood. It is clear, then, that there is a short time span which plays a part in all forms of life, economic, social, literary, institutional, religious, even geographical (a gust of wind, a storm), just as much as political.
> (Braudel, "History and the Social Sciences", 28).

Significantly, both Braudel and Wallerstein emphasize that events only assume the whole weight and density of their meaning and reality when and if situated both within their immediate contextual or *conjonctural* temporalities and the historical longue durée. As Braudel contends:

> At first sight, the past seems to consist in just this mass of diverse facts, some of which catch the eye, and some of which are dim and repeat themselves indefinitely. The very facts, that is, which go to make up the daily booty of microsociology or of sociometry (there is microhistory too). But this mass does not make up all of reality, all the depth of history on which scientific thought is free to work.
> (ibid. 28)

This insistence on the necessity of discerning the threefold structure of history, in conjunction with the dialectical dynamics and relationship among the three layers, also characterizes Lania's approach to history in both literature and reportage praxis and theory (see later). Significantly the development of world-systems theory – in its core form – coincided with the development of Lania's professional creative and journalistic practice during the 1920s and 1930s. As Braudel himself in his preface to Traian Stoinovich's book about the *Annales* paradigm reminds us, the development of the central ideas of his dialectics of duration occurred between 1929 and 1940 (Stoianovich 1976, 10).

Notably, Wallerstein's deployment of a certain mode of journalist discourse has been more consistent and extensive compared to Braudel. This is evidenced by his "Commentaries" – beginning in October 1998 and ever since continuing with unfaltering regularity twice a month and amounting to more than 250 so far. In "Commentaries", taking Braudel's

## 82 Conjonctural Cycles of Capitalist Oil Extraction

model of historical time (his dialectics of duration comprising the episodic, the cyclical, and longue durée) as his conceptual premise, and adapting it to his world-systemic vision of capitalist world-economy, Wallerstein seeks to develop a conceptually nuanced mode of journalism to analyze the significant events of his contemporary history from the perspective of his world-systems theory. Wallerstein's "Commentaries", however, are far from being a "draft of history" (a phrase usually utilized to describe journalism). "Commentaries", as Jose da Mota Lopez argues, are "neither a collection of disparate articles nor a simple practice of reflection about the contemporary" (238). Rather, they should be considered as a material-ist mode of dialectical thinking and writing about history that show us "how to do it . . . with intellectual and scientific rigour and in a way that is both highly creative and sociologically imaginative" (238).

Three characteristics of the "Commentaries", as elaborated by Jose da Mota Lopez, deserve to be emphasized. First, "in a very innovative format", they "bring together characteristics that are specific of journal-ism with what is basically an epistemological and methodological practice of analytical research that usually belongs to history and other social sciences" (226; "Journalism, History, and Eurocentrism" José da Mota Lopes, 225–240 in Longue Durée edited by Richard E. Lee. 2012). Sec-ond, the "Commentaries" are forms of "what is often called online or electronic journalism with a chronological difference; their beginnings are antecedent to the present practice of 'new journalism' by some years" (226). And thirdly, "the use of the longue durée both as a journalistic approach in the 'Commentaries' and as an essential method of world-systems analysis . . . makes possible an active, self-conscious, and practi-cal criticism" of Eurocentrism, "an integral part of the negative heritage of the European Enlightenment" and its concomitant "Euro-American universalism" (ibid. 228). As such, Wallerstein's world-systemic approach presents a vigorous critique of "a fundamental component of the domi-nant ideology of the capitalist world-economy" (ibid. 228).

Lopez in his elaborations on Wallerstein's "Commentaries" demon-strates the advantages of Wallerstein's world-systemic mode of journalistic discourse in the context of what he calls "crisis in journalism" (226–227). As Lopez expounds, the crisis in/of journalism Wallerstein discerns "is not a technical crisis of production or access to media channels" (227); rather, it is "a crisis of content and credibility, that is to say, it is first of all a political crisis" (227). Noting how this "critical situation" is "presently affecting both the social sciences and journalism", he adds,

> the reality is that not only does journalism today seem less able to give us meaningful and less parochial descriptions of our world, but also that the social sciences, in general, rarely seem able to question and coherently analyze it and its circumstances.
>
> (236)

*Conjonctural Cycles of Capitalist Oil Extraction* 83

He contends how adopting Wallerstein's world-systemic approach to history and the corresponding conception of the nature and functions of journalism within such a context can afford some efficacious solution or remedial measure for this crisis.

To this purpose, Lopez proceeds to underscore a determining point concerning the twofold or double-edged nature of journalism: "By its nature and development, journalism has always been simultaneously object and subject of the dominant culture of the world-economy: one of its sources and products" (230). On the one hand, as a historical scrutiny reveals, newspapers and journalism, more generally, "are imbedded in capitalism, and are usually an integral part of its structures of power" (298). Consequently, journalism is "intrinsically related to the existence and major objectives of the capitalist world-economy and the public affirmation of its social and political legitimacy" (298), thereby serving today, in all its media formats, as one of the "major instruments of its . . . hegemony" (230). On the other hand, however, this complicity does not sum up or exhaust journalism's nature and function. As he acutely indicates,

> Since their beginnings, newspapers and other channels of collective communication have equally been important instruments of anti-systemic struggle. They have been created and continue to be used with the specific objective of publicly denouncing, opposing, mobilizing, and confronting the negative outcomes of the domination of the modern world system at all levels of struggle.
>
> (239)

Attending to the specifically contemporary valence of such a function, he adds:

> journalism is today, as it has always been, an indispensable anti-systemic weapon, used by all kinds of social movements in the pursuit of their objectives and by all those who believe, individually, thar it is possible to construct a better world.
>
> (299)

Bearing in mind the foregoing points about both journalism's collusion in the promotion and perpetuation of the hegemony of the petro-capitalist system and its being an efficacious anti-systemic means, it is now time to see how journalism (and reportage) come to determine the dynamics of Lania's aesthetics and social-political praxis (as a journalist). We will see how a scrutiny of Lania's both journalistic and creative-literary works reveals striking affinities with the world-systemic conception of history and critique of world.

Journalism constitutes a crucial component of Lania's career and creative-critical activity. He wrote amply on the momentous events occurring

## 84 *Conjonctural Cycles of Capitalist Oil Extraction*

in Germany and elsewhere in Europe and beyond. Lania consistently contributed to such journals as *Die Weltbühne, Das Tage-Buch, Kunst und Volk*. By the mid-1920s he had already established himself as one of the chief exponents and practitioners of the genre of reportage – emblematically evidenced by the series of his reportage books (see Tatjana Röber 48–50; and Michael Schwaiger 72–134),[15] which significantly contributed to Lania's popularity, especially in the intellectual circles of the Weimar Republic. The chief functions of the press in a republican society, according to Lania, reside in enlightenment and pedagogy, manifested in their tendency towards "political education" and their motivation to actively participate in the socio-political process. Lania's own investigative expose and his critical political journalism was informed with a world-systemic vision which remains alert and attentive to the combined and uneven development dynamics of global petro-capitalism driving and informing it (see the Introduction to this very chapter). Lania posits a crucial task of the reportage is releasing individuals from their "private" isolation and mobilizing them to actively participate in the socio-political system by establishing "world references" [*Weltbezügen*] (see Schwaiger 10, 110, 310).

As a fleeting survey of the pieces and articles published in *Die Weltbühne* and *Das Tage-Buch* (to which Lania also contributed pieces) shows, not only is there an extensive coverage of the issues of energy (and their political-economic implications) in both national-local and global contexts. But, more specifically, one can also find there numerous pieces focusing on Albania and the question of oil in it. Notably, not only did Lania vigilantly pursue the pieces on Albania, but he was among the contributors too. One can find such striking pieces as the following in the newspaper *Die Weltbühne*; a piece which is not only concerned with the question of oil in Albania, but is also informed with a world-systemic consciousness and globally oriented scope:

> Around Valona [in Albania], barely 20 kilometers from the sea, petroleum sources have been discovered, and there are already two Italian companies – Ferrovie dello stato Italiano and the Miniere Bitume Selenitza – two English companies – Anglo-Persian and Ruston, the "Syndicat Franco" – Albania and the Standard Oil. *It will not be long and Valona, a dirty, miserable harbor village, will perhaps enjoy the dubious honor of being allowed to play a global political role and move from the simple name of a place to a concept like Mosul and Baku.* Then you will discover once again that there is an Albanian question, you will convene your own conferences and the prestige of the great European powers will once again be entangled in anxious worries. Petroleum is highly flammable, and what starts out as a harmless little fire in Valona can set half of Europe on fire.
>
> ("Im Lande der Silberkrone. Eine Autofahrt durch Albanien", LLC, B14/F3, 68; emphasis mine)

## Conjonctural Cycles of Capitalist Oil Extraction    85

This passage vividly illustrates Lania's method of reportage characterized by a critical intertwinement of a focus on the political-economic facts of his contemporary world history with a diagnostic critique of the ills of corporation capitalism tinged and combined with rhetoric sounding a note of foreboding about the Europe-wide catastrophes kindled by the rivalry over the appropriation of oil as the globally strategic commodity. Above all, it reveals Lania's world-historical and world-systemic approach manifested not only in his focus on a peripheral spot in Europe, but also in his attempt to show how that ostensibly peripheral spot (Albania) is already traversed with forces from the centre of the system (the global Anglo-American and European forces).

It was indeed the unrelenting pursuit of a fact-based, world-oriented, and objective kind of journalism – the pivotal values of which were social-political enlightenment, social mobility, social transparency, and praxis – that came to have a drastic impact on Lania's aesthetics. His aesthetics and mode of literary-journalistic praxis are socially oriented and politically engaged ones where, as will be delineated later, reportage, New Objectivity, and a critical realism feature as their premises. The following excerpt is an emblematic example of Lania's mode of journalism:

> Our present draws people today more under its spell than ever before, and this present is more exciting, more romantic, more colorful and more dramatic than the imagination of a poet could ever imagine. The *de-romanticization* of art paved the way for everyday romanticism, and this path leads from "pure" art to journalism and reportage, from poetry to truth, from the invention of sentimental fables or psychological secrecy to the relentless, true portrayal of the exciting mysteries of the prisons, the factory, the office, the machine, the surplus value, the class struggle.
>
> (Leo Lania, Entgötterte Kunst, Arbeiter-Zeitung, 20 June 1924; emphasis mine.)[16]

The term *"de-romanticization"*, as utilized here by Lania, should primarily be construed to designate an ideological-epistemological de-mystification and de-alienation. This should not be interpreted as Lania's wholesale rejection of German Romanticism since he was not utterly anti-Romantic in the strict sense of term. This arises from his approval of the revolutionary and humanizing aspects of German Romanticism – particularly as postulated by Schiller both in his creative work and his *Letters on the Aesthetic Education of Man* (see Michael 127, 248, 414). This passage also exposes some of the central values and criteria of Lania's aesthetics and politics. These include instigating social enlightenment, social mobility, and social transparency; promoting a focus on socially relevant and current topics characterized by a dialectical intertwinement of documentary "adherence to the fact" (embodied by the reporter) and

## 86  Conjonctural Cycles of Capitalist Oil Extraction

of creative-poetic vision that not only reveals the structural symptoms, social-political exploitations, and ideological blindspots but also provides a speculative account of the future implications of the current crisis.

In addition to Lania's basic socialist attitude, the previous passage evinces notable resonances between Lania and the "New Objectivity" ("Neuen Sachlichkeit"),[17] the aesthetics of which had a decisive influence on the literature and culture of the Weimar Republic. The aesthetics of the New Objectivity that emerged in the early 1920s was also described as a synchronization with the civilizing process (see Midgley, *Writing Weimar* 22–28, 35–41, 54–61) in connection with the various social modernization movements.[18] In addition to the democratically founded and unhindered publicly oriented journalistic work, the Objectivity program fostered a genre of realistic reporting that was to become a key genre of the 1920s, namely journalistic reporting. New Objectivity sought to achieve its goal by attending to the following: prioritizing the factual demands for objectivity, for a reference to contemporary reality and time. Similarly, Lania's incorporation of the elements of New Objectivity is evidently discernible in his interlacement of social-political critique with economic critique within the context of global capitalism, in conjunction with his deployment of journalism both as a counter-systemic apparatus and a discursive means oriented towards the events unfolding in the immediate contemporary history.

As will be demonstrated in my exploration of *Konjunktur* and *Oil Field*, what distinguishes Lania's use of reportage-based objectivity in his journalism and creative work is his conception of history which can be characterized as a multilinear and multi-scalar phenomenon. This is because for Lania history is a manifold where multiple non-synchronous presents interact – non-synchronous because of their belonging to different parts of the capitalist world system (that is, peripheral and central) and their being governed by the logic of combined and uneven development (see Koselleck 2002, 166; see also Trotsky 1962, 22, 130–135).[19]

Lania, however, identifies numerous drawbacks in New Objectivity – including its being non-political, non-dialectical, and bourgeois, but, above all, its conception of objectivity (as an aesthetic ideal), which involves a surface-bound focus on and a photographic reflection of/on reality. It is indeed in an attempt to remedy the deficiencies informing such strands as naturalism and New Objectivity that Lania dedicates his attention to the refinement of his Reportage Theory and practice into a full-fledged aesthetics. Reportage constitutes a conspicuous strand in Lania's career and thought both as a socialist journalist and a writer. The report books he published in the 1920s contributed significantly to Lania's popularity, especially in the intellectual scene of the Weimar Republic, and cemented his reputation as one of the most important exponents of the genre.

Upon closer inspection, many of Lania's aesthetic/artistic and journalistic essays and pieces manifest traces and echoes of the ideas elaborated

Conjonctural Cycles of Capitalist Oil Extraction   87

by the principal figures of Reportage Theory, including Egon Erwin Kisch and Max Winter, the founders of literary reportage and social reportage. The reason resides in the functionality of the report, which in Lania's understanding transcends the "factual" and "objective truth in the presentation" thereby ushering in another dimension that is ultimately decisive for the reporter's work. We will dwell on this crucial dimension later. Thus, Lania's conception of reportage should not be conflated with his postulation of a fully unmediated, impersonal, camera-like recording and reproduction of social-historical facts. Lania's repudiation of such a conception of reportage is not only attested by the explicit position he takes, in his "Reportage als soziale Funktion" (June 1926), against the photo-metaphor, thereby endorsing an in-depth and background-oriented analysis as the actual task of the reportage. It is also evidently reflected in his use of key terms such as the "revealing of the core" [die "Enthüllung des Kerns"] and "unmasking" (of social-political corruption and structural complicities) – utilized to capture the crux of the task of reportage. As he states: "Only he is with us who has the courage to tear the mask from his face and look into your face without looking down" (see 53).

Notably, the relationship between reportage and poetry was the centre of an intense debate in 1920s – where poetry was primarily associated with the criterion of "design/form" [Gestaltung] and reportage with "documentation". The noteworthy point about Lania's approach is his refusal to establish a dualistic or antithetical relation between reportage and poetry and instead insisting on them as two (not necessarily incompatible) modes of expression. The "literary basis" and the "stable foundation" of this factual documentary poetry [sachlich-dokumentarischen Dichtung], which enables "the artistic creation (or design) [künstlerische Gestaltung] of this time [contemporary history] and its social problems", remain the reportage.[20] According to Lania, it is not clinging to external facts that distinguishes the reporter from the poet. The characteristic that has traditionally been attributed to a poet is the poet's unfaltering valorization of "the design" (the rhetoric) – or the formal and ontological autonomy of the artwork – over and above the context or pre-text itself. What fundamentally distinguishes reporters is their ascription of primacy to the social-historical "object as it is" (in a dialectical, or at once personal and political mode). According to Lania, the reporter differs from the poet not only in that the latter "designs" the material while the former merely "documents" it, but primarily in that the material of the report is fundamentally of *general social interest* – the key concept in Lania that accounts for his divergence from Egon Erwin Kisch's stance toward Reportage. Lania defined reporting primarily as a "form of combat" ("Kampfform"), and only secondarily as an "art form" ("Kunstform") (see Schwaiger 97–99). As such, Lania supplements the contemporary debate about the relationship between reportage and literature – to which the principles of "documentation" and "design" were assigned – with an additional element that

## 88 Conjonctural Cycles of Capitalist Oil Extraction

puts this relationship on a fundamentally different level: the element of generally binding meaning, of general social interest, which is opposed to particular and singular self-interests.

The reporter, as Lania explains,

> does not take the position of the . . . observer as the object of his representation, whether it be a prison, a madhouse, a mine, a factory, but of the spy – he does not describe, he reveals – he does not show things as they are, but how they were and what will become of them.
> (Leo Lania, Reportage als soziale Funktion, in
> *Die Literarische Welt* 2 (1926) 26, 5f.
> See also Schwaiger 109–113)

As the son of a surgeon, Lania's conception of the diagnostic task of the reportage and a reportage-oriented aesthetics is couched in a critical-clinical rhetoric – informed by a surgical and surface-depth dynamics. Deploying the rhetoric of naturalistic aesthetics, Lania proceeds to utilize a noteworthy trope ("exposure of epidermis") to articulate the hermeneutics of truth at stake in the social politics of reporting (or journalistic praxis):

> he exposes the epidermis of his model, feels along the blood vessels, dissects meat, experiments with blood and bacteria. The reporter is not supposed to be just an internist, he is also a merciless surgeon, he has to cut to show the structure of the organism, or the ridiculous pus that disrupts all functions.
> (Lania, Reportage als soziale Funktion n.p.)

On this premise, reporting, to Lania, is not an aesthetic commodity for the marker ("not an aesthetic trade"), but rather the act of exposing pus and making the dirt (corruption) whirl up.

Lania's attitude is not only consonant with the Zeitgeist and the approach pervading the sociological and cultural-political studies at the time. The sociologist René König, for instance, utilized the analogy of a "doctor of society" ["*Arztes der Gesellschaft*"] to describe the role of the social researcher (54; see Schwaiger 117–118, 267). More importantly, such a stance derived its bearings from the "muck-raking journalism" (as the purest and most authentic form of reportage) which, according to Lania, found its most paradigmatic example in the American trend of Muckrakers. Lania's numerous reviews of the works of prominent American reportage writers (such as Upton Sinclair, Sinclair Lewis, and John Dos Passos) in the 1920s clearly show how lasting the influence of this American operational-practical and utility-oriented literature [*operativen Gebrauchsliteratur*] was on Lania and his work. Lania recognizes "muck-raking journalism" as an effective term. To him, it designates the practice of radical criticism aimed at the inadequacies of the political-economic

## Conjonctural Cycles of Capitalist Oil Extraction    89

establishment (including the oil industry and the meat industry – the focal points of two of Sinclair's prominent novels). The term and the mode/genre of writing to which it was ascribed gain such wide cultural currency and social-political impact that American President Theodore Roosevelt dedicated one of his speeches (April 14, 1906) to the topic and the issues this mode of writing raised. In his speech Roosevelt uses the term in a derogatory sense and delivers a caustic arraignment of the practitioners of the genre (see "Reportage als soziale Funktion"; see also Michael 115–116).

Lania explicitly mentions Upton Sinclair, George Kennan, and Albert Londres as "masters" of reportage genre [*"Meister des Reportagegenres"*] due to their exemplary contributions to investigative journalism and public effectiveness ("Reportage als soziale Funktion", see 52). Upton Sinclair, whose novel *Oil!* (as we will discuss later) came to provide ample insights into the technical details and intricacies of the corporation capitalist dynamics of this global commodity, was one of the most famous exponents of the Muckrakers. Deriving his insights and inspiration from the American Muckrakers (prominently, Upton Sinclair in such works as *The King Coal*, *The Brass Check*, and *The Jungle*), Lania, from 1926/27 onwards, increasingly dedicated his activities to socio-politically incendiary topics that had wide public appeal and promised to be commercially successful too. This strand of Lania's work places itself at the intersection of journalism/reportage and poetry. Among the works he produced in this strand are his documentary contemporary dramas for the Piscator stage, autobiographically coloured reportage poems (for instance, "Indeta, Die Fabrik der Nachrichten", 1927), and historical novels (including *Anita Berber – Der Tanz ins Dunkel*, 1929), in which fiction and fact permeate each other. The common thread binding all these works is their conformity to Lania's principle of a generally binding social interest.

The impact of America and American culture on Lania is not confined to a specific literary-journalistic genre. For Lania modern America and "Americanism" [*"Amerikanismus"*] (the terms he uses and invokes) denote a certain mode of social democracy characterized by the "practical" appropriation of public life by the individual, social transparency and social mobility (see "Reportage als soziale Funktion"; see also Michael 5–6, 27–33, 40, 72–75). Far from being an essentialist term restricted to certain historical boundaries or geographical entities (such as America or Germany re-built or modelled after America), "Americanism" is appropriated to be invested with Lania's ideal social-political condition or place where the private and public spheres, individual and collective, ultimately even the USA and Soviet Russia, merge, which, according to Lania, turned out to be the most American country ever in the 1920s. Elsewhere, Lania defines "Americanism" as "the visible workings of a collective consciousness" [*eines Kollektivbewußtseins*] that is fed from the sources of a strong, exuberant attitude towards life ("Reportage als

## 90   Conjonctural Cycles of Capitalist Oil Extraction

soziale Funktion"; see also Michael 121–122). Lania in a contentious move then proceeds to identify solely one country as qualified for the term "American": Russia. Lania explains the premise of his claim by referring to "Russia's relationship to technology, to the machine, to the things of daily life in conjunction with a modern novelty (arising from Russia's vastness and lack of tradition, Soviet Russia is American" (Leo Lania, "Maschine und Dichtung, Arbeiter-Zeitung", 1927).[21]

In the same vein, Lania's socialist conception of a society diverges from the typical communist doctrine wherein the individual is supposed to be dissolved in the collective or where the interests of the individual are supposed to be sacrificed for the interests of the collective (a view largely reflected in Brecht's earlier works such as his 1926 play *Mann ist Mann*). Lania diverged from the prevailing leftist trend both generally and as informing the aesthetic-literary field by underscoring the significance of the individual as an irreducible element in the establishment of the democratic society as a living organism driven by a dialectical dynamics (between the individual and the collective, between the classes and between the individual and the state). Lania's socialist vision of the society involves a holistic space as a living, collective organism, where a dialectical relationship bonds the individuals on the one hand and the individual and the collective and the state on the other hand. This stance is evidenced by the ensuing statement: "Nothing is more stupid than the unfortunately very widespread opinion . . . that socialism excludes any development of the individual, makes work animals out of all people, whose social function [kills] every private feeling, every individual life in them". He then proceeds to the crux of his vision: "To see how the new youth, the new person arrives at a synthesis of their social and private life interests, was my endeavor during my last trip through the Soviet Union" (see Schwaiger 64). Nevertheless, as is evident in his treatment of the characters both in *Konjunktur* and *Oil Field*, Lania's valorization of the individual should not be conflated with naturalistic attribution of primacy to psychological interiority. In Lania's materialist view, the individual is at once a source of agency/action and critical consciousness, and the "ensemble of social conditions" (see Schwaiger 65). In the light of the foregoing notions, it is now time to turn to an in-depth exploration of the ways in which Lania's materialist and dialectical aesthetics coupled with his reportage theory coalesce to inform his two petro-dramatic plays.

## IV.   From *Konjunktur* to *Oil Field*

*Konjunktur* and *Oil Field* – in conjunction with *Oil Islands* – are the only plays in this book that afford us ample insights into not only the determining role of oil in the global scene of economic and political modernization, profit, power-struggle, and global hegemony and rivalry over oil as a strategic commodity in the critical years between the two World Wars

## Conjonctural Cycles of Capitalist Oil Extraction   91

(1918–1935) – and into the years of Cold War, in the case of *Oil Islands*. *Oil Field* and *Konjunktur* also delve into the complex political-economic and social-cultural means through which the global petro-capitalist system – both through its imperial arms and monopoly corporation capitalism (with gestures towards multinational corporation capitalism) – seeks to exert its modes and relations of production, its social and political-economic logic, and establish its hegemony. As such, the plays depict the trajectory of petro-capitalism and illustrate the mechanisms and dynamics of the petro-capitalist system at the level of imperial (represented by Britain), global (represented by Italy, France, and USA) corporation operation and their activities in both core and peripheral countries. *Konjunktur* (*1*, *2*) registers the oil encounter in Albania which proves a junction in the global war and competition over cheap resource extraction. Whilst I will delineate here, by way of comparison, some of the salient features of *Konjunktur 1* and *2*, primacy will be accorded here to the thematic, aesthetic, and historical-geographical alterations the play underwent in its evolutionary transition from a China-focused, revolutionary work to an Albanian-set work with a world-historical and world-ecological focus to, ultimately, an allegorical work about the *conjonctural dynamics* of extractivist global capitalism set in an apparently indefinite country. One conspicuous change to the play involved its adoption of a materialist aesthetics – where not only the dynamics of oil (as commodity and social relation, as matter and mediation) comes to determine the form and dynamics of the text, but the infrastructural and material paraphernalia of oil and the oil industry are incorporated as pivotal thematic and dramaturgical constituents of the play.

The textual history of the play in both its manifestations and versions – *Konjunktur* (as produced by Piscator) and *Oil Field* (never produced as a staged performance) – is one of the most intriguing and subtly entangled ones among the texts under scrutiny in this book. Given that *Konjunktur* proves to occupy a juncture at the intersection between various contending parties at political and aesthetic levels/respects, a brief dwelling on its textual history will canvass the scene of cultural and social politics permeating the 1920s Germany and the various discursive-ideological tensions and power struggles raging amongst the contending parties.

Since its gestation as a preliminary outline and idea, the play appeared in three textual guises or forms – all in German and undergoing exceedingly drastic revisions – before it reached its drastically altered form in English – as *Oil Field* – more than six years later. The play began its itinerant life as *Red versus White* [*Rot gegen Weiss*] then evolved into *Konjunktur 1* (or pre-Piscator version) and finally, *Konjunktur 2* (or post-Piscator version). Though one could add a third version which is the one preceding the slight refinements made to it in consequence of the objections to it raised by the representative of the Communist Party among others (see later). However, to eschew confusion and given the

## 92   Conjonctural Cycles of Capitalist Oil Extraction

slight extent of changes I have decided to simply refer to the final text as *Konjunktur 2*. The latter is the one staged by Piscator at Piscatorbühne on the 10th of April, 1928. *Konjunktur 2* was substantially revised and rewritten in English (in collaboration with Charles Duff), hence accorded a new title: *Oil Field* (1934).

Although no published copy of the first version of the play (*Red Against White*) has survived, we can garner our inklings from several reviews and Piscator's own comments on the play, and collate them to develop a general outline of the story. There is just as little evidence of this play as of the changes to *K2* made shortly before the premiere. The most substantial clue to the content of this earliest, or the "original version" comes from Piscator's statements in *The Political Theater*. *Red Against White* was written as mainly a socialist comedy and was predicated on factual events in China. The core of *Red Against White* consists of a Chinese general who falls into the hands of an insidious manager in England who politically and financially exploits both him and the Chinese workers more generally. This, in turn, gives rise to a kind of civil horror. The comedy-like consequences of this business, in which the manager goes bankrupt, constitutes the overarching plot and framework of the play. Piscator's reminiscences and remarks on the draft can be illuminating:

> He had in mind to shape the bargain that is driven by revolutions, and to show how the idea triumphs against the personalities who want to abuse it. The comedy, whose provisional title was "Red versus White" followed on from the events in China and featured a Chinese general who fell into the hands of a busy manager in England and from him being financially exploited as a kind of civil horror, at the centre of the plot. The comedy-like consequences of this business, in which the manager went bankrupt, made the framework of the play.
> (Piscator 1929, 204)[22]

At the time when *Red Against White* was created, in the spring of 1927, the clashes between the Red Army and White Guards escalated in China. The English, represented in the play by the figure of the manager, became exceedingly embroiled in the fighting. At the beginning of 1928, ruminating on the past ten months of the Chinese civil war, Lania attributed the failure or "debacle" to the Soviet Union (the Bolsheviks) and their intrusive and oppressive methods of government in China (see Röber 353–359). At the end of *Red Against White*, revolutionary idealism was supposed to triumph over devastating imperial-global economic greed for profit (represented by the British Empire); but this first preparatory work on *Konjunktur* proved, according to Piscator, "a failure" since the basic idea did not "carry the whole piece" and the plot did not seem convincing. In this play, Lania derives part of the aesthetic and dynamics of his play from the theatre tradition of picaresque and salon comedy evidenced by

## Conjonctural Cycles of Capitalist Oil Extraction   93

his own allusion to Eugene Scribe's *Das Glas Wasser* (1840) [*A Glass of Water*] (11.17), which is a well-made historical comedy of intrigue where epic-scale historical events emanate from ostensibly trivial quotidian incidents (for instance, the Queen's simple request for a glass of water).

Piscator, however, criticized the interweaving of dramaturgy and comedy scheme as an unsatisfactory "compromise" (*Political Theatre*, 198). Piscator contended that the incorporation of comedy into the scheme of the play led to an attenuation of the other fundamental constituent of the play, to wit, the complex discursive and causal patterns permeating the social and political-economic realities of contemporary oil-driven history. In other words, Lania's choice of comedy (of manners) as form – which entailed a scheme-based treatment of the narrative and a typifying simplification of the psychologically complex characters – negates the subtleties of the global networks, national-global agencies, and political-economic dynamics underpinning the oil world and petro-capitalist discourse. As both Lania's and Piscator's commentaries on *Konjunktur 1* indicate, the other notable bone of contention or challenge in the collaborative process was the accommodation of the practical theatre considerations in order to make the play transcend the bounds of mere essayistic forms (see *Political Theatre*, 199; see Tatjana Röber 378–387). Piscator presented Lania with the aesthetic-dramaturgical manoeuvres which, he believed, would enable them to achieve the right balance between more "documentary" and "dramatic" forms; in other words, a diffusion of critical ideas and historical facts through the intricacies of aesthetic form and dramaturgical techniques of the Piscator stage (see *Political Theatre*, 205; see also Tatjana Röber 295–301). Spurred by the feedback and advice from Piscator, Lania embarked on a drastic rewriting of the piece to the extent that the outcome (*Konjunktur 1*) can barely be considered to bear any traces of the so-called original. Featuring oil as its thematic and diegetic spine, *Konjunktur 1*, subtitled "the comedy of economics" (*Die Komodie der Wirtschaft*), takes the discovery of oil in a peripheral Adriatic country (Albania) as its core. There is also a noteworthy aesthetic-dramatic change from salon comedy and mischief and charlatan to a more abstract, objectivist, and reportage-based mode.

Although Piscator (and the leading actress Tilla Durieux) found the first two completed acts of *Konjunktur 1* appealing and dexterously carried out, Piscator found the revised version still inadequate and incongruent with some of the aesthetic principles of his practice – emblematically his idea of "sociological dramaturgy" that valorized some quasi-Leninist intellectual and stylistic values, including objectivity, concrete and simple presentation of reality, factuality combined with a certain prophetic idealism, anti-decadence (that is, opposed to individualistic-anarchist needs of bourgeois artists which characterize trends such as expressionism and neo-romanticism).[23] This was not least because the revised version was still cast largely in the style of the conventional intrigue and salon

## 94  *Conjonctural Cycles of Capitalist Oil Extraction*

comedy of the 18th and 19th centuries. Accordingly, the most important deficiency was the gap between the thematics and aesthetics. In other words, *Konjunktur*'s failure particularly stemmed from its inability to formally tap into the potential possibilities of the "material" – to wit, oil in conjunction with the petro-capitalist logics and petrocultural dynamics surrounding it – with its conventional means of expression. Put more lucidly, despite the inclusion of oil as a thematic concern and intermittent references to it, not only did *Konjunktur 1* prove historically inadequate in its failure to take stock of the crucial role oil played in global political economy and modern history. *Konjunktur 1* also fell short in terms of its dramatic aesthetic (at formal, dramaturgical, and affective levels) by lack of engagement with oil as matter and mediation/mediator, as lifestyle and form of life, as commodity and social relation, and, finally, as a materially-biophysically unique, historically determining, and politically-economically strategic material/object with formidable agency.

Aesthetically, *Konjunktur 1* is streaked with strands of salon comedy, aborted love affairs, and gestures of erotic-political seduction and persuasion. Conceived as an "economic comedy", *Konjunktur 1* was specially developed by Lania for the Piscator stage according to the principles of "sociological dramaturgy" – which were starkly opposed to the majority of the traditional dramatic forms including comedy and realism. Piscator had already staged three successful productions, namely, *Hoppla, We're Alive!*, *Rasputin, the Romanovs, the War, and the People who Rose Up Against Them*, and *The Adventures of the Good Soldier Schwejk* – all produced between September of 1927 and April of 1928, during the exceedingly turbulent latter years of the Weimar Republic. Lania's *Konjunktur* was supposed to be the fourth production in the series where the principles of Piscator's objectivist dramaturgy, the reportage-based dramatic aesthetics, and new social-cultural sensibility were supposed to be paradigmatically illustrated (see Schwaiger 275–299). Accordingly, in working on *Konjunktur 1*, Piscator's foremost aim was to dissolve the comedy structure in a bid to reach a form in which human hero-individuals are replaced by the socio-politically overdetermined agential matter/material (oil, other resources, and the concomitant commodity culture), collective subjects, types, personifications, as strikingly emblematized by the mode of the first act.

Whilst one of Lania's crucial concerns was the generic cohesion and poetic consistency of the play, for Piscator the primacy had to be accorded to the "ideas", their objective concretization and their relational dynamics upon the stage. This is attested by Piscator's endorsement of an unsmoothed representation, a dynamic, "liquefied" [*verflüssigte*] aesthetic that emphasized the breakpoints [*die Bruchstellen*] (Lania, *Die Komödie der Wirtschaft*, 2; see also Röber 1999, 381). Lania's generic-poetic concern, however, revolved around the role of the human hero/protagonist (Claire Barsin) and the fact that in the new version whilst the (former:

## Conjonctural Cycles of Capitalist Oil Extraction    95

in *Konjunktur 1*) protagonist (Claire Barsin) looms large at certain parts of the play, she gradually vanishes towards the end. Hence, his main preoccupation in the diegetic-dramatic dynamics and economy of *Konjunktur 2*. As he avers, his desideratum was: "to translate the brittle, hitherto hardly worked on political material into poetry, to soak it up in the human" (Piscator, *Political Theatre*, 198). Piscator planned to open the Lessing Theater with the Lania script which marked his fourth main production. Ultimately the quandary was resolved when, under Piscator's direction, Lania composed a conclusion in which a Russian agent (Claire Barsin) gained control of a newly discovered oil field in Albania through inciting revolution. This conclusion, as we will see, will prove incendiary.

The textual history akin to its thematic crux – oil – features a situation where capitalist and communist, national and international, along with the values promoted by each, come into conflict. The play features as one of the most collaboratively composed pieces. As Lania avers, Erwin Piscator and his dramaturgical aesthetics exerted an indelible and formative influence on the thematics and dynamics of the text. As he recalls:

> His directorial suggestions have shown me the way on which I tried to realize those intentions that did not arise from a spontaneous idea or a momentary inspiration, but grew out of the tasks and ideas that this stage wants to serve. Fertilized by it, out of our collective collaboration, this comedy [*Konjunktur*] was born.
> (Leo Lania in the program booklet for *Konjunktur*)

Indeed, the collaboration with Piscator, as a socialist producer and director, proved formative and inspired a more politicized and socially-politically well-informed and well-structured play in that it placed the story in a more world-conscious context and pushed it beyond mere national preoccupation and borders and geographical myopia. One of the principal aspects of this influence was objectification (emphasis on the objects in conjunction with alienating process which lead to reification of human individuals) as a means of enhancing the social-political objectivity of the aesthetics and thematics of the play: "Piscator's staging was based on the assumption that the material in all its objectivity and totality would be vividly visible through the construction of the stage" (Leo Lania, *Die Komödie der Wirtschaft*, in: Der brennende Punkt, Blätter der Piscatorbühne [April 1928], 1–2; 2). Lania's *Konjunktur* (subtitled: *Economic Comedy*) provided the literary template for the fourth production of the Piscator stage, which premiered on 10 April 1928 in the Lessing-Theater.[24]

One of the most conspicuous outcomes of this collaborative process – particularly for a writer committed primarily to the socialist cause – was the shift of focus away from pure politics (evident in earlier versions of the *Konjunktur*) towards a more materialist vision and political economy. This turn, prompted mainly by Piscator and partly Brecht, is above all

## 96  *Conjonctural Cycles of Capitalist Oil Extraction*

manifested in the inclusion of the globally strategic fuel (driving wars, industrial nations, and the capitalist system simultaneously) and dominant global commodity par excellence: oil. It is indeed only in *K2* that the "substance oil", or more precisely: "the laws and phases of its economic development", assumes its true weight (*Political Theatre*, 198). Although the three-act structure of *K1* is retained in *K2* as its tectonics, the plot of intrigue remains partly the structural framework in the second version (*Political Theatre*, 204). As Brecht indicates:

> there was a play called *Petroleum* [*sic*], originally written by Leo Lania but adapted by us, in which we wanted to show exactly how oil is drilled and treated. The people here were quite secondary; they were just ciphers serving a cause.
>
> (Interview with a Danish Journalist 1934)

This collaborative dynamics, conspicuously, also involved contribution from Alfons Goldschmidt (the prominent Marxist economist and one of the founders of the League for the Proletarian Culture). His ideas and writings not only came to inform the political-economic and historical vision of the play and its treatment of various facets of oil. Goldschmidt also contributed an article to the performance booklet where he provided an extended account of the history of the commercial exploitation of oil, ranging from Titus Drake's discovery of how to engineer a fuel-burning engine in 1850 to Rockefeller's Standard Oil Trust and the inexorable escalation of international competition. Here he drew the audience's attention to the world-historical and world-economic significance of oil as a global strategic commodity:

> The history of this war is full of blood, stupidity, and corruption, of brutal attempts at monopolization. . . . Murders, abductions, desecrations, all manner of brutalities have been demonstrated in this imperialist economic battle, perhaps even more horrible than open warfare. The world war of 1914/18 was already an oil war. . . . It was carried out with and around oil, around the colonies as oil production and oil sales areas, around the security of the maritime oil bases.
>
> (Alfons Goldschmidt, "Petroleum!, in: Der brennende Punkt, Blätter der Piscatorbühne" [April 1928], 3–5)[25]

Some of the changes to the text, however, were more politically motivated and coercive and less aesthetically driven. One of the most fascinating parts of the textual history concerns the pre-premiere performance of the play for the representatives of the Communist Party of Germany, the Russian trade agency, and the Russian embassy, whose approval (in terms of the play's compliance with the party politics and its values) was a tacit necessity for the smooth continued life of the production. But the

## Conjonctural Cycles of Capitalist Oil Extraction    97

acceptance committee convened by Piscator before the premiere – which adumbrates the uncertainty of the "producers" with regard to the "political correctness" of their production – concentrated on the plot (rather than the aesthetics or underlying political critique of Anglo-American capitalism). Upon the performance of the preview, the conclusion of the play received a caustic criticism not only from the representative of the party (KPD), but also an influential segment of the Piscatorbühne's audience, the Russian embassy, and the reviewer of the German communist newspaper. In brief, they found the presentation of Soviet Union and its foreign policies outrageous and demanded the rectification of the text. In the pre-performance text of *Konjunktur 2* (which is almost identical with *Konjunktur 1*), the Soviet Union (and its foreign policies) is, metonymically, incarnated by a character, Claire Barsin, who embarks on an array of manipulative and interventionist activities (including leading an anti-state revolution) in an attempt to not only incite anti-imperial and anti-foreign sentiments and attitudes amongst common people and workers but she also relentlessly strives to gain monopoly over Albanian oil resources (as the disguised representative/agent of the Soviet Union). The (economic) policy of the Soviet Union, represented by Claire-Barsin, is based, akin to that of the capitalist countries, on a double strategy, which is kept secret until the end from those who were first affected, the Albanian workers and peasants. It was due to this (perhaps inadvertent) subversion of what was supposed to be antithetical differences between communism and capitalism (at ideological and political-economic levels) that the director had no choice but to alter the script (148). Part of the problem and the ire it provoked seems to reside in the fact that in *Konjunktur 1*, the oil power of the Soviet Union is used for the reputation of the system, political persuasiveness is substituted by economic assertiveness – an equivocal feature that unwittingly exposed ideological contradiction in the Soviet Union's treatment of other peripheral countries and the double-dealing nature of its policies.

Given Piscator's leftist allegiances, it mattered to him to dispel any issue that would taint his efforts. As Piscator indicates:

> The question was sensitive for us because it affects the position of the Soviet Union in this economic-political struggle for the sales markets for oil: its relations and contrasts with the oil producing and selling American and English corporations as well as its position as a competitor within of the capitalist world economy.
>
> (*Political Theatre*, S 200)

Given the urgency of the matter and the imminent premier, the rectification of the provocative depiction of the Soviet Union (in *Konjunktur 1*) was assigned to Bertolt Brecht, who through his judicious revision prevented the theatre from closing its doors. Driven by his characteristic

98   *Conjonctural Cycles of Capitalist Oil Extraction*

perspicacity, the experienced Brecht single-handedly rewrote the final act of the play to please all concerned by changing the Russian agent to an American spy in disguise, thus making it possible for the curtain to rise on the play. *Konjunktur* was eventually premiered at the Piscatorbühne in the Lessing Theater on the 10th of April 1928 (149).[26] I have delved into this issue through an extended comparison of the conclusions of both versions next.

## V.   The Birth of a Peripheral European Petro-State: The *Conjonctural* Dynamics of Oil Extractivism in *Konjunktur 1* and 2

The foremost point which needs elaboration is the very title of the play. Notably, the German word "Konjunktur" is etymologically derived from the Medieval Latin word "coniunctūra" which has in turn been derived from "conjunctus". In Latin, the word signifies connection, link, and conjunction. In German, Konjunktur is a polysemic, feminine, genitive noun (plural Konjunkturen) designating business/trade cycle (hence both an economic boom and bust), current economic situation (or current trend in the business outlook), upward trend or expansion, and a favourable turn of the market or a boom. Whilst almost all the foregoing meanings are discernible in the thematic preoccupations and political-economic dynamics of Lania's *Konjunktur 1* and 2, it is the "cyclical" dynamics – evoked by the term – which demands our attention. Crucially, the play's title, *Konjunktur* (which cannot be captured in all its complexity within the restrictive confines of one equivalent in English) conforms to the *conjonctural dynamics* that informs the play's vision of oil and the extractive logics of the global petro-capitalist system at historical and political-economic levels. This emphasis on cyclicality and phases-based boom and bust dynamics evident in the title *Konjunktur* evinces a crucial consonance with the Braudelian-Wallersteinian notion of *conjoncture*. As delineated, "conjuncture" (a barely approximate equivalent used as a translation of the French original "conjoncture") constitutes one of the models or pivotal components in Braudel's triadic world-systemic account of history. Braudel distinguishes between two kinds of "conjunctures": intermediate-term conjunctures and long-term conjunctures. The former refers to such matters as wars, rates of industrialization and price cycles; and the latter designates upheavals such as "long-term demographic movements, the changing dimensions of states and empires (the geographical conjuncture as it might be called), the presence or absence of social mobility in a given society, [and] the intensity of industrial growth" (1972, 899). Lania's world-oriented and world-systemic vision is attested by his notebooks where he articulated his conjonctural and materialist vision of history, geopolitics, and political economy by not only positing local/national history as inherently embedded within global history, but by establishing a

## Conjonctural Cycles of Capitalist Oil Extraction    99

causal and dialectical relationship between the core and the periphery, the local and the global:

> the bombings in China, the . . . signing of the Turkish-Russian alliance treaty – which hit the whole Balkans and make them tremble: change of government in Bulgaria, dynasty crisis in Romania, another revolution in Greece and the sky is full of thick clouds over Mosul from which lightning can come down at any moment.
>
> (Lania: "Die Geschichte eines Buches")

Lania continues: "No wonder that Europa Locarno, the League of Nations, almost forgets its own worries and needs and stares at the cloud bank with fear and shudders: it covers petroleum and that is known to be a highly flammable substance" (ibid.)[27] And this twofold dynamics – cyclical and uneven (or core-peripheral) – constitutes, in the play, the logics of the prevailing mode of the political economy, political ecology, and geopolitical dynamics informing both the discovery (extraction and production) of oil in Albania and the relationship between the national government of the peripheral country (Albania) and the international oil companies – and/or imperial-global forces – intervening in the country in pursuit of cheap resources. Noteworthy in the previous passage is Lania's reference to another peripheral European country which rose to global prominence and came to occupy a crucial position in the map and network of global capitalism solely due to the discovery of oil in it. Mark Biondich's comment is illuminating:

> Romania was an exception in so far as it managed to attract foreign investment for its lucrative oil industry – in 1914 Romania was the fifth largest oil producer in the world – which in turn stimulated the iron, machine, and timber industries.
>
> (2011, 50)

Indeed in Albania – and more broadly the Balkans – industrialization was fairly slow and hampered by the "overwhelmingly agrarian nature of Balkan societies, which lacked the necessary raw materials, technical skills, and domestic capital, the beginnings of industrial development date from this period" (50). Consequently, when the mechanical rhythms and logics of petro-industrial capitalism reached Albania (and the Balkans), it yielded a reproduction of a capitalist pattern of combined and uneven development (rather than national advancement and prosperity). As Mark Biondich explains: "The nature of modernization . . . entailed growing government indebtedness, eventually leading to greater foreign control over national budgets and economies" (ibid.) It is indeed in light of this globally connected and *conjonctural* dynamics that *Boom and Bust* can be proposed as an approximate descriptive translation of the title (*Konjunktur*).

100  *Conjonctural Cycles of Capitalist Oil Extraction*

Primarily, the very spatial and temporal (historical and geographical) descriptions and features of the setting attest to Lania's materialist vision and world-systemic critique. This critical insight is manifested in his discernment of the extractive logics of petro-capitalist economy and its historical dynamics – characterized by Lania in two interrelated terms: *conjonctural* and *longue durée*. As such, Lania associates the history of petro-capitalist interventions – into both intra-national and extra-national resource-rich territories – with the allegorical notion of *any* "Great War". Lania's deployment of the signifier "Great War", not restrictively in reference to the First World War, but rather to any resource-driven global war foregrounds the allegorical nature of war and its cyclical historical dynamics. Whilst *Oil Field* is set in a nearly indeterminate country (allegorically named Puritania – hence its being factually non-existing), *Konjunktur 1* and *2* are alternately set in the two Albanian cities of Valona and Durazzo. Both cities are coastal and port cities and are among the most significant cities both in terms of culture and their rich offshore oil and gas reserves. Both cities are exposed to the Adriatic Sea and located in the proximity of the Mediterranean Sea. Whereas *Oil Field* opens onto a setting which remains a countryside or marginal spot on the outskirts of an indefinite city, *Konjunktur* (*1* and *2*) explicitly situates the setting within a historically factual and recognizable country but specifically limns the contours of the places of action. As such, the explicit geographical mooring points the reader/audience are provided in *Konjunktur* establish the internationally exposed and connected accessibility of the two cities in Albania. As Piscator elucidates: "From the beginning, *Konjunktur* was to be understood not only in the narrow economic sense, but also in the broader social sense; Boom (or *Konjunktur*) for war uprisings, evangelizers, adventurers" (*Political Theatre*, 198).

Strictly in accordance with the historical facts, *Konjunktur* demonstrates how the questions of Albanian national independence and its recognition as a legitimate part of the international community through the endorsement of its membership in the League of Nations, on the one hand, and the political economy of oil and energy extraction, on the other, lie at the core of the tension-laden relationship between Albania and the world powers. The discovery of oil also accounts for the sudden looming presence of global powers and the League of Nations in Albania which, as a peripheral country in Europe, barely received any global attention before. *Konjunktur* thus demonstrates the status of oil as a globally strategic commodity. It does so by showing how national independence, international recognition, and political-national legitimacy of the ruling government in Albania (alternately led by Noli and Zogu) are not only indelibly intertwined with, but are also contingent on, the political economy of national oil and the national government/state's willingness to sacrifice and compromise its national interests and economic profits by granting the global powers access to its oil resources cheaply.

*Conjonctural Cycles of Capitalist Oil Extraction* 101

Lania's critical focus on oil and petro-capitalism in Albania is mostly predicated on historical facts. In fact, the Albanian history of the first two and a half decades of the 20th century offers a rich repository of issues which also constituted many of Lania's vexing concerns. The oil companies that feature and operate in *Konjunktur* (1 and 2) were actually present in Albania (with the exception of the Russian Naphta Syndicate, which is added in *Konjunktur 2*). The oil-determined Albanian history during the aforementioned period also acted as a laboratory, where Lania could not only put his world-economic and world-historical ideas to test, but could find the proof of them as well. These included the anti-imperialist movements and uprisings that were nationalistically bent, the activities of the Soviet Union represented by the 3rd International, the failure of the League of Nations, Albania (a peripheral European country) as a rendezvous of various oil companies contending for monopoly, the seizure of power by an unscrupulous dictator. Lania features the countries that had asserted claims to Albania's resources over the past two and a half decades as personifications or emblems of the global oil powers and imperial petro-capitalism. Likewise, he constellates opponents and allies according to historical circumstances. As Mark Biondich notes: "Albania's first genuine political parties emerged only after the Great War, but they represented prominent personalities and their cliques rather than clearly defined political ideologies" (2011, 119).[28]

The two chief leaders with competing claims to ruling Albania from the late 1910s to late 1930s were Ahmed Zogu and Fan Noli. Whilst both Noli and Zogu professed to be patriotic modernizers – asserting that "Albania needed a paternal government guiding it to modernity" (Biondich 2011, 119), Noli and Zogu pursued vastly different policies and ideologies to achieve this ostensibly laudable aim. In their modernizing ambitions, both Noli and Zogu were beset with two formidable forces: external (international-global powers) and internal (national-domestic conflicts). As Biondich explains: "[t]o achieve this they had to contend with political factionalism, clientelism, and deep social fissures, pitting the traditional Muslim landed elite [including local clan elders and feudal landowners] against both the nascent intellegencia and the bourgeois reformers in the Orthodox south" (119). Zogu, the more pragmatist one, came to power in early 1924 but was forced to resign given the scandal of the assassination attempt on Noli – his rival.[29] There occurred in June a revolution that culminated in the election of Noli – the Harvard-educated, Christian Orthodox Bishop of Durres and a fervent nationalist and an idealist. Albania under Noli, which had just got rid of foreign troops and elected its own government, was approached by interested parties in the country's newly discovered oil reserves, initially the British. In order to secure its peace, Albania, whose government was not recognized by the major European powers, sought membership in the League of Nations. However, when Albania appealed to the League of Nations for help after

## 102 *Conjonctural Cycles of Capitalist Oil Extraction*

the invasion of Yugoslav and Italian troops in 1921, the League declared itself "powerless" (see Chapter 4). The whole recognition was denied by major international powers (including Britain, Italy, France, and US) not only because of Noli's anti-imperialist stance, but also his reluctance to implement radical domestic reforms (including land reforms). Noli's anti-imperialist stance is conspicuously evidenced by his refusal to sacrifice the sovereign national control over its oil resources and his rejection of an oil concession for which Great Britain, Italy, France, and the United States were competing intensely (see Austin 2012).

Having been defeated in parliamentary election by Noli, Zogu fled to the Kingdom of Serbs, Croats, and Slovenes (Yugoslavia) where he embarked on the recruitment of a mercenary army. Five months later, Zogu returned with an army to oust Noli and seize power, establishing himself as an authoritarian dictator. In the meantime, aided by the Yugoslav army, Zogu invaded Albania and established an apparently Republican (but actually authoritarian) state as the first president of Albania. In contrast to Noli, Zogu was willing to yield to an oil concession with the British and two other countries. This time, Zogu's request for foreign help was supported by the British Foreign Office, which in return demanded the exclusive rights to the exploration and exploitation of the Albanian oil deposits for its state-owned Anglo-Persian Oil Company (APOC, today's BP). The trade took place and Albania became a member of the League of Nations. Ironically, none of the so-called Western democratic powers that were ambitiously pursuing an oil concession with Albania prevented Ahmed Zogu from overthrowing the democratically elected government in 1926. The invasion and the overthrow were carried out with a mercenary force paid mainly by APOC and Standard Oil (see Austin 2012, 134–138). Consequently, Zogu stood up as dictator and immediately started to implement and finance his agreed concessions with APOC and other global powers. Oil concessions were granted to APOC, Standard Oil, two Italian companies, and the French Syndicat Franco-Albanian. Significantly, all of these companies were also fighting over the oil in *Konjunktur* (1 and 2), but APOC had been replaced by Royal Dutch Shell. Akin to Goldstein who also tried to get rid of both in *Konjunktur 1* to the highest bidder, Zogu awarded the cigarette monopoly and the Albanian National Bank, among other things, to Italy and became so dependent on Italy that in 1926 he ratified the so-called Tirana Pact, which effectively made Albania an Italian protectorate.[30] Whilst initially Zogu (in the hope of receiving political and economic support) forged a close alliance (bordering on guardianship) with Italy, gradually Italy (under the dictatorship of Mussolini) started showing colonial ambitions by asking the Albanian schools to teach in Italian, for instance. This was faced with widespread public protests conducive to the development of an opposition movement of Albanian Communists. Later in 1939, when

Italy (under Mussolini) sought to make Zogu Italy's puppet, Zogu fled to Greece rather than complying. Albania was later occupied by the invading German army in 1941. Ultimately, with the fall of Mussolini in 1934 and the defeat of Axis Powers in the Second World War, a communist government rose to power in Albania in 1945 led by Hoxha.

This concise account of the national and political-economic life of Albania under Noli, Zogu, and the communists finds extensive resonances and reflections in the play. For instance, in *Konjunktur 1* the agitation of the liberation movement had the same success; the French and Italian governments withdrew their troops. Trebitsch has already promised all parties their share – above all Brown – though he ultimately flees the country leaving them high and dry and having to deal with the domestic and communist revolutionary forces led by the Soviet Union's agents. The other salient correspondence between real historical events/figures in Albania and the contextual-historical aspects of *Konjunktur* is the impostor figure in the play – embodied by Trebitsch in *Konjunktur 2* and only partially by Pusspad in *Oil Field* (since the latter character is far more rounded and multivalent than a stereotypical impostor). Notably, the Anglo-Italian and French-Yugoslav alliances are taken over in *Konjunktur 1*. The figure of the impostor (Goldstein/Trebitsch) alludes to various historical megalomaniacs in Albania, including the Albanian "little Mussolini" (Ahmed Zogu) as well as to Hitler. Similar to Zogu's escape to Yugoslavia and finally to Greece, Trebitsch (and/or Goldstein) leaves his power and position – notwithstanding global powers' promise of support for his dictatorship – for Munich at the end of *Konjunktur* (*1* and *2*). Finally, the crucial role of oil in determining the dynamics and fate of the political-economic life of Albania demonstrates Retort's argument to the effect that petro-capitalism has been founded on "corporate/state collusion, regulation of surplus and manufactured scarcity" (Retort 2005, 56).

## VI.  The Petro-State, Petro-Capitalism, and Petro-Communism in *Konjunktur 1*

To provide a lucid trajectory of this section, I will first present a succinct summary of the plot along with the chief aesthetic features and thematic preoccupations of *Konjunktur 1*. Secondly, I will delineate the chief thematic preoccupations and strands informing *Konjunktur 1* in order not only to achieve a lucid understanding of its world-systemic and world-historical vision, but also to establish the upheaval the play underwent in its transition from *Konjunktur 1* to *Konjunktur 2*. Finally, the third sub-section will comprise an extensive engagement with the materialist aesthetics of *Konjunktur 1* with a specific focus on its scenographic, semiotic, and dramaturgical facets both at textual and performance levels. This section will demonstrate how the manifold nature of

## 104   *Conjonctural Cycles of Capitalist Oil Extraction*

oil (as a "force field") upon its entry into the text came to transform the aesthetics of the play beyond a mere anthropocentric focus and realistic dynamics.

*Konjunktur 1* opens onto a landscape swarmed with signs of life in all its uneven dynamics by displaying a jarring juxtaposition of the local and global community. Alongside the local people with their primitive "barrel, sack, beam, shacks" and "small houses of a poor southern village" (meaning, Riva of Valona in Albania), we find interspersed across the stage hordes of tourists of various nationalities and industrial-technological wonders of the day (including cars, Kodak cameras, and binoculars). The most striking sight is a bunch of three Tibetan lamas led by Romney as the impresario of the scene. This scene of mundane casualness and carnivalesque diversity is ensued by a formal event attended by the Albanian Army General, Romney (a cosmopolitan businessman and impresario), Brown (the representative of the League of Nations in Albania), Rossi (the representative of the Kingdom of Italy), and Dubois (the representative of France). Rossi and Dubois also serve as the heads of the Italian Naphta company and Franco-Albanian petrol syndicate, respectively. Deftly navigating and negotiating her way through this medley of luminaries is Claire Barsin who is trying to gain their trust and forge ties with them, through seductive manoeuvring and flirtatious mannerisms, in the hope of manipulating their decisions and gleaning inklings about their intentions. Scattered among the snatches of conversations, we glean the news of the discovery of oil in Albania, permeated with a simmering sense of rivalry amongst the global forces over gaining monopoly over Albanian oil resources. Other characters include Goldstein-Franklin (a cosmopolitan impostor and disguiser), Jonny (an American engineer in the oil industry and Evelyn's former fiancé), Evelyn (Claire's daughter), Ahmed (a native Albanian revolutionary), Rifan-Bey (in *Oil Field* he is described as "a merchant of doubtful origins").

The keynote of *Konjunktur 1* – the struggle over gaining monopoly over Albanian oil resources by global powers – is sounded early in the play in the conversation between Rossi and Jonny. When Rossi indicates to Jonny, "We have to have the new drill holes up and running within 8 days", Jonny responds: "[the rights to drill those oil wells] Have been awarded to the French". Astonished yet undeterred Rossi responds thus: "You unsuspecting angel! That's why we have to have you. . . . Word will get around that there is not a drop of oil in your springs". Such a discovery, followed by the arrival of all global powers into the country, induces prospective cataclysms in Albania – ranging from industrialization, urbanization, birth of a new mode of globalized nation-state (as a petro-state) and its concomitant nationalistic political economy where oil features prominently along with the transformation of natural and social space as well as subject positions (for instance, the transformation of

*Conjonctural Cycles of Capitalist Oil Extraction* 105

peasants into labour force and oil workers). This fiery-paced transformation is captured, in *Konjunktur 1*, in the frenetic race over extraction of oil and its volume. *Konjunktur 1* thus illustrates how, due to the discovery of oil in this peripheral country, almost every element within the play – from the state (national government) structure, and infrastructure to global relations and social dynamics – is infused with instability, restlessness, and volatility.

In the same vein, *Konjunktur 1* reveals the precarious foundations on which the petro-modern Albanian state is going to be built. Relatedly, almost all scenes are punctuated by intermittent presence of the Loudspeaker. Throughout *Konjunktur 1*, the reader/audience is barraged with the Loudspeaker's announcement of the news of significant events occurring around the world, thereby establishing the significance of Albania as a globally connected spot on the world map. A cogent case in point is the report, delivered by the Loudspeaker, on the relational dynamics between Albania and the global economy: "From Paris: Reports of the development of new oil sources in Valona led to a stormy bull market in Franco Albania. Council of Ministers votes for flexible loans". This "worldly" situatedness tacitly betokens how Albania's domestic affairs are determined by global forces. It is on the basis of facts/occurrences (in this context) that the Albanian General avers to Dubois and Romney: "That's us. What, you can see from this pile of shacks that we are the center of world politics here in Valona!" As Graeme Macdonald cogently observes:

> As soon as oil is struck, its site is internationalized by virtue of the multinational capital and expertise required (often American) to set up the extraction infrastructure and the labor force, and to enable its immediate plunge into the world market.
>
> (7–31)[31]

Another testimony to the transformation of Albania into a globally connected zone of oil extraction appears when the Loudspeaker declares: "Caution! Here is Berlin, Havas reports from Rome; the Yugoslav-Italian conflict . . . has been tightened further since yesterday". Elsewhere the Loudspeaker declares: "When the Albania conflict was intensifying, the London nightborne reacted with lively fluctuations" (n.p.).[32] The Loudspeaker also plays an epic or meta-dramatic function. This is evidenced by the way it features at the end of Act One. Here Speaker announces: "Caution! Caution! Here Berlin, Paris, New York, Tokyo, Melbourne, Rome. Our comedy follows evening programs".

The vibrant diversity of the oil field and petrocultural frontier – at racial, national, and class levels – is evidently reflected in the conversation between Claire and her daughter Evelyn. When Evelyn laments/remarks: "in these four weeks I have already recognized what is blooming here:

106   *Conjonctural Cycles of Capitalist Oil Extraction*

drunken officers, oil agents with impossible manners, sweating Turks, dirty natives". Evelyn's remark here significantly reveals how the extraction of natural resources (raw material) from the peripheries runs parallel with the production of race. Claire's response is illuminating: "Natives! You speak as if they were Zuluneger [or Zulu negroes: a racial descriptor of a sub-group of Africans]"[33] to which Evelyn retorts: "Whether whites or negroes is not the decisive factor. In any case, they are all unsavory with one another". Another impediment of which Claire is acutely cognizant and tries to overcome is the racial politics which pervades the political economy and social discourse utilized by the global powers in the peripheral country (as a zone of extraction). An evident case in point is the recurring use of the highly racially charged term – "coolies" – invoked in reference to both native Albanian oil workers and foreign oil workers by various European and Anglo-American characters including Evelyn and Romney. The use of this term (which was a common element of the racialized cultural discourse of the time) not only reveals how the extraction of oil (and other natural resources) from a peripheral zone runs parallel with the production of race (and racialized cheap labour); it also demonstrates how under bourgeois capitalism, racialized prejudice, produced as hegemonic common sense, was rampant and normal at various (social-cultural, racial, and political-economic) levels.

Notably, *Konjunktur 1* is attentive to fashions of the day – including Zen Buddhism farcically represented (as a mode of naïve pacifism) by impostor Goldstein – and how they are being commodified as part of the fad and capitalist consumer culture. This is also reflected in Romney's sarcastic remark. When Johnny says: "You don't believe", he asserts: "Certainly, but you know, we are actually almost two years late. . . . Downfall of the Land of End Meditation – Fatalism – Immersion into oneself – fashion is a little passé. One prefers heavier food again". Shedding light on the racial and cultural politics of the day, the Buddhist lamas are referred to, by the passengers, as "yellow brothers" and "sluggish breed". Lania's depiction of the commodification of an earnest spiritual pursuit can be construed to betoken the historicity of ideologies and fashions in modernity, that is, how serious and lifelong spiritual-intellectual missions and commitments have turned into ephemeral interests.[34]

The foremost figure associated with lamas and Buddhism is Goldstein who has instrumentalized Buddhism as a disguise for placing himself in the centre of world news and contemporary global politics: Albania as a newly established oil frontier and zone of extraction. Indeed, one of the comical elements (verging on grotesque and black humour) in the play – which more broadly implies national and global politics as a realm driven by grotesque dynamics – is the figure of the impostor Goldstein. Goldstein was intended to evoke associations with not only the historical figure Ignaz Trebitsch-Lincoln but also with slightly coded Goldstein-Franklin (Trebitsch-Lincoln in *Konjunktur 2*). As such,

## Conjonctural Cycles of Capitalist Oil Extraction    107

Goldstein (as Trebitsch-Lincoln) also evoked the recent German past, since the historical Trebitsch-Lincoln had appeared in China as the general of the White Guards and previously in Germany as the press chief of the putschist Kapp. As is evident, therefore, Goldstein is an overdetermined figure who represents the individual variant of the amalgamation of politics and profit. In *Konjunktur 1*, we encounter Goldstein initially as the press chief of the manager Romney. On the way to power, Goldstein-Franklin transforms, reacting almost reflexively or instinctively to the situation – running the gamut from a peaceful, dispute-arbitrating monk into a combative Albanian freedom fighter (Act 1, Scene 10), "lawyer" and "advocate of the enslaved people" (Act 1, Scene 11), then to Claire's press secretary and manager (Act 1, Scene 14) who coldly and cynically calculates the war, then resumes the role of the Albanian freedom fighter (Act 2, Scene 14), and is at the same time a double agent (for Claire and Brown, Act 2, Scene 12), and finally soars to dictator (Act 2, Scene 17). Finally, there is the figure of Rifan-Bey (Beig/Bey in Turkish mean sir, master, herr), one of those who "draw the blood of our peasants", who allegorically refers to the agricultural and economic structure, which was still residually shaped by Turkish feudal rule (*Konjunktur 1*, 29). The global powers repeatedly succeeded in taking advantage of the national liberation movements, which were mostly advocated by right-wing circles.

Another comic element streaking *Konjunktur 1* is the comedy of manners, the principal portion of which is carried by Evelyn and Jonny. In this technique, a light comic effect (for critical and didactic purposes) is engendered through the juxtaposition of the trivial and the earnest, of casual leisure and pleasure with a serious national-revolutionary cause. In fact, *Konjunktur 1*, through Claire and Jonny/Evelyn, interweaves serious social-political issues with the private-personal and the familial thereby demonstrating how intertwined they are at the levels of libidinal and political economy. The following example is a case in point. When Evelyn says to her mother: "Revolution and humanity and politics – this idealism is quite nice, but not for mature people. Do you have at least one interesting friend here?", Claire responds: "Can't you really think of any other goals in life than tennis and flirting?" Relatedly, *Konjunktur 1* contains a number of extended quibbles and comic exchanges (reminiscent of the comic tradition of stichomythia) between the two former fiancés (Jonny and Evelyn) who seem to be still interested in one another. These exchanges, however, provide us with ample insight into broader and thematically crucial issues. *Konjunktur 1* contains numerous fairly long dialogues. Next is an illustrative example where in their conversation a fleeting and apparently casual reference is made to the merging of oil companies. In *Konjunktur 2*, similarly, we encounter a determining element within the dynamics of the play, namely, the merging of otherwise national oil companies and the consequent birth of multinational

108   *Conjonctural Cycles of Capitalist Oil Extraction*

oil corporations. The ensuing snatch from the Evelyn-Jonny conversation illustrates this point:

EVELYN: Will he pay more? You should be too good to be used as a coolie by this French corner company.
JONNY: Poor Franco-Albania! We'll see who will make the race.
EVELYN: Certainly not you, if you act so stupidly. Why haven't you been with Royal Dutch long ago? A completely different company!
JONNY: Just wait until we merge with Standard Oil. Dubois is negotiating with your mother.
EVELYN: I want to know what will look out for you. But you're not listening at all. What's going on?
JONNY: The boys here seem to be boiling something up, sneaking around like hungry droppings. Calculate it won't be long before guns pop here.

When Evelyn tauntingly asks: "Are you scared?", Jonny responds: "I'm a free citizen of the United States – what can this rabble do to me? The decision is up to us only". Evelyn's retort, however, is equally telling: "Don't imagine too much! Everyone else here understands their business better than you do". Significantly, "merging" (or the ability of the national and international oil corporations to merge with one another) further compounds the entanglements and complicities between the national and the international, the local and the global as well as oil corporations and states; it also foregrounds the polymorphous perversity of fossil capital and its attempt to gain global hegemony and perpetuate its extractive practices driven by the logics of combined and uneven development.

The theme of "merging" of oil corporations appears at critical junctures in *Konjunktur 1* and *Konjunktur 2*, ushered in to instigate a cataclysm in the dynamics and configuration of national-global dynamics of political-economic relationships between global powers and oil corporations on the one hand and between the peripheral nation-state (oil-rich Albania) and global forces on the other. Such a cataclysm is not only driven by utmost capital accumulation but also to cancel or disrupt the normal national laws and constitutional rights (to the global powers' favour) by creating a state of exception or an unpredictable situation where the peripheral country is left in a precarious state. One instance of such merging practice is indicated in the conversation between Rossi and Brown in *Konjunktur 2*:

ROSSI: Is that so sure?
BROWN: Absolutely. Do the rehearsals.
ROSSI: My company might be ready to merge with Royal Shell –

Elsewhere the Loudspeaker announces:

Royal Dutch merged with Italian NAFTA. Attention! Attention! London closes: Royal Dutch plus 5, Italian NAFTA plus 3 1/4, Franco

## Conjonctural Cycles of Capitalist Oil Extraction  109

Albania minus 11 1/2. Aftermarket reacts to the completely unclear situation in Albania with lively fluctuations, French oil papers falling. What will France do?

(*Konjunktur 2*, Act 2, Scene 7)

Later in the play when Jonny asks for his resignation, Dubois's response sheds further light on a highly volatile field of oil extraction aggravated by the phenomenon of "merging": "But young friend, don't get so heated, buy time! The Royal Dutch is heavy armor. The Standard Oil is no lesser caliber". When Jonny asks him in astonishment: "The – Standard –?" Dubois flaunts the chameleonic flexibility granted by the global and multinational dynamics of petro-capitalist extractivism thus: "We can also merge, the Americans use it as opening credits. Happy Barsin will not be averse. We'll make our race and you your record, don't worry –!"

Whilst Romney has no political ambitions and is rather merely a cosmopolitan businessman who is obsessed with money and profit, Claire harbours far-reaching and cataclysmic political plans. This becomes explicitly evident when Romney asserts:

Don't come at me with high politics. What's at stake here is a much simpler matter: the powers that maraud around there want to get at each other's throats because no one wants the other to have an Albanian bite. But openly admitting to being a robber – no, that's no longer appropriate today. So all the powers harangue about the solitude and independence of Albania, which has done so much to them. Let's take the gentlemen at their word.

When Claire tries to debunk his claims by indicating that his ultimate goal is the monopoly over cheap Albanian oil ("And the oil springs under your own direction?"), Romney states: "That will be found later. After all, we will not sit forever in this godforsaken corner. Once things are in order, we start to London". The details of his intention are further elucidated when he appoints Goldstein as the press chief and assigns him the task of promoting the leader of the freedom movement (Claire) marketed as "Jeanne d'Arc of Albania" in the European metropolises: "Paris, Berlin, New York. You will be amazed at the success you will achieve: As an Albanian Jean d'Arc, world lady and yet exotic, the modern woman, victory for feminism –". Interestingly, Romney's remarks – his reference to props, puppetry, and show in relation to the political-economic field unfolding in Albania – are amenable to being read in a meta-dramatic and allegorical manner. In an allegorical interpretation, *Konjunktur 1* adumbrates the puppetry-like logics of the political-economic relation between the core and peripheral regions of the petro-capitalist system. This is demonstrated by the way Albanian people of various political factions and fronts prove to be protégés and playthings in the game of global powers. As such, *Konjunktur 1* evinces

110   *Conjonctural Cycles of Capitalist Oil Extraction*

some affinities with *Trauerspiel* – as characterized by Benjamin (though partly anachronistically). Romney however perhaps unwittingly throws into relief one of the crucial concerns of the play, namely, the ways in which the petro-capitalist and petro-communist discourses blur the boundaries between politics and economics. As Romney explains to Claire: "Don't run away from me. They [*lamas*] are the pacifist slogan [watchword], you are the revolutionary one. One as good as the other – it just depends on the economy".

Claire Barsin is, on the one hand, a nationalist and revolutionary activist who seeks to regain national rights to the oil and improve workers' conditions. On the other hand, Claire is the undercover representative of the Soviet Union, a revolutionary who tries to establish the Soviet Union's communist ideology through the triumph of economic potency. Hence, although Romney funds Claire out of his voracity for financial gain, it is Claire who gradually takes the course of events and matters into her own hands rather than taking commands and directions from Romney. Consequently, Claire subtly manipulates various contending parties by pitting them against each other whilst simultaneously she is galvanizing and mobilizing the workers and other national revolutionary forces behind the scenes. This is evident in the end when Claire reminds Romney of his initial funding ("You and your lamas will bring in the loss, and then you may have the consolation that with the expenses for your revolution – ") then Romney retorts: "For your revolution". This imbrication of the politics and economics revolving around the question of oil, at national and global levels, is raised in *Konjunktur 1*, in the remark by Romney – the impresario of one of the contending political parties who intends to install a charlatan chameleon, Goldstein, as the Albanian president. When Goldstein, remarking on the role of oil and the representational and social-cultural power of the media, naïvely observes: "But the public opinion of Europe, on which we want to work –!", Romney drives a wedge between economics and politics by stating: "I will not swing myself, neither on a horse nor on a throne, because I don't feel like breaking my neck". No sooner has Romney reiterated his point ("Now it's not about politics, it's about business") than Claire, as the politically sophisticated thinker and prospective female revolutionary leader, tries to rectify this attitude by averring: "Doesn't that coincide?" (Act 2, Scene 6). The indelible intertwinement and co-determination of economy and politics is the thematic and dramatic core of *Konjunktur 1*. Indeed, historically, one of the principal reasons underlying both the conflict between and the entanglement amongst the political parties, global powers, and oil corporations in Albania in the 1920s and 1930s was the co-determination and interdependence of oil-driven politics and economics. More specifically, this co-determination gravitated towards and hinged on a contradictory situation where the apparently neutral and democratic global forces (Britain, France, etc.)

## Conjonctural Cycles of Capitalist Oil Extraction   111

would be willing to grant Albania their moral-political legitimation and international recognition on the condition that the Albanian state would be willing to grant them access to cheap oil and other Albanian natural resources; hence, politics as a camouflage for economic interests and vice versa. These demonstrate the disempowerment of politics by the business magnates in the course of the concentration of capital and labour. As such, Lania's *Konjunktur 1* presents economy as an extended arm of national politics under the conditions of globalization, a process that allows foreign policy and economic policy to become almost indissociably merged. Such entanglements between politics and economics in the case of oil-owning Albania were indeed consonant with the prevalent historical conditions of the inter-war period in Europe. As Gilbert Ziebura explains:

> Characteristic of the "interwar period" is a circumstance that was noticed with astonishment by contemporaries: the inextricable mutual interpenetration of politics and economy: politicization of the economy, but also, as a correlate, the economization of politics, both internally and externally, were, at least to this extent, new experiences.
> (Gilbert Ziebura, *Weltwirtschaft und Weltpolitik* 1922/24–1931, Frankfurt am Main 1984, S. 15f and 18)

Significantly the trope of the card game – allegorically capturing the arbitrary and abstracting rules and dynamics of the capitalist competition and profiteering "game" – is a recurring trope throughout both *Konjunktur* (1 and 2) and *Oil Field*. Romney states:

> Then; Albania! At the moment it seems like fashion again. I'm not a politician, but I'll give you ten to one: wherever these gentlemen from the oil have their hands in the game, the last card that flies on the table is just a Declaration of war.
> (Act 1, Scene 3)

Elsewhere Jonny in his conversation with Claire avers:

> Maybe tomorrow, maybe the day after tomorrow. So far one has hesitated because this freedom movement after all is a card in the game of power that everyone likes to save as the last trick. And because they knew that a Romney is still the best partner, otherwise you had been arrested four weeks ago.
> (Act 2, Scene 4)

Another prominent deployment of the game trope occurs in Claire's conversation with Ahmed and workers which I discussed earlier.

## 112 *Conjonctural Cycles of Capitalist Oil Extraction*

What sheds further light on both the intertextual nature and underpinning facets of the trope of card game or shuffling the cards is that it seems to have been derived from Upton Sinclair's *Oil!* (1927) which opens with the ensuing image:

> Shuffle the cards, and deal a new round of poker hands: they differ in every way from the previous round, and yet it is the same pack of cards, and the same game, with the same spirit, the players grim-faced and silent, surrounded by a haze of tobacco-smoke. So with this novel, a picture of civilization in Southern California, as the writer has observed it during eleven years' residence. The picture is the truth, and the great mass of detail actually exists. But the cards have been shuffled; names, places, dates, details of character, episodes – everything has been dealt over again. The only personalities to be recognized in this book are three presidents of the United States who have held office during the past fifteen years. Manifestly, one could not "shuffle" these, without destroying all sense of reality.
>
> (1)

Apart from the self-reflexive, aesthetic facet of this passage in relation to the narrative and characterological aspects of *Oil!*, this trope both in Sinclair and Lania accentuates the systemic rules and dynamics of the petro-capitalist logics and order and less emphasis on individual figures and names. The emphasis on a large degree of replaceability of names and fluidity of figures reveals the world-systemic nature of powers that determine the political economy and logics of this global commodity at the levels of extraction, commodification, and distribution. As indicated previously, during the Balkan War, for instance, Albania became a plaything of the interests of the Triple Alliance (Italy, Austria-Hungary, and Germany) and the Entente (England, France, and Russia), the country was divided up, offered for sale, or placed under a joint control commission.

Notably whilst, in *Konjunktur 1*, Albania seems to have a military chief commander (General), it seems bereft of a political leader or head of the state since no mention is made of such a figure in the play. This point attests not only to the political chaos and polarly divided condition prevailing in Albania at a national level, but also to Albania's vulnerability to being exploited as a zone of extraction by the global forces of the petro-capitalist system. In its frenetic pace, *Konjunktur 1* features a number of narrative strands running parallel with each other. On the one hand, we witness the arrival of the global forces (Britain, France, and Italy amongst others) and their efforts to obtain the authorization for the extraction of oil and, particularly, monopoly over it. On the other, we see a nationalist revolutionary movement (led by Ahmed, working-class people, and others) but lacking a firm leader and sufficient political-economic means. It is such a lacuna in nationalist and anti-imperialist leadership that Claire

*Conjonctural Cycles of Capitalist Oil Extraction* 113

comes to fill. Another strand that runs through the fissures emerging in the space of collision between these two principal opposing forces is represented by the self-propelling opportunist/charlatan – Goldstein – who lodges himself into the right place at the right moment thereby seizing the reigns of national political leadership – though for a transient period.

In the meantime, Claire negotiates her way and navigates a precarious and perilous path among the Italian (Rossi), French (Dubois), and the British (Brown) as well as national insurgents and Albanian state heads (including Goldstein and General) by (1) mobilizing and enlightening them, (2) making hollow promises to undermine their agreements and plans, and (3) by forging hollow alliances with them. The outcome of her relentless, yet covert, efforts is revealed when global powers try to suppress the revolutionary forces by deploying their own occupying armies situated in Albania. Having been persuaded by Claire (and her allies) to the effect that such wars are primarily class wars which claim innocent people of various parties and fronts rather than the people of power, the army forces of various factions refuse to wage war by defying the orders. Such an upheaval in the dynamics of the affairs primarily arises from Claire's unremitting endeavours to incite both a nationalist spirit and counter-capitalist class consciousness amongst various sides by alerting them to how they and their country's resources are pawns in the political-economic game of global powers.

On the cusp of the triumph of the revolutionary forces when the circumstances are ripe for a revolutionary leader like Claire or Ahmed to assume the control of the national state and economy, Goldstein disrupts all anticipated plans and dynamics by thrusting himself as the person who has got the unwavering support of the majority of political factions in Albania and Albanian people, thereby self-appointedly calling himself the legitimate national ruler. Goldstein, however, proves a dictator and inefficient ruler. Once in power, Goldstein explicitly identifies himself as a "dictator" and orders the suppression of nationalist revolutionary forces whilst keeping it secret from Claire. Consequently, for quelling and gaining economic favours from the global powers, he starts entering into negotiations for auctioning away national resources. The tragi-comic dynamics of both Goldstein's position and action as well as Albania's fate (in both cases verging on grotesque) is given a cogent characterization by Claire. Addressing Goldstein, she avers: "Yes, you have courage: not because you are brave, but cheeky. The recklessness of the coward. And therefore what you started as a farce can end in tragedy". Goldstein's policy consists of a noncommittal approach through which he pits the competing national parties against one another and plays contending global powers off one another; a policy which he enjoys as yet another frivolous adventure but one that ultimately ends up to the detriment of both Albanian people (and their political-economic interests) and Albania's natural and human resources. Later in the play when Goldstein has assumed his role as the authoritarian ruler of Albania and is striving to wrest as much economic

## 114  *Conjonctural Cycles of Capitalist Oil Extraction*

and political support from rival parties and powers as possible by making promises and commitments concerning oil extraction and other resources whilst holding their fulfilment in abeyance by postponing them to an indefinite future, Claire arrives to confront him and thwart his plans. Here, Claire's observation on Goldstein's actions and the consequent plights inflicted on Albania is psychologically insightful and revealing:

> No, I can't laugh at your masquerade or at your bluffs because (suddenly jumping up very bright, half into the audience) . . . Because this comedy that is being played here is bloody stupid. Because you fools and impostors and economic heroes have human lives on your conscience, happiness of families, the fate of countries, the peace of Europe. Because this harmless madness, once unleashed, is dangerous to the public. Listen, listen!!
>
> (Act 3, Scene 15)

Ironically, Brown, as the supposedly neutral representative of the League of Nations, turns out to be a corrupt British agent clandestinely advancing the petro-capitalist interests of Royal Dutch Shell (which was mainly owned by the British). It is Brown who through insinuations gives Goldstein reassurance (for the latter's violent suppression of the nationalist insurgents) and manipulatively gives him advice as to which political side and global power to turn to and trust (the British) and which to dismiss (the French and the Italians) all in return for his political-economic support and continuation of his dictatorship. The collusion of the international law and Anglo-European powers in the extractivist exploitation of the peripheral countries had already been insightfully discerned by Lania: "No wonder that Europa Locarno, the League of Nations, almost forgets its own worries and needs and stares at the cloud bank with fear and shudder: it covers petroleum and that is known to be a highly flammable substance".[35] Here Lania indicates how the global value and political-economic power of oil had blinded everyone including the League of Nations thus exposing the politically-economically corrupt and vested (neo-)colonial interest of the petro-imperial core (the global north) in the petro-peripheries.[36]

The ensuing exchange throws into relief the discursively subtle ways through which the abstract and the concrete, the ideological and the material were intertwined in the global petro-capitalist order. Significantly, the following conversation – occurring at a critical moment in the play – appears in both *Konjunktur 1* and *2* (with the slight difference of renaming Goldstein as Trebitsch in the latter play. Here Goldstein/Trebitsch is trying to persuade Brown to support him and provide him with torpedo ships by forewarning him that his fall will be followed by the rise of anti-British reds (communists in Albania). Brown, however, deflecting attention away from British Empire's economic interests (including oil and other resources), does not cease articulating his goal in humanitarian and

*Conjonctural Cycles of Capitalist Oil Extraction* 115

democratic terms; that is, for them it is not a battle over material resources but a battle over ideas (winning the heads of the masses):

TREBITSCH: Where the idea of revolution has to be confronted with an equally sparkling idea: dictatorship, fascism [*sic*]. I fall – a new wave of the red tide will hit the British lions – the foundations – the empire is shaken –

BROWN: We are only concerned with ideal goals: the consolidation of democracy and European culture, if we support you.

Towards the end, finding himself in a cul-de-sac between the powers and nationalist insurgencies and resistance (the Freedom Party), Goldstein first appeals to Claire for help, suggesting: "the fight is stopped, the Freedom Party officially recognizes me, I get my company with Brown in order and leave". Finding his offer rejected by Claire, Goldstein resorts to his last ruse by convincing Brown that he intends to suppress the rebellious forces of nationalist resistance and grant Brown monopoly over Albanian oil (and other natural) resources. Goldstein however reminds Brown that he lacks the necessary military means of accomplishing his plans, thus appealing to Brown to lend him the torpedo ship. Goldstein, true to his hollow nature and impostor trait, finding his life at stake and political ruling too overwhelming, decides to flee the Albanian scene by using the torpedo ship to get as far from Albania as possible and vanish once again into another disguised identity (akin to his former lama identity). Finding this moment of chaos and confusion amongst the global powers coupled with the lack of a central state power, Claire finds it a propitious moment to make a final foray into ousting the authoritarian and capitalist global power by leading the nationalist resistance forces and wins the battle, thus seizing control of the national ruling. *Konjunktur 1* concludes on an ambivalent, or mixed, note of revolutionary change and hope for the birth of a new socialist nation-state independent on the one hand, and with the brooding gloom of an impending collision between the national resistance and global powers looming over the horizon, on the other.

## VII. *Konjunktur 1* as Petro-Drama and Its Thematic Preoccupations

*Konjunktur 1* invokes an explicit thematic parallel or causal link between energy and autonomy at the level of nationalism, social equality, and working-class rights. There is also an emphasis on working-class solidarity, the necessity of historical consciousness in conjunction with structural alteration and systemic insight rather than immersion in remedying day-to-day struggle against the trials in a capitalist economic order. In keeping with its world-systemic and cognitive-mapping dynamics, *Konjunktur 1* weaves the foregoing concerns into a dense tapestry of other

116  *Conjonctural Cycles of Capitalist Oil Extraction*

interdependent issues. Some of the recurring and vexing concerns of the play include: oil workers, production of peripheral Albania as a resource frontier, pursuit of resource and political-economic monopoly, revolutionary nationalism and internationalism, anti-petro-capitalism and protégé national government, critique of international laws and neutrality. I have scrutinized these thematic concerns in three distinct yet interrelated sections.

## A.   The Production of a Resource Frontier, Petro-Revolutionary Nationalism, and Peripheral Oil Workers

One of the noteworthy facets of *Konjunktur 1*, which distinguishes it from the majority of the plays concerned with various aspects of oil and an oil-driven life of the individual and society, is its sustained attention to the life of oil workers. In the previous energy regime (coal), the capitalist rulers (at national and imperial-global levels) had already realized how worker power could be disruptive and threatening to the established order. However, coal workers' strikes and rebellions against the capitalist system were perceived by the economic-intellectual heads of fossil capital as so incomprehensible that workers were represented as fundamentally alien (see Elizabeth Carolyn Miller 2021; also see Michael Niblett 2020). In this light, the next extraction cycle or energy regime in the fossil capital – namely, the oil system – took a pre-emptive measure in this regard. As some scholars have already noted, what rather occludes the role of the workers in the petro-industrial and petrocultural world is that oil is far less labour-intensive and more capital-intensive at the point of extraction compared with other resources and fossil fuels, including coal (see Mitchell 2011, 20–39; see also Podobnik 2006, 47). Workers – both oil workers and mine workers – feature far more prominently in *Konjunktur* (*1* and 2), compared to *Oil Field*. The ensuing scene illustrates the point at issue. Whilst Claire and Rossi are engaged in their conversation, we see "A troop of workers, ragged men, are marching individually, heavy loads on the shoulder, over the groyne. Soldiers with planted Bayonets drive the people to one side. Workers stop, putting down loads, running out". This scene (along with many others) presents a palimpsestic and contrapuntal picture of the concurrence or coexistence of not only various classes within a nation but of local/national and global forces. Whilst Rossi invokes humanistic-civilizational mottos (which have already been revealed to be thinly disguised discursive codes for the continuation of colonial-exploitative presence) by stating "Italy is determined to continue its historical mission –", Claire acts as the voice of the oppressed, "as an advocate for the weak and under pressure". *Konjunktur 1* spares no efforts at exposing the underside of the smoothly flowing oil industry – one important constituent of which is "workers". In the heat of the tensions and rivalry over gaining monopoly over the oil wells and extraction

## Conjonctural Cycles of Capitalist Oil Extraction   117

amongst the French, Italian, and (disguised) English forces, the play makes numerous apparently casual and fleeting references to the workers as the material (under)ground of the petro-capitalist industry. For instance, we catch a glimpse into oil workers' conditions when Romney "pointing at the workers" asks Jonny: "where are these people being driven?" and Jonny responds: "Are workers from our oil wells". Gleaning our inklings from the workers' speeches as well as the descriptions of their conditions interspersed throughout *Konjunktur* (*1* and *2*), we realize how Lania seeks to demonstrate the lives of oil workers to be a life of social-political alienation and economic exploitation in a petro-capitalist system where the oil workers' alienated lives are enmeshed with the lives of commodities. Perhaps partly due to historical limitation, since although at the time oil as an energy regime had gained global primacy, petro-capitalism had not fully developed into a fully globalized and dominant cultural commodity permeating every fibre of the psychosomatic being of the society and individual – what *Konjunktur 1* does not attend to is the deep-seated ties between trade unions (and working class) and fossil capitalism (see Mitchell).[37]

Claire introduces herself thus: "I stand here before you as a representative of the revolutionary Committees of the Balkan Federation" (Act 2, Scene 1). Claire asks them to disrupt the flow of imperial fossil capital through labour militancy but also strategic patience, socialist consciousness, and solidarity. Whilst sparing no efforts to dignify the workers for their anti-capitalist and national resistance activities of collective nature, Claire's remarks reveal her emphasis on the necessity of recognizing the intertwinement between anti-capitalist nationalization of resources and decolonization. Claire's critical vision, in this regard, is evocative of Rosa Luxemburg who, in *Mass Strike* (1905), accentuates the necessity of engendering a coalescence and confluence between the economically based struggles of workers and the revolutionary political struggles in other sectors of society since, according to her, the various forms of the mass strike "run through one another, run side by side, cross one another, flow in and over one another [in] a ceaselessly moving, changing sea of phenomena" (29–30).[38] Whilst in keeping with her communist egalitarian ethos, Claire promotes working-class consciousness and the proletariat's rights to economic-political power, and she insightfully accentuates the significance of national self-determination and autonomy of resource management if any domestic revolution is supposed to take place. The glaring irony in such situations is Claire's own position as a disguised agent of the Soviet Union. In the meantime, she promotes the rights and working conditions of workers whilst insisting on the nationalization of oil for Albania.

The workers, however, distrust and suspect the foreign forces and want to go on a strike and take action whilst Claire is exhorting them to exercise some patience whilst she is conducting negotiations with both national and international forces. Claire remarks: "Still three days! I ask

118    *Conjonctural Cycles of Capitalist Oil Extraction*

you! I have certain news that things are brewing among the troops. We have to be patient" (Act 2, Scene 1). Significantly, Lania depicts the oil workers both as a monolithic unit (hence a manipulable mass) and as individualized voices by showing how they may have conflicting views and how different workers reckon different courses of action as the effective one. The first facet of the oil workers (as a monolithic voice and manipulable mass) features both in *Konjunktur 1* and *2*. In *Konjunktur 2*, for instance, we encounter a highly emblematic scene that illustrates this dynamic. Here whilst on strike workers have assembled to protest their exploitative working conditions. Evident in their mutable attitudes is their being liable to being deceived by the so-called leaders and intellectuals. First we see workers protesting:

Workers (in increasing numbers, very excited, gather)

OVERSEER: Don't worry, you won't starve to death.
1 WORKER: Shut up.
2 WORKERS First we toil –
3RD WORKER: And break our bones
1ST WORKER: Because things can't go fast enough.
3RD WORKER: And now we're on the street.
RUGE: Down with the strangers! – bandits! – Out with them! –

Subsequently, in this scene, we see Rifan-Bey arrive, presenting himself as a sympathetic proponent of the workers' rights and taking the initiative to guide them towards a rewarding course of action. Here we see how workers can be easily swayed and deceived. First we hear Rifan-Bey, "very ragged among the workers", state:

> Ha, ha, ha! Just scream, scream! Will be of much use to you. The strangers have deaf ears and their hearts are harder than the stones here. Yes, do you know why you are now on the street? Because the French want to bring foreign workers into the country.

This is then followed by the masses of oil workers' shouts: "Down with the French!" No sooner has Rifan-Bey resumed his incendiary Otherizing rhetoric ("This disgusting thing, more bloodthirsty than the mosquitoes, more cruel than the sharks are the French") than Dubois (the French representative) "meaningfully pulls his wallet in passing" and bribes him. This brings about a drastic shift of gears which produces nothing short of a tragi-comic sense of black humour verging on absurdism:

RIFAN-BEY (after exchanging a look with Dubois): – The French are not. Oh no, they are not the culprits. The Italians are to blame. They founded this business, they want to starve us.

*Conjonctural Cycles of Capitalist Oil Extraction*   119

SHOUTS: Down with the Italians.
RIFAN-BEY: They stole the ground from us, they called the foreign military
into the country.
SHOUTS: Hit them up!

As regards the second facet (oil workers as individualized voices), in *Konjunktur 1* the body of workers is represented by four workers, almost each of whom holds a different opinion about the critical matters and best course of action against their exploitative working conditions. *Konjunktur 1* features a number of scenes where oil workers have gathered to protest against the presence of foreign forces/companies. Their protest arises not merely from their nationalist fervour; but, more importantly, from the fact that they find their working conditions both physically and financially unbearable. We see them assembling, along with Ahmed and Claire, to discuss options and choices in anti-capitalist and anti-imperial reaction. The workers consider the following as possible remedies: going on a strike; turning from one exploitative foreign country/company to another apparently less exploitative country/company as the last resort; and, ultimately, even trusting and appealing to the head of the newly established Albanian state led by Goldstein – who is ironically a non-national dictator, that is, a British national who has assumed a nationalist-revolutionary posture – as a counter-force for ousting these international-imperial oil companies and, instead, taking the reigns of the oil industry and management of workers in a hopefully more benign manner. Whilst the workers deem "strike" an efficacious counter-move or remedial measure, Claire admonishes them to exercise more patience since, given the current dynamics of the affairs, energy-worker rebellion or strike may not be as rewarding as they anticipate.

One of the most vociferous and candid voices that advocate revolutionary socialism and the rights of the oil workers is Ahmed. Ahmed in his myopic, yet sincere and well-intentioned, vision also ardently believes that the remedy lies in the abolition of foreign exploitation and presence/interference:

> Yes! The open fight against the local and foreign printers, against the Begs, who draw our peasants' blood, and the French and Italians and English and Serbs, who steal our oil and break the bones of our workers in pieces.
>
> (Act 2, Scene 1)

Claire draws their attention to the futility and counter-productive nature of any however revolutionary action that takes nation as its sole focus and isolated scope of action. Instead, Claire insists on the necessity of considering the world-systemic dynamics informing the relation between the national and global sides coupled with the ways in which the persistence

120   *Conjonctural Cycles of Capitalist Oil Extraction*

of an uneven core-periphery and class-hierarchy dynamics would preclude the possibility of any structural change in Albania. This is evidenced in her conversation with Goldstein. Whilst Claire's critical vision is informed with a world-historical and world-economic approach – through which she tries to enlighten and incite the working class and native Albanians – Goldstein remains negligent/ignorant of the significance of Albania as a resource frontier and the determining ways in which it can affect the world economy and politics, that is, as regards the determination of energy regimes, the dynamics of power amongst global powers, and the distribution of wealth and accumulation of capital. The ensuing exchange illustrates the point at issue:

CLAIRE: They are by all means equal to the dictators who pillage the largest countries in Europe today out of stupidity or vanity, out of greed for fame or money – depending on the economic situation.
GOLDSTEIN: They overestimate the importance of Albania. The caricature of a state. What is happening here –

As such, Claire urges the workers to broaden their confined horizons beyond a local-national purview to understand how the situation plays out and is determined by twofold forces. On this premise, Claire advises a combination of nationalization and decolonization and revolutionary socialism within the nation. Claire emphasizes incisively the determining force of the global context:

> There is no other way to do it. As long as we are not safe from the occupying army, each of our actions, each revolution, each uprising will be exploited by one of the powers against the other, even a revolutionary Albania is only a laughable figure – in the game of the great. Fine freedom movement by the grace of Dubois or Rossi or Browns – thank you very much!
>
> (Act 2, Scene 1)

One of the revealing moments in *Konjunktur 1* is when Claire in her conversation with the workers, whilst accentuating the significance of countering and resisting exploitative political economy of global powers imposed on national labour force and resources, seeks to broaden their horizons beyond the immediate and the personal (*hic et nunc*) by alerting them to a far longer span and scope, that is, the longue durée of imperial-colonial occupation of the land and its exploitative extraction of its four cheaps: labour-power, energy, raw materials, and food (Moore 2015, 53). Claire also strives to imbue Ahmed's revolutionary idealism with some pragmatism. As she exhorts him:

> This open battle has been fought so often and has always ended in defeat. The rulership has changed, once it was Turks and once the

## Conjonctural Cycles of Capitalist Oil Extraction   121

Greeks and then the Austrians and now the League of Nations. What has remained is exploitation and hunger for the peasants, bribery and benefices for the rich and the country has the historical role of being a theater of war for all the powers of Europe.

Another salient moment that illustrates the world-systemic vision of *Konjunktur 1* transpires when Ahmed suspiciously probes Claire's motives. In response, Claire avers how she intends to counter this uneven history of colonial-imperial extractivism whereby peripheral countries (including Albania) are subjected to a hierarchical core-periphery logics at social-cultural and political-economic levels:

> I want this Albania no longer to be a European curiosity and a cheap material for operetta librettists, while dividends are minted from our oil and grain on the markets of the famous cities to finance the dreadnoughts and armies that carry the war across Europe from these ports and villages every 10 years. I don't want a revolutionary gimmick, but the bloc of the Albanian people with the workers and peasants of the Balkan countries, the closed front with the soldiers of the occupation forces.
>
> (Act 2, Scene 1)

### B.   Monopoly Petro-Capitalism

A conspicuous thematic component of *Konjunktur 1*, which also features as the common thread binding the imperial-colonial powers' treatment of Albania, is the question of monopoly. Notably, all global powers present in Albania strive to exploit Albania's politically-economically precarious and vulnerable position by offering international recognition and legitimization, military-political protection, and some basic economic reward in return for Albania's granting them the monopoly over its valuable and strategic resources – above all, oil. A more meticulous consideration of each proposal and interaction between the state and the contending global powers can be illuminating.

First we witness the proposal of oil monopoly offered by the Italian representative Rossi who, holding the draft of a proposal in his hand, reads thus:

> Albania immediately concludes a protection and alliance treaty with Italy. Your government grants the tobacco monopoly and the mining rights to the Banca di Roma, and the oil sources to the Italian oil syndicate. You will receive cash for the first time.

This is followed by the arrival of the French representative's offer. Dubois states:

> Albania places itself under French sovereignty, i.e. your government immediately concludes a protection and alliance treaty with

## 122  *Conjonctural Cycles of Capitalist Oil Extraction*

Yugoslavia. They lease all of the oil sources to our company for 99 years, a French consortium receives the tobacco monopoly and mining rights in the northern Albanian ore area, the management of the state bank is transferred to a mixed Yugoslav-Albanian commission chaired by a French.

The most egregious request for monopoly is made by the putatively neutral delegate, Brown, which is ensued by Goldstein's promise of its delivery contingent on Brown's provision of the torpedo ship to be deployed against the revolutionary forces. As Goldstein states:

> They explain that the revolutionaries had attacked the ship in the dark of night, so the captain was forced to intervene in the battle. By the time the case is settled, you will have your ship back, my government has been saved, you will have the oil monopoly, Albanian will come under English sovereignty, you will become a pair!

*Konjunktur 1*'s emphasis on the rampant rise in the global powers' pursuit of monopoly over raw materials and energy resources as one of the prominent features of the late 19th and early 20th century political economy is confirmed by Ernest Mandel, when he observes:

> It is not surprising this monopolization occurred more rapidly in the "new" branches of industry (steel, electric machines, oil) and in the "new" industrial nations (USA, Germany) than in the "old" branches of industry (textiles, coal) and the "old" industrial states (England, France).
>
> (*Late Capitalism* 1978, 188)

It is worth noting that the pursuit of capitalist monopolies led by both oil corporations and imperial powers – underpinned by the same logic and pattern as delineated by Mandel – is discernible across all three plays (*Konjunktur 1* and *2* and *Oil Field*). However, given that I extensively elaborated on the question of monopoly and the ways in which it features in or bears upon these plays, suffice it here to briefly address its historical facet. The plays' foregrounding of monopoly as a nationally determining political-economic element closely corresponds to the real historical conditions and facts in Albania's history. Whilst all global powers, above all England, withheld Albania an international recognition and legitimacy in the League of Nations during the reign of Noli (who adamantly refused to grant them monopoly over oil and other resources), England was quick enough to grant Albania recognition and membership in the League of Nations (based on the endorsement from other major powers) as soon as Zogu expressed willingness to endow the English and some other global powers with their share of the monopoly of various national resources at a cheap price. Significantly, this part of national

*Conjonctural Cycles of Capitalist Oil Extraction* 123

history is explicitly represented in *Konjunktur* (1 and 2) in the conversation between Brown and Goldstein. Here, when Goldstein insists on further supports from the British Empire or the League of Nations to maintain his dictatorship, Brown avers: "[the recognition and legitimization of your dictatorship] [w]ouldn't have come to us very cheaply either. The shouting that will then begin – you are not a protector to be honored with".

Integral to Lania's focus on the question of monopoly capitalism is his socialist critique of the colonialist-capitalist dynamics of the international law and its founders and guardians (England, France, Italy, the USA, and Germany). A glaring instance of how the allegedly neutral imperial democracies had in fact highly vested interest in the political-economic conditions of certain underdeveloped European and non-European countries is Mr. Brown, who features as a manifold figure whose various facets barely seem congruent with one another. Brown, who according to the play is "Royal Dutch", President of the English Oil Trusts, and the "Chairman of the Federation Committee for Albania" incarnates the overdetermined nature of the role of Anglo-American and central European forces as neutral arbiters in world political-economic affairs. The conflicted nature of the roles invested in one imperial nation or global power (in this instance, Britain) – symbolically embodied by Mr. Brown – is further accentuated here. This point finds an illuminating expression in Dubois who at a critical juncture in the play – where all their schemes and plots have collapsed due to Goldstein's betrayal and refusal to adhere to (conduct) the plan as coup d'état as planned by Brown – notes: "Are you making this statement on behalf of the League of Nations Committee or Downing Street or Royal Dutch?"; to which Brown replies: "I am convinced that you will convey this statement to the Quai d'Orsai[39] as well as to Standard Oil". This exchange serves indeed as a compelling evidence for the *conjonctural dynamics* of the colonial history of imperial interventions of the core countries into resource-rich peripheries.

As indicated, Goldstein is too much of a coward – hence given to self-preservation and self-interest – to jeopardize his life as a pawn in the abstruse schemes of the global powers. As a non-Albanian, he is not even sufficiently affectively-emotionally invested in Albania as part of his own history; a point which would otherwise galvanize him to cling to his position. When out of desperation Goldstein suggests he resign, Brown compels him to persevere by inexorably suppressing the revolutionary popular uprisings. When Goldstein asks for torpedo boats in order to allegedly launch a counter-revolutionary manoeuvre, Brown says:

> They weren't going to get it either. We recognized you, I can't go any further. I've already gone far. If you run off here, we will be one more embarrassment richer. Europe is patient, but we have been asking too much of it lately.

(Act 3, Scene 16)

124    *Conjonctural Cycles of Capitalist Oil Extraction*

As a last resort, Goldstein insists on abdication whilst astutely raising the question of oil resources:

> I don't need to take my skin to the market, I know other jobs than being a dictator. I can also abdicate – about the oil wells, your interests in Albania – whether those with the rebels or Mrs. Claire are willing to reach a concession –?

Brown, however, interjects to drive in another impossible divide between politics and economy: "The interests of the Royal Dutch do not have the slightest influence on the policies of my government and the League of Nations". Goldstein is too subtle to succumb to this ideological manoeuvre (Brown's claims about neutrality and the politics-economics dichotomy) and "more and more certain" debunks Brown's claims by accentuating the world-historical and world-economic significance of Albania for the British petro-capitalist system:

> I'm standing here on an outpost of the British Empire. The men of your government? They want to prove their energy by blowing up safes and stealing documents and looking for Bolshevik spies. When it is necessary to counter the idea of revolution with an equally sparkling idea: dictatorship, fascism. If my government falls a new wave of the red tide, the British lions – the foundations – the empire will shake –
>
> (Act 3, Scene 16)

After Goldstein's insistence on abdication is faced with Brown's foreboding dismissal: "That will not do. Think of the chaos this will unleash", Goldstein makes the following request: "Put the torpedo ship [an English warship] at my disposal, which is anchored in the roadstead of Valona"; a torpedo ship which he intends to use, as he claims, to open fire on the insurgents by bombarding Durazzo. Testifying to Goldstein's astute discernment, it is ultimately the alluring prospect of monopoly over Albanian oil resources that makes Brown ultimately acquiesce to grant Goldstein access to the torpedo ships. Subsequently, Goldstein lays out his plan thus: Goldstein's forces will spread the rumour that the revolutionaries had attacked the torpedo ship in the dead of night, so the captain was forced to intervene in the battle by massacring them and opening fire on them. Goldstein mentions the happy resolution of his tragic drama thus: "By the time the case is settled, you will have your ship back, my government has been saved, you will have the oil monopoly, Albania will come under English sovereignty, you will become a pair!" Brown's frivolous response is revealing: "Damn risky fun". Notably, whilst Brown still expresses his concession (concerning the torpedo ships) under the guise of ideas (democratic-humanitarian values), this time, however, Goldstein reminds him of the

## Conjonctural Cycles of Capitalist Oil Extraction    125

material-economic grounds of such ideological values: "Our very real cause will win! Culture and civilization and oil and democracy". The ultimate anti-democratic concession to guarantee the British Empire's brand of "oil democracy" attests to the anti-democratic, double-dealing, and anti-communist politics informing an ostensibly international and neutral organization (the League of Nations) and the allegedly democratic European countries. This interventionist politics, underpinned by a global struggle between Western liberal capitalism and Soviet Union communism, also reveals how these global powers' stance towards the (semi-)peripheral resource frontiers is premised on the perpetuation/ maintenance of resource monopoly, and political-economic hegemony of the core Western countries (including the US). This point finds cogent corroboration in the ensuing exchange between Brown and Dubois where both the world-historical vision underpinning *Konjunktur 1* and the world-systemic nature of oil extraction and production by the global powers are revealed. Here, *Konjunktur 1* shows how the repercussions of Albania's revolutionary movements, nationalization of natural resources (including oil) might instigate a wave of decolonization across the globe in other semi-colonies:

BROWN: Naturally. As a result of the mutiny, the prestige of Italy and France in the Balkans has received a strong shock anyway.
DUBOIS: (ironic): England too.
BROWN: Five cruisers of our D-class have already left for a fleet demonstration against the Albanian coast.
DUBOIS: England, too, will witness the retroactive effect of this revolution in Egypt, in Turkey.

(Act 3, Scene 1)

### C.  Revolution for or Against Oil and Its Logics?

Claire, initially unofficially and later officially, assumes the role of the leader of the national Albanian revolution (along with Ahmed) against the foreign powers and companies protesting the extraction of oil and the rights and conditions of the workers. Claire, as such, features as a twofold figure: at once allegorical and historical. She embodies the allegorical in terms of her representing the idea of a socialist-anti-imperial revolution; and as a historical figure in terms of her appearance as the disguised agent of the Soviet Union. Claire's inexorable anti-capitalist and revolutionary endeavours, extensively delineated earlier, culminate in a climactic moment when she storms into Goldstein's office (as the head of the state) catching him in the collusive act of reaching double-dealing politicaleconomic agreements (with oil monopoly as their core) with the British (Brown), French, and Italian representatives separately. Goldstein's surreptitious plans are sabotaged when Claire disrupts their predatory

126    *Conjonctural Cycles of Capitalist Oil Extraction*

schemes by divulging how they have been treacherously acting against one another behind one another's back. Ultimately, Goldstein, true to his impostor nature, utilizes the torpedo ship to escape the Albanian scene rather than confronting and suppressing the nationalist insurgents (as he has promised to Brown). The revolutionary forces, led by Claire, seize this moment and arrive in the capital to gain control over all the strategic sites of power. The play concludes with the reading of the declarations of the revolutionary forces through the radio and the global leaders' meeting to make decisions regarding this national upheaval by further plotting against the future of the country and planning how to counter the revolutionaries and to regain monopoly over its oil resources.

Perhaps the most conspicuous aspect of this climactic moment is Claire's observations concerning the nature of history, future, and revolution. In keeping with her socialist-communist ethos, Claire believes in historical-materialist determination of the mind-body of individuals and the possibility of revolutionary transformation of the content of the minds of the Albanian people. Notably, Claire rejects metaphysical determinism and embraces dialectical-historical constructivism, that is, class inequality as a historical capitalist-bourgeois construct rather than an eternal fact of human social organization. As she ardently avers:

> I have far too much faith in the relentless logic of this time, not to believe that people of the same kind, young, old, sooner or later have to stand where they belonged. The only thing that matters is that they are thoroughly turned inside out.[40]

Here the reverberating and key phrase is as much "the relentless logic of this time" as men to be "thoroughly turned inside out". The former phrase betokens a sense of dialectical dynamics and historical materialism – in other words, the historical dynamics stemming from the intersection of the local/national with the global at political-economic levels – coalescing to determine the course of events towards the emergence of a socialist, revolutionary order. The latter phrase hints at the violence and authoritarianism latent in such a "turning-out" of the man. Claire explicitly articulates her vision of this process of de-alienation and revolution thus:

> You are not born a revolutionary or a socialist. But neither is it because it just happens to happen. (presses Evelyn and Jonny's hand now) You should now – (breaking off, changing the tone)[41] Oh no, no philosophy – you should go to Durazzo by car and you to the radio station! You should work, then you will already prove what is your turn. (To Evelyn) And be careful not to get shot.[42] We still have too much work and too serious decisions ahead of us for us to have the right to be foolhardy today. So, let's start now.[43]

*Conjonctural Cycles of Capitalist Oil Extraction*   127

It would be illuminating to gauge the dynamics of the Albanian revolution – and, more particularly, Claire's vision of it – as depicted in *Konjunktur 1* against the classical account of proletariat revolution articulated by Marx to see to what extent they evince convergence or divergence. Marx succinctly sketches the process of working-class revolution in an industrially developed capitalist society as follows:

> Along with the constant decrease in the number of capitalist magnates, who usurp and monopolize all the advantages of this process of transformation, the mass of misery, oppression, slavery, degradation and exploitation grows; but with this there also grows the revolt of the working class, a class constantly increasing in numbers and trained, united and organized by the very mechanism of the capitalist process of production.
>
> (*Capital, Volume I* Marx 1976, 929)

He proceeds to explain how all these developments of productive forces and a united working class, over time, become "incompatible with their capitalist integument" (Marx 1976, 929). This culminates in the death knell of "capitalist [private] property" where the "expropriators are expropriated" (Marx 1976, 929). Marx elaborates on the dialectical dynamics of this process thus: "Capitalist production begets, with the inexorability of a natural process, its own negation. This is the negation of the negation" (Marx 1976, 929).

As is evident there are significant historical and ideological imbrications between Marx's account and Claire's vision enacted in the play. One of the chief differences concerns Albania's national history and political condition. More specifically, in *Konjunktur 1*, the occurrence of the socialist revolution in Albania was not preceded with a long history of the domination of a modern capitalist state or a bourgeois society. As such, both Claire's and Lania's vision at this stage seem to be inclined toward the early Gramsci's revolutionary vision of change rather than Marx's evolutionary/stagist account of it. This is attested by Claire's affirmation that their national-socialist revolution was not a bourgeois revolution (led by the elitist and mainly driven by minority bourgeoisie in their race for power), but the oil workers' (or proletariat's) revolution against both a colonial-imperial petro-capitalism's extractive exploitation of Albania and against a class-based dictatorship towards and hence as part of a universal socialist program. As such, Claire's speech is highly consonant with Gramsci who discerns the promise of the birth of a "New Man" in the event of the Russian Revolution. As he exclaims:

> As a result of the Russian revolution the man who was a common criminal has turned into the sort of man whom Immanuel Kant, the theoretician of absolute ethical conduct, had called for – the sort of

## 128   Conjonctural Cycles of Capitalist Oil Extraction

man who says: the immensity of the heavens above me. the imperative of my conscience within me. What these brief news items reveal to us is a liberation of spirit. the establishment of a new moral awareness. It is the advent of a new order, one that coincides with everything our masters taught us.

(1990, 28–30; see also 1975, 126–128)[44]

As a couple of other characters also indicate (including Claire's daughter), Claire-Barsin's socialist-revolutionary leanings (evocative of Leninism) are also inflected with a certain degree of subjective idealism and voluntarism. These features are also the critique of Lenin and Bolshevism that Gramsci sympathetically expressed. It is worth glancing at it since it elucidates Claire's socialist vision too:

He [Lenin] and his Bolshevik comrades are convinced that socialism can be achieved at any time. They are nourished on Marxist thought. They are revolutionaries, not evolutionists. And revolutionary thought does not see time as a progressive factor. It denies that all intermediate stages between the conception of socialism and its achievement must have absolute and complete confirmation in time and place. It holds that it is enough that these stages be realised in thought for the revolution to be able to proceed beyond them.

(1990, 32)

*Konjunktur 1*'s note of hope – which is missing in *Konjunktur 2* (the post-censorship text) – stems from the unblemished prospect of revolutionary change presaged by Claire's ascendency to power and the assumption of leadership where she features as an anti-capitalist, pro-proletarian socialist (as a Soviet Union agent). Claire's socialist-communist ideology – rendered explicit towards the end of *Konjunktur 1* – pertains to the pre-censorship state of the text (prior to the imposition of the revision). The climactic moment of *Konjunktur 2* (the post-censorship version) features a last-minute revelation of Claire's true identity where she avers to be an American and not a Russian representative who had been pretending to pursue communist goals whilst intending to gain and implement capitalist policies and profits (in relation to Albanian oil resources) on the national and international scene. This loss of textual and political ambiguity (stemming from the censoring of the scene) is ironically confirmed by Piscator's retrospective reflection on what the play should have conveyed, but – perhaps because of the incendiary reactions and censoring sensitivity it could have instigated – was unable to convey: "One could have shown [in *Konjunktur 2*] that the Soviet Union, precisely in order to maintain its importance for the international labor movement, consciously pursued capitalist world economic policy" (*Political Theatre*, 200).

## Conjonctural Cycles of Capitalist Oil Extraction   129

In *Konjunktur 1*, such moments of revolutionary hope and re-education of social ethos, historical consciousness (and the unconscious), and political spirit of Man should be considered in the broader context of the early 20th century when: "with the nineteenth-century political world reduced to ashes by the First World War, the Bolshevik Revolution appeared to be the phoenix-like expression of a new political destiny for all of Europe" (43).[45] By 1919, the British Socialists had already held a convention at Leeds which announced their intention to "do for Britain what the Russian Revolution has accomplished in Russia" and which passed a resolution calling for the establishment of worker and soldier soviets. Claire's petro-revolutionary goals – including her clarion call for the transformation of the mind of people and the spiritual rebirth – can best be understood in the foregoing context. However, what further complicates the situation in Albania is its being a rudderless oil-owning resource frontier in conjunction with Claire's status as an undercover Soviet Union agent.

True to its critical-materialist spirit, *Konjunktur 1* leaves as many questions unanswered as it has answered. Surely, what provides the impetus and propulsive source of hope and progressive social-political transformation is oil and the petroleum industry. However, it is not clear how and through which processes, social relations, and political-economic dynamics the birth of such a New Man is planned to be conducted. This lacuna (and the tenebrous prospect it portends) gains a bleaker shade when we consider Claire's status as a socialist foreigner (a Russian agent) with a disguised identity. As such, whilst the play concludes with the ousting of one mode of political-economic governance (capitalist imperialism and colonialism) and its supersession with a socialist-communist one, what remains unchallenged and unaltered is the more profound and structural-material ground, that is, the oil order – where oil, as a nationally and globally strategic commodity, is entrenched as the fulcrum around which the communist-capitalist and national-global relations and conflicts turn. *Konjunktur 1* concludes with an impending sense of further oil-centred tensions and struggle at national and international levels with the brooding prospect (further complicities and counter-moves to be forged by both the communist Soviet Union and the imperial Anglo-European forces looming over the horizon).

## Notes

1. "Albania should be taken seriously in terms of its oil resources" (Sali Berisha, Albania's prime minister).
2. See Robert Clegg Austin, *Founding a Balkan State: Albania's Experiment with Democracy, 1920–1925*, Toronto: University of Toronto Press, 2012, pp. 15–17.
3. Michael Ross, *The Oil Curse: How Petroleum Wealth Shapes the Development of Nations* (Princeton, NJ: Princeton University Press, 2012).
4. Fredric Jameson, "Culture and Finance Capital," *Critical Inquiry*, 24.1 (Autumn 1997), pp. 246–265.

## 130  Conjonctural Cycles of Capitalist Oil Extraction

5. Delineating the characteristics of the second "variant" of capitalism, Mandel explains them thus:

> [here] surplus profits can be realized by the introduction of technical innovation even in the absence of perfect mobility of capital. This is the classical case of monopolies, where there are decisive restrictions on the mobility of capital because of a combination of operative agreements between the most important owners of capital and massive installation costs – in other words a qualitatively higher level of concentration and centralization of capital. This combination results not only in temporary surplus profits, but also in the lasting surplus-profits which are a characteristic feature of the epoch of monopoly capitalism.
>
> (94)

6. See Moore's and Nixon's respective, and equally relevant, arguments in this regard as delineated in the "Introduction".
7. There have been two rigorous and extended studies of Lania's work by Tatjana Röber and Michael Schwaiger. Whilst neither work specifically focuses on the questions of oil, energy, or even nature or ecological questions (whether from the perspective of ecocriticism or that of Energy Humanities), but both dedicate some sustained critical attention to *Konjunktur*. In her doctoral thesis (titled: *Der Mensch steht in der Mitte, aber nur relative: Subjektivität und Wahrnehmung in Kulturtheorie und 'sachlichem' Theater der 20er Jahre*), Röber takes a selected number of dramatic works and their theatrical productions by Brecht, Piscator, and Feuchtwanger, among others, as her focal point and explores their politics of form and their political aesthetics from sociological and socio-psychological perspectives predicated on theories elaborated by Benjamin, Kracauer, Horkimr, and Sloterdjik. In his doctoral thesis (titled *Von der Kunst zur Reportage und zurück: Leo Lanias Konzept einer politisch operativen Literatur und Medienkunst*, 2014), Schwaiger more specifically concentrates on Lania's journalistic and dramatic career. The crux of Schwaiger's analysis are Lania's Reportage Theory and Piscator's influence on the aesthetics and politics of Lania's work particularly as developed through their collaborative work on the production of Lania's works. What both theses have in common is their focus on the earlier and German versions of the play (*Konjunktur 1* and 2) – hence the lack of any sustained engagement with *Oil Field* and the details and dynamics of the trajectory from *Konjunktur* to *Oil Field* in both works.
8. See "Der Hitler-Ludendorff-Prozess" (Verlag Die Schmiede, Berlin 1925 – Reihe: "Außenseiter der Gesellschaft – Die Verbrechen der Gegenwart"). See also Leo Lania, *[Wien 1924; Berlin 1925]: Gewehre auf Reisen* (München: Bilder aus deutscher Gegenwart, 2002). (Reprint).
9. Just to mention one of his daredevil adventures, in October 1923 (shortly before the "Bierhaus coup"), alerted by the advance of the Italian fascists, Lania went to Munich to the Volkischer Beobachter [Folk Observer], Hitler's headquarters at the time, in an act of investigative journalism. He disguised himself as an Italian: under a disguised identity he self-appointedly presented himself as a liaison between the fascist party and the German "brother movement" (WiU, 220).
10. For example, an article about the Consul organization "Spain – Das Arsenal Deutschlands" in the Berlin Borsen-Courier, September 1924; "Die deutsche Ochrana", all in LLC, Bl4lF3.
11. See "Prager Tageblatt"; see LLC, B14/F3; 2 and 10 as well as B13/F6; 76.

## Conjonctural Cycles of Capitalist Oil Extraction   131

12.

> Emigration – for me that meant the loss of all my tools: the German language. . . . I never spoke for a moment about the fact that I could never become a French writer. I was able to have my articles and books translated, but the isolationism of the French press and publishers could not be broken.
> (WiU, 310)

13. For an extended account of the affinities between world-systems theory and Lania's historical vision, reportage theory, dramatic aesthetics, and mode of journalistic practice see the first section of this chapter.
14. *Petrocultures: Oil, Politics, Culture* edited by Sheena Wilson, Adam Carlson, Imre Szeman.
15. The report books appeared in the following order: (1) *Die Totengräber Deutschlands. Das Urteil im Hitlerprozeß [Germany's Gravedigger. The Judgment in the Hitler Trial]* (Neuer Deutscher Verlag, Berlin 1924); (2) *Gewehre auf Reisen [Rifles on the Road]* (Malik-Verlag, Vienna 1924; a year later there was an edition by Malik-Verlag, Berlin); (3) *Der Hitler-Ludendorff-Prozess [The Hitler-Ludendorff Trial]* (Verlag Die Schmiede, Berlin 1925 – Reihe: "Außenseiter der Gesellschaft – Die Verbrechen der Gegenwart" [Series: "Outsiders of Society – The Crimes of the Present"]); (4) *Gruben, Gräber, Dividenden [Pits, Graves, Dividends]* (Malik-Verlag, Berlin 1925); (5) *Indeta, die Fabrik der Nachrichten [Indeta, the Factory of News]* (Verlag Die Schmiede, Berlin 1927 – Reihe: "Berichte aus der Wirklichkeit" [Series: "Reports from Reality"]).
16.

> Unsere Gegenwart zieht den Menschen von heute stärker in ihren Bann als je eine Zeitepoche bisher, und diese Gegenwart ist aufregender, romantischer, farbiger und dramatischer, als sie die Phantasie eines Dichters je ersinnen könnte. . . . Die Entromantisierung der Kunst hat der Romantik des Alltags den Weg bereitet, und dieser Weg führt von der "reinen" Kunst zur Journalistik, zur Reportage, von der Dichtung zur Wahrheit, von der Erfindung sentimentaler Fabeln oder psychologischer Geheimniskrämerei zu der unerbittlichen, wahren Schilderung der aufregenden Mysterien der Gefängnisse, der Fabrik, des Kontors, der Maschine, des Mehrwerts, des Klassenkampfes.

17. In contrast to Pictorialism, in the 1920s and 1930s, however, the Neue Sachlichkeit or New Objectivity movement in Weimar Germany, and the turn toward pure or straight photography in the work of such artists as Paul Strand, Eugène Atget, August Sander, and Fredrick H. Evans affected another reversal, and documentary styles became a dominant form in photography. See Alison Nordstrom, *Truth Beauty: Pictorialism and the Photograph as Art, 1845–1945* (Vancouver: Vancouver Art Gallery, 2008).
18. Surveying the various artistic instances and manifestations subsumed under the rubric of the Neue Sachlichkeit concept, David Midgley provides a general but illuminating definition:

> In terms of the history of art, "Neue Sachlichkeit" became a shorthand term for the variety of ways in which a rising generation of artists foreswore the confident personal visions and gestures of Expressionism and turned instead to constructing discrete images of a post-war reality they had experienced as profoundly fragmented.
>
> (26)

## 132 Conjonctural Cycles of Capitalist Oil Extraction

Midgley identifies anti-expressionism and collage as two other prominent features of the Neue Sachlichkeit trend in German art in the Weimar period.

19. Kosellech Reinhart, *The Practice of Conceptual History: Timing History, Spacing Concepts* (Stanford: Stanford University Press, 2002).
L. Trotsky, *The Permanent Revolution and Results and Prospects* (London: New Park, 1962).

20. See Michael Schwaiger, pp. 74–94; see also Leo Lania, "Die Erben Zolas," *Die Neue Bücherschau*, 9.3 (1927), pp. 111–115.

21. See "Is There Thought Control in America? The Lessons of Europe," 1947 (unveröffentlichtes Manuskript); LLP, B12/F9. See also Leo Lania, "Reminiscences of the Time When a Poet Could Not Be a Sergeant," *Free World*, 2.4 (1942), pp. 345–346, 346.

22. Erwin Piscator, *Das politische Theater* (Berlin, 1929).

23. Erwin Piscator, "Outline of Sociological Dramaturgy" (1929), in *On Essays on German Theater*, ed. Margaret Herzfeld-Sander (New York: Continuum, 1985), pp. 183–185, here p. 184. Ibid., pp. 9–10.

24. See Schwaiger, pp. 300–303.

25. See also *Konjunktur*, Erwin Piscator Sammlung 54, Erwin Piscator Center 138, Akademie der Künste.

26. Piscator indicates 8 April as the opening night of *Konjunktur* (*Das Politische Theater*, p. 204), but the *Deutsches Buhnenspielplan* lists 10 April as the premiere.

27. Pact of Locarno (1 Dec. 1925) involved a series of agreements whereby Germany, France, Belgium, Great Britain, and Italy mutually guaranteed peace in western Europe. The treaties were initialed at Locarno, Switz., on 16 October and signed in London on 1 December.

28. *The Balkans: Revolution, War, and Political Violence Since 1878.*

29. See Chapters 5 and 6 of Robert Austin, *Founding a Balkan State*. London: University of Toronto Press, 2012.

30. See Stefanq, *Pollo and Puto, Arben: The History of Albania* (London, 1981), pp. 101, 183, 196.

31. Graeme Macdonald, "Oil and World Literature," *American Book Review*, 33.3 (March/April 2012), pp. 7–31.

32. Throughout the ensuing two chapters I will not be using any page numbers when quoting passages from the two plays (*Konjunktur 1* and 2) since no page numbers appear in the archival manuscripts of the plays I have been utilizing as the premise of my analysis.

33. More strictly, Zulu designates a Nguni ethnic group in Southern Africa. The Zulu people are the largest ethnic group and nation in South Africa, with an estimated 10–12 million people, living mainly in the province of KwaZulu-Natal.

34. Deriving her insights from Benjamin and others, Buck-Morss acutely observes how the possibility of a real democracy has been exceedingly undermined and eroded since the late 19th century by the proliferation of a universe of commodities:

> by the late nineteenth century, the bourgeois dream of democracy itself underwent this form of censorship: freedom was equated with the ability to consume. Benjamin writes that egalité developed its own "phantasmagoria," and "la revolution" came to mean "clearance sale" in the nineteenth century.
>
> (Buck-Morss 1989, 284)

## Conjonctural Cycles of Capitalist Oil Extraction   133

35. See Lania: "Die Geschichte eines Buches" ["The Story of a Book"].
36. Pact of Locarno (1 Dec. 1925), series of agreements whereby Germany, France, Belgium, Great Britain, and Italy mutually guaranteed peace in western Europe. The treaties were initialed at Locarno, Switz., on October 16 and signed in London on December 1. The Locarno agreements consisted of (1) a treaty of mutual guarantee between Germany, Belgium, France, Great Britain, and Italy; (2) arbitration treaties between Germany and Belgium and between Germany and France; (3) a note from the former Allies to Germany explaining the use of sanctions against a covenant-breaking state as outlined in article 16 of the League of Nations Covenant; (4) arbitration treaties between Germany and Czechoslovakia and between Germany and Poland; and (5) treaties of guarantee between France and Poland and between France and Czechoslovakia.
37. Timothy Mitchell, *Carbon Democracy: Political Power in the Age of Oil* (New York: Verso, 2011), p. 18. For more recent instances of such ties between trade unions and fossil capitalism see Alexander Kaufman, "Democrats' Drama on Fossil Fuel Money Shows a Radical Green Jobs Plan Can Be a Win-Win," *Huff-Post*, 11 August 2018.
38. Rosa Luxemburg, *The Mass Strike* (Chicago: Bookmarks, 1986).
39. Both the French ministry and a place in France, The Quai d'Orsay, is a quay in the 7th arrondissement of Paris. It is part of the left bank of the Seine opposite the Place de la Concorde.
40. Ich habe viel zu starkes Vertrauen die unerbittliche Logik dieser Zeit, un nicht zu glauben, dass Menschen Fures Schlages, jung, ahrlich, fruher oder spater dort stehen mussen, wohin sie gchoren. Es kommt nur darauf an, dass. sie einmal tuchtig umgekrempelt werden.
41. Man wird nicht als Revolutionér geboren und nicht als Sozialist. Aber man ist es auch nicht, weil es sich zufallig gerade so trifft. (druckt Evelyn und Jonny jetzt die Hand) Ihr sollt jetzt – (abbrechend, den Ton anderd).
42. Ach was, keine Philosophie – Du sollst nach Durazzo mit den Auto und Sie zur Radiostation! Arbeiten sollt Ihr, dann werdet Ihr schon beweisen, was an Fuch dran ist. (Zu Evelyn) Und gib acht, dass Du nicht erschossen wirst.
43. Wir haben noch zu viel Arbeit und zu ernste Entscheidungen vor uns, als dass wir heute schon das Recht hatten, tollkuhn zu sein. So, und nun wollen wir anfangen.
44. Antonio Gramsci, *Selections from Political Writings 1910–1920*. Ed. Quintin Hoare (Minneapolis: University of Minnesota Press, 1990). See also "La Rivoluzione contro il Capitale," *Avanti!*, 24 November 1917 translated into English: *History, Philosophy. and Culture in the Young Gramsci*, trans. and ed. P. Cavalcanti and P. Piccone. St. Louis: Telos Press, 1975.
45. Walter L. Adamson, *Hegemony and Revolution* (London: University of California Press, 1980).

# 3 "On a Wave of Oil England Swam Towards Victory . . . Our Weapon of Choice Was Oil"

Oil Monopoly, Petro-Dramaturgical Aesthetics, and Capitalocene in Leo Lania's *Konjunktur 2*

The innovative nature and significance of *Konjunktur* – in aesthetic and political-economic terms – are cogently captured by Piscator when he states: "[*Konjunktur 2*] opened up whole new perspectives for the theater" (Piscator 1980, 274).[1] Coming to *Konjunktur 2* with a fresh memory of *Konjunktur 1* in mind, we discern how the former grants us a dialectical vision – by juxtaposing the micropolitics and macropolitics of oil and desire – in a way not to be found in the latter. Whereas *Konjunktur 1* utilizes fictional-allegorical (and still nationally recognizable) names, *Konjunktur 2* alters them all to the names of real historical-political figures. A salient case in point is the names of figures such as Sir Henry Deterding (the President of Royal Dutch), W. C. Teagle (the President of Standard Oil), and Lomow (the Chairman of the All-Russian Naphta Syndicate) of whom there is no mention in *Konjunktur 1*, whilst they, as will be expatiated later, feature prominently in *Konjunktur 2*. In this regard, *Konjunktur 2* can be argued to intend to present a historically more accurate and detailed picture of the co-implications and complicities between corporation petro-capitalism and nations that constitute the core of the imperial-colonial powers in the global north. In what follows, I will first present a detailed account of *Konjunktur 2*. I will then proceed to delineate what I will call the petro-dramaturgical and infrastructural aesthetics of the play. This includes an exploration of not only the dramatic-diegetic but also the semiotic-material components of the play including props, music, and its multi-media dramaturgy. It also involves an inspection of the ways in which petrocultural elements and signs (including oil wells, cars, and media) feature prominently throughout *Konjunktur 2*. Finally, the crux of this chapter is the focus on the three extended speeches delivered by the three global oil powers and heads of two globally extended oil-driven competing hegemonies. Scrutinizing the three speeches and situating them in their local-global contexts, it will be demonstrated how the play evinces a world-systemic vision of oil (as a strategic global commodity and a symbolic sign) and a Capitalocenic critique of the dynamics of its extraction, production, and consumption.

DOI: 10.4324/9781003134664-4

## "On a Wave of Oil England Swam Towards Victory" 135

### I. The Endgames of a Peripheral Oil Frontier

*Konjunktur 2* (like *K1*) is set in Albania. Act One opens onto a scene where we witness the adventitious discovery of oil by Three Tramps (or wandering figures) in a remote area. They sell the discovery (oil-rich lands) – in exchange for schnapps and a few coins – to two other obscure figures who immediately recognize the existence of oil and the corresponding value of the property. One of the three people who discovered oil in the land is stabbed to death by his buddies. A local feudal lord, Rifan-Bey, disputes with the two figures (who now believe they are owners) over the proprietorship of the land, claiming that he owns half of the property. The Italian Rossi visits the property on which Rifan-Bey has started building. Rossi knows that the land belongs to the Albanian Bianca Goxhomani and negotiates with Rifan-Bey to buy it from Bianca on his behalf. The Frenchman Dubois shows up with some surveyors and begins to stake out the fields on the other property. When the two drifters (who killed their friend – the third member of their bunch) insist on their claim, he lures them into playing a game of cards around the property and then swindles them by cheating in the game. Dubois promises one of them, a former German officer, a position in the Albanian army as compensation.

It turns out that instead of fulfilling his commission (buying the land from Oxhomani for Rifan-Bey), Rossi has deceived Oxhomani (about the value of the property) and bought the property cheaply himself. Rossi and Dubois introduce themselves as the plenipotentiary envoys from their countries. Gradually, there appears an upsurge of signs, plaques, and boards on the land – bearing such inscriptions as "Syndicat Petrolifere Franco-Albanient" and "Società Italiana Petrolifera" – serving both as an open declaration of ownership claim by each international/foreign company (run by imperial/foreign forces) and also portending the prospective oil companies to be established soon. We then witness the arrival of oil workers at the land. Bianca runs a canteen for the oil workers. She reclaims her field from her lover Rossi; but he then sunders all his ties with her, foregoing their friendship. Bianca's accusations that Rossi cheated on her induces the workers' wrath towards the foreigners. A monk (Monch) tries to settle the dispute. When that fails, adopting a nationalist rhetoric, the monk invokes the national hero (Skenderberg) and calls for a "holy war" for the freedom of Albania: "Im Namen Skanderbergs fur die Freiheit Albaniens! Albanien den Albanern! Auf zum heiligen Kriegi Kampf! Kampf!" (Act 1, Scene 10)

Brown, the chairman of the League of Nations Committee for Albania, arrives to resolve the predicament by demanding the use of military duress. Notably, Brown's speech illuminates the entanglements among politics, economy, and the colonial-imperial legacy of international law (embodied, in *Konjunktur 2*, by the League of Nations, now UN), where the League of Nations appears as a thinly disguised guarantor of the

136   *"On a Wave of Oil England Swam Towards Victory"*

imperial (British) interests and hegemony: "Das Leben koniglich britischer Untertanen ist in Gefahr. Kombinierte Formationen der alliierten Truppen besetzen das Land. Wer ist der Kowmandierende der einheimischen Armee?" ["The lives of royal British subjects are in danger. Combined formations of the Allied forces occupy the country. Who is the commander of the local army?"] (Act 1, Scene 12). When the commander of the local troops arrives to greet Brown, the latter states: "Ich hoffe, dass die albanische Armee in enger Kameradschaft mit den kombinierten Detachements der Besatzungs – truppen ihre Pflicht erfulen wird. Die Sicherheit der nationalen Produktion muss mit Waffengewalt –" ["I hope that the Albanian army will do its duty in close comradeship with the combined detachments of the occupying forces. The security of national production must be achieved by force of arms –"] (Act 1, Scene 12). The commander, an Austrian, then repels the insurgent local people.

Claire Barsin joins them and shows Brown, Rossi, and Dubois her letter of credit. She wants to negotiate with the oil companies present about a share in the financing of the oil transport. Claire asks Bianca, Goxhomani, and another Albanian, Ahmed Noli, for advice and help, as she seeks to establish some solid contact with the local population. The monk introduces himself to Claire as Trebitsch-Lincoln, a person with an eventful past, and proposes that she work as his press officer and launch an Albanian freedom movement with her as leader in order to consolidate a popular basis or force as means of gaining leverage in the negotiations with the global powers.

In Act Two, the competition between the Italian and the French oil companies, represented by Rossi and Dubois, flares up as to who will drill for oil first. Dubois demands a faster work pace from Jonny, the chief engineer of the drilling oil field, in order to reach oil before the Italians. Jonny complains about the poor and objectionable working conditions of the oil workers involved in the excavation/extraction work. Evelyn, Claire's daughter, incites Jonny's ambition to enforce the drill record. Meanwhile, Claire is negotiating with Rossi, regarding her interest in a joint sales organization to give her a monopoly on the Mediterranean markets, which would mean "challenging the Royal Dutch to a duel".[2] When Claire states: "Bestunde die Moglichkeit, unserem Öl ein Monopol auf den mittellandischen Markten zu schaffen Italien, Griechenland, Serbien, auch Spanien –" ["Seize the opportunity to create a monopoly for our oil on the Mediterranean markets – Italy, Greece, Serbia, also Spain"], Rossi replies: "Corpo di Bacco [by Jove]! Das heisst nichts anderes, als die Royal Dutch zum Duell herausfordern. Sie mussen sich sehr stark fuhlen". ["The body of Bacchus! That means nothing else than challenging the Royal Dutch to a duel. You must be feeling very strong."] (Act 2, Scene 3). In light of this pretension to monopoly, Rossi deems Claire, who doesn't want to name her client or authorizing source, to be an agent for Standard Oil. This is ensued by a spectacular outburst of oil from the ground. This

## "On a Wave of Oil England Swam Towards Victory"   137

consequential discovery of oil transpires as the material fulcrum of the play round which not only the political-economic and social dynamics of *Konjunktur 2* revolve, but also a relentless global competition over monopoly of oil extraction/production and markets is unleashed.[3] Claire however laconically intimates that her motives – contrary to all the other global parties involved – are far from capitalist. As she explains to Rossi: "Wir suchen jedenfalls keine Anlage fur Kapital". ["In any case, we are not looking for an investment for capital."]

Brown, who is both director of Royal Dutch and chairman of the League of Nations Committee for Albania, in his latter capacity orders a working time limit and prohibits unskilled workers from working on the machines. When Rossi complains, Brown proposes a cartel with Royal Dutch. The loudspeaker announces the merger of Royal Dutch with Italian Naphta. Dubois has the drilling stopped because he fears that Royal Dutch will dump prices. He orders 80% of the workers to be laid off. Rifan-Bey, who is bribed by Dubois, foments the disgruntled workers against the Italians and offers Rossi his services as a girl trafficker.

The revolutionary agitation among the occupation troops, which Claire had directed, flusters Brown and makes him see his oil-related profits jeopardized. Consequently, Brown bribes Trebitsch to instigate a small coup, which would give the League of Nations an opportunity to occupy the country militarily and to place the French and Italian oil wells under its administration. The agitation and insurgency instigated by Trebitsch and Rifan-Bey starts bearing fruit, particularly when the fomented workers vent their aggressive frustration on the foreigners and the oil machines, proceeding to set the drilling field on fire. Claire, who supports Ahmed and Bianca in the (non-nationalist) struggle for the interests of the locals and the working class, cannot restrain the machine attackers. The workers do not trust her because she does not want to reveal whose interests she represents and on whose behalf she is carrying out her mission in Albania. Claire hopes that her plan will work out by agitating to cause a mutiny among the military forces of various occupying forces in order to prevent them from entering into an actual multivalent war. All actors/sides meet at a festive evening party, where everyone conspires with everyone and against everyone. Rossi and Dubois have given their troops orders to advance against the troops on the other side in the next few minutes, but drink together to peace. Claire flirts with the men present, trying to hold them off and not let themselves be committed. Suddenly representatives of all the occupation troops enter the hall and announce their refusal to fight. Claire and Ahmed, who think they have achieved their goal, but also all the others present, are astonished to see Trebitsch declaring himself the president of Albania in a coup d'état. To the cheers of the local soldiers who have arrived, he declares that he is being supported by the Albanian national army.

138  *"On a Wave of Oil England Swam Towards Victory"*

In Act Three, the presidents of Royal Dutch, Sir Henry Deterding, of Standard Oil, W. C. Teagle, and the chairman of the All-Russian Naphta Syndicate, Lomow, give radio speeches on the importance of oil in the world and give instructions on the situation in Albania. Brown, Teagle, Rossi, and Dubois consult with each other in the government palace. Rossi and Dubois declare that their detachments will be withdrawn from Albania. Trebitsch, confidently, appearing in an elaborately embellished uniform acting as president, tries to play off the participants in the group, who have previously agreed on a common approach, against each other. He pretends to have Claire on his side. After the departure of the country and oil company representatives, the Austrian General Trebitsch informs that there is still a seething vexation among the people and that "in an emergency, you can put up a lot with the Albanian army". Claire asks Trebitsch to abdicate and disappear. Trebitsch is riven with hesitation as to how to cope with the current crisis and with the irreconcilable demands of contending parties in conjunction with the obligations he has incurred in relation to the global oil powers in his attempt to smooth his ascendancy to power with their help. What aggravates his situation is his lack of prospects. One after the other, Dubois and Rossi approach Trebitsch with an offer of cooperation. Their monopolizing and extractivist conditions are: a protection contract with their state, leasing of the oil wells, tobacco monopoly, administration of the state bank, and the right to mine in the ore area. When Brown enters, Claire reveals the secret of her "identity". She shows the contract she signed with Jonny, the Standard Oil representative, as an agent of the Soviet Syndicate. It includes: "Joint sales company for Russian and Albanian oil to conquer the Mediterranean and Asian markets".

Everyone present is stunned. Trebitsch has Claire arrested; Rossi, Brown, and Dubois take the side of the President. Claire and Bianca are tried in a court martial consisting of the general, the lieutenant, and Rifan-Bey. Brown accuses Claire of having instrumentalized her political work and also her comrades-in-arms, Ahmed and Bianca, for their economic goals. In the government palace, Trebitsch receives the message that the peasants from the area are armed and on the march to overthrow him. This shatters his confidence, leaving him no resort but to only think about saving himself by abandoning his luck-borne position. With his characteristic chicanery and nimble-minded alacrity, he strikes up a heroic posture and starts churning fascist phrases to persuade Brown to put a torpedo boat at his disposal. In prison, Claire and Bianca are waiting for the verdict to be pronounced, and they expect the death penalty. When the court has just announced the death sentence, the news comes that Trebitsch has taken a torpedo boat to Trieste and then travelled on to Munich. Then Ahmed and Claire exclaim: "We have won!" Dubois and Rossi ironically congratulate Claire, calling her a heroine. Finally, this flicker of national hope is dimmed with some sombre and dystopian streak (dark humour)

## "On a Wave of Oil England Swam Towards Victory" 139

when the issuing of three short statements by Brown, Teagle, and Claire comes to evoke the continued presence of the insidious imperial-neo-colonial powers struggling to gain monopoly over Albanian oil resources and the impending threat of an oil war.

## II.  Petro-Dramaturgy and Infrastructural Aesthetics

Lania's statement in the program note testifies to how crucial the semiotic and scenographic elements are to the politics and thematics of the play: "The decoration conveys not only the atmosphere, but also the content of the play" (201). Piscator's influence on the transformation of *Konjunktur*, as delineated earlier, is striking and substantial. This becomes evident through a mere juxtaposition of the two versions of the playscript. Oil does constitute the hinterland against which the whole dynamics of *Konjunktur 1* unfolds, but it rarely appears in its foreground. However, whereas oil has got a spectral, though pervasive, presence in *Konjunktur 1*, it is present in *Konjunktur 2* in all its hefty and clanky infrastructural paraphernalia. More importantly, in *Konjunktur 2*, oil is explored in all its contradictory overdetermination in the petro-capitalist world system as at once an abstract global commodity and a concrete, volatile substance which makes all the wheels and engines of the world (and, above all, those in the core Western, industrial world) move, thereby producing in its wake a social-economic order governed by combined and uneven patterns of development, extraction, and distribution of profit and wealth.

In its manifold and highly textured scenic and scenographic complex, *Konjunktur* (1 and 2 along with *Oil Field*) seeks to convey the afore-mentioned attributes and dynamics of oil by offering us what I will call a Capitalocene-oriented or Capitalocene-conscious dramaturgy, thereby providing a critical cartography of both monopoly and multinational petro-capitalism in conjunction with their core-periphery political econ-omy. In mapping a world in which even a peripheral European country is not spared the extractive tyrannies of this combined-and-uneven logics, both *Konjunktur* (1 and 2) and *Oil Field* present an anxious articulation of the human's relationship (both at national and transnational, both at private and public levels) with what is nonhuman. This nonhuman element includes not only nature and the peripheral country colonially reduced to a pre-cultural and pre-civilizational state. More importantly, the element of the nonhuman, in these plays, designates not just oil (both as a material and discursive-symbolic construct) but its concomitant infrastructural and political-economic system. Furthermore, due to its sheer size, expanse, and technical-technological complexity as well as abstract, alienating logics, oil and its infrastructural paraphernalia defy any attempts to represent its volatile, invisible, yet ubiquitous presence, that is, oil and what it materi-ally and metonymically represents: the global petro-capitalist system. This is a nonhuman petro-capitalist system with the social-economic logics,

140    *"On a Wave of Oil England Swam Towards Victory"*

global market forces, and industrial activities of which the humans interact and yet cannot fully assimilate into their human networks. Lania's allegorical and reportage-based aesthetic – enhanced by the application of Piscator's objectivist and sociological dramaturgy – translated this condition into a palpable experience in the theatre by utilizing and devising a number of striking techniques, including the use of music, film (projected onto screens), and props (infrastructural aspects of oil industry such as derricks, cars, a radio/loudspeaker, electrified billboards, and concomitant accoutrement of the petrocultural world).

More importantly, the non-realistic and materialist aesthetic – intertwined with Piscator's objectivist-relational dramaturgy informing the plays – is also evident in Lania's shifting of the focus away from the agency of the human subject to the attribution of primary agency to the object, to wit, oil and all the abstract and hierarchical processes that propel and govern the petro-capitalist system, an uneven system that, as *Konjunktur* and *Oil Field* show, is less driven by the material needs of the individuals, classes, and nations and more by the abstract processes of surplus accumulation through dispossession and uneven distribution. As a testimony to its materialist-objectivist approach, *Oil Field* and *Konjunktur* (*1* and *2*) are less human-subject- (or protagonist-) oriented and more object-oriented. Above all the other objects and commodities of the modern petroculture populating the stage of these three plays, the paradigmatic object is "oil" – where the object (oil) is revealed to be far more than a passive, inert entity. Here, oil is conceived as an always already natural-cultural and intrinsically relational entity with manifold agency, surrounded by gravitational pull of the conflictual forces of libidinal and political economy (at local-global and private-public levels). As such, all three plays varyingly reveal how oil – as a global commodity and an aporetic object of desire – reveals complex psychological fields of intensity, historically sedimented patterns of identification, the dynamics of desire, and the structures of phantasy and its concomitant petrocultural effects on the experience of subjectivity, space, time, relationality, and freedom/autonomy. This act of ascribing agency and centrality to oil – at thematic and psychodynamic levels – is underscored by Lania: "The hero of this comedy is petroleum. The aim is to show the complex of economic questions that this material dominates, the laws and phases of its economic development and their political effects" (Leo Lania, *Die Komödie der Wirtschaft*, in: Der brennende Punkt, Blätter der Piscatorbühne [April 1928], 1–2). Piscator's sociological dramaturgy also contributed to the enhancement of the materialist approach suffusing the play at semiotic and phenomenological (kinaesthetic and perceptual) levels. This makes the audience experience how oil permeates their life across its cognitive and sensorium spectrum. As Lania explains: "Piscator's staging was based on the assumption that the material in all its objectivity and totality would be vividly visible through the construction of the stage" (Leo Lania, *Die*

## "On a Wave of Oil England Swam Towards Victory"  141

*Komödie der Wirtschaft*, in: Der brennende Punkt, Blätter der Piscator-bühne [April 1928], 1–2).

Perhaps the most striking dramaturgical facet of the play that opens the audience's eyes to the sheer social, political-economic, and ecological upheaval a space can undergo in consequence of the discovery of oil and the emergence of oil industry is revealed in the early stages of the play. The first act of *Konjunktur 2* begins on an almost naked stage or field ["dem nackten Feld"] (see also Piscator, *Das politische Theater*, 208) representing a barren, deserted, undeveloped area in Albania. The discovery of oil makes the area valuable in one fell swoop. We witness the precipitous transformation of a pre-industrial, agriculturally structured land in an underdeveloped country into an incrementally industrialized landscape in an extremely condensed, concentrated, and "objective/factual" [Sachlich] form. This petroscape is populated simultaneously by capitalist forces and a proletarian "mass" society. The pace, dynamics, and configuration of this transformation was supposed to feel as if everything on the stage was in fast motion, thereby drawing the audience's attention to their condition of possibility: oil. This was thus intended to evoke the "avalanche" effect the global "fight/war for petroleum" ["Kampf um Petroleum"] triggers, involving a whole systemic chain of mechanization, industrialization, modernization, and globalization. *Konjunktur 2* illustrates how this war is fought on material-geopolitical as well as symbolic-discursive grounds. This is vividly illustrated by the conspicuous use of media (such as newspaper and radio) along with references to the questions of reporting/representation as a means of gaining hegemonic leverage, symbolic legitimacy, social advantage, and moral-political superiority. This demonstrates Lania's acute cognizance of the ethics and politics of media/representation since each instance of news/media representation of a certain historical reality is invariably inflected by the ideologies, economic interests, and the social-moral norms of the owner or agent of the means of production and representing agency. As Piscator himself explains:

> From the discovery of the petroleum source to the preparation of the wells, from the construction of the derrick to the commercialization of oil as a commodity, the plot – rivalry, murder, displacement, corruption, revolution – should unroll in front of the viewer, and thus dragging them into the whole gears of international petroleum politics.
>
> (Piscator 1929, 208. Lania 140 PT, S. 99)

As a result of this boom-like oil discovery, which establishes the connection between the European metropolises and this peripheral country, Albania becomes the "center of world politics" ["Zentrum der Weltpolitik"] and is thus made available now for being subjected to the extractivist logics of a globally extended petro-capitalist system. Accordingly, in

142 *"On a Wave of Oil England Swam Towards Victory"*

*Konjunktur 2*, while Rifan-Bey is erecting his barracks in front on the right, the fourth and fifth workers are building a primitive hut on the left. The large board on the right reads: "Land purchase and sale", and the sign on the left reads: "Land Recycling Company". Behind it, there is a proliferating number boards of various sizes: "Real estate broker" – "Agency" – etc." While the stage becomes the site of construction and is enriched with set pieces, it fills with people – notably a "Swarm of workers" (Act 1, Scene 8) the availability of whose cheap labour is one of the prerequisites for profitable oil extraction and oil industry. These wooden boards, which show the ownership structure, act as indicators of the increase in value. The next and final stage of development that can be visualized is the construction of drilling rigs:

> On the left and right in front the wooden frames of drilling rigs are set up, which slowly grow upward during the following scenes, while at the same time building is taking place in the background, the facilities for further drilling rigs are being built.
>
> (Act 2, Scene 1)[4]

The other pivotal dramatic-dramaturgical element is the "Loud-speaker". The installation of a loudspeaker adumbrates not only the formal and informal communicational and technological connection of Albania to the internationalized politics, but also the indispensability of information channels and networks for the global power in their attempt to maintain their hegemony over petro-modern economy and petrocultural society. Significantly, the functions of "Loudspeaker" by far exceed those of a semiotically manifold stage prop or symbolic media. The presence of Loudspeaker betokens how both global hegemonic powers and national dominant discourse own the means of representation and manipulation of facts and historical truths, thereby setting the discursive and political-economic norms and relational dynamics. Loudspeaker also reveals the global effects and social-cultural implications of the advent of oil in the quotidian life of the society, including time-space compression (see Harvey *The Condition of Postmodernity* 26–281, 288–306), a façade of cosmopolitanism and consumerism. These latter phenomena are illustrated by the staggering pace and the global scope and reach of the news thus evidencing the rise to global significance of the peripheral Albania due to its possession of a globally strategic resource/commodity: oil. This abrupt thrust into the global spotlight, however, proves to have counter-productive implications for the peripheral country at national and local levels in that by being placed within the global map of oil resources, Albania is subjected not only to a "produced" chaotic domestic/national condition but to the petro-capitalist logics of accumulation through dispossession. Importantly, the play shows how the news is not an objective reflection of the events in Albania or elsewhere, but rather inflected with

*"On a Wave of Oil England Swam Towards Victory"* 143

the political-economic interests and ideological sympathies of the global powers. Throughout *Konjunktur*, almost all conversations are punctuated with volatile news announced and released through "Loudspeaker". The news chiefly revolves around the oil market, political conflicts and upheavals around the world which are shown to be predominantly driven by oil and tensions over oil resources. One of the recurring refrains of the news is the proposed, conferred, and then withdrawn offers of various world powers (including Britain, France, and Italy) to grant Albania both independence and recognition in exchange for cheap access to its oil resources. This adumbrates the extent to which not only the quotidian lives of the individuals but also of nations, particularly at economic, social, and political levels, are susceptible to the volatile waves of the global oil market and its political-economic dynamics (reflected in and through the news).

As is evident, "Loudspeaker" not only acts as a character in *Konjunktur 2*, it also features as a condensed synecdoche for multi-media news agencies, intelligence agencies, and a whole chain of institutional-disciplinary discourses and apparatuses encompassed by the capitalist system (including stock markets). As such the Loudspeaker reflects both the national/domestic and global implications and reverberations of every single tension, conflict, and political-economic alteration step in the oil-possessing periphery (as an oil frontier) on economic dynamics of global economy – including the price of the most valuable energy commodity and strategic resource. The ensuing announcement – made in consequence of France's obtainment of a concession for extracting certain oil resources in Albania – is a salient case in point: "11 1/2 – New York reports: Standard Oil plus 3 1/2 – Standard Oil plus 3 3/4 Standard Oil plus – plus – plus". This economic piece of news is counterpointed with a political one: "Loudspeaker: Warning! [caution] Warning! This is Berlin! Serious confusion in Albania". Therefore, there incrementally appears in the play a parallel between the exponential spike or decline in the stock market shares, currency rates, and oil price throughout the play and the exponential rise and fall of tensions at national (amongst contending domestic factions and forces in Albania) and global levels (both amongst the global forces themselves and between the global forces and national Albanian state). As such, a parallel is gradually established, both in the dramatic-diegetic dynamics of the play and the mind of audience, between the volatile political-economic circumstances in Albania and the volatility of oil prices in the global market. This whole dynamics is established and orchestrated by Loudspeaker. Here is another illustrative example where an explicit parallel is evoked between the political crisis in Albania (as an oil frontier) and the crisis in oil prices in the global oil market. Loudspeaker announces: "The countermines as a result of the Albanian conflict were victorious. Oil market crisis exacerbated by rumors that Petrolifére Franco-Albania would join

144 *"On a Wave of Oil England Swam Towards Victory"*

Standard Oil – Royal Dutch 3 percent lower than Italian Naphtha Syndicate minus 4 1/4" (Act 1, Scene 2). And here is yet another announcement of the consequent fluctuations on the stock market and prices: "London closes: Italian Naphtha Syndicate 6 1/2 less, Royal Dutch minus 5 – Franco Albania plus 11 1/2 – New York reports: Standard Oil plus 3 1/2 – Standard Oil plus 3.3/4 Standard Oil plus – plus – plus" (Act 1, Scene 2). By foregrounding the pace at which these shifting political-economic waves ripple between the global centres and peripheries, *Konjunktur 2* adumbrates the advent of a new oil-induced phenomenon: "time-space compression" (see Harvey *The Condition of Postmodernity* 26–281, 288–306). Finally, Loudspeaker fulfils a cartographical – or, cognitive-mapping – function by evoking a total or overarching image of the far-flung oil frontiers scattered across the world in geographically disparate locations and yet concatenated by the extractive and uneven logics of the petro-capitalist system as an energy regime. Here is an example. Loudspeaker: "Stock market weak, oil papers falling, armor values in demand" (Act 1, Scene 2), later adding: "From Paris: Reports of the development of new oil sources in Valona led to a stormy bull market in Franco Albania. Council of Ministers votes for flexible loans" (Act 1, Scene 2).

The other prominent scenographic and dramaturgical element in *Konjunktur 2* (which is absent in *Oil Field*) is the multi-media nature of the production: use of photos, films, and newspaper headlines projected onto the screen, thus featuring as the "worldly" hinterland to the play or the world-systemic subtext underpinning it.[5] The use of film (as much a real-time as a media-dependent event) enhances the global dimensions of the play by picturing the broader global context in which oil has established itself as the foremost strategic fuel and commodity. It also illustrates the peripheral zone's (Albania's) being enmeshed into the globally extended network or map of the petro-capitalist system. As soon as the construction of the stage is completed with a plot point and the economic activity is taken to a new stage: a film shows the drilling of an oil well. With film recordings showing the initiation of oil drilling (Act 2, Scene 5), the technical (and visualizable) processes are completed, marketing begins, and an unremitting competition over oil monopoly (including cartel collusion and political subversion) is launched. These processes are conveyed to the audience via character speeches and loudspeaker announcements. For instance, a few scenes into the play, Loudspeaker announces the merger of Italian Naphta and Royal Dutch and, for the first time, these announcements appear in conjunction with the stock market reports (Act 2, Scene 7).

As Piscator put it, the film in *Konjunktur 2* was supposed to "fulfill a very special function in the play this time" since it was supposed to be "put together according to new criteria".[6] In its intended function, the film and its use were supposed to give the play a "fixed framework", and

## "On a Wave of Oil England Swam Towards Victory" 145

this framework should obviously be journalism or, to put it more casually, "the newspaper". As Piscator elaborates:

> the film should not only reveal and expand the background of the play, not just be an illustration, but a "fixed framework" in the true sense of the word. . . . This journalistic comedy was supposed to develop from the newspaper, that is, the entire section of the stage was closed off by a newspaper page, a canvas that, like a newspaper, was divided into different columns, each of which corresponded to a specific location on the stage.
>
> (*Political Theatre*, Piscator 1929, 208)

*Konjunktur 2* demonstrates how the media (including journalism) occlude boundaries between historical reality as reported and represented by the hegemonic media of the dominant discourse and historical reality as lived (fictional) experience. This was followed by the parallel between the political-economic and discursive-media competition between the global powers over gaining hegemony on Albanian oil resources – a competition partly carried out through public media. As Piscator explicates:

> While the struggle between the rival groups for the oil well developed on the stage itself, the struggle between the Italian and the French corporations, the press war between France and Italy raged on the screen, the global political contradiction was shown graphically both by cartoons and by writing enlivens. In this way I achieved an extraordinary simplicity and clarity of the processes, which, like in a textbook, were vividly illustrated.
>
> (Piscator 1929, 208)

As will become evident in our discussion of *Oil Field*, the features and thematic-historical content conveyed through the dramaturgical means (including film) here were superseded with a textual representation of them. In other words, the aforementioned details actually feature within *Oil Field* as part of the dramatic text rather than remaining an additional dramaturgical element added to (but not explicitly mentioned in) the text of *Konjunktur 2*.

This intertwinement of dramatic fiction with historical fact conducted through the use of multi-media dramaturgy, as an effective means of not only representing historical facts but exposing their logics and dynamics, is also in keeping with Lania's valorization of documentary aesthetics, his reportage theory, and his idea of revolutionary comedy as delineated in the preceding chapter. Piscator's elaboration of the intended functions of the use of film and news projected onto the screen can be illuminating:

> The newspaper page kept pushing forward, was repeatedly removed or pierced in a different place, then revealing the stage; the action

146 *"On a Wave of Oil England Swam Towards Victory"*

began at exactly the same point where the newspaper commentary had ended. Until in the end the newspaper went up in flames and the Albanian revolution reached its climax with the setting on fire of the oil wells. . . . In general, it seems to me that with the staging of *Konjunktur* . . . in the direction of a simplification of the stage means, the loosening of the form, the most complete achievement of the season was achieved.

(Piscator 1929, 208)

This efficacious and revealing use of various props and dramaturgical techniques to achieve aesthetic and political education and critical enlightenment is striking and testifies to how *Konjunktur 2* was indeed designed as a "deepening piece" thereby aiming to "get to the bottom of things" ["Dinge zu gehen"] (Lania in *Political Theatre*, 197) thereby showing "inner connections" ["innere Zusammenhänge"] (Lania in *Political Theatre*, 197).

Music and the use of song in the performance also complements the thematic concerns and dramaturgical aesthetics of *Konjunktur*. The production included incidental music by Kurt Weill and a condensed form of the chanson – titled "Petroleumsong" (also known as "The Margate Shell" or "Seashells from Margate") written by Felix Gasbarra – for which Weill composed music after the fashion of the theme song in "Hoppla". Given the revealing resonance between the thematic world-systemic and *conjonctural* vision of the play, it is worth mentioning one of the songs which depicts the global ubiquity and significance by presenting a cartographical account wherein the nodal points of petro-capitalism to date are referred to: "And as the sun / At the highest level / In Margate on the promenade / Then the oil began to burn / From Azerbaijan to Tibet / It set the world on fire / Our fatherland is called petroleum / Lady we tear our fur off / Shell! / Shell! / Shell!" (printed in: Leo Lania 1928). Weill set Gasbarra's satirical lyrics, about the discovery of oil in an English seaside town, in its epic-like dynamics. The song was performed – as an interlude and commentary – by the actor Curt Bois who acted as the impostor character (Goldstein and later Trebitsch-Lincoln based on the real-life Hungarian-English adventurer Ignaz Trebitsch-Lincoln) and the actress Tilla Durieux who played the "World Lady" style.

What further renders the visual-semiotic and dramaturgical aspects of *Konjunktur* in its treatment of the apparatus of oil industry and paraphernalia of oil culture distinctive is its use of cars, not only as iconic props/objects and petrocultural commodities, but also as significant thematic elements. Notably, in this regard, Lania (and Piscator) derived and adapted ample insights – including a considerable portion of the petrocultural and infrastructural details in conjunction with the oil-specific visual dimensions of industrialization – from Sinclair's novel *Oil!* (1927), which was published in Germany in the same year by Malik-Verlag under

## "On a Wave of Oil England Swam Towards Victory"  147

the German title *Petroleum*. This particularly included car culture and the technical details of the oil industry. Interestingly, not only had Lania read Sinclair's *Oil!*, but had in fact reviewed it (see, Die Neue Bücherschau 3 (1925) 5, 12–15; 13; see Piscator, *Political Theater*, 197). This use of Sinclair's *Oil!* and its influence on German petro-literature demonstrates not only the world-literary consciousness and relational dynamics that a topic like oil (facilitated by its actual infrastructure) fostered. It also attests to the global hegemony of the Anglo-American world system whereby Anglo-American literature/culture occupies the core (in terms of global cultural hegemony) thereby being endowed with canonical status, cultural capital, and material-symbolic value (including global circulation and translation). Furthermore, this unobtrusive detail anticipates the American Century where American culture featured as the quintessential model of commodity culture and progress sweeping across Europe and beyond (see Arrighi 2002, 21; see Arrighi 2007, 8–10, 155–162, 184–190; and see Arrighi 2009, 83).

In both *Konjunktur* and *Oil Field*, the car acts as a metonymy whereby the invisibility of oil and its effects are "concretized" or made objectively visible in terms of a highly rampant and readily recognizable commodity but also a new way of life and social-cultural symbol. In other words, through these objective dramaturgical means the plays reveal the new ontology made possible by oil, an ontology that can only be maintained in the global north by perpetuating a core-periphery dynamics of exploitative extraction where the leisure and comfort of one world is predicated on the exploitation of the natures, people, and resources of another (peripheral) world that can only afford to ride animals. In *Konjunktur*, the car is not only symbolic: a symbol of status, class, and self-expression and new social-cultural order and era. The car is also utilized metonymically, deployed to foreground the industrial-commercial complex, the commodity-consumer culture, Americanization as a global power thus acting as a sign of America's cultural hegemony, and the newly arisen interlacement of autonomy and automobility (see Huber 16–18, 28–31). In this regard, *Konjunktur 2*'s treatment of "car" as a symbolic and metonymic object/commodity is resonant with its historical functions in the later 1920s and 1930s culture in America and Europe. During the foregoing historical period, as various cultural historians have acutely delineated, the car proved not only an overdetermined object surrounded by cultural imaginaries, but also a magnate towards which the individual subject's desires gravitated. As such, the car was perceived both as a space for cathecting the subject's libidinal-political economy and a conduit for expression of the subject's racial, gender, and class identity and agency. (See my discussion of the car as a petrocultural commodity/object in Chapter 5 on *Oil Islands*). By the same token, the characters in the first scenes are on foot and Rossi rides in on a donkey. But later Dubois comes in a motorized vehicle and Rossi pulls in and drives in the car "tooting from the right"

148  *"On a Wave of Oil England Swam Towards Victory"*

(Act 1, Scene 7). And finally Trebitsch appears on stage with the car as a symbol of status and technology. Crucially, as a sign of her solidarity with the locals, Claire (like Ahmed and Bianca) has a horse as a means of transport. Correspondingly, the characters' social status and costume are adapted to the respective level of civilization. The crooks wear rags; later one of them appears in uniform as a first lieutenant. Rossi, a journalist at the beginning, and Dubois have a different appearance when they introduce themselves as representatives of their countries. (The direction is: "Both are now elegantly dressed, white trousers, black skirts", Act 1, Scene 8) As such, the stark presence of cars/automobiles in the context of a 1920s play serves a twofold purpose. Firstly, the existence of the automobile is intended to render visible not only its condition of possibility – oil and oil industry – coupled with the uneven political-economic logics of the extraction, production, and circulation of oil. Secondly, the automobile is also deployed to evoke the whole infrastructure in both of its manifestations: both physical equipment and technology and the labour force required to transport workers and resources to the mostly remote areas.[7]

In deploying all the material and dramaturgical measures and means, Lania and Piscator sought to concretize the otherwise invisible and abstract presence, force, and effects of oil as well as the political-economic logics underlying the petro-capitalist system's practices of extraction and distribution, and commodification (financialization, surplus value, and abstraction/commodification) of oil – phenomena that the audience would rather have experienced in the form of heat, light, electricity, energy/fuel (gasoline), and speed for the cars. In doing so, Lania and Piscator conjoined the semiotic and the phenomenological – where the former involves the audience's aesthetic experience based upon the reading of signs and the latter places the audience in a phenomenal "field" where signs and meanings are rendered perceptible through sensory experiences. This twofold aesthetics was also resonant with the avant-garde trends of the mid-1920s that were increasingly interested in exploring the sensory experience of modern urban life, a world in which industrial technology enabled a multiplicity of simultaneous perspectives to overwhelm the previous nature of lived experience. As such, the stage almost started looking like a live and living/lived photomontage (or nearly cinematic) with the crucial difference that the audience was not afforded the safe distance of the screen but was rather flung into a condition of immersion, involvement, and complicitous exposure. Consequently, going through the material density of such a dramatic field, the audience "moved" and "was moved" along with the mobile, fluid atmosphere of *Konjunktur 2* and its world – all driven by oil. This kinaesthetic dynamics engenders a mobile-fluid image (an image-movement) and a sense of unremitting and immersive motion (a time-movement, a la Deleuze). Such a dynamics is akin, in effect and function, to Piscator's treadmill-stage (his use of treadmills as vehicular in design and a means of accentuating an epic

## "On a Wave of Oil England Swam Towards Victory" 149

continuance) – a technique that reveals Piscator's awareness of his stage's symbolic suggestiveness, though barely evincing any critical attentiveness to the dangers of technology, reification, and societal collapse (see Michael Fried's 1967 essay, "Art and Objecthood"). As Piscator states: "The fact that this technique 'symbolized' a stage of society (the dissolution and decline of a social order) was secondary and fortuitous" (*The Political Theater* 180).

### III. Petro-Reportage and the Three Speeches of the Leaders of the Global Oil System

Perhaps the most salient part in *Konjunktur 2* – distinguishing it from both *Konjunktur 1* and *Oil Field* – is the array of speeches delivered by the leaders of the global powers and the heads of oil corporations which, whilst in fierce competition with each other over oil monopoly, together hold global hegemony over the capitalist logics and uneven dynamics underpinning their extraction, production, circulation, and evaluation of oil in the world. What distinguishes these speeches is the multiplicity of crucial functions they fulfil. Primarily, the speeches demonstrate the political-economic and social-cultural significance of oil at national and global levels. Secondly, the speeches disclose the world-systemic dynamics informing the oil corporations' competing claims and attempts at hegemony. Above all, they testify to the status of oil as the fulcrum around which the national, international, and corporation manoeuvres and relational dynamics – at political-economic and social-cultural levels – revolved in the interregnum period (1918–1939) and beyond. In other words, the speeches by various heads of the states and leaders of oil corporations accentuate the role of oil as both the driver of internationally determining decisions and the impetus of the capitalist world system.

Another noteworthy point here is the way these three speeches illustrate one of the distinctive aesthetic features of Lania's petro-drama: its combination of reportage and stylized/dramatized speech, a feature which also facilitates the combination of historical facts and fictional truth. None of the three figures (Lomow, Teagle, and Deterding) feature in the rest of the play. As such, their unexpected appearance and their speeches can be argued to serve a reportage function – driven by an epic dynamics – through which the hinterland action or Hintergrund logics of social and political-economic processes steering the petroculture and petro-capitalist system are foregrounded. Notably, Lania takes a formal measure to reflect the ideological divide and political-economic difference between the worlds of communism and capitalism. This is formally evidenced by the way in which Lomow's speech is not only accorded precedence (it appears earlier in the play), but also kept separate from the other two speeches delivered by the Western capitalist leaders.

150  *"On a Wave of Oil England Swam Towards Victory"*

The facts and points raised in the speeches closely correspond to the historical facts. During the late 1920s, world production of oil rose by 50% due to the discoveries in Texas (USA) and Venezuela along with the renewal of exports from the Soviet Union (see *Access to Energy: 2000 and After*, 30). The world consumption of oil also rose substantially. An emblematic case in point is the spectacular rise in the number of cars in the US. Whilst in 1900 there were nearly 8,000 cars in the US, by 1930, there were 26.5 million cars swarming the transformed landscapes of the US as a new carbon nation.[8] The early decades of the 20th century also witnessed the largest accidental oil spill in history: Lakeview Gusher. Lakeview Gusher Number One was an eruption of hydrocarbons from a pressurized oil well in the Midway-Sunset Oil Field in Kern County, California, in 1910, lasting 18 months and releasing 9 million barrels (1.4 × 10$^6$ m$^3$) of crude oil (115).[9] Perhaps the most conspicuous event with global implications was the decision of the two global superpowers of petro-capitalism – Britain and the USA – to convert the fuel of their military forces (above all navy and maritime) from coal to oil.[10] Indeed, 1914–1918 marks a critical juncture in world politics and resource history. This consequential decision was made in a bid to gain ascendency and advantage – in military and economic respects – over the other global forces (Brown 2003, 155). At the time, the US remained a neutral power, albeit openly supplying the Allies with resources, including fuel (Fordham 2007). Suffice it here to provide just a glimpse into what was sweeping across the globe (particularly US). Figure 3.1 explicitly illustrates this tidal shift (or transition) in the dynamics of the fuels and energy resource.

Secondly, these oil-focused speeches by the heads of multinational oil corporation companies serve both a cartographical and a historical – conjonctural – function. In their *cartographical function*, the speeches

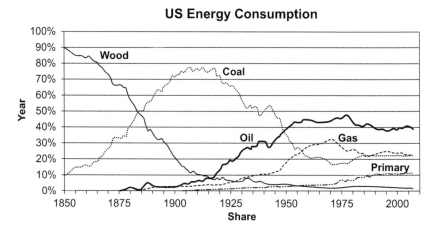

*Figure 3.1*

## "On a Wave of Oil England Swam Towards Victory" 151

provide the reader/audience with a fairly totalizing cognitive map into the nodal points of the petro-capitalist system in the 1920s and 1930s, thereby affording them an insight into the dynamics through which the peripheral countries (such as Albania, Iraq, Persia/Iran, Nigeria) are first "produced" as resource frontiers or zones of extraction by being incorporated into the petro-capitalist system. And, subsequently, these peripheries (or resource frontiers) are subjected to the extractivist core-periphery logics of global petro-capitalism in a systemic manner. This core-periphery dynamics is informed with the same political-economic logic of combined and uneven development which seeks nothing but the extraction of cheap raw materials – oil, above all – followed by the processes of commodification and abstraction (production of capital and financialization). These processes, in their own turn, were supposed to be conducive to the production of utmost surplus value and market monopoly by one imperial-global power or one multinational corporation company. In their *conjonctural function*, where both *Konjunktur 2* and the characters evoke a long, cyclical history of various resources (including wood, coal, minerals, agricultural-marine resources, and labour), the speeches draw the reader's attention to how such a capitalist system is driven by a cyclical dynamics of resource extraction and accumulation through dispossession. In this regard, Isser's delineation of the pervasive ways in which oil came to inform fundamental aspects of both infrastructure and the daily life of the society in the global north (particularly Western Europe and the US) in the late 1920s and early 1930s can be illuminating: "Competition for control of world oil became intertwined with national policy in the aftermath of World War I" (Isser 2016, 6–7). Isser underscores the importance of petroleum as follows: "supplying fuel oil for the fleet, aviation fuel for the air force, and gasoline for motorized vehicles made access to crude oil a military necessity" (ibid.). Notable in this regard is the considerable differences between the national government's treatment of their national oil corporation companies of various global powers and the oil corporations' global adventures. This difference was evident between the US, on the one hand, and Britain and France, on the other. The difference specifically stemmed from the dependency of the British and French on external oil supplies, whereas in the case of the USA "the existence of large domestic supplies had caused the US government to be complacent with regard to supporting American oil companies in their attempts to gain access to foreign oilfields" (ibid.). The perception of shortages after the World War I, however, caused a temporary change in the US government's attitude, "persisting long enough to apply sufficient pressure to enable the American companies to enter the Middle East fields" (ibid.).

Thirdly, the content of the speeches reveals not only tensions and conflict between the UK and the USA over oil resources in South Asia and Africa, but also a globally extended rivalry amongst the UK, Germany, and France over oil resources. More importantly, they also reveal the

152 *"On a Wave of Oil England Swam Towards Victory"*

complicity and alliance, despite intense competition, between these countries and their state-endorsed corporations. These complex entanglements led to a situation where the boundaries between not only national corporations and national governments (states) but also between the national and multinational corporations – by means of the formation of multinational corporations – were blurred.

Notably, this appearance of the three world-renowned leaders must have sounded reverberating chords in the audience's mind about their contemporary history. In 1927, the year before the premiere of *Konjunktur 2*, an international price war broke out between the Western oil companies and the Soviet Union, which urgently needed foreign currency and flooded the market with cheap oil. More specifically, in the world history of oil, 1928 is marked by two decisive events: The Achnacarry Meeting (or the unsigned "As-Is Agreement") and the Red Line Agreement. As regards the first event, the Achnacarry Castle event involved a meeting among Henri Deterding (Royal Dutch/Shell), Walter Teagle (Standard Oil of NJ), Heinrich Riedemann (Standard Oil of New Jersey's delegate in Germany), Sir John Cadman (Anglo-Persian), William Mellon (Gulf), and Colonel Robert Stewart (Standard Oil of Indiana). In the mid-1920s, these three companies formed the world's three leading oil companies and their successors are still the largest companies in the world today. At the Achnacarry Meeting, they decide to found a secret cartel that would not only tackle pricing policy and mutual interests in the international oil regions, but also manage the organization of the processing oil industry until long after the Second World War. The ultimate goal of the meeting was to find a solution to the dilemmas of overproduction and overcapacity in the industry compounded by the "ruinous competition" among the producing companies and countries. The crisis of divided markets, price instability, and decline in profitability had been exacerbated by the surge in oil production stemming from the Soviet Union, Venezuela, the US, and Romania, flooding the market, weakening the prices, and threatening the economic stability and monopoly. In a bid to remedy the excess supply problem, all the attending parties concurred on the following measures: the allocation of a quota in various markets to each company (excluding the domestic US market); reducing costs, sharing facilities, and the exercise of caution in building new refineries and other facilities; and, above all, the control of production. (See Chapter 14 in Yergin, Daniel 2008. As regards the second event, the 1928 "Red Line" Agreement (or the Group Agreement), on the other hand, was a deal struck between several British, French, and American oil companies concerning the oil resources within territories that were previously ruled by the Ottoman Empire (that is, the Middle East). The origins of the Red Line Agreement can be traced back to the initial formation of the Turkish Petroleum Company (TPC) in 1912. As Steve Isser indicates, the Red Line agreement "fit

## "On a Wave of Oil England Swam Towards Victory"   153

in with the attempts of the Majors to bring order to the world oil market [and] to avoid price wars" epitomized by the Achnacarry Meeting (see Isser 2016, 8).

This discussion illuminates the drastic ways in which oil came to determine the geopolitical, social, and economic life of nations and humans at national and international levels between the 1920s and 1940s. Now, in light of the foregoing facts, let us turn to each speech in *Konjunktur 2* to see not only how they critically resonate with and expand these facts but to also see the subtle ways in which Lania's choice of form and context helps expose the latent world-systemic dynamics informing the ideologically opposing oil-systems: Western capitalism and Soviet communism.

### A.   Oil and the Communist Soviet Union

The first speech is delivered by a figure – Lomow – who is introduced in *Konjunktur* as the Chairman of the All-Russian Naphta Syndicate. Lomow occupies the politically-economically opposite position – to that of Deterding and Teagle. This is starkly reflected in the political-economic dynamics and social-historical rhetoric permeating his vision and speech. The speech therefore affords a vastly different perspective onto the strategic-discursive ways in which oil is utilized as a fulcrum for shifting the balance in the wider global struggles between the capitalist and communist poles/powers – which respectively identify themselves as the proponents and opponents of the petro-capitalist world system.

Lomow's speech, along with the other two, serves a manifold function where, in conjunction with their diegetic role in the overall dynamics and context of the play, it provides ample historical information about the discovery of oil, the emergence of the industrial-financial oil system, and the development of a full-fledged petroculture. The speech also exposes the political-economic means and modes of production deployed by both the Allies and their opposing forces across the globe. Furthermore, Lomow's speech takes us to the alleged genesis of oil extraction and Rockefeller's rise at the paragon of the capitalist oil boom by hinting at his rise from lower-class roots, his later petit-bourgeois status, and ultimately his transformation into the wealthiest oil magnate and capitalist of all time as kerosene and gasoline gained widespread ground (see Ida M. Tarbell's *History of the Standard Oil Company*. See also Sonia Shah 2004, 6). Such a transformation also attests to the magic power of oil – in social and economic terms – through which oil became not only a means of transcending and traversing social-economic structures (including one's class), but became an integral part and expression of social desire. Significantly, utilizing various discursive strategies, Lomow's speech indicts Rockefeller as someone who betrayed his own working-class origins and by privatizing oil and seeking it through imperial-colonial means throughout the world, established

154 *"On a Wave of Oil England Swam Towards Victory"*

a capitalist and liberalist system. In keeping with his ideological tenets and communist convictions, Lomow also provides unique insights into the dispossessed and alienated conditions of oil workers – a crucial facet missing from the capitalist accounts of oil by Deterding and Teagle. As he exclaims:

> It's been 64 years since a small accountant at a small flour shop in Cleveland met a small worker who invented an invention for making purified luminous oil. That is when the oil industry was born. Five years later the little accountant had become their ruler. Over hundreds of oil companies, refineries, natural gas, sales, pipe, shipping, railroad companies, over billions of dollars, over millions of people, white, black, yellow races, over Chinese kushlis who feed their lamps with American oil and Mexican farmers [peasants] who have to lose their lives in the bloody battles of corrupt generals for the dividends from Standard Oil. John Rockefeller, the Caesar of petroleum, kept his word! He illuminated the world, erected the kerosene lamp as a symbol of his power in the jungles of Africa and in the rocky wilderness of the Himalayas. The flame of the kerosene lamp has faded in the glare of the electric light, but the hunger for oil has increased.

Lomow proceeds to reveal the ways in which oil was profoundly ideologized and thereby invested with symbolic power, that is, oil as a means through which the discursive and political-economic wars and rivalries between the capitalist-liberalist and the allegedly communist countries were conducted. Lomow's speech affords us a glimpse into the massive industrial and social-cultural modernization coupled with the infrastructural alterations instigated by the magic power of oil. And he starts his speech thus: "The world needs petroleum. From the hum of the engines, the rattle of the machines, the pounding of the locomotives, the roar of the propellers, a scream breaks out: Petroleum! Even more petroleum! Petroleum!!" (*Konjunktur* 2, Scene 1, Act 3).

Notably, with the occurrence of the Bolshevik Revolution and the subsequent nationalization of oil in Russia (Soviet Union), Royal Dutch/Shell lost 50% of their share of Russian oil at a stroke. The other major shareholder were the Nobles who fled the country and ultimately sold their oil shares to Deterding who purchased it on the assurance he received from Standard Oil of New Jersey concerning the political protection of the investment in the revolutionary Russia. In the second half of the 1920s, the left-liberal to socialist spectrum increasingly focused on the Soviet Union as an economic power. As an "oil force", Soviet Union was able to compete with the world powers – specifically, England and the USA. This oil-endowed leverage instigated a change or shift of focus in the rivalry between the Western capitalists and Soviet Communists, from the political

"On a Wave of Oil England Swam Towards Victory" 155

to the economic stage where the Soviet Union was able to compensate for foreign policy setbacks and diplomatic isolation.

In his contribution to the program booklet of *Konjunktur 2*, Alfons Goldschmidt explicitly alludes to this facet of the play by situating the political-economic dynamics of oil in its contemporary context, thereby accentuating how the historical resource struggle constitutes the crux of the play:

> It was a socialist process of rationalization that quickly made the Russian oil industry independent and powerful, much more important than before the war. So now there were three great oil powers in the world: U.S.A., England, and Soviet Russia. All three aspire to the market, albeit under different conditions and with different goals. The real competition for petroleum only began with the Russian Revolution. Leo Lania's play represents a phase of this struggle.
> (Der Brennende Punkt, S.5. See also Röber, Chapter 4, Part 2)

Indeed, the oil deposits on Soviet territory and the clever marketing coups of the Russian economic strategists had attracted international attention. This is evidenced by the fact that the energy policy of the Soviet Union was a pivotal feature of the country's planned economic boom from the time of Lenin (head of government until 1924) onward. The Soviet Union was virtually self-sufficient in energy; major development of the energy sector started with Stalin's autarky policy of the 1920s – where Stalin articulated the five-year plan in 1928 whereby Russia was supposed to rise to global power by outstripping the US (see Yergin, *The Prize*, 114–133). In *Konjunktur 2*, the profoundly ideological (communist) nature of Russian oil is nowhere articulated as vividly as in the ensuing part of Lomow's speech:

> Russia has petroleum. No Caesar commands it, and no Cromwell, no Rockefeller and no Deterding. His ruler? 130 million Russian workers and peasants. They will not abandon the oil as an important key to their power. With him they opened the bars of the hunger blockade and with him they will blow up the gates of the fortresses that British and American imperialism has erected in the five continents. The resources of all countries for the working people of all countries. So we declare: the Albanian oil springs belong to the Albanian farmers. In the name of the International. (Lautsprecher: Es spricht der Vorsitzende des Allrussischen Naphta-Syndikats.) (n.p.)

The invocation of an array of authoritarian leaders from across the history of the Western world with vastly different modes of political-economic governmentality – parliamentary elitism and quasi-republicanism (Cromwell), capitalism-democracy (Rockefeller), and imperialism

156 *"On a Wave of Oil England Swam Towards Victory"*

(Caesar) – and concluding with an oil figure is an important ideological gesture and reveals the play's *conjonctural vision*. In a notable discursive manoeuvre, Lomow underscores the socio-symbolic value of oil by pitting the Soviet Union – as a proletarian and communist liberator – against this longue durée of Capitalocene and its cyclical nature and extractivist dynamics. In Lomow's account, the Russian/communist oil is depicted not as a commodity and privilege of a certain economic, political, or social class. Rather, oil is the material lifeblood and sustenance of the people and a symbol of social-economic equality and liberty. Lomow's speech thus demonstrates how, far from being a neutral raw material or resource, oil is densely traversed and invested with ideology, racial, gender, and class politics and economy. This attests to the symbolic position oil occupied in the first half of the 20th century (and keeps occupying now) on the local and global scene.

Ironically, such a speech cannot but be haunted by the violent spectre of the Soviet Union's own treatment of the working class and resources (particularly oil) both domestically and internationally. In their political and economic dynamics, the Soviet Union implemented an extractive practice which evinced considerable affinities with the exploitative capitalist methods, though the Soviet Union pursued its extractive goals not through privatization but through the consolidation of political-economic power around a central state. Particularly when considered within the context of *Konjunktur 2* and within the broader historical context – where we can find in more detail the Soviet Union's treatment of its own workers and nationals as well as other sympathetic nations and allies (such as China) – Lomow's speech throws into relief the contradictions of this oil-driven petro-state as a political hegemony (to wit, Soviet Russian communism). As such, *Konjunktur 2* unwittingly shows how, whilst allegedly aiming to oppose the logics of petro-capitalist system at an ideological level, the Soviet Union ended up enacting, at a material level, strikingly similar extractive logics, core-periphery dynamics, and uneven developmental patterns not only domestically but across the world in China and elsewhere in Asia and Europe.

Furthermore, such antithetical positions and rivalries between the communist and capitalist forces in ideological-political respects should not mislead us into assuming the lack or eschewal of any entanglements or interactions on material and economic levels between them. Whilst Russia's oil production had dramatically declined in the 1900–1920 period (from 10 Mt/y to 3 Mt/y) both because of World War I and the domestic turmoil between the revolutionary Bolsheviks and the Tsarist state, by the establishment of the Bolshevik state and settlement of the chaos, Russia's oil production underwent an upheaval by having a soaring rise in production in the 1920–1930 period (see Babusiaux 2007, 9–10). Importantly, whilst "the import of Russian oil products met with greatest opposition in England and France", notwithstanding the political-ideological impediments,

Soviet oil "play[ed] an increasingly important role in the industry and commerce of European and Near Eastern nations" (Fischer 111). Predicated on detailed analysis of statistics, Fischer avers in 1927 that "incongruous though it may seem, it is nevertheless a fact that the Naphtha Syndicate of the Bolshevik state now supplies oil for the natives of four capitalistic Powers: Great Britain, France, Italy, Greece" (113). *Konjunktur 2*, therefore, can be argued to stage an oil-driven struggle not only between the national and international forces but between the capitalist oil and socialist-communist oil. This crucial facet of the play, however, was mainly occluded in the production by the intrusive censorship and surgical excision foisted upon the text, ironically, by the representatives of Communist Party in Germany (the Soviet Ambassador, the KPD, and Die Rote Fahne) who were attending the rehearsal and found the attribution of the complicity in the speculative dynamics of global economy to an agent of the Soviet Union sacrilegious. In Lania's original ending, Barsin was revealed to be simultaneously a spy for the Soviet state and a commercial agent of a Russian oil syndicate who had been given orders to strike a deal with the highest bidder. Brecht undertook the subtle task of revising the text – as a result of which Barsin – in a deus ex machina moment – was disclosed to be a South American spy acting under the guise of a Russian spy, who was posing as a Russian businesswoman (see Piscator 1980, 276–278).

## B.   Oil and the Capitalist-Imperialist System

### 1.   Great Britain

The second speech is by Deterding who rises from behind his desk in his office at Royal Dutch in London and delivers the following:

> Gentlemen, on a wave of oil England swam towards victory in the great war. Great Britain's victory – that is not the dethronement of the German emperor, not the breaking up of Austria, not Italy's increase in power and France's brokering – our victory is petroleum. Before the war we controlled a quarter of world oil production and today we control over two thirds of world oil, we have almost all – important European and Asian sources of petroleum in our hands, the Union Jack has even advanced into the heart of America, two fifths of the English Oil Capital operates in the United States' petroleum industry. Mexico and Persia, Mosul and Djambi are subject to us, whichever road an English ship wants to travel on, these are the stations of the Royal Dutch where it can dive in all corners of the world, they – the key positions of British power – are the foundation of the empire. So we decide: Mister Brown receives unlimited financial aid, a squadron of the English navy is commanded against Albania. All Albanian oil fields belong to the Royal Dutch. In the name of culture and civilization.

158 *"On a Wave of Oil England Swam Towards Victory"*

This speech not only identifies oil, contradictorily, as both the cause of war (World War I) and its cure, or at least a panacea for victory in it. It also delineates a cartographic account of the geopolitical scope of British petro-capitalist system. The two key phrases of this speech are "drive" and "driving in all corners of the world" – the agency of which is attributed to oil. Oil is thus presented not only as the cause of modernization and full-fledged industrialization, but also as the condition of possibility of new ecologies and nations, economic cycles, and social-cultural systems. Furthermore, what is evident in this ardent speech is not only how oil, as an artifact of global despoliation, appears as a world-ecological and world-economic force that spans a world-historical field by "producing" new *peripheral* racial and spatial categories and entities. It also evokes the outlines of a larger logistical transformation in British politics.

Deterding's speech presents us with a highly dense passage in that it assumes the reader's knowledge of the modern history as the history of oil. This is attested by the way the speech evokes and is underpinned by a whole history of colonial adventures, social-political upheavals, and carving out of new countries (as imperial projects) merely due to the countries' possession of rich oil resources (including Iraq, Kuwait, Nigeria, etc.). Historically, the 1890–1910 period marks a time when there was a raging contention and suspicions surrounding the viability, sustainability, and practical potential of oil in Britain and beyond, given oil's foreign origins, the high cost of the fuel, and the uncertainties about its supply along with the questions of class, culture, and national politics that the adoption of oil as the main national energy mode would usher in (Koselleck 1985, 239. See also Jones 1981, 42.)[11] Britain had begun its pursuit of oil already in the 1890s. As early as the 1880s, oil had turned into a locus of national debate. A paradigmatic case in point is Charles Marvin's flurry of writing where he warned that in case of the neglect of the global significance of oil by England, it would soon be relegated to a periphery of the geopolitics of oil. "The Petroleum Question" was indeed most vociferously posed in the mid-1880s by Marvin, an English emissary to Alexander II who had caught the popular attention by documenting the Russian oil trade. As he exclaims, the whole quandary boiled down to a blunt question: "Who is to boss the coming oil age?" (Marvin 1889, 31).[12] Consonantly, De Thierry forewarned that devoid of oil, the colonized and peripheral nations would "break up our empire as it has already broken up and sucked the sap out" of its colonies (de Thierry, *The Morning Post*, 178, 313 qtd. in Henry, *Oil Fuel and the Empire*). Such Jeremiad reckonings coupled with the exceedingly intensifying rivalry between Britain and Germany (particularly over military power, submarine rivalry, and resource monopoly) ultimately spurred Britain to take a "fateful plunge"[13] into oil in 1912. This is evidenced by the conversion of the fuel and military machinery in the navy from coal and coal-consuming warships to oil and oil-driven ones. This momentous

"On a Wave of Oil England Swam Towards Victory" 159

decision was made by Winston Churchill, the then head of the Admiralty. This mandatory transition to oil as "the fuel of the future" or "our future fuel"[14] – marked not only an upheaval in the cycles of resource extraction in the British capitalist world system. It also marked petroleum's emergence as a nationally indispensable and globally strategic geopolitical resource, as it required a stable supply chain to be built across the modern world system. This was realized by the British Empire having safely and cheaply tapped into oil fields in Persia, Iraq, Burma, Borneo, and India (see Ferrier 202–285).[15]

Deterding's speech in *Konjunktur 2* also betokens the historical and temporal fields opened by oil's formidable magic force, that is, oil both promised and delivering a realized present and a speculative future of imagining a collection of "futures past" or "superseded futures" (Koselleck 1985). Oil's association with temporality and finitude stems not only from its pre-historical origins (in human, and not geological, time) and its being a non-renewable resource with apparently incognito measure of its remaining amount at national and global levels (due its being globally kept a secret by the governments and corporations for strategic and national security reasons). It also arises from the transformative effect of oil on space, time, and environment, including time-space compression and the Anthropocene. The concern about finitude of oil as a resource came to determine England's inexorable treatment of even its closest political ally: the USA. As we will see, this noteworthy point is interestingly underscored in Teagle's speech later. This preoccupation with time, futurity, and finitude – that is, oil as a determinant of the future of the nation and its political-ideological values – coupled with all the geopolitical decisions (at imperial-international and national levels) it entailed – is vividly reflected in Churchill's cautionary note that, while "the advantages conferred by liquid fuel [oil] were inestimable", to "change the foundation of the navy from British coal to foreign oil was a formidable decision in itself" (Dahl 2001, 51).[16] The fate of Britain (both as a nation and a global force/hegemony) and its success at war – were contingent on its success in obtaining access to cheap oil resources from the "peripheries" (such as Iran, Iraq, Albania, etc.) through its long-standing colonial-imperial strategies and extractive practices. As Churchill explains:

> The oil supplies of the world were in the hands of vast oil trusts under foreign control. To commit the navy irrevocably to oil was indeed to take arms against a sea of troubles. . . . If we overcame the difficulties and surmounted the risks, we should be able to raise the whole power and efficiency of the navy to a definitely higher level; better ships, better crews, higher economies, more intense forms of war power – in a word, mastery itself was the prize of the venture.
> (Winston S. Churchill, *The World Crisis, Vol. 1*. New York: Scribner's, 1923, 133–136.)

160 *"On a Wave of Oil England Swam Towards Victory"*

In prospect of escalating tensions and competition with Germany and the US, in conjunction with Germany's technological superiority, the British government embarked on a series of globe-trotting campaigns not only to guarantee the security of its own oil needs, but to also hinder Germany's access to a stable source of petroleum by seeking to hegemonically "control the raw material on which . . . [it] must run" (Engdahl 2004, 28–29). Britain's oil-focused campaigns particularly concentrated on the Middle East and Mesopotamia, a move on which I elaborate later. Furthermore, Deterding's points about the abstract fluidity of oil as time, force, and energy anticipate the process of speculative financialization of both value/ wealth and a future where the capitalist system continues to hold hegemonic power in a different guise (see my discussion of Jeff Diamanti in my chapter on *Arctic Oil* in Volume Two).

## 2. *The USA*

The previous discussion both within the play and within the historical-political context leads us to the third prominent speech in *Konjunktur 2* by Teagle. Standing behind the desk in his office of Standard Oil, New York, he delivers the following lines to the world:

> Gentlemen, our victory in the great war, that was the victory of the truck over the locomotive. We vaporized it, and our weapon of choice was petroleum. Four fifths of the petroleum used to feed the tanks and cars, submarines and aircraft of the Allies during the war came from American sources. But while we were exhausting our fields, England took possession of new sources in all parts of the world, while English capital was working on American soil, the British oil regions were closed to us. We will break this blockade and we decide: Engineer Jonny Rogers is appointed as our representative and sent to the board of directors of the Franco Albanian, which has merged with us, he receives unlimited financial aid, two cruisers from our war fleet are running out against Albania. All Albanian oil fields belong to Standard Oil. In the name of culture and civilization. Italy doesn't want war. The Italian detachment is withdrawn from Albania by order of the War Ministry.
>
> (Act 3, Scene 1)

This snippet provides us with a glimpse into how, historically, the "Standard Oil Company of New Jersey" (from which Esso and Exxon Mobile later emerged) soon developed into the largest oil producer in the world under the direction of its manager. Notably, the mention of Walter Teagle's name as the head of Standard Oil Company situates the play within a critical juncture. The American troops engaged in the war in 1917 were the first fully motorized army in world history. The global race

*"On a Wave of Oil England Swam Towards Victory"* 161

for the raw material oil started before the First World War, but intensified considerably in the 1920s. After the collapse of the Ottoman Empire, the English and French split up the Middle East anew; indeed, some of the newly carved-out countries (such as Iraq and Kuwait) were founded chiefly to facilitate and enable the Western powers to extract oil. As Yergin accentuates, for both the Axis and the Allies, "oil was recognized as the critical strategic commodity for the war and was essential for national power and international predominance" (35). By the same token, a key word in Teagle's speech, here, is oil as the "weapon of choice" – a term that evokes how struggles over political hegemony both in Europe and globally were carried out through a focus on energy resources and, above all, oil. Focusing on the 1930s and 1940s, Walter Voskuil discerns a direct relationship between political power in Europe and the control of coal and oil resources (along with other mineral deposits). Voskuil demonstrates how both the "goal of Lebensraum" and that of the battle of the Atlantic was to gain control over resources. This included "Swedish iron ores, the ores of Lorraine, the Polish coal fields, the Romanian oil fields, Yugoslavian bauxite" and others (Voskuil 1942, 247). Noteworthy in this regard is Voskuil's description of different strategic roles coal and oil/petroleum played during the First World War – where coal came to be considered as the backbone of industrial production, or the thick, blunt, backside of the knife, and oil and its role in power projection is seen as the sharp cutting edge of the knife (ibid., 247–248).

A crucial mention is made, in Teagle's speech, of the opposite attitudes maintained by Britain and the US in relation to the global oil resources. Whilst Teagle's point particularly concerns the post-World War I context, this policy adopted by the UK extends back to the pre-World War I period as well. A prominent spot or resource was the oil that lay in Mesopotamia (particularly Mosul and Baghdad) which was considered "an indispensable commodity, indeed a strategic necessity" by the British navy (24). The area of Mosul was crucial to British war aims geo-strategically both in terms of the land war and in terms of the oil resources that lay there. The priority on control over Mosul by the British is demonstrated by several factors, including: British willingness to act in contrast to the Sykes-Picot Agreement of 1916 in their capture of Mosul, the British geological reconnaissance in February of 1916, and explicit statements on the part of the Admiralty that "physical control" over oil producing areas was necessary (25). Notably, Mejcher explains how the American "Open Door" foreign policy applied pressure on the British attempts to monopolize the resources found in the areas under their control. Britain's unabashed counter-manoeuvre to the American chants of "Open Door" was "Physical Control" (Mejcher 1976, 28–36).[17]

What partly altered Britain's exclusionary petro-politics was the fact that in the wake of World War I, Britain was one of the most heavily indebted nations in the world and the majority of it was owed to the US since

162 *"On a Wave of Oil England Swam Towards Victory"*

Britain had to ask the US forces to carry fuel and other strategic resources (such as food) through identifiably US marine transportation so that they would not be attacked by German forces. According to Broadberry and Howlett: "[t]otal overseas borrowing by the government during the war amounted to £1,365 million by the end of the financial year 1918/19, with 75 per cent coming from the United States" (2003, 17). Estimates of the total cost of war on the Allied and Entente powers show that Britain undertook the "lion's share" of the burden (Broadberry and Howlett 2003). However, where Britain accrued debt, the United States burgeoned on the boons of trade with a Britain in dire need: "The share of American exports going to the Allies rose from 61 percent before the war to more than 80 percent during the war" (Fordham 2007, 286). Fordham explains that with British military expenditure in the United States rising to some 40% of total expenditures, it was economically viable for the United States to keep its trade ties with the Allied Powers (2007, 286). This led to a drastic decline in American trade with the Central Powers. Such a rift in economic relations was ultimately conducive to a military confrontation between the Germans and the US.[18]

## Conclusion

Notwithstanding the victory of the liberation/resistance national forces (ironically led by a non-national: Claire Barsin), *Konjunktur 2* concludes on an inauspicious note which forebodes further war on ideological and material (over the strategic resource: oil) grounds pursued along geopolitical lines. Teagle's and Brown's simultaneously overlapping and jarring statements testify to this point at issue. Teagle avers to Jonny: "We have only one enemy: Russia, only one goal: Baku, only one task: arming ourselves for war. Only one solution: war! But first we have to beat England". And Brown avers: "We have only one enemy: – Russia, only one goal: Baku, only one task: arming ourselves for war, only one slogan: war! And double armor [or doubly arming ourselves] against America". The concluding words are accorded to Claire who wonders: "When – is [or comes] – the next war?" In the same vein, the final scene opens with a brooding *Stimmung* ("it is getting dark") and ends with a tentative twilight where we witness the continuation of the flow of oil extraction and capital flow across the networks of global petro-capitalism: "It is getting lighter below, the characteristic tanks of the Royal Dutch are growing in place of the derricks".

*Konjunktur 2*, compared with *Konjunktur 1* with its equivocally hopeful conclusion, limns a more bleak and sceptical picture of the status quo and the relations and power dynamics between contending global powers and national political parties, by unveiling complicities and collusions among them where the possibility of vertical integration of forces into one monopoly or hegemony overrides and undermines the possibility of a

## "On a Wave of Oil England Swam Towards Victory" 163

genuine national-revolutionary movement led by the Albanian people and dedicated to advancing their needs and interests. As such, the partly dystopian horizon *Konjunktur 2* evokes at the end arises from a global crisis of action; that is, the play leaves us in a situation where the tensions and conflicts between ostensibly opposite political parties and forces such as socialist and capitalist as well as national and international forces (despite their intense ideological differences) faint and blur and vanish – due to their extensive complicities, uneven power relations, and their ultimately capitalist motives – only to foreground the triumph of the world-systemic power of oil hegemony.

In keeping with its partly epic-style aesthetics, *Konjunktur 2* concludes with a meta-theatrical moment where Loudspeaker announces: "Achtung! Achtung! Hier ist Berlin. Das war der Schluss unseres Abendprogramms. Vergessen Sie bitte nicht, die Antenne zu erden! Auf Wiederhören bei der Bekanntgabe der politischen Tagesnachrichten". ["Attention! Attention! Here is Berlin. That was the end of our evening program. Don't forget to ground the antenna! Goodbye to the announcement of the daily political news."] This meta-theatrical announcement evokes multivalent resonances. Firstly, it fosters a sense of alienation or estrangement effect where the audience's attention is drawn to the theatrical-fictional nature of the theatrical event. Such V-Effekt dynamics is intended to alert the audience to the social-historical and political-economic logic informing actions and relations of the countries and characters surrounding the question of oil. On the other hand, such a reiteration of a historically factual phrase within the context of this apparently fictional-theatrical work blurs the boundaries between fact and fiction thereby engendering a mise-en-abyme moment where the audience is prompted to critically ponder how what they just witnessed unfold upon the stage was far from being a piece of fiction detached from the forces and structures determining their daily social and political-economic lives. Finally, this announcement/moment contains a coded cultural-historical reference which would have been readily recognizable by the audience of its contemporary history (the 1920s). Indeed, historically German radio history began with an identically phrased announcement on 29 October 1923 – a cultural signifier that enhanced the verisimilitude and historical factuality (reportage-effect) of the play.

As was demonstrated in my scrutiny of the various facets of the play, *Konjunktur 2* – as a work of petro-drama – is distinguished by a number of features, saliently including its development of a materialist and petro-aesthetic dramaturgy to depict the manifoldly agential nature of oil as a globally strategic commodity in the early decades of the 20th century. As was made evident in my detailed exploration, *Konjunktur 2* makes a consistent effort – evidenced by its aesthetics, thematics, and its political-economic vision – to expose not only the world-systemic dynamics and uneven (core-periphery) logics informing the extractive practices

164 *"On a Wave of Oil England Swam Towards Victory"*

conducted by both capitalist and communist oil powers in the global peripheries. It also exposes the material ways in which oil gradually came to both permeate culture and society as a force, commodity, and object of desire and to re-define the fundamental conceptions and experience of time, space, relationality, and identity in petro-modern societies. *Konjunktur 2* shows what links the petro-communist and petro-capitalist systems is the uneven and core-periphery mode of relationship between them (as hegemonic countries/forces) and peripheral countries (such as Albania, Iran, and Iraq).

## Notes

1. Erwin Piscator, *Gespräch zur Aufführung des 'Schwejk' in Berlin.* Erwin Piscator Center 2732 (Berlin: Deutsche Akademie der Künste).
   Erwin Piscator, Letter to Siebert, Ilse. Erwin Piscator Center 2305. Deutsche Akademie der Künste, 25 May 1959.
2. Historically, the Royal Dutch Shell group was owned 60% by Royal Dutch and 40% by Shell, a British company. Henceforth RDS.
3. Claire (to Rossi): "Wir suchen jedenfalls keine Anlage fur Kapital". ["In any case, we are not looking for an investment for capital."]
4. "Links und rechts vorne werden die Holzgerüste von Bohrtürmen aufgestellt, die während der folgenden Szenen langsam in die Höhe wachsen, gleichzeitig wird im Hintergrund gebaut, es entstehen die Anlagen zu weiteren Bohrtürmen" (Act 2, Scene 1).
5. This very same dramatic-aesthetic device was utilized in the production of *Oil* by Hickson (see Fakhrkonandeh, *Textual Practice* 2021).
6. Piscator himself expressly refers to the joint work with Lania on the film accompanying *Konjunktur*; see Piscator (1929, 208–209).
7. The metonymic and symbolic role of automobiles and cars both in the US and more broadly in Europe. See Matthew Huber, Lifeblood, Chapters 1 and 2.
8. See *Public Roads Administration, Federal Works Agency, Highway Statistics Summary to 1945* (Washington: US Government Printing Office, 1947), p. 18.
9. Dmitry Chernov and Didier Sornette, *Man-Made Catastrophes and Risk Information Concealment* (London: Palgrave, 2015).
10. See Peter A. O'Connor, "Energy Transitions," in "The Pardee Papers," (2010), p. 9.
    David Allan Snyder, "Petroleum and Power: Naval Fuel Technology and the Anglo-American Struggle for Core Hegemony, 1889–1922," Texas A&M University, 2001, pp. 53–54.
    Jon Tetsuro Sumida. *In Defence of Naval Supremacy: Finance, Technology, and British Naval Policy, 1889–1914* (Boston: Unwin Hyman, 1989), pp. 21–22.
    Vaclav Smil, *Energy Transitions: History, Requirements, Prospects* (Santa Barbara California: Praeger, 2010), p.225.
    Richard Heinberg, *The Party's Over: Oil, War and the Fate of Industrial Societies* (Gabriola Island: New Society Publishers, 2003).
    Robert O. Keohane, *After Hegemony: Cooperation and Discord in the World Political Economy* (Princeton: Princeton University Press, 1984).
    Bernard Mommer, *Global Oil and the Nation State* (Oxford: Oxford University Press, 2002).

## "On a Wave of Oil England Swam Towards Victory"    165

11. Reinhart Koselleck, *Futures Past: On the Semantics of Historical Time*. Trans. Keith Tribe (Cambridge, MA: MIT Press, 1985). G. Gareth Jones, *The State and the Emergence of the British Oil Industry* (London: Macmillan, 1981).

12. Charles Marvin, *The Coming Oil Age: Petroleum – Past, Present, and Future* (London: R. Anderson, 1889).

13. The term originates in Winston Churchill's comment that "the fateful plunge was taken when it was decided to create the Fast Division" of oil-fired battleships in April 1912. "Then, for the first time, the supreme ships of the Navy, on which our life depended . . . could only be fed by oil," he explained (Churchill, 1923, 131).

14. See Winston Churchill, *The World Crisis, 1911–1918* (London: Thornton Butterworth, 1923). See also I.C., "Our Future Fuel"; Richardson, "Petroleum" and "Petroleum as Steam Fuel"; Wilkins, "Rock Oil."

15. Ronald W. Ferrier, *The History of the British Petroleum Company Volume One, 1901–1932* (Oxford: OUP, 2000).

16. Erik J. Dahl, "From Coal to Oil," *Joint Force Quarterly* (*JFQ*), (Winter 2000–01), pp. 50–56.

17. See also Kellaway, "Mesopotamian Oilfields: Memorandum by the Minister in Charge of the Petroleum Department," 22 April [1920], C.P. 1118, CAB 24/104.

18. George E. Gruen points out how many countries were interested in the province of Mosul: as well as Britain and France, Germany and American investors tried to obtain railway oil concessions there. Kemalist Turkey attempted to retain it in 1923. This was largely due to the potentially huge oil reserves that the province contained (see G. E. Gruen, "The Oil Resources of Iraq: Their Role in the Policies of the Great Powers," in *The Creation of Iraq, 1914–1921*, ed. R. S. Simon and E. H. Tejirian (New York NY: Columbia University Press, 2004, pp. 110–123).

# 4 "Oil Is an Idea"

## From Production to Anti-Production in Leo Lania's *Oil Field* (1934)

## I. Introduction

The years intervening *Konjunktur* (1 and 2) and *Oil Field* proved replete with existential, political, and economic vicissitudes for Leo Lania. These include his travels to and sojourns in France and Britain as well as his immigration to the United States. In London, Lania worked intensely on the rewriting of *Konjunktur* when he also corresponded and met with Brecht, who partly worked on the revisions too; and in the United States, he finished the final version (titled *Oil Field*) in collaboration with Charles Duff. As a testimony to the prophetic vision of the play where war (politics) and oil (economy) are shown to be inextricably entangled, the rewriting of *Konjunktur* and its metamorphosis into *Oil Field* was completed in 1934, the eve of the Second World War.[1] Corresponding to Lania's peregrinations, the dramatic text underwent a cataclysm in its transition from *Konjunktur* (1 and 2) to *Oil Field*. This cataclysm consists not only of alterations to the historical-geographical setting, but also to the aesthetic and thematic features along with the narrative elements of the text. Whilst both titles – *Konjunktur* and *Oil Field* – evoke an allegorical dynamics in their avoidance of any historical and geographical specification, *Konjunktur* more specifically hints at the nature and dynamics of petro-capitalism (its conjonctural logics), whereas *Oil Field* adumbrates the systemic reproducibility of the petro-capitalist extractive practices in the peripheries almost regardless of the latter's national-local histories and identities. As such, the title of *Oil Field* is, lexically/semantically, more blunt, direct, and general thereby establishing an almost indexical relation between the title and the content/topic concern of the play: oil.

The longue durée and allegorical aspects of *Oil Field* are evidently manifested in its rendition of space, time, form, and props/costume. More specifically, geographically, the setting has altered from the historically specific Albania to the allegorically named Puritania. The other notable feature of the allegorical space/setting is its "periphery" status. As the stage directions indicate: "Action takes place in the small and hitherto quite unimportant Republic of Puritania" (n.p.). This choice of setting

DOI: 10.4324/9781003134664-5

*"Oil Is an Idea"*   167

testifies to Lania's critical consciousness of the ways in which a (semi-) peripheral country is targeted by global powers and capitalist corporation only to (re-)produce them as zones of extraction or a resource frontier by harnessing them to the world-systemic dynamics of capitalism where the peripheral country becomes one amongst a network of peripheries, the only binding strand of which is their being governed by the uneven rhythms of capitalist surplus production and economic-racial extractivism. Historically, too, *Oil Field* is set in an indefinite period. Although social-historical traces betoken a 20th-century world, according to the stage directions: "The period of the play is a few years after the latest Great War, not necessarily the 1914–1918" (n.p.). By evoking the memory of World War I in relation to oil, Lania accentuates how oil extractivism and oil (as a global strategic commodity and hegemonic energy resource) played a prominent role in the causes and outcomes of both World War I and, prospectively, World War II. More importantly, however, by situating the play in an indefinite inter-war period, Lania underscores how oil (and other fossil fuels), far from remaining limited, in its determining role, to the two world wars – will continue to be the cause of cycles of war in the future. Further enhancing the world-economic and world-ecological facets of both oil and *Oil Field*, Lania makes a point of establishing the ways in which such a peripheral region/space (Puritania) is always already traversed with imperial and global powers from the Western core. As the stage directions indicate: "Other countries concerned are the Powerful Powers – The Kingdom of Bolonia, Perfidia, the Empire of Fritzonia and Violonia, and the Republic of Lala" (n.p.). Along with the thinly disguised names of the imperial/global powers, the allegorical and world-ecological facets are further substantiated when the stage directions aver: "The uniforms of the soldiers etc. are quite unlike those of any known country – this is the only remarkable feature about them; but it is very important" (n.p.).

The substantial alterations to *Konjunktur*, however, extend far beyond the choice of the title and historical-geographical features. Other noteworthy differences include the removal of such main characters as Claire Barsin, the historically factual heads of oil corporation and states, and some of the native Albanian individuals such as Ahmed. The removal of Claire Barsin – who occupies a central position in *Konjunktur* – not only affords us a glimpse into an upheaval in Lania's stance towards the Soviet Union and its brand of communism in the years since the completion of *Konjunktur* in 1928 – during which Lania grew increasingly disillusioned with and critical of the Soviet Union's suppressive and authoritarian politics. It also reveals the extent to which *Oil Field*, ideologically (sociopolitically) and aesthetically, diverges from *Konjunktur* and pursues different aims through different dynamics. With the removal of Claire Barsin, the communist and pro-Soviet weight is shifted from the endorsement of socialist-communist revolution (as the ultimate solution or panacea to the pernicious poison of capitalism) to a meticulous inspection of the

168   *"Oil Is an Idea"*

dynamics through which capitalism not only uses oil as a strategic global commodity but also systemically produces resource frontiers and zones of extraction around the globe for accumulation through dispossession. Whilst some of the names of the characters used in *Konjunktur* (such as Riffan-Bey, Dubois, Brown, the workers, among some others) are retained, in *Oil Field* we encounter new characters such as Oxhumani and Pusspad. The other two conspicuous elements of *Oil Field* are, first, its sustained focus on the question of land where it depicts how a national-local and resource-rich land undergoes various stages of transformation – including individual dispossession, nationalization, internationalization, abstraction into a capitalist commodity, and its subjection to metabolic rift. The second is the play's scrutiny of the exploitative conditions of oil workers far more extensively than *Konjunktur*.

Aesthetically, *Oil Field* is distinguished by two concomitant facets: its generic hybridity and its formal (and dramaturgical) complexity. In moving from *Konjunktur* to *Oil Field*, we are moving from a historical quasi-realist play (streaked with elements of reportage, intrigue comedy, documentary, and Brechtian epic) to a mainly allegorical and partly social-realist work. Notwithstanding its mainly allegorical dynamics, *Oil Field* variously partakes of various aesthetic features and formal techniques including reportage, documentary realism, dark comedy, some Brechtian techniques (such as alienation effect). Furthermore, such generic and aesthetic alterations can be partly accounted for through a reference to the direct politicization of globally strategic commodities such as oil or coal – due to numerous reasons including their polluting properties, ties to colonialism, and fostering of addiction for non-renewable things. As was extensively delineated in the preceding chapters, *Konjunktur* (1 and 2) evinces elements of Objectivist realism (where oil/object features as the main character), intrigue comedy, comedy of manners, and allegory manifested in its depiction of characters either as ideological incarnations/mouthpieces, national-moral types, and/or puppet-like characters in conjunction with its presentation of a puppet-like array of pitiful human actions, a slapstick series of murders, national and international intrigue, the use of multinational corporations as shields for global-imperial forces, political-economic rivalry and geopolitical espionage between Russia and western European forces, illicit deals, and the looming prospect of a world war. Similarly, *Oil Field* contains both realistic (reportage and historical materialism) and non-realistic (allegory and dark comedy) elements. In *Oil Field*, the element of intrigue is almost entirely obliterated; for instance, there is no trace of the escape with torpedo ships by a cosmopolitan charlatan. The realistic facets of *Oil Field* are further enhanced through the removal of the picaresque and intrigue-comedy element of *Konjunktur* (though still a faint comic streak traverses *Oil Field*, chiefly embodied by Goldstein – who was a British cosmopolitan adventurer and charlatan and not a native of Albania hence why he decides to flee the country when in an imbroglio). The character that most closely (but solely very partially) fulfils the diegetic-dramatic and social-political functions occupied by Goldstein in *Konjunktur* is Pusspad. Pusspad, in contrast to Goldstein, is not only a native of Puritania, but is actually a lawyer though an opportunist one who is inclined towards corruption too. The difference between them is further thrown into relief in that Pusspad does not escape the country but rather perseveres through the national insurgencies and crisis and ultimately manages to establish some partial order at a national level by assuming the mantle of a dictator (endorsed by imperial-colonial powers) by betraying national interests (conceding the rights to national oil to foreign powers) and wreaking economic devastation on the nation for the sake of survival and retention of his position. Such are some of the aesthetic strategies that are devised to express the political-economic and ethical discourse in *Oil Field*, accompanied by the incorporation of various textual registers (dialogue, allegorical narrative, and a compilation of slogans, insults, and declarations) and an emphasis on the discursive-ideological and connotative power of language.

Whilst Lania endorsed some of the goals and causes of social realism, his rendition of the oil world is not marked with a naturalistic glorification of the grime of commodity extraction, but rather with dark comedy where absence of a democratic nation-state, a labour union power, and critically enlightened praxis and heroism (at social-political levels) leads to tragic loss and political-economic disaster. Lania diverges from many tenets of realism (particularly psychological realism) since it chooses not to confine his work to mere representation of the historical reality of the oil world, but to provide an insight into the structural dynamics of that reality as well as a systemic critique of that reality which it intends to "represent" by foregrounding various levels of the alienation (or estrangement) at stake in the re-production of the local-global reality wrought by petro-capitalism. As such, in *Oil Field*, Lania presents a more nuanced picture of the nature and dynamics of oil and its functions in the emergence, development, and expansion of the petro-modern powers, the (semi-)peripheral petro-state, and the dynamics of the encounter between the peripheral oil-possessing nation and global-imperial powers. This nuanced representation was achieved by adopting a rather different aesthetics, one that would both depart from the political dogmatism and historical determinism sedimented in the naturalist and committed socialist form, and the naïve appeal to the transparency of left-identified signifiers.

Lania's non-realistic aesthetics is vividly reflected in the play's eschewal of detailed characterological inspection and psychological depth in its rendition of characters. Instead, the play is inclined towards a pseudo-expressionistic, sociological typology. Whilst the socialist-realist frame has been a staple in tackling historical events, the aesthetics of commodities, and the abused and alienated life of the workers, Lania moves beyond

170   *"Oil Is an Idea"*

a realist aesthetics by incorporating elements of epic theatre, grotesque or dark comedy, and reportage aesthetics. In *Oil Field* many of the elements that partook of the Brechtian epic techniques of V-Effekt (including songs/choruses) as well as "reportage" (particularly announcements played through the radio or delivered by oil magnates and powers) have been excised. Nevertheless, *Oil Field* residually retains some of these epic and reportage techniques by including such media and dramatic elements as newspaper headlines and pieces (installed as banners, by Pusspad, outside his newsstand) and stage directions.

The allegorical status is further reflected in the choice of the names of characters and their descriptions in ways that imply their origin and nationality. Yubitch and Oxhumani (with European, particularly Eastern European associations); Nicholas Pusspad (an at once allegorical-descriptive and generic European name); Ruffian Bey described as "a merchant, of doubtful origin"; Freddy and Tom (with European and particularly Anglo-American associations) are described as "a couple of uncouth adventurers"; Dubois (with French connotations) as "an international gentleman"; Rotti (with Italian connotations) as "an international adventurer" (n.p.). The choice of names – culturally and etymologically – affords us some hints to their nationality. For instance, it would not be far-fetched to surmise that Dubois is French, Rotti Italian, and Brown Anglo-American; Freddy and Tom sound Anglo-American or German too. Trebitsch (in *Konjunktur 1 & 2*) corresponds to Pusspad. Whilst Trebitsch is rendered as an "impostor" character type, Pusspad is presented as less of a character type. Many of the main characters in *Oil Field* can be characterized in terms of Lukacs's notion of the type and typical character as a potent dialectical means of capturing the general and particular, the historical and the universal, the critical realist and psychological depth, particularly the characters caught between two and more fictions and factions (discourses/ideologies) (see Lukacs 1970, 124–146; see also Lukacs 1962, 62–71). More importantly, Lania deals with the dynamics and logics of oil (extraction) and its implications not merely as historical facts but also as social and political-economic problems. Whereas *Konjunktur 1* and *2* depict characters in broad strokes and partly as social or generic types and representatives of their ideological discourses, countries, or classes, in *Oil Field* not only do we witness a shift of focus away from salon comedy and swift movements between the physical spaces, social strata, and political parties. But, more importantly, we notice a sustained attention to the details and dynamics of oil as lived by common people. Hence whilst maintaining its allegorical dimensions/aspects, *Oil Field* evinces significant signs of "social realism" (though inflected with elements of V-Effekt) as elaborated by Lukacs.[2]

Lania's partial departure from realism can be argued to be partly impelled by the thematic fulcrum of his plays: oil – which as a potent "force-field" entering the dramatic-literary text – infuses the text with its

"*Oil Is an Idea*" 171

own psychodynamics, aesthetic features, and phenomenological structures.[3] The non-realism also arises from Lania's decision not to confine his work to mere representation of the historical "reality" of the lives of oil in Albania, but to provide a critique of that "reality" which it intends to "represent". Lania's choice of form shows how the petro-capitalist reality of oil battens on the de-realization of the periphery through various means including the abstraction of the resource (oil) through financialization and labour extraction, "alienation" at stake in the international-imperial forces' intervention in petro-capitalism, and finally, the consequent de-realization of the historical reality of the peripheral nation (Puritania) at local-national levels due to the social and political-economic estrangement from that reality wrought by the emergence of the oil order implemented by both the national petro-state and the global forces.

Indeed, scrutinizing various facets of oil – including the social, infrastructural, aesthetic, and political-economic – constitutes the crux of this chapter. In *Oil Field*, oil is shown to be the ground or substratum of all the transformations at individual, local, national, and global levels. Oil does not remain a subtextual element as was the case in *Konjunktur 1*, where oil – whilst depicted as the underlying cause of national-international conflicts – remains a hinterland or an atmospheric backdrop for the political-economic intricacies and diplomatic game of intrigues between global-imperial capitalist powers. In *Oil Field*, by contrast, far from occupying a marginal, subsidiary, or offstage presence, oil, as well as its infrastructural and discursive accoutrements, occupies the foreground. *Oil Field* stages oil in a variety of shapes: the fierce oil-frontier spirit of rivalry, petro-violence, land dispossession, the birth of the petro-state, the production of a resource frontier as a zone of extraction, the concomitance between resource extraction and racial production, the subtle processes through which oil is appropriated by the imperial powers and international corporation and subordinated to the logics of global petro-capitalism. By the same token, *Oil Field* gives the specifics of oil production a substantial verbal-visual weight by dramatizing the emergence of an oil-based national political economy (promising a swinging transition from an agricultural economy though proving impotent and abortive) and of an oil industry as an energy regime and a way of life at all levels. Lania's depiction of the dynamics of the transition from the agricultural to the oil-industrial nation-state evinces his acute cognizance of the structural dynamics and systemic features of the oil industry as a global industry. In this regard, he garnered his insights from Graf,[4] a succinct account of whose points and arguments was included in the program notebook of *Konjunktur*. Lania's critical engagement with oil, and its world-systemic dynamics in the 1920s and 1930s, was prescient for its time given that climate change had not spiralled into a global crisis. Lania's critical vision in his focus on oil is further corroborated when we consider that at the time most of the nations (particularly the industrialized ones in the global

172 *"Oil Is an Idea"*

north that were or had been engaged in one or both world wars) needed cheap oil to overcome the corrosive effects of the Depression and to further develop the middle class. As such, critiquing oil directly seemed to have no political backing until the environmental movement really took hold in the 1960s.

Accordingly, I will demonstrate how Lania delineates the dynamics of the petro-capitalist and (neo-)colonial extractive processes by presenting an in-depth dramatic account of the pivotal stages through which imperial-global powers gain monopoly over a global strategic resource (oil) found in a peripheral European country. As I will elaborate, five principal strategies are discernible in this complex extractive process implemented by the global petro-capitalist powers. These five, as they feature in *Oil Field*, include: (1) Extraction, (2) Abstraction, (3) Nationalization, (4) Anti-Production, and (5) Vertical Integration. It is worth concisely elaborating on these five crucial stages or components. *Oil Field* shows how the moment of the discovery of oil is almost immediately ensued by the land becoming the object of individual-local dispossession and its transformation into a matter of national security and international rivalry. As *Oil Field* illustrates, such a process is implemented not only through the spirit of frontier petro-violence, but also through the processes of nationalization (as a neo-colonial strategy) and abstraction (turning the land into an energy commodity). Subsequently, *Oil Field* reveals how global powers consent to facilitate the establishment of the peripheral nation as a petro-state – recognized as a legitimate state by the global powers and international law – contingent on a secret concession on the part of the peripheral nation (Puritania) to provide global powers with cheap oil and access to other resources such as labour. *Oil Field* depicts how the precarity of the peripheral petro-state and its exposure to the neo-colonial dynamics informing its relation to the petro-capitalist world system arises from not only the national chaos/instability, political rivalry at social and political-economic levels (largely instigated and aggravated by the global powers), but also the peripheral nation's lack of technological-industrial means of extraction and production of oil (and other resources). Consequently, the peripheral petro-state (Puritania) almost entirely depends upon the presence/contribution and intervention of the global powers. This renders the peripheral petro-state subject and liable to the logics and dynamics of global capitalism as a world system (and its vertical integration designates the establishment of hegemony through monopoly of strategic resources). Both processes of abstraction and vertical integration are conducted through a dynamics of accumulation-through-dispossession (of the national-local land and its subsoil resources). Notably, these five components constitute the five pivotal thematics and five points of diegetic dynamics of the plays as well.

There are a number of features that distinguish *Oil Field*'s engagement with the question of oil. However, the most prominent feature of the

"*Oil Is an Idea*"  173

play is its depiction of the production of a resource frontier or peripheral oil-possessing nation in terms of a fivefold process. The first component of this fivefold process is the process of "accumulation through dispossession" of land and resources. Secondarily, there is the play's exploration of the process of "abstraction" of such issues as value, oil (and other resources through a process of commodification and finacialization), neo-colonial political-economic interests of the global powers, and labour power not only through the capitalist processes of commodification but also through such ideological means as the production of social-political discourse. This is partly illustrated in *Oil Field* in the national and global powers' invocation of such ideas as the so-called global peace, global justice (a "Higher Justice"), and world order, all of which come to override the national-local interests. In this regard, we will also see how oil acts not only a symbolic incarnation of the logic of petro-capitalism, but as the catalyst for the illegitimate and capitalist/exploitative marriage of abstract and concrete. In the play, the abstract side is partly represented by the commodifying practices of the global petro-capitalist powers and partly by the notion of "national ideology" and national identity acting as a simultaneously objective and subjective agent. The concrete facet is embodied by the oil-rich land owned by a female individual. Such a marriage, thus, allegorically illustrates the manner a peripheral nation is commodified and harnessed to the rhythms of imperial and monopoly petro-capitalism (governed by the global powers) through the sham façade of nationalism and humanitarianism along with the installation of petro-colonial structures and a bureaucratic apparatus. As regards the third element, *Oil Field* presents "nationalism" (and the consequent nationalization of oil) as an ideological move galvanized and engineered mainly by global powers in a bid to establish their oil monopoly and their protégé petro-state in Puritania, which, due to its authoritarian and non-democratic nature, will invariably depend on international law and global powers' support to maintain its legitimacy and authority. *Oil Field* shows how nationalization under the black sun of oil entails adopting oil as a strategic national commodity, which, in turn, subjects the peripheral nation to being driven by the logic of the global capitalist market. As such oil, in a staple economy, is established as a means of defining national identity, history, and future as a technologically modern and progressive prospect forged as a discursive strategy by some of the imperial powers as a strategy to oust the other global rivals branded as outsiders and foreigners. Also, *Oil Field* shows how such an oil-dependent nationalist discourse is bound to produce an authoritarian and staple state. The other distinctive feature of *Oil Field* is its depiction of the other two crucial stages of the process of full assimilation of the peripheral oil-possessing nation into the political-economic logics of global petro-capitalism, namely: "anti-production" and "vertical integration", both of which are indelibly intertwined to the point where actually the former appears as a historical manifestation of

174  *"Oil Is an Idea"*

the latter. Conjoined, anti-production and vertical integration designate a political-economic strategy and a discursive measure through which a peripheral resource-rich country is subsumed into the global hegemony and economy and harnessed as a part of a network of the world-systemic (hence combined and uneven) dynamics of extraction, production, and consumption of resources and commodities. A paradigmatic evidence of this process of vertical integration is the imposition of an "anti-production" decree by the global powers (collectively running the newly forged amalgamated multinational oil company) where the desperate economic needs and interests of the nation (Puritania) are sacrificed to global rhythms of surplus extraction; an action which is justified by being ironically articulated in terms of a "higher global justice" and "world peace". More specifically, in *Oil Field*, the vertical integration dynamics involves a dynamics where Puritania becomes a rentier state when the amalgamated companies led by Brown appoint the head of Puritania state as the head of a national oil company which is supposed to "not" produce rather than produce abundantly and incessantly. *Oil Field* renders this evident by showing how, due to the overproduction and gluttony of oil in the later 1920s, the global powers decide to ascertain their profitability, monopoly in the global oil market, and surplus extraction by sacrificing the economic life of the peripheral, oil-possessing nation and exacerbating their economic and political crisis by coercing them not to produce their oil just to ensure their own surplus extraction in the global market by keeping the price of oil up by precluding overproduction. Significantly, all five stages and components are inextricably intertwined and nearly structurally synchronous.

Accordingly, this chapter will proceed in five steps – unfolding in two sections – where each delves into the dynamics of the aforementioned fivefold process and the ways in which they affect the individuals and the nations. Furthermore, the chapter explores the functions and perceptions of oil as well as how oil features as the magic transformer in contact with which everything undergoes upheaval. One of the focal points of the chapter will be the play's illuminating exposure of the dynamics of the transitions from monopoly capitalism to multinational corporation capitalism with oil as its impetus.

## II.  At the Oil Frontier: Land: Appropriation, Dispossession, Extraction

Akin to *Konjunktur 2*, *Oil Field* opens onto an unspoiled natural landscape, a topographically empty space devoid of any signs of civilized life. Here we are confronted with an uninhabited "idyllic" field in a peripheral nation where three ostensibly common people – named First, Second, and Third Man – who seem to be domestic/native explorers or adventurers are trudging on the land apparently in quest for something – though not oil. The three are described thus: "The first and second wear the wide, national trousers and fez of Puritania. . . . The third wears riding breeches slouch hat and coloured shirt, and has a large old-fashioned revolver. . . . All are dirty and ragged, carry pack, with shovels, oddments, etc." (1). The three men adventitiously notice a smelly liquid "flowing gently from the earth" (2). Upon dipping their fingers into it and smelling it, they realize, to their thrill and astonishment, that it is oil. They stake a sign there, "Claimed" (2) and they fill a water bottle of it perhaps as a sample to show it to the potential buyers. This is immediately ensued by a barrage of other – rival – parties. Consonant with the dynamics of the frontier, *Oil Field* confronts us with the cycles of expropriation, dispossession, erasure of the natural-ecological features and national-individual history of the land (particularly concerning ownership), and violence in the absence of the real owners: Ms Oxhumani, the shepherds, the peasants, and the national government/state.

Accordingly, the three men's foremost move is the appropriation of the land which does not belong to them, "While the other two are off-stage", the third explorer/adventurer "slinks quickly and nervously and nails a small board with the word CLAIMED on it" (2). Subsequently, we see Freddy and Tom who are brought by one of the three men (Third Man) to the site in the hope of a deal. Freddy is described as someone "who has once been a well-to-do aristocrat" and Tom as a "brutalized type" (2). Upon discovering that Third Man's claim is authentic, they, "gloating and amazed", exclaim: "PETRO – PETRO – LEUM" (2). And Third Man "drily" confirms: "Oil! Yes" (3). Freddy cunningly reminds them of all the legal and bureaucratic hassle that might await him: "Have you any idea of what kind of bother we're likely to have with the Government? Perhaps the ground belongs to . . ." (3–4). Then, making the three men drunk by paying for their whisky, Freddy bribes one of the three (Third Man) to sell the land for a paltry amount of money. Ultimately, Third Man is forced into selling the oil-rich land at a picayune price at gunpoint and under duress by Freddy and Tom. When Second Man notices how their friend (Third) has been dealing with Freddy and Tom over the land, he approaches Third and demands his share. In response, Third stabs him to death and escapes. When Freddy suggests they write "Oil wells" on the sign board, Tom remonstrates him thus: "You bloody fool. Do you want to have everybody about our ears?" proceeding to write on the board "Land Development Co. Ltd" (5). Similarly, in keeping with the murderous spirit of the resource frontier, after the deal, even the two accomplices/friends (Freddy and Tom), overcome with greed, threaten one another and draw revolvers on each other. What saves either from being killed is the appearance of Ruffian Bey. Indeed, the libidinal economy of this oil frontier is as revealing as its political economy. Here, Eros and Thanatos, biopolitics and thanatopolitics are indelibly intertwined (see Foucault, *Society Must Be Defended*, 241–254; see also Esposito 2008,

176  *"Oil Is an Idea"*

8–32).[5] It becomes clear how blood and oil go hand in hand from the outset. Previously we heard the ensuing exchange:

TOM: Damn! It looks very much as if instead of digging out Oil we shall have to start by digging in bones.

FREDDY: That's all right – it's nothing. Order must be maintained. Questions of ownership would often be complicated if a lucky little murder did not occasionally help to clear things up. Dead men tell no tales.

(5)

Notably, Ruffian Bey arrives along with a whole entourage of workers, peasants, paraphernalia, and foreman, and claims ownership of the land. Ruffian Bey is described as "a stout man, wearing a fez, a richly embroidered waistcoat and belt, with a rosary in his hand" (7). Such socially revealing character descriptions not only betoken how the cycles of expropriation incrementally take the question of oil beyond the common, lower-class explorers who discovered it, thereby ushering in the question of class power and social-political hierarchy. It also shows how oil incrementally expands its orbit of influence to the point where it reaches across and beyond class, racial and national lines and borders. When Ruffian Bey tries to stake his board/sign and remove the previous one, Freddy and Tom protest: "Hi, hi, blast you! Leave that board alone. Get out! This is our field". Ruffian Bey counters this by claiming to have owned the land "from time immemorial" (8): "Dear . . . A slight misunderstanding! You are standing on a field belonging to me – to me" (7). Later, their conflict spirals into drawing guns on each other. Ruffian Bey, however, who is equipped with surveying paraphernalia and accompanied by retinues (a small group of armed men) outweighs Tom and Freddy and forces them to move to a far-flung corner of the land. Defeated, they go to the extreme left of the field and stake their board there. Ruffian Bey's triumph is echoed in the music: we hear a "triumphant music".

The next scene features yet another stage in the transformation of the nature and value of the land – registered in semiotically and scenographically stark colours: "When the lights come on they show building operations Right and Left, small cottages, etc, being erected" (9). Whilst Ruffian Bey is busy enclosing the land by staking posts and barbwire, Rotti arrives and asks him about the operations. When Ruffian Bey claims to have purchased the land from Oxhumani and conceals his knowledge of the existence of subsoil resources, Rotti asserts that Oxhumani has not apprised him (her lawyer) of such a deal. Ruffian Bey pretends to have agricultural-herding plans in mind whilst striving to devalue the land by misrepresenting it: "They're not much – Not worth a hundred dollars, Stones, nothing but stones. It's only on account of my sheds. (Stops) Listen, I shouldn't mind offering two hundred – and fifty for you as commissions"

"*Oil Is an Idea*" 177

(10). When Ruffian unabashedly insists on his lies about his real plans to raise cattle there, Rotti hints at his real intentions by adding that instead of goats he needs to buy donkeys to help him with the "digging operations" (11). Astonished to hear of Rotti's knowledge of the existence of oil, Ruffian asks "What are you referring to?" – to which Rotti responds: "To what's underneath the stones" (11). Thus, Ruffian abandons his pretensions and appeals to Rotti to negotiate the purchase of the land from Mme. Oxhumani on his behalf and offers him money in return for his services: "I can give you spot cash, (does so) It's only a little friendly service" (10–11). Rotti leaves to apparently seek Oxhumani's consent to sell the land.

Consequently, we witness how the discovery of oil transforms the appearance and nature of the land, illustrating how oil has led to the "production" of a new space. The next scene features an outburst of a bureaucratic superstructure of the capitalist machinery: a nexus of real estates, legal institutes, and financial mediators that facilitate the construction of the infrastructure of oil extraction and petroculture. Correspondingly, there sprouts a riot of boards installed and staked by various contending oil extracting parties on the land:

> While Ruffian Bey is erecting his huts in front Right, FREDDY and TOM are building a primitive shed Left. To the right of it a large board "Land bought and sold", to the left a board "Land Development Company Ltd," Behind them small and large boards spread themselves, "Land Brokers", "Agency", &c "Lawyer".
>
> (12)

This dynamics attracts an onrush of new resource-seekers, each of whom produces a fabricated legal paper/document which testifies to the rightfulness of their ownership claim. Gradually we see the appearance not only of nationals of higher classes (such as the feudal-lord-sounding Ruffian Bey) but also international agents such as Dubois and Brown.

Next in the row is Dubois described as "another international gentleman who is not too scrupulous" (n.p.). Dubois arrives with explicitly recognizable purposes: as a surveyor and oil speculator. As he exclaims: "My instructions are to stake out the field" (13); he then "waves his hand, whereupon his assistant gets ready surveying apparatus, while he himself sits sideways on the saddle or the side-car and with ostentatious and noisy enjoyment begins eating" (13). Subsequently, Freddy and Tom approach him and claim that they had met him before in a gambling game where they lost money to Dubois. It is not clear whether Freddy is concocting a fake history in order to swindle and even murder Dubois or not; nevertheless, Dubois does not let himself be ensnared in their gambits. Freddy avers:

> Surely in Pienna! In 1913, May I – Freddy Urlowitz – Baron Freddy – (Laughing) In those days I was still in the Army. Third Cavalry. Of

178 *"Oil Is an Idea"*

course with my memory at Sacher's – What a mad night! You must remember, little Uschi, a real out-and-outer who was there. Really, isn't the world small.

(13)

Freddy then reminds him how at the pub Dubois "took him too high" that night when they met and robbed him of a substantial amount of money. Dubois confirms that he used to be a "vicious gambler" but adds that it is long since he quit the practice. Freddy, however, insists on having his revenge by suggesting that they play another round of card game. Dubois rises to their challenge and outmanoeuvres them. This is, more broadly, reminiscent of the recurring trope/motif of the political-economic dynamics of the oil field (oil system and oil frontier) as a card game involving a master-puppet dynamics – which pervades both *Konjunktur* (1 and 2) and Sinclair's *Oil!* (as discussed in the last two chapters).

In the meantime, Rotti returns to Ruffian-Bey with a legal document that bears his (Rotti's) name as the current owner (rather than Oxhumani's or Ruffian-Bey's), a fact that attests to how he managed to deceive Oxhumani about the true nature and value of her hand and convinced her to sell it to him at a very low price; and now instead of selling it to Ruffian Bey he asserts that he intends to keep it for himself. Rotti asserts how the land is originally owned by the local Ms Oxhumani and that it was left as a common where not only all passers-by could traverse, but Shepherds could bring their herds for grazing. Interestingly, a land which is evidently described as naturally rich and lush ("idyllic" and rich enough to yield crops for flocks) is later re-named as barren and wasteland – a neo-colonial discursive strategy for devaluation of material resources and de-realization of historical reality at the periphery. When Rotti asserts that "There's no talk of any commission now" (16), Ruffian Bey pleads that he reconsider. In response, however, Rotti breaks some bewildering news that reveals the international dimension of the oil matter:

Oh, I'm merely a journalist, I don't understand anything of business, Mme. Oxhumani asked me to do her a little favour, and of course I couldn't refuse. After all you can build your goat sheds anywhere, but there's an Italian Company which is in need of this field (Emphasising) This very field, end they have authorised me –"

(17)

The whole affair ends with an ironic bathos when Rotti gives him a picayune 20 dollars for the hovel Ruffian-Bey has already built there and then dismisses him.

The next scene features the resolution of the gambit between Dubois and Tom/Freddy. As soon as they embark on gambling, they realize Tom/Freddy have no money or guarantor to stake for the gambling. Instead,

"Oil Is an Idea" 179

they suggest to stake their land: "What'll you pay for the land with everything that's on it and in it?" (19) However, Dubois insidiously diminishes the value of the land by calling it barren. Tom contrarily avers: "In two years you'll be pumping oil out of the ground here – Oil I tell you!" (18); in response to which Dubois accentuates both the speculative nature of this claim and the challenges of oil extraction involved: "If the peasants haven't burnt the whole caboodle over my head before then. Meantime I can starve" (18). When instead of selling the field to Dubois for the purposes of gambling, Freddy suggests mortgaging it to Dubois, the latter agrees and asks him to show him the title deeds so that they can sign a contract. Freddy and Tom, however, have no official ownership documents. This further emboldens Dubois to assert: "Really? Perhaps you haven't even signed a contract to purchase? The field may not even belong to you? What then are you doing here?" (19). The tension flares up into drawing guns: Dubois, however, "(Gets ahead of him, and himself draws his revolver) Voila!" and offers them two hundred. In the heat of the dialogue it also becomes clear that Freddy used to be "First Lieutenant, . . . the Cavalry in Olmutz" (20). Notably, Dubois indicates a point that affords us an insight into the national and international implications of the oil discovery: nationalization of oil as a matter of national security and international politics: "The Puritanian Army is in urgent need of instructors, Peasants are getting out of hand and fields must be protected" (19). Ultimately, they reach a concession. They gamble on the field and given that Dubois is a professional swindler and hustler, he gives Freddy and Tom a rout – thereby appearing, allegorically, as the international capitalist who leaves the peripheral nation even more impoverished than the time preceding the discovery of oil in it. Dubois gives each of them a banknote and having forced the two to sign the contract, folds the paper and puts it in his pocket, saying "So, my dear friends, you've got rid of all your cares very easily. You have nothing more to worry about, I'll look after everything. The world is before you again" (20). The challenge that started with the vindictive intention of restoring justice and financial balance (regaining the last loss in the gambling) ends up with Freddy and Tom undergoing an aggravated instance of loss and dispossession. This grotesque irony is further intensified when Dubois hands them his pack of playing cards since their cards are no good. As Dubois states: "Too obvious. I'd like to present you with mine – they're good even for professionals, Please, as a memento" (21).

The next scene (Scene 9) depicts the confrontation between two major powers in *Oil Field*: Rotti and Dubois – who have both emerged triumphant in their dispossession of the true and false owners of the land. Here we witness: "Workmen are fixing boards Right and Left. On Dubois' house 'syndicat Petrolifere', on Rotti's house 'societa Petrolifera'. Music throughout the scene" (21). When Rotti impugns Dubois's ownership claim by revealing a piece of legal evidence,

180   *"Oil Is an Idea"*

> (Here's my contract for sale. It complies with all the necessary formalities of a convenance of real property according to Puritanian law. Look! Place, date, signatures of the vendor, purchaser and two witnesses, There's the purchase price in figures and words),

we see Dubois produce "an even more elaborate document", emphasizing that "[p]rospecting rights are vested in the finder and were legally transferred to me" (22). Finding a rival intolerable, they both start calling each other's documents fake: "Bah! A swindle. What crooks!" to which Dubois counters by: "We'll see what your contracts are worth" (22). This tension suddenly gains international proportions when Rotti introduces himself as "General-Consul of the Kingdom of Bolonia" and Dubois as "Authorized agent and accredited representative of the Republic of Lala" (21). The scene ends on a note of unresolved tension and conflict and with Rotti instructing the workmen: "This field must be staked out by to-night, Do you hear? Where's the barbed wire?" (22).

The next scene features the introduction of further expansions to the oil field with new technological and industrial paraphernalia of oil industry and extraction operations established: "A wireless installation has been fixed on the roof of Dubois's hut. Loudspeaker within bellows. Musical accompaniment from another loudspeaker" (22). Then we hear Loudspeaker make the following announcement: "London speaking. Serious disturbances in Puritania. Newly discovered oil wells –" (22). Significantly, this is the first scene which opens with Loudspeaker announcement rather than a character – which reveals the staggering pace at which the discovery of oil in Puritania has assumed national proportions and global implications. No sooner has the announcement been played than "three people have come forward from the backgrounds; ragged inhabitants of the districts; a little oldish peasant and two goatherds" (22). Equally crucially, Scene 10 introduces a revealing moment/move in the subtle ways through which international powers seek to gain monopoly over national oil resources. This is evidenced by how abruptly otherwise ordinary individuals with no international and political affiliations disclose their true identity and ideological affiliation by introducing themselves as reps of the global powers. This is vividly reflected in the intense and explicit rivalry between Rotti and Dubois. This becomes evident when, for instance, Dubois "shouts louder than the Loudspeaker" and exclaims: "The Republic of Lala is the traditional champion of democracy for the freedom of Puritania –" (23). Dubois is however interrupted by Rotti who harangues about democratic, humanistic, and civilizational values of his state thus: "In the interests of world peace The Kingdom of Bolonia guarantees the liberty of Puritania" (23). Evidently, global powers seek to simultaneously politicize, socialize, and moralize oil by investing it with certain (democratic, humanistic, and egalitarian) social-cultural, moral, and political-economic values, thereby making oil incarnate the magic

"Oil Is an Idea" 181

means of obtaining them. This frenetic outbreak of discursive battles as a means of gaining monopoly over cheap material (oil) resources of Puritania is followed by Loudspeaker's announcement: "The Council of the League of Peoples will hold an extraordinary meeting next week in which the crisis in Puritania (the rest cannot be understood)" (23). A noteworthy scenographic facet of *Oil Field*, which throws into relief the play's materialist and world-systemic vision, is its use of multi-media dramaturgy – including the use of photographs and films projected onto the screen hanging on the backstage wall. The most prominent amongst such elements is the use of Loudspeaker. Indeed one of the principal dramatic ways through which the nearly immediate dialectical-causal connection between the local (as an oil resource frontier) and the global (governed by the dynamics of petro-capitalism) – in the wake of the discovery of oil resources in Puritania – is established through the use of Loudspeaker. This is attested by the announcements made by Loudspeaker immediately in the aftermath of each crucial event or upheaval in Puritania. In one instance, Loudspeaker plays the following: "London speaking. Serious disturbances in Puritania, Newly discovered oil wells . . ." (22). In another we hear Loudspeaker announce: "The Council of the League of Peoples will hold an extraordinary meeting next week in which the crisis in Puritania" (23). This dramatic technique also illustrates not only the time-space compression in the transmission and experience of the rhythms of capital; it also illustrates how a peripheral country (Puritania) – otherwise entirely neglected and insignificant on the international scene – is suddenly thrown into the global limelight (of the news and media) due to its possession of oil.[6]

Scene 11 introduces some natives who return to see what has befallen what used to be their "common" lands or "natural" fields. Here, when a few Puritanian Shepherds approach the land, Rotti, pointing to "the boards which have in the meantime been erected", confronts them thus: "What do you want? Can't you read? . . . 'No admission except on business,' 'Trespassers will be prosecuted" (23). Then, First Shepherd's naïve reply sheds light on this exclusionary politics of space: "This is where they found the oil! There under the stone in our fields" (23). Rotti alerts them to the fact that the lands have now assumed national and international significance; and consequently they are no longer a communally shared, natural landscape. As he states: "The property is sold and there's work going on. Off you go!" (23) The issue of ownership is further compounded when the farmers/peasants and Shepherds come to Rotti and ask about the use function of the field claim: "This is where they found the oil! (to the Second Shepherd) There under the stone in *our* fields" (23; emphasis original). Significantly, Rotti draws a causal correlation between oil and civilization (and modernity). When Second Shepherd, referring to the fact that the appropriated fields have traditionally and historically been "common" lands where they have been allowed to graze their cattle, objects:

## 182 *"Oil Is an Idea"*

"We've always been allowed to pass over these fields", Rotti accentuates the prospective boons of such material dispossession ("But we're getting civilized"). This statement unveils a crucial point: the abstraction of oil (as a discursive-ideological move) manifested in the symbolic link established between oil (as a material resource and commodity) and modern culture and society, including all its associations: industrial and mechanized lifestyle, modern bureaucratic state, and enlightened political rationality. Rotti, nevertheless, makes a point of reminding them of the new foreign owner: "A Bolonian Company has taken over the exploitation of these oil wells, The Company is the sole and only proprietor of the piece of land –" (23).

Then the Shepherds and Peasants ask if the oil is a source of welfare and wealth and belongs to the nation and when their share reaches them. In response, Rotti asserts: "Of course the discovery will be to the advantage of the whole country. For all inhabitants, for the whole of Puritania. (pats the old Shepherd genially on the shoulder) you've got a direct interest there, my friends" (24). The Shepherds then ask about their share of this newly found national treasure specifically and its benefits for them whilst foregrounding the national and global significance and value of oil as a commodity: "How much do we get? We've been told that oil is worth more than all the money there is in Puritania" (24). Rotti assures them of the boons of national oil as a source of prosperity and welfare in the long run. However, he preaches patience and diligence. Rotti's explication of the preliminary stages of diffusion of the simultaneously abstract and material effects of oil in its production of a bureaucratic petro-state illuminates the point at issue: "Patience, my friends. First, the whole country must be developed, Then, if general prosperity, education, and civilisation come, money will flow freely too, Don't worry!" (24). Implicit in this passage is an inkling to how oil acts as a fluid thread through which territory, modernity, bureaucratic power and the petro-state (as a welfare state) are knotted together.[7] Here, Rotti's answer dispels the myth of the immediate and direct economic transformation wrought by oil by alerting them to the necessity of establishing a bureaucratic superstructure and petro-state apparatus as an essential condition of its possibility, that is, as a conduit or pipeline through which the refined rewards of oil can flow into the lives of the nation. These discursive apparatuses, as *Oil Field* shows, are the means of dispossessing the nation of its resources both by the state and the global powers complicitous with an authoritarian national despot/regime.

Contrary to Rotti's claims, however, *Oil Field* illustrates how the local habitat and the locals (including the peasants and shepherds) are undergoing a metabolic rift by being stripped of their traditional natural-ecological and social resources and conditions of their production, sustenance and existence: their livestock, their habitat, their Lebenswelt (life-world), and a meaningful relation to them. Furthermore, the consequent rift between the local experience of extreme economic-ecological degradation and the

"Oil Is an Idea" 183

production of surplus value through the capitalist abstractions of oil at a global scale is evident both throughout *Oil Field* and in the concluding scene. Significantly, *Oil Field* shows the discourse and process of nationalization and the consequent birth of the modern petro-state (as a neo-colonial project) to be an integral part of the abstracting effect of oil as a commodity. In *Oil Field*, as will be demonstrated, nationalism (and the nationalization of oil) is shown to be an ideology endorsed by the global and petro-capitalist powers as a means of gaining monopoly over Puritania's oil resources (by installing a protégé national government) and of ousting the global rivals.

As such, *Oil Field* affords us an insight into how the enclosure of the local-communal ethos, ownership, and social-historical past is implemented through the superimposition of nationalism, a nationalism defined as a unitary claim on identity and predicated on a shared resource – already expropriated by the global powers – rather than a historical consciousness, social-cultural spirit, or shared values. As we will see, this dynamics and logics of nationalization will become more explicit later in the play manifested in the proposed marriage of Oxhumani and Pusspad which is intended to symbolically seal the discursive (the modern petro-state) and the material, the culture and nature, the idea and the matter. Indeed, the dynamics of such a neo-colonially mobilized mode of nationalization is highly consonant with what Michael Watts explicates in the context of oil imperialism in the Niger Delta: "What we have in other words is not nation building – understood in the sense of a governable space – but perhaps its reverse: the 'unimagining' or deconstruction of a particular sense of national community".[8]

The Three Shepherds expose the paradox in Rotti's logic and the consequent ironic dynamics involved in his account of the anticipated outcomes of transforming the land into a site of extraction by accentuating how the discovery of oil has left the locals more profoundly dispossessed, impoverished, and alienated rather than endowing them with the riches of the welfare state. Relatedly, another conspicuous point raised in this scene is the petro-capitalist production of the wage labourer through dispossessing them of their land and stock as well as alienating them from their traditional skills and roles as shepherds and farmers. The poignant irony involved here is that, contrary to Rotti's promise of wealth and welfare, the advent of oil as the dominant economic force leads to the Shepherds' further impoverishment:

OLD PEASANT: (timidly) Can we work for you?
ROTTI: Why, of course.
1ST SHEPHERD: What do you pay?
ROTTI: 25 Cents a day.
2ND SHEPHERD: Food too?
ROTTI: Food? This isn't a Saloon. This is a factory.

184  *"Oil Is an Idea"*

1ST SHEPHERD: (Laughs) Formerly we had 20 cents and food. Now, when oil has been found under our fields, we get 25 without food?
ROTTI: I can't pay any more. If you like you can start at once. Otherwise clear out, I've no use for spectators.

(24)

Subsequently there arises the climactic encounter between Oxhumani and Rotti where she confronts him about his betrayal and her trust by swindling her lands out of her hands at a paltry price under the pretext that he was selling them for her and on her behalf. Marka Oxhumani is introduced as a "buxom Puritanian woman of peasant stock, who plies the oldest profession" (n.p.). She thus seems to be a promiscuous woman (if not a total prostitute). In keeping with the allegorical association of the names of the characters – which makes the place and the characters gain more universal and global resonances, Oxhumani as a name can be construed to not only imply humanity in general. Equally important is the first segment or morpheme in the name – Ox – which, given her gender and the social and racial aspects of her identity (a promiscuous woman from a peripheral country) evokes the associations with nature, a pre-modern and pre-civilizational state, irrationality, flesh, sexuality, instinct, and even animality (given the ox segment of her name). As a dispossessed female figure and the original and true owner of the land on which oil has been discovered, Mme Oxhumani, on the one hand, represents Puritania at an allegorical level, particularly enhanced given her initial presentation in *Oil Field* as someone who needs a legal representative to defend her rights and interests in conjunction with the traditional associations of femininity with passivity, nature/body, and vulnerability aggravated by her sensuous lewdness and moral laxity, and social notoriety, all of which are used by the national and global powers as a pretext for exploiting her. On the other hand, as will be extensively elaborated later, Oxhumani is discursively constructed, by the dominant national state and global powers, as the symbol of Albania.

When Oxhumani objects why Rotti abused the leeway allocated to him and sold the land at a far higher price and pretends to be the owner of the land, Rotti's answer is revealing:

Do you know why I advised you to sell the field? Because you must leave the country. You, a weak woman, alone amongst the mob, in this inferno of stench and madness. In a fortnight there won't be one stone left on the other, In two months we'll have the scum here, from the four points of the compass: in three months we'll have all hell let loose. In six months. . . . They would have taken the fields from you sooner or later. That's how it is! In two months you would have had to part with the field without compensation. What more do you want?

(27)

*"Oil Is an Idea"* 185

Here, significantly, Rotti posits national/local dispossession as an inherent and ineluctable part of the process of the development of a peripheral country (such as Puritania) as a resource frontier in the global map of petro-capitalist system – informed with an uneven logics/dynamics and driven by the logic of surplus accumulation through dispossession. When Oxhumani demands the return of the land, Rotti insidiously reveals his agential and mediatory role: "The only difficulty is that it doesn't belong to me either", adding that it now belongs to "a Bolonian Company". Oxhumani, however, does not relent: "I don't understand business. You said yourself that any rascal could swindle me, and you were right"; then adding, "It's a damned swindle! You wheedled the contract out of me, and its not even paid for" (28). Finding Oxhumani inexorable, Rotti resorts to manipulative means by claiming "That's just it – you don't understand me. And how I loved you!" (28). Seeing through him and his deceptions, Oxhumani insists on having her lands returned to her whilst acknowledging her abject status and precarious position: "Why? Because I'm a simple woman, because I am not so aristocratic as you – Director, President or whatever you are!" (28). Assuming a menacing tone and reminding her of her moral notoriety, condescendingly Rotti offers: "You can get the contract verified at my office" (28). Bewildered at hearing the word "office", Oxhumani laments the injustice inflicted on her and the criminality grounded in oil/land dispossession: "Office? You slave away for your whole life, for twenty years I've been living in poverty, and now this crook boasts of his office! Justice! Is that justice?" (28). Oxhumani's open plea for justice finds an equally deceitful response in the next scene.

Scene 13 ushers in two new stages in the international rivalry over Puritanian oil. Here, the play shows how the dispossessed natives (Puritanians) are targeted by the global powers as a means towards an end. A salient case in point is how the losers (such as the French: Lala Kingdom) and late comers (such as the British Empire represented by Brown) use Oxhumani's case as a oblique means of regaining ownership. A conspicuous example of this transpires when Dubois approaches Oxhumani with a gesture of magnanimous help, introducing himself thus: "I am the representative of the Lala Company which alone has the right – do you understand? The Republic of Lala will never allow a weak woman – a lovely woman –" (29). When Oxhumani dismisses him out of scepticism, Dubois insists: "But you shall have justice dear lady", adding: "You didn't know that there was petroleum in your soil, You believed that you were being paid two hundred dollars for stones and dried grass, So it's quite clear that you were cheated" (29). Seeing crowds of people who have been attracted to the place due to the commotion, Dubois seizes the opportunity to delegitimize and undermine Rotti and thrusts himself as an honest mediator and representative. Jumping on a log, Dubois exclaims:

> Good people, I understand your bitterness, You distrust us because we are foreigners, But there are foreigners and foreigners, I came to

186  *"Oil Is an Idea"*

you as a friend, as your benefactor. Come forward, sir, and tell your compatriots of the good luck that has befallen them.

(29)

This moment affords us a glimpse into the extent to which international oil companies have been purchasing all the lands surrounding the one in which oil has been discovered. An egregious case of dispossession is the field owned by *Yubitch. Singling out Mr Yubitch, Dubois avers: "This man owned a little piece of field. Field do I say? A dung heap! He came to me and asked if I'd like to buy it. Three hundred dollars he asked, And what did I answer, Mr Yubitch?" Wresting confirmation from Yubitch, Dubois shows himself overconscientious by underscoring how he cared about the seller more than himself (landowners) by expressing his keenness to overpay:

> Three hundred, I said – no! Of course there's no oil in your field, I don't know whether oil will ever be found in it. But you shall never think that I've tried to do you. Four hundred dollars I paid. Is that true?

(31)

The description of Yubitch's oil-rich lands in terms of wasteland and dung heap is a familiar orientialist-colonialist trope and rhetorical-discursive strategy undertaken in a bid to misrepresent and degrade the value of the natural resources of the peripheral country.

No other sign or object in the play foregrounds the uneven and dispossessing dynamics inherent in this capitalist exchange than Mrs Yubitch's silk dress. Pointing to Mrs Yubitch, Dubois says:

> Four hundred dollars for a heap of stones. Yesterday a poor man, today – . . . silk – all pure silk. (jumps down from the jog and turns her round like a mannequin. . . . Those who want to be sure that they will not be taken advantage of, those who want to get wealth and happiness quickly – come here.

(30)

It is through references to such unobtrusive details of quotidian life that Lania shows how the expropriative and dispossessing practices of petro-capitalism involve a double dynamics whereby not only the structural means of ensuring the extraction of oil at an undervalued and low price are implemented but also a commodity culture and consumerism is introduced through which the political-economic dispossession is doubled through a process of social-cultural dispossession and reification too (and a double process of dispossession at that) Mrs Yubitch's silk robe emblematically exposes the deceptive and dispossessive nature of an

"Oil Is an Idea" 187

exchange-value-based capitalist economy where one commodity (the silk robe) is nearly devoid of any surplus value whilst another commodity (oil) with which the silk robe has been exchanged through the mediation/abstraction of money does not cease gaining surplus value. This becomes evident when one considers the market value of oil and a silk dress and how the former keeps rising and the latter keeps plummeting due to the nature of the materials involved.

Dubois's publicity stunt instigates an eruption of price rivalry between him and Rotti. When pointing to Oxhumani, Dubois exclaims: "This Syndicate pays the highest prices. Let the horrible tragedy of this widow be a warning to you all, Beware of deceivers!" Rotti retaliates by asserting: "Beware of swindlers! My prices cannot be beaten!" (30). Then, Rotti points to Oxhumani and asserts: "Everybody knows that this widow is nothing but a loose woman" (30). Gradually the crescendo of tense political-economic rivalry between the representative of the two global powers (Italy and France) flows over into appropriating the questions of gender, justice, and egalitarianism as means of gaining hegemony. This is manifested in their definitions of national independence, social morality, and economic fairness in the following terms. Dubois claims: "The Republic of Lala which I represent will never permit national independence to be martyred" (30), prompting Rotti to respond: "Bolonia will never allow bad women to obtain national independence and –" (31). Ironically, the figure who has been used as the fulcrum of the discursive-economic debate is abandoned and neglected by both the national-global powers and the crowd as we see the people throng round the two men to sign contracts with them regarding their lands.

Scene 14 introduces a new character who will prove central both to the fate of certain individuals (including Oxhumani) and to the nation/Puritania. His symbolic role is proleptically manifested by the musical accompaniment to his appearance: "Pusspad sings parody on Faust song" (32). Indeed, as the future President of Puritanian, Pusspad will feature as a crucial agent in determining the dynamics and outcome of the competition over oil monopoly and the future of Puritania as a neo-colonial petro-state. Pusspad arrives at this pandemonium of intense rivalry, appearing as "a grubby and shabby man, who whoever by a stiff collar, bowler hat and despatch case, indicates he is a member or an intellectual profession. He forces his way through the haggling crowd up to Rotti obsequiously" (31). Pusspad introduces himself to the throngs of dispossessed landowners and common natives as a lawyer, well-versed in the subtleties of Puritanian law and constitution: "Nicolas Pusspad from Pureville, Notary. Here's my authority and confirmation by the District Court. (from his despatch case he takes documents which he gives to those standing near him)" (34). As such, Pusspad steps in to provide voluntary help and free legal service for remedying their predicament. Addressing the Puritanians

188   *"Oil Is an Idea"*

(including petit-bourgeois labourers and peasants), he invokes a nationalist rhetoric and spirit:

> Puritanians! Fellow-countrymen! You have met to consider what is to
> be done with your soil and your oil. You have recognised that if every
> one contracts for himself, every one will be cheated, You must stand
> together and appoint me your representative. Its the only safe way.
>
> (34)

Calling the foreign land speculators and oil companies "Capitalistic
sharks" (55), Pusspad proceeds to incite and galvanize people to take
arms and legal action against the expropriation and under-valuation of
their oil-rich lands by offering himself as their spokesperson and representative given his, allegedly, extensive knowledge of the intricacies of Puritanian law as a lawyer. Pusspad refers to how the oil companies stripped
the local/native owners off their lands without the owners' knowledge of
subsoil resources:

> What are you fighting about? (To one group) Have you received any
> sort of offer for your fields at all? No. But you (to another group)
> whose soil is of incalculable value, you have long ago had it taken
> from you at a ridiculous price. This woman here, Marke Oxhumani,
> was cheated in broad daylight. You have all been cheated in the same
> manner.
>
> (36)

Addressing a crowd of natives (including the Shepherds and Peasants) and
pointing to Oxhumani, Pusspad, exclaims: "Yes, look at this woman, It
is foreigners who are robbing us, If we Puritanians will hold together –"
(33). Then Pusspad exhorts them against selling "separately". People's
(particularly landowners') reaction, however, is driven by myopic considerations of individualistic self-preservation, self-interest, personal profiteering, and divisiveness. Accordingly, some of them believe that "First
we must get rid of those who have no business here"; and some believe
that "those whose fields aren't worth anything" should be excluded from
the cause/campaign against foreign oil companies (34). Even when Mrs
Yubitch suggests, "All the contracts which have been entered into up
to now must be declared invalid. Every one of them", her suggestion is
dismissed by her fellow townsmen. This lack of unity and solidarity is
discernible even among the working-class people. When First Shepherd
says "Union alone can bring us good results", Second Shepherd retorts:
"We don't want union. We want decent wages" (35). Ultimately, when
Pusspad draws up a legal document whereby he would be ratified as the
legal representative of the landowners, the people grow suspicious of the
abstruse, legal language used in the document. Subsequently, they tear

*"Oil Is an Idea"* 189

up the document, assault Pusspad, and beat him up. As is evident, due to sheer greed and internal dividedness and conflict, the anti-imperial campaign against the foreign oil companies proves impotent, thus yielding nothing but implosion and further dispossession.

Streaked with a note of grotesque irony and dark comedy, Lania's depiction of the interaction between people and Pusspad reveals not only peasants' and landowners' naivety and greed, but also their displaced distrust and misguided suspicion. The combination of their moral reification (that is, they only trust someone who also has an express economic interest in the issue) and ideological benightedness leads to their aggravated dispossession at personal, local, and national levels. *Oil Field* shows how such an ethos ultimately leads to the seizure and the prospective undervaluation of their lands. In this scene, incited by one another's distrust, the crowd of people eventually assault Pusspad and wreck his shanty office.

Disillusioned and having been beaten bitterly by the peasants and locals and his banner and booth battered, Pusspad is then approached by Brown – who is identified in the character descriptions as "Sam Brown, President of Puritanian Commission of the League of People" (n.p.). Notably, what is referred to in *Oil Field* intermittently either as the "League of Nations" or the "League of Peoples" corresponds to what is called the United Nations in contemporary history. In fact, Brown is one of the few characters whose name and role has survived the revisionary transition from *Konjunktur* to *Oil Field*. Initially, Brown laments the chaos of the situation and then subtly tries to manipulate Pusspad into being his protégé by calling Pusspad's work an "honourable effort", accentuating the national scale of the oil-induced crisis: "The state of your country is terrible. Puritania has become the scene of wild fighting between Oil Companies. An enormous responsibility rests on you, Mr. Pusspad" (43). Even as Brown extolls Pusspad's disinterested neutrality ("Your moral qualities also will be exposed to temptations of the most unexpected kind") he forewarns him that: "They will try to bribe the man who occupies this important post"; and ultimately insinuating himself as his ego ideal (super ego) by implying that amidst this moral wilderness, it is only Brown who stands aloof and unsullied by such filthy, materialist motives: "at every step which he undertakes at the prompting of his conscience" (43). Brown regurgitates all the tawdry discursive tropes and motifs of the colonial discourse, disguised by such unobjectionable and abstract categories as universal humanism, international law, and European civilization/enlightenment: "In this struggle for all the oppressed and the weak you will have the League of Peoples at your back" (43). Pusspad, however, proves to be far from a gullible and naïve person. This is evidenced by the paradoxical point he raises: "My incorruptibility has also to be paid for" (44). When Brown objects that "And you pretend to be the advocate of the weak!", Pusspad accentuates how not only does he need to sustain himself financially for his living but he needs an incentive to resist the temptation of

190 *"Oil Is an Idea"*

bribery from various political-economic sides and powers. Ultimately, they reach a concession in accord with which Brown provides him with the financial resources for establishing a newspaper.

Consequently, Brown and Pusspad forge an alliance whereby Pusspad establishes and runs a newspaper funded by Brown and in which Pusspad is assigned the task of disclosing the corruptions and exploitative treatment of the land, natural resources, and labour forces by the foreign oil companies. In return, Brown promises to support him financially. It soon becomes evident however that Pusspad's newspaper has the missions to not treat all parties neutrally but to exempt one party (the British) from criticism and to target and vilify the rest (the French, Italian, Yugoslavian, etc.). Here we witness the appropriation of media as a discursive-representational means of conducting the battle over material and political-economic hegemony as a means of reaching resource monopoly at a discursive level. When Brown insinuatingly asks Pusspad about the vision and mission of the newspapers, the latter articulates his vision in general moral terms: "Articles about right and wrong" (44). Brown then seeks to politicize and historicize it by inflecting it with political economic interests and orientations and adds: "And about the strong and the weak" (44). When Brown asks him: "And what would be published in such a newspaper?" Pusspad's answer is revealing:

> About the Republic of Lala and about the Bolonians and the Perfidians. I would put them all in their places. I would deal with the international situation. And (putting his hand on his heart) I would be the purest Puritanian – incorruptible to the grave.
>
> (45)

It takes merely a short while however until we find him entirely morally corrupted and politically converted but also complicit in all sorts of cross-collusions.

Suddenly there appears the news of Mr Yubitch's suicide – caused by his dispossession and his realization of how he has been deceived into selling his oil-rich land at a price far lower than its real price. Brown seizes this individual-local event, which would be otherwise of little consequence at the national scale and level, and declares a state of emergency. When Brown exclaims: "Conditions here seem to be quite appalling. The country is handed over without protection to the worst kind of profiteering. Hasn't the country produced even one man? Just one?" (42) Brown's use of national chaos as a justification for intervention through the declaration of a state of exception – based on which the national law and traditions are suspended – instantiates the use of neo-colonial strategy (under the guise of international law) as a means of establishing hegemony and monopoly over the political economy and ecology of a peripheral nation. This neo-colonial-imperial method is akin to the method British Empire

"Oil Is an Idea" 191

deployed in its creation and treatment of the oil-rich peripheral countries such as Iraq and Nigeria (see *Slow Violence* 105–127).

Subsequently, there transpires a crucial juncture in the dynamics of affairs in *Oil Field*. In a statement – where the links between politics, militarism, and economy (extraction of oil as a strategic commodity) become explicit – Brown (from the Perfidian State) declares a state of exception:

> At the request of the League of Peoples, to which the task is entrusted of settling the opposing interests in Puritania in connection with the newly discovered oil fields, I place the Fifth Perfidian Squadron at the disposal of the Puritanian Supreme Command (pointing to FREDDY) which has declared a State of emergency.
>
> (41)

Brown's declaration of a state of emergency on the pretext of Yubitch's suicide strikes us as a grotesquely comic moment whilst being suffused with poignant irony and black humour. This declaration, furthermore, discloses how the impetus and interest of the international law and global community in the national affairs of Puritania is merely driven by extractive incentives (monopoly over oil resources) rather than humanitarian values. Brown's disciplinary decree is readily implemented at a national level manifested in the Crier's announcement: "State of emergency! Anyone found in the streets after 8 o'clock at night will be shot, Anyone found in the neighbourhood of the oil wells without leave will be shot!" (41).[9]

Notably, Brown absolves himself of any imputation of economic investment in the situation: "I have no business interests" (42). Brown's assertion is faced with Rotti's and Dubois's request that he, along with the naval forces, leave Puritania if he has genuinely no economic interest in Puritania since Rotti and Dubois separately own the oil fields adding that: "it's lucky that the oil fields are already in firm hands" by which he means in the hands of the Bolonian/Italian and Lala/French forces as representatives of global powers. However, when the Naval Officer asks Brown whether they should leave or stay, Brown pinpoints a national lack/deficiency and crisis in Puritania and discerning the country as rudderless he declares it precarious and in dire need of international support and national consolidation as a lever to oust the other global powers: Rotti (Kingdom of Bolonia) and Dubois (Kingdom of Lala). As Brown avers: "Conditions here seem to be quite appalling. The country is handed over without protection to the worst kind of profiteering. Hasn't the country produced even one man? Just one?" (42). This is an interpellation and merely a rhetorical question with a double purpose: to seduce Pusspad into assuming the position as an inefficient and pliable protégé and to implement their neo-colonial restructuring of the political-economic conditions of the peripheral country to ensure continuous access to cheap oil and to oust other global rivals. The other reginal and global powers

192 *"Oil Is an Idea"*

express their vehement objections and helplessly leave the meeting whilst putting their military forces at a stand-by and alert position and not ceasing with their relentless attempts to gain monopoly and undermine the government which has granted monopoly over oil solely to the British (led by Brown disguised by his role as the representative of League of Nations). Rotti states:

> In connection with the landing of the Perfidian Naval Detachment I have to state in the name of the Bolonian Government, that the Bolonian Government is prepared to safeguard Bolonian interests in Puritania most decisively, The Cruiser "Liberty" and two torpedo-boats have received instructions.
>
> (41)

This is followed by Dubois's assertion: "In the name of the Government of Lala I solemnly protest against such a demonstration by the Bolonian Navy, and have to give notice that the Cruiser 'Equality' and three torpedo-boats-" (41).

Brown then entrusts Pusspad with the task of prioritizing Oxhumani's case as a nationalist/national case of dispossession. As was demonstrated, Oxhumani has already gained a symbolic status as a national symbol of dispossession, resistance, abjection, and precarity. Notably, the global capitalists' double move – simultaneous dispossession and assimilation/appropriation – finds a paradigmatic manifestation in Oxhumani's condition. First, she is stripped of her oil-rich land by Rotti as the agent of the Kingdom of Bolonia; then, she is appropriated as part of the oil company's rhetoric and discursive move.

## III. Nationalization as Internationalization?

Act Two opens onto a full-blown petroscape. *Oil Field* makes a point of foregrounding the "process" of the "production of extractive space", to wit, a petro-capitalist site of oil extraction:

> The scene has undergone a thorough change. Where formerly there were boards and fingerposts, there stand now the wooden scaffoldings or boring towers, which during the course of the next scene slowly rise in height. The whole of the background shows in perspective (preferably on the back cloth) similar boring towers.
>
> (46)

Here, by deploying an epic theatre technique (V-Effekt or alienation effect), the stage directions underscore the significance of "staging" to enhance critical detachment, thereby alerting us both to the national-international conditions and material-discursive forces that gave rise to

"Oil Is an Idea" 193

it and also the logics and dynamics through which such a new field or phenomenon emerges. As such, the scene blurs the boundaries between historical reality and ostensibly fictional nature of events unfolding upon the stage:

> It is advisable to carry out the change of scene airing the interval with the curtain up, to that the progressive transformation of the originally empty field into a huge mining installation may be seen. This scene changing should be regarded as part of the play.
>
> (46)

This overnight overhaul where a former (Ottoman) colony and a current (neo-colony or rentier) petro-state is morphed into a metropole is reflected in the swarm of native and international workers. And the wooden boards, which metonymically show the ownership structure, act as indicators of the increase in value.

Evidently, this scene illustrates one of the contradictory effects of oil, that is, the way oil totalizes and concretizes social space and social relations while simultaneously re-producing them within and subjecting them to the world of abstraction and infrastructural and economic concealment. Henri Lefebvre's definition of the social space can illuminate the dynamics informing *Oil Field*:

> Though a product to be used, to be consumed, it [social space] is also a means of production; networks of exchange and flows of raw materials and energy fashion space and are determined by it. Thus this means of production, produced as such, cannot be separated either from the productive forces, including technology and knowledge, or from the social division of labour which shapes it, or from the state and the superstructures of society.
>
> (85)[10]

By the same token, in *Oil Field* the social relation, ecological facts (including the condition of the land and natural landscapes) and the logic of self-identification (at personal, local, and national levels) become a symptom of the material, extractive production driving petro-modernity. Lefebvre's account of space can have a revealing bearing on the extractivist logics, uneven dynamics, and reifying effects of capitalist petro-modernity as depicted in *Oil Field*. A focus on the social space as an extractive site not only illuminates how individual and national ownership rights and relations, on the one hand, and national and international/global relations, on the other intersect and entangle. It also illuminates how "property relationships" (that is private or public land and the resources it holds/houses as property) intersect with "forces of production" (ibid. 85). As such, any attempt to ponder and unravel the logics underpinning these spaces entails

194 *"Oil Is an Idea"*

a world-systemic and dialectical thinking grounded in infrastructural and superstructural concerns.

By focusing on the moment of Puritania's transition from a pre-oil nation-state or society to an oil-possessing/producing one, *Oil Field* throws into relief the drastic social and ontological alterations wrought by the introduction of a new energy regime – including the production of a petro-modern nation as a resource frontier. As Bruce Podobnik argues, shifts from one energy system to another are catalyzed by three principal forces within capitalist cultures: commercial competition, geopolitical rivalry, and social conflict.[11] Notably, the three forces or premises coalesce into a recurring conceptual constellation that recurs with variations through the plays explored in this book. By the same token, *Oil Field* illustrates how the three forces play a determining role in the course and dynamics of events at national and global levels. In the play, the fledgling Puritanian petro-state, and the capitalists (and the corporations they form through amalgamation) are tied in an intense struggle with one another. More specifically, within the petro-state, oil inevitably intersects and interweaves the state space, bureaucratic power, and social-cultural forces. The state space encompasses the political space of statecraft (including Repressive State Apparatus), the land/territory, and subsoil deposits. The bureaucratic power encompasses the discursive forces, media, and the Ideological State Apparatus. And social-cultural forces include the elements of symbolization (for instance, Oxhumani as a national martyr and hero) and nationalization. Given the transformation of the peripheral space into a new social-political reality (a resource frontier), along with all due to new energy dynamics and political-economic realities that permeate it, there is no longer any space for the conventional forms of gamblers and traditional charades and charlatans characterizing salon comedy, grotesque comedy, and comedy of manners. Instead we have extraction/extortion of nature, alienation of people, and distortion of facts on a national and international level. Hence, we need a new genre to deal with this new social-historical reality and the political-economic and discursive dynamics permeating it. The formal/aesthetic implications of such political-economic and social-ecological features are attested by the play's combination of epic theatre, documentary (reportage), social and stereotypical realism, and grotesque comedy. A similar logic is discernible in Lania's treatment of characters in that *Oil Field* features no heroes and almost no sense of personal-subjective heroism and leadership.

In fact, the rest of *Oil Field* illustrates how Lania intends to represent the emergence of the petroscape in all its material and symbolic, disciplinary and discursive, as well as infrastructural and superstructural complexities by configuring a manifold space where the boundaries between the political-economic, ecological, representational-symbolic and social-cultural are blurred. This is partly illustrated by the juxtaposition of three

"*Oil Is an Idea*" 195

spatial objects that loom large in *Oil Field* – all three of which undergo an upheaval in the volatile trajectory of the fate of national oil and oil industry. These three include: the site of oil extraction (in the background), Pusspad's dual-function office (at once legal and journalistic), and oil companies' food store or café (in the foreground). The precipitous transformation is reflected not only in the way Pusspad's shanty office (bearing the banner "the Great Puritanian Observer") is

> transformed step by step during the progress of Act, the wooden shanty grows in height and breadth, till by the end of the Act it appears as the "House of Liberty", a palace of sham grandeur, which hides the boring towers which lie behind it from view.
>
> (46)

It is also manifested in the way the Inn Canteen (oil companies' shop) "become[s] equally grand and is transformed" into "Café International" (46). This attests to how in parallel with the development of oil extraction sites there flourishes all the accoutrements – including the consumer spaces and facilities – of the petroculture. The first few scenes of Act Two depict the spiralling rise of the sprawling petro-industrial landscape and extraction facilities. Evident in the hinterland is the extraction processes in full-blown form and the exploitative treatment of cheap labour force employed from among the dispossessed natives. Such a precipitous upheaval of the social-political space and ecological-economic landscape is reflective of the magic effects of oil – which partly stem from "the biotic concentration of time – the product of millions of years of concentrated solar energy, or what Jeffrey Dukes refers to as 'buried sunshine'" that "allows for the temporal acceleration of the pace and productivity of production" (Huber 2014, 7); a dynamics which, in turn, effected phenomena such as time-space compression (David Harvey) and the age of speed (Paul Virilio).

The first few scenes of Act Two primarily substantiate the deceitful strategies of oil companies and global powers by revealing how the lands (variously owned by Oxhumani and Yubitch) previously described as "dung heap" by Dubois have turned out to be "profitable oil field[s]" (49). As Ruffian Bey gloatingly observes to Oxhumani: "Today they (pointing to the workmen) have been digging at the spot where once your goats used to graze. (Pats the goats) Nice animals, They don't get anything either" (49). The tacit parallel here between the dispossessed natives and animals is revealing in biopolitical and existential-racial terms. Here we see the human and nonhuman (natural-ecological) cost of oil capital by witnessing how the oil industry has started its biopolitical ravages by sacrificing the lives of cheap labour forces as indispensable and replaceable means of production. Act Two also depicts the production of new social identities in the aftermath of oil discovery and the rise of the petro-state.

196  *"Oil Is an Idea"*

The play reveals this in a semiotically marked manner with their distinctive costumes. As the stage direction indicates:

> In a separate group the shepherds of the first act, now transformed into workmen. They wear proper labourer's clothes, and in dress and behaviour are distinguished from the peasants who, although very ragged, still keep alive in their comic frockcoats.
>
> (49)

Significantly, Mrs Yubitch's now shabby silk dress is described as "the memory of the rapidly departed days of their happiness" (49).

Running parallel with these operations we see how Pusspad strives to spread his political, social, legal, and economic tentacles as widely as he can by establishing not only a newspaper but also a food canteen for the workers and a legal office for the victimized and exploited. In fact, Act Two opens with Pusspad's account of the alterations that have occurred since the end of Act One. As he observes:

> A fortnight ago I decided to open this shop for food and drinks. The sale of spirits and beer, I thought, is a better source of profit than this fruitless legal business. . . . I hear now to my horror that the Oil Companies intend to open their own canteens. The only way of preventing this is to bring them to their knees.
>
> (47)

The first thought is the erasure of all the residues of the history of former forms of ecological, economic, and social life: "First of all the goats must get out" (47). In a revealing soliloquy, we hear Pusspad explain his machinations to take advantage of the harrowing conditions of the victims of the international oil companies by pretending to sympathize with the exploited workers and dispossessed native landowners. He seeks to wrest profit from the conflicts and tensions between the two parties by pretending to act as a neutral representative and caring mediator (and media representer) whilst remaining willing to compromise all his much-touted moral virtues by embarking on corruptions including bribery, hypocrisy, misrepresentation of the conditions of the workers and natives, and the displacement of responsibility. As he asserts: "it may be that all I have to do is to throw a little light on the utterly unheard of methods of these sharks, who are moreover strangers in this country, against their employees" (47). Indeed, Acts Two and Three more explicitly reveal the magnitude of the oil-induced ecological degradation, exploitation of the working class, and the alienation of the natives (including shepherds and peasants) by divesting them of their conditions and means of production: skills and lands. These points find an articulate expression in Pusspad's speech when he addresses the Puritanian people: "My dear friends, a strip

"*Oil Is an Idea*"  197

of our coast, once so idyllic, lies before you – desolate. Barely a month has been sufficient to turn you, once peaceful country-folk and happy goatherds, into joyless serfs" (47). Pusspad, then, appeals to them thus: "As editor of the Great Puritanian Observer . . . I would like to confide your grievances to me" (47).

Equally crucially, these early scenes feature a heterogeneous host of people – encompassing all the dispossessed landowners (Mrs. Oxhumani and Yubitch), common people (represented by anonymous and generically named men and women), workers (including peasants and shepherds), the exploited (oil workers), and claimants (Ruffian-Bey) – who have gathered at a space between the Inn-Canteen and Pusspad's office to lodge a complaint and voice their grievances against the oil companies' exploitative operations. Each group is encumbered with certain woes and plights. Primarily, the common people complain about the soaring prices particularly at the oil companies' grocery store (or supermarket) which charges the workers exorbitantly. As Worker laments: "at the 'Industrious Digger' prices are too high" (51). The second looming issue is the safety and well-being of the oil workers. Second Woman provides us with an illuminating account of the sheer extent and depth of this (a roster of predicaments):

> Owing to the terrible agitation and unrest more and more of our people are coming to harm. This is the fault of the company because it wants at any price to get oil. They've given up putting up supports, they don't damn off any more and don't put in enough planks, so that there are accidents every day. The pace of the work is inhuman.
> (48)

The oil workers convey to Pusspad their languishing under crushing working conditions inflicted on them by both oil companies: Lala and Bolonia. The oil workers complain about their low wage and overtime work – a situation which has arisen from the intense race, waged by foreign oil companies, over being first to extract oil in commercial quantities and also over gaining monopoly at the cost of jeopardizing the health and safety of workers as dispensable means of production (48). When in response to their complaints, Pusspad first suggests: "This overtime will have to be stopped – at once", the 4th Workman objects: "In that case there won't be enough even for drinks" (48). Importantly, here we see how energopolitics and biopolitics are indelibly intertwined (economic and social-existential precarity). As the 3rd Workman says: "And then we can't take sufficient care, because we are utterly worn out by the long overtime" (48). This betokens the contradictory situation the workers are hurled in by the capitalist system where they need to overwork if they intend to survive. Pusspad crookedly manipulates the Workers' grievances. When they complain about the barely sustainable and outrageously low wages, Pusspad's proposed remedy is telling: "you should be able

198 *"Oil Is an Idea"*

to work overtime and that's your right and you should not be deprived of that right and freedom". Then with a note of striking dark irony and humour, he adds: "Correct. It would be an unheard of attack on the liberty of workman if he were robbed of the right to work overtime" (48). Subsequently, Pusspad takes the workers' details and promises them to publish a critical and scathing indictment of it.

The biopolitical logics and exploitative conditions inflicted on the workers by the petro-capitalist industry and energy regime can be illuminated by considering Marx and Weber's complementary accounts of the reifying effects of capitalism on the labour force. Marx elaborates how to make capital "rich in social productive power, each labourer must be made poor in individual productive powers". Quoting Adam Smith, Marx explains how, for instance, the detail labourer "becomes as stupid and ignorant as it is possible for a human creature to become" (*The Wealth of Nations Smith* (1776) vol. 2, pp. 782–783.) Such a division of labour "attacks the individual at the very roots of his life" by inscribing the logic and dynamics of capital in the very bodies of workers. Consequently, the detail labourer becomes a "crippled monstrosity", "his detail dexterity [forced] at the expense of a world of productive capabilities and instincts" (1967 [original 1867], 360–363). As Marx argues,

> under the present system, if a crooked spine, twisted limbs, a one-sided development of certain muscles, etc., makes you more capable of working (more productive), then your crooked spine, your twisted limbs, your one-sided muscular movement are a productive force. If your intellectual vacuity is more productive than your abundant intellectual activity, then your intellectual vacuity is a productive force.
>
> (1845, 285)

Max Weber's incisive observation can further reveal the anatomo-politics of capital. According to Weber, in the modern capitalist factory, "the individual is shorn of his natural rhythm as determined by the structure of his organism; his psycho-physical apparatus is attuned to a new rhythm through a methodical specialization of separately functioning muscles" (1968, 38). The converse, of course, is the disembodiment of intellect.[12]

Subsequently, *Oil Field* confronts us with one of the most compelling manifestations of the effects of the processes of capitalist abstractions of oil as a commodity in the context of the transition from monopoly to market capitalism, namely, the notion of "shares" (50–52). When Ruffian Bey acridly reminds Old Peasant (who is flaunting the boons of oil capital for himself): "But you're just as much a beggar as we all are", Old Peasant replies: "Beggar? I have shares. They're worth millions" (50). The poignant irony of the situation, however, does not elude First Peasant who seizes it to accentuate: "And with all your millions you can't even pay for a drink" (50). Old Peasant, however, believes that the abstruse

"Oil Is an Idea" 199

mechanisms of the capitalist order (including the world of shares and stock market) elude the knowledge and understanding of the peasants: "You don't understand. Mr Dubois, who gave me the shares for my field, said that they are more valuable than gold, he said, so he did" (50). This is given its final blow revealing its hollowness and sham fluidity by 2nd Peasant: "Then why won't Mr. Dubois give you even 50 dollars for the beautiful shares? Eh? You've been nicely had, you old idiot, (All laugh)" (50). Mrs Yubitch who is present at the scene establishes a contrast between the finite logic of solid commodity/capital (land) and the ostensibly infinite logic of fluid commodity/capital (oil). Then Mrs Yubitch boasts that she has ben shrewd enough to use her money to purchase another land:

> But I've been smarter. Yubitch sold the oil in the field. The oil keeps on coming, so the fellows from Lala can take away as much of it as he likes and it doesn't grow any less. But the money melts away. That's where the swindle comes in. That's why Yubitch shot himself. But with the money he got I've bought myself another field.
>
> (50)

This passage sheds ample light on the dynamics of the process of capitalist abstraction and the fantasy of oil as an infinite resource and an inexhaustible source of capital – a point which evokes the alleged characteristics or claims of capitalism, that is, the phantasy or myth of infinite growth, which Harvey identifies as one of the contradictions of capitalism (see *Seventeen Contradictions of Capitalism* 222–239); however, others alert her to the fact that the remaining un-sold lands are the ones which oil companies were sure to not contain any oil. As Third Peasant counters:

> Yes – and in that field there isn't one drop of oil, and it is so stony that even the donkeys get the dumps when they're driven there. You've got your silk dress as a memento. That's something, Mrs. Oxhumani has only got her two goats.
>
> (50)

Crucially, various characters (particularly landowners) lament how their "solid" lands and their subsoil riches (including oil), once exchanged for money, underwent a magic transformation whereby they turned into evanescent entities which evaporated into the abstract realm of consumer culture, finance capital, and stock market shares. The phantasmatic, abstract, and spectral logic informing the value and dynamics of the characters' stock market shares, consumer commodities, and even money here anticipates the full-fledged features of finance capital which started dominating the scene of global economy from the 1930s (and particularly from 1970s) onwards. More strictly, the logic evoked in this scene of *Oil Field* is in fact readily reminiscent of the characteristics of finance capitalism as

200    *"Oil Is an Idea"*

articulated by Fredric Jameson in "Culture and Finance Capital".[13] Deriving his premises from Giovanni Arrighi's *The Long Twentieth Century*, Jameson underscores the significance of Arrighi's identification of a "dialectical transformation" at the core of the financialization of capital flows whereby "the effects of exchange value and monetary equivalence" cause "a withdrawal from older notions of stable substances and their unifying identifications" ("Culture", 151). Whilst the crux of Jameson's argument in this essay is the demonstration of the causal-dialectical correlations between finance capital's abstract money flows and the increasing abstraction of artistic forms, for the purpose of my argument, I solely focus on his characterization of financialization. The ensuing characterization is illuminating:

> Capital itself becomes free-floating. It separates from the concrete context of its productive geography. Money becomes in a second sense and to a second degree abstract. Now, like the butterfly stirring within the chrysalis, it separates itself from the concrete breeding ground and prepares to take flight. We know today only too well (but Arrighi shows us that this contemporary knowledge of ours only replicates the bitter experience of the dead . . .) that the term is literal. This free-floating capital, in its frantic search for more profitable investments . . . will begin to live its life in a new context: no longer in the factories and the spaces of extraction and production, but on the floor of the stock market, jostling for more intense profitability.
>
> (251)

Identifying the logic of this new form of capitalism as "the form of speculation", Jameson further elaborates how this new mode of capitalism is different from its predecessors: "it won't be as one industry competing against another branch, nor even one productive technology against another more advanced one in the same line of manufacturing" (251). Jameson then proceeds to explain how this abstracting process of financialization in the form of speculation involves a logic where "specters of value, as Derrida might put it, [vie] against each other in a vast, worldwide, disembodied phantasmagoria. This is of course, the moment of finance capital as such" (251).

This scene culminates in a reverberating note – Oxhumani's unremitting gesture of resistance: "And that's why I shall sit here and not go away with my goats till they eat grass again where my land is being torn up now" (50). Having listened to all the grievances of various social groups, Pusspad thus assumes the mantle of the *vox populi* and the popular "representative" of the people thereby mediating between the workers/people and the capitalists (companies and authorities) in his simultaneously imperially inscribed (by Brown) and self-appointed role as the proponent of truth, freedom, and justice. Pusspad promises to workers to be their

"Oil Is an Idea" 201

"speaking tube" (51) and strive to subvert the exploitative political and economic structures: "through that speaking tube your voices will resound with such force that these boring towers will begin to tremble" (51). Subsequently, compiling a terse account of all the afflictions and grievous conditions bred by the oil companies, Pusspad installs the draft of the forthcoming issue of his newspaper like a "poster" outside his booth. The launching headline he chooses for his first issue is an incendiary one: "The Great Puritanian Observer: published Monday. Appalling conditions in the oilfields. Who is responsible?" (51). No sooner has Pusspad hung the poster of the first issue than does the barrage of visits from the heads of oil companies start. Notably, the reactions it provokes in the oil companies' representatives and the information that it consequently elicits from the characters – whilst they are ardently haggling over the ways of camouflaging their exploitative practices and the amount of the bribe – attest to the rampancy of corruption and complicity. It also provides us with illuminating insights into various facets of the exploitative conditions of oil workers and oil extraction sites.

The first to arrive at Pusspad's office in a flustered and furious manner is Dubois. Pointing to the poster, Dubois – as the representative of "the Syndicate Petrolifere" – bluntly asks: "What does that cost?" Taking advantage of Dubois's desperation, Pusspad gloats: "That'll be expensive. The grievances of your workmen fill columns, it may even be said that they cry out to heaven" (51). Trying to diffuse the crisis, Dubois explains how his company intends to redress its operations and improve the conditions: "Our company has therefore decided to meet the workmen still further and to canteens on their own property where we shall sell food and drink to our employees at cost price" (52). Pusspad, however, adds another plight to the roster: "and the people are underfed and cannot keep up the proper rate of work because they are no longer able to pay for the expensive food stuffs" (52). Ventriloquizing the workers, Pusspad further asserts: "the wages are insufficient", adding that "Everyday men are injured because the safety measures are insufficient" (52). Ironically, Dubois weaves his voice into Pusspad's criticism and echoes him as a means of both conscientious acknowledgement and voiding Pusspad's critique of its force. Then he suggests that the oil companies establish their own canteens to provide the workers with food at "cost price". As a last resort, Dubois feels compelled to cut to the chase and disclose their true crude intentions to the detriment of human-nonhuman natures in the periphery and resource frontier (Puritania), whilst once more accentuating the global dimensions of oil as a commodity: "Now then Pusspad, be sensible. All we want here is to get oil out of the ground, nothing else. What the world expects from us is oil and not weakly sentimentality" (52). Then coaxingly trying to mitigate the charge of exploitation, he antagonizes the rival company: "Just between ourselves, we are really not the worst; I could understand it if you were going for the Bolonians, With them it's

## 202   *"Oil Is an Idea"*

the purest profiteering". And finally he proposes a definite solution – bribery: "But we . . . (he pushes a bundle of banknotes towards PUSSPAD) for charitable purposes" and leaves. Pusspad confirms the obliteration of the scandalous truth thus:

> It is a real stroke of luck that my paper will appear as early as Monday, and it remains to be seen whether after my sensational disclosures the workmen will feel any inclination to make the purchases from their murderers.
>
> (52)

The second representative of the international oil companies to arrive at Pusspad's office is Rotti. Acutely cognizant of the reasons underlying Rotti's visit, Pusspad pretends to be "busy with the first number of my paper". With undented self-righteousness, however, Pusspad asserts:

> You are really going too far. No one has the slightest feeling of honour left can possibly keep silent. If ever the Press had a message to give, it is there. A journalist who is conscious of his responsibilities has much sympathy with business, but this particular business is going too far. The country is bound hand a foot and handed over to the worst type of profiteering.
>
> (53)

Then, without any prevarication Pusspad hints at the condition and cost of his silence: "You will be good enough to give up the plan of installing your own canteens. What's written there (pointing to the strip of paper) is, amongst brothers . . . – worth quite a lot" (53). Confronted with Pusspad's question ("Who will speak if I keep silent?") and finding him adamant in his pretentious and strident in his ambitions, Rotti "abandons hope of getting a word, chucks a bundle of bank notes on the table" and shouts suggestively, "Nobody" (53). Then, whilst similarly projecting the exploitative treatment and responsibility onto the rival company ("If you want to talk of profiteering, just go for the Lala Company. You've got a mission there!"), Rotti offers the bribery money (53). The consequent gestural and dramaturgical dynamics of the scene is revealing: Pusspad "cuts off a further big piece from the strip of paper crushes it and throws it into the wastepaper basket" (53), Indeed, the "SHRINKING STRIP of Paper" – the stage direction's description of the draft of the forthcoming issue of the newspaper hung outside his stall by Pusspad as a work-in-progress to provoke and lure the targeted parties – is an allegorical instance of media/news corruption and their collusion in the occlusion of the social-historical facts and their misrepresentation.

The last person drawn to Pusspad's office due to the forthcoming issue is Brown. As indicated earlier, Brown (who seems to be almost certainly

# "Oil Is an Idea" 203

British with some American associations too) paradoxically embodies a double identity and, accordingly, speaks in a double voice. Indeed, Brown's position not only reveals the colonial nature and roots of international law (see later). Equally importantly, it also discloses a discursive strategy through which the boundaries between the League of People/ Nations (of which he is a delegate) and the Empire of Perfidia (of which he is a national and secret agent) are blurred. As we will see, what further compounds this double dynamics is the act of amalgamation of national oil companies into a multinational corporation in a bid to gain monopoly over the world market and guarantee surplus production.

Barraged with Brown's tirade of criticism, Pusspad attempts to morally justify his actions by giving an account of his intentions:

> I started from the point that the eyes of the workers must be opened as to the terrible position into which they have been brought by the Companies. In this way alone is it possible to extirpate the whole profiteering root and branch.
>
> (54)

Then he adds: "The position of the workers is appalling because the Oil Companies think of nothing but their own advantage" (54). Insidiously and subtly Brown starts undermining Pusspad's rational assumptions about the "facts" of oil extraction/production and his moral position as the truth-teller. Brown asks: "And what advantage do you mean by that, Pusspad?" (55). No sooner has Pusspad uttered the words: "Why, [the advantage] from the oil" than Brown assails his position thus: "Has any been found yet?" (55) Whilst acknowledging that not a considerable amount of oil seems to have been found yet, Pusspad nevertheless asserts that "the Companies are raking in money" (55). Infuriated, Brown turns the tables by making an ironic claim: "I thought that those who had done the 'raking in' up to now had been the workers, and those who had done the paying out were the Companies" (55). Finding himself disarmed, Pusspad objects: "But once it [oil] comes –" only to face Brown's harsh interjection:

> Once it comes! Now in the first place it isn't at all sure yet that oil will be found. Secondly, if oil should be found, whether there will be enough, Thirdly, if there is enough, what are we going to do with the oil? Just look at this paper (unfolds a newspaper) which reports that the prices of oil are falling.
>
> (55)

Brown's fallacious remarks here concerning the speculative nature of the amount, market, and value of oil (making it appear as a barely cost-effective undertaking) are part of his deceptive attempts to exaggerate

204 *"Oil Is an Idea"*

the risks and costs involved in the extraction/production of oil to historically confuse, causally complicate, and economically occlude not only the political-economic value of oil on the global scene, but to deflect attention away from the conditions and implications of the oil companies' extractive practices. They are also reflective of a broader concern of the period (1900–1930) regarding oil as discussed in Chapters 1 and 2 regarding the durability, viability, and feasibility of oil as a fuel and energy resource.

Moving beyond the concerns over discovering an inadequate amount of oil, its financial feasibility, and under-production, Brown proceeds to underscore the polar opposite – that is, overproduction – as another risk involved:

> Then if enough oil is produced, there remains fourthly the questions whether the wells are not producing too much. Whoever goes in for higher for oil risks boots and snow-shoes. That, Mr. Pusspad, is where your heroic pioneer work will come in. And then you dare (reads from PUSSPAD's notes) to talk of capitalistic sharks? Have you ever seen wage-paying sharks? (Indignantly) Unless business flourishes here, then your merry goat herds can go back to the morass from which they are most anxiously trying to extricate themselves.
>
> (55–56)

What renders this passage illuminating is its historical accuracy in its reflection of the concerns and discursive measures and political-economic strategies deployed by the international oil companies at the time not only to ascertain the perpetuation of their monopoly and their capitalist mode of production/extraction, but also to maintain the status of oil as the dominant global commodity and strategic resource (see J. H. Bamberg 300–342).[14] Importantly, however, the fallacious reasoning deployed here by Brown to lower the value of the appropriated lands, to cast doubts on the speculatively calculated amount of existing Puritanian oil, and to degrade the value of labour wage on the pretext of the feasibility of economic investment in Puritanian oil and the uncertainty of the future of oil is highly consonant with the ones presented to the Iranian/Persian government at the time by APOC (later BP).[15]

Finding the magnitude of the oil issue (at once national and global) overwhelming, the stakes of the situation dauntingly high, and the logic of Brown's apparently paradoxical demands unfathomable, Pusspad suggests:

> To speak quite frankly, I had my doubts all along. This political struggle is not for me. If you look at things from a higher point of view – objectively – so to say – it will be better if our paper leaves the Oil Companies alone, and I should prefer to write about the beauties

"*Oil Is an Idea*"  205

of the country. I shall write something about sunsets and landscapes and about the cultivation of flowers.

(56)

Brown's response to Pusspad's suggestion of his withdrawal from political-economic issues is explicitly menacing, thus exposing the coercive and military-repressive side of the oil issue. As Brown asserts: "And I shall have you arrested for embezzlement. Did we give you money so that you should write poetry" (56). Then nonplussed – and resonant with Worker's complaint about the contradictory logic of price rise in his conversation with Ruffian Bey – Pusspad moans: "If I write about oil, you're not satisfied, and if I don't write about oil you're not satisfied" either, (56). Revealingly, here Brown reprimands Pusspad for having grossly given material form to, garnering our inklings from Brown's statements, what can be described as the sublime ("ineffable" and transcendental and volatile) abstractness of "oil". As Brown elaborates:

Is this what you call writing about oil? oil is – an idea. And what is it you have made of this great idea? A question of food and drink. Do you know what that is? Utter materialism. Less work and higher wages. As if that were the point now, and not the loftiest possessions of your nation; honour, liberty, independence. It is possible for a nation to attain its ideals through starvation. You must think in terms of politics, of statesmanship, and drink – the crassest nonsense.

(56)

Brown's characterization of "oil as an idea" not only exposes one of the crucial features of oil: its associations with modernity, freedom, and progress, on the one hand, and with magic, the sublime, and the transcendental, on the other. It also reveals one of the pivotal processes – namely, "abstraction" – through which extractive petro-capitalism turns oil into a complex commodity. This abstract quality – effected through a process of abstraction – is amenable to being construed in at least three interrelated senses. As *Oil Field* also illustrates, it is the coalescence of the three under the capitalist mode of production that comes to determine oil as the insurmountable horizon of being in the petroculture. As Coronil acutely argues: "Oil, more than any other commodity, illustrates both the importance and the mystification of natural resources in the modern world" (Coronil 1997, 49).

Primarily, the first facet of abstraction of oil as a commodity and its extraction/production involves its transformation not only into a resource for surplus value, but also a "source value" in its own right (like gold before 1930s and 1970s – when gold was the standard material ground for the stability and assessment of the global value of dollar as the hegemonic currency). This first facet of abstraction can be elucidated if we

## 206 *"Oil Is an Idea"*

consider it in light of Marx's deployment of "abstraction" as a descriptor for the notion of commodity form. Elaborating on the scale and complex dynamics of 19th-century industrial capitalism, Marx scrutinizes the transformation of useful objects into commodities and how the assessment of value in a commodity becomes more complex following its entrance into the capitalist marketplace. Marx claims that this is due to the way in which "the commodity-form, and the value-relation of the products of labour within which it appears have absolutely no connection with the physical nature of the commodity and the material . . . relations arising out of this" (23). As such, part of the abstraction process resides in the schism between the use-value of a commodity and the exchange value imposed upon it by the market – a process which entails the abstraction of a commodity's exchange value from the material circumstances of its production. As Marx explains, this abstraction process is conducive to the emergence of the "phantom quality" which comes to suffuse commodities. This "phantom quality", in turn, obliterates the circumstances of that commodity's creation. Elaborating on the social, ethical, and psychological ramifications of this process of abstraction (commodity-production) and fetishization, Marx explains how this "fetishism" – which "attaches itself to the products of labour" – entails the supersession of the "social relations between men" with the "fantastic form of a relation between things" (168). Marx then indicates how this process occludes the material (natural and labour) history of the commodity's production and distribution, leaving the buyer solely with a price tag to conjecture the value of a product. The outcome of this process is the transformation of a commodity – such as oil – "into social hieroglyph" which leaves the buyer in the position of a speculator attempting to decipher its true value (169). This fetishistic confusion, as Derek Sawyer acutely explains, engenders the "universalisation of the historical":

> To comprehend social properties of objects as deriving from their material attributes is at the same time implicitly to universalise them. Thus, value . . . becomes a property products possess transhistorically, irrespective of their particular modes of production. . . . Capitalist conditions are thereby covertly taken as premises of any and all human sociation.
>
> (Sawyer 1987, 91)

In brief, fetishism (including what Huber calls "petro-fetishism"),[16] according to Marx, pivots on an inversion whereby the social is perceived as material and the historically dependent is perceived as universal and immutable. Marx's critique is particularly relevant when considered in relation to oil and fossil energy more generally because oil – as *Oil Field* strikingly depicts – is also subjected to potent forms of fetishism, abstraction, and reification.

*"Oil Is an Idea"* 207

The second facet of Brown's statement – "oil as an idea" – is concomitant with the first facet (the process of abstraction, commodity-production, and fetishization), namely, double alienation and metabolic rift. As both Marx and contemporary eco-materialist scholars consonantly argue, with the emergence of capitalism – which simultaneously instigates the dissolution of landed property – labour becomes alienated from its "prior communal relation to the Earth", which, under the capitalist mode of production is "'historically dissolved' in its entirety" (Marx, quoted in Foster et al. 2010, 283; see also Marx 1973 [1857/58], 497). As Foster elaborates, the metabolic rift reached a climactic phase during the "second agricultural revolution" (ca. 1830–1880), evidently manifested in both the local (the "antagonistic division between town and country") and the global as "whole colonies saw their land, resources, and soil robbed to support the industrialization of the colonizing countries" (1999, 384; cf. Marx 1973 [1857/58], 485). Foster attempts to specify the tension between capitalist production and the natural environment by emphasizing the contradiction between use-value and exchange value. Foster elaborates on the growth imperative of capitalist production thus:

> It is not use value, fulfilling concrete, qualitative needs, that constitutes the aim of capitalist production, but rather exchange value, generating profit for the capitalist. The abstract, purely quantitative nature of this process, moreover, means that there is no end to the incentive of seeking more money or surplus value, since M' leads in the next circuit of production to a drive to obtain M", followed by the drive to obtain M''' in the circuit after that, in an unending sequence of accumulation and expansion.
>
> (Foster 2013, 2)

In other words, the tendency toward rising productivity and ever-greater expansion is contingent upon the increasing exploitation of resources (such as oil), land and labour, which in capitalism are regarded as "free" gifts of nature. The concept of rift thus illustrates how labour exploitation and environmental degradation are co-determined by the same historical process; namely, capital's unending quest to accumulate and expand.

Thirdly, Brown's invocation of "oil as an idea" can be interpreted to designate how oil has made possible our perception and conception of a whole host of ostensibly abstract ideas, social categories, social-political structures and experiences – an assemblage which altogether we designate as petro-modernity and petroculture. Such conceptions of oil (and fossil fuels, more generally) not only reveal how oil came to feature as the condition of possibility of modern life as we know it (in all its consumer, technological, and infrastructural manifestations), but also how oil came to alter the late modern human's conception of the future too.[17] As indicated in the Introduction of this book, the articulation and conceptualization

## 208 *"Oil Is an Idea"*

of the abstractions that oil makes possible for capitalism is a primary goal of the cultural critique of oil in petrocultural studies. Notable in this regard is Mitchell's incisive argument to the effect that not only was the modern financial system made possible by oil but also the very discipline of "the economy" itself as we know it now, which emerges discursively as an object of knowledge at the historical juncture when oil's elastic and plastic character paved the way for the golden era of capitalist growth. As Mitchell explains, the economy "was an object that no economist or planner prior to the 1930s spoke of or knew to exist"; until then, economic analysis used to solely apply to "government, or the proper management of people and resources, as in the phrase 'political economy'" (Mitchell 2011, 124). When considered more specifically in relation to the petrocultural effects of such a dynamics, Labban's explication of the two pivotal facets of oil – which due to co-extensive existence intensify the abstracting dynamics of oil-driven capitalism – can be illuminating: "Introducing financial logic to the study of oil engenders a space-time parallax between oil's representation as a physical commodity circulating in physical (and financial) markets and its representation as a financial asset circulating in financial (and physical) markets". As Labban further elaborates: "Both are real enough and have their own materiality, but each alone is an abstraction incapable of standing in for the oil market, whose objectivity is produced from the incessant displacement between two space–times of circulation" (Labban 2010, 542).

As such, this description ("oil as an idea") foreshadows the oft-invoked trope of the invisibility yet ubiquity of oil and petroculture (in all their permutations), a phenomenon which is itself an outcome of the capitalist process of abstraction. Indeed, critiquing oil, as Brent Ryan Bellamy and Jeff Diamanti argue, entails including in the discourse its concrete human cost and its apparent immutability:

> You cannot see energy in the way that you can see a barrel of oil, because energy in the concrete is still abstract, and an energy system fuelled by fossil fuels is more abstract still, even though it is determinate of virtually all economic and political capacities today. The critique of energy is . . . a critique of the many barbarisms that flow from the contradictions of late fossil capital; and it is a critique of a fossil-fuelled hostility to the very notion of social revolution – and hence of the very notion of structural dependence too.
>
> ("Phantasmagorias of Energy", xxv–xxvi in *Materialism and the Critique of Energy* edited by Bellamy and Diamanti)

*Oil Field* thus seeks to counter this process of de-materialization not only by exposing the material – that is, social, cognitive-affective, and political-economic – changes it effects at the level of class, race, gender, and nation; but also through its materialist aesthetics and dynamics.

*"Oil Is an Idea"* 209

Notably, what remains latent and silenced in all three international representatives' speeches and their ostensibly rational request for a simple exchange – oil, extracted from Puritania, in exchange for some picayune money given to the oil-owning periphery – is the logic underpinning such a demand (for the extraction and production of a commodity which is globally hotly sought for), that is, the international division of labour – or, what I have been referring to as combined and uneven development – pervading the mode of relationship between the cores and peripheries of the petro-capitalist world-system. As Trotsky indicates:

> Marxism takes its point of departure from world economy, not as a sum of national parts but as a mighty and independent reality which has been created by the international division of labour and the world market, and which in our epoch imperiously dominates the national markets. The productive forces of capitalist society have long outgrown the national boundaries.
>
> (Trotsky 1962, 22)

When in response to Brown's "oil as an idea", enunciation, Pusspad bemusedly observes: "But you said that I was to write about right and wrong, about strong and weak –", Brown abandons all pretension and abstract speech about national rights and moral values and dictates his targets: "About the Lala and the Bolonians. About nothing else. It doesn't matter under what torment the workers produce the oil –" (57). This statement, in contradiction to Brown's former promotion of the newspaper as an "independent speaking tube" (56), attests to the appropriation and deployment of the media and journalism – by the (neo-)colonial and capitalist forces – as a discursive means of naturalizing and legitimizing the hegemony of the dominant forces and their extractive practices. Here, Brown also reveals how far he is from being a representative of a neutral international humanitarian agency (League of Nations); he valorizes the interests of a national side and a certain oil company. Continuing his petro-imperialist catechism, Brown insinuates:

> An enormous responsibility rests on the man who is called upon to write here as the pioneer of a new era. And the maturity of his moral character must correspond to the importance of responsibility. The Lalas and the Bolonians do not possess these moral qualities. Why not?
>
> (57)

When Pusspad intuitively responds: "Because they pay their workers badly", Brown vehemently repudiates a point that is historically factual and morally accurate and, instead, avers: "[no, because] they do not respect the national feeling of the people. That's why the Lalas and the

## 210    *"Oil Is an Idea"*

Bolonians must leave the country" (57). Following the previous indoctrinating statement, Brown continues his ideological inculcation by posing a rhetorical question to Pusspad: "All this merely in the interests of the foreign wirepullers. In this hour Puritania needs – what?" Pusspad too foregoes all pretensions and responds: "The protecting hand of – Mr Brown" (58). Interestingly, Brown does not entirely dismiss such a possibility; nevertheless, he answers: "Not for the moment". So, whilst a now fully indoctrinated Pusspad is eager to succumb to Brown's logic and ventriloquize him by becoming his direct speaking tube or ideological arm, Brown prefers to utilize a less direct and an ideologically subtler manner of achieving his petro-imperial goals.

Brown then proceeds to dictate the two premises, or essential conditions, of achieving the goal established earlier. The foremost necessity for remedying the national catastrophic circumstances is posited by Brown to be a nationalizing movement instigated and led by the media and an "independent" newspaper (run by Pusspad under Brown's directions). As Brown inculcates: "First of all a slogan which shall unite the country. A newspaper which shall stand above all classes and parties, independent of all powers, impervious to all influence" (58). The second essential necessity is an independent national leader according to Brown: "And a leader who by his example shall lead his country to the glorious future which history has reserved for it" (58). This indeed marks the first step towards promoting Pusspad as the first national leader/dictator of Puritania, which is going to transpire slightly later in the play. However this gesture corroborates not only the non-national – more strictly, neo-colonial – origin of the notion of nationalism in Puritania as a discursive move by the petro-imperial power (Perfidia) intended to engineer hegemonic consent over the vilification of specific "foreign powers and oil companies". This national agreement would also facilitate Perfidia's attainment of monopoly over the national resources of Puritania by installing a protégé national dictatorship (headed by Pusspad). Furthermore, by predicating the battle for power on abstract and dynamically manipulable and volatile phenomena – such as nationalist fervour and vilification of the foreigners – the global petro-imperialism (represented by Brown) deflects the nation's attention away from its resources and their material practices and effects (including the question of labour exploitation, class inequality, and nationally-globally uneven nature of extractive practices, oil economy, and resource and wealth distribution) – which is Brown's next move.

Brown is seeking to not only undermine and stigmatize the rival companies (Lala and Bolonia); he is also trying to deflect the public attention (of Puritanians) away from the oil extraction practices entirely, thus ousting the international rivals. Brown is carrying this out through de-materialization and abstraction, that is, away from concrete material political-economic circumstances (including the treatment of the workers, their low wages, the extractive practices) and instead emphasizing the vague/

"Oil Is an Idea" 211

abstract and universally humanistic notion of morality and conscience. "About the Lalas and the Bolonians. About nothing else. It doesn't matter under what torment the workers produce the oil –" (57). Brown urges Pusspad to manipulate the workers by indoctrinating them into a particular mode of national consciousness: "Your country which was once a paradise for innocent peasants has become the cockpit of the sort of profiteers. Lala and Bolonians try to obtain influence over the inhabitants" (57). More specifically, Brown asks him to discursively exploit the notion of nationalism and nationalization as a general, abstract, and mystifying concept under which all genders, races, and classes can be subsumed. The ensuing example corroborates the issue at stake. When, inspired by Brown's provocations Pusspad sees his mission to "open the workers' eyes", Brown, crucially, instructs Pusspad to "not" open the "workers' eyes" (to the material shortages, inadequacies, and deficiencies), but to rather open the "workers' hearts" (58). This point once again throws into relief the politics of emotion as a means of manipulating people, creating abstruse social waves and waves of social feelings whose origin seems to be simultaneously too deep (mythically rooted in the pre-history of a people or nation) and too unconscious – hence at once authentic, too non-rational, and incognito – to define or identify (see Sarah Ahmed 2–18, 42–93).[18]

What further corroborates Brown's political-economic bias – his nationally vested interest and ideological allegiance, rather than being the neutral agent of the international League of Nations – is his exemption of "Perfidians" from any economic corruption and political collusion: "And that's where the Perfidians must take their place" (57). Notably, Brown avers the Perfidians to be "the only safeguard for a true communion between the workers and employers, between foreigners and natives, between burgesses and the peasants –" (57). Brown shows how he is entirely indifferent to the conditions of lower classes, the nation, and the natives and is only preoccupied with ousting the rivals so that the Perfidians can continue the same logics and dynamics of production with monopoly unrivalled. A revealing passage here is "Per ardus ad astra!" (58) – invoked by Brown as a gist of his idea – since it affords us an inkling to the country Brown seems to represent: the British Empire (of which this passage is part of its national motto).

Invoking the mythical logic of the frontier spirit, Brown in effect is asking Pusspad to implement the (il)logic of a state of exception where any sense of legal, moral, and historical "right", law, and "proprietorship" and "history" is suspended in favour of an authoritarian rule of the exceptionalist state (national dictator or the imperial/neo-colonial order) which expropriates and re-defines everything in its own image and favour (see earlier). Furthermore, Brown's (neo-)colonialist rhetoric here becomes more explicit, attested by his use of the word "morass" in relation to the native Puritanians thereby associating the natives with primitivism

212 *"Oil Is an Idea"*

and chaos (lack of rationality, modern order, and civility). This moment vividly exemplifies the petro-state's act of epistemic and material violence in relation to Oxhumani (as the symbol of Puritania – her victimized and subaltern condition – and later as a martyr) conducted through an act of symbolization and discursive assimilation.[19]

## IV. Nationalization Through Petro-Symbolism: The Birth of Mother Nation and/as Petro-State, the Alliance of National Spirit and Natural Matter

The first step towards nationalization is taken by Pusspad by having an earnest conversation with Oxhumani in a bid to convince her to allow Pusspad to present her case – her being swindled out of her lands by the foreign oil companies – in his newspaper as a case of national crisis and dispossession. Oxhumani, however, is highly suspicious of Pusspad's allegedly humanistic motives:

> why do you take on all this trouble and worry? You're not honest. . . . I've never yet been able to get any thing by a swindle yet either. I've never had anything given me in my whole life, Mr. Pusspad. Every coin I've earned honestly. That's why I won't let myself be had.
>
> (62)

Such attitude of cynicism towards gestures of help – particularly when couched in terms of humanitarian and non-materialist motives – is a prevailing attitude among the native Puritanians. As such, *Oil Field* depicts how the reification of social relations is already a rampant feature of the early 20th-century European society where, symptomatically, only those offers of help are trusted which are proposed not under the guise of humanitarian gestures. Finding Oxhumani impervious to his claims about his impersonal sense of duty and sincere motives, Pusspad affirms having a personal interest in her case: "Your field is very valuable now. If you get it back through my help and let me have a share of your profit?" (63). Hearing a familiar note of self-interested profiteering, Oxhumani relents and acquiesces to have her documents photographed and her case presented through Pusspad's newspaper: "If you think it'll lead to business – all right. But I won't let go of the paper" (63).

Another salient point raised in the conversation between Oxhumani and Pusspad is the glimpse it affords us into the infrastructural magnitude of the oil field and its ecological implications. At two points in their conversation, these conditions are vividly illustrated. Firstly, when Oxhumani wonders how it would be possible to have the oil companies removed from her lands whilst "already there are seven drilling machines on my field", Pusspad replies:

*"Oil Is an Idea"* 213

You haven't ordered any drilling machines, Mrs. Oxtumani. You're going to claim that they shall be pulled down within 12 hours, and you will even claim that your field shall be restored to the same condition as before. With all the grass and thistles on it.

(60)

And secondly when Oxhumani forewarns that she cannot afford to defray the costs of Pusspad's offered services as a lawyer whilst expressing her misgivings about the efficacy and viability of such a prosecutor and litigation act ("The companies will never give in"), Pusspad reassures her: "We shall compel them! It's really too insane. Here we have these outsiders with their fat pocketbooks, who place twenty hundredweight of iron on the landscape, shout that they are pioneers, and search for oil" (61).

Furthermore, what this scene renders palpable is the role and function of newspaper as a means of moulding public consciousness; journalism as a conduit through which the war of discourses over material resources (oil, in particular), the politics of representations, and social hegemony is waged. This is corroborated in the world-historical dimension of journalism as reflected in Pusspad's remark:

and your papers – your title deeds – your documents? No one takes the slightest notice of them! We shall show these gentry what a document is. We shall photograph it! I tell you, the World will stare, (in a matter-of-fact tone) Just give me that document of yours.

(61)

As has become evident by now, *Oil Field* shows various functions of journalism. This is variously demonstrated by the identification of two main characters' professions as journalists: Pusspad and Rotti. We recall Rotti's self-description when feigning ignorance about the existence of oil in the land: "I? Oh, I'm merely a journalist, I don't understand anything of business" (17). The politically-economically determining role of journalism and media – at national and global levels – is most prominently illustrated through a focus on Pusspad. As extensively elaborated in Chapters 1 and 2, journalism was not only one of Lania's professional engagements, but also came to structurally inform his aesthetics, particularly manifested in his theory of reportage. Accordingly, journalism features prominently in both *Oil Field* and *Konjunktur* (1 and 2) and fulfils significant thematic, critical, and aesthetic functions. Some of these functions include: journalism as a recorder of and critical commentary on daily, short-term "events" of the petroculture; journalism as a discursive force and means of establishing the values and norms of the petroculture; journalism as a means of critiquing and exposing the exploitative extractive practices at national-global levels; journalism as informed with a world-systemic critique of the extraction and production practices of oil; journalism as

214 *"Oil Is an Idea"*

a means of misrepresenting and disguising the real motives and dynamics of the neo-colonial-imperial practices and intentions of international powers. Indeed, a cogent testimony to the role of the media (including newspapers, periodicals, advertisements) is the extensive manner Standard Oil Company resorted to media and publicity promotion in order to establish an oil-driven and oil-dependent lifestyle (including automobiles) as an indispensable component of the cultural-social ethos, manner of self-expression, and habits of consumption between the 1880s–1920s. This is a period that witnessed the exceeding ascendancy, expansion, and centralization of the oil industry – considerably facilitated by the media and related discursive conduits: an oil industry that pursued the promotion of a "vital car and automobile" culture in the US (see Barrett 2014, 52–62).

Crucially, the mode of journalism practiced by the likes of Pusspad (in their service to the imperial and petro-capitalist powers) runs counter to Lania's vision of the historical and political-economic missions of journalism as well as its functions when deployed as an aesthetic-political method in his plays. Contrarily, in his focus on journalism as a chief means of ideological manipulation and discursive rivalry over political hegemony and economic monopoly, Lania shows his critique of non-independent modes of journalism which we extensively discussed in Chapter 1. In his critical treatment of the nature and functions of journalism and media in the first half of the 20th century, Lania maintains a double focus: simultaneously on the ways in which journalism directs and is directed by the flux and chaos of immediate events of the contemporary history, and on the historically extended and geographically expansive waves of political-economic forces – that is, a world-systemic vision. Such a vision lends us an insight into their logics in the context of conjonctural and longue durée histories.

The next scene features a parallel upheaval not only in Pusspad's position, but also in the fate of the nation, that is, the unfolding of the dynamics towards full assimilation of national oil resources of the peripheral Puritania into the global petro-capitalist network/market through the processes of "vertical integration" and "anti-production". A spatial manifestation of this upheaval is illustrated by Pusspad's office – an alteration which betokens his rise in power in his move towards being appointed as the head of the nation-state (the Puritanian dictator). As the stage directions indicate: "Pusspad's office – now the editorial office of the 'Great Puritanian Observer' – has become a real house. On the walls are large posters, on which Marka is depicted exactly as she was photographed in the last scene" (63). This scene opens onto a world where not only is Pusspad's newspaper (as the dominant news agency that gained ground) hotly sought after, but where the incendiary news of Oxhumani's dispossession and exploitation by the oil companies has been spreading like wildfire. We hear: "Ragged newspaper vendors run across

*"Oil Is an Idea"* 215

the stage shouting 'Great Puritanian Observer's sensational disclosures'. They distribute the newspaper amongst the workmen and peasants who are crowding before the canteen" (63). Significantly, the publication of the issue and the subsequent publicization of Oxhumani's case results in national agitation and insurgency led by the media and the emergent national government appointed by the neo-colonial petro-imperial power (Perfidia represented by Brown). The target of this nationalizing pseudo-revolution is twofold: at once the nationals who are protesting the crippling economic conditions and the "foreign companies" that are extracting cheap oil from Puritania.

Relatedly, throughout *Oil Field*, the banners/billboards (installed mainly by Pusspad and Ruffian Bey) as well as the alterations and revisions to them play a metonymic role in that they betoken larger, national-international, ideological, political-economic, and discursive shifts and developments in the course of the events. Accordingly, the banner/billboard's declarations reveal two concurrent stances. On the one hand, the domestic economic agents who take advantage of the nationalist cause and the vilification of the foreigners for making profit through increasing their prices. On the other, these banners are expressive of the Puritanian people's deep distrust of and critical posture toward foreign oil companies – if independence can be achieved only through expropriation, then corporation control over the industry is revealed as highly undesirable. One salient instance of the use of banners is the one installed by the profiteer Ruffian Bey: "in front of the canteen, a great notice board is being hoisted: PURITANIANS, BUY ONLY FROM PURITANIANS" (66). The installation of this sign has been coeval with – even caused by – Pusspad's publication of a special issue on Oxhumani's case and a clarion call for a national revolution against the foreign companies. Amongst the Newspaper Vendor's shouts ("Sensational disclosure! Tragedy of a widow!"), we gather however, and as anticipated and indicated earlier by Pusspad, Pusspad has utilized Oxhumani's condition to promote and pursue his own profits and political ambitions. As one of the Workers incisively observes later: "Oh, he's great at making promises, but in reality he only wants to make money out of it, just the game as that rogue Ruffian Bey" (67). Here, we witness how other profiteers are seizing the revolutionary moment of "nationalization" as an excuse for increasing the prices and co-opting the market in their own favour. When the Workman objects to the exorbitant price, "Why are you putting up prices?", Ruffian Bey responds: "Look in the newspaper, It's all there" (64). Finding such an explanation absurd, Workman objects: "Now just listen, what has the story of Mrs. Oxhumani to do with the price of bread and whisky?" To which Ruffian responds: "Everything, my friend, everything. Don't you see we are going to be a nation? Haven't you read that? (unfolding a paper, reading) new times are dawning" (64). Adopting a more explicitly nationalist and anti-colonialist rhetoric he avers: "Everybody must contribute his mite, seeing that our

## 216  *"Oil Is an Idea"*

future is at stake – our liberation from the Lalas and the Bolonians" (64). Worker, however, proves perceptive enough to discern the contradictory logic of the situation:

> First of all the price of bread went up because the Lalas and the Bolonians came into the country now it's going up because they've got to be turned out. When no oil is found you put prices up, and if there's any found you'll put them up again.
>
> (64)

This scene depicts the doubly exploitative dynamics of the oil frontier imposed by both the domestic/national and international capitalists and opportunists.

Correspondingly, in parallel with the focus on the macro-economic and macropolitical moves (undertaken by Pusspad and Brown) Lania also a focuses on micro-economic and micro-social issues. A conspicuous element in this regard is the economic crisis which features as a recurring and looming preoccupation of *Oil Field*. The national economic crisis in Puritania – characterized by simultaneous recession and inflation – arises from a host of issues: the political and economic crisis at a national level, including a lack of leadership and an independent national government; Puritania's peripheral-precarious status and its being vulnerable to the exploitative treatment of globally hegemonic powers; the crisis and conflict over Puritanian oil resources between Puritania and international powers, on the one hand, and amongst the international powers themselves on the other.

Few instances so poignantly illustrate the contradictory situation in which the native Puritanians are caught as the act of self-amputation carried out by Old Peasant out of desperation and in anticipation of reward and effort-free charity. The ensuing conversation can shed light on some of his personal motives and their contextual causes. When a dispossessed Old Peasant blurts out: "That's it. Lucky. Now I've done it. Now it can't be undone, That's why I did it", the people surrounding him (including Freddy, other peasants, Mrs Yubitch), agape, ask: "you cut – ?" (72). Contrasting the useless, abstract shares papers with the materiality of bread (of which he is bereft and to which the former – stock market shares – provide no access), Old Peasant then asserts how neither the national economic conditions nor the working conditions are less crippling than self-mutilation:

> My field has gone, and as for the papers which the Lala fellow gave me, I can't even get a piece of bread. Am I to go and work in the pits? No rest by day or night. No proper sleep, no pleasure in the food. If you lie down in the sun the overseer is after you at once. So I said to myself, No. I'll cut off my arm. Then I'll be rid of all worries. Now

*"Oil Is an Idea"* 217

I can't dig any more. (to Freddy) Can't carry a gun either and now I can lie in the sun all right. Let those dig and shoot who like.

(72)

When Mrs Yubitch wonders then how he is going to earn a living, Old Peasant responds:

I don't want anything. I go along by the pits, look at the others slaving, the overseer comes along, gives me money to go away. They don't want to have any cripples standing around the pits. This is enough for cheese and whisky.

(73)

This act of self-amputation indeed serves as an allegorical picture of Puritania and how it feels to see its natural sources exploitatively extracted by the global forces and how it feels to be obligated – due to being under duress – to treat its own natural resources (akin to Old Peasant's treatment of his own body), that is, to let them be cut off and taken away at a cheap price with detrimental ecological and political-economic ramifications.

At an allegorical level, this act of self-mutilation evokes the notion of *oil as curse* which has been widely shared and debated in the national-cultural context of the peripheral countries such as Iran, Venezuela, Nigeria, and Iraq (amongst others).[20] The idea of oil as curse designates a situation where the possession of oil resources – as a valuable globally strategic energy resource – by the peripheral or underdeveloped countries yields "generally perverse outcomes" (Terry Lynn Karl, The Paradox of Plenty, 1997, xv) rather than endowing them with the anticipated unfettered socio-economic progress. The production of this reverse, or perverse, dynamics – evoked by the trope of oil as curse – partly stems from the lack of adequate and efficient political-economic modes of governance at a national level. More importantly, however, it arises from the way the possession of rich oil resources renders the peripheral countries victims and vulnerable to the violent forays of global-imperial powers, including severe sanctions, invasions, and neo-colonial practices, national dictatorships supported by global powers. As a consequence, the "end of oil", as Pérez Schael puts it, is regarded as a happy ending since it made the "blonde man" – Shell and Creole men – leave so that waters could become pure again (1993, 147). Consonantly, discussing the notion of oil as curse in the context of Venezuela, Penélope Azuaje acutely argues:

The modernity brought by oil was viewed through a moral light that construed oil as the destructive agent of nature and culture. And here lies a primordial ambivalence behind the national paradigm: a lingering nostalgia about a lost agrarian past that created a discursive

218 *"Oil Is an Idea"*

tension of simultaneously embracing and demonising the modernising magic powers of oil, as it created prosperity and poverty in the same degree.

(Azuaje 2019, 24)

In a similar vein, this dystopian stance towards the possession of valuable natural and energy resources – such as oil – by a peripheral country finds a cogent corroboration towards the end of *Oil Field* when we are confronted with the self-mutilating Old Peasant once again to learn more about the consequences of his action.

## V. Nationalization, Abstraction, and the Birth of the (Neo)Colonial Petro-State

Subsequently, *Oil Field* depicts the next move – planned by the petro-imperial power (Brown) and performed by the protégé national state (Pusspad). Pusspad conducts his nationalizing mission in a bid to undermine the currently dominant international oil-producing companies (Bolonia and Lala) to supersede them with the petro-imperial force: Perfidia. Pusspad starts manipulating the minds of lowly people – such as Tom and Freddy – by vilifying the foreign companies and identifying them as the source of all miseries within the country. In his attempt to recruit as many people as possible, Pusspad deploys an incendiary nationalist rhetoric to foment the militia and people. Consequently, the people attack the sites of foreign companies and sabotage their infrastructural facilities. There breaks out a violent conflict and an explosion of bloodshed. The process of infusing a spirit of nationalism both through the media and through the military is replete with dark comedy and black humour – an aesthetic inflection that illustrates the grotesque/ absurd and sham nature of a discursively forged national consciousness, and a nationalizing movement by the emergent national state (under the directorship of the global powers).

A brief look at one instance of Pusspad's attempts to proselytize and ideologically convert the people in order to establish an antagonistic spirit of nationalism can illuminate the logics of his discourse. In Act Two, Scene 11, we see Pusspad approaching the two whom we earlier met as amongst the first profiteers of the oil field: Freddy and Tom. Promoting the due rights of the nation now trampled by the foreign oil companies, Pusspad ardently exclaims:

This disgrace must stop. First the cursed foreigners steal our land, and now they steal our money. They must be made to feel the just wrath of the people, Prices will not be lowered. Send me over two honest patriots – immediately!

(65)

## "Oil Is an Idea" 219

Having gathered the former adventurers and thugs – including Freddy and Tom – Pusspad entrusts to them the mission of recruiting an army of committed mercenaries and soldiers (68). Notably, Pusspad's words are couched in a nationalist rhetoric which re-defines not only its social-historical context (Puritania as a unified yet victimized nation) but also its addressee as national subjects and compatriots whose duty it is to defend their nation. These acts of ideological interpellation conducted by Pusspad in his recruitments are consistently punctuated and interlaced with the pervasive presence of drunkenness. On the one hand, drunkenness serves as an element of grotesque comedy which obliquely exposes the sham and hollow nature of the whole process of nationalization and emergence of the national petro-state as an autonomous entity. On the other, drunkenness serves a symbolic role by revealing the people's condition of ideological illusion and false consciousness partly wrought on them by the petro-imperialist ideology. An illustrative example is when Pusspad, finding the mercenaries drunk, exclaims: "So you gentlemen, are the representatives of the patriotic population of Puritania, whose faces flush with shame". When they try to conceal their flushing cheeks (caused by drunkenness) by referring to the "so hot" weather, Pusspad translates their terms into a nationalist ideology thus: "when in your righteous thirst for liberty – drunk with enthusiasm –" only to be interrupted by the naïve commoners who miss his metaphor thus: "(offended) Drunk? I beg your pardon, we are certainly not the least bit drunk. . . . Just on a few whiskies, ridiculous!" (68). Pusspad then solemnly asserts: "In one word, you burn with anger. Your souls are boiling" (68).

Subsequently, Pusspad turns to Freddy – who is an expelled Colonel of the Puritanian Army and sympathetically indicts his expulsion from the army. After drinking to one another's heath and chanting "Long live Puritania", Freddy grabs Pusspad's arm and curses "Those Perfidians that League of People's Army" because they treat him dismissively as a drunkard. Approving Freddy's claim, Pusspad affirms that Freddy is in fact "elevated" not only because of his fervour for his country, but also because "From your youth up your suffered from the shame of your oppressed country" (69). Another moment of bathos and grotesque comedy occurs when the drunkard Freddy and Tom mistakenly refer to Puritania as Fritzonia. Pusspad however reminds them how their parapraxis is because of their national concerns: "You've spent many sleepless nights. Now your patience is at an end" (69). Consequently, the now fully interpellated Freddy and Tom are recruited to carry out the military order and lead the Puritanian army in its confrontation with the forces of foreign oil companies: "For every bullet a dead enemy. Down with the enemies" (69). Then Pusspad explicitly commands them:

> Turn out the foreigners! That's it! If they won't leave the country willingly, they must be made to feel the power of an embittered people,

220 *"Oil Is an Idea"*

You will collect the patriots, men athirst for liberty like yourselves. . . .
And you will storm the oilfields. Violence against violence.

(70)

These scenes evince a mélange of tragic violence, moral gravity, and grotesque comedy. This is reflected in how nearly every ardent and earnest
statement made by Pusspad is punctuated with a comic misapprehension
or hilarious comment by the two drunk officers. Perhaps one of the most
ironic and grotesque moments – evincing the indelible concomitance of the
sublime national spirit and the mundane everyday life and needs – is when
Pusspad utters: "Your whisky or your life! Stick them up!" (70). And later
he adds: "every patriot will join the National Guard! Pusspad will give every
man a gun, a green belt, brown boots and half a bottle of whisky a day"
(71). By imbuing Pusspad's nationalist rhetoric with a commodity logic
(evident in numerous references to market and commodities), Lania intends
to expose not only the intertwinement between politics and economics, but
also how the chief propelling force behind this nationalization movement
is an interest in material resources (above all, oil); in other words, this is
a battle for the monopoly over the national market and resources. The
following example testifies to the point at issue. When Ruffian Bey moans:
"They're not going to buy from us any more. The workmen are going over
into the foreign canteen", Pusspad – consonant with his earlier assertion:
"They know their duty to their country. Puritanians, drink nothing but
Puritanian whisky" – responds: "The workmen aren't such disreputable
scamps as you are" (65). Notably, Pusspad's nationalist ideology leads to
an intensification of domestic or native people – a point which reveals the
boundaries between critically vigilant and false consciousness into relief.
The following moment when Workers and Peasants find Ruffian Bey's profiteering increase of prices all in the name of a nationalist cause unbearable
and some try to justify it is an emblematic case in point:

WORKMAN: Oh, he's great at making promises, but in reality he only
    wants to make money out of it, just the game as that rogue Ruffian
    Bey.
3RD PEASANT: You're a low down agitator! Just look at all the stuff
    that's being served to Oxhumani. And Ruffian Bey isn't even taking
    any money for it.
1ST PEASANT: Just because he is a true-born Puritanian, Not a foreigner,
    Not a Lala or a Balonian.
2ND PEASANT: (to the workmen) You, you've been bribed by the foreign-
    ers to set us against our brothers. Get out of this, (the WORKMAN
    is bundled off)
3RD PEASANT: Come, let's sit down here. We mustn't desert Ruffian Bey
    just when he is making such great sacrifices for us.

(67)

*"Oil Is an Idea"* 221

Lania's rendition of the manner this national consciousness as a neo-colonially induced ideology re-inscribes and re-defines the individual's relation to their local and historical reality – by deploying an array of discursive moves, including interpellation, the development of national consciousness as an ideology, subjectivation, and ideological training – anticipates Althusser's characterization of ideology as something that "represents the imaginary relationship of individuals to their real conditions of existence" (Lenin 109). The other crucial affinity between Lania's and Althusser's conceptions of ideology is their insistence on the "material" basis and nature of this "imaginary relationship". As Althusser explains: "Ideology has a material existence" (Lenin 112) because "an ideology always exists in an apparatus, and its practice, or practices" (ibid.). Ideology always manifests itself through actions, which are "inserted into practices" (Lenin 114), for example, rituals, conventional behaviour, and so on. Indeed, Althusser goes so far as to adopt Pascal's formula for belief. Emphasizing the role of performance and ritual – reflected in his reference to Pascal – "Pascal says more or less: 'Kneel down, move your lips in prayer, and you will believe'" (Lenin 114). Althusser further adds: "all ideology hails or interpellates concrete individuals as concrete subjects" (Lenin 115).

Spurred by Brown's instructions, Pusspad leads the nationalization cause by conducting a military manoeuvre against the Bolonian and Lala oil companies. The next scene exhibits the outbreak of violent conflicts between national and international military forces. In front of Pusspad's house, we hear a fusillade of "Shots off" ensued by a distraught Pusspad who "runs to and fro in great excitement, starts at every shot, gazes out in the direction of the noise" (73). When some workmen "bring in a stretcher with wounded", Pusspad fervently calls them "Victims of liberty" (73). Having violently suppressed the resistances against the exploitation of workers and extraction of oil by the nationalist and socialist groups, Pusspad's authoritarian and protégé government starts emerging and gradually consolidating itself. When all the representatives of the global powers and international oil companies simultaneously visit Pusspad to express their commiseration and sympathy over the violent conflicts, the bloodshed, and the distressing national catastrophe, fomented by one of them – Perfidia – in the first place, Pusspad, ironically, insists on having his state leadership authority and presidential role legitimized through democratic means, that is, by holding a general election: "But not until you have by a general election expressed your entire confidence in me will I accept the heavy burden of power. Puritanians, proceed to the vote" (74). Accordingly, the next scenes feature a furore of national election. Then we see the administration of a general national election which is a show with the international powers (Perfidia, Lala, and Bolonia) as its impresarios and Pusspad as its puppet/protégé. The results are announced. The results – as Pusspad had "predicted" – are 95% in favour of Pusspad.

222 *"Oil Is an Idea"*

Pusspad's subsequent moves towards national leadership role as a dictator are election, marriage with Oxhumani, and the nationalization of the oil fields. All these grand moves, however, ironically culminate in a bathos: the submission and abandonment of national interests in favour of the surplus-extraction logics of global petro-capitalist forces which dictate the cessation of production on Puritania due to the glut and overabundance of oil production around the world and as a pre-emptive move to prevent a price plummet.

The dynamics and historical circumstances surrounding the emergence of two very different political figures at national levels are evocative of Gramsci's account of leadership in similar circumstances. In *Oil Field*, these two figures are represented by a lawyer – supported and installed by the global powers – and by an independent common woman (Oxhumani) whose conditions I have pondered and probed in detail later. My concern here is the striking relevance of Gramsci's characterization in relation to Pusspad, and at an allegorical level the political apparatus in a peripheral petro-state. As Gramsci observes:

> Failing to give [spontaneous movements] a conscious leadership . . . or to raise them to a higher plane by inserting them into politics, may often have extremely serious consequences. It is almost always the case that a spontaneous movement of the subaltern classes is accompanied by a reactionary movement of the right-wing of the dominant class . . . to attempt coup d'eta [sic].
>
> (Gramsci 1971, 199)[21]

In a similar vein, we see how Pusspad – who rose to power under the spurious enterprise of nationalizing oil resources – at once parasitically battens on national oil and an oil-driven nationalism and yet suppresses the spontaneous national resistance movement of common people (symbolically led by Oxhumani) – evidently reflected in his ruthless acts of massacre, imprisonment, and collusion with the global powers. In other words, Pusspad assumes the mantle of a full-fledged dictator even as he appropriates Oxhumani as a national symbol for enhancing the popular legitimacy of his petro-state.

## VI. The Allegorical Marriage of Oil and Idea/Ideology

In his endeavour to fully establish his military dictatorship, Pusspad seeks to nationally consolidate his power and gain public approbation by pursuing a symbolic marriage with the now national figure: Oxhumani – well-known as the "hero" and the "martyr of Puritania". When Pusspad proposes to Oxhumani, however, he encounters a resounding rejection. When he seeks an explanation, Oxhumani replies that Pusspad does not have a basic material income to afford a married family. Flustered,

Pusspad then boasts about "My power" as a solid pivot and evidence of his position and authority. Oxhumani perceptively alerts him to the transient and borrowed nature of it: "A uniform. And that can be taken from you again. But you only want to marry me so as to get my field. I'm not quite such an idiot as that" (77). Then Pusspad refers to his second simultaneously symbolic-material testimony to his wealth/power: "I am the proprietor of the greatest newspaper in Puritania" (77); in response to which Oxhumani contrasts the transience of the newspaper to the permanence of oil as sources of capital: "Today they are reading the paper – tomorrow nobody will want it any more. What will you do then? Oil always has its value" (77). Oxhumani who is now acutely cognizant of her own national symbolic status as well as her presumption of the prospective retrieval of her oil field, asserts: "You see you can't answer me. To marry Marka Oxhumani is a thing that everyone would like to do today" (77). What makes this conversation ironic, however, is Oxhumani's ignorance of her being a discursive-symbolic means in the national-global game. This point is latent in Pusspad's forewarning that "Your field! You haven't got it yet" (76). This is further evidenced by the clandestine agreement between Brown and Pusspad over the appropriation of Oxhumani's case as a pretext or winning card in the struggle over oil resources and political-economic hegemony. As a last resort, Pusspad conveys the news of his soon-to-become-thriving canteen shops and business. On hearing this, Oxhumani avers: "Why didn't you tell me that at once? The shop, that's something definite, That's a business. A thing like that is worth real money" (77). This reaction attests to one of the vexing concerns of *Oil Field*: a belief in materialistic attitude and scepticism towards (however candid) humanistic motives as a rampant trait of the inhabitants of Puritania. Eventually, to Pusspad's proposal of an at once symbolic and material marriage Oxhumani bluntly says: "Your shop and my field – it could be done" (78).

The extended conversation between Pusspad and Oxhumani – where Pusspad vaunts his heroic role in endorsing and advancing Oxhumani's denied rights and promises their restoration and reparation by pursuing revenge on international oil companies – is suffused with a sense of irony, tragic poignancy, and dark comedy. This complex ambience emanates from the audience/reader's (and even Pusspad's) acute cognizance of the deceitful nature of the marriage and of the fact that Oxhumani's oil lands will never be returned to her. What further compounds the sense of tragic irony here is Pusspad's own ignorance of the hollow nature of nationalism and the anticipated wealth promised by the oil nationalization.

The next scene features Pusspad and Oxhumani hand in hand. This, however, should not be construed as merely a marriage of comfort and mutual profiteering. This marriage – a marriage of politics and economics – indeed marks a dialectical synthesis of dichotomies driven by the "rule of capture", national ideology of a petro-state, economic interests, and

224 *"Oil Is an Idea"*

profiteering. This is a symbolic moment that features a synthetic union of Pusspad – as the male agency, as the idea and the spirit or political head of the nation – and Oxhumani – as the female agency, as the nurturing ground on which a nation is based; in other words, Oxhumani/woman as the mother nature or as the mater/matter which provides the nation with its nurturing milk: oil (or an oil-rich ground and its subsoil riches. It is through giving Oxhumani not only a national symbolic status – the "martyr of Puritania" (66) – but also the free lavish indulgent treatment (conferred on her by Ruffian Bey and Pusspad) that common people start believing the fabricated narrative about Oxhumani's status and the authenticity and efficacy of the nationalization movement and story and buy into it. As one of the common people says: "She [Oxhumani] is the richest woman in the country now" (67).

In the meantime and behind the scenes, the play discloses how Pusspad, in his meeting with Brown, already betrays his agreement and bond with Oxhumani by pledging the oil lands as the security for a national loan taken out from the petro-imperial power (Perfidia represented by Brown). As will become evident later, this is indeed what provokes Oxhumani into defiance and resistance; a gesture which, in turn, garners popular support and turns into a national insurgency later. As such, the allegorical status of Mrs Oxhumani and her oil-rich land gains further corroboration in that the acts of betrayal and dispossession – at a national level – are carried out through her and her land. This becomes manifest not only when she is appropriated as a symbol of the oil nationalization enterprise, but also when the land (originally pertained to her) is used as a guarantor and bond for taking out an enormous loan on a national level. When Brown asks "What security do you offer?" Pusspad replies: "The Oil Field of Puritania" (79).

## VII. The Emergence of the Oil Nationalism and the Puritanian Petro-State

The next pivotal stage in the unfolding of the oil-driven national events is the birth of the national petro-state and the nationalization of Puritanian oil resources. This moment is distinctly marked by Pusspad's speech on oil. However, what undermines the validity and viability of Pusspad's ambitious declaration is the historical reality illustrated by the stage direction which precedes his speech and serves as a haunting hinterland against which his speech is set. The ensuing stage direction depicts a scene of international global conflicts and claims staked in the forms of flags on a peripheral ground:

> The Oil Wells. Over the boring tower left floats a Lala flag, over the boring tower right, a Bolonian flag, the whole workings are closed towards the front by a boarding in the middle of which a wide double

"*Oil Is an Idea*"   225

gate is open. At the beginning of the scene workmen are swarming round the boring towers. The gate has sentries in the National Puritanian uniform. In front of the gate a small platform is erected on which sits [Pusspad in full uniform].

(80)

By spectacularizing petro-modernity, this site reveals the marginalization of the human subject – particularly that of a peripheral country (Puritania). This scene vividly manifests oil as the overdetermined fulcrum round which the confrontation and complicity between the national and global forces are formed and revolve. More specifically, this scene illustrates the intensely contested nature of Puritanian oil fields, the current mode of petro-capitalism (namely, monopoly capitalism) pervading the field, and the way the nationalization of oil, ironically, is conducive to the birth of a rentier petro-state. Slightly prior to the birth of the petro-state, as a military-industrial complex, we see Pusspad making a pledge to Brown: "My first law will enact that the Field and Wells are national property. I'll pledge them to you" (79). This moment accentuates how the nationalization of Puritanian oil – ironically – is predicated on and concomitant with the dispossession of the national locals (represented by Mrs Oxhumani) since it is Oxhumani's oil fields – expropriated by international oil companies and then national state – that Pusspad uses as the security bond for his loan from Brown.

Immediately after this we find Pusspad "arm in arm with Oxhumani". Pusspad sits on a platform next to the oil wells, fully clad in the appurtenances of the state apparatus: "full uniform, white tunic, gold epaulets, helmet, decorations, surrounded by several officers" with Oxhumani seated next to him "in magnificent toilette" (80). In his speech Pusspad establishes an inherent intertwinement between soil, oil, and nation based on natural and mythical roots. Notably, he refers to minerals and natural resources as "the rich treasures" and "these [natural] treasures" of the country (81). In his political discourse, Pusspad invokes all the entrenched tropes of petrocultural logic by positing a correlation between nationalization of oil, on the one hand, and national autonomy, culture, modernization, material progress, civilization, and a brilliant future, on the other. In accord with the petrocultural discourse of the 20th century, in Pusspad's speech, progress is tied to material resources and access to them rather than an endogenous and immanent movement arising from the history of the nation (as a polity and ecology), its social-historical forces, and evolution.[22] In this discourse, we discern the interweaving of nation and nature (capitalized and commodified already), between soil (at both material and symbolic levels) and oil:

This is an historic moment for the world, The day of liberty, awaited for centuries, has at last dawned for Puritania. The time of oppression

226    *"Oil Is an Idea"*

has gone for ever. The people of Puritania is now taking its destinies into its own hands. Today we are a small and poor people, but the rich treasures which the soil of Puritania holds are the guarantee of future prosperity. These treasures it is our intention to use in the furtherance of culture, civilisation and the progress of the human race. And I hereby solemnly state that I shall lead Puritania forward towards a brilliant future.

(80–81)

Pusspad's speech provides us with an illuminating instance of the "abstraction" mechanism – as a discursive and political-economic strategy. Through a process of abstraction and sublimation, oil is equated with and transformed into such abstract socio-political ideas and phenomena as democracy, civilization, freedom, and progress – notions which (as simultaneously abstract and concrete, hollow and substantial) are invoked as means of alienation, expropriation, and dispossession.

This is in fact a meta-dramatic moment in that Lania illustrates how the petro-state resorts to dramaturgical techniques and rhetorics to articulate its magic ability to transform a nation from an agrarian stage, to conclude all global oppression, and remedy all economic plights (including unemployment, recession, inflation, and poverty) through the magic power of oil. This situation is reminiscent of the process of the nationalization of oil by various freshly born petro-states which have often had authoritarian national governments in various parts of the world, including Saudi Arabia, Kuwait, Persia/Iran, Venezuela, and Nigeria. A brief consideration of Fernando Coronil's *The Magical State: Nature, Money, and Modernity in Venezuela* (1997) can elucidate some of the imbrications between the situation in Puritania and that in the aforementioned countries. Here, Coronil argues that the Venezuelan petro-state exercised its monopoly over the oil rent dramaturgically, enacting collective fantasies of progress by way of spectacular projects of development and infrastructure to seize its subjects through the power of marvel rather than with the power of reason: "the state seizes its subjects by inducing a condition or state being receptive to its illusions – a magical state" (1997, 5). In reality, however, the Venezuelan petro-state – akin to its Puritanian counterpart in *Oil Field* – "came to be viewed as an enormous distributive apparatus of oil rent money, increasingly hollowed out by a breach between authority and territory, modernity and modernization" (4). As is evident in Pusspad's speech earlier, there is a striking affinity between the conception of oil as a national magic force/commodity by the Venezuelan state (as elaborated by Coronil) and the logics informing Pusspad's invocation of oil as a force underpinning nationalization and national prosperity. As we will see, however, whilst Pusspad harbours highly similar ambitions with regards to oil and its functions for Puritania and himself as its national leader, the global forces come to subvert all his naïve aspirations.

"*Oil Is an Idea*" 227

Coronil explains how the extraordinary oil wealth converted the Venezuelan state into "a magnanimous sorcerer" thereby "inducing a condition or state of being receptive to its illusions – a magical state" (3–5).[23] Underscoring the unviable and unsustainable nature of this dynamics and such an oil-based national identity, ideology, and political economy, Cronin explains how, for instance, the oil crisis of the 1980s dissipated not only the magic power tied to oil but also the "magical spell of the indebted state, delegitimizing its parochial authority and constraining its power over the nation; the president is no longer the magically endowed agent of progress" (392). In a similar vein, we will see how Pusspad's ambition of founding a magic state on the boons of oil is illusory and will only lead to a state of implosion and abortion at personal and national levels – in that rather than culminating in the anticipated national autonomy, prosperity, and progress, the nationalization and production of oil leads to dictatorship, state of emergency, and suppression – all coalescing to make the country devolve into a neo-colonial rentier state.

## VIII.   Anti-Production on the Waves of Oil

Notably, this national moment of the nationalization of oil and the birth of the Puritanian petro-state is ensued with a moment with international and global significance, that is, the speech on oil delivered by Brown. Indeed, this moment not only provides us with one of the most extended insights into the historical conditions of oil and oil production in the early decades of the 20th century. It also marks a critical juncture in the course of the narrative as well as the dynamics of political-economic power in the world of the play. Here explicit references are made to World War I, thereby establishing a link between the whole cataclysmic national events in Puritania (surrounding the question of oil resources) and the actual recent historical event at a global scale. The semiotic and scenographic configuration of the scene is illuminating too. Here, Brown's address to the Puritanian President (Pusspad) and Puritanian nation is delivered from a deserted room in the government palace with the oil fields featuring as the hinterland to this speech: "in the background there is a view of the oil fields" (82). Then we hear Brown deliver the ensuing lines:

> Gentlemen! On a wave of oil that the Allies were carried to victory in the latest Great War to end war. It was the victory of motor lorries over railway engines. Not the abdication of the Emperor of Fritzonia, not the dismemberment of Violinia, not Bolonia's increase in dominion (bows towards Rotti) and not the conquests of the Republic of Lala (bows towards Dubois) – it was oil which was the crown of victory. Before the war the Royal Cockle controlled a quarter of the world produce of oil, and today that Company has at its command more than two-thirds of the world's oil. Such a power confers rights,

228    *"Oil Is an Idea"*

but it also imposes on the men who have the management of that valuable treasure, special duties – above all the duty of unity, of solidarity, of serving the common weal. I am happy to find that we all here are animated by the same feelings.

(82)

Lania's materialist approach to historical events – attested by the primacy he accords to the political-economic agency of oil in global history – is discernible in this passage. We remember from Chapter 1 the remarks included in the program booklet for *Konjunktur* written by the journalist Alfons Goldschmidt: "The world war of 1914–18 was already an oil war. It was carried out with and around oil, around the colonies as oil production and oil sales areas, around the security of the maritime oil bases".[24] Here Brown affirms the strategic value of oil as a global commodity and as an infrastructural and politically-economically determining factor in national and global affairs. In Chapters 1 and 2, I extensively delineated how various global powers – including Britain, the US, France, Italy, and Netherlands – sought to consolidate their monopoly of oil extraction, production, and evaluation processes in the global market through concurring on merging their respective national or private companies into a limited number of companies, including Royal Dutch Shell. I also provided a detailed account of the crucial historical role of oil in determining the course of world wars. This, as we recall, prominently included the use of oil-driven machinery and military-industrial means of transportation as a means of gaining political and military advantage. As we recall, Churchill's conversion of coal-driven ships into oil-fuelled ones was a conspicuous example. Therefore, here I will confine my elaborations to the key term in this speech on oil, namely, the term "wave". It is my argument that wave here has more than a literal and/or metaphorical denotation. The invocation of wave in relation to oil primarily evokes the fluid dynamics, the volatile nature (as a biophysical property), and viscous and volatile materiality and biophysical properties of oil. More crucially, however, the term "wave" here betokens the political-economic logics and historical dynamics of both oil and capitalism. More specifically, the term "wave" designates the scope and mode of relationship between capitalism and nature (including the material/natural resources and energy resources) across the longue durée of capitalism, namely, its wave-like or cyclical movements. In order to discern the implications and the full meaning of the term invoked here by Brown in relation to oil and oil history, it is worth considering the wave-based account of the dynamics of capitalism as variously elaborated by various leftist thinkers.

Many leftist thinkers have already striven to conceptualize the historical dynamics and political-economic logics of capitalism in terms of waves and surges. Prominent amongst them are Kondratiev, Ernest Mandel, and Carlota Perez. Kondratiev's theory of long waves of capitalist

*"Oil Is an Idea"* 229

development, for instance, argues that capitalism moves in waves of 40 to 60 years' duration. And Mandel defines "long waves" of capitalism as cycles of "successive acceleration and deceleration" of capital accumulation (*Long Waves of Capitalist Development: A Marxist Interpretation* 1995). Most recently, and in the context of Energy Humanities and Petrocultural Studies, Andreas Malm conjoins the compelling facets of these theorists to elaborate a wave-based theory or model of conceptualizing this history of dynamic non-equilibrium and articulating an account of fossil capitalism. As Andreas Malm avers: "Capitalist growth is a singularly turbulent process. It moves in spurts and slowdowns, creates and destroys, accelerates and decelerates, clears the ground of established structures for the building of higher stages and tumbles, without fail, into depressions" (162). Providing the periodization of the waves of capitalism from Table 4.1, Malm contends: "The history of the fossil economy takes the concrete form of a sedimentation of layers upon layers – not through gradual accretion, but through successive alluvial deposits from discontinuous, often violent long waves" (165).

Notably, considering the periodization delineated in Table 4.1, *Oil Field*'s inclusion of the political-economic necessity of "anti-production" is a historically accurate depiction of this phenomenon since its historical context (1930s) coincides with the "Downswing" (1914–1945). More specifically, the implicit evocation of the history of capitalism as a wave-based history of uneven resource extractivism, Lania alerts us to the necessity of considering capitalism in the context of its longue durée in order to discern its uneven dynamics and its ecological effects.

The other facet of the trope of the "wave" – namely, the volatility of oil as a material, energy resource, and capitalist commodity – becomes evident in the volatile waves it creates at personal, local, national, and international levels. More particularly, this wave-like volatility is reflected in the paradoxical logics of oil discovery for the nation which endows them with nothing but further dispossession, exploitation, and recession. For the national state and people, the oil production ultimately leads to anti-production, neo-colonization, and the domination of an authoritarian national government. At an allegorical level, this wave-like volatility

*Table 4.1* Upswing and Downswing, *Oil Field* (1934)

|  | *Upswing* | *Downswing* |
| --- | --- | --- |
| First long wave | ca. 1780–1825 | ca. 1825–1848 |
| Second long wave | ca. 1848–1873 | ca. 1873–1896 |
| Third long wave | ca. 1896–1914 | ca. 1914–1945 |
| Fourth long wave | ca. 1945–1973 | ca. 1973–1992 |
| Fifth long wave | ca. 1992–2008(?) | ca. 2008–(?) |

230 *"Oil Is an Idea"*

of the nature and the boons of oil when handled by the petro-capitalist system – in the hands of which "all that is solid melts into air" – is attested by the nature of exchange value as experienced by the characters in *Oil Field*, that is, their selling of their oil-rich land in exchange for money and commodities as a result of which, according to Lady Yubitch and the workers, the money and the wage earned from oil work evaporates and vanishes easily whilst, magically, oil continues to flow and produce surplus value unceasingly. These conditions correspond to the social and political-economic conditions prevailing from the 1920s onward. Also, this condition is reminiscent of Zygmunt Bauman's characterization of the term "liquid modernity" (an emblematic descriptor of the age of oil par excellence) as an age characterized by the radical instability of political-economic structures and logics, cultural forms and social institutions, a reality "never before encountered" (1–2, 69–79).[25] Predicated on these points, we can see how *Oil Field* hints at how oil is only one wave – among many others – on which capitalism moves and has historically moved as the dominant political-economic form and force.

## IX. Amalgamation and Anti-Production

Whilst the national agitations gain momentum in the hinterland – mainly led by Oxhumani as a leading figure who feels doubly betrayed and dispossessed in consequence of Pusspad's refusal to fulfil his promise to restore her lands, the climax emerges when Pusspad, reckoning himself in an advantageous position, approaches the companies with the offer of a new lease for the oil fields, whilst acknowledging that "I am of course prepared to consider the interests of the foreign companies, if Mr. Rotti is willing to pay an adequate sum as indemnity" (82). Pusspad suggests to all three an agreement or contract which involves a combination of leasing the oil fields to them (on the condition of shared profits) and a national loan taken out from international oil companies with the Puritanian oil field as the security or deposit. When Pusspad turns to the heads of oil companies (who are simultaneously the representatives of global powers), he finds himself facing new identities and entities, that is, individuals with new political-economic roles, discursive titles, and ideological alliances. This becomes poignantly evident when turning to all of them, Pusspad says: "Puritania has oil (pointing to Rotti) You want oil – (pointing to Dubois) You want oil – (pointing to Brown) You – please make your tenders" (83). Pusspad is confronted with the disillusioning news that he is dealing with new personal-symbolic identities (as representatives with vested interests) and political-economic entities with new affiliations. Subsequently, to Pusspad's consternation they disclose and disown their former affiliations along with their agreements with Puritania by simply declaring the oil companies null and void due to their being merged into a new entity. As Rotti avers: "I am no longer interested in the business

*"Oil Is an Idea"* 231

of the Bolonian Oil Company", Dubois similarly asserts: "I have nothing more to do with the Lala Oil Company" (83). And ultimately Brown delivers the final blow: "The Petrolifora Bolonian and the Lala-Puritanian no longer exist" (83).

This gambit ushers in a turning point in the dynamics of the power relations and the nature of political-economic entities in *Oil Field*. Pusspad is entirely out-manoeuvred by all the foreign companies when confronted by a whole array of drastic upheavals in the positions and policies of the foreign companies and their heads: their decision to merge into one multinational oil company called the Royal Cockle (a thinly disguised name/code for Royal Dutch Shell). Consequently, Pusspad sees all the promises and anticipated utopian plan evaporate before his eyes. Initially, Brown seeks to justify the decision concerning amalgamation and anti-production as a remedial measure to the sheer inner turmoil at political and economic levels. As he explains to Pusspad:

> The position was really too difficult. The land is in a ferment. Production requires not only large financial means, but also a strong political and military support, and above all unity of leadership. It will be a comfort to you to learn that from now on you will have but a single partner – the Royal Cockle – in other words, the Kingdom of Perfidia.
>
> (84)

The paradox here resides in the equivalence or identity established between a multinational company (Royal Cockle) and one single nation (Perfidia) which implies how that one nation should hold the position of a global empire for this formula to make sense. Then out of desperation Pusspad appeals to Brown as the representative of the League of the Nations (or Peoples) – which is allegedly a humanitarian and neutral organization willing to provide the countries in crisis with help. As Pusspad avers: "You are the representative of the League of Peoples, you are responsible to the League for the protection and the interests of my country – the League of Peoples will not tolerate that Perfidia should swallow us up" (84). Brown however delivers yet another crushing piece of news: "You are addressing yourself to the wrong quarter. Since the Board of the Royal Cockle has asked me to join it, I have, out of loyalty, resigned my position in the League of Peoples. At present I am nothing but a simple Perfidian citizen" (84). This moment reveals the porous lines between the ostensibly neutral international organizations (such as the League of Peoples) and national or international political-economic entities with vested interests – thereby highlighting the colonial roots and neo-colonial goals of the so-called international law (see later). It also throws into relief the volatility of the oil world and the arbitrariness of political and international legal roles and agreements.

232 *"Oil Is an Idea"*

Initially, Brown affords us an insight into the determining role of oil in the fate and outcome of the Great War: "Before the war the Royal Cockle controlled a quarter of the world produce of oil, and today that Company has at its command more than two thirds of the world's oil" (82). Then Brown proceeds to elaborate on the legal and political-economic implications of such a global monopoly endowed by magic powers as incarnated by oil in conjunction with the uneven extractive logics deployed by petro-capitalist system for its "cheap" extraction and production:

> Such a power confers rights, but it also imposes on the men who have the management of that valuable treasure, special duties – above all the duty of unity, of solidarity, of serving the common weal, I am happy to find that we all here are animated by the same feelings.
>
> (82)

Of consequence and note here are the value-laden notions "international law" and "higher justice", both of which involve a discursive gesture of self-appointed and self-assumed position of authority and moral righteousness where an exploitative use of power is recast and disguised in the discourse of "rights", "duties", and "unity and solidarity" along with a rhetoric of "exceptionalism" ("special duties") which practically designate subsumption and devouring of smaller companies countries and areas – which need to be construed and unravelled as designating merely in the exploitative extractivist and imperialist right for one small group in the Western core to decide for the rest of the world. The event of amalgamation delineated in the earlier passage also evidently corresponds to the historical facts of the oil production. As a result of concessions like the ones achieved in Persia/Iran, Iraq, Nigeria, and Albania, "the Big Three oil cartel came to control 70 percent of global oil output by the 1930s" (56). Notably, however, was the infrastructural and discursive (petrocultural) means through which such a global political-economic hegemony was maintained: "By the end of the Great Depression, the foundations of the modern international oil system – corporation/state collusion, regulation of surplus, and manufactured scarcity by means of interlocking partnerships – had been laid" (56).

When Brown starts speaking in the naked language of finance capitalism – utilizing lingos such as "speculative" – "The amalgamation is not carried out for the speculative, but solely for economic ends" (85) – Pusspad feels disarmed and mystified. On the other hand, however, he realizes how he has been blindly ensnared in the globally extended game of capture and uneven extraction like a pawn from the outset whilst being kept under the illusion of gaining political legitimacy, economic authority, and national autonomy. Michael Watts's remarks can illuminate the mode, dynamics, and purposes of such a complicity between the formerly imperial companies (governed at national levels) and the peripheral petro-state (as the resource frontier): "multinational corporations came to be both the objects and agents of what has come to be called 'transnational governance'" ("The Oil Archives" 97; in *Subterranean States: Life Worlds of Oil and Gas* edited by Hannah Appel, Arthur Mason, Michael Watts). Watts defines "transnational governance" as an "array of overlapping laws, voluntary guidelines, and standards, the development of which has been driven by the combined force of professional communities, national governments, and a range of international organizations, NGOs and activists" (97). This is indeed the mode of governance we see to have prevailed in Puritania by the end of *Oil Field* – paradigmatically manifested by the act of "vertical integration".

The logics steering the anti-production decision adopted by the global oil powers in *Oil Field* closely accords with the dynamics of the oil field specifically in the 1930s. Steve Isser identifies this dialectical oscillation between overproduction and scarcity as the "rule of capture" – which as he posits is an integral feature of the petro-capitalist system. As he explicates, the rule of capture had "a strong influence on the structure of the producing sector of the petroleum industry". The "basic pattern" of this rule of capture "was a spasm of overproduction in newly discovered fields, followed by a rapid decline in output as reservoir pressure was depleted" (2016, 4). Isser delineates two reasons underlying such a "production cycle". First, "the common-property nature of oil reservoirs under the rule of capture" and second, "the lack of available credit for the small producer" (4). As he further elaborates, the other challenge was that under the rule of capture the oil firms – and national oil companies by extension – are affected by it in three ways. Firstly, "the value of a unit of reserves declines since if it is not produced today it may not be available tomorrow". Secondly, there are "rapidly increasing marginal costs of production as other firms deplete the reservoir, independent of the individual firm's production decision". And thirdly, considering the surge in production,

> unless the reservoir is amply served by suitable transportation (i.e., pipelines) the high marginal cost of transporting surge production to markets will cause the price at the wellhead to decline even when this additional production is insufficient to effect market price.
>
> (4)

As Isser elucidates, the first two factors "encouraged each firm to maximize its short-run level of production, usually at the expense of long-term production from the reservoir and certainly with regard to the optimal path of production" (4). The third factor however "left the small producer at the mercy of the larger (4). Notably, the position of the minor producer and the fate of the smaller oil firm companies caught in a field monopolized by the main oil companies bears a striking affinity with the fate

234 *"Oil Is an Idea"*

of a peripheral oil-rich country (such as Puritania). Similarly, Puritania lacks not only the technical knowledge, expertise, and facilities for the extraction of oil, but also the production and distribution as well as the transportation facilities for exporting oil as a commodity. These structural inadequacies coalesce to render Puritania (as a peripheral resource frontier) subject to the rhythms and extractive logics and uneven dynamics of the system. I will explore this issue in more depth later.

## X. Petro-Stasis and Anti-Production

If either Pusspad or we (the readers) deemed the news of the dissolution of all the former agreements and identities – in the aftermath of the formation of the multinational oil corporation – as the worst news, we would be mistaken. When everything seems ripe for Pusspad to reap the harvest of his enterprises – both personally and nationally – even under the rubric of a new agreement – he is confronted with yet another foreboding hurdle. Making a further hopeful foray into establishing a contract for oil production, Pusspad naïvely wonders:

> But surely you yourself are interested that the production from your works should proceed without any stoppage or friction. (a saving thought occurs to him) Especially just now when you expect from the amalgamation an increase in production – you surely want to work properly, to work quickly, get a lot of oil – more oil,
>
> (84)

In response, Brown breaks the news of anti-production: "It means that we are blindly chasing after money, but that with a heavy heart we have decided in the interests of a whole-hearted fight against the world crisis to make a sacrifice. We are stopping work" (85). Brown subsequently delivers an extended speech where the naivety of both the logic and ontology predicated on which Pusspad has been proposing his plans collapse:

> The whole world is athirst for oil. It is easy to understand the effort to help to satisfy that thirst. But likewise dangerous. For the world consists not only of those who are athirst, but also of those who have had enough, and the command of justice requires that those who have had enough and those who are athirst, the poor and the rich, should receive the same measure of justice. In this alone lies true democracy. In the interests of that higher justice we have set aside all separate interests, combined ourselves into one sole Company, and have nominated you, Mr. President Pusspad, our first Chairman with an annual salary of 5000 gold ducats. Puritania is a small country, but on the Board of the Puritanian Oil Trust we have given to the Leader of that country the same rights as to the representatives of the

*"Oil Is an Idea"* 235

Powerful Powers. We shall proceed to the vote. The Amalgamated Cockle resolves to stop the production of oil in order to restore the balance between supply and demand which has been upset by the world crisis. Those in favour raise their hands.

(85)

Along with the invocation of oil as a "world driver" – attested by such passages as: "on a wave of oil" and "the whole world is athirst for oil" – which illustrates the global currency of oil as the commodity, what distinguishes this passage is the use of the orally charged word "thirst" which is revealing since it evokes the associations of addiction to oil, oil as a natural or energy resource which is as vital as water, and the overdetermination of the oral zone in hysteria where the drive (as a form of desire) reveals the coexistence of Eros and Thanatos. The second noteworthy point is that "democracy" is here characterized as a means of redressing the law and dynamics of combined and uneven development and distribution of resources – produced in the first place by petro-capitalism itself – whilst in reality it is being utilized as a means of intensifying this uneven dynamics due its reinforcement of global petro-capitalism. As such, this is a characterization that exposes the neo-colonial and ideological nature of international law – and its concomitant institutional arms and legal-political forms such as human rights and democracy – through which the currently global powers (former colonial-imperial powers) seek to perpetuate their hegemony over the rest of the world and its human-nonhuman resources. By the same token, Brown is here camouflaging how this cul-de-sac of recession and crisis (instigated by the acts of amalgamation and anti-production) is not only engendered by the capitalist extractive regime but is actually a preparatory move towards further surplus production.

To justify his apparently illogical decision (which is nothing short of a revolution in the dynamics of oil production), Brown here appeals to the colonial tropes of the "Higher Justice" – decreed by the global order, international law, and humanity at large (as a world category). This is evidenced by his spurious reference to unequal relations "between the poor and the rich" at national and international levels and the necessity of remedying them; a point that evokes the questions of race, gender, class, and ecology. We are nevertheless acutely cognizant of how the notions of Higher Justice and International Law (a re-encoding of the imperial-colonial rule of the West) are deployed as a new discursive guise for the imposition of a state of global emergency whereby the global oil game can be turned in favour of Western powers. The ultimate goals of these petro-capitalist powers are to guarantee the perpetuation of the capitalist system through the continued flow, to ensure surplus extraction, and to maintain monopoly over global market. Consequently, the Royal Cockle company looms large and is assigned a determining role in shifting and tipping the balance in favour of the multinational oil company (which has the global monopoly over oil

236 *"Oil Is an Idea"*

extraction and production) to the detriment of the national interests. The Royal Cockle thus bribes Pusspad into a concession whereby he would fully halt the national production of oil. This concession – which includes an annual salary for Pusspad and reinstating him in his presidential position – in effect renders the Puritanian national oil and national oil company a branch of the petro-capitalist order represented by the multinational oil company. The relational dynamics at stake here is readily reminiscent of the monopoly mode of capitalism characterized by Fredric Jameson:

> It is only with the second or monopoly stage of capitalism, and the emergence of a classical imperialist system beyond the confines of the various national experiences, that a radical aesthetic and epistemological doubt about the possibility of grasping society as a whole begins to be felt: and it is precisely this radical doubt that inaugurates modernism as such and constitutes the representational drama.
>
> (Jameson 1990, 244)

The necessity of prioritizing the global dynamics and logics of the oil market entails the imposition of the cessation of oil-production at a national level. Such a sacrifice of the political-economic life of a peripheral nation in the interests of the global petro-capitalist order is determined by the capitalist concerns of the multinational oil corporation – including the reinforcement of the global value of oil as a commodity, ensuring the cost-effectiveness of its production, and the creation of new market needs by producing new technologies and forms of life. This new global petro-capitalist order comes not only to override the former international agreements, but to transform the whole logics of production and consumption. Correspondingly, rather than chronicling the immense social and economic alterations unfolding in Puritania due to the oil discovery, *Oil Field* shows how almost nothing happens by way of the oil-induced promises of progress, economic plenitude, and social welfare; and "almost" no improvement transpires in the wake of oil discovery. This ironic stasis and political-economic catastrophe (at a national level) arises not merely from the incompetence or corruption of the national government of Puritania, but from a condition imposed on it by the imperial or corporation powers dominating and governing the global petro-capitalism.

It will be illuminating if we consider this counter-intuitive move from the perspective of a Deleuzian characterization and critique of capitalism. In Deleuze's triadic characterization of capitalism – comprising: territorialization, de-territorialization and axiomatization – this moment of anti-production can be considered an integral stage or component of the late capitalist system. As Deleuze and Guattari write:

> the forms of social production, like those of desiring-production, involve an un-engendered nonproductive attitude, an element of

"Oil Is an Idea" 237

anti-production coupled with the process, a full body that functions as a socius. This socius may be the body of the earth, that of the tyrant, or capital. This is the body that Marx is referring to when he says that it is not the product of labour, but rather appears as its natural or divine presupposition. In fact, it does not restrict itself merely to opposing productive forces in and of themselves. It falls back on all production, constituting a surface over which the forces and agents of production are distributed, thereby appropriating for itself all surplus production and arrogating to itself both the whole and the parts of the process, which now seem to emanate from it as a quasi-cause.

(Deleuze and Guattari 1983, 10)

This passage cogently captures the dynamics informing the multinational Cockle Shell's actions concerning the cessation of production. Such an anti-production moment, as Deleuze explains, is a precondition for boosting surplus extraction through the introduction of new and more profitable modes and means of production. This theoretical insight is substantiated by the manner the petro-capitalist order acted in the 1930s right in the midst and aftermath of the Great Depression (as an instance of anti-production). Significantly, the 1930s has been identified, by Matthew Huber, as "the last time the sociospatial organization of life – and energy consumption – was profoundly reorganized" in the USA (2014, 26). Notably, The notion of anti-production as one of the pivotal moments in the life and operational dynamics of capitalist order is highly consonant with the more recently proposed notion of "disaster capitalism" (Klein 2008).

By the same token, there is a subtle but determining falsification in Brown's ostensibly rational argument – that is, there will be no supply without demand. The policy adopted by the multinational alliance and oil corporation concerning anti-production and merging alliances subverts the common-sensical and customary assumption (Say's law) that as long as there is demand there will be supply and capitalist production will continue. The justification proposed by Brown, as an arch-capitalist, is reminiscent of Say's law – which argues that the supply of goods in the market engenders the demand for them – which was vehemently repudiated by Marx (Marx 1973, 94; Harvey 1982, 76). Marx contends how consumption, distribution, and exchange are actually moments of production. In other words, needs (hence demand) are "produced" by the capitalist system. As such, we can argue that Brown is simply deceiving Pusspad about the reasons underlying the decisions made about both the amalgamation and anti-production. Whilst Brown articulates his explanation in the moral-legal terms of "HIGHER JUSTICE", a world-systemic scrutiny of this moment discloses how this decision is propelled by a twofold reason: firstly, to conquer the inner limits of petro-capitalism at

238   *"Oil Is an Idea"*

its stage of development at the time; and secondly, to conduct a radical transformation of the petroscene in the hope of boosting the surplus production and countering resistance. Such a dynamics had already been discerned by Marx when he states: "the true barrier to capitalist production is capital itself" (Marx 1981, 350, 358). Another contradiction besetting both Brown and Pusspad here has been acutely articulated by Mandel: "the supreme contradiction of the capitalist system [is] that between the effective socialization of production and the private, capitalist form of appropriation" (Mandel 1968, 170).

Historically, these two phenomena very closely correspond to the fact of oil production and oil capitalism in the world of the 1930s. On the one hand, there are the issues of boom-bust dynamics, amalgamation of national oil companies into multinationals during the 1920s and 1930s. As Isser explains:

> After WWI the major oil companies became international, integrated giants (Exxon, Mobil, Texaco, Chevron, and Gulf), while a second tier of major companies emerged during this period. . . . Finally, the cycle of recurring gluts on the market during the 1920s, by driving prices down and stocks up to the point where even the integrated firms wanted regulation, would result in the formation of the pro-rationing system. It was the need to protect this system of production control, and those interest groups whose fortunes were tied to it, that would prompt the Eisenhower Administration to establish restrictions on the importation of oil.
>
> (Isser 2016, 3)

On the other hand, what sheds ample light on the lived and petrocultural ramifications of such boom-bust and anti-production vs overproduction rhythms is Huber's elaboration on the latent facet of this anti-production logics delineated in the previous speech:

> While we often think of oil crises in terms of scarcity, the problem of the 1930s (and indeed even parts of the 1980s and 1990s) was the abundance of oil on the market – that is, overproduction, glut, and prices falling below the standards needed for profitable accumulation in the oil sector. This overproduction had a lot to do with the tensions between the subterranean geologies of petroleum and the capitalist system of private property rights that chaotically attempted to delimit access to it.
>
> (2014, 30)

Whilst emphasizing the necessity of accommodating the question of the New Deal as a crucial element for understanding such an upheaval, Huber proceeds to explain how the politics of oil overproduction "paralleled

*"Oil Is an Idea"* 239

the wider politics of the Depression era in that it called into question the viability of the capitalist mode of commodity production for profit" (30). Yet these struggles over oil production can only be understood in the context of the wider New Deal efforts to provide the basis for a new "way of life" underwritten by oil consumption (30). Huber adds a crucial point that helps us establish the otherwise unobtrusive link amongst incompatible phenomena: the unemployment of workers, the abundance of cheap oil, and the introduction a new petro-capitalist logic and a concomitant petrocultural discourse, the latter of which included a new lifeform which included commodity culture, lightening of automobiles, technological facilities. Huber explains how the new technologies – which were part of the new oil order and petrocultural lifestyle – were concomitantly developed with the availability of abundant oil resources and in a bid to create a market for it. As Huber perceptively explains: "'cheap energy' [available in the 1930s] was not simply waiting to be consumed by masses of worker – consumers" but "broader struggles over the production of 'a way of life' in the 1930s were contingent on concomitant struggles with the materiality of petroleum itself" (30). Huber adds how just as "mass unemployment illustrated a dramatic breakdown in labor markets on a national scale, collapse also lurked for the oil industry" (30). This dialectical dynamics leads to the questions of labour force, workers, and employment in Puritania in consequence of the event of "vertical integration".

## XI.  Oil Workers, Global Petro-Capitalism and the National Petro-State

The oppressive restrictions imposed by global forces, operating now under the new guise of multinational oil corporation, breeds a new crisis and wave of national predicaments – which saliently includes a labour crisis. Absolute unemployment reigns in Puritania. The sign board vociferously announces: "NO HANDS REQUIRED. WORK STOPPED" (86). The consequent economic scarcity, and impoverishment reach such a peak that workers and other lower-class people start sabotaging the pipelines in the hope of getting some oil – which, ironically, they will not be able to sell. In the wake of the declaration of the state of emergency, we see the soldiers marching around the oil field and besieging it to protect it and impede any possible mutiny or insurgency.

This situation poignantly demonstrates the native workers' extremely vulnerable and precarious positions: oil workers and lower-class natives whose lives have been entirely left at the mercy of the rhythms and logics of production in the global petro-capitalist system beyond their immediate local world. One of the workers cogently expresses the contradictory vicissitudes of the oil-bound nation: "At first it was impossible to go fast enough for them. Work, work, day and night. I'd almost forgotten what the sky looks like, And now –" (86). And then the Second Shepherd

## 240 *"Oil Is an Idea"*

complements the point: "now you've nothing else to do but look at the sky, the whole day long" (87). Ruminating on the ruin of their former work life as peasants, farmers, and skilled workers (lost in the advent of oil discovery) and the loss of their current work life as oil workers and labour force of the oil industry (lost in the wake of anti-production decision), one of the workers utters: "Formerly there were nothing but fields here, It was not worth much, and the soil. It was poor, but it did give bread. It was poor pasture, but it was enough for asses and goats" (87). Another oil worker states: "Once I was a peasant – but they took my land away, I became a workman – now they've taken away my work" (87). Here the discovery of oil and the advent of international/foreign oil companies are described as a revolutionary moment of alienation, dispossession, and abstraction registered at social, ecological, and economic levels:

> Then they found oil. All at once the soil was worth a lot. Instead of poor corn these fine houses and factories have grown on it, instead of lean grass it has given fat oil, And now? It isn't field any more, it isn't pasture any more, we're not allowed to cultivate any of it, and we mustn't dig either.
>
> (87)

The condition of native and transnational labour force (workers) in the Puritanian oil industry run by the global petro-capitalist powers is consonant with the conditions elaborated by Moore's account of the labour movement and world-ecological and world-economic processes through which capital accumulation is conducted through appropriative forays into uncapitalized or under-capitalized zones and re-producing them as commodity frontiers. In such a frontier space, human and nonhuman nature and lives – indispensable to securing cheap energy, raw materials, food, and labour power – matter only as much as they can be assimilated for the purpose of accumulation (see Moore 2015, 53). Such extractive dynamics are conducive to a precipitous exhaustion of ecological and social-economic conditions upon which their productivity depends; hence the wave-like and periodic movement of capital across the globe from one frontier to another. As Moore elaborates, the world-ecological dynamics of this petro-capitalist system pursues "developments that reward the rapid exhaustion of nature (including human nature), so long as external supplies can be secured" (Moore 2011, 19).

This quote also demonstrates how fossil capitalism as a value system (of exchange and surplus value) works. Here, whilst the value of the land, both as a resource and an asset, and that of the commodity it contains (oil) keep rising, the value and relevance of the labour force keeps plummeting. Marx cogently articulates these contradictions:

> machinery in itself shortens the hours of labour, but when employed by capital it lengthens them; . . . in itself it lightens labour, but when

"Oil Is an Idea"    241

employed by capital it heightens its intensity; . . . in itself it is a victory of man [sic] over the forces of nature but in the hands of capital it makes man the slave of those forces; in itself it increases the wealth of the producers, but in the hands of capital it makes them into paupers.

(Marx 1867/1990, 568–569)

Equally importantly, we should be acutely attentive to the technical and infrastructural modes and conditions of production in oil industry – an industry which was not only far less heavily dependent on labour force, but gradually even reduced this dependency. This dynamics is reminiscent of the mechanical nightmare envisaged by Marx in *Grundrisse*, where the machine "possesses skill and strength in place of the worker" and labour is reduced to "a conscious organ . . . a mere living accessory" (Marx 1939/1993, 693).

The tragic irony of such contradictory capitalist logics is further thrown into relief when the trope of "oil as magic" is invoked. Indeed, throughout *Oil Field*, oil is not only depicted as an abstract commodity and a natural mater, but is also perceived to act as a magic agent endowing the nation with a windfall of effortless wealth and magic transformation into modernity. One of the ways through which the manifold relationship between the nation and nature, between oil and nation, and between oil and nature is depicted is through the correlation between oil and soil – where oil features as a surplus-producing commodity and soil as its at once natural and symbolic container. Amongst its numerous functions, such a parallel serves as a way of accentuating the corrosive and pernicious effect of oil (and, concomitantly, oil industry and capitalist oil extraction) on soil/land – synecdochically representing non-Capitalocenic nature. Notably, the reference to oil in terms of magic or sorcery here is intended to foreground the ironic absence of such an anticipated result or function in the peripheral Puritania despite the fact that, as the 2nd Shepherd objects, "Yet it's still the same soil. And the oil hasn't grown less" (87).

The deconstructive inversion of the trope of "oil-as-magic" – through presenting it as oil-as-tragic when placed in the hands of a petro-capitalist extractive regime – finds its most extended and explicit articulation in Tom's remark:

There's some sorcery about it all, I don't understand it either, Yet I understand all about cards, But to cheat at cards, is no sorcery. And one can do it. Just let somebody show you the trick, and you can copy it. But let one of us copy this; first they dig for oil and get rich on it. Now they don't dig, and get richer still, That is sorcery, if you like.

(87)

Pusspad declares a national revolution and a state of emergency to justify the contradictory decisions and politics which he has been

242 *"Oil Is an Idea"*

instructed to make. Here the workers are invoking the widespread trope or petrocultural imaginary of equating the possession and discovery of oil (by a nation-state) with not only oil windfalls but also its capacity to magically endow great wealth without work. This is indeed the "enchanted" experience promised or evoked by oil and petro-economy. The ensuing arguments proposed by Andrew Apter – in his reflections on Nigeria's oil boom of the late 1970s, elucidate this social-cultural myth: "oil replaced labour as the basis of national development, producing a deficit of value and an excess of wealth, or a paradoxical profit as loss" (2005, 201). This is obviously a paradoxical situation which Apter ascribes to the fact that the value created by oil was "based not on the accumulation of surplus value" but on the circulation of externally generated oil rents and revenues (2005, 14, 201).[26] *Oil Field*, similarly, demonstrates how any national development in Puritania is affected by the overdetermining logic imposed by the global petro-capitalist powers and by the booms and busts of the oil sector. A cogent case in point is the abrupt way everything (including the wheels of the petro-industry) come to a grinding halt, all work ceases, and workers dismissed.

## XII. The Sacrifice of National Oil, Execution and Dispossession of the Mother Nation

The disastrous economic conditions (including recession, inflation, unemployment, and the scarcity of basic material needs) prevailing in Puritania leaves the common people no resort but to take arms against both the petro-state and the foreign forces. The peasants, workers, and shepherds intend to trespass and enter the oil field and sabotage the oil extraction facilities. A conscious hostility towards the "machines" is palpable in these scenes. Consequently, Oxhumani is pushed to a limit where she unwittingly takes on the leading role, and accentuating her claim to her land, the crowd now fomented and spurred raid the oil field and shots are heard. Amidst this pandemonium, Oxhumani is urgently approached by Pusspad in the hope of reaching a concession and of quelling the national turbulence. The ensuing statement by Oxhumani cogently captures the history of personal-national dispossession, the contradictory logics of exploitative core-periphery dynamics in conjunction with the precarious and vulnerable state of a peripheral country subsumed in the pernicious networks of global petro-capital:

> That's my field. They stole it from me because they wanted the oil. Now they don't want the oil they'll have to give it back to me. (to the crowd) I only want the bare field, I'll make you a present of the damned oil. Everybody may carry away as much as he wants.

(89)

*"Oil Is an Idea"* 243

What renders this moment distinctive is the dawn of a new socialist voice and nationalist consciousness – whilst we are poignantly aware of the tragic fate and outcome of nationalization (leading to anti-production stasis and slump) – but nevertheless a faint flicker of a new consciousness and resistance is audible here.

The revolutionary movement and the violent conflicts between the opposing sides gain momentum reaching a liminal point where, if not violently suppressed, the revolutionary forces will gain ascendancy over the state and foreign forces. Consequently, Brown holds an emergency meeting with Pusspad. The stage direction's description of Pusspad is illuminating: "Under that look [Pusspad] is like a schoolboy who, half sulkily half frightened, awaits a severe reprimand" (90). This implies both a childish foolishness (lack political rationality) and a childlike innocence – both of which would be accurate description of Pusspad's simultaneously naïve, self-interested, and nationalist attitude. Finding Pusspad in a defiant spirit and ready to abdicate, Brown in a colonially infantilizing and coaxing manner tries to wheedle Pusspad into exerting utmost military force to suppress the national revolutionary forces by already calling him the "Hero" of a national "Tragedy" (90). Pusspad, however, refuses to follow this oppressive order and delivers an ardent reply which nearly sums up the principal events of the play:

> did you really believe that Pusspad could be bought like the first backstreet attorney you meet! On your instructions I supply a little revolution, so that you may settle your affairs more easily. I am satisfied with being your obedient servant, I arrange to get the land into your hands, put you in possession of the treasures of our soil, I deceive the population, betray the ideas in which it believes, I risk my head – isn't that how you expected things? Yes, and what do I get? It is possible that I may be a scoundrel, but you'll find that Pusspad definitely is not an idiot.
>
> (91)

Then Pusspad declares his resignation saying "I am going back to my native village" (91) only to face Brown's grimly menacing note: "The penalty for desertion is death. It's in the penal code of every State" (92). When Pusspad deems this merely a threat or joke, Brown expresses the order more bluntly: "There is no question of wish – it's a question of must" (92). Importantly, Brown reminds Pusspad of a compromise global powers made in favour of Pusspad: the recognition of Puritania as an independent nation-state and of the legitimacy of Pusspad's government:

> That is why we have recognized you, given you our support, political, military, and financial – and so we must look to you. Your retreat

244  *"Oil Is an Idea"*

means chaos, and chaos means the destruction of our property. That
is why you cannot go back.

(92)

As we may recall, the interdependence of access to cheap oil and national
recognition by global powers is resonant with what happened in Albania –
as depicted in *Konjunktur* (1 and 2) and discussed at length in Chapters
1 and 2. What remains latent in Brown's reminder, however, is how such
an agreement (between him and Pusspad) was in fact cemented, that is,
in exchange for providing global powers with access to cheap oil; an
agreement which, ironically, exposes the neo-colonial nature of the international law presided over by the hegemonic powers.

When Pusspad laments: "You are to blame. The stopping of the works"
(93), Brown once again utilizes the abstract and mystifying rhetoric
of objective economics to justify the global system's petro-capitalist
rationality:

[The stopping of the works] was the imperative command of rational
economics, You may condemn this policy and upset it if you like.
Then your place is out there (pointing out of the window) From that
point you must go ahead, Take our fields away, divide the land among
the population.

(93)

Brown exhorts Pusspad to abandon "jests and bluff" since "the hour is
too serious" (93). Subsequently, Brown strives to establish the legitimacy,
necessity, and moral righteousness of the suppression of the national resistance forces (led by Oxhumani) as an ineluctable step by de-historiciz-
ing and de-individualizing the dynamics and agency of this act. Brown
accomplishes this through a discursive sleight of the hand: by couching his
rationalization in a rhetoric that borders on Buddhist fatalism or cosmic
determinism, thereby absolving not only himself and Pusspad of moral-
legal responsibility but the entire system of its acts of violent dispossession
and suppression:

It wasn't I who put the oil into your soil. It wasn't Royal Cockle
which invented capitalism and it's not your fault that man is born
with the longing to get out of the post of small attorney and rise to
be President of the State, and the people out there are not to blame
because they are hungry.

(93)

Here various parties' attempts to attain political-economic ascendancy
has been justified in terms of them being invariably driven by an inherent
cosmic drive or desire for accumulation, progress, and self-improvement –

"Oil Is an Idea" 245

thus dispelling the questions of morality, legality, and justice. Knowing Pusspad as a person given to self-preservation and cowardice, Brown dismisses the possibility of his resignation and insists that Pusspad has solely two options: either to join the revolutionary Puritanian forces in their battle against the dictatorial petro-state and foreign powers or (the far easier and safer choice) to maintain his complicitous alliance with the global powers and multinational oil company by using the advanced military weapons they provide ("our magnificent armaments") to "back us [global powers] against poorly equipped peasants" (93). Brown adds how Pusspad's opting for the former would make him a revolutionary (nationally) and a criminal (in the eyes of the international law). When Pusspad objects that this is bound to be a bloody war since "Marka is a symbol for the people. They revere her" (94), Brown seizes this as a compelling reason for her suppression: "That's why she is so dangerous. I know – mustn't make martyrs – a symbol survives even in its tomb" (94).

Another crucial point is raised in Brown's speech, that is, the boom and bust dynamics of oil production as well as the dependency of the value of oil on a whole petrocultural infrastructure. As Brown explains:

> but here it's a question of gaining time. It's impossible to sit on bayonets. We in Perfidia have found out that it is possible to put up for three hundred years with this admittedly very unpleasant seat. You may perhaps be able to manage it for – five years.
>
> (94)

Whilst trying to kindle a spark of hope in Pusspad about the promises of an indefinite future thus evoking the discursive concomitance between oil and futurity, Brown disarmingly adds:

> Five years is a long time. We don't know what may happen in five years. Perhaps there will be a new invention which will raise the consumption of oil to undreamt of figures. There'll be a boom. We shall resume production – a stream of gold will flow into your country. So gain time. Have this woman shot. It will clear up the position and you will have the possibility of being allowed to hope for better times. More than this vague possibility Perfidia hasn't got either, I have given you friendly counsel. You need not take it. But you are shrewd enough to find out for yourself that there could be no better solution.
>
> (94)

The dialectical dynamics invoked by Brown here – comprising dichotomies or poles of production and anti-production – has in fact been one of the established and oft-invoked features of the world of capitalist oil production. As Isser explains: "From the beginning the industry was characterized by a cyclic pattern of boom and bust, with most of the risks

246 *"Oil Is an Idea"*

incurred by producers, especially independents. The producers' weakness was due to a combination of physical and legal factors" (2016, 3). The historical facts, approximate dates and timeline, and the historical trajectory of the oil production – as depicted here – all closely correspond to the historical of facts and vicissitudes of oil world during the 1920s and 1930s.[27]

Crucially, this moment marks the full assimilation of not only the present history and political-economic dynamics of the peripheral nation into the logics of the global petro-capitalist system but its future as well. As such, this moment can be explicated in terms of "vertical integration". In fact, vertical integration was one of the chief strategies deployed by oil companies particularly during the first half of the 20th century. A salient case in point is Rockefeller's treatment of Standard Oil Company and its smaller dependent companies. Rockefeller integrated them horizontally and vertically. And this dynamics – when translated into a multinational scale – is exactly what happens at the end of *Oil Field* where all apparently international oil companies – each of which is a national one in itself – merge to give birth to a multinational oil corporation to the triumph of finance capitalism in its global reach and success. Distilling Tarbell's chronicling of the history of oil in early 20th-century America with a particular focus on the subtle ways in which Standard Oil monopolized oil through the systemic dynamics, Frederick Buell refers to a crucial notion that can also be appropriated to describe the political-economic manoeuvre imposed on the peripheral Puritania by the multinational oil company (Royal Cockle): "Rockefeller transformed extraction culture into a vertically integrated monopoly that stifled this resurgence of American individualism and frontier spirit. Oil, once systematized, began transforming social life – sending out tentacles into people's private lifeworlds to change them" (*Oil Cultures* 76).

Brown's next move is to grant Pusspad sovereignty and unrestrained leeway to exert all his military might to suppress the national uprisings and to declare a state of emergency as a consequence of which both national and international law can be suspended. Brown however conducts this in a double-handed way; on the one hand he intends to absolve international law/community and himself (as a world power) of any taint of the imputation of endorsing egregiously anti-democratic and anti-authoritarian measures in a foreign country; on the other hand he exhorts Pusspad that he has no choice but to follow the dictatorial course already charted for him:

> Right. Internal policy is a matter which Perfidia will not influence. With whatever means you may master the revolution out there – that's your own private affair. But the maintenance of peace and order, the protection of our property, those are not questions of interior policy, they concern the vital interests of Perfidia and of the whole Continent. For this peace and order you are responsible to us.

(92)

*"Oil Is an Idea"* 247

The juxtaposition of the "internal" and "interior" – as two nearly synonymous words which however in the context of Brown's speech denote two vastly different entities – is highly evocative here. Indeed, the simultaneously drastic separateness and yet inextricable entanglement between the "internal" and "interior" creates an aporetic situation for the president of the peripheral country (Pusspad) – a country of which the infrastructure and vital economic force (oil) belongs to and is run by the international oil companies. It is under the duress of such an aporetic situation that Pusspad finds no resort or remedy but to succumb to its tragic logic.

As a consequence, given the manner Brown has been abusing his position as the representative of the League of Nations (or Peoples), Brown can be argued to symbolically embody "the colonial legacy of international law" (see Shafiee 102). What Katayoun Shafiee argues about Iran can be applied to Germany in the late 1920s, and 1930s Germany and Albania as depicted and as they feature in *Oil Field* and *Konjunktur* (*1 and 2*):

> In the period between the signing of the first oil concession in 1901 and its revision in 1933, AIOC's organizational work involved transforming the oil regions into a laboratory for managing power relations between the British oil corporation and the national Iranian state's claims to sovereignty. These activities were an integral part of, indeed indistinguishable from, its in-house scientific work.
>
> (71)

This argument illuminates how the much-touted values and alleged intentions of the global core powers (the European and Anglo-American countries) – including the promotion and expansion of democracy, liberty, humanistic equality, and national autonomy – prove to be far from true. This is starkly evidenced by the global powers' exploitative interventions in a peripheral country – a move which is driven not by the alleged democratic and humanistic incentives, but by their economic and political interests, including the promise of a cheap resource.

More specifically, *Oil Field* (and *Konjunktur*) illustrate how global-imperial powers and (multi-)national corporation capitalist forces (both of which predominantly coincide and are identical) in their approach to the peripheral part of the world endorse political stability, nationalization of resources, and recognition of the ruling party as a legitimate, democratically elected power and part of the international community *only insofar as* such peripheral countries conform to their extractivist logics and dynamics; otherwise, the profit of global powers resides in the perpetuation of political, social and economic turmoil and instability (upheaval and cataclysm) in such peripheral countries. The depiction of the emergence of the multinational oil company – as a strategic means for the perpetuation of the petro-capitalist system and guaranteeing its

248 *"Oil Is an Idea"*

surplus production – is one of the crucial features that distinguishes *Oil Field* from *Konjunktur* (*1* and *2*). As we witnessed *in Konjunktur* (*1* and *2*), the attempt to link economy and politics at national-global levels and to gain access to cheap oil resources was made through the quest for "monopoly" over oil in the form of separate companies run by national-imperial countries. In *Oil Field* by contrast all those countries now merge and combine shares to engender a new entity called the multinational oil corporation (Royal Cockle).

## XIIII.   A Lover's Execution or a Symbol's Sacrifice?

The next crucial encounter is that between Pusspad and Oxhumani. Here Pusspad visits Oxhumani in the hope of convincing her to leave the country ("you must go abroad") in order to escape the execution. Oxhumani, however, remains imperviously insistent on the restoration of her rights and those of others. Pusspad remonstrates: "Here am I fighting for your life, and you. . . . You are taking part in acts which amount to high treason. . . . Revolution! Civil war! Dead and wounded, storming of the oil wells, destructions of foreign property" (95). When Oxhumani tries to explain how all the events were unpremeditated and spontaneous – partly in response to the violent treatment the people received from soldiers: "The soldiers have been shooting. I don't know myself how it came about so quickly. Quite suddenly it started. Those soldiers will have to be punished" (95). Pusspad then tries to give Oxhumani a hint into the sheer gravity and proportions of the issues at stake: "Surely you don't expect us to go to war for the sake of your wretched field" (97). Oxhumani is awe-struck at the sheer dimensions of the issue which have been eluding her entirely:

> War – for the sake of my field? What on earth do you mean? . . . I haven't the remotest intention. How ridiculous. What should I do abroad, now that I have got my field back? Balderdash. The people merely want their fields back. If they get them tomorrow, the day after everything will be over.
>
> (96)

To which Pusspad bursts out: "Your field – your field – always the same stories. That in itself is a criminal, treasonable statement" (96). Pusspad, however, insists that the lands are now "foreign property". When Pusspad asks Oxhumani to ask people to return the lands and oil fields, Oxhumani reminds him of the local and national nature of the ownership (including her land): "Your duty is to give me back my field. That's the very reason why you became President" (97). She then adds how this plight has been erupted due to unemployment and anti-production. When Pusspad tries to regurgitate Brown's abstruse and abstract justification,

"*Oil Is an Idea*" 249

Oxhumani counters what Pusspad (ventriloquizing Brown) calls economic "rationality" (as a justification for the anti-production) by calling it "irrational" and detrimental at least in the context of Puritania and its national economics: "The foreigners don't want them at all. They have no use for them. They're letting the factories and towers and chimneys fall into ruins – in a few months every thing will be rusted away" (96). Oxhumani laments how the allegedly nationalist Pusspad has proved nothing but a puppet and a pale reincarnation of the foreign plunderers: "Rotti stole my field and you're trying to drive me out of the country. But there's nothing doing. If I were to go out into the street now –" (98). Oxhumani reminds Pusspad of his promises as a leader and lover and his subsequent betrayal of them: "You lied to me. You lied to the whole of the people. (Goes up to him) You are a scoundrel, like Rotti" (97). Finding the conversation with Oxhumani futile, Pusspad orders her arrest and imprisonment thus leaving her awaiting the implementation of her imminent death sentence.

What we anticipate in the conclusion of the play is a tragic-heroic climax – the execution of Oxhumani. However, *Oil Field* – in keeping with its ironic mode – brings about a reversal which is nevertheless nothing short of a tragedy in another key. The climactic moment depicts Oxhumani exposed in all her precarity and abjection standing against a group of officers pointing at her with loaded guns on the verge of shooting at her whilst the commotion of the people in the street pour into the prison walls: "Cheers for Marka! Liberty! Justice!" (98). Immediately after officer – in charge of the execution – finishes reading the conviction sentence ("because of incitement to armed rebellion she is here by sentenced to death by shooting. In the name of the Republic. Signed, Pusspad, President"), we see Oxhumani collapse and succumb under the sheer pressure of the liminal situation. She screams: "I'm afraid! Oh, don't – I am afraid I don't want the field! I don't want the field!" (99). This moment is significantly ensued by "complete darkness"; then we hear officer saying "Shoulder Arms! About turn! Quick March! they tramp off. Puritanian National Anthem heard in the distance" (99). Evidently, Oxhumani is coerced into an act of self-disownment and self-dispossession – highly akin to the decision into which Pusspad was coerced under the duress of the global forces. Indeed, this marks the climax of the allegory of national dispossession, the triumph of global oil powers and the process of integration under the black sun of petro-capitalist oil hegemony.

Towards the end of the play, in accord with its dialectical vision, Lania zooms out to yet again provide us with a long shot where the barometer of the spirit and consciousness of the nation – that is, lower-class and ordinary people – is canvassed to demonstrate the tragic and ironic outcome of the discovery of oil in a peripheral nation and its transformation into a resource frontier through its being subjected to the logics of the global petro-capitalist system. In other words, the devolution of Puritania

250  *"Oil Is an Idea"*

into a "zone of sacrifice". The last scene of *Oil Field* confronts us with a dystopian, dismal, and highly evocative scene:

> Daylight grows. The scene is the same. Bright sunlight. Lounging against the hoarding are the former peasants and shepherds as out-of-works as in the 3rd scene of the Act, only they are still more ragged, and the whole scene shows the utter neglect of boring towers and installations: the hoarding is broken in many places, the scaffolding is rotten in parts and has fallen in. The sentry guards this picture or defeat, and desolation.
>
> (100)

What is evidently discernible in this scene is the preponderance of the signs of oil allegory: the state of fallen nature, depleted human life left in a creaturely state, and infrastructural ruins (of the oil sites and oil factory) which feature as the shattered promises of the magic of national oil; what was supposed to be progress, prosperity, and promise of transformation towards a glorious future ends up in a rusty backyard of world history or a dump ground of the global economy. Instead, we encounter an allegorical ruin (in the Benjaminian sense of the word): apocalyptic but bathetic since the dereliction is not even the outcome of the heroic action of the people or leaders. The devolution of Puritania into a zone of sacrifice illustrates how this resource frontier is turned into a barometer and pacemaker of global petro-capitalism. Amongst the debris of this wasteland – which was once pristine natural landscape and a common source for agriculture and herding – one cannot but hear the ironic reverberation of the naïve and deluded claim made by the workers and peasants earlier in the play: "we are a free country now" (88).

What further corroborates the allegorical dynamics of *Oil Field* is the allocation of the concluding word to a tragically grotesque figure whom we have already met: the self-amputee Old Peasant. Previously the self-amputee Old Peasant explained to others how he did this act of self-mutilation out of desperation (the unbearably exploitative work conditions) and with the wish to gain some effortless profit, sustenance by leading a parasitic life as a disabled. Ironically, however, he has now been left in a more profoundly abject and dispossessed condition of bare life than when he worked as an oil worker under abusive conditions both due to the dismissive treatment he has been receiving from various parties and the catastrophic economic circumstances aggravated by the cessation of production. As he explains:

> After all it hasn't brought me luck. If I think it over quietly to myself – not to work and not to run after the oil and only to sit here and beg – there was no need to cut off my arm for that. They're all doing it now and yet they have kept both their arms. It doesn't even run to

"*Oil Is an Idea*"  251

dry bread and hard rind of cheese. There are too many of them at it. Why did I cut off my arm? It was waste of a good arm.

(100)

The grievous loss suffered by Old Peasant in conjunction with its two-fold cause (both self-inflicted and induced by the unendurably alienating circumstances) make the self-amputee assume allegorical dimensions and represent Pusspad and Puritania. Pusspad similarly in an act of national self-amputation initially sacrificed national oil resources (by leasing the oil resources to foreign companies through outrageously cheap and disproportionate concessions) and betrayed his own people. Subsequently, he found himself coerced into cutting his limb off by acquiescing to the cessation of production to the detriment of his own nation.

The final moment, accordingly, evinces a tragi-comic dynamics which corresponds to the aesthetics of the play and the political-economic dynamics, including the fate of Puritania and its historical condition. The final aural element is cast in the register of tragic irony and parody. As the stage directions indicate, we hear a "parody of Puritania national anthem [which incrementally] gets louder" (100) attesting to how the nationalization of the oil resource and the birth of the national petro-state of Puritania were a neo-colonial and capitalist project rather than one driven by immanent historical-social consciousness and spontaneous endogenous movement of the people. This verbal and aural crescendo culminates in a reverberating and rather explicit motto-cum-topos that crystalizes the critical thrust of the preoccupations of the play. As the curtain falls slowly, on it is written in large characters: "THIS IS WHAT IT COSTS – NOT TO PRODUCE OIL" (100). The ambiguous voice and register of this passage further accentuates the allegorical dimensions of *Oil Field* – that is, its critical applicability to all the peripheral oil-rich countries which have been subjected to similar capitalist logics – by casting the passage in an impersonal voice where it is not clear whether it is a human voice (one of characters' or the author's) or a sign/banner.

## Conclusion

Informed with a world-systemic vision, and through its partly tragi-comic and partly socialist-realist aesthetics, *Oil Field* presents a symptomatological portrayal of the political-economic fate of an oil-possessing peripheral nation-state by focusing on the uneven entanglements between the local/national and the global powers revolving around the question of oil in the context of a globally extended petro-capitalist system in pursuit of extending its resource monopoly. It vividly depicts how the world powers (mainly the European and Anglo-American) – notwithstanding their pretentious claims to such values as international law, human rights, democracy, and civilization – exploit their superior power and hegemonic

## 252 *"Oil Is an Idea"*

position to gain political-economic monopoly, to perpetuate their logics of extraction (monopoly capitalism) and to guarantee surplus production in their interactions with a resource-rich peripheral country. They achieve their goal by producing the peripheral country as a resource frontier and subsequently a zone of sacrifice. *Oil Field* thus demonstrates how petro-capitalism has been founded on "corporate/state collusion, regulation of surplus and manufactured scarcity" (Retort 2005, 56). *Oil Field* demonstrates how "Capitalism is a world historical phenomenon and its uneven development means that individual nations cannot be at the same level of economic development at the same time" (Antonio Gramsci, 'The Return to Freedom . . .', Avanti! 26 June 1919), a situation which testifies to the fact that "Capitalism is not a mode [mode] of production it is a production of worlds [mondes]" (Lazzarato 2004, 96). Finally, whilst all three plays are informed with a dialectical vision, *Oil Field*, more specifically, presents a view of the lived effects of oil-driven life from below whilst *Konjunktur* (*1* and *2*) presents a view from above. As such, whilst maintaining its focus on the political-economic dynamics and the extractive logics of the production of oil, *Oil Field* affords us a more intimate, extended, and detailed insight into the psychological, ecological, ethical, and social-cultural effects of oil on the lives of the people of a peripheral nation.

## Notes

1. See Tatjana Röber, pp. 399–404.
2. Georg Lukacs. *History and Class Consciousness*. London: Merlin Press, 1971, pp. 130–161.
3. As Patricia Yaeger acutely indicates:

> perhaps energy sources also enter texts as fields of force that have causalities outside (or in addition to) class conflicts and commodity wars . . . each resource instantiates a changing phenomenology that could recreate our ideas about the literary text's relation to its originating modes of production as quasi-objects.
>
> (Patricia Yaeger 2011, 444)

4. The study "Erdöl, Erdölkapitalismus und Erdölpolitik", published in 1925 by Georg Engelbert Graf.
5. Roberto Esposito Biopolitics and Philosophy, Timothy C. Campbell 2008.
6. Leslie Sklair, *The Transnational Capitalist Class* (Oxford: Blackwell, 2001), p. 3.

> The world of British Empire one hundred years ago, too, was wired as never before – at that time by telegraph cables, and, more metaphorically, by railway networks and steamship travel. Moreover, British and colonial subjects at the time imagined themselves in this way, as interconnected, cross-cabled, while many of their activities and aspirations were informed by the existence of cross-empire networks. The world order may not have been as saturated with communications nexuses as

*"Oil Is an Idea"* 253

now, but, significantly, looking from the point of view of then, it was saturated as never before.

7. For an extended explication of a similar case of the structural intertwinements between oil and these four phenomena, see Penélope Plaza Azuaje, *Oil in Venezuela Culture as Renewable Oil How Territory, Bureaucratic Power and Culture Coalesce in the Venezuelan Petrostate* (London: Routledge, 2019), pp. 7–9, 54–65, 79–88.

8. Michael Watts, "Violent Environments: Petroleum Conflict and the Political Ecology of Rule in the Niger Delta, Nigeria," in *Violent Environments*, ed. Nancy Lee Peluso and Michael Watts (Ithaca: Cornell University Press, 2001), pp. 292–293.

9. Agamben's gloss on this is that

> the exception does not subtract itself from the rule [regola]; rather, the rule, suspending itself, gives rise to the exception and, maintaining itself in relation to the exception, first constitutes itself as a rule. . . . The sovereign decision of the exception is the originary juridicopolitical structure on the basis of which what is included in the juridical order and what is excluded from it acquire their meaning.
>
> (1998, 18, 19)

He concludes from this that "what emerges in the limit figure is the radical crisis of every possibility of clearly distinguishing between membership and inclusion, between what is outside and what is inside, between exception and rule" (25).

10. Henri Lefebvre, *The Production of Social Space*. Trans. Donald Nicholson-Smith (New York: Blackwell, 1991).

11. Bruce Podobnik, *Global Energy Shifts: Fostering Sustainability in a Turbulent Age* (Philadelphia: Temple University Press, 2006), 1–17.

12. Weber 1968; Marx and Engels 1975; Marx, Karl 1845; Marx, Karl 1967[1867a].

13. Fredric Jameson, "Culture and Finance Capital," in *The Cultural Turn: Selected Writings on the Postmodern, 1983–1998* (London: Verso, 1998).

14. J. H. Bamberg, *History of British Petroleum, Vol. One* (Oxford: OUP, 1982).

15. See Katayoun Shafiyee, *Machineries of Oil* MIT 2020, pp. 40–46; see also Ross Barrett, "Picturing a Crude Past," pp. 54–55.

16. See Matthew Huber, "Refined Politics: Petroleum Products, Neoliberalism, and the Ecology of Entrepreneurial Life," *Journal of American Studies*, 46.2 (2012), pp. 295–312, 297.

17. For an extensive explication of the various facets of petroculture in the long 20th century along with the relationship between oil and futurity see Chapter 5.

18. Sarah Ahmed, *Cultural Politics of Emotion* (Edinburg: Edinburgh UP, 2014).

19. Discussing the oil industry and corporations in relation to the political-economic dynamics of their extractive practices along with their treatment of workers in the middle of the 20th century (1930s–1950s) both in the context of US and Saudi Arabia and the world more broadly, Brian Black argues that in this emerging industrial form, not only was the frontier myth of the wildcatter neutered, but Big Oil constructed the biggest façade of all: "there was no free market for oil. Instead, petroleum became the most managed, controlled, and industrially manipulated commodity of the modern era. None of these details, however, was part of the popular image projected by the industry" (Brian Black 2012, 88).

## 254 *"Oil Is an Idea"*

20. See Michael Watts and Ed Kashi's photo-essay book *Curse of the Black Gold* (2008) and Michael Ross's *The Oil Curse: How Petroleum Wealth Shapes the Development of Nations* (1993).

    Janet Stewart, for instance, contends that: "The resource curse formulation reproduces this dialectic [the complicit relationship between Enlightenment and myth, between reason and its irrational other] by combining the abstractions of commodity capitalism with awe for the magical power of the material object" (Stewart 2017, 287).

21. In *Reflexive Representations: Discourse, Power, and Hegemony in Global Capitalism* edited by Johannes Angermuller, Dirk Wiemann, Raj Kollmorgen, Jorg Meyer. Munster: Verlag, 2004.

22. Improve social conditions or to foster economic growth (Yúdice 2003, 10–11).

23. Fernando Coronil, *The Magical State: Nature, Money, and Modernity in Venezuela* (Chicago: University of Chicago Press, 1997), pp. 3, 5.

24. See Alfons Goldschmidt, "Oil-Lmperialismus," *Die Weltbuhne. Jg.*, 23 (1927), Nr. 31. See also Alfons Goldschmidt. "Petroleum!". In *Der brennende Punkt.*

25. Zygmunt Bauman, *Liquid Times: Living in the Age of Uncertainty* (Cambridge: Polity Press, 2007).

26. Apter, Andrew. *The Pan-African Nation: Oil and the Spectacle of Culture in Nigeria*. 2005, Chicago: University of Chicago Press.

27. See Mandel, *Late Capitalism*, p. 190.

# 5 "It's Not Easy to Make Oil and Love Run in Harness Together"

"Petroleum Odes", "Oil Odour", and "Odious Coolies" in Lion Feuchtwanger's *Oil Islands*

## I. Prelude

No other play in this book drenches us in oil – in all its materiality, infrastructural complexity, magic intoxication, and toxicity – as relentlessly as Lion Feuchtwanger's *Oil Islands* (1927) does. Indeed, *Oil Islands* takes us to one of the repressed sites of the historical and cultural unconscious of Western petro-capitalist modernity: a peripheral oil-rich island in an un-identified US-governed Caribbean region where neither the international nor national rules, which otherwise apply on the land, are in force. The aforementioned sense of being afloat and immersed in oil – evoked by *Oil Islands* – is conducted through a twofold means: cognitive and affective. Far from launching its presentation of oil's looming presence on the island merely through a number of discursive dialogues or detailed stage directions and scene descriptions, *Oil Islands*, from the very outset, wraps us into a dense weave of sensory perceptions, semiotic details, songs, music, conflictual oral and official histories, and rumours where various affective, historical, ideological, and cognitive layers collide and imbricate. In the same vein, far from affording us the knowledge about the nature, effects, dynamics, and history of oil extraction and production, both on the island and more generally in the world, merely through abstract and intellectual means – such as reportage, discursive speeches (by characters), stage directions, and descriptions – *Oil Islands* enables us to garner that knowledge through perceptual, affective, and more material means. A salient case in point is our first encounter with the main character at the manifold core of the play – Miss Deborah Grey, the Oil Giant on both the island and the world who acts as the head of the apparently multinational (but actually chiefly American) oil company. *Oil Islands* ascertains that this first encounter is, both materially and metaphorically, mediated through and preluded with a thick pall of oil smoke, a miasmal mesh of oil reek, and a swirl of gothic-inflected rumours about her – including discursive accounts of her and her individual history as well as other characters' impressions of and experiences with her.

DOI: 10.4324/9781003134664-6

256 *"It's Not Easy to Make Oil and Love Run in Harness Together"*

There is a host of features that renders *Oil Islands* unique amongst the plays under scrutiny here. Primarily, there is its choice of a peripheral island as its setting: a Caribbean/Venezuelan island located somewhere just south of the United States. Conjoined with its world-systemic vision, the play's choice of setting not only helps reveal the "multi-scalarly" uneven political-economic dynamics of the petro-capitalist system at the levels of nature, race, gender, and class. It also foregrounds the allegorical nature of the play whereby it seeks to limn – in miniature, multi-scalar form – the world-ecological logics of this extractivist system in its global scope and longue durée span. The second distinctive feature is its extended focus on the question of nature as affected by the global oil industry and petro-imperialism due to its being commodified into a *Gestell* or energy resource. By showing how the island is growing exceedingly uninhabitable and arid – evidenced by the rampant air, soil, and water pollution – *Oil Islands* depicts how the extraction of oil on a formerly idyllic island inflicts a "metabolic rift" or irreparable loss of human-nonhuman nature on it. The third distinguishing feature of *Oil Islands* is its sustained focus on the vicissitudes of the transnational labour force, the link it draws not only between the production of race (and racialized cheap labour) and resource extraction but also between colonial slavery and neo-colonial handling of oil workers (petro-precariat). It also includes the question of the working class in the oil industry at national and transnational levels. As such *Oil Islands* reveals the entanglements between racial politics and economics of petro-labour and working force under global capitalism. The fourth distinctive facet of *Oil Islands* is its demonstration of the ways in which desire and death, and, correspondingly, libidinal economy and political economy are intertwined. This twofold vision is carried out through the multivalent associations evoked around two principal characters – Miss Grey and Miss Peruchacha – in the play in conjunction with their symbolic roles and associations with toxic desire (hence Thanatos) and natural desire (hence Eros) respectively. The final salient feature of the play is its dramatic aesthetics, that is, its aesthetic hybridity and manifold form. *Oil Islands*, whilst appearing mainly naturalistic in form, is streaked with the elements of allegory, tragedy, Brechtian epic, grotesque, and black comedy.

Lion Feuchtwanger (1884–1958) wrote *Oil Island*'s predecessor – *Die Petroleuminseln* (*The Petroleum Island*) – in 1926. *Die Petroleuminseln* was premiered at the Deutsches Schauspielhaus in Hamburg on 31 October 1927, directed by Erich Ziegel and featuring Maria Krahn and Maria Eis in the leading roles.[1] The play proved successful and garnered much public and critical acclaim and attention, though not primarily for its playtext. The play was also staged on 28 November 1928 (director: Jürgen Fehling; starring: Maria Koppenhöfer and Lotte Lenya) in Berlin (with a jazz band in front of pictures of car races) and was set to premiere at the Staatstheater on 28 November 1929.[2] *Die Petroleuminseln* was

*"It's Not Easy to Make Oil and Love Run in Harness Together"* 257

translated into English – as *Oil Islands* – by Willa and Edwin Muir in 1929. Whilst the original *Die Petroleuminseln* appeared in conjunction with two other plays within the same volume (Kalkutta, 4. Mai. Drei Akte Kolonialgeschichte and Wird Hill amnestiert? Komödie in vier Akten),[3] *Oil Islands* appeared along with *Warren Hastings* within a volume subtitled: *Two Anglo-Saxon Plays*.

*Oil Islands* opens onto a pollution-ravaged and crisis-ridden world. The Brown Islands is currently dominated by an American oil company (with international alliances) managed by Deborah Grey (The Chimpanzee or Monkey) who is grappling with an array of crises on various fronts. *Oil Islands* indeed confronts us with a dense weave of interlacing narrative strands, all of which are traversed with various imbricating thematic, psychological, and political-economic elements. There are five pivotal crises round which the main thematic and dramatic dynamics of the play revolve. First and foremost is the ecological crisis (egregiously manifested in the pervasive pollution) on which I elaborated previously and will extensively probe later. The second crisis concerns the oil extraction and production on the island in political-economic terms. A chief part of this crisis stems from the national US ban on the use of transnational labour force (including on the island) – a law that has brought the production to a grinding halt due to the question of profitability and production prices. Concomitant with the second crisis is the crisis of the transnational labour force – or cheap labour as a form of modern slavery – which unfolds round the question of the Immigration Bill in the play. The fourth valence of the crisis arises from the haunting possibility of imminent oil scarcity, that is, the exhaustion of oil resources both on the US land and on the Brown Islands. This concern, however, is dispelled with the discovery of the new oil fields and resources both on the island and elsewhere. The fifth crisis arises from the fraught relationship between Miss Grey and Lady Peruchacha (henceforth Grey and Peruchacha) and the intense rivalry between them propelled by both personal, political-economic and social-cultural reasons. This is partly personally rooted in the feminine sense of jealousy and rivalry. However, this rivalry – given the social-cultural positions of the two women coupled with their symbolic and historical associations – assumes both symbolic (at a textual-dramatic level) and allegorical (at a meta-dramatic level) dimensions and implications too. In this allegorical reading, the hideous Grey "embodies" the oil world in all its toxicity, its (infrastructural) monstrosity, its moral and political-economic corruptions, and its exploitation of human-nonhuman nature, labour force, and peripheral countries. The gorgeous Peruchacha, on the contrary, represents the traditional nature-friendly lifestyle and values that are more humanistic and less exploitative. Miss Grey pursues an extractivist approach and Peruchacha promotes a preservationist approach in relation to nature, humans, and natural resources. This rivalry is further compounded due to the exceeding encroachment,

258 *"It's Not Easy to Make Oil and Love Run in Harness Together"*

restrictions and impediments foisted by Grey on Peruchacha's business (tourism and agricultural extractivism) and Peruchacha herself as an exotic beauty and appeal.

The other source of suspense in the global game of oil rivalry is the representative of the Soviet Union, Mr. Ingram, who arrives on the island with the offer of an oil concession between the US and the Soviet Union. Ingram is over-ambitious, morally-financially corrupt, and ruthless. Interestingly, Grey falls in love with Ingram and treats him favourably. Brandishing the crisis-ridden situation in which Grey is caught, Ingram suggests that he be personally (rather than as the representative of Soviet Union) endowed with some substantial money and shares in Grey's oil company and in return Ingram would establish a low-priced and profitable oil concession with Russia for Grey. Grey asks him for some time to ponder the offer. Meanwhile, Grey has been striving to overcome the crisis and turn the threat posed to her oil hegemony by the American company, "the Trust", as well as other international rivals by conceiving an Immigration Bill through which the use of foreign, cheap labour would be prohibited on the US land but permitted on the island: a measure that would considerably increase the cost of production on the US land whilst keeping the production costs low thereby maintaining the hegemonic dominance of Grey's oil company. To facilitate the passing of the Immigration Bill, Grey sorely needs to improve her public profile in terms of moral and familial values. Consequently, she makes a wily move by arranging an interest-based marriage with the Viscount of Westmoreland to obtain some symbolic social capital and restore her reputation blemished with her own perverse political-economic practices and the pernicious effect of her exploitative petro-extractive operations on human-nonhuman nature on the islands. Through a highly elaborate network of schemes and power games – including complicity, bribery, and sham marriage – Grey manages to have the Immigration Bill passed whereby the use of the transnational labour on land is banned and its employment on the island is authorized. Consequently, not only does she win the national rivalry over oil monopoly and transnational labour, but the intra-islandic battle with Peruchacha on the same matters. Whilst striving to win the favour of the senior employees and the public against Grey, Peruchacha decides to take some of the confidential documents she has obtained – concerning Grey's corrupt and collusive agreements with some American politicians about the Immigration Bill and double-dealing measures regarding the exploitative employment of transnational labour (in violation of the national law) – both to the Japanese and the US Congress in order wreak havoc on Grey's political-economic plans and to ruin her current monopoly and future extractivist plans.

Amidst the intense rivalry between Grey and Peruchacha, there occurs another traumatic experience when Grey realizes that Ingram also finds her features loathsome and is merely using her as a means to his own

*"It's Not Easy to Make Oil and Love Run in Harness Together"* 259

ends, and she withdraws her supports from him. Subsequently, a critical juncture arises in the relationship between Ingram and Grey when Ingram publicly humiliates Grey at Peruchacha's gathering. Wounded by Ingram's act of public humiliation of her at Peruchacha's villa – when he reveals how Grey calls him "H. B. my own sweet love" and thus taking Peruchacha's side in the public. Grey fully ruptures her relations with him, annuls all agreements with him, and strips him of all her protection against the Russian agents who believe Ingram has betrayed their trust and are therefore seeking to arrest and prosecute him. Ultimately, with the successful passing of the Immigration Bill and establishing the Russian Concession through means other than Ingram, Grey finds herself triumphant. There remain two more hurdles on her lap of victory: convincing the Japanese to agree with the employment of cheap, foreign labour on the island and to totalize her oil ontology and narcissistic psychic space by eliminating Peruchacha from the islands. Ultimately Grey accomplishes this task by upstaging Peruchacha as the traitor by imputing to her an act of national high treason for disclosing confidential documents to the Japanese) and having her arrested and executed. Grey's billet-doux achievement is clinched when, having subtly gained the acquiescence of the Japanese, she manages to have the double Immigration Bill approved whereby the employment of transnational workers on the land is prohibited but on the island legally permitted. Grey has Peruchacha arrested and asks her to sell her lands and villa to Grey and leave the islands. When Peruchacha refuses to reach a compromise, Grey has her murdered whilst being acutely cognizant of how she is jeopardizing her reputation, the status and fate of the oil company and the value of the shares of the oil company. Ultimately *Oil Islands* leaves us with a Grey over-bedecked with her trophies, that is, a now triumphant but self-professedly "barbaric", lovelorn, undesirable oil Duchess/Queen. The conclusion evokes a dystopian future looming over the island's horizon. *Oil Islands* concludes with an explicit declaration of plans by Grey which presages nothing but the aggravation of the ravages of the current extractive petro-capitalist practices by the oil company at national and global levels.

Feuchtwanger is primarily known as a prominent novelist and only secondarily a dramatist. He has been described to be "more than most authors . . . the mirror of his times" (Lothar Kahn *Insight and Action*, 1975, 17). Lothar Kahn describes him as not only a "studious sage and a man of action, skeptic or believer, democrat or communist" (1975, 17) but also "the greatest historical novelist of modern times and one of the truly sophisticated vivifiers of the past" (19). As regards the itinerary of Feuchtwanger's personal and professional life, Feuchtwanger's mid-life, akin to Lania's experience of various plights (including persecution), was beset with agonizing vicissitudes. Whilst himself a staunchly secular person, Feuchtwanger was of Jewish descent. A Bavarian Jewish novelist and playwright and a prominent figure in the literary world of

260 *"It's Not Easy to Make Oil and Love Run in Harness Together"*

Weimar Germany, he exerted considerable influence on his contemporaries, including Bertolt Brecht. Feuchtwanger's Judaism and tenacious criticism of the National Socialist German Workers Party made him a target of government-sponsored persecution after Adolf Hitler's appointment as chancellor of Germany in January 1933. Suffering an onslaught of harrowing persecutions, Feuchtwanger fled Germany to spend a brief period of internment in France. Ultimately, he found asylum in the United States, where he stayed until his death in 1958.

In his lifetime, Feuchtwanger was both a successful dramatist and best-seller novelist. One of the most determining upheavals in Feuchtwanger's life was his conversion from Jewish Orthodoxy to Buddhism, which he encountered during his student years in Munich as a student of Sanskrit secular education. Feuchtwanger's encounter with the sacred language of the East, Sanskrit, indeed proved a paradigmatic experience for him and fostered his devotion to Buddhism as a redeeming and saving cause (see Sebastian Musch 2020, 106–111, 125–134). As a sweeping survey of Feuchtwanger's both fictional and dramatic works reveals, the geographical scope and historical span of his work evince a concern with the world rather than being confined to bounds of merely the recent history and a nation (Germany) or even a continent (Europe). They also show a world-oriented aesthetics as well as a world-oriented social-cultural and political-economic consciousness. This is not only vividly discernible in his choice of settings for his works: the Caribbeans (*Oil Islands*), Ancient Rome (*Der falsche Nero*), pre-revolutionary America (*Wahn oder der Teufel in Boston*), or 18th-century *Baden-Württemberg* (*Jud Süß*). It is also discernible in his attention to the structural political-economic and historical forces that form cultures and societies along with his emphasis on the necessity of treating cultures and nations as systems that need to enter into dialogical and dialectical processes of historical synthesis in order to expand and improve towards a more holistic, enlightened, and humanistic condition. Two prominent examples of his world literary approach are his 1917 adaptation of an Indian classic titled *Der König und die Tänzerin* and his 1915 adaptation of Sudraka's *Vasantasena*, one of the classic Sanskrit plays, which according to Musch, was "a showstopper and remained so during the Weimar Republic" (127). Both plays were intended to foreground the contrast between "Indian wisdom on stage with the cruel reality of wartime Germany" (Musch 127) where Indian philosophical insight and wisdom comprised "infinite kindness, calm wisdom, and closeness to nature" (*Insight and Action*, 79). Next to these two plays on the futility of war and violence, Feuchtwanger's cosmopolitan spirit is most saliently attested by his convictions about the efficacy of Buddhism and the sacred yet secular wisdom of the East (Buddhism and India) as a panacea for the ills of the Western world and its modern times (technology, alienation, violence, etc.).

## "It's Not Easy to Make Oil and Love Run in Harness Together" 261

Perhaps the most cogent testament to Feuchtwanger's fascination with the East, Buddhism, and India is his play *Warren Hastings* (1915 and in English 1929) where he depicts an Eastern way of thinking as both diametrically opposed and even somehow superior to the Western way. Propelled by his idea of "humane colonialism", Hastings assumes the role of an over-ambitious Governor, a "man of deeds" whose attempts to reconcile both Europe's demands and India's needs lead him into personal tragedy. The play shows Hastings embroiled in a grave predicament, that is, his charge of bribery and treason. He cannot let go of his desire for power and his political vision. The victory of his foes, a delegation from London, which tries to have him tried and found guilty, will have grave consequences for Hastings: Hastings's reputation will be irreparably tarnished. His lover must be sent back to England, and he loses his best friend. And yet, according to Feuchtwanger, "Hastings' true opponent is India" (Feuchtwanger 1984, 377).[4] Hastings is depicted as a tragic figure or struggling soul between the East and West trying to mediate or reconcile them, whilst incurring detrimental ramifications both for himself and people of India, evidenced by how Hastings lets the people of Rohilla starve so that he can extort money from their enemies to be able to mollify his English prosecutors. Hastings reluctantly orders the execution of the Maharaja. Consequently, his hamartia is compounded by his blindness to Buddhist enlightenment ironically provided to him by his victim, the Maharaja:

> The world is not shaped in the manner dreamed up by white people. You cannot conquer it. You cannot keep it. The one who does not attempt to keep it shall be victorious. The one who does not resist shall be victorious. The one not tempted by it shall be victorious.
> (Feuchtwanger 1984, 377)

Feuchtwanger's ontological binarism along Orientalist-Occidentalist lines constitutes one of the pivotal features of his work and is embedded in the value-structure and ethical-existential dynamics of his world. In Feuchtwanger's view, the redemptive moment lies in a reconciliation between or recognition of Eastern and Western moral and ontological features. This is evident in his elite or gentile characters' struggle to strike a reconciling balance between the Eastern (Buddhist) and Western worldviews. These include Varro from the novel *Der falsche Nero*, Margarete Maultasch from *Die häßliche Herzogin*, and Hastings from *Warren Hastings*. Whilst there is no trace of Buddhism whatsoever in *Oil Islands*, there is an attention to the racialized Otherization and abjection of the non-Western people – the Caribbeans, Latin Americans, and transnational (African and Asian) workers – and their use as sources of extraction.

As Musch notes, Feuchtwanger's approach to Buddhism entails "an ontologization of political and geographical entities" (2020, 129). This

262 *"It's Not Easy to Make Oil and Love Run in Harness Together"*

ontologization as a static form of othering distinguishes itself by its explicitly conscious deployment, yet it does not attempt to overcome its blind spots. The East as imaginative geography exhibits specific characteristics that transcend historical and cultural contexts. Feuchtwanger showed no interest in practically experiencing the East or Buddhism, either through travel or through religious practice. The East, in Feuchtwanger's account, simply offers attributes complementary to those of the West. As is evident, tokens of orientalism are discernible in Feuchtwanger's conception of the East. Not only does the East as such remain a phantasmatic or transcendental idea rather than a practically experienced phenomenon in all its historical-geographical reality/materiality. This is a further testimony to the allegorical and transcendental predilections permeating Feuchtwanger's treatment of such notions and concepts as well as historical facts. The ensuing statement corroborates the dialectical nature of his focus on historical subjects and the nature of history more generally: "While the popular historical novel's main purpose is to entertain, it lacks any relevance for the present day, whereas a serious historical novel would combine entertainment with a historical mission and thus 'give meaning to history'" (Faulhaber 1972, 67–81). In his essay, "Vom Sinn und Unsinn des historischen Romans" ["On the Meaning and Meaninglessness of the Historical Novel"] (1935) Feuchtwanger writes that he uses historical facts as a means of creating distance between himself and the immediacy of the present; historical material becomes "ein Gleichnis" (510; an allegory) for his representation of the now (1956). More specifically, Feuchtwanger conceived of his historical writings as a contribution to the struggle "against historicism, relativism, and historical skepticism. The triad of progress, history, and reason – those ideas that he saw as the guiding star of humanity – had come under fire" (Musch 2020, 130). Notably whilst the majority of Feuchtwanger's fictional and dramatic works take relatively distant historical times and non-German geographical settings as their context, *Oil Islands* is an exception to this aesthetic strain or rule. Indeed, such an ontological vision along with a dialectical conception of history renders Feuchtwanger's historical preoccupations highly allegorically inflected – a link that serves as a common binding thread between the aforementioned works and *Oil Islands*: a work which as I will demonstrate is highly allegorical in a world-ecological and world-systemic sense.

Of salient significance is Feuchtwanger's own preface to the volume (the English translation that pairs *Warren Hastings* with *Oil Islands*). In this preface, addressed specifically to the "English reader", Feuchtwanger dismisses the ascription of any hermeneutic primacy or phenomenological value to the production of and the experience of watching a play as a more authentic or comprehensive way of understanding it. Instead he accentuates the necessity of a first-hand engagement with the text: "If you should have seen these plays produced, then please let the impression subside

*"It's Not Easy to Make Oil and Love Run in Harness Together"* 263

before you read them" (v). Ironically, whilst appraising the productions of these two plays, he avers how the production proved a distortion of the authorial intentions, thus repudiating the enhancing effect of the mediation of director and the whole theatrical troupe on enhancing the effect and accessibility of a play: "Several excellent producers have put them on the stage and a host of accomplished actors have played various parts. Unfortunately the majority of those producers have had their own interpretation" (v). A chief portion of Feuchtwanger's discontent stems from the reviewers' myopic focus on the historical content of the play and its accuracy rather than the aesthetic-formal features and the critical vision of the play:

> the pieces revealed themselves as symbolical statements of particular conceptions of the world or as definite pronouncements on America, Imperialism and sociological problems. It was only the plays themselves – whose simple intention was to express adequately what was in them – that remained unnoticed.
>
> (vi)

Judging by Feuchtwanger's own admonition, we – as the 21st-century readers separated by nearly a century from the publication of the text – should not reckon ourselves in a disadvantaged position in relation to the playtext. Articulating this hermeneutic-aesthetic concern as a historical problem, he avers: "In an age when it is difficult to make oneself understood on the simplest question even to one other person, to think of reaching one's interlocutor through thirty or forty collaborators is a precarious business" (v). Indeed, Feuchtwanger's disavowal of historical accuracy and historiographical fidelity as his foremost preoccupation enhances the allegorical, tragic and psychologically oriented facets of the play. As he explains: "Warren Hastings was not understood in Germany twelve years ago and failed. Now it is a success, and is not understood" (vi). Commenting on the reception of *Oil Islands*, he states: "*The Oil Islands* is not understood in Germany even now, and is a success" (1928, vi). He proceeds to make an even more contentious and radical claim which reflects his novelistic vision and his idealist expectations of the theatrical production of a play:

> Anyone who sees a production of that play to-day will gain as little understanding of it, so far as I can see, as a man who eats an excellently cooked rump-steak in a first-class restaurant will gain of a picture of cattle by Potter.
>
> (vi)

Ultimately, appealing to the reader, he demands that the reader produce the play in the ideal, abstract space of their imagination where the

264 *"It's Not Easy to Make Oil and Love Run in Harness Together"*

imaginative production is hoped to be far closer to the authorial intentionality due to its being unrestrained by the material limits of theatre and unmediated by the "interpretative distortions" of the director: "Act the two plays to yourself, I beg you, alone, on the stage of your mind. Then I shall have the rare luck of only having to come to an understanding with one collaborator instead of with fifty" (vi). As Feuchtwanger's embittered tone indicates, he was dismayed by the reviews the German version of the playtext received and vehemently attributed such a negative evaluation to the critics' failure to understand his play. As I will argue in the ensuing sections of this chapter, where the focus is mainly on the English version of Feuchtwanger's *Die Petroleuminseln* (*Oil Islands*), the play is thematically rich, intellectually nuanced, and aesthetically manifold and accomplished.

## II. The Argument

My exploration of the crucial facets of oil as depicted in *Oil Islands* will be predicated on a cluster of intertwined concepts, including the Capitalocene, petroculture, metabolic rift, commodity frontier (and/or extractive zone), and allegory. Delving into the world-systemic vision informing *Oil Islands* and its critique of the logics of petro-capitalism as a world-ecological force, in this chapter I will demonstrate how the play confronts us with the operations of Capitalocenic ravages of a US-led petro-capitalist company propelled with a world-ecological dynamics in full operation on a US-dominated Caribbean island in the first half of the 20th century. *Oil Islands* accomplishes this task by taking into account the ecological, racial, and material conditions of oil production by an extractivist regime that thrives on the dispossession of cheap nature, cheap labour (national and transnational workers, the poor and the marginalized), and cheap raw materials obtained through the exploitation of peripheral points (at national and global levels) by producing them as resource frontiers and zones of sacrifice. It will be demonstrated how this is not only discernible in the uneven ontological, racial, and political-economic mode of relationship between the American core and the Caribbean periphery. It is also evident in the uneven – in fact, disparate – nature of legal measures and political-economic logics informing the life on the (American) mainland and on the (US-governed) island as well as the relational dynamics between the two. This uneven dynamics on a world-systemic scale attests to how the surplus production and American ascendancy and monopoly in the world market are guaranteed by drastically different legal measures on land and island. This issue, in turn, illustrates the dynamics through which globally yet unevenly connected spaces in core and resource peripheries are produced; a dynamics that involves a globally extended configuration of laws, nature, movement of human labour and commodities which assures the attainment of surplus production, oil-dependent futurity, and perpetuation of the capitalist mode of production.

*"It's Not Easy to Make Oil and Love Run in Harness Together"*  265

Probing the ways in which the oil world as depicted in *Oil Islands* is traversed with globally and structurally uneven logics and world-ecological forces in various respects, we will deliberate on how the play stages a dialogue with the global by addressing itself to the oil infrastructure in that environment. In this world-systemic dialogue, the relational dynamics between the core (the American Empire and American mainland) and periphery (the Caribbean Island) is not only characterized by an uneven, extractivist logics (with the intricate exchange and complicities of the international forces in the hinterland). It will also be shown how *Oil Islands* compels us to ponder locality and geopolitics as possible sites of conflict, as sites of understanding the symbolic and material power as well as the kinds of agency that they enable in the environments where oil is extracted to feed global consumption. As such, this chapter will demonstrate the ways in which *Oil Islands* illustrates how already in the 1920s oil was emerging as ubiquitous as the primary energy form, fuelling the motion of both the petroculture and a global capitalist society. More specifically, we will see how *Oil Islands* also renders visible the "order" of oil's functioning thereby throwing into relief the logics and dynamics through which an alienation of the commodity from its methods of production is established in petro-capitalism.

As regards the aesthetics of the play, I will try to reveal how this world-ecological critique is evidenced by the aesthetics and form of the play: allegory as elaborated by Jameson and DeLoughrey. Ultimately, I will delve into the entanglements of desire (beauty, nature, fulfilment) and death (oil, ugliness, toxicity) in conjunction with that between libidinal economy and political economy. This crucial entanglement is evidently reflected in the subtle ways in which ecological/natural energy, capitalized (or commodified) energy, and psychic energy (the unconscious desire and repressed drives) are indelibly intertwined in each character – most saliently in Grey and Peruchacha. I will explicate the dynamics and implications of such entanglements by drawing on the arguments elaborated by Lyotard, Deleuze, Lacan, and Mbembé.

## III.

### A.  *The Songs and Sirens of the* Oil Islands

At the very outset, we find ourselves on board of the Steamship "Peruchacha" where the Passengers are playing the "Song of the Brown Islands" on a gramophone. In the performance the song was set to music by Kurt Weill and sung by Lotte Lenya as Peruchacha. This steamship (Peruchacha) does not belong to the oil company run by Grey, but rather to Peruchacha and a transportation and tourism company that she runs. Notably, this is the main non-industrial transportation company that runs the ships and ferries between the mainland US and the Brown Islands. The voyage to the

## 266 *"It's Not Easy to Make Oil and Love Run in Harness Together"*

Brown (or Oil) Islands is presented in highly allegorical terms evidenced by the title of the scene: "On the Way to Oil Islands". Amongst the passengers are both the employees of the Oil Islands company, the invited visitors and guests invited by Grey to attend her annual party held to celebrate her ancestor and his founding role in the establishment of the island, and Ingram the Russian emissary visiting for negotiations concerning the Russian Concession. *Oil Islands* thus opens with a tension-laden conflict between tourists, visitors, and passengers aboard a ship. More specifically, this conflict arises between those passengers who are playing a disc on a gramophone and chorally singing it and those who are offended by it and air their grievances. Initially, this contrapuntal configuration of voices, opinions, rumours, and snatches of the songs are interspersed throughout the conversations among the characters who are polarized into the proponents and opponents of Miss Grey's practice as the head of the islands' oil company.

The songs at the beginning and throughout serve an epic function. They not only foster the possibility of critical distancing from the world and character thus drawing our attention to the political-economic logics and governing dynamics informing the movement of this world and the relationship between its characters. They also reveal the struggle over hegemonic power and social-cultural legitimacy not only between the polar forces on the island (Peruchacha and Grey), but also between common people and the sovereign power on the island. *Oil Islands* orchestrates these layers of voices initially through an alternation between the song played on the gramophone and the songs chorally sung by the Passengers aboard the steamship. The play opens with the following lines: "This is the song of the Islands of Oil, / The women are sick and the men n.b.g. / The very trees rot where they stand in the soil, / And they all belong to a Chimpanzee" (5). Then the Chorus of Passengers sing: "Are you, going, Freddy? / I don't think, Teddy; / I want something else than dollars to woo, / And I'd rather make love to a chimp in the Zoo" (5). Only to be followed by the song played from the gramophone: "The men are a bad lot, the women are sick; / That's what the Islands are like, my lad. / It's a Chimpanzee that has the big stick, / And if you go there, you'll go to the bad" (5–6). And finally we hear from the Chorus an explicit portrayal of the effects of oil on the island:

> And if you go there, you'll go to the bad, / For the Chimpanzee's boss of your bed and your job / There is no law or money but hers to be had. / And you've got to submit in your bed and job.
>
> (6)

This chorally expressed line of critical insight culminates in a highly evocative piece where various thematic strands coalesce: "There's a stink of petrol and other things, / For there's Chinks and niggers of every degree: /

## "It's Not Easy to Make Oil and Love Run in Harness Together"    267

But the dollars don't stink that the petrol brings, / And you can't knock spots off the Chimpanzee" (6).

Upon closer inspection of the dense weave of the song, the ensuing chief strands can be teased out. The principal strand revolves around the motif of oil in relation to the oil tycoon (Deborah Grey) and the manner oil has been adversely affecting the life on the island. As a scrutiny of these songs demonstrates, the motif of oil vs nature has been aestheticized and moralized in public imagination and judgement. Aesthetically, the un-natural (monstrous), alienating, inhuman/dehumanizing, and toxic effects of oil on human-nonhuman natures have been associated with the repulsive ugliness of Grey; and the original, authentic, and pristine condition of nature are associated with the dazzling beauty of Peruchacha. Morally, the toxicity of oil and the corresponding ugliness of Grey's are construed to be a testimony to her morally monstrous and corrupt nature; whereas Peruchacha's advocacy of a preservationist approach to nature coupled with her embodiment of the traditional values and nature-oriented lifestyle is perceived to be morally noble.

Equally significant is the reverberating rhyming of "bad" and "bed" in the song since it already accentuates the entanglements between Eros and Thanatos, between desire and death, between private and public, and between ethics and biopolitics in the play at various levels. First, as the agent of oil and death on the islands, Grey is perceived, by the public imagination, as a sexually voracious, cannibalistic, and emasculating force. And more objectively in the play, Grey is depicted as a woman who longs for being desired and loved for her own sake and not for the money or power she possesses. Secondly, her morally corrupt, socially adversarial, politically unconscionable, and emotionally vindictive character as well as her ruthless destruction of the native human-nonhuman nature (sacrificed for the surplus extraction by the petro-capitalist system) renders her Eros (or desire) as a force which is inextricable from Thanatos (associated in *Oil Islands* with death, trauma, pain, and punishment). Thirdly, Grey's association with death/Thanatos is further enhanced given the almost identity between her and oil in conjunction with oil's whole infrastructure: oil industrial complex, ecological degradation and pollution, and settler colonialism. The fourth indeed stems from the third element, that is, the intimate intertwinement between two ostensibly polar forces with antithetical dynamics, namely, the libidinal economy and political economy. More specifically, the association established between "bad" and "bed" is evocative of Stephanie LeMenager's description of the modern and contemporary world's addictive attachment to oil in terms of "bad love" – a highly reverberating motif throughout *Oil Islands*.

LeMenager elaborates four reasons for such a symptomatic attachment to oil in terms of "bad love". Primarily, this is because "it has supported overlapping media environments to which there is no apparent 'outside' that might be materialized through imagination and affect as palpable

268 *"It's Not Easy to Make Oil and Love Run in Harness Together"*

hope" (2012, 70). Two, this is because of "the mystified ecological unconscious of modern car culture, which allows for a persistent association of driving with being alive" (80). Three, the investment in oil is an instance of bad love because "its biophysical properties have caused it to be associated with the comic 'lower bodily stratum,' in Mikhail Bakhtin's phrase" (117). LeMenager proceeds to add:

> Oil has been shit and sex, the essence of entertainment. The biophysical properties of oil made it difficult to demystify, especially in the 1920s when the United States approached peak oil discovery with the excitement attributable to other mining events, like the Gold Rush.
>
> (92)

Interestingly, the fourth reason is left intentionally indeterminate ("We gather to watch") in order to account for and leave room for the unanticipated effects of oil in the future: hence the link between oil and futurity (101). In the play, this association between bad and bed, between libidinal and political economy, between desire and death is inflected with a gothic register. More specifically, such songs evoke a sense of macabre and foreboding which congeals around Grey and the Oil Islands. Steward's remark exemplifies this point: "Nobody goes to the Islands if they can help it, sir" (9). This sense is further compounded when elements of the gothic – deadly desire, sexual voracity, the living dead, and mortal eroticism – are explicitly indicated. Tinctured with gothic colours, Grey is presented as an emasculating and voracious vagina dentata in the following instances: when in Scene 2, a bunch of people who have gathered close to the harbour address Ted Kelvey (who has been summoned by Grey to her dazzlingly illuminated yacht) and derisively say: "She's busy . . . she's had a gay young man sent out to her from Europe, a parlour bird" (19), then adding: "She has a lot to think about. She needs her big head to market so much oil through the world" (20). When Ted Kelvey goes to Grey's yacht, the Crowd taunt him in highly sexualized terms thus: "He's got broad shoulders, and good-looking legs, and nothing of the highbrow about him. That's the kind of thing chimpanzees like" (20). Another member of the group harangues: "Hey Ted, you've still got some juice to you, but you'll come back squeezed dry!" And couched in animalistic and highly racialized terms, they add: "Shame on you, Ted Kelvey! – You'll get a nasty little monkey baby, Ted!" (21).

Equally crucially, these songs – as a recurring motif – are invoked throughout the play by the dispossessed public as a counter-discursive means of both coping with the pernicious effects and encroachments of the oil regime on the lives of the inhabitants and of passing moral judgement on it. The songs also serve as a carnivalesque space for creating heteroglossia, expressing resistance and forming a counter-hegemonic space and ethos for practicing agonism and antagonism through which

*"It's Not Easy to Make Oil and Love Run in Harness Together"* 269

hierarchies and exploitative oppression of the petro-capitalist system headed by Grey. Bakhtin's remarks on the nature and function of carnivalesque can be illuminating:

> to consecrate inventive freedom, to permit the combination of a variety of different elements and their reproachment, to liberate from the prevailing point of view of the world, from conventional and established truths and cliches, from all that is humdrum and universally accepted. This carnival spirit offers the chance to have a new outlook on the world.
>
> (Bakhtin 1984, 34)[5]

By the same token, the oil song also serves a Brechtian function too whereby the audience is afforded the critical distance through which it can maintain its critical-dialectical consciousness about these conflictual forces and discourses, But also as a means of drawing the reader's attention to the causal relationship and the dialectical dynamics through which not only nature/energy, labour force, and the dominant petro-capitalist regime on the island (Grey's oil company) but also economy and politics are related. In these popular oil songs of Brown Islands, the oil-affected island is associated with decay, rottenness, natural degradation, dirt and pollution, and a fallen state – all coalescing to signify the metabolic rift in the cycles of capitalist extractive practices: when we conjoin all the snatches of the song, we palpably notice their revelation of a symptomatic miasmal condition in which both the human and the nonhuman natures are blighted and blemished by the toxic effects of the oil industry and extractive practices in the Island. Notably, what has been depicted to emerge clean out of this stench and filth is "dollar". The dollar is clean and stink-free because it is oil-turned-capital or a capitalist commodity; in other words, the stink-free dollar betokens oil after it has undergone the process of abstraction (and financialization) and has transformed into a commodity with an abstract exchange value.

The "Song of the Brown Islands" (in all its variations and permutations) is also reflective of the historical consciousness and social-cultural imaginary of the people affected by Grey's petro-capitalist extractivism and how they think of or perceive oil and oil industry and weave other issues into it as a clustered configuration of values for themselves. Later when Viscount, upon hearing the song, wonders why Grey should be so venomously vilified despite her services to the islands (including modernizing it) – "I don't understand it. It was Debsy who instituted the profit-sharing. It was Debsy who had Prohibition postponed. And Debsy set up the workmen's stores" – Sniffkins' response illuminates the counter-hegemonic nature of this song: "And if you were to fix up every workman in a special heaven of his own with a marble swimming bath and a private W.C., still you'd have the song of the Oil Islands round

270 *"It's Not Easy to Make Oil and Love Run in Harness Together"*

your neck" (78). The song links Grey (the oil magnate) to the polluted island and the coloured workers through the stigma of the smell, thus subjecting both ends of the oil world and social-economic hierarchy to a process of abjection thereby occluding the asymmetries of power. The synecdochic status of the song as a reflection of petrocultural and social-cultural consciousness of and reaction to the ravages of petro-capitalism is further corroborated by the Passengers' diatribe to Sniffkins' vehement objection to the playing of the song from the gramophone: "If you want to keep people from singing the 'Song of the Brown Islands, you'll have to turn all the fishes in the sea into policemen, and then you won't be able to do it" (7).

Crucially, these songs (including the "Song of the Brown Islands") do not merely disclose the public perception of and counter-hegemonic reaction to the ecocatastrophes wrought by the oil company. They also provide ample hints to the cultural politics and social norms of the time – regarding such issues as race, gender, and class – predominant in the Western world both at its core (particularly its Anglo-American part) and at its peripheries (in a Caribbean setting). A conspicuous case in point is the manner the simultaneously abject and abjecting stink of oil is associated with Grey, not only as an oil tycoon and the head of the Island Oil Company, but as a Jewish woman. As the song says: "The very trees rot where they stand in the soil, / And they all belong to a Chimpanzee" (16). As such, this abjecting association between the stink of oil and the perceived stink of a female Jewess illuminates the antisemitic and misogynous norms and ethos of the 1920s–1940s in Germany and the Western world, more broadly. Notably, the use of the "olfactory" sensory perception as a register of disgust, abjection, and animalization is consonant with the antisemitic language of the time which used "smell" as one of the markers of its anti-Jewish projections.[6] This is further corroborated when a young journalist explains: "In the stories about the Chimpanzee is a different smell than is usually found in the two-cent stories of the newspapers" (*Petroleuminseln*, 291). Elsewhere we hear: "She [Grey] is being choked by her own stink [in the original which has been altered to 'stinking oil, in the translation], the bitch" (*Petroleuminseln*, 304; *Oil Islands* 32). Such passages reveal the cultural-racial logic underlying the recurring association between Grey and contagious infection, venereal disease, voracious sexuality, and contaminating stain/stench (hence the juxtaposition of bad and bed). Equally notably, and in keeping with the toxic sublimity of oil and the psycho-symbolic aporias embedded in it – the oil woman figures in the play as "queer". As Patrick states: "Why, I guess there's more there than can be put into plain figures. There's something mighty queer in all the stories about the Chimpanzee, something quite different from what the papers usually feed you" (11). Such a cultural label exposes the social-cultural process of abjection at work here. The perceived nature and position/character of Grey as "queer" reveals her dual status as

*"It's Not Easy to Make Oil and Love Run in Harness Together"* 271

simultaneously animal (or monstrous) and superhuman. Both her animal (or monstrous) and superhuman status/character emanate from her association with and possession of oil and its manifold and overdetermined nature: an at once demonic and divine substance and source of energy, enlightenment, progress/movement. What further compounds this attribute of "queerness" is the ascription of a "maternal" role to Grey (as the "Mother" of the Brown Islands); an attribute which when juxtaposed with her reveals the perceived, or phantasmatic, role of Grey as a phallic mother. This point gains further corroboration when we accommodate the persistent way in which Grey (the Chimpanzee) is perceived (by the public) and depicted in phallic terms (with a "big stick") and masculinized due to her embodiment and possession of oil-driven power and capital. As Steward utters: "I wouldn't dream of it. If you have any savoir-vivre you lose nothing by giving the Islands a miss. The Chimpanzee once sent for a good-looking young mate of mine, and he disappeared in very suspicious circumstances" (9). Another example occurs at the car race when one of the spectators states: "I've always maintained that as a woman Debsy may be a chimpanzee, but as a business man she's a fox that makes Morgan look like a clumsy bear" (80). As will be demonstrated, this symptomatic and impossible desire of being a phallic mother adumbrates and emanates from the perceived nature of oil as the *objet petit a* or impossible object of desire. Grey's ambivalent image – as a phallic mother to be simultaneously abjected and glorified: an abjecting and abjected mother – is consonant with Kristeva's account of the social and psychological dynamics through which the process of abjection is carried out. Kristeva explains how the process of abjection is evidently at work in such phenomena as food loathing, maternal rejection, defilement rites, corpse, skin of the milk, Freud's theory of phobia, and Oedipus complex; adding how in encounter with the abject the emerging subject is at once constituted and plunged into crisis in encountering the threat of abjection and in undergoing the experience of the abject.[7]

Another noteworthy point manifested in these songs is the association between specific races and the stink of oil. This becomes evident when the "Song of the Brown Islands" is sung once more by the Crowd with a slight variation: "There's a stink of petrol and other things, / For there's Chinks and niggers of every degree; / But the dollars don't stink that the petrol brings / And you can't knock spots off the Chimpanzee" (82). Crucially, these lines expose a hitherto latent strain in the racial politics of oil: the racially other or peripheral as cheap coloured labour force (or oil workers). The song attributes this odour to the imported, non-white workers when it says: "They [the island natives and workers] stink of a yellow and black man" (ibid., 287), so that, according to a common strategy of devaluation, strangers and women are stylized as abjects because of their apparently distasteful smell. The transnational oil workers thus feature as modern-day slaves exploited as de-subjectified and stripped of

272 *"It's Not Easy to Make Oil and Love Run in Harness Together"*

any sovereignty and autonomy. It also reveals the racism of the tourists and passengers which seem to be predominantly Anglo-American and European. This is evidenced by their use of the word "niggers" and their "abjection" of the non-white races by associating dark-skinned people (black and brown) with dirt, stink, and waste material. As such, it is clear how both in the racialized cultural hegemony of the Westerners and in the racial politics of the extractive regime dominant on the island, humanity is bifurcated into "men" (humans: American and Anglo-Europeans) and "natives" plus Coolies (African Asian and other peripheral geographies/ regions) (see Jean-Paul Sartre 1961, 7). Other compelling evidence to the way the perception and representation of oil stink is inflected with the questions of race, gender, and other forms of ontological otherization in the cultural imaginary and racialized value structure of the Western (Anglo-American) world is manifested where the vilification of the toxicity of oil runs parallel with racial production and abjection of people of colour (labour force), particularly Africans. Some guests at Peruchacha's part sing: "There's stink of petrol and other things, / For there's Chinks and niggers of every degree" (25). The racial dynamics delineated demonstrates how the "I" of the modern Western world establishes its ontological-racial superiority and global hegemony (driven by the uneven extractive dynamics of petro-capitalism) by "abjecting" and "ejecting" the Other. The dynamics of this process are resonant with Kristeva's account of the notions of the abject and abjection (1982).

The rest of the scene is mainly caried out in the form of stichomythia-like conversations between the passengers who variously align themselves with the polar powers on the Oil Islands, namely, Grey and Peruchacha and what they symbolically stand for. Slightly later, the choral song is interrupted by Sniffkins (an inhabitant of the islands and an employee of the oil company) who, impugning the legitimacy and legality of the operation of the ship belonging to Peruchacha's company – describing it as "a company with such a doubtful charter" (7) – urges the passengers to stop the gramophone and the "libellous song" (7). Sniffkins ultimately smashes the gramophone into pieces only to face the ensuing reaction from the passengers: "Since the record's broken, let's sing the 'Song of the Brown Islands' as a Male Voice Choir" (8). When the Captain threatens to take legal action against him and other passengers try to punish his insolence by beating him, Captain's utterance illuminates the oppressive social-ecological conditions of life on the island: "Leave him alone. He has a' rotten enough life as it is, if he's from the Brown Islands" (8).

### B. *The History of the* Oil Islands

The poetic descriptions and choral songs through which both the social-cultural affects and impressions and the historical-narrative knowledge are conveyed are soon counterpointed with more accurate historical

*"It's Not Easy to Make Oil and Love Run in Harness Together"* 273

knowledge (obtained through the Murray guidebook). The latter method both evokes the broader historical hinterlands and affords more accurate information about the world of the play. As such, prior to even meeting the two main characters, we glean some inklings not only to who the two main characters are (Grey and Peruchacha), in terms of their psychodynamics, ethics, and historical origins, but also to their relation to the Brown Islands. In this regard, *Oil Islands*'s method for presenting history comprises a multiplicity of formal techniques, including allegory, reportage, and quasi-documentary (since some of the details of the historical records which are read are partly fictional). One illustrative example is Patrick's reading from Murray presented as a piece of documentary history and in the form of reportage. As Patrick reads reportage-like from the guidebook:

> The Islands were annexed by Spain in 1587, and used as convict settlements until the eighteenth century. In the nineteenth century the "Islands were taken over by the United States" and large plantations were created, chiefly by the Peruchacha family; but in spite of all efforts malaria was never quite suppressed. In 1887 Governor Daniel M. Grey discovered petroleum wells, the systematic development of which made him the first oil magnate in the States.
>
> (10)

What is crucial about this passage and which more broadly distinguishes the play is its longue durée approach whereby the island is situated within its *conjonctural cycles* and histories of extraction, colonization, and exploitation. Given the colonial roots and ancestral line of Peruchacha, it is evident that Feuchtwanger is perceptively eschewing any racial, ontological, and social-cultural essentialism by avoiding a blunt binary in which nativism, purism, and natural authenticity would be ascribed to Peruchacha and rapacious colonialism, and un-natural (monstrous) extractivism would be attributed to Grey. So, genealogically, both Peruchacha and Grey's familial history (ancestral lines) and their current practice can be characterized as two different modes and historical manifestations of the same phenomenon (namely, colonialism); one in the form of petro-capitalism and the other in the form of settler colonialism. The chief differences lie in their modes and means of exploiting the native land, its ecological/natural resources (agricultural and petrochemical, farming/agriculture through plantationism and oil extraction), and their form of governmentality. Such a difference is also illustrated by the choice of the names each main character (and people in their social-economic circle, respectively) adopts for identifying and referring to the islands: the Brown Islands and the Oil Islands. Whilst the native name "Brown Islands" signifies the history of the founders and the quasi-native people (evocative of associations with brown skins and being in touch with soil and nature of this tropical and

274 *"It's Not Easy to Make Oil and Love Run in Harness Together"*

exotic island), the more recent and functional name "Oil Islands" entirely obliterates that history and identifies the island as merely a resource frontier and a zone of extraction. As such, *Oil Islands*, evidently, refuses to paint an antithetical, or black-and-white, picture of the worlds and forces at work on Brown Island. Both characters have got their own social-political and psychological subtleties and discursive apparatus for their reciprocal battle.

Subsequently, we are afforded a more extended account of the contemporary ramifications of the aforementioned history. As Patrick observes:

> Today his granddaughter Miss Deborah Grey controls the great part of the oil production of the world. The Islands now appear as barren tracts of yellowish and greyish brown slime, with the sole exception of those parts still belonging to the Peruchacha family, where the original character of the scenery, reminiscent of California at its most beautiful, has been preserved. All ships which touch at the Islands belong to the Island Oil Company and the passengers are not permitted to land until after the observance of scrupulous formalities.
>
> (10)

This vignette confronts us with oil-driven Capitalocene as a site-specific local catastrophe or profound actuality of place now lying in a nearly resource-depleted and ecologically degraded condition. It also affords a glimpse into how on this islandic or peripheral oil site both human-nonhuman nature and the possibilities of life have perished or are crumbling under the sign of oil. It thus portends the almost apocalyptic end of the natural and human lives on this island, transpiring at the end of the play, caused by the Capitalogenic devastation and pollution of the island by Grey's energy regime. The description of Grey as the head of the greatest producer and owner of oil resources in the world readily establishes not only the global underpinnings of such a petro-matrix but also its world-ecological implications. Grey's voracious overreach for oil in this peripheral/islandic site finds a psycho-sexual equivalent and translation in the play's attribution, to her, of an orally sadistic (devouring) and emasculating (biting) inclination towards men. Indeed, the de-realization of the nature and the surreal or irreal phantasies and perceptions surrounding the oil figure (Grey) are inextricably intertwined and account for the presence of the elements of grotesque in the play (see also Lowy's notion of critical irrealism).[8] Considered slightly anachronistically, this scene presages contemporary formerly oil-rich sites now wastelands, such as Maracaibo in Venezuela, Baku in Azerbaijan, Gulf of Mexico (Deepwater Horizon), and Niger Delta in Nigeria.

From the very outset a starkly dystopian strain comes to imbue the ambience of the play thus foreshadowing the looming oil-stained world awaiting us on the island and ultimately the doom impending in the air

## "It's Not Easy to Make Oil and Love Run in Harness Together" 275

and awaiting the ecological life of the island, the oil workers, and Peruchacha. We are afforded abundant glimpses into the degraded state of nature (and the sheer scale of pollution) in this scene which I have probed next. The oil company's infliction of metabolic rift on the islands finds a cogent articulation in Sniffkins' account of the ecologically degraded condition:

> The air of the Oil Islands isn't healthy for everybody, my good sir, and if you are ever in a position to sample it – which I hardly expect – I should recommend you to keep a still tongue in your head. I have known people in the prime of life who were fatally affected by the climate of the Brown Islands.
>
> (18)

We can garner more specific insights into the ecologically degraded "climate" of the islands (including a reference to oil spills) from the ensuing description: "The water looks as thick as pea soup. It's a wonder they'd put such a yacht out on it" (19). As is evident, the lived/perceived and imagined effects of oil have been registered in highly affective-sensorial terms – particularly the olfactory, tactile, and the visual. In *Oil Islands* – given the rampant presence of pollution and toxic materials – the term "climate" gradually accrues a concrete material and transsubjective affective force and autonomous agency. In the psycho-symbolic and oil-saturated petroscape of *Oil Islands*, not only all interpersonal, social, and human-nonhuman relations are mediated by oil, but it is as if anyone who is associated with oil is physically and metaphysically infected with its contagiously corrupt nature and corrupting influence.

In the final moments of the first scene, when the steamship eventually reaches the smog-covered edge of the harbour, we start sensing the brooding presence of petro-capitalism's disciplinary regime and Grey's sovereign power. No sooner has the ship cast anchor than it is approached by the police asking it to return, refusing the passengers (the majority of whom have been invited to attend Peruchacha's annual party) on the Oil Islands, and exerting the implementation of a sovereign and exclusive regulation on mobility and space. The form of governmentality imposed by the oil company on various social-economic and infrastructural facets of the human-nonhuman life on the islands becomes evident when after 11 days of sea voyage to reach the Oil Islands the passengers are told: "Captain, I regret that I can't give you permission to land". To which Captain objects thus: "But your consul assured us we could land. This is a most high-handed, unwarrantable proceeding" (16). Each and every passenger starts airing their vehement grievances and vigorous objections. Ingram states: "I have important business with her" and Patrick asserts: "A little bird tells me I'm going to see Miss Grey in spite of all this damned mysterious island" (17). Passengers and visitors of various ranks and orders unanimously describe Peruchacha's party as "a celebration

## 276 *"It's Not Easy to Make Oil and Love Run in Harness Together"*

of national importance" (17) and call the interception of the steamship a "worldwide scandal" (17). We then hear more explicitly of the intense hostility and rivalry between the two chief figures (Peruchacha and Grey) on the island (hence their competitive claims to the passageways and mobility). And Ingram accentuates how Grey holds the monopoly in this power struggle: "If you are really keen on visiting them, you shouldn't have taken this steamer. The Chimpanzee always downs her rivals. It was sheer folly of Miss Peruchacha to set up an opposition line" (13). Such a disciplinary control of space and of the mobility and transportation of humans, commodities, and vehicles attests to the status of the Oil Islands as a resource enclave where not only does Grey's oil company hold monopoly over mobility, visibility, public access, passageways, and transportation. It also imposes a state of exception through which Grey can abuse her sovereign power to foist an extra-legal measure to vindictively disrupt her rival's (Peruchacha's) ceremonies and operations. What illustrates this extra-legal exercise of sovereignty is the court warrant Police Officer holds despite the legal agreements between Peruchacha's tourism and sugar-exporting company and Grey's oil company over transportation and passageways. As Police Officer says: "Decree of the Supreme Court. Would you care to look at the warrant?" (16).

Ultimately Grey's disciplinary staff remain relentless and none of the passengers are allowed to leave the ship to visit the island and attend Peruchacha's anniversary ceremony – except for Grey's own visitors (Ingram, the movie star, and a few others) – and forced to return to the U.S.A. Passengers' choice of response to this denial of entrance is important: a snatch from the prohibited "Song of the Brown Islands". They sing: "There's no law or money but hers to be had, / And you've got to submit in your bed and your job" (17). Interestingly, this opening scene also gives us a glimpse into one of the dominant petrocultural elements and its icon: the pervasive presence of automobiles as the symbolic markers of the 20th-century consumer culture and the era of Americanization. This is evidenced by Patrick's remark: "I'm a free-born American citizen, and I don't give two hoots for the gloomy remarks of that pessimistic guy. Do you see a single policeman anywhere on the quay? I see only automobiles in Miss Peruchacha's colours" (15).

Importantly, we are afforded a glimpse into the panoptic nature of Grey's disciplinary regime on the Oil Islands. This is evidenced by Patrick's astonishment at the obtrusive ubiquity and jarring visibility of the structures of the oil industry on the island: "Aren't those oil shafts over there?" Ingram responds: "The crew don't like to talk about the Islands. They think the Chimpanzee has ears everywhere" (9) – a remark which reveals the system of surveillance established by Grey's petro-regime. Subsequently, Steward adds: "And that's not a nigger superstition either, sir. There's wireless and all kinds of things. When you're in sight of the Islands the best savoir vivre is silence" (9). The ubiquity of Grey's disciplinary and

## "It's Not Easy to Make Oil and Love Run in Harness Together" 277

surveillance system is coupled with her near invisibility to the public – two attributes which commingle to render her the figure of the sovereign par excellence. This point is touched upon by Sniffkins when he emphasizes the public's lack of accessibility to her: "Miss Deborah Grey isn't exactly a museum exhibit, gentlemen, and I imagine you'll find it difficult to take a good look of her" (11). These two features indeed intensify the formation of a whole nexus of cultural phantasies about her real nature.

Importantly, however, the aforementioned conditions and concerns are conveyed through an affective-sensory register in *Oil Islands*, including the visual, olfactory, and aural. This affective-linguistic configuration (the oil song, the odour, etc.) also induces in us an affective anticipation of the components of the petro-industrial complex operating on the island, including Grey (with her psychological, ethical, and sexual characteristics), the oil workers, and ecological devastation. Upon closer inspection, we notice how the cultural climate, individual affective states, and the climatic-environmental conditions prevailing on the Oil Islands are indelibly intertwined and co-determining. All three also evince a symptomatic condition of suffering an ontological rupture and a metabolic rift, that is, de-naturing, depletion, and degradation. Due to its allegorical aesthetics, world-ecological (core-periphery) vision, and oil-saturated ontology, *Oil Islands* demands a repositioning of hermeneutics appropriate to a particular context without falling into the trap of an epistemology that is purportedly petrocultural and world-systemic but represents other interests. The unravelling of the dynamics of such aesthetic and its concomitant petro-ontological features demands the adoption of what Felski has called an "affective hermeneutics". Affective hermeneutics designates a method of analysis where the questions of affectivity, sensory perceptions, and (the hermeneutics of) reading serve as means through which we gain a more material and phenomenologically oriented grasp of how it feels to live and represent a world which witnesses the emergence of oil as the globally dominant means and medium of experience and lifeform, the material conditions of oil extraction/production, its ecological implications, dynamics of desire, and configuration of political-economic strata within this islandic petroscene.[9] Similarly, and in the context of petrocultural analysis, LeMenager utilizes the notions of "affective context" and "emotional geographies" to describe the embedded presence of oil in our quotidian life at the levels of habitual body (or perception), cognition, and representation. LeMenager indicates how raw materials such as oil and coal "produced" entire environments and were deeply integrated into the self-image of Western modernity (see LeMenager 2012, 60). By the same token, we can argue that if part of our energy unconscious and habits of consumption are repressed or invisibly cathected, then by raising them to the level of consciousness (with a focus on our petro-affective dynamics and their conditions of possibility), not only a genealogical account of the causes of current ecological ravages

## 278 *"It's Not Easy to Make Oil and Love Run in Harness Together"*

can be provided, but also a symptomatological account of our currently hegemonic modes of perception and representation that help perpetuate them. This task can be accomplished by showing how the structures of our unconscious phantasies, feelings, our experience of ourselves and the world are determined by a certain energy resource and a certain (petro-cultural) mode of extraction/production/consumption; a move which can pave the way for altering them (partly by re-coding emotions/affects) and moving beyond an oil-bound horizon.

One effective way of undertaking an affective hermeneutic approach in relation to *Oil Islands* is to concentrate on the questions of mood (or Stimmung), sensory details, and affective-cognitive (and/or psychosomatic) states as they feature in the play. As Heidegger explains:

> What we indicate ontologically with the term attunement (*befindlichkeit*) is ontically what is most familiar and an everyday kind of thing: mood, being in a mood. Prior to all psychology of moods . . . we must see this phenomenon as a fundamental existential and outline its structure.
>
> (1996, 126)

By the same token, a mood-oriented analysis of *Oil Islands* will reveal the affective-cognitive and relational effects of the individuals' "thrown-ness" into an oil world or petroscape. A compelling elaboration on the notion of "mood" and "affect", particularly in relation to atmospheric and ecological conditions permeating the world of a literary work – in the context of phenomenological-hermeneutic tradition, and in relation to literary analysis – has been proposed by Gumbrecht who explicates the advantages of such a mood-oriented approach thus:

> [T]he dimension of Stimmung discloses a new perspective on – and possibility for – the "ontology of literature." . . . [A]n ontology of literature that relies on concepts derived from the sphere of Stimmung does not place the paradigm of representation front-and-center. "Reading for Stimmung" always means paying attention to the textual dimension of the forms that envelop us and our bodies as a physical reality – something that can catalyze inner feelings without matters of representation necessarily involved.
>
> (2012, 5)[10]

The term "climate" here comes to signify a concrete, material, and trans-subjective affective impact on the subject. A *Stimmung*-oriented analysis of *Oil Islands* will enable us to discern how oil transpires as a tangible material affect that is both immanent to the individual and transcends them. A *Stimmung*-oriented approach will thus enable a material – that is, ecologically and phenomenologically oriented – reading/experience of

## "It's Not Easy to Make Oil and Love Run in Harness Together" 279

the oil ontology and oil affect that permeates the islands. In incorporating the questions of atmosphere/climate, mood/*Stimmung*, affective dynamics, and ambience in our world-systemic and petrocultural analysis of *Oil Islands*, the felt, unconscious, and psychosomatically registered effects and affects of oil (on the body of human and nonhuman nature) will be rendered legible and palpable. As will be shown later, this focus reveals how oil has created an "epochal climate" or *Grundstimmung* (the term proposed by Dreyfus and derived from Heidegger) identifiable as the Capitalocene. In this regard, it would be illuminating to utilize the notion of an epochal climate or *Grundstimmung* to delineate the concrete physical (to wit, climatological-ecological and affective-psychological) actuality of oil and petro-capitalist infrastructure operating on the island and to capture the material and affective structures pervading Feuchtwanger's petro-drama.[11] Such an approach will afford us an insight into the affective and material structures of consciousness, cognition, and perception along with the modes and economies of relationality, self-identification, and investment that an ontology of oil, an oil-driven lifeform, and a petrocultural discourse engender at personal and social-historical levels – particularly in the context of the early 20th century. The particular climate, infrastructure, and social dynamics of the Oil Islands exert a sense of gloom and sickness on their characters which is symbolically expressed through pervasive stink of oil, grotesque facial ugliness of the oil magnate, and the images of contagion, illness, and pathological behaviour recurring throughout. As such the reader is enveloped in the fluid folds of oil ontology of the play which is fraught with a sense of foreboding, a barbaric terror, sickness, and alienation. Such an aesthetics helps reveal how oil, far from being confined to an infrastructural dynamics, is enmeshed with and infuses the affective-cognitive structures of the individual subject as well as the atmospheric and environmental conditions of their being.

### C. Island and Allegory

The very choice of island as the setting of *Oil Islands* not only affords a unique opportunity for a cognitive mapping of the global reach and scope of the American oil empire. It also enables the reader to expose the ontological dynamics of petro-imperialism and reveal new facets and logics of petro-capitalism as an uneven global system, including its extractive-discursive strategies for neo-colonization of a resource-rich island, transportation of transnational labour as precarious cheap labour (approximating modern-day slavery), and its infliction of metabolic rift on the peripheral island. In the more extended three-volume scope of this book, it is only *Petrol Station* that matches *Oil Islands* in terms of liminality, that is, not only its being located both in a ecologically and ontologically liminal spot but also geographically liminal; in other words, the setting (the exotic Oil Islands) in the play features as an almost indefinite border between history

280  *"It's Not Easy to Make Oil and Love Run in Harness Together"*

and fiction, between the visible and the invisible, between consciousness and the unconscious. Due to its allegorical style, its use of a language uncoloured by local dialects, and its use of generic (almost stereotypical) names coupled with the dearth of historically-geographically specific and recognizable/identifiable places and figures that would contribute to grounding the text in a concrete historical reality, *Oil Islands* is a play that resists historical-geographical specificity and purely local readings. Instead, it insists on embodying a model of relational dynamics between the core (with its extractive logics) and periphery (as a resource for the four cheaps). As such, *Oil Islands* in its thematics, ontological logics, and political-economic dynamics claims to be globally extendable to a variety of other places and times across the historical span and geographical spectrum of the petro-capitalist system, thereby appealing to a globally inflected sensibility. The passengers on the ship and the inhabitants of the islands (including the transnational labour force) thus become subject to what Foucault calls "an economy of suspended rights" (1977, 11), given that to all of them various modes of a state of exception is applied as they are precluded the possibility of visit and coerced to return to the US mainland. As such, the political, racial, and libidinal economy prevailing on the islands becomes all the more morbid and macabre and all the more mystified and spectral.

*Oil Islands* inverts the generic expectations and cultural phantasies surrounding the figure of the exotic islands.[12] Rather than presenting, through the symbolic codes of primitive cultural tropes, the mosaic of a pastoral landscape and its palimpsest richness, it shows how such prelapsarian, though phantasmatic, bliss has long been gone and is now at once evaporating into toxic fumes and dissolving into a viscous soup due to the extraction and production of oil on this formerly idyllic island. As such, in *Oil Islands* we find ourselves in a fluid dreamscape where death and desire, love and hatred, nature and industry/technology, pollution and paradise coexist and even commingle. It is the death figure (the oil magnate) who presides over this landscape driven by the desire for the surplus production of capital and the desire for rewriting her face or being reborn into a desirable beauty through the power oil capital (see later). During the main narrative-dramatic time in which the play unfolds, it is set on a Caribbean island which was initially occupied by the Spanish pirates due to its idyllic nature and was subsequently converted into a sugar plantation where nature as a resource was extracted not merely as a source of agricultural subsistence, but rather as a source of capitalist production. More recently, the island has been appropriated as part of American territory and dominated by an American oil company (led by Deborah Grey) for the extraction of its oil resources. *Oil Islands* features a multi-tiered social and economic system and environments, consisting of the traditionally dominant class (the Peruchachas), the oil magnate and her company (Deborah Grey), the native locals and inhabitants, the

*"It's Not Easy to Make Oil and Love Run in Harness Together"* 281

transnational laborers, and the oil company staff. These points fall within three key cross-cutting themes: one, the universalization of sacrifice zones; two, extractive necropolitics; and three, political geo-ontologies. In its geography and the psycho-geography it evokes, *Oil Islands* is embedded in a weave of various geographical points: an exotic island, Russia, America, Japan. More specifically, taking an indefinite (un-specified) Caribbean island as its setting – and as a landscape in which quotidian life and the oil infrastructure are intimately intertwined – *Oil Islands* provides us with insights both into the longue durée of global extractivism and into the logics and form of globalism that operates within the industrial complex through which oil is extracted. Formally, not only does the play alternate between the two poles of social-economic power on the islands who have significant ontological and psychological differences: Peruchacha and Grey. *Oil Islands* also alternates between zooming in and zooming out. In zooming in, the play focuses on private scenes of business, ethical-psychological intricacies (including insights into the questions of desire, love, and hatred) and interpersonal relations; and in zooming out to reflect the social ethos and cultural consciousness. As such, Feuchtwanger partially provincializes the universalizing discourse of Europe concerning Anthropocene and concomitant matters.

The spatial, geographical, and ecological conditions described earlier attest to how the environment in which crude oil is extracted is not only "heterogeneous" and "international", but also "lacking in a sense of place" (Amitav Ghosh 2002) and an "insular and socially thin neoliberal landscape of deregulated enterprises" (James Ferguson 2006). Accordingly, Feuchtwanger's island can be described as a heterotopos, because with its contradictory properties it renders various forms of rift (including metabolic rift), and displacement inflicted by global petro-capitalism on the peripheries tangible. As will be shown, such dynamics is illustrated by the description and depiction of the island as a barbaric and animalistic space whilst maintaining a tacit critical dialogue with the Darwinian paradigm as part of its subplot and its characterization of the characters. The choice of setting itself to some extent discloses Feuchtwanger's latent political and racial leanings: even though the island seems to also include (pre-Peruchachan) natives, we are not afforded a glimpse into their lives; nor do we hear from them directly at all. Furthermore, the formerly Edenic island is not depicted as having been outside capitalist relations of extraction and production prior to the establishment of the oil company. In not choosing an island inhabited by truly aboriginal natives whose dwelling can be traced back to non-colonial or at least non-extractivist and non-violent origins and roots, the play places petro-imperialism as the latest cycle in an extended array of cycles of colonial extractivisms but also exploitation of human-nonhuman nature and peripheries as an inherent and transhistorical aspect of human life, sociality and mobility. Equally notably the island setting not only enhances the allegorical facets

282 *"It's Not Easy to Make Oil and Love Run in Harness Together"*

of the play, but evokes a long durée of colonialism, imperialism, and extractivism as well as labour movements and slave ships. The islandic setting is also consonant with the material and medium of oil: its fluidity, its volatility, its tidalectic dynamics.

As some scholars have argued, an efficacious representation and critique of the multi-scalar nature of both the Anthropocene/Capitalocene and the capitalist methods of extractivism "demands a multiscalar method of telescoping between space (planet) and place (island) in a dialectic or 'tidalectic' way to see how they mutually inform each other" (DeLoughrey 2019, 2). Fredric Jameson, since the 1980s, has been perceptively emphasizing the efficacy of allegory as a rigorous means of presenting a "totalizing" registration of the various levels of the capitalist system, but also as master narratives (imbricated in tradition) in which our collective fantasies about history and reality are reflected.[13] Most recently in *Allegory and Ideology*, Jameson re-affirms the advantages of allegory in terms of the world "allegoresis" by accentuating not only its capacity to capture the continuities and discontinuities (or disjunctions) between the local and the global, between the material and the abstract, between materialism and idealism (subjectivity and utopian thinking); but also its self-reflexive nature – hence its ability to alert us to the material conditions of possibility of emplotment and narration. According to Jameson, in an allegorical model, the

> gaps between these zones . . . constitute the empty spaces across which the attractions and repulsions (or identity and difference) pass. Such gaps thereby offer a convenient figure (in the absence of figuration) for the identification of incommensurables, as well as their differentiation.
>
> (xvii)

Jameson proceeds to add a crucial point by identifying "the gaps between the levels" as

> the place in which libidinal investment takes place . . . this concept designates a transfer of vital energies and of an almost obsessional attention from its source to another, less richly nourished area; or, . . . a distraction of one form of libidinal immediacy from its initial object to a less threatening or dangerous one.
>
> (xvii)

Such an interpretative and ontological model closely corresponds to the psychodynamics and aesthetics informing *Oil Islands*. One of the advantages of the allegorical model is the ways in which it enables a combination of the abstract and the concrete which in the context of a work concerned with oil and petro-capitalism could be translated into

## "It's Not Easy to Make Oil and Love Run in Harness Together" 283

abstractions of capitalism (through, for instance, commodification and financialization) and its concrete ecological affective-cognitive effects on human-nonhuman natures.

Allegory has recently been recognized as an effective aesthetic means of providing not only a genealogical critique of capitalism but also of the multi-scalar nature of the Anthropocene. Predicating her argument on Édouard Glissant's notion that the erasure of the postcolonial past is the reason or impulse underlying "an 'obsessive' desire on the part of the writer/artist to excavate the ruins of empire", DeLoughrey underscores the "importance of allegory in addressing the irruption into modernity" (2019, 3). The importance of allegoresis, to DeLoughrey, resides in its serving as an efficacious dialectical method and means for critically capturing the manifold and multi-scalar relations between past, present, and future as parts of a disjunctive and heterogeneous constellation. Having demonstrated the ways in which the "totality of ocean space is necessarily rendered in its smaller allegorical parts through the ship, the shore, and the body, particularly a sea creature" (166), DeLoughrey proceeds to focus on the allegorical significance of the island thus: "Next to the ship, the island is perhaps the most essential constellation for figuring the planet. Due to the part-for-whole function of allegory the island concept of bounded space has been a popular synecdoche for our 'Earth Island'" (166). Situating such allegorically significant implications in the context of the Anthropocene, she states: "This spatial allegory of finitude has become all the more relevant in an era in which Anthropocene scholars warn of humans reaching the limits of their 'planetary boundaries'" (166). Due to its deep entanglements with a long colonial history, the allegorically inflected notion of the island continues to be an effective constellation or means of revealing the dynamics of the capitalist world system. As Fredric Jameson observes, "in order to understand the world, . . . a being of such enormous complexity that it can only be mapped and modelled indirectly", we need "a simpler object that stands as its allegorical interpretant" (1992, 169).

If we consider the ensuing characterization of the customary or traditional conception of the island in Western literature, we will discern how Feuchtwanger's depiction of the Oil Islands and his act of situating it in a longue durée of colonial extractivism runs against this grain. As DeLoughrey elaborates:

> western discourse has configured the tropical island in terms of vulnerability, isolation, remoteness, nonhuman nature, and historical "purity" in terms of species development and of a culture isolated from the flows of modernity. The two powerful allegorical modes that are closely tied to islands, utopia and dystopia, arose from a long history of European colonization.
>
> (2019, 166–167)

## 284 *"It's Not Easy to Make Oil and Love Run in Harness Together"*

Equally importantly, the phenomenon/figure of the island has been wielded and recognized as a paradigmatic example of an allegorical rendition of the world and the forces informing its various parts driven by a *repetition-with-difference* petro-capitalist logic. As Richard H. Grove explains:

> The isolated oceanic island, like the frail ships on the great Scientific circumnavigations of the seventeenth and eighteenth centuries, directly stimulated the emergence of a detached self-consciousness and a critical view of European origins and behaviour, of the kind dramatically prefigured by Daniel Defoe in Robinson Crusoe. Thus the island easily became, in practical environmental as well as mental terms, an easily conceived allegory of a whole world.
>
> (1995, 8–9)

What distinguishes Feuchtwanger's island from the majority of Caribbean islands represented in literary-dramatic works (where the focus is primarily on various kinds of plantations and products such as cocoa, coffee, etc.) is its depiction of an oil island. Given the global scope and world-systemic dynamics of the extraction of oil – all of which entail a multi-scalar encounter between various geographical entities/forces, predominantly between the core and peripheries, informed with uneven relational dynamics at various levels of ontology, political economy, race, gender, and class – allegory offers itself as an efficacious form in tackling and depicting the dynamics of this world-systemic network of oil extraction – particularly given the historical-cultural ties between the form and empire.

Indeed, the encounter with the hitherto undiscovered lands and islands led to the formation of a new self-consciousness and a new unconscious among the Western subjects. As Jason Moore notes: "The Columbian rupture of 1492 marked not only the 'discovery' of the Americas, but the 'discovery of Mankind' – and with it, Nature" (Jason Moore, "Nature/Society & The Violence of Real Abstraction" in https://jasonwmoore. wordpress.com/2016/10/04/naturesociety-the-violence-of-real-abstraction/. See also Albuafia 2008; Mumford 1934). These sites of "utopian nature" however were soon turned into sites of ecological rupture due to violent extraction (of human-nonhuman resource) and experimentation; a systemic, imperial violence which was repressed, buried and mystified through misrepresentation – that is, through romance, sentimental travel stories, plantation georgics, and island idylls. More specifically, a noteworthy testament to the ways in which these peripheral islands were wielded not only as "laboratories" for implementing scientific and technological experiments but also – as *Oil Islands* illustrates – as laboratories for extractive practices and the study of their effects on human-nonhuman natures is Grove's study. Here Grove rigorously

*"It's Not Easy to Make Oil and Love Run in Harness Together"* 285

establishes how the tropical island colonies were utilized (or "instituted") as laboratories for the earliest European conservation practices, including botanical and other kinds of experimentation. As he demonstrates, the rise of ecological degradation ties very closely in the historical record with utopian island narratives, a "paradox" he relates to the "full flowering . . . of Edenic island discourse during the mid-seventeenth century" (Grove, *Green Imperialism*, 5).

Whilst the specific identity of the island remains indefinite, we can conjecture, with fair accuracy, its identity by garnering our inklings from numerous facts and references to the historical and geographical aspects of the island interspersed throughout *Oil Islands*. These pivotal features include not only the abundance of oil reserves on an island (the Brown Islands) which is located just south of the United States and only 11 days from its closest coastal point. It also includes ample information provided about various neighbouring countries, the racial identifications, and ethnic specificities, including characters' names and descriptions – such as the reference to Peruchacha as "salta atras". Add to this the references such as the Immigration Bill (to be approved by the US Congress), transnational labour, Japan's involvement in the transnational labour movements, and references to Murray's guidebook. These crucial clues, upon being juxtaposed, coalesce to provide us with a fairly coherent configuration and evoke a geographically more specific image of the island. Premised on these points, coupled with the historical facts delineated later, we can infer that Oil Islands is most probably a Caribbean island situated in the proximity of US borders. Such a focus takes us beyond the British and European focus evinced in the other three plays under scrutiny in the other chapters and affords us a rare insight into the operations of United States' petro-imperial and neo-colonial oil operations in a liminal area.

To establish this point, it is worth very briefly dwelling on the historical situation of Trinidad, Mexico, and the Caribbean Venezuela on the global oil market in the early decades of the 20th century. To begin with Trinidad, Walter Darwent drilled the world's first continually productive oil well in Trinidad in 1866 (Hughes 2017, 2; also see 7–10). The extraction process then burgeoned into the establishment of refineries and an increase in the production of commercially profitable quantities of oil. This trend reached a culminating point in the 1920s. This led to the establishment of Trinidad Leaseholds Ltd.'s Cat Cracker Unit at Pointe-à-Pierre in 1921. Notably, in 1930 the production of crude oil increased to 10 million barrels per year. More importantly, 1930 marks the very year in which Trinidad started to become a site for the refinement of oil imported from Venezuela. Gradually, more technological developments to the extraction and refinement of oil were introduced, including electrical well logging in 1932 and gas injection in 1933. And 1937 marks a juncture in the history of oil in Trinidad since this year witnessed widespread labour unrest in the oilfield area (see Hughes 2017, 6–10). However, there

286 *"It's Not Easy to Make Oil and Love Run in Harness Together"*

are two noteworthy points that render Trinidad a far less likely option for being the indefinite setting of *Oil Islands*. On the one hand, given that in the late 1920s Trinidad was producing nearly 38% and in the 1930s over 40% of the British Empire oil, considering the setting of the island in the play to be Trinidad would be far less likely. On the other hand, given the monopoly US held, historically, over oil extraction/production in the Caribbean Venezuela in conjunction with the explicit and extensive territorial and political-economic ties invoked between the US mainland and the Oil Islands in the play, it is highly likely that the setting is the Caribbean Venezuela.

As regards Mexico, whilst both Mexico and Venezuela experienced an oil boom (in terms of discovery and extraction/production), Venezuela seems a more likely option for the setting of *Oil Islands* because the first oil discoveries in Mexico occurred in 1900 whilst in Venezuela in the mid-1920s. So the latter historically also seems a more compelling match or correspondence.[14] This is further substantiated and corroborated when we take into account the facts concerning oil industry and oil production in the 1920s and 1930s both in a global context and more specifically within the US context. In the 1920s Venezuelan oil fields were perceived as a panacea for the crisis of prices and fear of peak oil and shortage (altogether described as "chaos in the domestic market" 10) besetting and haunting the US. As Isser explains:

> The fear of a crude shortage in the US, which had enabled the US Majors to enlist the US government in supporting their entry into the Middle East, was due partially to projections by the US Geological Survey (USGS) and the Bureau of Mines. The USGS had projected a total of little more than nine billion barrels of recoverable oil in 1920, and rising prices and increased imports from Mexico reinforced this perception of impending exhaustion.
>
> (2016, 10)

The United States' approach, however, was not purely economic, but – as has been the customary staple of resource colonialism – was informed with racial politics where resource extraction and racial production ran parallel in a hierarchized ontological and social-economic order underpinned with the same dichotomizing trope of nature-culture and modern-pre-modern. Underscoring how Venezuela was "economically and politically attractive at the beginning of the 1920s" to the United States, Garavini illuminates the racial politics latent in such an interest:

> US elite had long held a racist and patronizing attitude towards the Latin American neighbors. The US Council on Foreign Relations founded in 1921 argued that if the native inhabitants were not

## "It's Not Easy to Make Oil and Love Run in Harness Together" 287

capable of developing their natural resources, somebody else would have to intervene "regardless of the ethics".

(in Garavini 2019, 18)

One of the fascinating historical documents that illustrates such a racialized intertwinement of race, labour regime, and resource extractivism (under the rubric of neo-colonial governance and relations) is the following. A US report on Venezuela produced in 1924 argued that "the major proportion of the population is degenerating in its thought physically, morally and mentally"; this is justified on the basis that the "amalgamation of white, negro and several Indian stocks" tended to adulterate or attenuate the purity of the race (quoted in: Tinker Salas, 2009, 35). The following statement sheds lights on the dynamics and mechanisms of such a twofold discourse: "Weakening racial stock aside, Venezuela had become attractive at the precise moment when the Mexican revolution was endangering the position of the international oil companies there" (Garivini 18).

The Venezuelan and Caribbean were critical to US-imperial petro-imaginary, which was partly codified through the 1934 Petroleum Act. Such a neo-colonial encounter/contact between the American Empire and the peripheral Venezuela left an indelible mark on their national economy and ecology, turning Venezuela into a monoculture. The upheaval in Venezuela's staple economy is evidently reflected in the trajectory of the commodities produced and exported during the 1913–1940 period. A scrutiny of the 1913–1940 interval vividly illustrates how within the space of 20 years oil moved from playing no role whatsoever in the national economy of the Caribbean Venezuela in 1913 (where cocoa and coffee occupied the predominant position) to becoming by far the dominant staple and product in 1940 when it occupied nearly 95% of the export and national income (see Table 5.1).

Table 5.2 illustrates the trajectory through which Venezuela rose to become the dominant oil producer, along with the US, in the world during the 1920–1940 interval; hence Venezuela's significance to the political economy of the global oil market and to the world energy market but also to the maintenance of its infrastructures.

Situating *Oil Islands* and its longue durée critique of extractive capitalism (comprising Peruchacha's sugar plantations and Grey's oil extraction) in a comparative context can be highly illuminating. Pondering the effects of the oil discovery and production in the context of Angola and placing it in the longue durée of the encounter between the peripheral Angola and the British Empire (core), Reed observes how "Oil reinforced the extractive political institutions established under Portuguese colonial rule and added fuel to the fiery contests for control of the Angolan state after independence" (2009, 18). A testimony to the allegorical (in the sense of world-systemic dynamics and its more global geographical-historical

288 *"It's Not Easy to Make Oil and Love Run in Harness Together"*

*Table 5.1* Main Commodities Exported by Venezuela from 1913 to 1940[15]

| Year | Coffee and Cocoa | | Petroleum | |
|---|---|---|---|---|
| | Value | % | Value | % |
| 1913 | 109,1 | 71,4 | – | – |
| 1921 | 84,7 | 63,4 | 11,8 | 8,8 |
| 1929 | 158,0 | 20,3 | 593,6 | 76,2 |
| 1936 | 51,1 | 6,7 | 684,2 | 89,0 |
| 1940 | 27,2 | 3,2 | 809,0 | 94,0 |

Source: Miguel Izard, *Series estadisticas para la historia de Venezuela*, 1970.

*Table 5.2* Foreign Oil Production by Region (Thousand Barrels)

| Country | 1920 | 1925 | 1929 | 1932 | 1940 |
|---|---|---|---|---|---|
| Mexico | 157,069 | 115,515 | 39,530 | 32,805 | 44,036 |
| Venezuela | 457 | 19,687 | 137,472 | 116,541 | 185,570 |
| Other S.A. | 6,611 | 21,119 | 53,295 | 51,219 | 83,194 |
| Iran | 12,230 | 34,038 | 42,145 | 49,471 | 66,317 |
| Other M.E. | 0 | 0 | 798 | 837 | 31,929 |
| Far East | 29,145 | 35,868 | 55,339 | 53,244 | 81,740 |
| United States | 442,929 | 763,743 | 1,053,128 | 785,159 | 1,353,214 |

Source: DeGoyler and L. W. McNaughton, *Twentieth Century Petroleum Statistics* (Dallas 1950).

extendability/applicability) nature of the setting of *Oil Islands* and the uneven relational dynamics it exposes between the peripheral Caribbean island and the US core concerning the issue of oil is the treatment of similar peripheral zones and regions as resource frontiers by other European imperial-colonial forces. Furthermore, the two islands of Curaçao and Aruba, just off the coast and part of the Dutch Antilles, "offered a guarantee of political stability (they were part of the Dutch empire) and a perfect geographical location to build refineries" (18). Most importantly, "the waters and delta of the vast estuary-lake of Maracaibo were home to gigantic and hyperproductive deposits, such as the one mentioned in La Rosa, that promised lower extraction costs when compared to US oil fields" (Garavini 2019, 18). As Garivini further adds: "Geographically, Maracaibo was close to the potential export markets, in particular to the United States and, in Western Europe, to Great Britain" (18).

## "It's Not Easy to Make Oil and Love Run in Harness Together" 289

Considering the conspicuous allegorical aesthetics of *Oil Islands* in conjunction with the disciplinary dynamics implemented by Grey's oil company (on space, mobility, and biopolitics), it would be safe to argue that Oil Islands feature as a resource enclave in the play. Garnering my bearings from Watts (2004) and his emphasis on both commodity determinism and enclave politics, I would argue that in both *Oil Fields* and *Oil Islands* we see how both the centralized government and transnational oil corporations collude to perpetuate uneven petro-capitalist dynamics as well as economic and institutional reliance on oil. As Reed explicates:

> The enclave is not only a geographic descriptor for walled-off oil bases, it is also the conceptual site of partnership between the government and oil corporations. Each partner relies on the other for legitimacy. Government and corporate officials operate in tandem to manage resource control through co-optation and violence. The enclave is the structuring force behind petrocapitalism and petro-violence.
>
> (Reed 2009, 19)[16]

As *Oil Islands* extensively and explicitly illustrates, another function of the resource enclave and its production of the peripheral regions/countries as zones of sacrifice is the facility of keeping them invisible and out of public scrutiny to evade any accountability for the social-ecological devastation and human-nonhuman sacrifice they inflict on these zones. Drawing on the production sites of the American mid-Atlantic region, Christopher F. Jones gives further insight into this geopolitical perspective of oil:

> The production of oil came at great environmental cost. But users who lived hundreds and even thousands of miles away did not need to worry about oil flowing into their streams or ruining their soil. . . . For the most part, the users of oil gained the benefit of cheap energy without assuming responsibility for its environmental damage. One of the reasons that fossil fuel energy production has been so environmentally destructive is that those who benefit from energy sources rarely have to live with the environmental damages associated with its production.
>
> (143)

As *Oil Islands* unfolds, we glean insights into the extent to which the oil island is a world unto itself where through policing and disciplinary forces all spaces, mobility, and transportation (of people, passengers, visitors, and native inhabitants) are controlled and are under the monopoly of the oil company and its head: Grey. As such, the Oil Islands strikes us as an "enclave". By depicting in detail how a peripheral oil-rich region in the Caribbean Venezuela is first de-territorialized (through eradicating and appropriating its local nature and history as well as its social-cultural

290 *"It's Not Easy to Make Oil and Love Run in Harness Together"*

structures) and subsequently re-territorialized as part of the planetary or global petro-capitalist system – by being grounded in the "operations of capital", as an immense global assemblage of oil extraction, logistics, finance, and corporation power – Feuchtwanger shows how oil fields should be treated as planetary phenomena (Mezzadra and Neilson 2019; 25–48, 56–87; see also Labban 2014; Arboleda 2020). The petro-capitalist system as its features in *Oil Islands* – in all its extractive, logistic, disciplinary, and discursive complexity and multivalence – as operative in the Venezuelan/Caribbean oil frontier of Brown Islands resembles an astounding spatial patchwork, a quilt of multiple imbricating and intersecting spaces of territorial concessions, pipelines, rigs, flow stations, and export terminals. As Watts acutely notes: "Spatial technologies and representations are foundational to the oil industry: seismic devices map the contours of reservoirs, and geographic information systems monitor and meter the flows of products within pipelines" (22). Watts then proceeds to elaborate on the significance of the processes of discursive acculturation, assimilation, disciplinary organization (cartographical practices), expatiating how such apparently hard-science areas and activities are simultaneously historical-geographical (hence horizontal and locally-globally extended, informed with uneven dynamics) and geological (hence vertical, associated with deep time, and trans-historical). As he notes:

> Hard rock geology is a science of the vertical, but when harnessed to the marketplace and profitability, it is the map that becomes the instrument of surveillance, control, and rule. The oil and gas industry are a cartographer's dream-space: a landscape of lines, axes, hubs, spokes, nodes, points, blocks, and flows.
>
> (222)

The crucial point, as Watts accentuates, however, is that as "a space of flows and connectivity, these spatial oil networks are unevenly visible (often subsurface and virtual) in their operations" (222).[17]

By the same token, Feuchtwanger's play superimposes what social discourse usually separates, namely Western modernity's Thanatotic economics: its dark, atavistic downsides (cf. Johnson 2010, 270), which include the spatially marginalized places of cheap energy and cheap labour extraction as well as metabolic rift (resource depletion, ecological degradation, and pollution). *Oil Islands* also indexes the disjunctions and rifts attendant upon the Caribbean's violent integration into the capitalist world-ecology. It stages the process and dynamics of "petro-barbarization" – comprising a triadic petro-capitalist process of de-territorialization, re-territorialization, and axiomatization – of the Caribbean oil island and its production as a resource enclave. This barbaric resource frontier accomplishes this by exposing its latent phantasmagoric stage on which death and desire coexist and commingle. It thus figures the disruption to

"It's Not Easy to Make Oil and Love Run in Harness Together" 291

local nutrient cycling systems and food regimes caused by the reorganization of human and extra-human nature in line with the demands of the core whereby the sugar plantation is remade to facilitate the workings of an externally oriented neo-colonial petro-economy.

The striking irony at the climactic end of the play is that Peruchacha – as the proponent of natural conservationism on the island and the symbolic embodiment of unblemished beauty and spirit of nature but also a traditional eco-friendly form of life – is extirpated and excluded from the island as the outsider and as the unwelcome intruder by Grey, an event that allegorically illustrates how the chemical-industrial petro-capitalism primarily expropriates nature and natural resources only to divest nature of its *élan vital* and deplete it of its ontological integrity and biophysical features by converting it into commodified form. Such an act of exclusion at the climax in conjunction with Grey's symptomatic act of aestheticizing the birth of the island as a now fully "barbaric" and "toxic" petroscene betokens how the formerly partial resource enclave has now come full circle. The oil company's totalization of its ontological-ecological monopoly over the island is resonant with how James Ferguson describes African oil zones as "enclaved mineral-rich patches" where "security is provided . . . by specialized corporations while the . . . nominal holders of sovereignty . . . certify the industry's legality . . . in exchange for a piece of the action" (Ferguson 2006, 204).

### D.   Oil, the Oil Monstress,[18] and the Anti-Oil Queen

*Oil Islands* stages oil in a variety of forms – ranging from the menacingly moving oil ships and gigantic, standing oil tankers to the legions of oil-stained oil workers marching across the lawns, to the omnipresent oil-induced pall of smoke and foul oil stench. Oil provides the impetus not only for the whole ontology of the play, but for its narrative logics, dramatic dynamics, and its characters' psychodynamics. The most salient embodiment of oil in *Oil Islands* is Miss Grey who is depicted as the representative of petro-modernity, and its sadistic voracity, who spares no effort at razing the habitation and extracting the resources of the disenfranchised. Yet, oil's insidious presence is felt most discernibly in its effect on nature, on transnational cheap labour regime and its petrocultural effects (commodity culture, transportation, car race, mobility) on the human-nonhuman lives it seeks to dismantle. This petro-matrix thus encompasses an immense swathe of transnational labour that is drawn on the grids of an international division of labour, concealed at the site of production, and embodies a "commodity fetishism" that makes invisible the human cost of a petro-economy. Crucially, and this is what distinguishes the overarching vision prevalent in *Oil Islands* from the one informing a play like

292 *"It's Not Easy to Make Oil and Love Run in Harness Together"*

*Oil Field*, oil itself as it features in *Oil Islands* is not necessarily vilified or demonized. It is the logics of dynamics of extraction and the mode of production which are depicted (arraigned and underscored as the sources of the predicament). This world-systemic vision informing *Oil Islands* is consonant with the arguments articulated by some of the political economists and historians of energy. As Kristin Reed incisively notes:

> Though it may spark visions of grandeur and finance extensive arsenals, however, oil is not a conjurer of kleptocrats or warlords. Oil should not be seen as an excuse for poor governance or violent repression. Such deterministic thinking creates the temptation to attribute all ills to oil, obfuscating the agency of individuals and their ability to uphold or dismantle degrading, violent, and exclusionary processes and institutions.
>
> (2009, 18)

Accordingly, in *Oil Islands*, we are confronted with a world profoundly divided along various axes: ontological, psychological, ecological, social-cultural, and political-economic. On the one hand, we witness the incremental and detrimental activities of a petro-capitalist system headed by Miss Grey and its devious manoeuvres for expansion, success, and monopoly over oil extraction and production. On the other, we observe the endeavours made by the traditional heir to ruling the island and the more historically grounded inhabitant to counter the corrosive infringements on the island's natural environment by Grey's petro-capitalist oil company. At one level, the play depicts the intense personal rivalry between the two main characters and chief forces on the islands: Miss Grey and Miss Peruchacha – whose presence polarizes its world and people. This battle is highly psychologically and libidinally inflected. Grey is the sovereign head of the oil company who possesses immense political-economic power/clout and but has an unbearably hideous face and appalling physical features. Due to her unfavourable physical features – aggravated in light of Peruchacha's dazzling beauty and the disarming erotic-amorous appeal it exerts on the men within Grey's entourage – she harbours an intense grudge and malice against her and spares no efforts to wreak havoc on her personal, social, and economic life. On the other hand, Peruchacha is a captivatingly beautiful woman and native to the island ever since her ancestor colonized the island more than two centuries ago. The world associated with each female character (Grey and Peruchacha) is dominated by a drastically different set of social, ecological, ethical, and economic values though certain imbrications are also discernible between them. As such, in *Oil Islands* we witness an inversion of traditional gender dynamics at stake in the representations of the oil world and oil industry as a phallogocentric and male-intensive one –

## "It's Not Easy to Make Oil and Love Run in Harness Together"   293

where it is men who feature as frontier figures and the chief figures in charge of the oil-driven enterprises, both in the sleek corporation offices and the blood-ridden extraction sites (see Rebecca Golden Timsar 2015, 72–89). In the ensuing sections I will delve into the aforementioned facets and manifestations of oil in four distinct yet inextricably intertwined sections for the sake of argumentative and structural clarity.

*Oil Islands* depicts oil primarily as implicated in a capitalist world-systemic dynamics; it also features oil as a point of convergence between two ideologically-politically opposed orders/systems: the United States (as the paradigmatic example of Western liberalism and capitalism represented by Grey) and the Soviet Union (as the epitome of communism represented by Ingram). In other words, oil appears as "a secular mode of theology – promising an infinite and transformative flow of jouissance and semiosis" (Deleuze 2006, 22) – or secular mecca (or sacred totem) round which the opposite ideology solemnly converges and prayerfully revolves. Another pivotal facet of oil is the play's rendition of oil as a site of the intertwinement and collusion between the metaphysical and the physical. The former includes the idea of God, the transcendental, the church, the sacred, and a telluric totality; and the latter designates the idea of oil as matter and commodity and petro-capitalism as the mode and logics through which oil is produced and distributed. In other words, *Oil Islands* not only presents oil as the *objet petit a* (that sacred and phantasmatic object of desire through which the individual's impossible desires are promised to be fulfilled); but also as the transcendental signified (see Fakhrkonandeh Aporias of Oil as an Object of Desire" in College Literature, 2022). This renders explicit the latent premises or cognitive metaphors in the cultural imaginary of such a petro-capitalist world: oil is capital, oil is both the abject object of desire and the transcendental condition of possibility of desire, oil is God in the sense that oil appears as the point of confluence between Phallus (the signifier of unity, identity, sovereign socio-symbolic power) and Logos (both the name of the father and in the sense of Nomos: law, the hegemonic social-cultural and political-economic source of value, energy, and condition of possibility of movement). This characterization of oil in the petro-capitalist order is in keeping with the characterization of capitalism, variously by Derrida and Deleuze and Guattari, as an Oedipal economy and steeped in the principles of phallogocentrism (see Philip Goodchild 2009, 11, 17–18, 25; see also Mark Taylor *Altarity* 1987, 255–278). One of the moments in which such an intimate intertwinement between oil (in the form of petro-capitalism), religion (Christianity), God, and authority converge into an overdetermined apparatus comes to the fore when the Preacher – employed by Grey's petrocultural apparatus – is menacing the Crowd who are vilifying Grey. "[P]utting up his fist", the Preacher says:

> And if any of these same sewage merchants are crazy enough to splash their filth on the Viscountess by hinting that she's pushing the

294 *"It's Not Easy to Make Oil and Love Run in Harness Together"*

Immigration Bill from any but the purest, most philanthropic and most Christian motives, I'll put them wise to the fact that God has fitted out his representative, Eddy Maxwell, for this tough job not only with words that have a kick to them and not only with a mighty powerful grip on lost souls, but also with a remarkable biceps.

(76)

Crowd's response is equally revealing: "What did I tell you? Any proposition that has five hundred millions behind it has God behind it too" (76).

### E. The Petro-Queen and the Sacrificial Lover: Deborah Grey

No engagement with oil would be possible without delving into the psychological, ethical, and political-economic subtleties of Grey, given the position she occupies not only in the petro-dynamics of the narrative but also in the public perception of oil on the island and the social imaginaries surrounding oil and oil industry. In contrast with *Oil Field* – where in accord with his principle of objectivity and eco-materialist vision, Lania seeks to present a less subjectified conception of the nature of oil (as a strategic and overdetermined global commodity) – in *Oil Islands* oil is highly individualized and personalized through the character of Grey. In other words, if oil is the so-called hero of *Oil Field*, it is Grey who features as the (anti-)hero of *Oil Islands* not merely as a female human subject, but as a liminal being partaking of both human and nonhuman, female and male, deadly and lovely characteristics. More strictly, it is not so much the fact that, in *Oil Islands*, the character is accorded primacy over and above the material object (the energy resource), but rather that Miss Grey is so indelibly merged with oil and its concomitant social, metaphysical, and political-economic implications that it is difficult to distinguish between the two and determine which one is the subject and which one the object and to determine where one ends and the other begins.

Some critics have mentioned *Die Petroleuminseln*, and thus *Oil Islands*, as a partial adaptation from Feuchtwanger's novel *The Ugly Duchess* (1923; translated 1927) – particularly given the conspicuous link between the two main characters at the core of both works: the ugly duchess or the ugly woman of power. The novel confronts us with a binary ontology where physical, on the one hand, and psychological, moral, and intellectual values, on the other, have been assigned to, and are embodied by, the characters along binary or dichotomous lines. The lady who has a hideous face is intellectually efficient and has practical prowess and industrial resourcefulness. She is striving to modernize the country by ushering in the forces of modernity, progress and mechanization/industrialization whilst the beautiful lady is an indolent and incapable woman and yet is cherished and favoured by people. Regardless of how such a novel is amenable to a possible allegorical interpretation where industrialization and fossil

## "It's Not Easy to Make Oil and Love Run in Harness Together" 295

fuel modernity despite their ugly (machinic and dirty/sooty) features and pernicious effects actually act as a boonful and beneficial force of progress and facilitation, the novel also sheds light on social-cultural and moral biases, misconceptions and myopias of the public/people where physical and metaphysical lines are literalized, conflated, and misconstrued.

*Oil Islands* retains certain historical and personal configurations and traces from Feuchtwanger's novel *The Ugly Duchess Margarete Maultasch*. Both texts – incidentally also the "Anglo-Saxon" piece *Calcutta, May 4th* – deal with a social upheaval, the transition to a complex society with a growing population, which is accompanied by the disempowerment of traditional oligarchies and elites and an expanded infrastructure, capital, and a pragmatic and flexible government oriented towards the common good, which is not hindered by abstract or individual-oriented (humanistic-legal) principles. There are substantial differences between the two works in various pivotal respects. For instance, not only are the settings of the novel and the play different, but also the characterization of Grey in each work. However as specifically regards the bearing of the novel on *Petroleuminseln* and *Oil Islands*, whilst still traces of *The Ugly Duchess* are discernible in the German version of the play *Die Petroleuminseln*, the novel barely has any bearing on the English version of the play, *Oil Islands*, to the point where the novel can be argued to serve as a faint and receding template for it. Feuchtwanger himself in a personal comment published in *Die Weltbühne*, makes it clear that his novel *The Ugly Duchess* can be considered preparatory work for the theatrical version, because the focus of the plot is again the fight of a strong, talented woman against her ugly face, only he has the Tyrol of the 14th century exchanged for "a somewhat legendary island in the southern area of the USA and the twentieth century way of life" (1927). The most conspicuous difference between the two works is that there is no oil in the novel and here the ugly duchess is simply the head of an engineering industry and a harbinger of industrial modernity. In Feuchtwanger's play (*Oil Islands*), on the contrary, not only does oil feature as the fulcrum of the thematics and dynamics of the play, but also the ugly potentate embodies the stinking island polluted by oil mining, thereby establishing an allegorical relationship between the ugly oil magnate and the environment. What further distinguishes the play from the novel is the way the blunt binaries (informing the novel) are compounded and blurred between the ostensible poles of the play (Grey and Peruchacha) by exposing co-implications and affinities in psychological, ethical, and economic respects between them.

The novel, contrary to the play, presents a sympathetic portrayal of the ugly duchess where she is depicted as a motherly figure in a symbiotic relation with the country and its natural landscape where nature of the nation and the duchess (as a maternal figure) mutually nurture one another (see Feuchtwanger 1998, 114). In the novel, the unsightly woman of industrial-economic power identifies with the magnificently unfolding

## 296  "It's Not Easy to Make Oil and Love Run in Harness Together"

state of Tyrol in the sense of a compensatory act that lets one forget the deficient physical features and creates satisfaction. About the wisely governing duchess it is said: "She dug her way into the country. . . . The land was their flesh and blood. Its rivers, valleys, cities, castles were part of her. The wind of his mountains was their breath, the rivers their veins" (Feuchtwanger 1998, 114). The novel thus depicts the duchess enveloped with an aura of motherliness that literally "flows" into the country (ibid., 118) and causes the protagonist's ugliness to disappear through a second beautiful body. The novel thus evokes the idea of the Magna Mater, which was persisted in the cultural discourse until the 17th century and which imagines the earth as a maternal, sexualized living being in the sense of the traditional micro-macrocosm concept. In this narrative of sexualization and feminization of nature, caves and subterranean passages are considered places of birth where, for example, metals (like embryos) grow (cf. ibid., 12). Feuchtwanger's novel is reminiscent of this tradition, when the prosperous landscape rises as *pars pro toto* in the womb of the ugly potentate. In the play this maternity is rendered as intellectual and economic motherhood rather than affective emotional nourishing and replenishing. In the novel, Margarete's negatively portrayed opponent, the beautiful Agnes von Flavon, embodies the "semblance" of the good old days. She is in alliance with the enemies of the Jews, inciting pogroms that sabotage the urban life Margarete has created. The "stupid, instinctless" (182) people succumb to the beautiful appearance, idolize the useless Agnes (183) and misjudge the achievements of the ugly, but maternal, fluent Duchess for her country (184). As is evident, then, in the novel, the ugly duchess has the sympathies of Feuchtwanger, notwithstanding her monstrous deeds – she has her first husband and her lover Chretien killed in order to nullify their national policy plans apparently due to their attempts to sabotage their national interests – which are depicted to be motivated by the welfare of the nation.

In *Oil Islands*, Deborah Grey, called "The Chimpanzee", is president of the world's largest oil company on the Brown Islands, somewhere in the Pacific Ocean. She is unbearably ugly, but tries to gloss and compensate for what nature has denied her with a veneer of toughness, intelligence, and the will to power. The Miss Grey in *Oil Islands* – as an arguable adaptation of *The Ugly Duchess* – is a drastically revised and altered figure with her psychodynamics and ethics reversed. If in the novel she was the wronged woman who suffered injustice, in the play, whilst betrayed by some of her employees and close allies (such as Lelio and Ingram), she features as an inexorable and unconscionable capitalist profiteer – not to say an arch-evil – who not only wreaks havoc on nature and the environment, but also exploits the native and transnationally imported workers and in her racialized petro-extractivist regime. Furthermore, with *Oil Islands*, we are in an ethically, psychologically, and diegetically far more nuanced world – compared with the antithetical world of the

## "It's Not Easy to Make Oil and Love Run in Harness Together" 297

novel with its predictable and crudely simplistic dynamics. In the play, Feuchtwanger renders Grey as a psychologically nuanced and existentially manifold character. Grey strikes us as an intellectually subtle, morally ambiguous, emotionally vulnerable, and economically ruthless woman. Still, she cannot remove the influence of a beautiful rival, Miss Perucha-cha, on men and public opinion; though Grey ultimately eliminates her through an act of murder.

Grey is also explicitly referred to as a symbolic mother: "beautiful she is not, but she's the mother of the Brown Islands" (48) – an inversion of the Magna Mater trope, which expresses the destruction of the mother earth by the phallic oil. The apostasy – that is, the taboo of mining and extracting underground resources – of reifying the virgin body of mother nature is inscribed, in *Oil Islands*, not in terms of matriarchal discourse but, as I will demonstrate, in terms of a "phallic mother" (see Kristeva 1984, 45–48, 75–79; see also Marcia Ian 1993, 1–57). Put pithily, Grey as a monstrous, phallic mother (due to her embodiment of oil and petro-capitalism) serves as an expression of the voracity of petro-capitalist modernity with its energy-intensive technologies and its ecologically detrimental resource extraction practices. As such, viewed from an ecocritical perspective, the islandic idyll appears as a projection of modernity. On the other hand, however, Grey is described by other characters in highly masculine and even phallic terms. She is repeatedly described to work as a man and as a "man of action" and thus as a type in which Feuchtwanger was emphatically interested. Feuchtwanger's power-thirsty character, Grey, is not only a symptom of the much-discussed crisis of masculinity in the inter-war period (see Kimmel 1987, 121–153; see Baron 1987, 61),[19] but she too is a "new woman" and subverts the traditional images of femininity by representing the "behavioural theory of the cold". As such, Deborah Grey comes to embody the monstrosity of American capitalism, which Feuchtwanger treats with irony and sarcasm in his collection of poetry *PEP* (a key term from Sinclair Lewis's novel *Babbit*). The associations of the oil-industrial woman of political-economic power (Grey) with maternity/motherhood can also be found in *Oil Islands*. Importantly, however, given the way her maternal character is defined and described along with the associations they evoke, as I will demonstrate more extensively, Grey strikes us as a phallic mother.

A condensed account of the manifold nature of Grey as an oil giant is provided by Obadiah who is the recruited poet and rhetorician of Grey's petrocultural apparatus (its poet laureate). In a vocal-poetic dynamics which is both reminiscent of and tries to counter the "Song of the Brown Islands" (delivered both chorally and via gramophone), Obadiah presents Grey as an arch-capitalist here:

> Who was it introduced profit-sharing on the Brown Islands? Deborah Grey. Who has increased the world's production of oil by sixty per

298 *"It's Not Easy to Make Oil and Love Run in Harness Together"*

cent? Deborah Grey. What would technical science look like today without Deborah Grey? Beautiful she is not, but she's the mother of the Brown Islands, Deborah Grey.

(48)

Elsewhere, Grey is described in masculine terms as a male boxer, "a heavyweight" by Colonel Monsoon and others (71). Similar to the popular non-fiction books about "raw material miracles" mythicizing the great oil magnates and stylizing them into mysterious and power-obsessed personalities – a form of fetishization that dissimulates the hard work of mining – Grey is called "Napoleon of oil" on the island. Uncle Obadiah utters: "You're the loveliest woman in the Islands, Miss Charmian. But the feminine Napoleum / With her dollars and petroleum / She has the monopolium" (88–89). One of the moments that affords us a glimpse into how she is predominantly perceived by the public in masculine terms – that is, physically unappealing but intellectually capable and in keeping with the gender politics of the culture of the time – is when upon disclosing her incisive idea of the double-edged bill and the concession with the Japanese (whereby Japan protests the incongruent law between the authorization of the use of coloured labour on the island but its prohibition on the US mainland), the astonished Colonel Monson calls her a world-class political-economic mind and juxtaposes her with an all-male host of world-prominent figures: "This Japanese idea of yours puts you in the same class as Roosevelt, or Shakespeare, or Edison, or Darwin" (113). Equally notably, the near identity of oil, the Oil Islands, and Grey is not only conjured up by other characters, but by Grey herself. In her conversation with Ingram – in a critical juncture when Ingram has not only lost all his credibility, trustworthiness, and emotional-affective capital with Grey, but is also being persecuted by the Russian emissaries – Ingram, pale and distraught, asks: "Has Moscow struck me off?" Grey's response attests to the point at issue: "Yes, but they don't remember that in the Oil Islands nobody can be struck off without Deborah Grey's consent" (70). As will become evident she identifies her desire and gender identity (her feminine quality) in terms of capital and oil.

Despite her position of power, however, Grey is doubly marginalized, because she is not only a woman (in an otherwise male business), but also ugly and thus not perceived as a desirable woman but more importantly not a "proper" or real woman or a deficient in the normative and typical gender characteristic of the time which constituted the definition of woman. However if we strip Grey's character of the traits and features attributed to her by other characters and consider her through her own verbal, affective, and behavioural patterns, she turns out to be far subtler than the alleged figure of a cold and merciless monster ascribed to her. The ensuing moment is emblematic in that it juxtaposes one character's impression of her with Grey's actual attitude and conduct,

## "It's Not Easy to Make Oil and Love Run in Harness Together" 299

that is, her interest in an apparently trivial matter (Lelio's hair) amidst the earnest discussion of negotiations around oil business:

INGRAM: The way you set about things, Debsy Grey goes to a seasoned business man's head.
OBADIAH: Wireless from the Island, Miss Grey that the delegation from Chicago is arriving tomorrow morning early. Will you turn back, or shall we tell them to keep the delegates waiting?
GREY: You have damned soft hair, Lelly.
INGRAM: In the States long hair on a grown man's head is as popular as dishonoured cheques or lyrical poetry.

(50)

As will be demonstrated more extensively, whilst the play spares no effort to explicitly render and expose the detrimental, immoral, and exploitative nature of Grey's extractive practices at social, ecological, and political-economic levels, it also makes a point of showing Grey's emotional vulnerability, her traumatized desire, and intellectual perspicacity as well as her fidelity to those who serve and stay faithful to her.

### F. Peruchacha

To capture a more vivid and accurate picture of the relational dynamics of the forces prevailing on the island, we need to more closely consider the other pole of the world of the play: Miss Peruchacha. The foremost feature with which Peruchacha is identified is her beauty, her erotic appeal, her seductiveness. At the car race, when Peruchacha, having lost the race to Grey, approaches Grey to tell her that she is going to the United States to implement her plans to abort Grey's attempts to have the Immigration Bill passed, Grey introduces Peruchacha to the Viscount thus: "This is Miss Charmian Peruchacha, the first lady in the Brown Islands" (83). Rebuffing Grey's epithet, however, Peruchacha prefers to be referred to with a name that accentuates her historical roots and a sense of authentic belonging: "Oh, just say a native, and be done with it. You folks in Europe, Viscount, can't have any idea of what it means to be a back number like me. You see, I'm a *salta atras*" (83). What is significant here is Peruchacha's act of self-identification in a racially self-conscious manner – that is, in terms of a "*salta atras*" (83) – which in the racial taxonomy of the colonial era was a highly charged term steeped in sexual and racial-cultural phantasies. Elsewhere Uncle Obadiah provides us with an extended elucidation of the term thus: "A Spaniard and a negress produce the mulatto, a mulatto and a Spaniard the Morisco, a Morisco and a Spaniard the *satta atras*, the 'throwback'" (83). At a maternal level, Peruchacha is perceived by the public to be a natural mother embodying and giving birth to natural beauty whereas Grey is

300 *"It's Not Easy to Make Oil and Love Run in Harness Together"*

deemed a sadist and tyrannical mother giving birth to a monstrous baby: the voracious oil industry.

As a fleeting glance at various speeches delivered by crowds of people attests, in the cultural imaginary of the inhabitants of the island, Peruchacha features as a force of grace, virtue, health, and salvation. To other characters and the public, Peruchacha seems to allegorically embody the formerly pristine natural richness and beauty of the island and its natural life. At Peruchacha's garden party held as the annual celebration of her ancestor, Lelio says: "Your park makes one feel a different being. When there's a west wind blowing the whole island simply reeks of oil, except in your park, Miss Peruchacha" (25). The ascription of such traits to Peruchacha by the public is further illustrated by the ensuing moment when the Preacher vociferously promotes Grey and menaces to beat Peruchacha's proponents and those who scandalize Grey, and the Crowd's response is telling: "Give him hell! Tar and feather him!". The Crowd then provide us with a more detailed insight into the material motives underlying their staunch support of Peruchacha: "Charmy fixed up our profit-sharing for us! He can be as funny as he likes, but he's to keep his dirty tongue off Charmy" (77). The Crowd further harangue: "Charmy saved us from Prohibition [of the importation of the coloured labour onto the island]". Other people in the Crowd add: "We want Charmy, the good angel of the Brown Islands" (77). Ironically, the play shows how later when Grey manages to have the Immigration Bill approved whereby the use of cheap coloured labour on the island will be permitted, the Crowd starts changing its view and perception and starts showing inner rifts and divisions. One member of the Crowd (named Gomez Frink) says: "Well, the Chimpanzee's a hard-boiled case, sure enough, but there's something to be said for her. Look at how she managed to get Prohibition put off for five years on the Islands" (73). Equally notably, however, *Oil Islands* shows Peruchacha's mercilessness and unconscionable ethos in her battle with Grey and her efforts to preserve the island against the pernicious forays of Grey's oil industry and extractive practices. This ethos is reflected in her relentless efforts to inflict social-cultural and political-economic loss, humiliation, and ruination on her rival – a move not solely driven by conscientious concerns over preservation of nature but also her personal interest and financial profit and narcissism. Grey, on the other hand, reveals an ambivalent moral and emotional attitude. As such, Grey shows an inclination to relent what she is invested in either in terms of love or eros/desire. A salient example is her treatment of Ingram. When she experiences emotional and social betrayal by Ingram, although she can hand him over to the Soviet state (in which case he will be executed), she spares his life and saves him from the persecutory Russians whilst simultaneously stripping him of all the financial gains he had reaped during her cooperation with Grey (including the major portion of his financial assets and shares in the oil project concession and as secretly invested in

*"It's Not Easy to Make Oil and Love Run in Harness Together"* 301

National Bank held somewhere apparently in the US). Accordingly, *Oil Islands* shows how the opposite party (Peruchacha and her social circle) who are rather associated with the naturistic, humanistic, and socialist, can be morally unconscionable in their battle.

Equally crucially, the play shows how the opposite party is a settler-colonialist and an extractivist of a less rapacious kind: piracy and running sugar plantations. Indeed, the nuanced vision of the play is not only reflected in its counterpointing one mode of extractivism with a more modern one. It also resides in its eschewal of establishing a dichotomous relationship with two principal parties/characters – where one would represent the metaphysical-mythical qualities of oil as a commodity and the abstractions of capital and the other party the material appeal of an exotic ontological order, the physical plenitude of a pristine, pre-modern nature, innocence, and beauty. As such, Feuchtwanger unremittingly shows the imbrications and affinities between the two extractive regimes by evoking the recent shift away from raw material extraction and sugar plantations towards the Anglo-European capitalist hegemony in coal and oil energy regimes and by exposing how each of these ostensibly binary categories battens and impinges on the other. The depiction of the extended (neo-) colonial history of the island in its origin enhances its allegorical facet. It also foregrounds the world-systemic approach informing the play evidenced by the way *Oil Islands* confronts us with the longue durée of colonial and capitalist modernity along with its cycles of extraction – ranging from the early modern period dominated by Spain and Portugal to the play's contemporary history (the age of fossil capital) dominated by the Anglo-American hegemony. That is why Peruchacha is referred to in racial register as *salta atras* or Mountback – a title which partly reveals her Spanish-Portuguese origins.

Significantly, we are afforded a retrospective glimpse, by Peruchacha, into the history and genealogy of the Peruchacha family on the island which they entered and inhabited as a settler colony. In her historical account of the social-economic dynamics pervading the time of her family's rule on the island, Peruchacha conjures up what the utopia and idyllic looked like and involved an unadulterated natural resort and a state of cohabitation:

> Ladies and gentlemen! The man in whose honour we are holding this celebration was an out and out robber, but he was something else besides. His place was neither a prison nor a workhouse for the people who lived on it. His people drank pulque and whisky and had time for recreation; they were plumped out with fruit and wine, and there was no reek of sweat or reek of oil on the islands. That is why, ladies and gentlemen, we are assembled to honour my great ancestor, who was a gentleman, pleasant in the sight of God and of men.
>
> (32–33)

302 *"It's Not Easy to Make Oil and Love Run in Harness Together"*

What is significant in this regard is Peruchacha's unabashed acknowledgement of the predatory profession of her ancestor. The realistic picture Peruchacha presents of her ancestor unwittingly reveals not only the settler-colonial roots of their mode of relation to the island and its natural resources; it also betokens the longue durée vision of the play where the Peruchachan order is implicitly presented as one cycle in the extractive practices of Western capitalist modernity in the peripheries and in relation to cheap nature, cheap labour, cheap raw materials. This historical-ecological dynamics is resonant with Blechmar's observation: "For the Columbian conquests were not merely exterminist and plundering; their epochal significance derives also from ambitious imperial projects to map and catalogue productive natures of every kind" (see Jason Moore. "NATURE/SOCIETY & THE VIOLENCE OF REAL ABSTRACTION". 2016. https://jasonwmoore. wordpress.com/2016/10/04/naturesociety-the-violence-of-real-abstraction/).

Interestingly, subsequent to the presentation of Peruchacha's account, Colonel tries to preclude the perception of the Peruchachan order as any sense of pre-modern backwardism associated with the sense of idyllic pastoralism (hence associated with stasis and stagnation and refusal) by assimilating it as part of the cycles of capitalist modernity. This is evident in his presentation of Grey's petro-capitalist order as a logical continuity or a social-political continuum of Peruchacha's ancestral (settler-colonial) order. Indeed, my aforementioned point about the imbrications and continuities between the two families' rule as two cycles within the longue durée of the capitalist modernity (thus rendering the island as a manifestation of the operations of the Capitalocene) finds an articulate expression in the revealing parallel Colonel draws between Peruchacha's ancestor and Columbus:

> If Mr. Juan Peruchacha were alive today, the Island would look precisely as it does now, just as Columbus today would set out on a modern vessel and not sail in a corvette. And that is why we honour Peruchacha, the gentleman, most sincerely in recognizing that he laid the foundations which made possible the present developments on the Island.
>
> (33)

Peruchacha, however, interjects and cuts him short by expressing her vigorous objections (to his attempts to blur the boundaries between the two orders (the Peruchachas and the Greys)) by insisting on the ontological and socio-economic differences between the two social-political orders: "Stop, Colonel Monson, I won't have that. I repeat, Peruchacha, the farmer, the founder and governor of the old Brown Islands, not the Oil Islands" (33). Here we witness the ideological and material-legal struggle over the representation of the history on the island. As such, we see how the rivalry between Peruchacha and Grey is that between two systems of colonization and extraction – one is ecological and in terms of scale less detrimental and aggressive (energy-intensive) and the other far more

*"It's Not Easy to Make Oil and Love Run in Harness Together"* 303

exploitative and devastating. In fact, the rest of the play illustrates the escalation of the conflict between the two social-political poles over the appropriation and ownership of the history and resources of the island and is relentlessly conducted through various symbolic and discursive means – saliently including the name of the island and the car race.

A remarkable occurrence arises when we hear "agitation among the guests as another gang of coolies is taken past them" (33). Outraged by this attempt to disrupt her party and the heinous human cost of the petro-capitalist regime, Peruchacha points to the coolies and protests: "What does this mean? What are these coolies doing here?" to which oil company's Overseer explains that they are the newly imported "gang for shaft thirty-seven" (33). Interestingly, Peruchacha's attitude towards the intrusive presence of the "coolies" is primarily informed with aesthetic sensibility and couched in highly racialized terms; put more lucidly, rather than arraigning the socially and economically exploitative treatment of the coloured oil workers, she is offended by the way the "coloured" oil workers blemish the pristine beauty of her party evidenced by her reference to their "ugly" and "dirty" features which besmirch the ostensible idyllic and prelapsarian vision of her world. When Peruchacha remonstrates to the affrontery and offense of this intrusive presence of the coolies, Colonel Monson reminds her of the historical legal agreements, indicating that "I regret this inconvenience. But according to the contract of 1899 the Island Company is entitled to a right of way between the harbour and the oil shafts in sector three" (34). Whilst acknowledging the existence of such a contract, Peruchacha nevertheless objects: "Contract? 1899? And you choose tonight for fishing up this contract?" (34). So gradually we realize how Charmian is also implicated in and unobtrusively feeds on and contributes to this state of turning nature into capitalized commodity (for instance, attested by her business of renting her steamships to the oil company) despite the apparent animosity and opposition between the two parties. Furthermore, Monson's reply is revealing in numerous respects. It betokens how Peruchacha's attempt to maintain the image of the Peruchachan patch of the island as unadulterated nature is a phantasy – or an ideological illusion – not only because the island's nature was already turned into commodified nature (sugar plantations) under her great ancestor's political-economic order, but also because, given the systemic and holistic nature of the ecosystem on the island, now nearly the entirety of the island has been raped and appropriated by being converted into a fully "functionalized" zone of extractive sacrifice and a resource frontier with its strict disciplinary and biopolitical regimes in place. Monson's reminder confirms the point at stake: "It's a ruling principle on the Islands that work comes before pleasure" (34).

Monson's remark here reveals the hegemonic reality principle dominating the island as subjected to the petro-capitalist logics of an advanced industrial society (US). This reality principle can be identified in terms of

304  *"It's Not Easy to Make Oil and Love Run in Harness Together"*

the "performance principle" as elaborated by Herbert Marcuse. Marcuse defines the Performance Principle as "that of an acquisitive and antagonistic society in the process of constant expansion, [that] presupposes a long development during which domination has been increasingly rationalized: control over social labour now reproduces society on an enlarged scale and under improving conditions" (1974, 45). Under the rule of performance principle, according to Marcuse, "society is stratified according to the competitive economic performances of its members" (44). These conditions are indeed consonant with the contrasts and drastic differences Peruchacha persistently accentuates to exist between the current oil-driven political-economic order and economic regime (biopolitical order) and the former one ruled by her family. These differences, as delineated by Peruchacha and other characters, involved not only ecological, ontological-existential, and biopolitical differences, but also differences in social ethos and the ethics and economics of work. Similarly, in the industrial capitalist regime driven by the "performance principle", as Marcuse explains, treats the questions of the senses and receptive faculties that seek fulfilment dismissively. This treatment arises from the hegemonic valorization of the disciplinary norm of repressive reason which reigns in instinctual drives for pleasure and enjoyment. The features and values of such a hegemonic order bear striking affinities with the conditions prevailing on Oil Islands:

> profitable productivity, assertiveness, efficiency, competitiveness; in other words, the Performance Principle, the rule of functional rationality discriminating against emotions, a dual morality, the "work ethic," which means for the vast majority of the population condemnation to alienated and inhuman labor, and the will to power, the display of strength, virility.
>
> (Marcuse 1974, 282)[20]

This thematic preoccupation finds a striking expression in Obadiah's remark when he facilely considers the age of oil – with all its technological facilities and mechanization of life – as promising more leisure and free time than their preceding social-economic orders: "If our era left men more time for reading I would write an epic called 'The Chimpanzee' and the theme would be the struggles and triumph of a great woman fighting against the ugliness bestowed on her by Nature" (31). Interestingly, the play itself provides a tacit and ironic meta-dramatic commentary on the fatuousness of Obadiah's hope when immediately subsequent to this comments we witness how "A gang of coolies is driven past" (31). The poignant irony of this passage can be acutely discerned historically too as various critics – above all, Marx – have argued too. In practice, industrial capitalism (including petro-capitalism) proved to be more exploitative in relation to human-nonhuman natures than the preceding paradigms. This

## "It's Not Easy to Make Oil and Love Run in Harness Together" 305

contradiction had already been predicted by Marx when he contended how

> machinery in itself shortens the hours of labour, but when employed by capital it lengthens them; . . . in itself it lightens labour, but when employed by capital it heightens its intensity; . . . in itself it is a victory of man [sic] over the forces of nature but in the hands of capital it makes man the slave of those forces; in itself it increases the wealth of the producers, but in the hands of capital it makes them into paupers.
>
> (Marx 1867/1990, 568–569)

Subsequently, we witness the adumbration of a new turn in the course and dynamics of the events couched in symbolic terms. When Lelio, as the chief oil engineer of Grey's oil company, intervenes to ask the oil company's overseer to take the transported coloured workers through another route, Peruchacha extolls his gallant favour thus:

> Thank you, Lelly. Well, ladies and gentlemen, since it appears that in my grounds you are still on the old islands, I ask you to join with me in giving three cheers for Peruchacha the farmer, the founder of the old islands!
>
> (35)

When Lelio blithely reiterates her words then Ingram states: "Now there's a smell of oil here too", followed by Monson's remark "Yes, the wind has changed" (35). The sensory trope of now-ubiquitous oil odour and "wind-change", indicated here, presages the exceeding domination of the oil ontology and the escalation of the tensions between the two symbolic representatives of the two orders: Peruchacha and Grey. This portentous event gains further resonances when we juxtapose it with an earlier dialogue. When Lelio asks Obadiah – who has been advising Lelio a moment ago: "I should advise you to stick to your intellect" – "Is there anything particular in the wind?", Obadiah's response has both literal (ecological) and symbolic significations: "No, but my eye's watering as if the wind were going to change" (29). Apart from the shift in wind portending the unfavourable turn in the course of events for Lelio (due to his support of Grey's opponent), more broadly and in the allegorical framework of the play the shift in the nature (given its new foul scent and toxic nature) and direction of the wind presages the brooding gloom of metabolic rift looming over the horizon of the island, the realization of which we witness in the conclusion.

Notably, whilst the questions of death, destruction, and deadly effect are primarily associated with Grey (partly emanating from her association with oil and its effect on human-nonhuman nature), a different kind deadliness is also associated with Peruchacha. Peruchacha's distinctive

306 *"It's Not Easy to Make Oil and Love Run in Harness Together"*

deadliness is attributed to her seductiveness which in turn induces Grey's mortal malice and vindictive rage. This siren-like seductiveness is most vividly articulated by Uncle Obadiah who associates Peruchacha's deadly beauty and erotic appeal with the Greek Helen. Finding Lelio (as one of the main engineers working at Grey's oil company) present at the garden party held by Peruchacha, Obadiah forewarns:

> When Helen went walking on the walls of Troy even the elders were stirred at the sight of her. That passage comes out very well in my translation. . . . But none the less it makes me uneasy to watch this youngster Lelio Holyday, for instance, committing suicide for her sake. You'll see, my dear sir, that that boy, who has a good head and a possible career, will ruin his chances tonight for good.
>
> (30)

\* \* \* \* \* \* \* \* \* \* \* \* \* \* \* \*

Premised on the earlier detailed exploration of the characters, what will illuminate not only the psychological and symbolic aspects of the play and characters, but also the gender, political, and ecological dynamics surrounding the overdetermined question and figure of oil let us scrutinize the intertwinement between psycho-symbolism of oil (within the petro-capitalist order/ontology) and psychodynamics of the characters and their investment in oil as well as their ecology and economy of desire. From the very outset a problematic parallel is established between physical and metaphysical, or between inner and outer or essence and appearance, which manifests itself in various guises: face vs force, beauty vs ugliness, physical appearance vs intellectual canniness, truth vs falsehood. These imbrications become evident, for instance, when Ingram, remarking on Grey's notorious unfavourable features/face, mischievously observes: "There are photographs which have earned for her all over the world the nickname of the Chimpanzee". Sniffkins (who is an ardent proponent of Grey's) replies: "There are lots of reasons for thinking a fine and intelligent face not particularly attractive, for instance when one is neither fine nor intelligent oneself" (12).

This association between the physical and psychological, and between material-physical and moral-metaphysical, is explicitly established by the play itself in the form of a meta-dramatic comment (a la Brechtian epic technique). When the curtain drops at the end of Act Two, the Producer (as a fictional character) appears and recites the following passages:

> Ladies and gentlemen, you have noticed, I dare say, / That in this play a heroic struggle is depicted, Waged by an indomitable woman day by day / Against the ugliness with which she is afflicted. / Watch the fight closely till the issue's clear, / And you will share in a valuable

*"It's Not Easy to Make Oil and Love Run in Harness Together"* 307

experience I / You cannot refuse sympathy to Debsy Grey's career / Provided that our claim wins your adherence, / To wit, that it is a career representative of our time, / And eminently fitted to portray human splendour, / Since upon this stage we assume that it's a crime / To let oneself be crushed or forced into surrender.

(94–95)

Equally illustrative in this regard are the titles of the scenes which also attest to such an entanglement and relational dynamics between the physical and psychological, between the libidinal and political economy and between death/oil and desire. Two salient cases in point are the titles of Scene 3 ("The Market Value of a Dazzling Beauty") and Scene 7 ("Beauty Is Stronger Than Truth"). The allegorical link between physical and symbolic as well as the libidinal and political economy is illustrated in Scene 3 when Ingram explains how he is "on a business footing with the Chimpanzee. And surely I can allow myself the pleasure of visiting a lady who would be a queen of beauty in any society" (56). When Peruchacha wonders: "What effect do you think her marriage will have on the oil crisis?" Ingram's response corroborates the gender politics of the oil field and petro-capitalism as delineated later: "Oil crisis? Fancy your being interested in that!" (56).

More broadly, as a sweeping survey of the play demonstrates, oil and the political-economic process of its extraction/production appear as strictly gendered matters. More specifically, both oil and petro-capitalism transpire as phallogocentric phenomena traversed with a phallocratic gender politics. In cases where the sexual identity of the oil potentate happens to be female (as is the case with Grey), the individual needs to implement phallic norms and embody a phallocratic economy of desire if they intend to be successful. This point is explicitly acknowledged by various characters, and most saliently by Ingram in his conversation with Peruchacha. When Peruchacha asks Ingram: "If you were stock-taking, now, what value would you set on a woman's good looks in business?" Ingram's reply evinces the gender politics indicated earlier: "I would enter it as an enormous liability. If Miss Grey: for example, didn't look like a chimpanzee she would certainly not have been able to run the Island Company successfully" (57). Finding such a crudely gendered treatment offensive, Peruchacha states: "If you weren't so fresh, and had more understanding, I would give you a convincing instance to prove how conceited and untrue to life your ideas are in this matter" (57).

Indeed, the link between the physical-psychological as well as the libidinal and political is not confined to Grey and the questions of ugliness, death drive, and oil. Notably, they encompass Peruchacha's beauty and erotic appeal too – perceived traits which she exploits very consciously. Significantly, such a reductively dichotomous and gendered contrast between body and mind, ugliness and beauty is persistently subverted

308 *"It's Not Easy to Make Oil and Love Run in Harness Together"*

by Peruchacha herself throughout the play, evidenced by the way she subtly wields her beauty and erotic appeal as a means of gaining socio-symbolic, social-political leverage and economic clout – gaining favours. An evident case in point is the rest of the aforementioned conversation between Peruchacha and Ingram where Peruchacha objects:

> You've only refused to discuss the oil crisis with me because you've been beating your own brains in vain for an explanation of what this marriage has to do with it. What will you bet that I can tell you exactly what it means?
>
> (58)

Ingram ironically finds Peruchacha's claims as hollow and facile – hence his remark: "I'd rather you rang for your nigger. I can't stand any more of this nonsense" (58). The infuriated Peruchacha, however, makes a point of debunking his gendered presumptions, particularly at the gramophone and party scene where Ingram loses all his credibility and capital. As Peruchacha forewarns: "I won't be considered stupid just because I'm not so hideous as the Chimpanzee. You can fling vitriol in my face if I don't give the Chimpanzee the knock-out on her own ground" (59).

Significantly, the implications of Peruchacha's seduction-based attempt to gain support and counter Grey's plans prove far-reaching, specifically due to the naïvely dichotomous gender politics informing the social-cultural dynamics prevailing the world of the play. Later in the play, we see the haughty and over-virile Ingram in a meeting with Peruchacha. Here Ingram is still ignorant of Grey's secret schemes to attain a double triumph by having the Immigration Bill passed whilst keeping Ingram in abeyance in order to obtain the Russian Concession at a much cheaper price and is still awaiting his profits and the final decision concerning the Concession from Grey. Peruchacha, however, by disclosing Grey's manoeuvre regarding the Immigration Bill to Ingram, shows the spurious nature of his claims about the gendered nature of intellectual-mental acuity. Adopting an ironic tone, Peruchacha states:

> I'm not such a great woman as Debsy Grey, but you have as much imagination, Mr. Ingram, as a hippopotamus. If I don't open your eyes she'll get your concessions from you for an old song. I only wanted to point out that there are women who know how to use the pretty faces that God has given them to get hold of things that would be extremely useful to lots of men, if they only knew. Information, for instance, which couldn't be got at in any other way.
>
> (59)

This utterance confirms Peruchacha's conscious exploitation of her beauty to achieve economic advantage, social-cultural capital, and

*"It's Not Easy to Make Oil and Love Run in Harness Together"* 309

political ascendency over Grey's ever-encroaching petro-sovereignty. Another illuminating comparison between Grey's and Peruchacha's extent and modes of power respectively is made by Lelio. Here, whilst acknowledging the drastic differences between the two, Lelio hints at the mysterious lure and seductive appeal Peruchacha exerts on others (particularly men): "Intellectually I am convinced that to compare Debsy Grey with Charmian Peruchacha is to compare a twenty-thousand-ton steamer with a pleasure yacht. But that *salta atras* has something about her which makes a fool of my intellect" (29). Elsewhere Lelio adds: "In any case, Miss Peruchacha is a dazzling beauty. It's interesting to watch her detaching men from your Chimpanzee" (28). *Oil Islands* thus features an inversion of the traditional gender politics by showing how women are equally, if not more, perceptive and perspicacious in strategic thinking and political-economic manoeuvres.

Equally importantly, this link between the ugliness and oil, between the physical and psycho-symbolic, and between the libidinal and political economy (desire and oil) is invoked consciously by Grey herself. In her conversation with Ingram, Ingram perceptively indicates the entanglements between the psychological and material (financial) by uttering, "The money that comes into my pocket is only half the fun" (69). When Grey describes this attitude as a frivolous act of sentimentality ("I hardly believe that any sane man would fling away his bank balance out of sheer sentiment"), Ingram repudiates such a description and avers it to be existentially and psychologically profound and serious (the question of desire, *objet petit a*, and one's identity): "Bank balance? That's not the question". Then he hits the nerve by saying:

> Debsy. A woman like you who has had to fight against her appearance all her life ought to know what it means to be always cold-shouldered. You can call me sentimental for once, if you like; but what I want is prestige, trust, simple good fellowship.
>
> (70)

Even more revealing is Grey's explicit indication of the parallel between the libidinal and political economy: "Did you say anything, Ingram? It seems to me that even an ugly woman becomes tolerable when she has power. Doesn't she?" (70). Such a relational dynamics between desire and capital, in a symptomatological reading, can be interpreted as a symptom of reified desire and relationality.

A striking illustration of the aforementioned entanglement and relational dynamics between the libidinal and political economy (oil/death and desire) appears in the confrontation between Grey and Ingram after the latter has betrayed Grey by disclosing their emotional-sexual affair,

310  *"It's Not Easy to Make Oil and Love Run in Harness Together"*

thereby making her an object of public scorn and derision. Here, Grey justifies her punitive action against Ingram by explaining:

> That's just why I couldn't have you laughing at me. And you knew that beforehand. But didn't you do it in spite of me? Didn't you make a vaudeville of words which should never have been repeated? Didn't you think you had only to put your arm round my waist to have me trembling and saying "H. B., my own sweet love?" Well, there's nothing doing! You've come a cropper, my own sweet love. A cropper, you common bully!
>
> (103)

Ingram, in response, explicitly mentions Grey's attempt to use her oil-based power as a means of covering her undesirability and ugliness: "Do you imagine you'll ever get anybody to sleep with you for love of your face? An Atlantic Ocean of oil wouldn't make you anything but the Chimpanzee" (103). Then more explicitly he invokes the parallel between political economy (capital, oil) and libidinal economy (the unconscious dynamics of desirability and facial-physical features):

> It's an idiotic world in which a man like me can come to grief because of a woman who makes capital out of her ugliness. You know yourself that you've only got the better of me because you're not a woman, but a monstrosity.
>
> (103)

As is evident, upon closer inspection, a persistent and explicit link is invoked between Grey's perceived "ugliness" and undesirability, desire (as a psychosomatic force), oil (as magic and transformative force), and oil-endowed capital throughout *Oil Islands*. The conjunction of these elements constitutes a Thanatotic constellation or matrix that is deemed by the characters to be the cause of the death of nature, people, and labour force.

The next compelling evidence to the indelible intertwinement between the desire and oil (petro-capitalist) as a means of beautifying herself (oil as a condition of possibility of the phantasy of beauty) is invoked by Grey herself. The ensuing soliloquy illustrates this dynamics where Grey self-consciously calls herself an oil creature. Here we find Grey alone in her office after her meeting with Ingram and engaged in reading the contract:

> This contract is pure extortion. And now that I am buying myself an expensive title, I who am hideous to look at, living entirely on oil, creating wealth for myself out of society's blunders, quite unmoved

*"It's Not Easy to Make Oil and Love Run in Harness Together"* 311

by the thrills of the class war, and uninterested in God, what is my next step to be?

(64–65)

Then Grey revealingly adds:

This man Ingram is a born horse-dealer. But he has a good jaw. Yet it's difficult for me to keep even a man like him. True, he says that a sea of oil can rouse many a man's ardour, and that gold can fire the blood as well as a smooth skin.

(64–65)

The hint that completes our vision of her phantasmatic libidinal economy and her psychodynamics is the parallel she draws between maternal/feminine feeding (traditionally associated with breast-feeding and sex) and money (including the petro-capitalist contract). As she explains: "Food is the only thing that never palls. One feeds the people one wants to keep: in many different ways. The usual feminine way is easier. But this is how I do it. (She signs the contract.) Deborah Grey" (65). Put more lucidly, she sees the contract with Ingram as her way of fulfilling him libidinally-erotically and as her way of expressing and investing her affective and sexual desire in Ingram.

A noteworthy yet poignant evidence to the intertwinement of the private and public, desire and oil, business and emotions, economics and erotics, both in the play and in Grey's case in particular becomes evident towards the end of the play when in her conversation with Colonel Monson whilst discussing the issue of and the crisis surrounding the impending Immigration Bill. This passage also reveals her poignant frustration at being denied love, affective-erotic bond, and recognition of desirability by nearly all males around her. When Grey wistfully reminds Monson of a memory of a perhaps fleeting affair – "That was a glorious time we had in Hawaii. A certain globetrotter can say what he likes about windbags, but we had many an ardent night. Do you remember, Freddy?" (113) – Monson gives her an evasive answer by changing the subject and refusing to remember. When Grey corners him by ruefully insisting: "It's a pity, Freddy that you don't want to remember that trip to Hawaii" (113), Monson, feeling under duress, ultimately avers: "No, I don't remember it. But whatever happens, I'm as happy as a drunken sailor to think that Debsy Grey, the mother of the Brown Islands, should hit on such a great idea" (114).

The aforementioned points concerning the relationship between oil and desire, between ugliness and beauty, and between desire and death find a paradigmatic corroboration in a moment when Grey establishes an explicit link between "oil as capital" and "oil as an overdetermined *objet*

312  *"It's Not Easy to Make Oil and Love Run in Harness Together"*

*petit a"* (or a phantasmatic-material force) through which she desires to de-territorialize her current physical-facial features and re-territorialize them as a divinely beautiful and irresistible (see Anti-Oedipus 84–106, 139–145, 184–192). An emblematic illustration of this point can be found (is discernible) in the moment when entirely alone Grey is suffused with a sublime sense of jouissance and transcendence:

> I find suddenly that I've got all the cards in my hands. It will become clear enough that power, when I happen to have it, is a part of myself and can transform my lips into the mouth of a Lilian Gish. God of Israel! How lazy I feel now!
>
> (68)

This euphoric laziness betokens the sense of replenishment, fulfilment, phantasy of primary narcissism when the individual (Grey, in this instance) is overwhelmed with a sense of oceanic omnipotence, transcendence of the material limits (including one's body and ugliness), and oneness with *objet petit a* (see Winnicott; also see Lacan 1998). This moment also marks the body of the oil despot (see *Anti-Oedipus* 186–195).

Importantly, in the psycho-symbolic structure of the play, Grey's ugliness (as an instance of protean physiognomy) is resonant with her psychological, emotional, and moral complexities and even contradictions she embodies throughout. If, as Theodor Adorno and Geoffrey Harpham have separately argued, both aesthetically and from a social-cultural and historical perspective, beauty is associated with formal completeness, unity, cyclicality, and the stable and identical form of a circle; and ugliness is associated with inner-outer multiplicity and division, grotesque, abject, caricatural, burlesque, and a shapeless mass of heterogeneous and conflicting attributes caught in "a civil war of attraction/repulsion" (Harpham 1982, 9). By the same token, *Oil Islands* not only demonstrates how the aforementioned features are respectively attributed to Perucha-cha and Grey at literal, symbolical, and psychological levels. Importantly, however, and as delineated previously, *Oil Islands* compounds this dichotomous and reductionist postulation of correspondence between formal-physical features and moral-psychological ones. Citing Rosenkranz, Theodor Adorno argues that, in the dialectics of the beautiful, ugliness was appropriated through negation where the sheer opposition of ugliness to the urge toward beauty engendered an inherent tension within the work of art that was a pivotal, if implicit, component in the production of its structural harmony: "the ugly is that element that opposes the work's ruling law of form; it is integrated by that formal law and thereby confirms it."[21] Adorno equated beauty with unity, rationalism, and coherence. In contrast, ugliness represented the "primacy of the particular" and of the individual (see Adorno 1997, 46–47). Indeed, the more nuanced and subtle account of the nature of beauty Adorno insightfully presents is

## "It's Not Easy to Make Oil and Love Run in Harness Together" 313

highly consonant with the moral-psychological complexities and imbrications between the two apparently opposite characters. As Adorno states: "Beauty is not the platonically pure beginning but rather something that originated in the renunciation of what was once feared, which only as the result of this renunciation . . . became the ugly" (Adorno 1997, 49–50).[22] Therefore, considered aesthetically, ugliness – akin to oil which according to Yaeger enters a text as a force field (2011, 306, 309) – enters *Oil Islands* as a force thereby exerting a psycho-symbolic influence on the form (which is primarily associated with beauty) and configuration of other elements. This link between ugliness and oil enhances the link between the ecological and moral-economic effects of oil where the environmental implications and the moral-economic dynamics of the petrocapitalist processes through which oil is extracted and produced cannot but be ugly, corrupt, and pernicious practices. Ugliness also corroborates the intimate interweaving between desire and death as embodied by Grey and as associated with oil.

## IV. Desire, Capitalism, Animality, and Naturalism

What further compounds the entanglements between libidinal and political economy, in the oil-driven dynamics of *Oil Islands*, is the introduction of a "naturalistic" strain which seems to usher in a tacit evocation of a certain strain of evolutionary ethics, animalism/animality, and instinctual inevitability and determinism. This naturalistic stain very specifically revolves around the relationship between rational and ethical norms and values, on the one hand, and the physical and psychological needs and features, on the other. More specifically, this naturalism involves a tension-laden relation between ostensibly less rational and more emotional, instinctual and urgent bodily-psychological needs and predilections, on the one hand, and more civilized, rational, and normatively humanistic inclination driven by the powers of consciousness, reason, and will. This strain is specifically introduced through a reference to a scientific experiment recounted by Lelio in "Scene 1: A Sexual Experiment with Rats", the title of which has been couched in starkly naturalistic terms. As Lelio explains:

> Two years ago in Ohio some people made an experiment with rats. Six male rats were confined in a box with an electric plate separating them on the one side from food and on the other side from females. After being deprived of food and of sex for seventy-two hours, five males died trying to get at the food and only one trying to get at the females.
>
> (47)

When Grey asks: "So out of the six only one went the way of honour and of Lelio Holyday", Lelio responds: "When they reversed the experiment

314 *"It's Not Easy to Make Oil and Love Run in Harness Together"*

and confined six females, only one female went for the food, and five for the males" (47). Grey's reaction to this is revealing: "Miss Grey bursts into tears". Subsequently Lelio adds a barbed and incendiary remark that corroborates the points we have been making: "The coolies, when they go home again from our island across two oceans, forget their eleven years' exile from home, their fear of cold explosions, the everlasting stink of oil, and remember a certain ugly face". Yet again, Grey's reaction reveals the deep-seated trauma involving the combination of her sore need for love and her lack of physical appeal. As Ingram says: "She's crying" (47). The scientific experiments on mice counterpoint physical need with psychological need evidenced by involving and specifically focusing on food and sex. As such, the experiment shows how for the female mice (and female humans – by extension) – the fulfilment of sexual desire, affective-emotional attention, and desirability are psychosomatic and existential needs even more vital than food (physical need). Importantly, no one embodies the fraught battle between will and instinct, erotic desire, and desire for capital (through the death-laden oil as commodity) as intensely and persistently as Grey does.[23] The poignant affinity – not to say near identity – Grey senses between herself and the female rats (instinctively seeking emotional-sexual fulfilment as an existential-psychological priority over and above the physical), is in keeping with her deep-seated experience of trauma concerning her physical-facial features and her perceived undesirability which she experiences very palpably at numerous points in the play. What distinguishes her from the rats is her conscious struggle to overcome this instinctual inclination toward "being desired" by restraining her inner urges to do so along with her use of capitalized oil and herself as the embodiment of its phallic and phallogocentric power as a (de)sublimated substitute. Furthermore, the indication of this scientific experiment enhances the aforementioned associations of the island itself as a laboratory – in ecological, biopolitical, and economic respects – for the extractive practices of petro-capitalism.

Correspondingly, there is also a salient anti-naturalistic streak in the play both at formal and psychological levels. This is vividly reflected in the extended scene of confrontation between Grey and Ingram where, reminding Ingram of his analogical logic in relation to women generally and Grey more specifically (namely, that man rides the horse – meaning the animalistic woman – and not vice versa), she expresses her unflagging determination to defy such a naturalistic logic and its postulation of humans as predictable deterministic machines or beings. In this scene, which marks a critical juncture in the dynamics of *Oil Islands* too, Grey confronts Ingram for his act of betrayal and inflicting emotional degradation on her at Peruchacha's party. When in a conciliatory and sycophantic manner Ingram tries to mitigate and alleviate the wound he has inflicted ("Do we raise a cheer for Deborah Grey and H. B. Ingram?"), Grey chooses a particular naturalistic discourse to

## "It's Not Easy to Make Oil and Love Run in Harness Together" 315

articulate her dismissal by explicitly alluding to the scientific experiment, an act which reveals her psychodynamics in a language which tries to defy a naturalistic and deterministic logic rather than the love or betrayal of merely one specific individual such as Ingram. Grey adamantly avers:

> Turned down. That's where you've made a mistake, Ingram. It's true that five female rats out of six try to get to the males, but you trusted in that too confidently; you didn't take it into account that I might be the sixth.
>
> (102)

Bewildered by Grey's reference to rats, Ingram wonders:

> The sixth? I took it for granted that you were the five in one. But let's stop this nonsense. The men in Moscow aren't given to joking, and it's only half an hour to twelve o'clock [the deadline at which Ingram will either be handed over to the Russians to execute him or be redeemed by Grey].
>
> (102)

Then, in the hope of quelling Grey's fury and cajoling her into acquiescence, Ingram even, seductively, offers to have sex with her. Whilst slightly tempted and evincing a lingering and faint emotional-sexual interest in Ingram, Grey remains resolute to dismiss her desire in order to defy the deterministic logic invoked by Lelio and Ingram earlier in the play by demonstrating the triumph of her rational will over her instinctual desire for sexual fulfilment and love.

Elsewhere, in keeping with the ambience and logic of naturalistic determinism – driven by the forces of a petro-capitalist, reified milieu, and hereditary forces (registered at an unconscious level as instinctual drives), Lelio recounts a parabolic anecdote which depicts a capitalist world and an exceeding process of interminable surplus accumulation, global expansion, and self-perpetuation of capitalism at planetary and extra-planetary levels – a dynamics reflected in the analogy of the grotesque physical bloating and bulging of the businessman. Lelio's parabolic vision foreshadows Grey's condition at the very climactic conclusion of the play. Here, Lelio's account depicts a fully reified ontology and human consciousness where money (as a metonymy for capitalism) has replaced both nature and human relationship. The businessman cannot think of anything but money and business since in his fully rationalized and reified world, there is no ontological category or definition for anything else. Lelio relates the parable thus:

> When he had made such an enormous pile / That he could have paved every room in his house with gold, / He saw that he hadn't anything

316   *"It's Not Easy to Make Oil and Love Run in Harness Together"*

really worth while / In all the various markets he controlled. / He was fifty-seven and he needed little sleep / His digestion was bad, but otherwise he was quite sound, / And he still had twenty-six teeth that he meant to keep, / His only defect was his tummy which was rather round. / It vexed him to find that not a client offered / To sell him the sea, the sky, the mountains and God, when he wanted to buy. / It vexed him that no one would take the cheques he proffered Or treat his signature respectfully. / He waved his cheques at the mountains to make them sit up and pay attention, / But they never even noticed that he beckoned; / Business was the only thing he had learned to mention, / And God wouldn't speak of business, and the sky remained vacant. / So there he sat with twenty-six teeth of his own and six golden ones, wasn't it funny? / A first-class magnate, with a bank balance in the very grandest style, / And couldn't get what he wanted, although he was willing to plank down the money, / So what was the use of his having made an enormous pile?

(44–46)

Read metaphorically, if God in this anecdote signifies both phallus and the transcendental spirit or principle of nature (both of which seem to be incongruent with the fully reified and capitalized world of the businessman) the moral lesson of the parable, poignant for Grey, seems to be that money (or the capital derived from oil) cannot buy one desire/desirability but rather intensifies solipsism, implosion, and a near-psychotic narcissism. The businessman's world in the previous parable is highly akin to and anticipates Grey's world at the end of the play – with the noteworthy difference that Grey's petro-capitalist world is a secular world where capital has fully superseded the transcendental Logos and God (see Peter Goodchild 2009, 75–104, 171–185, passim).

It is worth indicating that this naturalistic strain in the play runs parallel with the ideological attempts, made by agents in Grey's circle, at "naturalizing" Grey's toxic and monstrous petro-capitalist extractive practices and its treatment of nature, labour force, and the people. The paradigmatic evidence of such attempts is the act of calling Grey "the mother of the Brown Islands" by Monson and Obadiah. This attempt at naturalization should be read as an inherent act of dispossession and appropriation. Furthermore, there are also signs of a naturalistic treatment and perception of the coloured, non-native as non- or sub-human and part of nature. I have expanded on this point at length next.

\* \* \* \* \* \* \*

Crucially, a pivotal part of this entanglement between desire and oil (as capital or commodified material resource) – where the former

## "It's Not Easy to Make Oil and Love Run in Harness Together" 317

is traditionally associated with the private/personal realm of libidinal economy and the latter with the more public and socially oriented realm of political economy – arises from the dynamics of capitalism as illustrated by *Oil Islands*. Conceptually, these dynamics have been rigorously elaborated by Deleuze and Guattari (and, more recently, by Hardt and Negri). Repudiating the efficacy of any social-political theory or philosophical analysis that splits the psychic and the social, Deleuze and Guattari posit them as inherently intermeshed. For Deleuze and Guattari, desiring production is one and the same thing as social production since desire produces reality: "If desire produces, its product is real. If desire is productive, it can be productive only in the real world and can produce only reality" (*Anti-Oedipus* 28). Identifying the commodity culture prevailing in the capitalist mode of production as a culture of cruelty, Deleuze and Guattari define it thus: "This culture is not the movement of ideology: on the contrary, it forcibly injects production into desire, and conversely, it forcibly inserts desire into social production and reproduction" (*Anti-Oedipus*, 159). One of the crucial premises of their account of the overdetermined nature of desire in capitalism is their establishment of a relationship between social-production and desiring-production: "The truth of the matter is that social production is purely and simply desiring-production itself under determinate conditions" (*Anti-Oedipus* 29). This explicates how the social field is affected by the combined yet unequal differentiation of matter prior to its representation in subjects. Expanding on the relationship between desire, the body, and sign (as simultaneously material and linguistic), Deleuze and Guattari argue that the difference cannot be understood in terms of a language system into which the body is born:

> [Desire] makes men or their organs into the parts and wheels of the social machine. The sign is a position of desire; but the first signs are the territorial signs that plant their flags in bodies. And if one wants to call this inscription in naked flesh "writing" then it must be said that speech in fact presupposes writing, and that it is this cruel system of inscribed signs that renders man capable of language, and gives him a memory of the spoken word.
>
> (*Anti-Oedipus*, 159)

Predicated on the points delineated here, we can argue oil to be a material sign – simultaneously territorial, territorializing and de-territorializing – which can organize individual and social bodies into new units of value, meaning, and function – particularly within the late capitalist petrocultural context. In such a context, desire is primarily defined and fulfilled through oil (the despotism of the signifier) – or an oil-driven libidinal-political economy – at the levels of consciousness and the unconscious. Such a possibility arises from the nature of the unconscious itself: "The unconscious poses no problem of meaning, solely problems of use. The question posed

318 *"It's Not Easy to Make Oil and Love Run in Harness Together"*

by desire is not 'what does it mean?' but rather 'How does it work?'" (*Anti-Oedipus*, 119). One of the ways through which such a despotism of the petro-phallic signifier can be de-capitated (that is, decapitalized) is through the production of non-oedipal desiring machines: "How do these machines, these desiring-machines, work – yours and mine? . . . Desire makes its entry with the general collapse of the question 'What does it mean?'" (68). In this regard, Deleuze and Guattari distinguish between two modes of desire or desiring-production and libidinal investment: the fascist-paranoid and the schizo-nomadic modes of desire-production. The fascist-paranoid mode is a totalizing, past-oriented process whereby desire is coded and given a fixed use; it "subordinates desiring-production to the formation of sovereignty and to the gregarious aggregate that results from it" (*Anti-Oedipus* 376). The schizo-nomadic mode, on the contrary, is heteronomous, future-oriented, and "brings about the inverse subordination, overthrows the established power, and subjects the gregarious aggregate to the molecular multiplicities of the productions of desire" (ibid.).

A cogent testimony to the aforementioned entanglements between desire and capital, desiring-production and social-production in *Oil Islands* is discernible in the perceived necessity of Grey's marriage with Viscount of Moreland and its effects on the capitalist oil and stock market. In order to capture a glimpse into the reasons underlying such an important decision, we need to consider it in the context of Grey's unremitting endeavours to gain national and global monopoly over the production of oil and oil prices, particularly in its competition with its national rival: the Trust Company. A conversation between Grey, Monson, and the Directors of Grey's oil company provides us with ample insight into the broader national-global dynamics of the petroscene. First the First Director alarmingly states: "The new oil fields of the Continental Trust produce sixty per cent more than our previous estimates. So the Trust will be able to swamp our total production within eleven months" (36). Subsequently, Second Director tentatively adds:

> If the Trust produces more oil than we do, it will be in a position to dictate prices. Whether the acquisition of the Russian concessions will enable us to keep abreast of the Trust's expanding markets is open to question.
>
> (36)

And finally,

> in the most favourable circumstances, that is to say, supposing the Russian concessions enable us to produce oil in a ratio of 55 to 45 against the Continental Trust, we should pay for that advantage by a sum so large that our capital reserves would be seriously weakened.
>
> (37)

*"It's Not Easy to Make Oil and Love Run in Harness Together"* 319

Importantly Ingram proceeds to accentuate two crucial issues which are the focal points of our discussion here: the phallogocentric gender politics informing the petro-capitalist world and of her moral status and social reputation, Monson asks:

> Will you permit me a relevant question, Miss Grey? Have you allowed in your project for the damaging effect of your reputation as a woman? Have you considered that the Trust, in the event of such a bill being brought in, will certainly exploit in its favour your alleged immorality?

He then adds the other complicating factor: "The men in Moscow and their agent Mr. Ingram are well aware of the situation" (36). Grey's response attests to the extent to which the ostensibly distinct issues of the private and public, the libidinal and the political economy are inherently linked. In response, Grey confidently adumbrates: "I expect my reputation to be above suspicion by the time the Immigration Bill comes up for discussion, so that wouldn't cut any ice" (38). When Monson wonders: "I don't quite see how you're to manage that", Grey discloses her charade thus:

> you won't deny that I can hardly be saddled with a bad reputation when I'm the wife of the Viscount of Westmoreland. My agent in London cables me that there will be no further objections on the part of the old Earl.
>
> (38)

This act of political ingenuity compels the astonished Monson to confirm Grey's symbolic status:

> I always knew that you could make the Continental Trust look like a pack of curs yapping at the moon, but I must say you have risen to this dangerous situation in a manner which puts Edison in the shade. Hurrah for Debsy Grey, the mother of the Oil Islands!
>
> (39)

The play shows how the symbolic marriage releases the political-economic codes from the previous structures and logics, sending them on the crests of new speculative waves where gradually there appear new structures that try to re-code the de-territorialized flows of capital and libidinal energies. The upheaval that Grey's marriage induces in the capitalist order (metonymically represented by the stock market in *Oil Islands*) acts as a moment of what Deleuze calls "disjunctive synthesis" or "deterritorialization" through which the codes, evaluation logics, and alliance patterns are decoded, dismantled, and released as libidinal energies, flows of intensity, and capital leading to a new re-territorialization. The entanglements of

320  *"It's Not Easy to Make Oil and Love Run in Harness Together"*

market and marriage, private and public, libidinal and political economy, desire and oil find a paradigmatic illustration in the way Wall Street and the American stock market undergo drastic fluctuations in consequence of the news of Grey's marriage with the Viscount. In Act Two, Scene 2 – titled "The Retreat from the Stock Exchange New York 'Star'" – we witness the indelible entanglements between "social-production" and "desiring production". This scene opens onto the Financial Editor's Office and depicts the sheer chaos and confusion wrought by the news of Grey's marriage on the value of stocks including those of the oil companies. This is evidenced by the distraught Editor's frantic phone calls in the hope of gleaning an inkling to whether the news is fake or genuine, his nearly delirious speech, and his consternation at the unpredictable manner in which the stock market is undergoing volatile alterations. As he harangues on the phone in conversation with various colleagues:

> The Chimpanzee's marrying the Viscount of Westmoreland. I don't know what she means by it. Can't see through it at all. (Picks up telephone.) That the Stock Exchange? Yeh. Market's jumpy because of Chimpanzee's wedding? You don't say. Opening tendency: Island Company falling, Continentals rising. Thanks. Fairbank Brothers bearing Islands? You too? Do we know anything? Like hell we do. Go to it, anyway. (Hangs up the receiver). The boys don't know anything either. Damn it. Can't see through it at all. (Picks up telephone.) That the Chief speaking?
>
> (53)

Consequently, Financial Editor plaintively acknowledges the failure of his speculative attempts to elicit some data and prospective direction in which the stock market is moving: "Sickening to be expected to put people wise when you know about as much as a sucking infant" (53). Even when the manager of the agency arrives to ask Editor:

> Say, what about this marriage of the Chimpanzee? Are you on to it? . . . We reckon it's a bluff. Got hold of a Continentals 43. 19.6 . . . They think on the Street that she's bluffing. Want to know our clue? Oh, you're on to it yourself?
>
> (54)

Editor expresses his profound scepticism of the far-fetched possibility of this marriage and goes to any lengths to justify the fallacy of the rumour:

> He can't see through it either. I reckon I'll bank on a bluff too. (Picks up telephone.) Gimme the Chief. Yes, clear as crystal. The Chimpanzee's on her last legs and is pulling a bluff. But the boys in Wall Street aren't having any.
>
> (55)

*"It's Not Easy to Make Oil and Love Run in Harness Together"* 321

Left desperately clueless, Editor laments: "Can't see through it at all. (Telephone rings.) What? Islands rising again? (Hangs up receiver.) Still paddling. Well, this fourth of April will see many a good man digging his own grave" (55). As such, *Oil Islands* gives the vivid and striking picture of the behavioural pattern of the market (as a barometer of finance capitalism) in reaction and relation to the socio-symbolic as well as private aspects of the capitalists' lives. The stock market, as depicted in *Oil Islands*, evokes the image of a nervous system (of capitalism) where every libidinal or political-economic signal instigates a reconfiguration of elements, forces, and their value. This scene also illustrates the stock market and media (including the newspapers) as the discursive apparatus of petro-capitalism and the implementation of its triadic dynamics: connective synthesis, disjunctive synthesis, and conjunctive synthesis (see *Anti-Oedipus*). Finally, the dynamics of the scene shows both the media and the market to be nodal points where the private and public life of the individual and socius as well as the libidinal and political economy are imbricated. This is attested by how an ostensibly highly personal and private matter as marriage creates volatile ripples in something as highly abstract, quantitatively rational, and strictly regulated as the economic space of the stock market.

The next scene confronts us with a detailed and intimate view of Grey's marriage as a transaction. Here, the content of the conversation between Grey and Viscount reveals the truth of the event: a financial interaction devoid of any emotional content whereby they become business partners rather than marital partners. Whilst still befuddled with the reasons why a woman with the status of Grey has decided to marry such an economically unequal man, Viscount welcomes Grey as his bride and adds: "I don't know what prompted you to choose me, but I assure you that I greet you with all the respect due from an insignificant young man to the head of such a gigantic business" (61). Grey's response corroborates the commodified and symbolic nature of the marriage: "Your father, who has a keen eye for business, has gone over the settlements very thoroughly, with the result that both parties to the transaction are satisfied". Grey then proceeds to propose to give Viscount "a yearly income of sixty thousand pounds" and "a highly paid position at your disposal" if the Viscount happens to be interested in Grey's oil business (61). Having received the confirmation from Viscount that "with the sixty thousand pounds I shall do my best to live in a style worthy of you", Grey adds the conditions of the marital contract: "I ask you to stay on the Island for about six weeks after our marriage, and for about a fortnight every year after that" (62). Importantly, Grey underscores two other crucial points, both of which corroborate the point at issue concerning the indelible intertwinement of the libidinal and political economy (or the desiring-production and social-production). The first she indicates is: "My private life is a matter of public interest, and it

# 322 *"It's Not Easy to Make Oil and Love Run in Harness Together"*

would be misconstrued if we were to live continually apart" (62). And secondly, she adds:

> There is a lady on this island, a certain Miss Peruchacha, who is very pretty and amusing. Unfortunately, for reasons of which I am ignorant, she is unfriendly to the Oil Company. It is not of any importance, but I should be obliged if you would have as little to do with her as possible.
>
> (62)

## V.  Oil as a Complex Theme

What further enhances the aura of mystery not only surrounding Grey, but also the nature and future of oil on the island, along with the spiralling conflict between Grey and Peruchacha, is the question of the oil crisis and its tenebrous nature. From the very outset, the nature of the oil crisis and its veridicality is riddled with ambiguity and doubt. On the one hand, some people (among the rival parties and common people in the public) believe that Grey has confronted a scarcity of oil resources and a depletion crisis. On the other hand there is the rumour that Grey has discovered new oil resources. In this regard, the public refer to the fanfare of celebratory events and the extravagantly illuminated spectacle of Grey's yacht as a testimony to this point: "The Chimpanzee has had her yacht illuminated every night for three nights now. But she hasn't gone aboard" (19). As one member of the public says: "Oh, it isn't the parlour lizard, nor yet the hot nights – it's because new oil fields have been discovered on the mainland that she can't sleep. The yacht's brighter than ever now; they've turned on all the lights" (20). Another member of the crowd however mentions a different sort of crisis that is different from peak oil concerns or depletion crisis on the island, namely, the crisis of market for abundant oil discoveries: "She has a lot to think about. She needs her big head to market so much oil through the world" (21). And, finally, there are also people who, correctly, believe that the crisis arises from the imminent rout of Grey at the hands of her rival company, the Trust, in their competition to gain monopoly over access to the production and prices of oil. Early in the play, at Peruchacha's party when the Butler announces, "Mr. Overweek, the film actor, has sent to inquire if he may still accept your invitation", Peruchacha once more explicitly refers to the oil crisis and Grey's ensnarement in it:

> What, is the Chimpanzee letting him come? Has she no time to spare for Harry Overweek? Then the oil crisis must be really serious! She must be in it up to her neck! She's being choked by her own stinking oil, the bitch! I beg your pardon, gentlemen, but I am so overjoyed!

## "It's Not Easy to Make Oil and Love Run in Harness Together"    323

And even though she has turned away my guests, my garden party is now going to be a gaudeamus.

(32)

As such the play at this stage leaves us in abeyance as to whether there is an excess of oil due to new discoveries or a dearth of oil due to shrinking of the existing resources.

*Oil Islands* shows how the oil crisis is being fought at national and international fronts. The rivalry over national monopoly is reflected in the rivalry between Grey's oil company and the Trust Company. And the international competition over global monopoly over oil extraction-production is evidenced by the rivalry between the American oil companies (particularly Grey's) and not only those of the Soviet Union, but also those of other European rivals. At the national level, the succuss at gaining monopoly is determined by such questions as access to cheap resources, access to cheap labour, the production cost, and the price monopoly. It is premised on such dynamics that Grey intends to secure and win the national rivalry against the Trust Company over monopoly by passing the Immigration Bill.

Early in the play we find Grey in a meeting with the senior members of her oil company discussing various possible remedial measures to the current oil crisis. When Grey seeks their suggestions ("Your diagnosis, gentlemen, agrees with with mine. What do you recommend?"), it receives three propositional solutions by the three members. Initially, First Director states: "The purchase of the Russian concessions, even at a sacrifice" (37). Then Second Director adds: "The saturation of all available markets while we can do it" (37). Finally, Colonel Monson observes: "In a situation like this every decision is a risk with a minimum chance of success" (37). All the while, we later retrospectively gather that Grey has been running these sessions with some Socratic irony in the sense that she has already incisively found a remedy for this quandary and yet has been concealing it from others. Ultimately, Grey reveals the crux of her plan thus:

And what if we can force the Trust to increase their running costs to fifty per cent more than ours? . . . What if we can put through a bill for prohibiting the importation of coloured labour on the mainland, while allowing it in the Islands? I have put out feelers, in New York and in Washington. I have letters from Senators, both Republicans and Democrats. I have even sounded the White House.

(37)

Indeed, the implementation of such an exceptional legal measure authorized by the Central American state not only manifests the status of the Oil Islands as a peripheral heterotopia and a resource enclave where the state of exception is deemed the rule and not the exception as a modus

324 *"It's Not Easy to Make Oil and Love Run in Harness Together"*

operandi. It also demonstrates the transcendental status of oil in the phallogocentric economy: oil as Logos and Mythos at the same time and thus standing beyond law (or human Nomos). As Mbembé argues, the colony is the ultimate space of exception; it "represents the site where sovereignty consists fundamentally in the exercise of a power outside the law (*ab legibus solutus*) and where 'peace' is more likely to take on the face of a 'war without end'" (2003, 46). Stunned at the ingenuity of Grey's idea, one of the Directors ruminates on the possible ramifications of such a plan: "If the Trust could be deprived of its coloured labour, of course its new oil fields wouldn't be worth a damn" (37–38). And subsequently Monson adds: "And the Russian concessions would slump like a barometer before a storm. It would be a picnic for me to deal with Mr. Ingram then" (38). I will extensively delve into the details, dynamics, and outcome of this double-barrelled Immigration Bill scheme of Grey's and its political-economic, racial, and ecological implications later.

One of the fundamental facets of petro-capitalism as an extractivist and self-perpetuating order/ideology – which is one of its contradictory premises too – is raised in *Oil Islands* through Grey's reference to the idea of infinite growth and expansion through surplus extraction. This becomes apparent when Grey states: "Do you believe in short-sighted measures, gentlemen? I run the Oil Company as if it were going to last till the Judgment Day" (50). Here, Feuchtwanger exposes and presents a potent critique of the capitalistic fantasy of an inexhaustible expropriation that thrives on the incessant supply of an exploitable environment and disposable labour. This diagnostic approach to a petro-capitalist conception of history and nature is endorsed by Harvey's identification of the idea of infinite growth as one of the contradictions of capitalism (see Harvey's *Seventeen Contradictions of Capitalism* ??). It also finds corroboration in Andreas Malm's theory of fossil fuels as "the general lever for surplus value production" (Malm, Fossil Capital. Verso, 289).

### VI.  The Arrival of the Petro-Communist Link: Ingram and the Russian Oil Concession

One of the pivotal figures who arrives on the scene of the Oil Islands principally due to the question of the oil crisis is Ingram. Crucially, the aforementioned intertwinement between libidinal and political economy and between the private and public (both involving convoluted imbrications among oil, desire, death, and nature), ironically, serves as Grey's point of vulnerability and one of the principal ways through which she suffers emotional-sexual trauma, social stigmatization, and public humiliation. Notably, this is a trauma that she suffers in her rather unilateral love-sexual affair with the Russian emissary and agent: Ingram. Ingram, described as a "stout man in his mid thirties" (8), arrives as the official delegate from the Soviet Union to negotiate a contract regarding the Russian

## "It's Not Easy to Make Oil and Love Run in Harness Together"   325

Oil Concession with Grey based on which Grey would be able to have access to the extraction of certain oil resources within the Soviet Union. Finding Ingram's virile boldness, economic perspicacity, and flirtatious forays appealing, Grey nearly falls in love with him whilst concealing it. Ingram is a wily man who is acutely aware of Grey's needs, flaws, and weaknesses – in political-economic, social, and psychological-bodily terms – and seeks to exploit them through an array of manoeuvres, such as an offer of business cooperation, seduction, and bullying.

On the other hand, and as a disarming gesture, Grey evinces an incisive cognizance of how Ingram may be presuming Grey to be in a desperate and crisis-ridden situation and himself as the person who is on islands to "sell [her] the remedy" (40). When Grey however as a counter-manoeuvre shows him ample knowledge of Ingram's personal life, professional history, and private scandals as a means of maintaining her upper hand. Notably, a crucial though fleeting point is raised by Grey, which reveals the world-systemic nature of both the petro-capitalist and petro-communist ideologies and their forays into the resource frontiers around the world in pursuit of finding new cheap zones of extraction through establishing their political-economic hegemony by instigating various cataclysms including political-social revolutions and governmental changes. As Grey observes: "My agents are inclined to think that you are the same emissary from Moscow who started the revolution in Iraq" (40). Ingram, interestingly, considers that intervention as a failure: "It's hardly courteous to remind a business man of his failures, Miss Grey". When Grey bemusedly asks: "I have been told that the revolution was not at all unskillfully planned", Ingram's response demonstrates how for him economic outcomes are more important than the ideological-political ones: "The only test of affairs like that is their success" (40). Astonished at Grey's extensive knowledge about various facets of his personal and professional life, calling Grey a "business woman of the first rank", Ingram adds: "It's flattering for a business man who is not exactly of the first rank to find his private tastes of interest to [you]" (40). It becomes evident from their first meeting that Ingram is corruption-prone and willing to compromise his national allegiance and ideological fidelity and duty in exchange for personal profit. Ingram acknowledges that the proposed price he is demanding for the Russian Concession includes "a margin for fair bargaining" for himself too (40).

A compelling testament to the capitalist process of the abstraction of oil as a commodity with a volatile exchange value used as a means of surplus production is Ingram's remark about the value of Russian Concession (39). When Grey asks Ingram, "These said windbags [her advisers] inform me that you are asking three times as much for your concessions as they are worth". His response cogently demonstrates this point:

> The absolute value of my concessions cannot be determined even by Professor Einstein or the University of Cambridge. But at this moment

## 326 *"It's Not Easy to Make Oil and Love Run in Harness Together"*

your Company and the Continental Trust need them as much as an elephant needs his trunk, and as I have some brains in my head, I make my price accordingly.

(39)

This remark vividly manifests the volatility and fluidity of the commodity value of oil which remains contingent not merely on the use-value of oil and its production costs at a certain historical point, but on far more complicated dynamics and a globally extended host of political, economic, and ecological issues. Grey tries to turn the tables by indicating that it is actually the Soviet Union that is more desperately in need of the profits from the oil concession for their globally extended ideological purposes; a point which throws into relief the entanglement between politics and economics at a global level around the question of oil – particularly reflected in the global rivalry between the communist Russia and the capitalist Anglo-American hegemony. As Grey remarks: "As men of the world you and your Moscow employers must have observed that people who are fighting for power pay more for it than those who have it already. Why haven't you gone first to the Continental Trust?" (39). Finding Grey in a crisis-ridden situation on multiple fronts – both nationally and internationally (over global market monopoly and transnational coloured labour force) – Ingram seeks to exploit his advantageous position by demanding three times as much as the value of the concession. In the meantime, Grey and her team are acutely aware of the extortionist approach both Ingram and Soviet Union have in their identification of the value and price of the contract concerning the Russian Concession. As Colonel Monson explains the situation lucidly:

The men in Moscow and their agent Mr. Ingram are well aware of the situation. Mr. Ingram is exploiting it by asking three times the real value of his concessions. In the most favourable circumstances, that is to say, supposing the Russian concessions enable us to produce oil in a ratio of 55 to 45 against the Continental Trust, we should pay for that advantage by a sum so large that our capital reserves would be seriously weakened.

(36–37)

Repudiating such an imputation of profiteering, Ingram asserts the Russian Concession as a valuable and mutually profitable opportunity that will redeem Grey from the trials of the crisis: "It would be a piece of luck for you if I were to hang up my hat in your business now" (64).

Significantly, as is evident, Ingram's evocative and seductive combination of the sexual-libidinal and political-economic forces and suggestions, his ambiguous gestures and metaphors are among Ingram's characteristic moves through which he tries to harp and capitalize on Grey's sore spot

## *"It's Not Easy to Make Oil and Love Run in Harness Together"* 327

(her perceived ugliness and undesirability) though latently harboured need for sexual-emotional fulfilment. For instance, Ingram tries to render the prospect of their sexual-financial union as a sublime union cast not in aesthetically beautiful terms but in capitalistically sublime terms, making them reach new physical and metaphysical heights. This is reflected in Ingram's juxtaposition of God and capital:

> if you and I were to come to grips we wouldn't be exactly a couple for a Raphael to paint, but we'd make a partnership that could bring God himself to take a new interest in this degenerate planet. As a businessman I can tell with the naked eye that you're a heavy weight, Miss Grey.
>
> (41)

Unwittingly, and in a bid to wheedle Grey through into agreement, Ingram once more invokes the mind-body and libidinal political economy dichotomy as a recurring motif throughout *Oil Islands*: "Miss Peruchacha is certainly a dazzling beauty. One can always find women to sleep with, but very few to discuss business affairs with" (42). Ingram drops a hint to his knowledge of Grey's grappling with an oil crisis as part of his savvy negotiations. When Grey invites him to join in "an excursion on my yacht the day after tomorrow", Ingram acutely indicates: "I am glad to see you can find time for excursions in spite of the oil crisis" (42). Their first meeting ends inconclusively with Grey insisting on being given "six weeks" to ponder on the offer (a suggestion that he rejects) and Ingram demanding "partnership" with Grey's oil company whilst enticingly "tapping her on the knee" (41). Later on Grey's yacht, when amidst the hubbub of the party, Grey offers to pay Ingram "Twenty per cent?" of the profits of the oil contract, Ingram adds, "I reckon by that means to recover the twenty-eight per cent which Moscow was going to pay me for putting the screw on you". And then he pushes his ambitions to the extreme by proposing: "sixty percent". Uncompromisingly, Ingram insists on nothing short of "personal co-operation" and Ingram proposes the following:

> I'll make you a counter-offer. Take me as a partner into your business, with a seat and a vote on the Board of Directors, and I'll give you the Soviet concessions for twenty per cent less than the Trust will bid.
>
> (41)

Bewildered by Ingram's audacity, Grey states: "H. B. Ingram can ride the high horse all right". Here, seductively "caressing" Grey, Ingram suggestively utters: "I believe you'd rather be reduced to scraping out all the empty oil cans in the States before you'd admit that it's the man who rides the horse and not the other way about" (51). This observation once more manifests Ingram's phallocratic and macho ethos, but also gender politics

# 328 *"It's Not Easy to Make Oil and Love Run in Harness Together"*

of the time and in keeping with the naturalist strain (human as evolved animal) underpinning the play. Crucially, Grey's response to this bold remark prove a reverberating word and motif: "submission". As Grey avers: "There's no such thing as submission, Mr. Ingram" (51).

Crucially, from the very first meeting with Ingram, Grey reveals how traumatized and obsessed with her facial-physical features (as well as the others' perception/impression) she is. This is attested by her intense curiosity *to see how "the other" sees her* whilst unconsciously desiring the other to see her as she wishes herself to be seen – to wit, the very dynamics of phantasmatic desire as elaborated by Freud and Lacan (see ???). Grey seeks Ingram's view of her features and whether he finds her desirable:

> I know that I look something like my photographs in the illustrated papers, which are usually simply entitled 'The Chimpanzee.' None the less I prefer not to sit at table with men who find that the sight of me takes away their appetite. Tell me frankly as one man of business to another: could you enjoy a dinner in my company? Think before you answer.
>
> (42)

In response, and apparently as a gesture of compliment, Ingram states: "Three continents suffer from the delusion that women are only for the nighttime. But you are for the daytime, Miss Deborah Grey" (42). Here, once more, we encounter an observation that not only reveals the cultural politics of gender of the time, but corroborates the psycho-symbolic and libidinal-economic attributes of Grey I have been delineating earlier.

In the next meeting we find Ingram impatient and feeling deceived by Grey. Finding Grey's constant postponement of the finalization of their contract concerning the Russian Concession suspicious, Ingram asks for either the clinching of the concession contract and his fair share of the profit or a clear annulment of the agreements. Notably, Ingram attends the meeting with Grey fully armed, given that Peruchacha, in a bid to undermine Grey's plans, has now revealed Grey's secret attempts to have the Immigration Bill approved (which, if successful, will considerably reduce the value of the Russian Concession) to him. When Ingram discloses his knowledge of the Immigration Bill, it leaves Grey consternated and speechless. When Ingram says: "Miss Deborah Grey, I'm fond of you personally. But you can't expect me to sit still and smile until the first press notices of your Immigration Bill turn my concessions into waste paper" (62–63), Grey, "turning pale", wonders: "How did you get that information? (63). Subsequently, Grey asks for a bit of more time. However, sensing that Grey is playing fast and loose with him to gain some time for the outcome of the Immigration Bill (the establishment of which would place Grey in an advantageous position to decide about the value of the Russian Concession), Ingram parries her efforts by forewarning

*"It's Not Easy to Make Oil and Love Run in Harness Together"* 329

that: "You have an hour's time to consider it. After that either I'll have the contract or I'll be on board ship" (64). When Grey bluntly asks him: "How much do you cost, Mr. Ingram? . . . You gave me a hint earlier that you drew a distinction between Ingram the Moscow agent and Mr. H. B. Ingram in person" (63). Confirming his ambitious and self-interested inclination, Ingram affirms his willingness to compromise the national interests of the Soviet Union in exchange for a substantial personal profit: "Naturally I'm more on the side of Mr. Ingram in person. We can be said to have come to an understanding so far" (50). Ingram, however, alerts Grey to the fatal costs and implications of any such collusion: "Even on the Oil Islands you must have heard it rumoured that anyone who shakes too many juicy plums from the Moscow tree into his own lap isn't likely to have a long time to enjoy them in" (63). Ingram then menacingly adds:

> I don't want something that's only rumoured, I want something that's actually a fact. . . . My full and undiminished share. The day before yesterday, for instance, you concluded that important transaction with Chicago, and I wasn't told a word about it beforehand. That's a contravention of our contract. If I were to let your political associates know the way you honour your secret contracts, my beloved, you wouldn't find it easy to get your Immigration Bill carried.
>
> (69)

Ingram and Grey ultimately concur that Grey take a few hours to ruminate on Ingram's proposed terms of agreement. Ingram seductively adds: "Then we'll sleep together on it! (Laughs anil goes.)" (64).

Notably, *Oil Islands* provides us with a bifocal perspective/view in this regard however. That is, not only do we capture a glimpse into the negotiations between the Russian agent and the American oil potentate but we are also afforded an insight into how the Russian side views the affairs. This is provided in Scene 5 – titled "The Shadow of Moscow" – set in "Moscow. The central office of the Secret Service". Here we hear three Commissars talking about the profits of selling their oil resources to the American in the hope of gaining economic and political advantage over them. First Commissar observes:

> As our comrade the Minister for Foreign Affairs tells us, the favourable opportunity for selling our oil concessions has been missed in a most irritating manner. They will have to be got rid of now at a third of the price which might have been obtained earlier. Our agent general was Mr. Ingram.
>
> (66)

One of the most interesting points raised in this scene is the Russian's description of Ingram. As Second Commissar observes: "Mr. Ingram is

330 *"It's Not Easy to Make Oil and Love Run in Harness Together"*

described in our books as follows: energetic, unprincipled, pleasure-loving, cynical, very capable" (66). The scene concludes with the committee concurring on trusting despite his tardiness and delay (protracted practice). Later when all three Commissars arrive on the island on a mission to investigate the case and arrest Ingram to prosecute him, they aver: "Mr. Ingram should be struck off" (67). As we will see later, however, Grey intervenes and tries to abort their plan due to her lingering interest in Ingram. As she instructs her adviser who is also acting as the intermediary: "The Russian is to do nothing for the present. He is to be prevented from meeting Mr. Ingram at all. Is that clear?" (68).

Grey's quasi-amorous relationship with Ingram reaches a critical juncture at Peruchacha's party. The party, held at Peruchacha's garden, occurs in the interval between two pivotal events – Peruchacha's defeat at the car race and her departure to the US to sabotage Grey's attempts to have the Immigration Bill passed. Whilst the party seems to be partly tarnished by the now-ubiquitous reek of oil (94) and low-quality cocktails (94), in her taunting conversation with Grey and Ingram, Peruchacha unleashes a tirade of taunting, derisive remarks on Ingram, particularly targeting his virility and will in relation to Grey and daring him to speak the truth about whether, as the rumour (reflected in the "Song of the Brown Islands") goes, Ingram – like all other employees of Grey's – submits to her in bed and job or not:

> Mr. Ingram, this is supposed to be an evening of men's talk, where a spade is called a spade, and as I'm a *salta atras* I can talk like a man too. So tell me, do you submit, for instance, in your bed and your job? (88)

Undented by Peruchacha's challenge and calling the party "an evening of plain speaking" where Grey on behalf of herself and her entourage affirms, "We'll play our part", Peruchacha, derisive, teases and quips, particularly targeting his virility and will (90). This leads to a slight tension and bickering between Grey and Ingram where Grey insists that Ingram speak the truth and yet Ingram is averse to sabotage all his financial prospects and profits by speaking the truth. Peruchacha intensifies the challenge by asserting: "Have we got guys here who are struck dumb by the presence of a Viscountess?" to which Grey retorts: "Surely Mr. Ingram isn't struck dumb by my presence?" (90).

Bitten to the quick by Peruchacha's unremitting claims (to the effect that he is a sexual slave to Grey's sexual and materialist/financial voracious forays) in conjunction with Grey's relentless insistence on Ingram answering Peruchacha's quips frankly, Ingram feels stung into response – a response which costs him everything short of his life. Ingram blurts out: "Very well, I'll hold forth on the subject. I'll give you a sermon on the word 'submit.' I'll tell you who submits. And if you like I'll tell you

## "It's Not Easy to Make Oil and Love Run in Harness Together" 331

the actual words of submission" (93). Then he adds: "Yes, a man of my character does retail such words. They are words of the utmost power and penetration. Such words as "H.B., my own sweet love" when said by a certain person are absolutely convincing" (93). Whilst laughing in a stentorian and withering manner, Peruchacha echoes Ingram's words: "'H. B., my own sweet love!' To you Ingram? That's really comic!" – thereby searing the traumatizing words into Grey's memory and psyche as well as the public's memory (93). The duel-like party ends with Grey and her husband (the Viscount) leaving the party in rage.

Immediately subsequently to this critical clash, we find Grey in her villa rehearsing her vehement dismissal of Ingram before she actually summons him to enact her intentions: "Here and now I withdraw my protection from the man H. B. Ingram, once dear to me, because he stuck to his facts" (96). Equally importantly, here we are afforded an insight into the sheer magnitude of Grey's panoptic disciplinary regime, that is, her espionage system and the near-ubiquity of surveillance technology installed by her on the island. This is evidenced by her having the voices of all the people present at the party recorded on a gramophone disc. Above all, the gramophone scene takes us to Grey's psychic catacombs and to her traumatic crypt concerning the question of her ugliness and lack of desirability. The presence of the recording replayed numerously on the gramophone serves as a striking externalization of the obsessive compulsive dynamics of her trauma and the way she has been re-enacting it on the scene of her unconscious. The scene also affords an insight into the profound ways in which her psychosomatic desire (for love, affective bonds, desirability) is bound up with her investment in oil. Here we see how she obsessive compulsively returns to the recording of the scene and replays it for herself numerous times, thereby digging herself up into an aural ambience of Thanatotic trauma, hatred, and delirium – crystallized by the "ringing laughter". As Grey puts on a gramophone record and sets it going, we hear: "Yes, a man of my character does retail such words. They are words of the utmost power and penetration. Such words as H. B., my own sweet love' when said by a certain person are absolutely convincing. (Ringing laughter)" (96). Agonized by the reverberation of this aurally registered trauma, Grey feels compelled to adopt a new "barbarous" measure in relation to this act of "barbarity": "A barbarous island. And contempt will pierce even the shell of a tortoise. The most zealous saint could not require me to sleep in peace with such loud and genuine laughter in my ears" (96–97). It is indeed this collective jouissance at the cost of Grey that is seared into her consciousness as a resonant trauma. The ensuing lamentation discloses the profundity of her anguish and vindictiveness:

> It's mean, it's mean. Mean curs that you are. You'll stop laughing, you curs. The sun will not warm me while she can laugh. There is no

332  *"It's Not Easy to Make Oil and Love Run in Harness Together"*

tang in the sea, no ease in sleep, and no relish in food for me so long as such vulgar laughter goes ringing into the world.

(97)

Noteworthy in this regard is the symbolic role of the sun in this passage. Here, the sun not only symbolizes phallus and phallogocentrism, but bears a metonymic relation with oil and its phantasmatic promise of power, autonomy, and sovereign identity.

## VII.  An Hour of Reckoning: Death vs Desire, Grey vs Ingram

The moment of the rupture of all emotional-financial ties with Ingram is conducted in a highly ritualistic manner by Grey. Here Grey invites Ingram for the delivery of a full-blown divestment and psychological-affective self-defence. Struck by the sheer ritualistic pomp of the spectacle, Ingram wonders:

Why all these candles, Deborah, when you have electric light? . . . Why are we having this solemn music? Why is the table covered with white flowers as if this were a funeral? . . . Why have you got yourself up in such state? What's all this Ku-Klux-Klan flummery for, Deborah?

(98)

Grey's response is multifaceted where the affective, historical, and psychological appear as indelibly intermeshed:

Perhaps it's all rather in bad taste. But what else can you expect? This is a barbarous island; its traditions were founded by transported convicts. In any case, I didn't want two giants like you and myself to say good-bye to each other as casually as two herrings.

(99)

Grey maintains an emotional and sympathetic tone only to deliver the mortal blow towards the end:

Look at this cheque, please. It's the result of my long and wearisome negotiations with Moscow about Mr. H. B. Ingram. They are now at this point, that if I hand over this cheque before twelve o'clock tonight to the gentlemen in Moscow, proceedings against the said Mr. Ingram will be dropped.

(99)

Grey then "tears up the cheque" and explains to a flustered Ingram: "It means that I discard you. I leave Moscow a free hand" (100). Still

# "It's Not Easy to Make Oil and Love Run in Harness Together" 333

striving to maintain his equanimity and a sense of dignity whilst refusing to realize the entanglements of the libidinal and political economy as well as the depth of the traumatic wound he has inflicted on Grey's sore spot, Ingram says: "I refuse to play a part in your ridiculous melodrama of murdered paramours. I have other fish to fry" (100). Grey however asks him to cease with his pretentious self-ignorance and blindness. Ingram tries to blunt the edge of his public humiliation of Grey by describing it as something trivial, implying how the realm of political economy (including his business with Grey) is the realm of "real" facts and that the realm of desire and sex is the realm of near fiction and non-reality:

> You're too well versed in human nature not to know that every woman enjoys hearing other women run down. Charmy would have kept it up against me for ever if I had held my tongue, but who would have imagined that Debsy Grey would take a thing like that seriously?
>
> (101)

Countering this logic, Grey asserts how the questions of carnal-affective desire and sex are "real", "vital", and "concrete" phenomena for her: "I was mistaken enough to take you seriously, Ingram. I told you before that I probably wouldn't be able to stand it if you were to laugh" (101). Ingram tries to mitigate the thrust of his withering conduct at the party by resorting to the traditional trope or logic of desire as evanescent, immaterial, and thus positing sex and sexual desire as ephemeral and frivolous phenomena – as something nearly non-real and barely leaving any material traces on the substance/ground of memory – and politics-economics as the realm of reality and materiality:

> I'm not going to plunge into metaphysics. I've no gift for lyrical outbursts. . . . Quite seriously, of course a man sleeps with a beauty, if she hasn't too many objections. But out of bed, out of mind. You and I, Deborah, that's quite a different thing, that's something real. I only did a bit of clowning, for five minutes, and now I'm sorry for it. And that's all there is to the silly affair. It's wiped out. Forgotten.
>
> (101)

Grey – for whom desiring-production and social-production are indelibly intertwined – repudiates it by reminding him of the real and material effect Peruchacha's seductive allure and erotic appeal exerted on his rationality to the point of him jeopardizing the loss of his business profits and agreements with Grey: "You found plenty to say on that evening anyhow" (101). Then giving Ingram's fact-fiction binary logic an ironic twist: "People who indulge in the sport of telling the truth must be prepared to stand the consequences" (102). Counterpointing her allegedly "ugly face"

334 *"It's Not Easy to Make Oil and Love Run in Harness Together"*

with Ingram's "ugly heart", Grey implies how the latter is morally more condemnable and capable of inflicting harm:

> Even if it is true, it's my turn now to laugh. I love you, Ingram, but I won't hand out that cheque. I love you because you have an ugly heart; but the Moscow people are going to chew you up and I can laugh!
>
> (104)

Grey asks him to "give up, of course, and this time finally, your total, claims under our agreement" (105). Subsequently, Grey discloses how she is aware of all his clandestine bank accounts and complicities with Russians and rival companies and further demands that "Also you'll pay back the amounts you have received from us since you were admitted into partnership" and adds, "Of course it is. Further, you'll transfer your account in the National Bank" to the Island Oil Company. When Grey asks him to transfer all his money held in his various accounts to the Island Oil Company, Ingram calls it "pure extortion" and insists that if he does so "I'll be a beggar" (106). The outcome, pithily, is that Grey gets "the Russian concessions very cheap" and Ingram "will leave the Island alive" (106). After "cleaning out" Ingram "in such first class style", Grey acquiesces to give him ten thousand dollars when faced with his desperate pleading. Consequently, Grey gives the Soviet agents the check at the last minute and redeems Ingram's life. Ingram's last words are worth quoting:

> My good concessions gone. My connection with Moscow gone. I can't even draw a profitable conclusion from it all, for you're an abnormality, an exception. I was puffed up with well-founded hopes when I set foot on these Islands, and now I am leaving them as bare as a plucked chicken.
>
> (107)

Ingram tries to touch her soft spot by pretending to love her and even offering to have sex with her just to let her have a sense of gratification. Grey, however, rebuffs the enticement and refuses to play the pliable role: "There's your ten thousand. It'll take you. sometime, my lad, to fatten them up again" (108).

\* \* \* \* \* \* \* \* \*

The paradigmatic illustration of the inextricable enmeshment between desire and oil (that is, between the material and psycho-symbolic, the libidinal and the political economy, and the public and private) occurs towards the end of *Oil Islands* when Grey risks the loss of her political-economic position, her contracts with the Russians, and her credibility by

# "It's Not Easy to Make Oil and Love Run in Harness Together"  335

having Peruchacha murdered. Here Monson alerts Grey to the exorbitant cost of such an "instinctive" – that is, too personal and irrational – decision by reminding her of the global implications and the historical dimensions of the emergence and establishment of the oil company/industry on the island. As Monson avers: "Since your grandfather sank the first shaft here, the blood and sweat of three generations have gone into making these Islands the oil centre of the world. You, Debsy Grey, have done more yourself than any of them". He then proceeds to forewarn her:

> And now you're flinging away the whole Company simply for the sake of giving a silly goose a headache for a night or two! This is the first time, Miss Grey, that you've allowed your private affairs to interfere with business.
>
> (111)

Grey, however, demonstrates how acutely self-conscious of her decision and its underlying reasons she is by affirming her awareness of her "instinctive" flaw: "Oh, not the first time, Freddy. You're forgetting about H. B.". Monson, however, disagrees by insisting that "But that was a good stroke of business" (111). Whilst revealing how the loss of the possibility of a love relation with Ingram is poignantly rankling in her mind-body, Grey acknowledges the "greater loss" involved in the decision concerning Peruchacha: "I'm sorry to say it was. This time it's a bad one. I admit that this time I'm risking a pretty high stake for my own amusement" (111). Grey's use of a bathos, or understatement, to present a deflected and underestimated account of the deep-seated psychosomatic reasons underlying her decision is striking. Prior to leaving the scene in resentment, Monson insists: "A high stake? God of Israel! You've simply wrecked the Island Company". Nevertheless, Grey counters this by drawing his attention to the trump card she has up her sleeve: the double-edged Immigration Bill. As she states: "For a man of your years, Freddy, don't you think you're a bit rash in your conclusions? Perhaps we can save the bill yet" (111–112).

Grey's soliloquy-like speech on the value and nature of desire – in contrast to capital/oil – is revealing:

> He's rather upset because I'm playing ducks and drakes with the Company in order to dispose of Charmy. The old boy can't understand that it's worth risking all that oil simply to gladden one's heart. H. B. would have understood it. The said H. B. was quite right: Freddy is a windbag after all.
>
> (114)

This murderous desire marks the site of confluence between desire-as-wish and desire-as-force (see Lyotard *Discourse, Figure* 14–15, 161–194).

## 336 "It's Not Easy to Make Oil and Love Run in Harness Together"

Equally notable is the reversal of the customary dynamics of the use and perception of oil in the play in this scene, that is, rather than oil appearing as a means of fulfilling or even a metonymic replacement for it, oil is jeopardized "irrationally" in order to fulfil a personal desire which will incur politically-economically detrimental consequences. I have elaborated on this point more extensively. Then, finding herself alone she proceeds to unfurl her subconscious crypt and express her Thanatotic desire thus: "One thing is certain: I can't sleep while Charmy is able to laugh, while she can think of the stories of my friend Ingram". Then, finding herself obsessively enveloped in the aural memory of her trauma, she adds: "Her laughter won't be much longer in this world. Her laughter won't be in the world much longer. No, not much longer will her laughter be in the world" (109–110). Significantly this nearly delirious piece of speech – evidenced by the presence of repetitions in it and Grey's bodily expression where she "walks about with dancing steps" as she utters these words, which in turn reveals the obsessive compulsive nature of Grey's fixation on Peruchacha underpinned by the death drive – is amenable to an allegorical interpretation where the toxic petro-capitalism (in its Capitalocenic mode) obsessively seeks the extraction of natural resources (in this case oil) at the ecological-ontological cost of devastating nature to the point of its depletion and extinction.

Eventually, the time for the confrontation between Grey and Peruchacha arrives, a moment which features as the culmination of their fraught and symbolic conflicts. This moment indeed constitutes the final climactic moment which determines the fate of the main characters but also the islands and the human-nonhuman nature on it. Here in Act 3, Scene 3 – the title of which has been couched in at once Brechtian and naturalistic (nearly Darwinian) terms: "Struggles between a Chimpanzee and a Wild Filly and Apotheosis" (109) – we witness how the recondite and convoluted entanglements between death and desire and between nature and oil appear to fully unfold their underlying logics. As Grey delineates her plans to Monson, she, in coordination with the chief of the police, intends to hold an informal interrogation meeting with Peruchacha concerning the charge of "high treason" laid against Peruchacha due to her disclosure of confidential governmental information ("a secret telegram") to the Japanese "at a critical moment" (111). In this meeting, Grey intends to present Peruchacha with two propositions from which she is supposed to choose one. The first is to ask her to sell all her properties and belongings (including her symbolically charged garden) to Grey and leave the island forever – a decision which will relieve her of the penal consequences of her charge. And the second, if she rejects the first proposal, is to go to be tried and be either imprisoned or executed. Behind the scenes and prior to the meeting, however, Grey has instructed her agent, Sniffkins, to follow her cryptically coded message and carry out the instructions thus:

*"It's Not Easy to Make Oil and Love Run in Harness Together"* 337

I shall ring for you. If I say: "We have finished," then you will convey the lady to prison as quickly as possible. But if I say: "Please carry out your instructions," you will drive the car straight to the harbour. If there should be any attempt there to rescue her, you must frustrate the attempt at all costs, even at the cost of the lady's life.

(115)

Subsequently we are exposed to the full-blown spectacle of the confrontation between Grey and Peruchacha. Upon her arrival, Peruchacha calls Grey's act of "forcing me to visit you like this" as a "queer joke" (115). Grey's solemn response affords Peruchacha an inkling to the earnestness of the situation:

Not so queer, Miss Peruchacha, as your joke in handing over certain State papers to Japan. In Washington they appreciate your joke so little that they are instituting proceedings for high treason against its author. As I wish to avoid a scandal in the Brown Islands I have deferred to the wishes of the chief of police, and have consented to talk it over with you personally and confidentially.

(115)

Peruchacha, however, barrages Grey with ironic quips evidenced by her calling Grey as someone who has done "nothing but to scandalize the whole world" (116). When Grey cuts to the chase by asking: "Why did you hand over these papers to Japan?", Peruchacha unabashedly asserts: "To smash up the damned bill and the Island Company along with it" (116).

A psycho-semiotic scrutiny of the content of their conversation provides further compelling corroboration of my argument concerning the entanglements between physical and psychological, between death (oil, ugliness, hatred) and desire. Both Grey and Peruchacha invoke the indelible enmeshment between Grey's ugliness, her oil regime, and her erotic voracity (evidenced by her predatory ensnarement of men through her oil-endowed power). In other words, they confirm one of the crucial motifs which recurs throughout *Oil Islands*: oil as a means of wish-fulfilment and a phantasmatic object through which Grey can beautify herself and make herself desirable. Peruchacha constantly poses the questions of ugliness vs beauty and desire vs disgust. Of significance is the discursive register of each rival. Whilst Grey's language is steeped in references to facts, power, abstract references to finance and capital, and oil, Peruchacha's language abounds in references to desire, sex, and sexual appeal (bed), facial features, and nature. In the same vein, the direct yet subtle entanglements between death and desire as well as the libidinal economy and political economy become apparent when we consider the explicit mentions (by Grey herself, Peruchacha, and other

338 *"It's Not Easy to Make Oil and Love Run in Harness Together"*

characters) of how the oil magnate Grey strives to compensate for her lack of erotic capital (facial-physical desirability) with political-economic and symbolic capital; and how she seeks to compensate for her lack of beauty with the sense of sovereign power, autonomous agency, and global monopoly in the oil production endowed on her by oil and her relation with it. When Peruchacha flaunts her triumph both regarding men and the subversion of the Immigration Bill and gloats over Grey's symbolic, libidinal, and materialist fiasco – "Then I'll give you a few facts, Debsy Grey. Bankruptcy's one of them. You're ruined. You won't be able to buy yourself any more men. You've lost all your oil. You've got nothing left but your face" (116–117) – Grey's response illuminates my discussion of the manner that she has been trying to re-territorialize her physical-facial features through the mystical-mythical power of oil as capital. "I've got the better of my face all my life. What have you got the better of, Charmy Peruchacha?" (117). As a means of reinforcing her erotic power and social-cultural superiority, Peruchacha hits Grey's traumatic nerve when she utters: "Whenever I said 'my own sweet love' to a man, he trembled. None of them found it easy to laugh whenever I said that" (117). When Grey wonders: "If I was so ridiculous, why did you hate me then, Charmy?", Peruchacha replies: "Because you spoilt the Island for me with your face and your oil. And now the oil's gone. And there's nothing left but laughter" (117). Still concealing her triumphs (regarding the Immigration Bill) and refraining from delivering the final blow, Grey probes Peruchacha's motives more deeply. When Grey ironically asks Peruchacha: "Do you enjoy your triumph, Charmy?", Peruchacha reveals all the agony and vengeful feelings she has been harbouring all along due to the pernicious presence of the coloured oil workers, the polluting effects of oil on island's nature, and Grey's petro-capitalist mode of exploitative extractivism and blithely adds:

> Yes, I do. I enjoy it better than men. I enjoy it better than anything else in the world. What will you do now, Debsy? You won't be able now to send your filthy coolies through my garden, and the sea wind will blow away the reek of oil forever. You won't be able now to wheedle men into your bed with your damned dollars.
>
> (117)

Grey, however, suddenly gives a twist to the apparent dynamics of the situation by hinting at the trauma that particularly impelled her to take this vindictive course of action, that is, Peruchacha's sexual-emotional blow to Grey at the party: "Contempt will pierce even the shell of a tortoise. Have you considered that, Miss Charmian?" (117). When Peruchacha once more draws a parallel between the political economy of capital (economic success) and the economy of desire/desirability (to wit, facial-physical beauty and erotic appeal) by stating "anyone with a face like yours needs

*"It's Not Easy to Make Oil and Love Run in Harness Together"*   339

to be successful, at least. You're not even successful", Grey begins to give her a hint into her tragic ignorance of the truth of the situation: "Perhaps you've traded on your beauty to no avail" (118).

Grey then breaks the news to her: "Even if the Brown Islands are freed from the reek of oil, you're under arrest meanwhile" (118). Confronted with Grey's menaces and still being under the illusion that the Immigration Bill scandal will wreak havoc on Grey (both as a person and as the representation of the toxic dynamics of petro-extractivism), Peruchacha brings up the traumatic memory of the garden humiliation:

> Every day's a red-letter day for me, prison or no prison, as long as I know that the Oil islands are being wiped off the map. Your villa's as good as ruined, Debsy Grey, and the old Brown Islands are springing up again round your tanks and your stinking oil-shafts.
>
> (118)

Grey's response provides us with crucial insights in that not only does it reveal the sheer intensity of each character's psychosomatic cathection (investment) in – or near identification with – the island, thereby enhancing the symbolic and allegorical dimension of the island and the characters. It also exposes the ontological and social-economic differences between their two visions of the island – including its nature and its functions. As she avers:

> Don't say anything against my Island. It's a good island, an island of work, and very dear to me. I quite admit that you don't fit in with the Island. Your villa's a disturbance, and your lovers are a disturbance. The scent you use doesn't go with the reek of oil. You can draw your own conclusions. As surely as I am called the Chimpanzee you will never be called the mistress of the Brown Islands.
>
> (118)

Grey then proceeds to propose an opportunity to save her life:

> Do you want to waste your best years in prison? Today it's still possible for me to get you off. I have a fair bargain to offer you. Sell me the Villa Peruchacha, and quit the Island, and I'll settle your affair for you.
>
> (119)

When in response to her offer Grey faces Peruchacha's dismissive and "infectious laugh" (119), Grey wonders whether there is any message that she can convey on Peruchacha's behalf before her being sent to prison (which is in fact her murder before she even reaches the police station), "You shouldn't meddle with politics if your nerves are no better than that. Wouldn't you rather abandon the Island?" Even at

340 *"It's Not Easy to Make Oil and Love Run in Harness Together"*

the last moment, whilst naïvely affirming that she finds the "duel amusing", Peruchacha inexorably seizes the opportunity to renew her blow: "If you want to deliver a message for me, remember me to our friend H. B. Ingram, if he's still to be found" (119).

The tragic and dystopian end of the play features Grey alone in her Villa at night brooding over the whole roster of her achievement leaving nothing but human and nonhuman debris in their wake. Primarily, it is striking that Grey still insists on articulating the dynamics of her actions in anti-naturalistic terms – evident in her reference to the rat experiment. Besides, the psychosomatic economy of Grey's speech manifests how the memory of a traumatic loss (of the phantasy of gratifying her sexual-emotional desire in her relationship with Ingram) is still smarting in her:

> It's a pity I had to get rid of that man Ingram. My body remembers many men, my eyes remember many men, but my heart remembers only this man Ingram. He had a good strong jaw, and he went down fighting. It's not easy to make oil and love run in harness together. But since we're human beings and not rats, there must be some way of combining the desire of the five with the desire of the one.

Then she adds:

> This night will see the fate of Charmy Peruchacha decided, and also the fate of the Island Oil Company. The island is no good without its oil. The Island is no good with Charmy Peruchacha on it. Very few people will understand why I am taking the risk of pouring all the oil on the Island into the sea only for the sake of sweeping Charmy away with it. Perhaps Lelly Holyday will understand it.
>
> (109)

This dense soliloquy consists of a number of crucial stands. Primarily, it shows a process of de-sublimation and transference of love where she consciously seeks to defy the naturalistic logic of determinism (at the levels of hereditary, humanistic, or milieu forces and predilections) and a Darwinist conception of the human. As is evident, the strategy Grey adopts entails transferring her affective-libidinal force and investment (in terms of love and desire) toward oil – as an incarnation of economic sovereignty, autonomous power, and the possibility of self-transformation. Though these concluding remarks presage a dreary future for the oil – it is finalized here through the elimination of Peruchacha as the symbolic representation of the conservationism and old-style settler colonialism as well as Grey's explicit identification of the island as an "oil island", marking the totalization of Grey's petro-capitalist sovereignty and full commodification of nature and natural resources.

## "It's Not Easy to Make Oil and Love Run in Harness Together"  341

Secondarily, this climactic moment when Grey hazards losing all her oil capital, authority, and credibility by having Peruchacha murdered just to fulfil her vengeful desire against Peruchacha seems to evince a rupture in her commitment to the restrictive economy of petro-capitalism in that her actions (in relation to Ingram and Peruchacha) evince a dynamics where subjective will overcomes the reifying force of the acquisition drive and the material commodity (oil). This inclination towards a general economy of excessive expenditure, loss, and sacrifice is also vividly discernible in the ensuing assertion by Grey: "One should never be parsimonious, Freddy, either with one's nerves or with the lives of one's nearest and dearest, or with one's own life. But least of all with one's dollars!" (112). Upon closer inspection, however, Grey's actions can be described as a moment of ritualistic or transgressive sacrifice carried out within the confines and by the agent of the restricted economy – rather than a moment of general economy (loss of self, jouissance) (see Bataille).[24] This is in keeping with the insidiously dialectical logic informing the act of ritualistic sacrifice within the bounds of the restricted economy legitimized by it. So far we have been witnessing how *Oil Islands* renders a highly individualized-personalized picture of oil in relation to Grey – a feature which is evidently discernible not only in the persistent ways in which oil and its toxic effects are primarily associated with and identified with Grey by the public, but also in how Grey appropriates oil for her as not merely an object of desire per se but as a means of fulfilling her desires. In the final scenes of the play the relational dynamics between Grey and oil are pushed to new limits. The ensuing soliloquy by Grey not only evokes a parallel between the "ugliness" and "filthiness" of oil and Grey's perceived ugliness and corruption. It also renders explicit the process of de-cathecting her libidinal-affective investment in men (including Ingram) and re-cathecting (or re-investing) them in oil – hence the full-fledged birth of oil as the object of love and desire in Grey's psyche. This moment illustrates the totalization of the body-mind of the oil despot. As she intimates:

> And now even if the Oil Islands do go up in smoke over this affair, my pulse is steady and I am breathing regularly. It's a good thing that I've got rid of this thorn in my flesh. – So now she's being driven to the harbour. She steps out of the car. There's a strong smell of oil-in the harbour. There are one or two black ships loaded with barrels. I admit that they're ugly, these ships of mine, Charmy. But they can't be made to look pretty. Oil makes everything filthy.
>
> (120)

Whilst Grey's act of de-sublimation may foster cathartic effects for her by purging her of the fire of her "instinctual and irrational" passions, but it produces contrary results for the human-nonhuman nature on the island in that her act sets the island on a literal and metaphorical

342    *"It's Not Easy to Make Oil and Love Run in Harness Together"*

fire of devastation and ruination. Equally crucially, this act of sacrificing Peruchacha with all her symbolic accoutrements (as an incarnation
of nature, the sacred, beauty, and non-capitalist form of life) even at
the risk of losing all her capital by Grey (as an incarnation of industrial
petro-capitalism) can be construed to evoke the sheer spectacle of human-
nonhuman sacrifice and economic loss wrought by the two world wars,
both of which transpired after nearly a century of unremitting wealth
accumulation and economic-industrial growth. Notably, Bataille reckons these two historical events as an evidence to his dialectical theory of
restricted economy and general economy by positing them as expressions
of the inherent predilection towards general economy: "the two world
wars organized the greatest orgies of wealth – and of human beings – that
history has recorded" (1988, 37). By the same token, Grey's act of sacrificing Peruchacha (bordering on near self-sacrifice given the sheer degree of
risk at stake in it) is an allegorical evidence to how the emergence of capitalist economy (closely associated with Protestant asceticism) "destroyed
the sacred world, the world of non-productive expenditure, and handed
the earth over to the men of production, to the bourgeois" (127).

In contrast to *Oil Field*, where it is the objectivity of the oil commodity
and petro-capitalist system that prevails, here in *Oil Islands*, it is the human
will (of an oil magnate, though) that prevails oil in its various guises – as
an objective sublime force, as an abject taboo force, and as a divine magic.
This is evidenced by the way Grey jeopardizes her oil-endowed power,
position, and company just to demonstrate two contradictory urges: her
rational will to overcome her desire for sexual-emotional fulfilment (and
prove the naturalist logic wrong by refusing to be the human counterpart
of a female rat) and her blind desire for revenge propelled by hatred and
jealousy (in relation to Peruchacha). Though, one could equally argue
that the psychodynamics and the physical-facial features embodied by
Grey, both allegorically and symbolically, are nothing but the effect of
her relation with oil, as an oil creature. The conclusion offers both the
rebuttal and a confirmation of naturalistic logic – underpinning the play
at anthropological and psychological levels – where humans are subject to
the determinations of impersonal forces – either at personal (one's unconscious drives and instinctual forces) or trans-personal (forces arising from
one's hereditary/genetic constitution or one's milieu) levels. Grey's ethics
of action can be identified in terms of "ressentiment" in that both are
negative acts or driven by a reactive rather than an affirmative dynamics
(see Nietzsche 1969, 36–37). In other words, in case of her two actions
(in relation to Ingram and Peruchacha), she is driven by an eradication
of the "difference" or the other – be them desire, nature, or the human
Other – inside herself rather than affirming such a self-difference – an act
entailed by an ethics of self-overcoming (see Nietzsche 1972, 113, 173; see
also Nietzsche 1978, 14–15, 139, 202). Consequently, her will-to-over-
coming her all-too-human drives and needs is conducive to the birth of the

## "It's Not Easy to Make Oil and Love Run in Harness Together" 343

monstrous inhuman or the body of the oil despot rather than the birth of the "overman" – as a Nietzschean ethics of self-overcoming would yield (see Nietzsche 1974, 88, 137; see Nietzsche 1967, 339; see Nietzsche 1969, 86–87). More specifically, whilst Grey vigorously exercises her will-to-self-overcoming (reflected in her will to resist and overcome her instinctual wish to be sexually-affectively desired and in explicit indication that she is not a rat being attracted to Ingram), her murder of Peruchacha is an emblematic example of her succumbing to her instinctual urge toward vindictive elimination (of unbearable beauty and desirability) and acquisition (of Peruchacha's property and nature). Hence the conclusion of the play illustrates the triumph of Thanatos over Eros at two levels: the triumph of Grey the oil magnate over her relationship of love and desire with Ingram; and the triumph of the petro-capitalist system's oil extraction on the island and in the world over a non-oil-based mode of life pursued by human-nonhuman natures. As will be demonstrated, the Thanatotic aspect is also entangled with necropolitical facets of petro-capitalism and its treatment of human-nonhuman natures.

The conclusion sees the triumphant continuation of Grey's oil industry and oil discourse over the naturism and conservationism of Peruchacha's. In fact, one of the most revealing passages in *Oil Islands* is the concluding speech by Grey uttered in the wake of a whole litany of plights and scroll of triumphs:

> I feel in great form, Freddy. True, Uncle Obadiah has deserted me, but my appetite is excellent. I'll go sailing in the yacht, I'll enjoy myself, and I'll sleep soundly. Contempt will pierce even the shell of a tortoise; but I think that from today people will consider twice before they look down on me. My new workers are coming. They won't smell good, these white workers of mine and these hordes of coloured ones; the whole island doesn't smell good; it's a barbaric island. But it suits me.
>
> (123)

The picture this passage paints is dystopian and bleak through and through – evidenced by the continuity of the pervasive presence of "coloured oil workers", "the reek of oil", and the monopoly of the American oil company. Crucially, "barbaric" is the term with which *Oil Islands* concludes, utilized by Grey herself to identify the oil-saturated world or island she has created where barbarity is found back in the heart of petro-modernity and its logics and dynamics. Her invocation of "barbaric" (along with the cognate word – "barbarous" – used elsewhere in the play by various characters) triggers far-reaching reverberations in relation to the politics of gender, race, and class throughout *Oil Islands* – associations on most of which I have already elaborated earlier. Bearing in mind how the two charged terms "barbaric" and

344    *"It's Not Easy to Make Oil and Love Run in Harness Together"*

"barbarous" are variously used by characters in relation to native people, oil, and oil industry, and the island, suffice it here to explicate one more crucial implication of it in light of its use in this specific passage. By exposing us to Grey's use of the term "barbaric" in relation to her oil-saturated island, the play depicts the reversal of values and herein resides its critical edge where barbarism rather is shifted and projected back onto the discourse that uses the term to dispossess and dehumanize in order to extract and objectify both human and nonhuman nature in peripheral regions. The murder of Peruchacha serves as an allegory for the destruction and devastation of nature and natives by the exploitative practices of Grey's petro-capitalist regime governed by a racialized extractive logics. Primarily, and at a subjective-psychological level, the invocation of barbarism by Grey here attests to the prevalence of the death drive (Thanatos) over life drive (Eros). Allegorically, this evinces the identification of the establishment of full-fledged industrial petro-modernity and concomitant modern Western civilization as a barbaric one (see *Dialectic of Enlightenment*, Adorno and Horkheimer, pp. 1–15) which, according to Marcuse, pivots on "the ontological affirmation of death" (1974, 17, 25–29, 79, 126, 236).[25] This moment of ostensible political-economic progress for the American oil imperialism – carried out through eliminating all rivals through the acts of primitive accumulation and full appropriation of oil resources and other human-nonhuman natures – marks a humanistic-civilizational and psychological regression into a near-psychotic narcissism and despotic barbarism (see Deleuze and Guattari, *Anti-Oedipus*).

This moment marks the birth of Grey's petro-polis as one governed by the principle of necropolitics, that is, a form of life that produces death, governs the death and life of the subject and the object along with determining their value and meaning. In other words, a necropolitical order that thrives on the death of the human-nonhuman natures. Such an ontological and ecological dynamics is highly akin to the one described by Achille Mbembé. Mbembé presents a blunt definition of the necropolitical as the "power and . . . capacity to dictate who may live and who must die" (2003, 43). Emblematic examples of such a politic of death management places Mbembé's notion of necropower not only within the state's prerogative to wage war but also, and equally importantly, within the neoliberal market technologies whose purpose and goal is "the generalized instrumentalization of human existence and the material destruction of human bodies and populations" (44). Significantly, adopting a Thanatotic approach Mbembé defines the racialized political economy of colonialism and capitalism not in terms of the uneven distribution of life and wealth and pleasure, but of death and argues, "in the economy of biopower, the function of racism is to regulate the distribution of death and to make possible the murderous functions of the state" (45). One of the subtle strands of Mbembé's argument

## "It's Not Easy to Make Oil and Love Run in Harness Together"   345

is his identification of the function of racism as a discursive means of naturalizing and focalizing certain aspects of racism (for instance, its social-cultural politics) and of excluding or marginalizing its equally crucial dimensions (including its political economy of not talking about migrants – the labour force that played a crucial part in the revitalization of the post-Nazi, post-World War II Western Europe). In such settings, necropolitics is a structure; the

> sovereign right to kill is not subject to any rule. . . . In the colonies, the sovereign might kill at any time or in any manner. Colonial warfare is not subject to legal and institutional rules. It is not a legally codified activity.
>
> (47)

Mbembé delineates an account of the structural conditions of production of the necropolitical space by establishing parallels between early modern colonial occupation and its late modern neo-colonial counterparts and the contemporary warfare in which state actors are incrementally superseded by war machines. As he explains:

> I have put forward the notion of necropolitics and necropower to account for the various ways in which, in our contemporary world, weapons are deployed in the interest of maximum destruction of persons and the creation of death worlds, new and unique forms of social existence in which vast populations are subjected to conditions of life conferring upon them the status of living dead.
>
> (48)

The condition of living death cogently captures the condition of a transnational coloured labour force but also other components of human-nonhuman nature on the island affected by the ravage of petro-capitalist dynamics of the extraction and production of oil.

What distinguishes *Oil Islands*, in its materialist and world-systemic critique of the necropolitical and Thanatotic practices of petro-capitalism, is that it personalizes these necropolitical dynamics by presenting a highly psychologized and psychologically inflected portrayal of them and the manner they are subjectivized. This Thanatotic psychodynamics is not only evidenced by the economy of Grey's phantasies and desire for desirability and power. It is also evidenced by how, in Grey, moments of jouissance (or surplus production) coincide with or are identical with the moments of the death or destruction of the other, including other humans and other as nature (the nature on the islands). Finally, *Oil Islands* depicts how this necropolitical oil order partly implements its hegemony by exerting its laws on the movement and flow of humans, capital, desires, labour forces, desires, and materials.

346 *"It's Not Easy to Make Oil and Love Run in Harness Together"*

## VIII. Petrocultural and Infrastructural Faces of Oil

None of the plays under scrutiny in this volume engage with the petro-cultural facets of oil – that is, its cultural and social manifestations – as extensively and explicitly as *Oil Islands* does. *Oil Islands* features not only aspects of *the life of oil* at national and global levels both in its core and peripheral regions. It also depicts *life in oil, life through oil*, and *life with oil* – to wit, oil as a capitalist commodity, oil as a globally strategic energy resource, oil as the driver or motor of society and social-cultural phenomena and events, and oil as an indispensable element of normal functioning of the urban and suburban life, that is, oil as a fundamental component of lifestyle and form of social-cultural ethos. *Oil Islands* exposes the sheer extent to which the petro-capitalist system has appropriated and controls almost all discursive and disciplinary means of communication, transportation, and expression. The hegemony of the oil order becomes all the more evident when we consider its cultural ubiquity and its "new microphysics" of control (Foucault 1979, 139). Indeed, a salient facet of the oil industry's expansion of its hegemony and disciplinary power is through biopolitical and anatomo-political dynamics whereby it gives shape to the private thoughts, personal phantasies, cultural imaginaries, the economy of desire, embodied social practices, and the modes and conduits of the investment of time, interest, and energy by the individual and the collective (see *Energy Culture* 1–17, 148–153, 233–243; Foucault 1979, 139–147). Furthermore, a significant mention is made of "public opinion", showing already the crucial ubiquity and extensive presence of media and the "public" as determining forces in the urban petrocultural life in both democratic and socialist societies. As Sniffkins states: "Since opinion all over the world can be bought for considerably less than Miss Grey has paid for other things, it looks as though she doesn't care what the world thinks" (12).

Significantly, *Oil Islands* depicts the oil industry in all its discursive and symbolic webs and paraphernalia. More specifically, the play intermittently affords us a glimpse into the pervasiveness of energy culture as a large-scale apparatus including its entanglements with the film industry, car industry, visual culture and entertainment (for instance, advertising), and cultural, religious, and artistic institutes and media – such as literature/poetry and cinema. In this section we will explore *Oil Islands'* depiction of the ways in which the industrial-infrastructural facets of oil extraction-production are inextricably intermeshed with the production of an array of new petrocultural discourses through which the American oil boom of the early decades of the 20th century unfolded and found its lived forms through its transformative life-making and environment-making practices. As Ross Barrett and Daniel Worden, in their introduction to their edited volume *Oil Culture*, state:

> oil culture encompasses the fundamental semiotic processes by which oil is imbued with value within petrocapitalism, the promotional discourses that circulate through the material networks of the oil

*"It's Not Easy to Make Oil and Love Run in Harness Together"* 347

economy, the symbolic forms that rearrange daily experiences around oil-bound ways of life, and the many creative expressions of ambivalence about, and resistance to, oil that have greeted the expansion of oil capitalism.

(xxvi)

Whilst an emblematic illustration of the aforementioned petrocultural practices is the car culture, these practices also include the kinds of narratives required as part of the petro-capitalist efforts to create a national identity in energy. The play shows how oil (and the oil boom) reorganizes the existing social relations – though not without facing extensive public and private resistance, tensions, and conflicts; a reorganization that leads to the development of a new cultural politics of life. Viewed from a perceptual-phenomenological perspective, such petrocultural practices can be considered as modes of "humanizing oil". However, if viewed meta-dramatically, the humanization of oil by Feuchtwanger can be construed as a way of representing oil and its effects on human-nonhuman natures that can contribute to meaningful forms of action. As such, in Feuchtwanger's petrocritical account of the petroculture, we see not only how humans extract and produce oil but also how oil produces humans.

One of the earliest references to the petrocultural aspects of oil is the one to Uncle Obadiah, who is a full-time oil poet employed by Grey. As Monson observes: "Your petroleum odes are excellent, sir" (121). Obadiah, however, despite his staunch fidelity to Grey eventually quits his job when he gathers the news about Grey's arrangement of Peruchacha's murder. As he says to Grey, "I have proved to you that there isn't anything in the world I can't turn into a rhyme about dollars, but I won't write a line about Charmian's death. I'm through with all that" (121). A second example is the presence of Overweek, the movie star (whose name designates his ephemerality as an actor in the consumer culture and whom Ingram describes as the one who "looks like an advertisement for shaving soap" (12). Patrick indicates "the Chimpanzee has booked him", that is, invited him to the island apparently for promotional purposes (12). Ingram further adds how "the sweet creature [meaning Overweek] costs a good deal in hard cash" (13). As Overweek himself explains: "I have an engagement with Miss Grey to discuss a propaganda film for the Oil Islands. I don't know that I can spare the time to avail myself of Miss Peruchacha's kind invitation" (14). Then flaunting his value in capital, he adds: "Miss Grey sets such a high-price on my cooperation that I could not possibly expect to get the same generous remuneration from anyone else" (14) – to which Ingram replies by using a revealing analogy:

The men fight the Chimpanzee for profitable markets, and the women fight her for the men. Would you have thought it possible for anyone

348   *"It's Not Easy to Make Oil and Love Run in Harness Together"*

to prefer a crocodile to a wild filly? But our young Adonis is shying away from the filly.

(14)

A third instance of Grey's petrocultural apparatus is the Christian preacher who is in effect an ideologue and proselytizer of petro-capitalism, or an oil preacher. The Preacher arrives on the island fairly late in the play. On one of the few occasions when he appears on the stage we see him confronting the public (a group of people) who are singing the "Song of the Brown Islands". First we overhear the crowd's conjectures regarding the reasons of his presence on the island – particularly given that the Preacher speaks in two tongues: simultaneously vehemently indicting the effect of oil on nature and yet ardently advocating Grey and the Immigration Bill. Initially we find Preacher Maxwell roving around the island preaching – reminiscent of colonial missionaries and evangelists, though here he has not been dispatched and deployed by the Church but by the secular God of the island: Grey and oil money. Indeed he is simultaneously part of the Evangelist Church of spiritual salvation and of the Ideological State Apparatus of Grey's oil regime. As he declares: "Listen to the Reverend Ed Maxwell if you care two hoots for your soul. He'll undertake to snatch even desperate cases out of Satan's claws at specially reduced rates for a large turnover-only five dollars a theory!" (73). Crucially, however, this minor character affords us an illuminating insight into the degraded condition of the nature on the island. Preacher Maxwell:

> It's hard to believe that in this civilized country with its water power and its hot baths and its automobiles there are still some guys who let Satan get busy putting dirty garbage pails into them instead of souls. And yet when a man of God hits this burg, the first thing he hears is a so-called song that just about burns the cars off him and makes him wonder how the sanitary authorities in the Brown Islands can keep going with such rivers of muck pouring out all over the place.

This vignette affords us an insight into the metabolic rift in its full reign pervading every fibre of human and natural life on the island. This rampant pollution attests to the colonial dynamics of the oil regime inflicted on the human-nonhuman nature on the island.[26] The Preacher, however, proves more of a propagandist disguised by religious righteousness. This becomes clear when, in protest to the crowd's singing of the Brown Islands song, the preacher exclaims:

> So if I hear another syllable of that obscene product miscalled a song, I'll take the slavering skunk that spits it out and lam the truth into

*"It's Not Easy to Make Oil and Love Run in Harness Together"* 349

him with my good Christian fists until he sets up a new trip record for his return trip to hell.

(76)

As one of the members of the public surmises, "He's hired by the Chimpanzee. She only let him come because he'd make a good publicity agent" (76) whilst another member adds: "She's not such a damn fool. It must have been her European husband did it; but his fancy European ideas won't cut any ice here" (76).

*Oil Islands* also shows the pervasive presence of the culture industry and the Americanization of the native culture – attested by saturating it with American cultural commodities – above all, cinema. For instance, we overhear how some people in the crowd say "meant to go to the pictures and see 'The Smuggler's Girl.' You've done the proprietor out of seventy-five cents, Ted!" (20). Another instance of this Americanization and commodification of culture is illustrated by the pervasive presence of cars in the play (used by both opposite parties). As early as Scene 1 we find the signs of automobile culture. As Patrick says:

If you want to know, this child is banking on shaking Miss Grey by the hand very soon. I'm a free-born American citizen, and I don't give two hoots for the gloomy remarks of that pessimistic guy. Do you see a single policeman anywhere on the quay? I see only automobiles in Miss Peruchacha's colours.

(15)

It is through its petrocultural presence that the oil regime can subconsciously establish its conscious and subconscious need for it and its structural inevitability thereby creating new cognitive and affective habits and deep-seated cathections – to the point of identification – in the components of the petroculture. Few other phenomena illustrate such a dynamics than the car culture and the individual's perceived economy of relationship with their car – a point which finds its paradigmatic manifestation in the car race in *Oil Islands*. As Amitav Ghosh's observation illuminates the dynamics:

Culture generates desires – for vehicles and appliances, for certain kinds of gardens and dwellings – that are among the principal drivers of the carbon economy. A speedy convertible excites us neither because of any love for metal and chrome, nor because of an abstract understanding of its engineering. It excites us because it evokes an image of a road arrowing through a pristine landscape; we think of freedom and the wind in our hair.

(2002, 9–10)

350  *"It's Not Easy to Make Oil and Love Run in Harness Together"*

In a similar vein, indeed the car race serves as a compelling evidence to the fact that oil has become such a hegemonic means of self-expression and establishing social capital – that is, the race car as a ubiquitous and an indispensable part of cultural expression and personal expression of power, identity, and in that the two starkly adversarial characters – Grey and Peruchacha – notwithstanding all their antithetical views on many fundamental issues (including nature and oil) choose a car race as a means of giving public expression to their rivalry and a symbolic manner of settling their antagonism. At the car race Peruchacha endorses and promotes the car Humphrey (driver: Lelio – the former oil engineer at Grey's company who has been expelled now and harbours an infatuation with Peruchacha) and Grey endorses the car Gloria (driver: Wentley). As becomes evident as we move further into the scene, the car race is steeped in the racial politics of race, class, and gender. Notably, the objective, baser, more material aspects of oil (an oil extraction) associated with the earth, the ground, subsoil, nature, materiality, instinct and irrationality, and bodily passions are associated with women and people of colour and lower classes, whilst the more civilized and more rational facets are associated with the white race and higher classes. Colonel Monson's remark is a case in point: "They talk about the brutality of bullfighting, but these people who rejoice at the downfall of a fine sportsman are a hundred times worse" (84). Later Monson adds: "That woman will tumble over head first. These coloured people have absolutely no self-control" (85).

The economy and dynamics of the public's investment in the race more generally and in each car (respectively owned and endorsed by Grey and Peruchacha) more specifically reflects the cultural ethos and social morality of the public but also their utilization of the car race as a collective, social space for the expression of their opinion and grievances against the pernicious effects of Grey's oil empire. This is primarily reflected in the crowd's unremitting singing of the "Song of the Brown Islands". The second instance of such a critical consciousness is discernible in a remark made by a spectator: "It was a great idea of the Chimpanzee's this race by night. But it's tempting Providence to run in it. . . . All this racing in the dark reminds me of the oil crisis" (79). Furthermore, the ensuing exchange is a salient case in point. When one of the spectators asserts: "Of course the Chimpanzee will come out on top with Wentley driving her Gloria. . . . God himself in a racing six couldn't hope for more than the fourth place", another spectator responds: "But you can't help liking her. Do you know she's going to the States early tomorrow to wreck the Chimpanzee's bill?" (84). The race concludes with Grey's car in the first place and Peruchacha's in the second. Illuminated Sign announces the winner thus: "I., Wentley; Gloria. 150 miles in 2 hrs. 40 min. 23 secs" – which is the car endorsed by Grey (85). In keeping with the previously mentioned point concerning the public's appropriation of the car race as a social-political space for the expression of their counter-hegemonic views, when

*"It's Not Easy to Make Oil and Love Run in Harness Together"* 351

a "Voice through a Megaphone" announces: "Three cheers for Wentley. Three cheers for the Viscountess of Westmoreland [meaning, Grey]" and "Grey's flag is hoisted", the sole reaction we notice from the crowd is a "faint cheering" (85).

One of the remarkable components of the car race is the advertisements which not only reveal the cultural imaginary and politics but full capitalization of the social-cultural field. A meticulous exploration of the advertisement can be illuminating and rewarding. The first advertising sign we encounter bears these words: "Free-will, the Bible, and the Gloria, the three highest achievements of humanity" (80). By putting human will, divine Word, and a cultural commodity (car) on a par, this sign is consonant with the pervasive parallel historically drawn among oil and petro-modernity, the humanistic culture as well as the moral and democratic values, and, finally, oil as transcendental origin of life and the source of divine energy and magic transformation (enhanced by its chthonic associations, partly stemming from its coming from the bowels of the earth). The second advertisement banner says: "See the Gorgon and petrify! / See Naples and die! / See the Gloria and buy!" (85). And a third advertisement sign says: "On the sixth day God saw the Gloria and he saw that it was good. Then he decided that the Creation was finished and invented the week-end, which can only be properly celebrated in a Gloria" (79). Such descriptions are consonant with the identification of the perception of oil as fetishized and a "powerful thing-in-itself" (Huber 2014, 36). One striking example of the link between oil (as chthonic and commodified matter) and the religious/spiritual matters is the way American spiritualists and practitioners of so-called psychometry of the early 20th century were deemed as credible contributors to early oil-field exploration, a fact that testifies to the magical aura ascribed to oil from its early beginnings. Elaborating on this link, Rochelle Zuck explains: the promotion of this mode of practical spiritualism was conducted through the mobilisation of these figures to establish

> "a rhetoric of correspondence between the physical and spiritual worlds that allowed the excitement and pursuant dangers of drilling and speculation to be recast in terms of 'discovery' and divine revelation, languages of frontier exploration that resonated with the . . . American national psyche"
>
> ("The Wizard of Oil" 36)

One of the noteworthy points discernible in the public's interest in the car race and cars present in it is the economy and gender politics of their mode of investment in them. As the previous passages vividly illustrate, the spectators refer to cars predominantly in feminine terms and as means of enhancing their sense of masculine/phallic agency, autonomy, and potency. Focusing on the symbolic alignment of women and cars in media

## 352  *"It's Not Easy to Make Oil and Love Run in Harness Together"*

and in popular representation and the relationship of "contemporary ideologies of femininity to a commerce in cosmetics", Devereux scrutinizes the hegemonic gender politics driving the representation and performance of femininity underpinning these social-cultural manifestations and means of the petroculture (including cars, cosmetics, and advertisements) in the 20th and 21st century (2017, 163). Identifying the "petroculture's mobilization of the standard commodity figures of femininity" and their "aligning of women and cars in media and popular representation", she underscores a crucial characteristic that permeates them, namely, the petroculture's "sustaining of a symbolic economy that depends on women's not having the capacity to be self-propelling or self-determining: not to be driving but to be driven, not to be subject but object" (164). Whilst this argument does not hold exactly true of the thematics and dramatic dynamics, it is resonant with the cultural imaginary of the audience as depicted by *Oil Islands*.

Cars, however, were not merely used as means of self-expression. Due to extensive and relentless efforts made by the advertising industry and car and oil production companies, cars assumed highly gender-specific and racialized associations and values in the public consciousness and cultural imaginary. On the one hand cars were eroticized as the objects that enhanced the sexual appeal of men for women but also phallicization. The car also has an essential "factual" dimension; Paul Gilroy describes cars as "the ur commodity": "as such", he suggests, "they not only help to periodize our encounters with capitalism as it moves into and leaves its industrial phase, they also politicize and moralize everyday life in unprecedented configurations" (89).[27] An illustrative case in point is the car culture of the US between the two World Wars. As Huber shows, the "mass consumption of oil only emerges out of a wider social context through which massive amounts of workers can actually afford single-family homes, automobiles, and the multitude of other petroleum-derived products that saturate everyday life" (2014, 28). As Huber contends, any attempt to explain the widespread use and popularity of cars/automobiles – along with the social capacity to consume the mass quantities of oil – "within the confines of a single industry or set of industries manipulating the market" would be inadequate (28). Automobility, and the consumption of oil to fuel it, as Huber incisively argues "is much more social than a corporate plot" (28). Huber shows how due to highly manifold, complex, and intense/extensive media and discursive attempts, having a car became one of the definitions or condition of possibility. In other words, we need to see the mass consumption of oil as emerging not only out of narrow elite conspiracies but out of a wider cultural politics of, literally, the meaning of "life", how life should be lived, and what constitutes "the good life".

A historical reference to the conditions of oil industry and its petrocultural measures and strategies contemporary to *Oil Islands* can be

*"It's Not Easy to Make Oil and Love Run in Harness Together"* 353

illuminating. There is extensive historical evidence of the extent to which the oil companies, particularly BP and American oil companies (Exxon and Chevron), found it a vital necessity to invest in publicity and advertisements, producing short informative public-oriented films and documentaries (a conspicuous case in point is the one by Bertolucc's *La via del petrolio*).[28] Due to an array of crises and scandalous incidents arising from the oil industry and committed by oil corporation – ranging from the 1911 Standard Oil monopoly case to the Teapot Dome scandal of the 1920s – "the ethics of the oil industry were a common topic of conversation" (Jeremy Groskopf: 34).[29] In order to rectify the public perceptions about the oil industry and corporation as corrupt, the oil industry and its corporation arms made extensive efforts evidenced above all by their public-oriented media campaigns. As an article in the *Evening Star* observes:

> The United States Government . . . has made extensive use of films, nearly all of its departments having utilized them in educational and industrial work. . . . The oil industry has been particularly responsive, moved by a desire to have the public fully understand its problems and processes.
>
> ("How a President Started a World Film Exchange",
> Peekskill Evening Star, January 5, 1927: 5)

These double-edged efforts, whilst ostensibly intended to impart educational content "by describing the 'problems and processes' of oil" extraction, production, and circulation, were in fact covert attempts intended to present a glossed image of the industry. This is attested by their choice of "a hagiographic frame in a manner that idealizes the behavior of the [oil] men and machines" (35). As such, these oil films, circulated by the United States Bureau of Mines, were therefore "related solely to the physical toil of draining oil from the ground and the complexity of refining" rather than dealing with the oil crises and predicaments that had transpired (Groskopf 2021, 34). As is clear, thus, "the films were not designed to foster 'full understanding'; they were rhetorical constructs – institutional advertisements – designed to increase understanding in one area (the complexity of the task) while whitewashing a secondary problem (ethical lapses)" (Groskopf 2021, 34).

The oil corporations' attempt through petrocultural and discursive means to establish oil as a life force, a lifestyle, and a life (social-cultural logic and mode of relationship evaluation and communication) can be further explicated through the notion of "cultural fix". Put more lucidly, such attempts to entrench the invisible ubiquity of oil and to implicate all social-economic classes in it by not only making it the basis of the infrastructure but also synonymous with and a condition of possibility of the experience of autonomy, freedom, and power, which can be considered as a pivotal component of the capitalist system's attempt to establish

## 354 *"It's Not Easy to Make Oil and Love Run in Harness Together"*

what Stephen Shapiro, expanding on David Harvey's "spatial fix", calls "cultural fix". Shapiro defines it thus:

> This cultural fix broadly includes Gramscian hegemony and all forms of cultural and social customs, institutions and identity-formation. The cultural fix covers the moments of class compact, as well as mechanisms by which the working class is pitted against [itself].

On this premise, cultural fix serves as a critically disarming means deployed by stripping the working class of their means of critique, resistance and by implicating them into the dynamics of petrocultural patterns of a commodity chain. Shapiro further adds that

> The role of the cultural fix [designates, moreover, those] social and cultural matters involving the reproduction of class identities and relations over time-lengths greater than a single turnover cycle [of capital] are intrinsic, not superficial, to the [accumulation] of capital.
>
> (ibid.)

Notably, Moore also draws on Shapiro's "cultural fix" to capture how culture is required to uphold neoliberal capital by normalizing increasingly flexible and invasive forms of energetic extraction and naturalizing not only unpaid human work. As Moore elaborates: "If cultural fixes cement successive hegemonic agreements between capital and the direct producers, they also extend beyond the sphere of direct production". Observing how cultural fixes, necessarily, "transcend the wage-relation's double boundary with unpaid work", Moore explains how such "fixes naturalize not only capital's appropriation of unpaid work by humans – above all the reproduction of labor-power – but also new epoch-making practices of appropriating unpaid work by extra-human natures" (2015, 201). As such, both Moore and Shapiro underscore the considerable contribution of culture and cultural production to the cyclical continuity of capitalism (and specifically to the current circuit of capitalist accumulation: neoliberal capital).

When the car supported by Grey wins, there is a feeble cheer and barely any enthusiasm from the crowd of people. Ingram describes the moment palpably: "That's not a noise that would scare anyone into a fit. A debacle" (85). However, he proceeds to provide a capitalist term where lack of social capital can be compensated with and indeed arises from finance capital: "It was a debacle, Debsy, but don't let that bother you. When you're hated by the rabble, it only means that your credit's good" (86). The car race culminates in two determining events: Peruchacha's garden party and her announcement of the new of her trip to the US. When the

*"It's Not Easy to Make Oil and Love Run in Harness Together"* 355

Viscount asks her: "Why are you going to the States, Miss Throwback?", Peruchacha's manifold reply is illuminating: "I'm going to the States, Viscount, to engineer that Immigration Bill in such a manner that this island will once more become what it was in my forefathers' time's paradise with little to do and plenty to enjoy" (83–84). Viscount proves unwittingly prescient in his indication of the naïvely idealist and phantasmatic nature of Peruchacha's intentions and visions: "A poetical idea, Miss Charmian. Very prettily and poetically expressed" (84).

## IX.   Coolies of Petro-Capitalism on *Oil Islands*

The fulcrum of *Oil Islands* round which its whole precarious dynamics and narrative hinges is the passing of a bill on which the whole fate of Grey's economic-political life and her company (as the world's biggest oil producer) is contingent. The Immigration Bill is a double-barrelled move in that it is supposed to legalize the importation and employment of a transnationally imported cheap coloured labour force on the island and prohibit its use on the US mainland. The implications of this twofold Bill finds an articulate expression in the conversation between Grey, Monson, and the company's directors. When one of the Directors says: "If the Trust could be deprived of its coloured labour, of course its new oil fields wouldn't be worth a damn", Monson adds: "And the Russian concessions would slump like a barometer before a storm. It would be a picnic for me to deal with Mr. Ingram then!" (38). *Oil Islands* demonstrates how oil and oil industrial and corporation forms – particularly in the peripheries – command an extractive ecology of its own, spawning a capitalist system that thrives on multifarious forms of labour exploitation beyond those at the site of production. Like other extractive economies, such as mining and plantation agriculture, oil's transnational presence not only invokes a complex web of production and consumption affecting a vast geopolitical grid of military power. It also spans across a global network of labour, usually precarious, whose routes are often drawn along imperial histories of human migration. This petro-matrix thus encompasses an immense swathe of transnational labour that is drawn on the grids of an international division of labour, concealed at the site of production, and embodies a "commodity fetishism" that makes invisible its deadly ecological and political-economic dynamics and effects. As such, *Oil Islands* exposes the conditions under which both capital/capitalism and race are concomitantly produced in a peripheral geography and different temporality underpinned by an uneven dynamics. It also reveals the ontological and social-economic hierarchy entrenched in the uneven extractive practices of such a system. Similarly, Patel and Moore also assert the intricate relationship between cheap labour and "the racial orders by which bodies were read, categorized, and policed at the boundaries of Society and Nature" (68).

356  *"It's Not Easy to Make Oil and Love Run in Harness Together"*

The crucial questions of oil workers and labour force loom large from the very outset of *Oil Islands*. Upon scrutiny, there are few central scenes in *Oil Islands* that are not haunted by the presence or passage of oil coolies in their hinterland. For instance, not only is the first scene replete with references to the transnational oil workers on the islands in highly racialized terms. But also this issue comes to occupy the foreground in Scene 2 where we see the main action being constantly interrupted due to the passage and arrival of "throngs of coolies" across the stage. In Scene 2, set at night and at the quay when the crowds of people have gathered for some bantering and also to jeer at Grey's extravagantly illuminated yacht, a member of the crowd beckons to a ship and says: "There's a ship coming. A labour transport", another person in the crowd adds the clandestine – and at this stage illegal – aspects of the business of coloured oil worker importation: "[the ship] Comes by night, probably, so that you can't see how few coolies she gets in; for lots of people say she's having to economize" (19). The conversations are punctuated by the intermittent passing of foreign oil labourers: "Another gang of coolies" (22). As another character states: "There's another gang of coolies. I don't see any signs of cutting down expenses". And the other responds: "That transport was never meant to be hidden, for she was packed full" (22). Slightly later, in the midst of the jeer and jibe between Ted and the girls (and their exchange of sexual innuendos in relation to him and Grey the Chimpanzee) we see the grim face and facts of the oil life and oil island: "A gang of barefooted coolies glides noiselessly over the quay" (23). A little later we once more witness the passing of "Another gang of barefooted coolies" when a character gawping at the unceasing flow of the importation of coloured labour force says: "Say, here's the third gang of coolies!" (23). In another scene, upon coming across another striking sight of the dispossessed workers, a person from the Crowd avers: "But that's quite a fair-sized gang of coolies" and another accentuates the vital role of the cheap coolies in Grey's attempt at maintaining her rate of surplus production: "Well, in the manager's office they say the Chimpanzee can't keep it up, and that she'll have to cut down expenses somehow" (21).

A crucial facet of the question is the use of the term "coolies", a highly racially codified term. As Ashutosh Kumar explains (2007, xiii–xv), the use of the overdetermined term "coolie," which was also used for plantation slaves and cheap contracted workers on farms in postcolonial contexts and capitalism's exploitative conditions, serves to register the longue durée of capitalism (in its being a historically coded and semiotically overdetermined term). As various historians of culture and energy have indicated, "coolie" was a term widely in use since the 18th century and particularly utilized in reference to the Asian workers who worked on plantations and later in oil extraction sites. As such, the genealogy, social-cultural history, and economic dynamics involved in the term and

## "It's Not Easy to Make Oil and Love Run in Harness Together" 357

condition of the "coolie" has profound affinities with the term "slave". This association finds further corroboration in Stephanie LeMenager's argument: "oil literally was conceived as a replacement for slave labor" (2014, 5). *Oil Islands* describes the workers in the oil fields not only as "yellow" or "black" workers, but also as "coolies", thereby invoking an international system of forced labour that was established after the end of the slave trade in order to compensate for the lost workforce and to continue to guarantee economic "progress". "Coolies" come primarily from Asia (see Nitin Varma 2017, 43–56; see also Touraj Atabaki 2018, 189–226) and are primarily recruited by colonial powers, who mainly kidnap young men under duress – the contract workers often died on the crossing or took their own lives. On a meta-dramatic level, although Feuchtwanger depicts the racial politics and economics of capitalism and oil industry with a specific focus on transnational labour trade, nevertheless he does not give voice to the striking oil workers as Lania does in *Konjunktur* and *Oil Field*. This adumbrates the class-based textual economy as well as the class and racial politics of its author. This social and dramatic feature (vocally-linguistically registered) is vividly illustrated by the following where coolies are depicted as silent ("muted") and other characters as fully vociferous. When the stage direction says: "A group of coolies, bare-footed, noiseless, cross the quay" one of the characters states: "But it is a very impressive herd of coolies that they bring over there" (21).

The important point which is treated rather tacitly in *Oil Islands* is the subtle ways through which Grey engineers the approval of the Immigration Bill. Along with the question of bribery and corruption which Grey exploits to her advantage – as Monson says: "Everybody in the States who could be bought has been bought already" (112) – the more latent yet far more crucial cause of success in the establishment of the Bill (and Grey's winning of the fight for oil and oil production) is Grey's wily move by taking advantage of the xenophobia that accompanies the work of "coolies" from the start. Notably, Feuchtwanger's focalization of the transnational, coloured workers (with a specific focus on the Chinese) is fully predicated on historical facts. In the USA, the import of Asian workers at the time was accompanied by xenophobic propaganda that warned of the "yellow danger" – a catchphrase that prevailed in Europe from the 1890s (*Social Work Practice with Immigrants and Refugees* 30–35) – and led to anti-Chinese legislation. The Chinese Exclusion Act of 1882 prohibited the immigration of Chinese for ten years and excluded them from American citizenship (see Wong 2016, 107). In 1908, Japan and the United States reached a "gentlemen's agreement" whereby Japan stopped issuing passports to laborers wanting to emigrate to the United States. And in 1924, all Chinese were fully prohibited from entering the US because Immigration Act declared no one ineligible for citizenship may immigrate to the United States, thereby ending Asian immigration completely. Interestingly, in the Germany

358    *"It's Not Easy to Make Oil and Love Run in Harness Together"*

contemporary with the play, Chinese workers were seen as needless and disciplined on the one hand, and on the other hand they were perceived to be hardly suitable for "German" work and were sometimes equated with Jews (see ibid., 193–197). The strategically skilful oil magnate, Grey, reckons with this xenophobic attitude and taking advantage of it actually enforces the ban on employing "coolies" on the US continent. Through her political intervention, Grey secures a reserve army of foreign workers who also demand low salaries.

The workers on the Oil Islands function – akin to the landscape and its resources – as mute, raw material to be exploited. Significantly, the oil labourers – whether native or transnational – have been lent no voice of their own in Feuchtwanger's play. Recurringly, we see them haunting the central scenes and with their jarring presence when they are led across the stage as faceless masses. A noteworthy point concerning the dramatic and thematic function of the "coolies" or "labour force" is the manner they serve to evoke links (or act as a copula) between ostensibly contrasting, but in fact complicitous and imbricating, spaces of Grey's and Peruchacha's realms when they cross the boundaries between landscape park and industrial sites. As such they evoke links between the sugar plantation slavery and exploitative labour and the use of cheap coloured labour in the oil industry. As Donna Haraway incisively observes, the slave plantation system "was the model and motor for the carbon-greedy machine-based factory system", and it "continues with ever greater ferocity in globalized factory meat production, monocrop agribusiness, and immense substitutions of crops like oil palm for multispecies forests and their products" (2016, 206 n5). As such, the workers in Feuchtwanger's play remain the dark background or animal-like, silent objects; the text defies the attempt to give subaltern a voice and to deal with the problem of othering. In one reading, this can be construed to be an attempt by Feuchtwanger to show the bare life and abject conditions of the oil workers or petro-precariat at the hands of the extractive petro-capitalism where, as Moore explains,

> Most human work was not labor-power and therefore most humans within capital's gravitational pull were not, or not really, Humans. This meant that the realm of Nature encompassed virtually all peoples of color, most women, and most people with white skin living in semi-colonial regions (e.g., Ireland, Poland, etc.).
>
> (Moore 2016, 91)

Accentuating the uneven dynamics of such a racialized political economy, Moore adds: "The cheap nature strategy [becomes] pivotal to the audacious restructuring of human relations along modern – and powerfully dualist – lines of class, race, and gender" ("World-Ecological Imaginations" n.p.)[30] As he further adds:

*"It's Not Easy to Make Oil and Love Run in Harness Together"* 359

capitalism's Cheap Nature strategy, and the recurrent cyclical movements in favor of ever-cheaper nature until 2003, may be understood in relation to the cyclical threat of the Four Cheaps turning dear. Costly nature turns cheap through appropriating unpaid work on the commodity frontiers inside and outside the heartlands of commodification. These frontier movements counteracted the capitalization of global nature and its obverse: the tendency of the ecological surplus to fall. Frontiers made it possible for capital to voraciously consume both the geological accumulations and biological configurations of unpaid work without a ruinous increase in the costs of production.

(2015, 177)

The question of oil workers' resistance and the racial segregation and racial politics informing the petro-capitalist dynamics of their work finds a striking, though fleeting, representation in *Oil Islands*. In *Oil Islands*, races and ethnic groups are associated with a sense of riskiness, disease, and being sub-human, pre-civilizational, and closer to nature. On this basis, they are assigned a strictly segregated order, as the following radio communication read by Uncle Obadiah reveals: "Wireless from the head office: the white mechanics in the electric refineries are going on strike tomorrow because in Refinery Twenty-Three the coloured worker Puang Wu is still employed in a position reserved for whites" (49). Vaunting her prowess and alacrity, Grey states: "I settled that affair before we set sail in the yacht. . . . The coloured worker Puang Wu is to be removed" (49). When Ingram objects that the discriminatory decision is not judicious ("So that the white mechanics may spit in your face next time?"), Grey explains her broader plan:

The white mechanics in all the electric refineries, who are, of course, perfectly within their rights this time, will be replaced by other white mechanics on the first of the month after next. There should be two transports already under way.

(49)

As Lelio comments: "That must have cost you a good round sum" complemented by Ingram's plaintive caveat: "Which will be sorely needed during the oil crisis" (49). Grey's response, however, reveals not only temporal dynamics but historical vision driving the oil order in that it reveals not only the systemic (capitalism as a self-perpetuating system) but also future-producing facets of petroculture (see Chapter 5): "Do you believe in short-sighted measures, gentlemen? I run the Oil Company as if it were going to last till the Judgment Day" (51). In other words, in order to obliterate the very memory of the resistance and to preclude the very possibility of strike as an effective course of action for the workers in the future, Grey takes a drastic disciplinary course by expelling the "yellow

360 *"It's Not Easy to Make Oil and Love Run in Harness Together"*

worker" but also the striking whites even at the cost of short-term loss and financial sacrifice.

The total appropriation of the "coloured" bodies by Grey's Oil Company hinges on their precarity in their predicament as disposable bodies of the oil economy's "necropower", or what Mbembé calls "the capacity to define who matters and who does not, who is disposable and who is not" (61). The powerless bodies of oil workers are assimilated/employed for maximum extraction of force (productivity) only for a stipulated time. In such a dynamics, the labouring bodies are meant to be consumed and then wasted by "the logic of human disposability, . . . at accelerated rates in order to secure the most profit" (Michelle Yates 2011, 63). Notably, a scrutiny of Grey's language – her description of the coloured, or transnational, workers – reveals how the extractive violence – inherent in the process of the transportation of transnational workers coupled with the method of incorporating them as part of the production machine and their evaluation – is couched in an abstractly economic and even scientific language. Such a linguistic-discursive measure normalizes the necropolitical violence of the oil system through the rationale of the sovereign company/state's legal "right to kill" the spent or abjected bodies (64). In its critique of the existing petro-capitalist system, Feuchtwanger's *Oil Islands* accentuates the racial dimension of the expropriated petro-labour – where capitalistic development and colonial expansion (the exploitation of the populations on the periphery) are shown to be dialectically linked. Expounding the imperialist characteristic of expropriation, Fraser states:

> Far from being sporadic, moreover, expropriation has always been part and parcel of capitalism's history, as has the racial oppression with which it is linked. No one doubts that racially organized slavery, colonial plunder, and land enclosures generated much of the initial capital that kick-started the system's development.
>
> (67)

The facility and ease with which the strikes and protests of oil workers, both white and more technical oil staff and coloured and unskilled workers, are handled is a testament to the crucial difference between the political possibilities of action and social praxis afforded by each form of energy resource (coal and oil, in this instance) and respective extraction regimes as identified by Timothy Mitchell. The coal industry, due to the physical-topological features of coal and infrastructural properties of coal industry, was particularly dependent on the labour force (miners) and susceptible to disruptive action and industrial stoppages. As Timothy Mitchell has observed, the technicalities of "moving carbon stores from seam to surface created unusually autonomous places and methods of work" (2011, 20). In the oil industry, on the contrary, oil energy networks were "less vulnerable to the political claims of those whose labour kept them running"

## "It's Not Easy to Make Oil and Love Run in Harness Together" 361

(Mitchell 2011, 38–39). As Podobnik puts it: "Whereas large numbers of coal miners came to occupy strategic positions within centralized mining operations, the occupational characteristics of oil served to dampen labour militancy. Oil production involves a wide variety of distinct tasks, including drilling, pipeline construction, well maintenance, transportation, and refining. Each of these categories of work requires specific kinds of labourers and tends to result in distinct modes of labour control that reduce the capacity of workers to create unions and engage in strike activity" (2006, 47).

Earlier we witnessed how Grey's attempts to have the double-barrelled Immigration Bill approved was received with misgivings. When Grey asks Monson: "What if Japan decides to withdraw her protest against the immigration restrictions provided that the Oil Islands are left free?" she receives nothing but Monson's deep scepticism: But that's out of the question (112) only to receive Grey's incisive assertion that:

> Nothing's out of the question. Because of Mr Ingram's departure and the acquisition of the Russian concessions we have many posts to fill in the directorate and the departments. Now, since we have so many coloured workers already, why shouldn't we fill these vacancies with gentlemen from Japan?
>
> (113)

Ironically, Grey's strategic and intellectual perspicacity brings her nothing but another masculinizing compliment: "You're a heavyweight, Debsy" (113). Ultimately, however, and notwithstanding the earlier caveats and forewarnings expressed by Ingram and Monson – when the news of the final outcome of the Bill is broadcast from the radio, the astounded Monson exclaims: "Japan is going to intervene! God of Israel! Debsy, your technique is marvelous! Three cheers for Debsy Grey, the mother of the Brown Islands!" (123).

In focusing on the essential role of maintaining the national and global monopoly by Grey's oil company in the early decades of the 20th century, *Oil Islands* shows how the extractivist regimes thrive on the dispossession of the poor and marginalized. Asserting that petro-economies essentially replicate slave economies through overt parallels of borderless labour extrication from the global fringes, the play shows how petro-capitalism is mired in a crisis of "cheap labour" and "cheap nature" by illustrating how the prospective loss of the frontiers in cheap labour, energy, food, and resources threatens the decline of the world's largest oil company thereby fuelling its attempts to legalize its colonial-imperial forays and extractive accumulations in forms and phases. Andreas Malm and the Zetkin Collective unravel the premises of these systemic relations thus:

It is here, in acts of mobile combustion, that we shall look for a history of that primary level on which interpellations in the core can build. It is a history tied up with frontier racism, but it has spread

## 362 *"It's Not Easy to Make Oil and Love Run in Harness Together"*

broader and sunk deeper than acts of drilling. Focus will have to be shifted away from primitive fossil capital. An exhaustive investigation is obviously outside the scope of this work: what we shall offer are rather two vignettes. One concerns a primary vehicle in the nineteenth century, the steamboat, as deployed by the leading fossil economy of that period, the British Empire; the other, the automobile in the mid-twentieth-century US.

(2021)

In a similar vein, *Oil Islands* illustrates how the American-led petro-capitalist empire and its ecological regime is riven by mounting contradictions: metabolic rift/shift hence unsustainability of its operations, oil crisis, pollution, climate crisis, environmental degradation, the stagnation of agricultural productivity; climate volatility; geo-technical challenges to extraction of energy, minerals, and water; and deposit of wastes and pollutants. *Oil Islands* depicts the biosemiotic entanglements (37) between human (slaves and labour forces and natives) and nonhuman nature in a peripheral Oil Islands where both are vulnerable to the ravages and utilized as sources for surplus extraction.

In *Oil Islands*, the Brown Islands are depicted not only as a peripheral commodity frontier but also a nodal point and mid-point in the globally extended and unevenly combined network of American petro-capitalism. *Oil Islands* draws our attention as much to the strategic political-economic and social-culturally transformative force and power of oil (as a substance/material, means, and commodity) as it does to the conditions under which it is extracted. Most saliently, *Oil Islands* accentuates the global network – along with its relational dynamics and world-systemic logics – through which a resource (oil) frontier is produced. Such a resource frontier is informed with an uneven relational dynamics in that it entails a constant negotiation that is between the mainland and the peripheral island, between the national and the global and between the political-ideological rivals (the United States and the Soviet Union). This is in keeping with Moore's world-ecological approach and its relational dynamics/vision. Far from maintaining a dualistic focus – which would involve the identification of the environmental implications of political economy or, alternatively, the political-economic dimension of environmental issues – Feuchtwanger's *Oil islands* illustrates how a historical system such as capitalism needs to be comprehended as an immanently ecological project. This petrocritical vision is resonant with Moore's argument in which with the rise of the modern world-economy

> varied and heretofore largely isolated local and regional socio-ecological relations were incorporated into – and at the same moment became constituting agents of – a capitalist world-ecology. Local socio-ecologies were at once transformed by human labour power

*"It's Not Easy to Make Oil and Love Run in Harness Together"* 363

(itself a force of nature) and brought into sustained dialogue with each other.

(2003, 447)

*Oil Islands* reveals the aforementioned entanglements and dynamics by showing how the uneven core-periphery dynamics of the petro-capitalist world system – which partly depends on its access to cheap labour – to which the petro-precariat are subjected is reinscribed on a trajectory of America's neo-colonial use of transnational labour migration – the servitude of indentured laborers that form a post-slavery but nevertheless racialized mode of expropriation.

## Notes

1. Lion Feuchtwanger: Die Petroleuminseln, in: ders." Dramen II, hg. Und met einem Nachtwort von Hans Dahlke, Berlin 1984, pp. 248–358.
2. Feuchtwanger himself mentions 1923 and another time 1924 as the completion date of *Oil Islands'* source and predecessor: *Die Petroleuminseln.* A number of critics including Dahlke state that the play was sketched in 1924 and finished in Berlin in 1925 (see the Afterword to the German version of the play by Hans Dahlke, Berlin 1984, pp. 285–358).
3. *Calcutta, May 4th. Three Acts of Colonial History and Will Hill Be Amnestied? Comedy in Four Acts.*
4. Lion Feuchtwanger, *Ein Buch nur für meine Freunde* (Frankfurt a.M.: Fischer Taschenbuch Verlag, 1984c).
5. Mikhaïl M. Bakhtin, *Rabelais and His World.* Trans. Hélène Iswolsky (Bloomington/Indianapolis: Indiana University Press, 1984 [1968]).
6. More broadly, Janice Carlisle's perceptive argument concerning the use of smell as a means of racial, gender and class distinction, subjectification, and territorialization is illuminating: "Within the context of an olfactory encounter . . . class is a practice of everyday life, a way of comprehending quotidian, individual experience . . . it is a process of setting one person in comparative relation to another" (2004, 12–13).
7. As Kristeva elaborates:

> The abject has only one quality of the object – that of being opposed to I. . . . Not me. No that. But not nothing, either. A 'something' that I do not recognize as a thing. A weight of meaninglessness about which there is nothing insignificant and which crushes me.
>
> (1982, 1–3)

8. Michael Lowy, "The Current of Critical Irrealism: A Moonlit Enchanted Night," in *Adventures in Realism*, ed. Matthew Beaumont (Oxford, UK: Blackwell, 2007), 193–206.
9. Valorizing the notion of "mood" over and above "affect", particularly in the field of literary studies, Rita Felski and Susan Fraiman accentuate the potential that the concept of "mood" has for reconceptualizing dichotomous models of experience, knowledge, and relationality (including modes of thinking about the notion of "attunement"):

364　"*It's Not Easy to Make Oil and Love Run in Harness Together*"

> The concept of mood . . . circumvents the clunky categories often imposed on experience: subjective versus objective, feeling versus thinking, latent versus manifest. The field of affect studies is some-times taken to task for reinforcing such dichotomies, creating a picture of affect as a zone of ineffable and primordial experience that is subsequently squeezed into the rationalist straitjacket of language. The concept of mood, for the most part, avoids such difficulties. Definitions of mood often emphasize its role in modulating thought, acknowledging a dynamic and interactive relationship be-tween reason and emotion. Mood is tied up with self-understanding and shapes thinking rather than being stifled by thinking. It makes intellectual work possible and inflects it in subtle and less subtle ways, informing the questions we ask, the puzzles that intrigue us, the styles and genres of argument we are drawn to. Mood impinges on method.
>
> (2012, vi)

10. Hans Ulrich Gumbrecht, *Atmosphere, Mood, Stimmung: On a Hidden Potential of Literature*. Trans. Erik Butler (Stanford: Stanford University Press, 2012).
11. Dreyfus, *Being-in-the-World* p. 170 MIT Press, Cambridge MA 1991 Commentary of Heidegger's Being and Time Division I.
12. See Elizabeth DeLoughrey, *Allegories of the Anthropocene.*
13. Fredric Jameson, *The Political Unconscious: Narrative as a Socially Symbolic Act* (London: Routledge, 1983), p. 19. Consonantly, DeLoughrey describes allegory as "a mutable and often paradoxical mode of representation" that "reflects a disjunction between part and whole and an aporia between the continuity of the self and the world" (*Allegories of Anthropocene ???*).
14. As . . . indicates: "Although Mexico had been open to all comers because of private ownership of mineral rights, its production peaked early in the 1920s".
15. Anand Tropani, *Oil and the Great Powers: Britain and Germany 1914–1945* (Oxford: Oxford University Press, 2019).
16.

> Petro-capitalism denotes the interplay between politics and economy in oil-dependent states. As the basis for government access to foreign exchange and recognition in the international economy, the "structuring impact of oil" enables the Angolan state's survival – and success – despite government officials' failure to execute basic state functions.
>
> (Reed 2009, 19)

17. Michael Watts, "Securing Oil: Frontiers, Risk, and Spaces of Accumulated Insecurity," in *Subterranean Estates: Life Worlds of Oil and Gas*, ed. Hannah Appel, Arthur Mason and Michael Watts (London: Cornell University Press, 2015), pp. 211–237.
18. One of the principal sources of oil's status as an aporetic object of desire – that is, as a simultaneously transcendental cause of jouissance and a traumatic *objet petit a* – is its embodiment or evocation of a chain of master signifiers (phallic or paternal metaphors), such as freedom, agency, Enlightenment, and sovereign subjectivity. As Slavoj Žižek explains, in Lacanian terms the Master Signifier "brings about the closure of an ideological field by way of designating the Supreme Good (God, Truth, Nation, etc.)" (2003, 217). However, these master signifiers, as Lacan explains, are also empty signifiers because they do not have a concrete referent or fixed meaning. They, thus, embody

## "It's Not Easy to Make Oil and Love Run in Harness Together"  365

this ineffable surplus of jouissance; Lacan's explanation illuminates the logic underlying this: "because inexplicably I love in you something more than you – objet petit a" (Lacan 1998, 268).

19. See A. Baron, "Contested Terrain Revisited: Technology and Gender Definitions of Work in the Printing Industry, 1850–1920," in *Women, Work and Technology*, ed. B. Wright (Ann Arbor: University of Michigan Press, 1987), pp. 58–83. Also see M. S. Kimmel, "The 'Crisis' in Masculinity in Historical Perspective," in *The Making of Masculinities: The New Men's Studies*, ed. H. Brod (Boston: Allen and Unwin, 1987), pp. 121–153; J. A. Allen, "Men Interminably in Crisis? Historians on Masculinity, Sexual Boundaries, and Manhood," *Radical History Review*, 82 (2002), 191–207.

20. Herbert Marcuse, *Marxism and Feminism*, Women's Studies (Old Westbury, NY: The Feminist Press, 1974).

21. Peter Uwe Hohendahl, "Aesthetic Violence: The Concept of the Ugly in Adorno's Aesthetic Theory," *Cultural Critique*, 60.1 (2005), pp. 170–196.

22. Theodor W. Adorno, *Aesthetic Theory* (Minneapolis: University of Minnesota Press, 1997).

    Geoffrey Galt Harpham, *On the Grotesque: Strategies of Contraction in Art and Literature* (Princeton: Princeton University Press, 1982).

23. Ian Roberts, "Determinism, Free Will, and Moral Responsibility in American Literary Naturalism," pp. 121–138.

    The *Oxford Handbook of American Literary Naturalism* Edited by Keith Newlin.

24. Establishing an inherent link between energy and economy, Bataille distinguishes between two principal modes of economy: the restricted and the general economy. These two economies are different in ontological, temporal, social, and psychosomatic respects (*Accursed Share*). The restricted economy, according to Bataille, is driven by the principle of utility and acquisition where capital or money is relentlessly accumulated and invested in an indefinite future, which promises a "later" moment of jouissance if the entirety of "now" is dedicated to work. Such a dynamics is variously exemplified by communism, capitalism (that developed after the Middle Ages) and the liberal economies (developed in the late 18th and 19th century). General economy, on the contrary, is driven by the principles of loss, excess, and unrewarding expenditure. General economy involves an ethics of self-loss, transgression, sacrifice, pleasure, idleness, unemployability, and nothingness (see *Accursed Share*, Volume I. 10–11; 12, 22, 33–4; Accursed Share II.84–5). In Bataille's vision, the core ontological principle of the world is excess rather than scarcity. And the paradigmatic illustration of this principle is the sun in all its incessant self-expenditure. All human organizations and organisms are driven by these two conflictual forces which are dialectically related. Hence, the recurring pattern of the human world or systems oscillating between peace and war, between growth and squander, between accumulation and non-productive expenditure.

25. As Marcuse argues:

> In a repressive civilization, death itself becomes an instrument of repression. Whether death is feared as constant threat, or glorified as supreme sacrifice, or accepted as fate, the education for consent to death introduces an element of surrender into life from the beginning – surrender and submission.
>
> (1974, 236)

26. In *Pollution Is Colonialism*, Max Liboiron posits pollution as a historically situated colonial technology of Indigenous dispossession. Here, Liboiron explores the ways in which pollution, particularly plastic pollution, has acted as a form of colonialism. Pollution, as he contends, should not be posited merely as a "symptom of capitalism"; rather pollution is colonialism (51). Arguing for anticolonial sciences as knowledge systems that "function more like infrastructures" (133), here Liboiron elaborates a framework to demonstrate how scientific research methods can be considered as practices that can align with or against colonialism. Pollution is not only an act of environmental violence against indigenous lands, but it also assumes access to land to use for disposal. "[A]ssumed access to land is foundational to so many settler relations" (2021, 68). Yet science does not have to be colonialist; it can be anticolonial.
27. Paul Gilroy, "Driving While Black," in *Car Cultures*, ed. Danny Miller (Oxford: Berg 2001), pp. 81–104. See also Cara Daggett, "Petro-Masculinity: Fossil Fuels and Authoritarian Desire," *Millennium: Journal of International Studies*, 47.1 (2018), pp. 25–44.
28. See Georgiana Banita, "From Isfahan to Ingolstadt: Bertolucci's La via del petrolio and the Global Culture of Neorealism," *Oil Culture*, pp. 145–168.
29. "'All the Earmarks of Propaganda' Teapot Dome, the World Struggle for Oil, and Defining Corporate Rhetoric," *Jeremy Groskopf*, pp. 33–50 in Petro-Cinema Bloomsbury 2021.
30. https://jasonwmoore.wordpress.com/page/3/.

# Works Cited

Abulafia, David. *The Discovery of Mankind*. New Haven: Yale University Press, 2008.

Adamson, Walter L. *Hegemony and Revolution*. London: University of California Press, 1980.

Adorno, Theodor. *Aesthetic Theory*. Minneapolis: University of Minnesota Press, 1997.

———. *Negatic Dialectics*. Trans. E. B. Ashton. London and New York: Routledge, 2004.

Adorno, Theodor and Max Horkheimer. *Dialectic of Enlightenment: Philosophical Fragments*. Ed. Gunzelin Schmid Noerr. Trans. Edmund Jephcott. Stanford: Stanford University Press, 2002.

Agamben, Giorgio. *Homo Sacer: Sovereign Power and Bare Life*. Trans. Daniel Heller-Roazen. Stanford: Stanford University Press, 1998.

Ahmed, Sara. *Cultural Politics of Emotion*. Edinburgh: Edinburgh University Press, 2014.

Allen, Judith Alison. "Men Interminably in Crisis? Historians on Masculinity, Sexual Boundaries, and Manhood." *Radical History Review*. 82, 2002, pp. 191–207.

Althusser, Louis. Lenin and Philosophy and Other Essays. New York: Monthly Review Press, 2001.

Amitav Ghosh. *The Great Derangement: Climate Change and the Unthinkable*. Chicago: University of Chicago Press, 2016.

Angus, Ian. *Facing the Anthropocene: Fossil Capitalism and the Crisis of the Earth System*. New York: MR Press, 2016.

Ansell-Pearson, Keith. "Deleuze and New Materialism Naturalism, Norms, and Ethics." *The New Politics of Materialism*. Eds. Sarah Ellenzweig and John H. Zammito. London: Routledge, 2017, pp. 88–108.

The Anthropocene: The Promise and Pitfalls of an Epochal Idea in Future Remains: A Cabinet of Curiosities for the Anthropocene. Edited by: Gregg Mitman, Marco Armiero and Robert Emmett. London: The University of Chicago Press, 2017.

Apter, Andrew. *The Pan-African Nation: Oil and the Spectacle of Culture in Nigeria*. Chicago: The University of Chicago Press, 2005.

Arboleda, Martin. *Planetary Mine: Territories of Extraction under Late Capitalism*. London: Verso, 2020.

Arrighi, Giovanni. *The Long Twentieth Century: Money, Power, and the Origins of Our Times*. London: Verso, 2002.

———. *Adam Smith in Beijing: Lineages of the Twenty-first Century*. London: Verso, 2007.

## 368 Works Cited

———. "The Winding Paths of Capital: Interview by David Harvey", *New Left Review*. 56, 2009, 61–94.

Atabaki, Touraj. "Indian Migrant Workers in the Iranian Oil Industry 1908–1951." *Working for Oil: Comparative Social Histories of Labor in the Global Oil Industry*. Eds. Touraj Atabaki, Elizabetta Bini and Kaveh Ehsani. Basingstoke: Palgrave Macmillan, 2018, pp. 189–226.

Atkinson, Ted. "Blood Petroleum: True Blood, the BP Oil Spill, and Fictions of Energy/Culture." *Journal of American Studies*. 47:1, 2013, pp. 213–229.

Austin, Robert. *Founding a Balkan State*. London: University of Toronto Press, 2012.

Azuaje, Penélope Plaza. *Culture as Renewable Oil: How Territory, Bureaucratic Power and Culture Coalesce in the Venezuelan Petrostate*. London: Routledge, 2019.

Babusiaux, Denis. *Oil and Gas Exploration and Production: Reserves, Costs, Contracts*. Trans. Jonathan Pearse. Paris: Editions Technip, 2007.

Bakhtin, Mikhail M. *Rabelais and His World*. Trans. Hélène Iswolsky. Bloomington: Indiana University Press, 1984.

Banita, Georgiana. "From Isfahan to Ingolstadt: Bertolucci's La via del petrolio and the Global Culture of Neorealism." *Oil Culture*. Eds. Ross Barrett and Daniel Worden. Minneapolis and London: University of Minnesota Press, 2014, pp. 145–168.

———. "Sensing Oil: Sublime Art and Politics in Canada." *Petrocultures: Oil, Politics, Culture*. Eds. Sheena Wilson, Adam Carlson and Imre Szeman. Montreal & Kingston, London and Chicago: McGill-Queen's University Press, 2017, pp. 431–457.

Barad, Karen. *Meeting the Universe Halfway: Quantum Physics and the Entanglement of Matter and Meaning*. Durham: Duke University Press, 2007.

Baron, Ava. "Contested Terrain Revisited: Technology and Gender Definitions of Work in the Printing Industry, 1850–1920." *Women, Work and Technology*. Ed. Barbara Drygulski Wright. Ann Arbor: University of Michigan Press, 1987, pp. 58–83.

Barrett, Ross. "Picturing a Crude Past: Primitivism, Public Art, and Corporate Oil Promotion in the United States." *Oil Culture*. Eds. Ross Barrett and Daniel Worden. Minneapolis and London: University of Minnesota Press, 2014, pp. 43–68.

Barry, Andrew. "The Oil Archives." *Subterranean States: Life Worlds of Oil and Gas*. Eds. Hannah Appel, Arthur Mason and Michael Watts. Ithaca: Cornell University Press, 2015, pp. 95–107.

Bartosch, Roman. *Literature, Pedagogy, and Climate Change: Text Models for a Transcultural Ecology*. Cham: Palgrave Macmillan, 2020.

Bataille, Georges. *The Accursed Share: An Essay on General Economy, Vol. 1: Consumption*. New York: Zone Books, 1988.

———. *The Accursed Share: An Essay on General Economy, Vol. 2 and 3: The History of Eroticism and Sovereignty*. Trans. Robert Hurley. New York: Zone Books, 1991.

Bellamy, Brent Ryan and Jeff Diamanti (eds.). *Materialism and the Critique of Energy*. Chicago and Edmonton: MCM Prime Press, 2017.

———. "Phantasmagorias of Energy: Toward a Critical Theory of Energy and Economy." *Mediations*. 31:2, 2018, pp. 1–16.

Bennett, Jane. *Vibrant Matter: A Political Ecology of Things*. Durham: Duke University Press, 2010.

Biemann, Ursula and Andrew Pendakis. "This Is Not a Pipeline: Thoughts on the Politico-Aesthetics of Oil." *Imaginations*. 3:2, 2012, Web (Accessed 22.03.2022), pp. 6–16.

# Works Cited    369

———. "This Is Not a Pipeline: On the Politico-Aesthetics of Oil." *Energy Humanities: An Anthology*. Eds. Imre Szeman and Dominic Boyer. Baltimore: Johns Hopkins University Press, 2017, pp. 504–511.

Biondich, Mark. *The Balkans: Revolution, War, and Political Violence Since 1878*. Oxford: Oxford University Press, 2011.

Black, Brian C. *Crude Reality: Petroleum in World History*. Lanham: Rowman & Littlefield Publishers, 2012.

Bleichmar, Daniela, et al. (eds.). *Science in the Spanish and Portuguese Empires, 1500–1800*. Stanford: Stanford University Press, 2009.

Bloch, Ernst. *Heritage of Our Times*. Trans. Neville and Stephen Plaice. California: University of California Press, 1991.

Braudel, Fernand. "History and the Social Sciences: The Longue Durée." *Review*. 32 (2), 2009, pp. 171–203.

Brech, Bertolt. *Brecht on Theatre: The Development of an Aesthetic*. Ed. and Trans. John Willett. New Delhi: Radha Krishna, 1978.

Broadberry, Stephen and Peter Howlett. *The United Kingdom during World War I: Business as Usual?* 18 June 2003. http://piketty.pse.ens.fr/files/Broadberry-Howlett03.pdf

Brown, W. M. *The Royal Navy's Fuel Supplies, 1898–1939; The Transition from Coal to Oil*. Unpublished doctoral dissertation. London: University of London, 2003.

Buck-Morss, Susan. *The Dialectics of Seeing: Walter Benjamin and the Arcades Project*. Cambridge: The MIT Press, 1989.

Campbell, C. J. *Oil crisis*. Essex: Multi-Science Publishing Company, 2005.

Carlisle, Janice. *Common Scents: Comparative Encounters in High-Victorian Fiction*. Oxford: Oxford UP, 2004.

Casanova, Pascale. "Literature as a World." *New Left Review*. 31, 2005, pp. 71–90.

Chakrabarty, Dipesh. "Postcolonial Studies and the Challenge of Climate Change." *New Literary History*. 43:1, 2012, pp. 1–18.

———. *The Climate of History in a Planetary Age*. Chicago: The University of Chicago Press, 2021.

Cheah, Pheng. Spectral Nationality. New York: Columbia University Press, 2003.

Cheah, Pheng. What Is a World? USA: Duke University Press, 2016.

Chernov, Dmitry and Didier Sornette. *Man-Made Catastrophes and Risk Information Concealment*. London: Palgrave, 2015.

Christofis, N. *World-Systems Theory*. London: Palgrave Macmillan, 4, 2019.

Churchill, Winston. *The World Crisis, 1911–1918*. London: Thornton Butterworth, 1923.

Clark, B., & York, R. Carbon Metabolism. *Theory and Society*, 34:4, 2005, 391–428.

Clark, Timothy. "Derangements of Scale." *Telemorphosis: Theory in the Era of Climate Change*. Vol. 1. Ed. Tom Cohen. Ann Arbor: Open Humanities Press, 2012, pp. 148–166.

———. *Ecocriticism on the Edge: The Anthropocene as a Threshold Concept*. London: Bloomsbury, 2015.

Colebrook, Claire. *Death of the Post-Human*. Ann Arbor: Open Humanities Press, 2014.

Coronil, Fernando. *Magical State: Nature, Money, and Modernity in Venezuela*. Chicago and London: University of Chicago Press, 1997.

## 370   Works Cited

Crist, Eileen. "On the Poverty of Our Nomenclature." In *Anthropocene or Capitalocene? Nature, History, and the Crisis of Capitalism*. Ed. Jason Moore. Oakland: Kairos, 2016, pp. 14–33.

Daggett, Cara. "Petro-Masculinity: Fossil Fuels and Authoritarian Desire." *Millenium: Journal of International Studies*. 47:1, 2018, pp. 25–44.

Dahl, Erik J. "From Coal to Oil." *Joint Force Quarterly*. Winter 2000–01, pp. 50–56.

Damrosch, David. *What Is World Literature?* (Princeton and Oxford: Princeton University Press), 2003.

Davies, Jeremy. *The Birth of the Anthropocene*. Berkeley: University of California Press, 2016.

Deckard, Sharae and Stephen Shapiro. "World-Culture and the Neoliberal World-System: An Introduction." *World Literature, the Neoliberalism, and the Culture of Discontent*. Eds. Sharae Deckard and Stephen Shapiro. London: Palgrave, 2019. pp. 1–49.

DeGoyler, E. and L. W. Naughton. *Twentieth Century Petroleum Statistics*. Dallas: DeGolyer and MacNaughton, 1950.

Deleuze, Gilles. *Difference and Repetition*. Trans. Paul Patton. New York: Columbia University Press, 1994.

———. *The Logic of Sense*. Trans. Mark Lester and Charles Stivale. London: Athlone Press, 1990.

Deleuze, Gilles and Guattari Félix. *What Is Philosophy?* Trans. Hugh Tomlinson and Graham Burchell. New York: Columbia University Press, 1994.

———. *Anti-Oedipus: Capitalism and Schizophrenia*. 1983, trans. Robert Hurley, Mark Seem and Helen R. Lane, Minneapolis: University of Minnesota Press.

DeLoughrey, Elizabeth M. *Allegories of the Anthropocene*. Durham: Duke University Press, 2019.

Derrida, Jacques. *Signature Event Context* (17–18) "Signature Event Context" (MP, 307–30; LI, 1–23).

Devereux, Cecily. "'Made for Mankind': Cars, Cosmetics, and the Petrocultural Feminine." *Petrocultures: Oil, Politics, Culture*. Eds. Sheena Wilson Adam Carlson and Imre Szeman. Montreal & Kingston, London and Chicago: McGill-Queen's University Press, 2017, pp. 162–186.

Diamanti, Jeff. *Climate and Capital in the Age of Petroleum: Locating Terminal Landscapes*. London: Bloomsbury Academic, 2021.

Dipesh Chakrabarty, "The Climate of History: Four Theses," *Critical Inquiry*. 35, 2009, p. 208.

Dreyfus, Hubert L. *Being-in-the-World: A Commentary on Heidegger's Being in Time, Division I*. Cambridge: MIT Press, 1991.

The Ecological Rift: Capitalism's War on the Earth. By John Bellamy Foster, Brett Clark, Richard York. New York: New York University Press, 2010.

Engdahl, W.F. *A Century of War: Anglo-American Oil Politics and the New World Order*. London: Pluto Press, 2004.

Esposito, R. *Bios: Biopolitics and Philosophy*, Campbell, T. C. (trans.), Minneapolis, MN: University of Minnesota Press, 2008.

Evans, Mel. *Artwash: Big Oil and the Arts*. London: Pluto Press, 2015.

*EveningStar*. "How a President Started a World Film Exchange." 5 January 1927, p. 5.

Fakhrkonandeh, Alireza. "Oil Cultures, World Drama and Contemporaneity: Questions of Time, Space and Form in Ella Hickson's Oil." *Textual Practice*, 36:11, 2022.

## Works Cited 371

Fakhrkonandeh, Alireza. "'As an Illuminator the Oil Is without a Figure: It Is the Light of the Age': Traumas and Aporias of Oil as a Global Object of Desire in Ella Hickson's *Oil*." *College Literature*. 49:1, 2022, pp. 103–137.

Faulhaber, Uwe K. "Lion Feuchtwanger's Theory of the Historical Novel." *Lion Feuchtwanger: The Man, His Ideas, His Works*. Ed. John M. Spalek. Los Angeles: Hennessey & Ingalls, 1972. pp. 67–81.

Felski, Rita and Susan Fraiman. "Introduction." *New Literary History*. 43:3, 2012, pp. v–xii.

Ferguson, James. *Global Shadows*. Durham: Duke University Press, 2006.

Feuchtwanger, Lion. "Zu meinem Stuck *Die Petroleuminseln*." *Die Weltbuhne*. 23:46, 18 October 1927.

———. "Preface." *Two Anglo-Saxon plays: The Oil islands, Warren Hastings*. New York: The Viking Press, 1928.

———[RefCheck306] . "Vom Sinn und Unsinn des historischen Romans."

———. *Centum opuscula*. Ed. Wolfgang Brendt. Rudolsctadt: Gereifneverlag. 1956, pp. 508–515.

———. *Ein Buch nur für meine Freunde*. Frankfurt a.M.: Fischer Taschenbuch Verlag, 1984.

———. *The Ugly Duchess*. Translated by Willa and Edwin Muir, New York: Viking, 1928.

Fordham, Benjamin O. "Revisionism Reconsidered: Exports and American Intervention in World War I." *International Organization*. 61:2, 2007, pp. 277–310.

Foster, John Bellamy. "Marx's Theory of Metabolic Rift: Classical Foundations for Environmental Sociology." *American Journal of Sociology*. 105:2, 1999, pp. 366–405.

———. "The Epochal Crisis." *Monthly Review*. 1 October 2013. https://monthlyreview.org/2013/10/01/epochal-crisis/

———. *Marx's Ecology*. New York: Monthly Review Press, 2000a.

———. The Great Capitalist Climacteric. *Monthly Review*. 67:6, 2015, 1–18.

Foster et al. *The Ecological Rift: Capitalism's War on the Earth*. Eds. John Bellamy Foster, Brett Clark and Richard York. New York: Monthly Review Press, 2010.

Foucault, Michel. *Discipline and Punish: The Birth of the Prison*. Trans. Alan Sheridan. New York: Vintage Books, 1979.

———. *Society Must be Defended: Lectures at the Collège de France, 1975–76*, Macey, D. (trans.), London: Penguin Books, 2004.

Garavini, Giuliano. *The Rise and Fall of OPEC in the Twentieth Century*. Oxford: Oxford University Press, 2019.

Geo, Takach. *Scripting the Environment: Oil, Democracy and the Sands of Time and Space*. London: Palgrave, 2016.

Ghosh, Amitav. "Petrofiction." *The New Republic*. 2 March 1992: 29–33.

———. *Petrofiction: The Oil Encounter and the Novel*. New Delhi: Ravi Dayal Publishers, 2002.

Gilroy, Paul. "Driving While Black." *Car Cultures*. Ed. Danny Miller. Oxford: Berg, 2001, pp. 81–104.

Goldschmidt, Alfons. The program booklet for Konjunktur written by the journalist.

Goodchild, Philip. *Theology of Money*. Durham and London: Duke University Press, 2009.

Gramsci, Antonio. *Selections from the Prison Notebooks of Antonio Gramsci*. Eds. Q. Hoare and G.N. Smith. New York: International Publishers, 1971.

## 372  Works Cited

———. *Selections from Political Writings 1910–1920*. London: Lawrence and Wishart, 1977.

Groskopf, Jeremy. "'All the Earmarks of Propaganda': Teapot Dome, the World Struggle for Oil, and Defining Corporate Rhetoric." *Petro-Cinema: Sponsored Film and the Oil Industry*. Eds. Marina Dahlquist and Patrick Vonderau. New York: Bloomsbury, 2021, pp. 33–50.

Gruen, George E. "The Oil Resources of Iraq: Their Role in the Policies of the Great Powers." *The Creation of Iraq, 1914–1921*. Ed. Reeva Spector Simon and Eleanor H. Tejirian. New York: Columbia University Press, 2004, pp. 110–123.

Gumbrecht, Hans Ulrich. *Atmosphere, Mood, Stimmung: On a Hidden Potential of Literature*. Trans. Erik Butler. Stanford: Stanford University Press, 2012.

Haraway, Donna J. *The Companion Species Manifesto: Dogs, People, and Significant Otherness*. Vol. 1. Chicago: Prickly Paradigm Press, 2003.

———. "Staying with the Trouble: Anthropocene, Capitalocene, Chthulucene." *Anthropocene or Capitalocene?: Nature, History, and the Crisis of Capitalism*. Ed. Jason Moore. Oakland: PM Press, 2016, pp. 34–76.

Hardt, Michael and Antonio Negri. *Empire*. Cambridge: Harvard University Press, 2001.

Harman, Graham. *Object-oriented ontology: A New Theory of Everything*. London: Penguin Random House, 2017.

Harpham, Geoffrey G. *On the Grotesque: Strategies of Contradiction in Art and Literature*. Princeton: Princeton University Press, 1982.

Harvey David. *The Limits to Capital*. Oxford: Basil Blackwell, 1982.

———. *The New Imperialism*. Oxford: OUP, 2003, pp. 1–26.

Heinberg, Richard. *The Party's Over: Oil, War and the Fate of Industrial Societies*. Gabriola Island: New Society Publishers, 2003.

Hitchcock, Peter. "Oil in an American Imaginary." *New Formations*. 69, 2010, pp. 81–97.

Hohendahl, Peter Uwe. "Aesthetic Violence: The Concept of the Ugly in Adorno's Aesthetic Theory." *Cultural Critique*. 60:1, 2005, pp. 170–196.

Huber, Matthew. "Refined Politics: Petroleum Products, Neoliberalism, and the Ecology of Entrepreneurial Life." *Oil Culture*. Eds. Ross Barrett and Daniel Worden. Minneapolis and London: University of Minnesota Press, 2014.

Hughes, David McDermott. *Energy without Conscience: Oil, Climate Change, and Complicity*. Durham and London: Duke University Press, 2017.

Ian, Marcia. *Remembering the Phallic Mother: Psychoanalysis, Modernism, and the Fetish*. Cornell: Cornell Cornell University Press, 1993.

I.C. "Our Future Fuel." *Intergovernmental Panel on Climate Change Report*. Web. www.ipcc.ch/report/ar6/wg1/ Accessed 10.08.2021.

Imre, Szeman, Jennifer Wenzel and Patricia Yaeger (eds.). Fueling Culture 101 Words for Energy and Environment. New York: Fordham University Press, 2017, pp. 39–42.

Isser, Steve. *The Economics and Politics of the United States Oil Industry, 1920–1990: Profits, Populism, and Petroleum*. New York: Routledge, 2016.

Jameson, Fredric. *The Political Unconscious: Narrative as a Socially Symbolic Act*. London: Routledge, 1983.

## Works Cited    373

———. *Late Marxism: Adorno, or, the Persistence of the Dialectic*. London: Verso, 1990.

———. *Archaeologies of the Future: The Desire Called Utopia and Other Science Fictions*. London: Verso, 2005.

———. "How Not to Historicize Theory". *CriticalInquiry*. 34, 2008, pp. 563–82.

———. *The Antinomies Of Realism*. London: Verso, 2015.

———. *Allegory and Ideology*. London and New York: Verso, 2019.

Johnson, Bob. *Carbon Nation: Fossil Fuels in the Making of Modern Culture*. Lawrence: University of Kansas Press, 2014.

Jon, Gordon. *Unsustainable Oil: Facts, Counterfacts, and Fictions*. Edmonton: University of Alberta Press, 2015.

Jones, G. Gareth. *The State and the Emergence of the British Oil Industry*. London: Macmillan, 1981.

Kahn, Lothar. *Insight and Action: The Life and Work of Lion Feuchtwanger*. Rutherford: Fairleigh Dickinson University Press, 1975.

Kaposy, Tim. "Petroleum's Longue Durée: Writing Oil's Temporalities into History." *Petrocultures: Oil, Politics, Culture*. Eds. Sheena Wilson Adam Carlson and Imre Szeman. Montreal & Kingston, London and Chicago: McGill-Queen's University Press, 2017, pp. 389–405.

Karl Marx. *Capital, Volume One*, translated by B. Fowkes, Harmondsworth: Penguin Books, 1976.

Kashi, Ed. *Curse of the Black Gold: 50 Years of Oil in the Niger Delta*. New York: Power House Books, 2008.

Kaufman, Alexander. "Democrats' Drama on Fossil Fuel Money Shows a Radical Green Jobs Plan Can Be a Win-Win." *Huff-Post*. 11 August 2018.

Kelly, Jason. "Anthropocene." *Rivers of the Anthropocene*. Eds. Jason M. Kelly, Philip Scarpino and Helen Berry. Oakland: University of California Press, 2018.

Kennedy, Melissa. *Narratives of Inequality: Postcolonial Literary Economies*. Basingstoke: Palgrave Macmillan, 2017.

Keohane, Robert O. *After Hegemony: Cooperation and Discord in the World Political Economy*. Princeton: Princeton University Press, 1984.

Kershaw, Baz. *Theatre Ecology: Environments and Performance Events*. Cambridge: Cambridge University Press, 2007.

Kimmel, Michael S. "The 'Crisis' in Masculinity in Historical Perspective." *The Making of Masculinities: The New Men's Studies*. Ed. Harry Brod. Boston: Allen and Unwin, 1987, pp. 121–153.

Klein, Naomi. *The Shock Doctrine: The Rise of Disaster Capitalism*. New York: Picador, 2008.

———.*This Changes Everything: Capitalism vs The Climate*. New York: Simon & Schuster, 2014.

Körber, Lill-Ann, Scott MacKenzie and Anna Westerståhl Stenport (eds.). *Arctic Environmental Modernities*. Cham: Palgrave Macmillan, 2017.

Koselleck, Reinhart. *Futures Past: On the Semantics of Historical Time*. Trans. Keith Tribe. Cambridge: MIT Press, 1985.

Kristeva, Julia. *Powers of Horror: An Essay on Abjection*. Trans. Leon S. Roudiez. New York: Columbia University Press, 1982.

———. *Black Sun: Depression and Melancholia*, trans. Leon S. Roudiez. New York: Columbia University Press.

## 374  Works Cited

Kumar, Ashutosh. *Coolies of the Empire: Indentured Indians in the Sugar Colonies, 1830–1920.* Cambridge: Cambridge University Press, 2017.

Labban, Mazen. "Oil in Parallax: Scarcity, Markets, and the Financialization of Accumulation." *Geoforum.* 41, 2010, pp. 541–552.

———. "Deterritorializing Extraction: Bioaccumulation and the Planetary Mine." *Annals of the Association of American Geographers.* 104:3, 2014, pp. 560–576.

Lacan, Jacques. *Seminar XI: Four Fundamental Concepts of Psychoanalysis.* Trans. Alan Sheridan. New York: W. W. Norton, 1998.

Lania, Leo. *Die Komödie der Wirtschaft, Der brennende Punkt.* Blätter der Piscatorbühne Bepa Verlag, April 1928.

———. *Konjunktur (Re-Titled Prosperity) Prosperity* held at Wisconsin Historical Society Library and Archive in Box 5 Folder 13.

———. Konjunktur, Theatersttick in 3 Akten, Komddie, 2. Fassung U9271281 Materialien: ms. Msk., Pag. nach Akten, insg. 62 S., deutsch (2. Fassung) (B5/13). UA: 10.4.1928 Erwin-Piscator-Bi.ihne im Lessing-Theater, Regie: Erwin Piscator, Btihnenbild: Traugott.

Latour, Bruno. *We Have Never Been Modern.* Cambridge: Harvard University Press, 1993.

Latour, Bruno. "Morality and Technology: The End of Means." *Theory, culture & society.* 19 (5–6), 2002, pp. 247–260.

Laurie, Roberta. "Still Ethical Oil Framing the Alberta Oil Sands." *The Rhetoric of Oil in the Twenty-First Century: Government, Corporate, and Activist Discourses.* Eds. Heather Graves and David Beard. London: Routledge, 2019, pp. 169–188.

Lazzarato, Maurizio. *Les Révolutions du Capitalisme.* Paris: Le Seuil, 2004.

LeMenager, Stephanie. "The Aesthetics of Petroleum, after Oil!." *American Literary History.* 24:1, 2012, pp. 59–86.

Leo, Lania. "Die Komödie der Wirtschaft." *Der brennende Punkt, Blätter der Piscatorbühne.* Berlin: Bepa-Verlag, 22 November, 1927.

———. *Existence and Existents.* Trans. Alphonso Lingis. Pittsburgh: Duquesne University Press, 2001.

Levinas, Emmanuel. *Totality and Infinity: An Essay on Exteriority.* Trans. Alphonso Lingis. Pittsburgh: Duquesne University Press, 1969.

Lewis, Simon and Mark Maslin. "Defining the Anthropocene." *Nature.* 519, 2015, pp. 171–180.

Liberate Tate. "Disobedience as Performance." *Performance Research.* 17.1, 2012, pp. 135–140.

Liboiron, Max. *Pollution Is Colonialism.* Durham and London: Duke University Press, 2021.

Logar, Ernst. *Invisible Oil.* Vienna: Ambra Verlag, 2011.

Lowy, Michael. "The Current of Critical Irrealism: A Moonlit Enchanted Night." *Adventures in Realism.* Ed. Matthew Beaumont. Oxford: Blackwell, 2007, pp. 193–206.

Lukacs, Georg. "Critical Realism and Socialist Realism" in *The Meaning of Contemporary Realism.* London: Martin Press, 1962.

Lukacs, Georg. *Writer and Critic: And Other Essays.* Edited by Arthur David Kahn. London: Martin Press, 1970.

Luxemburg, Rosa. *The Mass Strike.* Chicago: Bookmarks, 1986.

# Works Cited    375

Lyotard, Jean-François. *Discourse, Figure.* Trans. Antony Hudek and Mary Lydon. Minneapolis and London: University of Minnesota Press, 2011.

———. *The Postmodern Explained.* Trans. Julian Pefanis and Morgan Thomas. Minneapolis: University of Minnesota Press, 1993.

Maass, Peter. *Crude World: The Violent Twilight of Oil.* New York: Vintage, 2009.

Macdonald, Graeme. "Research Note: The Resources of Fiction." *Reviews in Cultural Theory.* 4 (2), 2013, pp. 1–24.

———. "Containing Oil: The Pipeline." *Petrocultures: Oil, Politics, Culture.* Eds. Sheena Wilson Adam Carlson and Imre Szeman. Montreal & Kingston, London and Chicago: McGill-Queen's University Press, 2017, pp. 36–77.

Malm, Andreas. *Fossil Capital: The Rise of Steam-Power and the Roots of Global Warming.* London and New York: Verso, 2016.

———. "Long Waves of Fossil Development: Periodizing Energy and Capital." *Mediations.* 31:2, 2018, pp. 17–40.

Malm, Andreas and The Zetkin Collective. *White Skin, Black Fuel: On the Danger of Fossil Fascism.* London and New York: Verso, 2021.

Mandel, Ernest. *Marxist Economic Theory.* London: The Merlin Press, 1968.

———. *Late Capitalism.* London: Verso, 1975.

———. *Long Waves of Capitalist Development: A Marxist Interpretation.* London and New York: Verso, 1995.

Marcuse, Herbert. *Eros and Civilization: A Philosophical Inquiry into Freud.* Boston: Beacon Press, 1974.

Marvin, Charles. *The Coming Oil Age: Petroleum – Past, Present, and Future.* London: R. Anderson, 1889.

Marx, Karl. "Draft of an Article on Friedrich List." *CW.* 4, 1845.

———. (1939/1993). *Grundrisse: Foundations of the Critique of Political Economy* (Rough draft). (M. Nicolaus Trans.). Penguin.

———. *Capital.* Vol. 1. London: Lawrence and Wishart, 1967.

———. *Grundrisse.* New York: Vintage Books, 1973.

———. *Capital.* Vol. 3. New York: Vintage Books, 1981.

———. *Capital.* Vol. 1. 1867/1990. Capital. Volume 1. London: Penguin, pp. 568–569.

———. Das Kapital. Band 1. MEW, Band 23. Berlin: Dietz,1867.

Marx, Karl and Friedrich Engels. *Collected Works.* London: Lawrence and Wishart, 1975.

Martin Heidegger. *Being and Time.* Translated by Dennis J. Schmidt. New York: SUNY Press, 1996.

Mbembé, J.-A. and Libby Meintjes. "Necropolitics." *Public Culture.* 15:1, 2003, pp. 11–40.

McLean, Duncan. *Plays One: Julie Allardyce, Julie Allardyce, One Sure Thing, Rog Comes to Shuv, Blackden, I'd Rather Go Blind.* London: Methuen, 1999.

Mejcher, Helmut. *Imperial Quest for Oil: Iraq 1910–1928.* London: Ithaca Press, 1976.

Mezzadra, Sandra and Brett Neilson. *The Politics of Operations: Excavating Contemporary Capitalism.* Durham: Duke University Press, 2019.

Michael T. Klare. "A Tough Oil World: Why Twenty-First Century Oil Will Break the Bank—and the Planet," *Huffington Post,* posted March 13, 2012. http://www.huffingtonpost.com//.

Michael Truscello. *Infrastructural Brutalism.* Cambridge: The MIT Press, 2020.

## 376  Works Cited

Mitchell, Timothy *Carbon Democracy: Political Power in the Age of Oil*. London: Verso, 2011.

———. *Carbon Democracy: Political Power in the Age of Oil*. London: Verso, 2011.

Mitman, Gregg, Marco Armiero and Robert S. Emmett (eds.). *Future Remains: A Cabinet of Curiosities for the Anthropocene*. Chicago: University of Chicago Press, 2018.

Mommer, Bernard. *Global Oil and the Nation State*. Oxford: Oxford University Press, 2002.

Moore, Jason. Capitalist World-Ecology." *Journal of Peasant Studies*. 12:1, pp. 1–46.

Moore, Jason W. "Capitalism as World Ecology: Braudel and Marx on Environmental History." *Organization and Environment*. 16:4, 2003, pp. 431–458.

———. "Ecology, Capital, and the Nature of Our Times: Accumulation & cRisis in the Capitalist World-Ecology." *Journal of World-Systems Research*. Vol. XVII, No. 1, 2011, pp. 108–147.

———. "From Object to Oikeios: Environment-Making in the Capitalist World-Ecology," 2013. http://www.jasonwmoore.com/uploads/.

———. *Capitalism in the Web of Life: Ecology and the Accumulation of Capital*. London and New York: Verso, 2015.

———. "The Rise of Cheap Nature." *Anthropocene or Capitalocene: Nature, History, and the Crisis of Capitalism*. Ed. Jason W. Moore. Dexter: PM Press, 2016, pp. 78–114.

———. "The Capitalocene, Part I: On the Nature and Origins of Our Ecological Crisis." *The Journal of Peasant Studies*. 44, 3. 2017a, pp. 594–630.

———. "Metabolic Rift or Metabolic Shift? Dialectics, Nature, and the World-Historical Method." *Theory and Society*. 46, 2017b, pp. 285–318.

———. "The Capitalocene Part II: Accumulation by Appropriation and the Centrality of Unpaid Work/Energy." *The Journal of Peasant Studies*. 45:2, 2018, pp. 237–279.

———. "World-Ecological Imaginations." Web. https://jasonwmoore.wordpress.com/page/3/

Moretti, Franco. "Conjectures on World Literature." *Debating World Literature*. Ed. Christopher Prendergast. London and New York: Verso, 2000, pp. 148–162.

———. "Conjectures on World Literature." *Debating World Literature*. Ed. Christopher Prendergast. London and New York: Verso, 2004, pp. 149–150.

———. *Graphs, Maps, Trees: Abstract Models for Literary History*. London and New York: Verso, 2005.

Morton, Timothy. *Ecology Without Nature: Rethinking Environmental Aesthetics*. Cambridge: Harvard University Press, 2007.

———. "The Dark Ecology of Elegy." *The Oxford Handbook of the Elegy*. Ed. K. Weisman. Oxford: Oxford University Press, 2010, pp. 251–271.

———. "Ecology as Text, Text as Ecology." *Oxford Literary Review*. 32:1, 2010, pp. 1–17.

———. *Hyperobjects: Philosophy and Ecology after the End of the World*. Minneapolis and London: University of Minnesota Press, 2013.

Mtiller, Darsteller. Tilla Durieux, Curt Bois u.a. (siehe Besetzungsliste in Anhang IV).

———. *Konjunktur 1 & 2*. US MSS 27AF Prosperity play, 1927 Box 5 Folder 13.

# Works Cited 377

———. *Oil Field: A Satire in Three Acts.* (in collaboration with Charles Duff). Occasional Music by Hans Eisler. 1934 (B5/F11). Materialien: ms. Msk., 100 S. (Pag.), engl.

Mumford, Lewis. *Technics & Civilization.* London: Routledge and Kegan Paul, 1934.

Musch, Sebastian. *Jewish Encounters with Buddhism in German Culture.* London: Palgrave, 2020.

Niblett, Michael. "World-Economy, World-Ecology, World Literature." *Green Letters.* 16:1, 2012, pp. 15–30. 10.1080/14688417.2012.10589097

———. *World Literature and Ecology: The Aesthetics of Commodity Frontiers, 1890–1950.* Cham: Palgrave Macmillan, 2020.

———. *On the Genealogy of Morals.* Trans. Walter Kaufmann. New York: Vintage, 1969.

———. *Gay Science.* Trans: Walter Kaufmann. New York: Vintage Books, 1974.

———. *Thus Spoke Zarathustra: A Book for None and All.* Trans. Walter Kaufmann. New York: Penguin, 1978.

Nietzsche, Friedrich Wilhelm. *The Will to Power: An Attempted Transvaluation of All Values.* Trans. Walter Kaufmann and R. J. Hollingdale. New York: Random House, 1967.

Nixon, Rob. *Slow Violence and the Environmentalism of the Poor.* Cambridge: Harvard University Press, 2011.

———. "The Anthropocene: The Promise and Pitfalls of an Epochal Idea." *Future Remains: A Cabinet of Curiosities for the Anthropocene.* Eds. Gregg Mitman, Marco Armiero and Robert Emmett. Chicago: University of Chicago Press, 2018, pp. 1–18.

———. "Anthropocene 2." *Fueling Culture: 101 Words for Energy and Environment.* Eds. Imre Szeman, Jennifer Wenzel and Patricia Yaeger. New York: Fordham University Press, 2017, pp. 43–46.

O'Connor, Peter A. "Energy Transitions." *The Pardee Papers.* December 2010. www.bu.edu/pardee/files/2010/11/12-PP-Nov2010.pdf

Orsato, R. *Sustainability Strategies: When Does It Pay to Be Green?* London: Palgrave, 2016.

Paul J. Crutzen. "Geology of mankind" in *Nature.* 415, 2002, page 23.

Pendakis, Andrew. "Being and Oil: Or, How to Run a Pipeline through Heidegger." *Petrocultures: Oil, Politics, Culture.* Eds. Sheena Wilson Adam Carlson and Imre Szeman. Montreal & Kingston, London and Chicago: McGill-Queen's University Press, 2017, pp. 376–388.

Pérez Schael, M. S. *Petróleo, cultura y poder en Venezuela.* Caracas: El Nacional, 1993.

Petrocultures Research Group. *After Oil.* Edmonton: Petrocultures Research Group, 2016.

Piscator, Erwin. *Gespräch zur Aufführung des 'Schwejk' in Berlin.* Erwin Piscator Center 2732. Berlin: Deutsche Akademie der Künste.

———. *Das politische Theater.* Berlin, 1929.

———. "Letter to Siebert, Ilse." Erwin Piscator Center 2305. Deutsche Akademie der Künste. 25 May 1959.

———. *Das Politische Theater: Fraksimiledruck der Erstausgabe* [1929]. Henschelverlag Kunst und Gesellschaft Berlin, 1968.

———. *The Political Theatre.* Translated by Hugh Rorrison. New York: Methuen, 1980.

## 378 Works Cited

———. "Outline of Sociological Dramaturgy." *Essays on German Theater*. Ed. Margaret Herzfeld-Sander. New York: Continuum, 1985, pp. 183–185.

Podobnik, Bruce. *Global Energy Shifts: Fostering Sustainability in a Turbulent Age*. Philadelphia: Temple University Press, 2006.

Priest, Tyler. "The Dilemmas of Oil Empire." *The Journal of American History*. 99:1, 2012, pp. 236–251.

Public Roads Administration, Federal Works Agency. *Highway Statistics Summary to 1945*. Washington: US Government Printing Office, 1947.

Rancière, Jacques. *Dissensus: On Politics and Aesthetics*. Ed. and Trans. Steven Corcoran. London and New York: Continuum, 2010.

———. *The Emancipated Spectator*. Trans. Gregory Elliott. London: Verso, 2009.

———. *The Future of the Image*. Trans. Gregory Elliott. London: Verso, 2007.

Reed, Kristin. *Crude Existence: Environment and the Politics of Oil in Northern Angola*. Berkeley: University of Carolina Press, 2009.

Retort collective. *Aflicted Powers: Capital and Spectacle in a New Age of War*. London: Verso, 2005.

Richardson, C. J. "Petroleum." *The Times*. 3 September 1866.

———. "Petroleum as Steam Fuel." *The Times*. 24 July 1865.

Ricoeur, Paul. *Time and Narrative, Volume 1*. Trans. Kathleen McLaughlin and David Pellauer. London: The University of Chicago Press, 1983.

Rigby, Kate. *Dancing with Disaster: Environmental Histories, Narratives, and Ethics in Perilous Times*. Charlottesville: University of Virginia Press, 2015.

Roberts, Ian. "Determinism, Free Will, and Moral Responsibility in American Literary Naturalism." *The Oxford Handbook of American Literary Naturalism*. Ed. Keith Newlin. Oxford: Oxford University Press, 2011, pp. 121–138.

Ross, Michael L. *The Oil Curse: How Petroleum Wealth Shapes the Development of Nations*. Princeton and Oxford: Princeton University Press, 2012.

Tatjana Röber. "Der Mensch steht in der Mitte, aber nur relativ": Subjektivitiit und Wahrnehmung in Kulturtheorie und 'sachlichem' Theater der 20er Jahre. Doctoral Dissertation. Hamburg University, 1999.

Salas, Miguel Tinker. *The Enduring Legacy: Oil, Culture, and Society in Venezuela*. Durham: Duke University Press, 2009.

Salvaggio, Ruth. "Imagining Angels on the Gulf." *Oil Culture*. Eds. Ross Barrett and Daniel Worden. Minneapolis and London: University of Minnesota Press, 2014, pp. 384–403.

Sartre, Jean-Paul. "Préface" in *Frantz Fanon, Les damnés de la terre*. Paris: F. Maspero, 1961.

Sawyer, Derek. *The Violence of Abstraction*. Oxford: Blackwell Publications, 1987.

Schwaiger, Michael. Von der Kunst zur Reportage und zurück: Leo Lanias Konzept einer politisch operativen Literatur und Medienkunst. Dissertation. University of Wien, 2014.

Schwarz, Roberto. "National Adequation and Critical Originality." *Cultural Critique*. 49:1, 2001, pp. 18–42.

Shafiyee, Katayoun. *Machineries of Oil: An Infrastructural History of BP in Iran*. Cambridge: MIT Press, 2020.

Sinclair, Upton. *Oil!* London: Penguin, 2007.

Works Cited 379

Sklair, Leslie. *The Transnational Capitalist Class*. Oxford: Blackwell, 2001.

Smil, Vaclav. *Energy Transitions: History, Requirements, Prospects*. Santa Barbara California: Praeger, 2010.

Snyder, David Allan. "Petroleum and Power: Naval Fuel Technology and the Anglo-American Struggle for Core Hegemony, 1889–1922." Diss. Texas A&M University, 2001.

Social Work Practice with Immigrants and Refugees 30–35.

Sonia Shah. *Crude: The Story of Oil*. New York: Seven Stories Press, 2004.

Stacy, Alaimo. *Bodily Natures: Science, Environment, and the Material Self*. Bloomington: Indiana University Press, 2010.

———. "Trans-corporeality." *The Posthuman* Glossary. Eds. R. Braidotti and M. Hlavajova. London: Bloomsbury Academic, 2018.

Stewart, Janet. "Resource Curse." *Fueling Culture: 101 Words for Energy Humanities*. Eds. Jennifer Wenzel, Patricia Yaeger and Imre Szeman. New York: Fordham University Press, 2017, pp. 285–288.

Stoekl, Allan. "Foreword." *Oil Culture*. Ed. Ross Barrett and Daniel Worden. Minneapolis and London: University of Minnesota Press, 2014, pp. xi–xiv.

Stoianovich, Traian. *French historical method: the Annales paradigm*. Cornell: Cornell University Press, 1976.

Sumida, Jon Tetsuro. *In Defence of Naval Supremacy: Finance, Technology, and British Naval Policy, 1889–1914*. Boston: Unwin Hyman, 1989.

Szeman, Imre. System Failure: Oil, Futurity, and the Anticipation of Disaster. *South Atlantic Quarterly*. 106 (4), 2007, pp. 805–823.

Szeman, Imre and Dominic Boyer (eds.). *Energy Humanities: An Anthology*. Baltimore: Johns Hopkins University Press, 2017.

Szeman, Imre and Jeff Diamanti. *Energy Culture: Art and Theory on Oil and Beyond*. Morgantown: West Virginia University Press, 2019.

———. "Nine Principles for a Critical Theory of Energy." *Polygraph*. 28, 2020, pp. 137–159.

Szeman, Imre. "Introduction: A manifesto for materialism." *Essays on Canadian Writing*. Toronto Iss. 68, (Summer 1999), pp. 1–18.

Szeman, Imre and Jennifer Wenzel. "Literature and Energy Futures." *PMLA*. 126:2, 2011, pp. 323–325.

———. "Crude Aesthetics: The Politics of Oil Documentaries." *Journal of American Studies*. 46, 2. *Oil Cultures*, 2012, pp. 423–439.

———. "How to Know about Oil: Energy Epistemologies and Political Futures." *Journal of Canadian Studies/Revue d'études canadiennes*. 47:3, 2013, pp. 145–168.

———. "What Do We Talk about When We Talk about Extractivism?" *Textual Practice*. 35:3, 2021, pp. 505–523.

Taylor, Diana. *The Archive and the Repertoire: Cultural Memory and Performance in the Americas*. Durham: Duke University Press, 2003.

Taylor, Mark C. *Altarity*. Chicago and London: The University of Chicago Press, 1987.

Thomlison, Adam. "From Pipeline to Plate: The Domestication of Oil Sands through Visual Food Analogies." *The Rhetoric of Oil in the Twenty-First Century: Government, Corporate, and Activist Discourses*. Eds. Heather Graves and David Beard. London: Routledge, 2019, pp. 189–210.

## 380 Works Cited

Timsar, Rebecca Golden. "Oil, Masculinity, and Violence." *Subterranean Estates: Life Worlds of Oil and Gas*. Eds. Hannah Appel, Arthur Mason and Michael Watts. London: Cornell University Press, 2015, pp. 72–89.

Tropani, Anand. *Oil and the Great Powers: Britain and Germany 1914–1945*. Oxford: Oxford University Press, 2019.

Trotsky, Leon. *The Permanent Revolution*. London: New Park Publications, 1962.

———. *The Permanent Revolution*. London: New Park Publications, 1975.

Van Dooren, Thom. "Nature in the Anthropocene? A Reflection on a Photograph." *The Yearbook of Comparative Literature*. 58, 2012, pp. 228–234.

Varma, Nitin. *Coolies of Capitalism: Assam Tea and the Making of Coolie Labour*. Oldenbourg: De Gruyter, 2017.

Vivasvan Soni, "Energy," *Fueling Culture: 101 Words for Energy and Environment* 133.

Voskuil, Walter H. "Coal and Political Power in Europe." *Economic Geography*. 18:3, 1942, pp. 247–258.

Wallerstein, Immanuel. *World-Systems Analysis: An Introduction*. Durham and London: Duke University Press, 2004.

Walonen, Michael. *Contemporary World Narrative Fiction and the Spaces of Neoliberalism*. Basingstoke: Palgrave Macmillan, 2016.

Warwick Research Collective. *Combined and Uneven Development: Towards a New Theory of World-Literature*. Liverpool: Liverpool University Press, 2015.

Watts, Michael. "Violent Environments: Petroleum Conflict and the Political Ecology of Rule in the Niger Delta, Nigeria." In Liberation Ecologies: Environment, Development, Social Movements, edited by Richard Peet and Michael Watts, 273–298. New York: Routledge, 2004.

Watts, Michael John. "Oil as Money: The Devil's Excrement and the Spectacle of Black Gold." *Money, Power and Space*. Eds. Trevor J. Barnes, Jamie Peck, Eric Sheppard and Adam Tickell. Oxford: Blackwell, 1994, pp. 406–445.

———. "Violent Environments: Petroleum Conflict and the Political Ecology of Rule in the Niger Delta, Nigeria." *Violent Environments*. Ed. Nancy Lee Peluso and Michael Watts. Ithaca: Cornell University Press, 2001, pp. 292–293.

———. "Securing Oil: Frontiers, Risk, and Spaces of Accumulated Insecurity." *Subterranean Estates: Life Worlds of Oil and Gas*. Eds. Hannah Appel, Arthur Mason and Michael Watts. London: Cornell University Press, 2015, pp. 211–237.

Weber, Max. *On Charisma and Institution Building*. Ed. S. Eisenstadt. Chicago: Chicago University Press, 1968.

Wenzel, Jennifer. "How to Read for Oil." *Resilience: A Journal of the Environmental Humanities*. 1:3, 2014, pp. 156–161.

Westall, Claire. "World-Literary Resources and Energetic Materialism." *Journal of Postcolonial Writing*. 53:3, 2017, pp. 265–276. https://doi.org/10.1080/174 49855.2017.1337671

Wihstutz, Benjamin. "Anticipating the End: Thoughts on the Spectator and the Temporality of Dasein." *Theatre Research International*. 34:2, 2009, pp. 109–115.

Wilke, Sabine. "Theatre and Performance." *The Cambridge Companion to Literature and the Anthropocene*. Ed. John Parham. Cambridge: Cambridge University Press, 2021.

Willett, John. *The Theater of Bertolt Brecht*. New York: New Directions, 1968.

## Works Cited 381

Williams, Raymond. *Marxism and Literature*. Oxford: Oxford University Press, 1977.

Willmott, Glenn. "Oil Tragedy as Modern Genre." *Petrocultures*. Eds. Sheena Wilson, Adam Carlson and Imre Szeman. Montreal: Mcgill-Queen's University Press, 2017, pp. 187–196.

Wilson, Sheena. "Oil Ethics." *American Book Review*. 33:2, 2012, pp. 8–9.

———. "Energy Imaginaries: Feminist and Decolonial Futures." *Materialism and the Critique of Energy*. Eds. Brent Bellamy and Jeff Diamanti. Chicago and Edmonton: MCM Prime Press, 2017, pp. 377–411.

Wong, K. Scott. "East Asian Immigrants." *The Oxford Handbook of Asian American History*. Eds. David Yoo and Eiichiro Azuma. Oxford: Oxford University Press, 2016, pp. 104–115.

"Working Group on the 'Anthropocene'." Subcommission on Quaternary Stratigraphy, 23 February 2016. quaternary.stratigraphy.org.

Yergin, Daniel. *The Prize: The Epic Quest for Oil, Money, & Power*. 2008. New York: Free Press.

Yaeger, Patricia. "Editor's Column: Literature in the Ages of Wood, Tallow, Coal, Whale Oil, Gasoline, Atomic Power, and Other Energy Sources." *PMLA*. 126:2, 2011, pp. 305–326.

Yates, Michelle. "The Human-As-Waste, the Labor Theory of Value and Disposability in Contemporary Capitalism." *Antipode*. 43:5, 2011, pp. 1679–1695.

Yúdice, George. *The Expediency of Culture: Uses of Culture in the Global Era*. Durham: Duke University Press, 2003.

Zapf, Hubert. *Literature as Cultural Ecology: Sustainable Texts*. London and New York: Bloomsbury, 2016.

Ziarek, Krzysztof. "The Limits of Life: A Non-anthropic View of World and Finitude." *Angelaki: Journal of the Theoretical Humanities*. 16:4, 2011, pp. 19–30.

Ziebura, Gilbert. *Weltwirtschaft und Weltpolitik 1922/24–1931*. Frankfurt am Main: Verlag 1984.

Žižek, Slavoj. *Tarrying with the Negative: Kant, Hegel, and the Critique of Ideology*. Durham: Duke University Press, 1993.

Zuck, Rochelle Raineri. "The Wizard of Oil: Abraham James, the Harmonial Wells, and the Psychometric History of the Oil Industry." *Journal of American Studies*. 46, 2012, pp. 313–336.

# Index

abstraction 15, 25, 29, 31, 43, 148, 151, 168, 171–173, 182, 193, 205, 206, 208, 218, 226
affective context 277
affective hermeneutics 277
Albania 66–67, 69, 72, 76–77, 84, 99, 100–106, 109, 111–113, 120–124, 135–137, 143
allegory 59, 168, 250, 256, 262, 264–265, 279, 282–284
anthropocene 9–18, 38–40, 50, 53, 56–57, 281–283
Arrighi, Giovanni xxiv, 23, 200
artwash xii–xiv

bad love 5, 267–268
Bakhtin, Mikhail 268–269
Bellamy, Brent Ryan xvii–xix, 208
Brecht, Bertolt 36–37, 70, 73, 97–98, 157, 168, 170, 260, 306, 336

capitalism 2–4, 9, 16–32, 61, 68, 91, 167–168, 174, 198–200, 207–208, 228–229, 252, 283, 313–315, 356
Capitalocene xiv, 15–19, 24, 139, 262, 274, 279
Chakrabarty, Dipesh 10, 13–14
coal 22, 40, 43–46, 116, 150–151, 161, 360
Colebrook, Claire 38–39
commodification 77, 106, 112, 148, 151, 173, 283, 349, 359
commodity 50, 56–57, 67–68, 77, 85, 88–91, 94, 96, 139–140, 142–144, 147, 161, 163–164, 167–169, 182–183, 187, 199, 204–209, 239–241, 351–352

commodity fetishism 291, 355, 361
crisis of representation 35, 48

death 256, 267, 305, 307, 309, 324, 332, 337, 344–345, 366
Deleuze, Gilles xxv, 148, 236–237, 293, 317–319, 344
DeLoughrey, Elizabeth 58–59, 282–283
desire 6, 35, 51, 63, 134, 140, 235, 244, 256, 265, 267–268, 271, 280–281, 293, 300, 306–307, 309–318, 333–345
Diamanti, Jeff xvii–xix, xxv, 2–3, 208
dramatic form xx, xxv, 37, 41, 52, 93–94

emotional geographies 277
empire xvi, 32, 98, 158, 231
energy unconscious xxviii, xxv, 7, 62
England 67, 71–73, 122–123, 125, 154–160, 162
environment 15–18, 21–22, 28, 41, 46, 50, 57, 70, 159, 207, 265, 281, 289, 292, 295–296, 324, 346

Feuchtwanger, Lion 255–256, 259–264, 281, 290, 295–297, 301, 324, 347, 357–358
First World War 71–73, 76, 100, 129, 151, 156, 158, 161, 167, 227

Germany 70–71, 73–74, 79, 84, 89, 91, 96, 107, 112, 123, 151, 157, 160, 247, 260, 263
global warming xi, 8, 14, 22, 38, 41, 48, 56

## Index 383

Haraway, Donna 57, 358

infrastructural criticism xxv
infrastructure xxv, 1, 3–4, 6, 42,
  55, 105, 147–148, 151, 177, 226,
  245, 247, 265, 279, 281, 287,
  295, 353

Jameson, Fredric xxi–xxii, 58–59, 68,
  200, 236, 282–283

Kershaw, Baz 41
Konjunktur 66–70, 76, 79, 80, 90–98,
  100–105, 107–109, 115–116,
  118–119, 127–128, 134, 139,
  146–148, 166–168

labour 2, 17–19, 25, 27, 32, 46–47,
  55, 68, 77–79, 120, 171–172, 198,
  206–207, 209, 239–242, 256–259,
  264, 279, 291, 300, 324, 345,
  355–358, 360–363
Lacan, Jacques 8, 265, 312, 328
Lania, Leo 68, 70–80, 83–90, 93–96,
  100–101, 166–167, 169–172,
  213–214
LeMenager, Stephanie 2–5, 57,
  267–268, 277, 357
Liberate Tate xi–xiv
libidinal economy 175, 256, 265, 267,
  280, 310–311, 317, 337
longue durée xvi–xvii, xxiv, 2, 14–15,
  17, 20, 23, 30, 49, 54, 58, 69,
  78–82, 100, 120, 156, 228–229,
  273, 281, 283, 287, 301–302, 356
Lyotard, Jean-François 52, 265, 335

Marx, Karl xxii, xxiv, 24–25, 27–29,
  42, 127, 198, 206–207, 237–238,
  240–241, 304–305
Materialism 43, 205, 282
Materialist Ecocriticism 9
Mbembé, Achille 265, 324,
  344–345, 360
metabolic rift 15, 24–31, 70, 168,
  182, 207, 256, 264, 269, 275, 277,
  279, 281, 290, 305, 348, 362
metabolic shift xxii, 24, 27, 30

Mitchell, Timothy 39, 55, 116–117,
  208, 360–361
Moore, Jason 15–32, 77, 240, 354, 358
Morton, Timothy xiv, 36, 45,
  51–52, 59

Nixon, Rob 14–15, 40, 50, 53, 58

objet petit a 6, 8, 41, 56, 271, 293,
  309, 312
Oil Field 66–68, 70, 76, 79–80,
  90–91, 166–174, 191, 193,
  233, 252
Oil Islands 255–257, 262, 264–266,
  272, 275, 277–281, 289, 294–296,
  346
oil workers 105–106, 116–119, 197

Pendakis, Andrew xiv, 7, 36, 51
petrocapitalism 171, 186, 343, 346,
  358, 362
petroculture xvii–xviii, 352

race 36, 46, 54, 62, 106, 208, 256,
  272, 287, 359
racial politics 106, 256, 271–272,
  286, 357
reportage theory 71, 76, 86–87,
  90, 145
resource enclave 289–291, 323

Second World War 74, 76, 103, 152,
  166–167
Shapiro, Stephen xxiv, 78
Shell 2, 73, 102, 114, 152, 154,
  228, 231
Sinclair, Upton 2, 39, 88–89, 112,
  146–147, 178, 297
Szeman, Imre xxv, 1–3, 5, 35–36,
  43–44, 55, 57, 59–62

Wallerstein, Immanuel 17, 76, 78,
  80–82
Wilke, Sabine 46
world-ecological xxv, 9, 15, 18,
  20–24, 46, 62, 167, 240

Zapf, Hubert 44–45

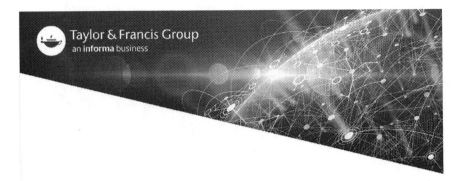

# Taylor & Francis eBooks

www.taylorfrancis.com

A single destination for eBooks from Taylor & Francis with increased functionality and an improved user experience to meet the needs of our customers.

90,000+ eBooks of award-winning academic content in Humanities, Social Science, Science, Technology, Engineering, and Medical written by a global network of editors and authors.

## TAYLOR & FRANCIS EBOOKS OFFERS:

- A streamlined experience for our library customers
- A single point of discovery for all of our eBook content
- Improved search and discovery of content at both book and chapter level

### REQUEST A FREE TRIAL
support@taylorfrancis.com

Printed in the United States
by Baker & Taylor Publisher Services